Composing from Sources

ASSA

Composing from Sources

James D. Lester
Austin Peay State University

New York San Francisco Boston
London Toronto Sydney Tokyo Singapore Madrid
Mexico City Munich Paris Cape Town Hong Kong Montreal

Senior Vice President and Publisher: Joseph Opiela
Acquisitions Editor: Susan Kunchandy
Marketing Manager: Deborah Murphy
Development Manager: Janet Lanphier
Development Editor: Barbara Conover
Senior Supplements Editor: Donna Campion
Media Supplements Editor: Nancy Garcia
Production Manager: Joseph Vella
Project Coordination, Text Design, and Electronic Page Makeup: Electronic Publishing Services Inc., NYC
Design Manager/Cover Designer: John Callaghan
Cover Illustration: Christie's Images/SuperStock
Manufacturing Buyer: Alfred C. Dorsey
Printer and Binder: R.R. Donnelley & Sons Company
Cover Printer: Phoenix Color Corporation

For permission to use copyrighted material, grateful acknowledgment is made to the copyright holders on pp. 535–540, which are hereby made part of this copyright page.

Library of Congress Cataloging-in-Publication Data

Lester, James D.
    Composing from sources / James D. Lester.—1st ed.
      p. cm.
    Includes bibliographical references and index.
    ISBN 0-321-10826-4 (paperback)
       1. English language—Rhetoric. 2. Research—Methodology. 3. College
    readers. 4. Report writing. I. Title.

PE1478.L39 2003
808'042—dc22

                                    2003056483

Please visit our Website at www.ablongman.com/lester

ISBN 0-321-10826-4

4 5 6 7 8 9 10—DOC—11 10 09 08

Brief Contents

Detailed Contents

3 Strategies for Critical Reading   64

4   Writing a Summary   128

8   Writing the Single-Source Essay   260

10 Writing a Paper Using MLA Style   335

11 Writing a Paper Using CMS Note Style 386

Preface

My goal in writing *Composing from Sources* is to help you understand and use the basic skills of academic research and writing so that they become routine. With these at hand, you can then concentrate fully on developing *your* theories and ideas, as supported by the sources and your gathered evidence, to compose both single-source and multi-source assignments.

Your instructor for this course and many other instructors during the next few years will ask you to share your ideas in written discourse. However, you will quickly discover that your basic personal knowledge is broad and general, but you need specialized information for your college papers. Thus, *Composing from Sources* offers specific advice, numerous writing examples by both professionals and your student peers, and exercises and assignments.

Among the skills and strategies you will learn are:

- Use of your own background and knowledge as fertile ground for exploring a topic and for filtering the ideas of others.
- Methods of searching for sources via library networks, the Internet, and the field.
- Ways in which to locate specific sources of information, and to judge a source for its intellectual value to your project.
- Strategies for critical reading, such as making marginal annotations, drawing inferences, and finding a writer's basic argument.
- Techniques for writing passages that paraphrase a source, summarize an entire piece, or quote directly.
- Methods of providing citations to your sources in the correct form and in the assigned academic style.
- Ways in which to avoid plagiarism and to honor the property rights of others.
- Methods for writing a single-source essay that interprets, makes a rebuttal, or provides an evaluation.
- Methods for writing the multi-source essay that will synthesize outside materials into your discourse.
- Use of appropriate format and style for the different academic disciplines, particularly MLA, CMS, and APA style.
- Techniques for writing essay examination answers of quality and precision.

In this age of technology, students more than ever need guidance in identifying the best sources and in drawing paraphrases and quotations from them. Thus, *Composing from Sources* will take you through a series of steps as you discover the best sources, read with a critical and discerning eye, draw from the sources in a variety of effective ways, and build an essay that displays your own wisdom as supported by an intelligent blending of outside sources.

Chapter 1 explains that a good early source of information often exists within you. You are encouraged to consider yourself not only as a source of information but also as the filtering agent that digests information, selects appropriate ideas, and merges them into a powerful combination of convictions and supporting evidence.

Chapter 2 addresses two questions frequently asked by students: *How do I determine the best sources? Are these sources authoritative?* Because it is easy to be caught in an Information Age web of confusion, this chapter explains the use of library sources, Web sources, and field research. It focuses heavily on Internet material and makes clear the distinctions between the library's Internet databases and those sources gathered by a general browser. This chapter and the one that follows offer you clear guidelines for identifying credible sources.

Chapter 3, covering the various strategies for critical reading, goes beyond the usual techniques of highlighting and annotating to explore ways of determining the validity of a source and the methods for testing assertions, inferences, and implications. It also explores logic and the ebb and flow of inductive and deductive reasoning.

Chapters 4, 5, and 6 offer training in developing three types of notes: summary (including how to write plot summaries, annotated bibliographies, and abstracts), paraphrase (including how to paraphrase from an interview, how to handle a writer's irony, and how to provide a citation), and direct quotation (including selection, proper introduction, and a formal citation).

Chapter 7's discussion of academic integrity is essential in this multimedia age of easy downloads, scanned text, and "copy/paste" features. The chapter stresses the importance of placing a source correctly in a proper context. It explores common-knowledge exceptions and methods for academic citations. The exercises will help you avoid any hint of plagiarism by blending paraphrases and quotations properly with an accompanying citation to the source.

Chapter 8 explores the single-source essay and the methods for discovering ideas by responding to another person's work. It gives separate treatment to essays of interpretation, rebuttal, evaluation, and review.

Chapter 9 explores the multi-source essay. It first stresses that you establish your own point of view before reading critically from numerous sources. It then explores methods for discovering different implications by writers and the techniques for grouping multiple sources for analysis and synthesis.

Chapters 10, 11, and 12 explain the style guidelines of the Modern Language Association, the University of Chicago Press, and the American Psychological Association. The chapters are grounded in fundamentals as established by the *MLA Handbook for Writers of Research Papers*, Sixth Edition, 2003; *The Chicago Manual of Style*,

Fifteenth Edition, 2003; and the *Publication Manual of the American Psychological Association*, Fifth Edition, 2001.

Appendix A explains the special skills necessary for writing essay examination answers.

Appendix B briefly reviews the style guidelines of the Council of Science Editors (CSE).

Appendix C provides a set of additional readings—on a variety of subjects and in a variety of forms and styles—that can be the basis for either a single-source or a multi-source essay.

Boxed Guidelines and Tips appear throughout the chapters. Marginal icons refer to specific readings, exercises, and audiovisuals in the companion website. Every chapter closes with a chapter review, a major assignment, and, usually, an installment of the special feature "Tracing the Work of Two Students," which follows the progress of two students as they each research and write a paper. Their completed papers appear in Chapters 10 and 11.

The Ancillary Package

The publication package includes these additional features:

Integrated Website: A Companion Website (http://www.ablongman.com/lester) provides students and instructors with activities specific to each chapter's contents, including additional writing assignments, links to research and writing sources, and instructional audiovisuals. Throughout the text, marginal icons will direct you to the Companion Website.

Instructor's Manual: This manual, written by Teresa Thonney and Gwendolyn James of Columbia Basin College, will assist instructors using *Composing from Sources*. In the manual, instructors will find chapter summaries, teaching suggestions, answers to exercises, and class activities.

Acknowledgments

The Preface would not be complete without the acknowledgment of many people who served in the development of *Composing from Sources:*

The students who have always inspired me, particularly Kaci Holz and Halley Fishburn, who provided the samples of their work in progress at the ends of the chapters.

The staff at Longman Publishers, especially acquisitions editor Susan Kunchandy; development editor Barbara Conover; and Teresa Thonney and Gwendolyn James, the authors of the Instructor's Manual.

The following instructors who reviewed this text and helped improve it at every pass:

Marty Brooks, John Tyler Community College

Walter Everett, University of Southern Indiana

Judith Gardner, University of Texas at San Antonio

Catherine H. Houghton, Point Park College

Maurice Hunt, Baylor University

D. G. Miller, Mississippi College

Lyle W. Morgan, Pittsburg State University

Suzanne Patterson, Arkansas State University, Beebe

Teresa Thonney, Columbia Basin College

Linda Woodson, University of Texas at San Antonio

To the readers of this text, I wish you well on your adventure into critical thinking, careful selection of sources, wise and prudent borrowings, precise citations, and fully developed and well-defended essays.

JAMES D. LESTER

Why We Compose from Sources

From your earliest years onward, writing is an ever growing part of your world: Letters and words scribbled on a lined piece of paper. A homemade birthday card for a parent. School assignments and tests. A college or job application. Perhaps even a love letter or two. These and numerous other examples make clear the significance of writing to your life.

Writing takes on further importance as a part of your academic world. You will write lengthy papers and answer essay test questions for almost all of your courses—whatever the discipline. Because such writing often requires the use of source materials and their citation, your understanding of these procedures and your ability to apply them to your writing are important steps to your academic success.

In this first chapter we will consider the basic methods for drawing upon yourself (personal sources) and drawing upon the wisdom of others (outside sources) as you write an assignment. Although the focus of this text is on the use of outside sources that require formal citation, we will consider first a strictly personal autobiography without the use of sources and then an essay—conversational in tone—that uses magazine style for quoting sources and thus requires no formal citation. A final example of personal writing—a student assignment—combines personal ideas with those of sources. Each of these selections provides a helpful stepping stone to discussion of the use of formal sources in the chapters that follow.

Personal Sources

At times, college writing assignments will allow you to draw information from your memory and experiences in order to write personal narrative and opinion papers. You will be responding to private sources, such as a turning point in your life, an interview with your grandfather, or a personal perspective on fraternity life. You will be arguing in a subtle way that *your* life has rich connotations worthy of consideration by others. You are not writing from a blank slate but from those memorable encounters of danger, hatred, love, triumph, and even failure.

Outside Sources

Many college writing assignments require you to respond in some manner to sources beyond your personal knowledge: a biography, a lecture or textbook chapter, a poem, a history book, and even a lab experiment. You will be required to reach beyond yourself not only to absorb new information but also to interpret it and make it a part of your presentation.

For example, in the classroom your instructor will lecture and conduct a discussion to open your mind to new ideas. Later, during a quiz or test, your answers will draw upon the lectures to demonstrate how well you have absorbed the information and made it a part of your thinking. Drawing information from outside sources, you will also move beyond the library and classroom as you search out articles from the Internet and go into the field for observation or interviews.

An assignment to compose from sources takes two forms, one fairly easy and another more difficult. The easy task, a summary of a source, briefly describes the contents of a passage or describes an entire work. The difficult task, interpretation and evaluation, requires critical reading, constructive thinking, and the precise reporting of your findings.

G U I D E L I N E S

Why We Write from Sources

- To discover ourselves and the ideas hidden in our minds.
- To find new ideas and issues by reading texts that others have written.
- To develop a critical eye with constructive thinking.
- To find various ways of interpreting a piece of writing.
- To locate the issues of importance.
- To develop skills in paraphrasing and quoting from sources.
- To learn the techniques for acknowledging the sources that we cite.

This chapter will introduce three methods for building a paper.

Method one uses personal experience as the only source. The excerpt from *Zoya's Story,* beginning on page 3, demonstrates this method. The marginal notes highlight various writing issues we shall discuss in other chapters of this textbook.

Method two uses a response to outside sources. William Speed Weed in "Circles of Life," pages 8–11, borrows from the scientific work of astronomer Parren Williams. The essay by Weed, published in *Discover* magazine, demonstrates how interpretation can bring complex topics to a general audience. Marginal notes with the essay explain issues to be discussed in future chapters of this text.

Method three uses a combination of methods one and two. Latoya Waller in her essay "Freedom of Speech on Campus," pages 14–17, draws from personal experience as a woman of color to frame a rebuttal of a published article by Nat Hentoff.

G U I D E L I N E S

Sources for Writing

Personal Sources

Memory

Experiences

Conversations with others

Outside Sources

Books

Articles from the Internet, newspapers, magazines, and journals

Lectures

Television programs

Interviews and surveys

Using Personal Experience as a Source for Writing

Zoya is an Afghan woman who lost her mother and father under the Taliban rule in Afghanistan at the turn of the century. As a youngster, she was forced to flee into neighboring Pakistan. In *Zoya's Story: An Afghan Woman's Struggle for Freedom*, published in 2002, she tells her story to writers John Follain and Rita Cristofari. Her source, of course, is her life and her memories, both the bittersweet and the horrifying. Dressed in a burqa and confined with others in a minibus, Zoya returns to her homeland. The burqa becomes a clear symbol of the Taliban's oppression of Afghan women. The marginal notes explain points that we shall examine in more detail in various chapters of this text.

Prologue to *Zoya's Story*

At the head of the Khyber Pass, when we reached the border with Afghanistan at Torkham, our car stopped short of the Taliban checkpoint. Before getting out of the car, my friend Abida helped me to put the *burqa* on top of my shirt and trousers and adjusted the fabric until it covered me completely. I felt as if someone had wrapped me in a bag. As best I could in the small mountain of cheap blue polyester, I swung my legs out of the car and got out.

The burqa *covers every part of the woman's body. It serves as a symbol for one aspect of her life. For another example of a writer using symbolism, see the Sager essay, pages 405–411.*

The checkpoint was a hundred yards away, and I stared for a moment at my homeland beyond it. I had been living in exile in Pakistan for five years, and this was my first journey back to Afghanistan. I was looking at its dry and dusty mountains through the bars of a prison cell. The mesh of tiny holes in front of my eyes chafed against my eyelashes. I tried to look up at the sky, but the fabric rubbed against my eyes.

The *burqa* weighed on me like a shroud. I began to sweat in the June sunshine and the beads of moisture on my forehead stuck to the fabric. The little perfume—my small gesture of rebellion—that I had put on earlier at once evaporated. Until a few moments ago, I had breathed easily, instinctively, but now I suddenly felt short of air, as if someone had turned off my supply of oxygen.

The burqa *is like a prison cell or a shroud that denies her oxygen or feels like shackles on her legs. You, too, can use comparisons to enrich your personal narration (see pages 101–103).*

I followed Javid, who would pretend to be our *mahram*, the male relative without whom the Taliban refused to allow any woman to leave her house, as he set out for the checkpoint. I could see nothing of the people at my side. I could not even see the road under my feet. I thought only of the Taliban edict that my entire body, even my feet and hands, must remain invisible under the *burqa* at all times. I had taken only a few short steps when I tripped and nearly fell down.

When I finally neared the checkpoint, I saw Javid go up to one of the Taliban guards, who was carrying his Kalashnikov rifle slung jauntily over his shoulder. He looked as wild as the Mujahideen, the soldiers who claimed to be fighting a "holy War," whom I had seen as a child: the crazed eyes, the dirty beard, the filthy clothes. I watched him reach to the back of his head, extract what must have been a louse, and squash it between two fingernails with a sharp crack. I remembered what Grandmother had told me about the Mujahideen: "If they come to my house, they won't even need to kill me. I'll die just from seeing their wild faces."

I heard the Taliban ask Javid where he was going, and Javid replied, "These women are with me. They are my daughters. We traveled to Pakistan for some treatment because I am sick, and now we are going back home to Kabul." No one asked me to show any papers. I had been told that for the Taliban, the *burqa* was the only passport they demanded of a woman.

If the Taliban had ordered us to open my bag, he would have found, tied up with string and crammed at the bottom under my few clothes, ten publications of the clandestine association I had joined, the Revolutionary Association of the Women of Afghanistan. They documented, with photographs that made my stomach churn no matter how many times I looked at them, the stonings to death, the public hangings, the amputations performed on men accused of theft, at which teenagers were given the job of displaying the severed limbs to the spectators, the torturing of victims who had fuel poured on them before being set alight, the mass graves the Taliban forces left in their wake.

These catalogs of the crimes perpetrated by the Taliban guard's regime had been compiled on the basis of reports from our members in Kabul. Once they had been smuggled to the city, they would be photocopied thousands of times and distributed to as many people as possible.

But the Taliban made no such request. Shuffling, stumbling, my dignity suffocated, I was allowed through the checkpoint into Afghanistan.

As women, we were not allowed to speak to the driver of the Toyota minibus caked in mud that was waiting to set out for Kabul, so Javid went up to him and asked how much the journey would cost. Then Abida and I climbed in, sitting as far to the back as we could with the other women. We had to wait for a Taliban to jump into the minibus and check that there was nothing suspicious about any of the travelers before we could set off. For him, even a woman wearing white socks would have been suspicious. Under a ridiculous Taliban rule, no one could wear them because white was the color of their flag and they thought it offensive that it should be used to cover such a lowly part of the body as the feet.

The longer the drive lasted, the tighter the headband on the *burqa* seemed to become, and my head began to ache. The cloth stuck to my damp cheeks, and the hot air that I was breathing out was trapped under my nose. My seat was just above one of the wheels, and the lack of air, the oppressive heat, and the smell of gasoline mixed with the stench of sweat and the unwashed feet of the men in front of us made me feel worse and worse until I thought I would vomit. I felt as if my head would explode.

We had only one bottle of water between us. Every time I tried to lift the cloth and take a sip, I felt the water trickle down my chin and wet my clothes. I managed to take some aspirin that I had brought with me, but I didn't feel any better. I tried to fan

She returns as a member of a secret revolutionary group, the RAWA. She risks her life, and you, too, should write about a moment of your life that has deep inner meanings (see pages 260–268).

Zoya explains Taliban rules to show their absurdity, just as you might comment on oppression that has affected your life and colored your point of view (see pages 12–17).

myself with a piece of cardboard, but to do so I had to lift the fabric off my face with one hand and fan myself under the *burqa* with the other. I tried to rest my feet on the back of the seat in front of me so as to get some air around my legs. I struggled not to fall sideways as the minibus swung at speed around the hair-pin bends, or to imagine what would happen if it toppled from a precipice into the valley below.

I tried to speak to Abida, but we had to be careful what we said, and every time I opened my mouth the sweat-drenched fab-ric would press against it like a mask. She let me rest my head on her shoulder, although she was as hot as I was.

It was during this journey that I truly came to understand what the *burqa* meant. As I stole glances at the women sitting around me, I realized that I no longer thought them backward, which I had as a child. These women were forced to wear the *burqa*. Otherwise they faced lashings, or beatings with chains. The Taliban required them to hide their identities as women, to make them feel so ashamed of their sex that they were afraid to show one inch of their bodies. The Taliban did not know the meaning of love: women for them were only a sexual instrument.

She again focuses on the burqa *as a symbol for women subjugated by the Taliban men.*

The mountains, waterfalls, deserts, poor villages, and wrecked Russian tanks that I saw through the *burqa* and the mud-splattered window made little impression on my mind. I could only think ahead to when my trip would end. For the six hours that the journey lasted, we women were never allowed out. The driver stopped only at prayer time, and only the men were allowed to get out of the minibus to pray at the roadside. Javid got out with them and prayed. All I could do was wait.

T I P   *Write with a Mission*

Zoya has a mission in telling her story. She is not deeply interested in narrating the events of her life; instead, her goal is to address the travails of Afghan women under the rule of the Taliban. Seen through her eyes, the oppression of Afghan women under the Taliban becomes a powerful argument. This lesson provides a rhetorical principle for any writer: Write with a mission when you narrate your life, tell a story, or describe a member of your family. The events of your life make a statement, maybe one not as forceful as Zoya's, but one that, written from the heart, can provoke profound reactions from your readers.

It was not necessary for Zoya to visit a library to gather information. She had merely to look into her own heart. You, too, might be able to tell powerful messages

WEB LINK
to Reading
1.1
http://www.
ablongman.com/
lester

about child abuse, poverty, drug addiction, parental neglect, and other troubles in a list that could go on and on. Of course, personal topics need not be negative. You might narrate the nurturing value of a grandmother's kitchen, which was a testing ground for life and its adventures, or you might describe the triumph of training for and winning an athletic competition. In every case, you will be making a point—that your grandmother's kitchen, for example, gave you the strength of body *and* mind to persevere in your pursuit of a medal in freestyle swimming.

A reason exists for telling any story; that reason is like an underlying argument. For example, the back cover of the book by Zoya features a long list of Taliban rules that Zoya wishes to expose. Here are just a few:

- Ban on women being treated by male doctors.
- Ban on women studying at schools, universities, or any other educational institutions.
- Requirement that women wear a long veil *(burqa),* which covers them from head to toe.
- Whipping, beating, and verbal abuse of women not clothed in accordance with Taliban rules and women unaccompanied by a *mahram.*
- Whipping of women in public for having exposed ankles.
- Ban on women wearing shoes that produce sound while walking. (A man must not hear a woman's footsteps.)
- Ban on the photographing or filming of women.

This partial list demonstrates clearly that Zoya is not merely telling her life's experiences; she is making an argument against the exploitation and mistreatment of women in *all* cultures of *all* countries.

Zoya's essay demonstrates these ideas on using one's life as a source:

WEB LINK
to Exercise
1.1
http://www.
ablongman.com/
lester

- Write with a mission.
- Understand your reasons for using a scene from your life.
- Don't be afraid to show your emotions.
- Create a symbol that helps you focus the writing.
- Use concrete words and detailed images to paint pictures for your readers.

Researching and Composing from Sources: Analysis and Interpretation

Let's look now at a different kind of writing, one that uses ideas from textbooks, lectures, books, and scholarly articles. William Speed Weed's essay first appeared in the November 2002 edition of *Discover,* a scientific magazine that you can find at most newsstands. As you will see, Weed's writing differs greatly from that of Zoya. In brief,

WEB LINK
to Chapter 1
Related Web
Destinations
http://www.
ablongman.com/
lester

it summarizes scientific research, analyzes it, and interprets it for a lay audience, you and me, so that we can understand a little more about the way planets orbit the sun.

This assignment to read Weed's essay is relevant to your work, for you will also read complex essays and will need to find ways to summarize the material in capsule form. After all, you might one day be a law clerk helping to compose a piece of legislation for a state senator, who will ask you to write a brief research report on the pertinent laws and regulations. Or your work for a local chamber of commerce might require you to research the potential for growth of a local industrial park.

Weed's sources are scientific articles and an interview with the astronomer Parren Williams. In reading his essay, you will learn something about the methods writers use to explain and evaluate sources as well as the techniques for acknowledging borrowed ideas and for quoting or paraphrasing. However, the formal methods of citation that we will discuss in later chapters are not necessary here, as in quoting his sources Weed uses a magazine style, which does not require in-text page citations. Marginal notes to the essay comment on techniques used by Weed and direct you to discussion elsewhere in this text.

Circles of Life

William Speed Weed

Earth is a Goldilocks kind of place. Not too hot, not too cold. Things here are just right. We have a solid rock to stand on, liquid water to sustain us, and an atmosphere to shield us from radiation. Our cozy planet happens to lie just the right distance from the sun, in what astronomers call the habitable zone. But that's not all. On a larger scale, we live in a galaxy that is not too young, not too old. For a few billion years after the Big Bang there was nothing but hydrogen and helium in the cosmos— nothing to make up terrestrial planets. It took the first few generations of stars to forge heavier elements like oxygen, iron, and uranium, which may power Earth's churning, molten interior. By the time our sun formed 4.5 billion years ago, there was plenty of planet-making material around. But the universe is aging, and astronomers predict it will run out of radioactive uranium, potassium, and thorium, and planets that form later will be as dead as the moon.

Within our just-right galaxy, we also live in a just-right spot, about halfway out from the center—not too far in, not too far out. At the core of the Milky Way, the stars are packed together so tightly that they nearly collide with one another, and interstellar radiation would make life—or at least complex life as we know it—impossible. Out at the rim of the galaxy, there aren't enough stars to produce the heavy elements needed for terrestrial

In the opening three paragraphs, Weed uses a conversational tone to explain the topic—the Earth moves in "a nearly perfect circular orbit." You, too, will need to explain early and clearly the subject to be examined (see pages 307–314 for more tips on writing this type of introduction).

planets. Out there, you might get a rocky Mercury, about one-twentieth the size of Earth, but its gravity would be too weak to hold on to an atmosphere.

Here in our solar system, in the just-right spot around a just-right star, our Goldilocks planet runs laps around the sun in a nearly perfect circular orbit, always staying 93 million miles from the fire. For decades, astronomers assumed that an orbit like this was essential to habitability. A planet that moved in an oval or ellipse would swing too close to the sun at one end of its orbit and sail into the chilly beyond at the other end. If elliptical orbits prohibit life, it means that astronomers searching for Earth-like planets have fewer candidates to choose from. It also means that Earth is vulnerable. If a wandering star or a rogue black hole were to perturb the orbit of Jupiter, deforming Earth's orbit in turn—an extremely unlikely event, but astronomers estimate there are 10 million rogue black holes in the Milky Way—life on the planet would be destroyed.

Or maybe not. Astronomer Parren Williams and his colleagues at Pennsylvania State University at Erie have been studying elliptical orbits recently, and they think life on Earth can withstand a lot more tumult than scientists previously guessed. They have been running sophisticated computer models of planets in orbits of varying eccentricity circling suns of various sizes. "High eccentricity does not critically compromise planetary habitability," Williams says. Then he drops the astrobiology lingo and translates with a boyish smile: "These planets will still support life."

Weed introduces the theories of an astronomer, paraphrasing and quoting Parren Williams. You, too, will need to know these techniques, which are explained in Chapters 5 and 6.

With his dimpled cheeks, handsome face, and wardrobe of quiet collared shirts, Williams looks like a man who might draw his circles round. It was his mentor, renowned geoscientist Jim Kasting, who first defined the "habitable zone" in which planets could support life. The idea had been floating around since the 1960s, but in the early 1990s, Kasting used computer modeling to determine the zone's exact dimensions: between 79 million and 140 million miles from a star (farther out for hotter stars, closer in for cooler stars). Outside that narrow path, Kasting argued, "planets will overheat or freeze."

At the time, astronomers knew only of planets with fairly circular orbits. But when the first extra solar planets were discovered in 1995, some of their orbits were highly elliptical. Williams decided to see how life would fare in this unknown territory—and if his mentor's formula would hold. He teamed up with Penn State colleague David Pollard, a paleoclimatologist who has developed a respected computer model he uses to study Earth's ancient climate. The model, known as GENESIS2, is made up of 70,000 lines of computer code that mimic Earth's atmosphere, oceans, ice sheets, and a host of other factors, including the shape of its orbit. To push Earth into an oval orbit, all Pollard had to do was plug in a new number.

If an orbit is perfectly circular, in the model it is said to have an eccentricity of 0; a straight line has an eccentricity of 1. Earth's orbit is very close to the former—0.0167. Pollard and Williams decided to stretch it toward the other extreme. They ran models for eccentricities of 0.1, 0.3, 0.4, and 0.7. In each case, they kept the average distance of the orbit the same: Earth still made one lap of the sun in 365 days. They let each simulation run for 30 theoretical years and then looked to see what Earth's climate was like in the brave new orbits.

Weed summarizes the work of Williams and David Pollard. You, too, will need to use summary (see Chapter 4).

The least eccentric orbit—0.1—kept the planet inside the habitable zone all year long; not surprisingly, there was barely any change in climate. At higher eccentricities, though, things got interesting. As astronomer Johannes Kepler explained in 1609, the more elliptical a planet's path, the closer it gets to the sun at one end of its orbit (known as perihelion), and the farther from the sun it goes at the other end (known as aphelion). At an eccentricity of 0.3, the planet's orbit would pass inside the orbital path of Venus at perihelion and fly within 20 million miles of Mars at aphelion. In Pollard's model, though, even when Earth drew closer to the sun than Venus, it didn't develop a Venus-like climate. "Water has a very high heat capacity," Williams says, "so the large amount of water on Earth is slow to warm up." And the heat wouldn't last long. As Kepler also explained, planets on eccentric orbits travel fastest at perihelion, accelerating furiously. "Well before the oceans start boiling," Williams says, "the planet is racing away."

The magazine style for quoting sources, as used by Weed, requires no in-text page citations, but academic research papers will require them (see Chapters 10–12). A bibliography is also standard for research papers, but not for magazine articles.

At the other end of an eccentric orbit, Earth slows down again. But here the climate model takes a strange and welcome turn. The planet absorbs so much heat during its brief trip around the sun, Williams explains, that its coldest months out by Mars are still warmer than winter months on a circular orbit: The average global temperature is 73 degrees Fahrenheit, versus 58 degrees on Earth now. It's not a perfectly regulated system: Some parts of the African, South American, and Australian interiors heat up to 140 degrees at perihelion. But the extreme temperatures only last a month or two. . . .

. . . In the past seven years, more than 100 extra solar planets have been detected through a method known as radial velocity. Astronomers can't actually see these planets, only a telltale wobble in the stars that the planets are orbiting. But the amplitude and timing of the wobble can reveal a planet's size as well as the shape of its orbit. One star, 16 Cygni B, has a planet with

WEB LINK
to Reading
1.2
http://www.
ablongman.com/
lester

an eccentric orbit of 0.67; another star, HD222582, has a planet with an orbit of 0.71. Both these stars are brighter than our sun, but their planets have a wider orbit than Earth, so they pass straight through the habitable zone. The planets are gas giants like Jupiter and thus less likely to harbor life. But according to Williams's climate calculations, if they have large rocky moons, those moons could be habitable.

Here Kasting sounds a note of caution: "It's going to be very hard to detect those moons if they exist," he says, and the total population of planets in eccentric orbits may be small. Solar systems with elliptical orbits tend to be less stable than systems with circular orbits: Their planets can cross one another's path and bang into each other.

When astronomers get better at detecting planets, Kasting suspects, they will find a host of Earths out there, running circular orbits inside his habitable zone. Still, he says, Williams's work is "one more reason to be optimistic" that we can find another Earth—even if it is a bit more eccentric.

In a conclusion, Weed must arrive at a clear reason for the research and his own analysis. He shows how the work of Williams and others will help later scientists find "a host of Earths out there." In your own endings, you, too, must arrive at a clear conclusion about the subject (see pages 320–328 for an example of how one student synthesized his sources to reach his conclusion on mountain climbing).

T I P *Write to Explain and Even Simplify a Complex Subject*

William Weed had a mission in writing his article: to explain the work of astronomer Parren Williams and to show how Williams, on the cutting edge of paleoclimatology, provides models for variation in Earth's orbit. The work advances theories on the means of finding other habitable planets in the solar system. Thus Weed has done something that you will be asked to do—summarize a complex topic, borrow from the sources, acknowledge what you have borrowed, and make the subject *understandable* to your reader.

WEB LINK
to Exercise
1.2
http://www.
ablongman.com/
lester

Unlike the personal writing of Zoya, Weed had to study his sources carefully, read the scientific papers, and interview Parren Williams, David Pollard, and Jim Kasting, as well as read the ancient theories of Johannes Kepler. After gaining an understanding of the subject, Weed needed a reason for writing the article, and he found two topics particularly interesting: (1) the Earth can get knocked out of its orbit yet life will survive, and (2) habitable planets need not have a near-perfect elliptical orbit.

Thus, Weed's essay demonstrates these ideas:

- The writer must gain an understanding of the subject.
- The writer must summarize and simplify various concepts for a lay reader.
- The writer can quote phrases and sentences from the sources.
- The writer must explain the significance of the subject and justify the essay's message.

Writing to Combine Personal Experience and Outside Sources

WEB LINK
to Reading
1.3
http://www.
ablongman.com/
lester
You will soon be asked to write a paper that draws upon the ideas found in another source, and you may react personally to sources because of your experiences. To demonstrate the demand of such a writing assignment, let us look at the work of one student—Latoya Waller. An assignment in one of her college courses was to read an essay by Nat Hentoff entitled "Free Speech on Campus," originally published in *The Progressive* and republished in the reader being used in the course. The instructor then asked her to write an essay on Hentoff's idea. In the essay, Hentoff debates the forces of bigotry and racial attacks in conflict with free speech and open expression. Hentoff asks,

> What is to be done, however, about speech alone—however disgusting, inflammatory, and rawly divisive that speech may be?

He answers:

> At more and more colleges, administrators—with the enthusiastic support of black students, women students, and liberal students—have been answering that question by preventing or punishing speech. In public universities, this is a clear violation of the First Amendment.

Latoya Waller was given these specific directions by her instructor:

> Consider the stereotyping, the economic deprivations, and the personal slurs that many members of minority groups continue to suffer. Then decide which you believe is more important: totally free speech or the protection of the rights, feelings, and status of groups that have been discriminated against. Write an essay in which you argue that on college campuses protecting "equality and justice" either is or isn't more important that protecting freedom of speech. Provide specific examples to defend your position.

Waller faced two distinctive tasks—investigating the subject and writing the paper.

The Investigative Stage

The preliminary work for Waller and any other writer consists of three parts:

- Reading the source with a critical eye.
- Summarizing the basic ideas of the source.
- Thinking constructively about what you wish to do with the source.

Reading the Source

Critical reading and listening means that you must discriminate between useful information that contributes to and extends your understanding of the topic and triv-

WEB LINK
to Audio-
video 1.1
http://www.
ablongman.com/
lester

ial items or nonessential information. For example, your notes during a lecture reflect critical choices, as does your underlining and highlighting of material in a textbook. You are making logical choices about what you hear or read. In effect, you sit in judgment of the wisdom of the source, borrow details from it, and ultimately share that wisdom with your readers. In another example, you might search the Internet for articles on a topic, such as Legal Rights for Noncitizens, but you will probably dismiss some articles as trivial, read only parts of others, and download a few for close examination. Your investigative skills are at work. Waller focused on Hentoff's support of free speech no matter how inflammatory that speech might be. She had her focus and her mission—to disagree with Hentoff's position.

Summarizing the Source

You will begin to understand the words of another if you take the time to put the source into a capsule form that frames the basic ideas. Here is Waller's brief overview of Hentoff's position.

> Hentoff cites instances of racial bigotry but focuses heavily on institutional punishment against those making racist remarks, which punishment he views as a violation of the Constitution's amendment on free speech. He argues that free speech must not be tempered by groups promoting "equality and justice." Thus, the conflict pits open expression against sensitivity and racial awareness.

Note: Later sections of this textbook, especially Chapter 4, will help you write effective summaries.

Thinking Constructively

Constructive thinking requires you to absorb the information and make it a part of your presentation. You will learn new words and bring them into your discussion, such as *civil liberty, visa system, naturalization,* and *due process.* You will confront issues that force you to make choices (*liberal* vs. *conservative, civil rights* vs. *federal authority*). In addition, you will learn to write with sound reasoning. Constructive thinking answers a basic question: What does this material mean? For example, you might explain a term, such as *civil liberty,* and apply it to your discussion of the problem at hand.

Waller uses constructive thinking to relate her own experiences with bigotry. For her, the key terms were *equality and justice* in conflict with *freedom of speech.* To be fair, she had to think constructively about both terms, but ultimately she favored one side at the expense of the other. As you will see, she chose *equality and justice.*

The Performance Stage

Composing an essay from sources will require these tasks:

- Finding your own position.
- Selecting items for summary and quotation.

WEB LINK
to Informa-
tion on the
Writing
Process
http://www.
ablongman.com/
lester

- Introducing the topic in an inviting way.
- Writing a body that mentions the source often for support or rebuttal.
- Writing a conclusion that nails down the central mission of your work.

Now, let us read and analyze Waller's essay. Marginal notes describe the writing techniques and direct you to discussions elsewhere in the text.

Freedom of Speech on Campus

Latoya Waller

I was born in Clarksville, Tennessee, and the farthest I have traveled from here has been Southern Kentucky. Growing up, I did not experience much racism. I guess I was just lucky. However, at sixteen I worked through the summer at Opryland theme park in Nashville. My best friend at the time, a white guy named Josh, lived in Portland, Tennessee. One day during casual conversation, I had asked him for his home phone number. He then told me, "I can't give it to you; I'm not allowed to talk with black people." His parents were racists! Immediately, I was shocked and angry. Later, I was ashamed for my friend; I thought he had the perfect life. Nevertheless, what really surprised and disturbed me was the continued existence of people, like his parents, who condemned me to their son because of the color of my skin. I had lived in a naive world back then. Now that I am older, I know that racism remains a major problem in the United States.

Drawing on her personal experience as evidence, Waller opens with an anecdote (a brief story) to demonstrate a point. See pages 311–314 for more details about framing an initial statement of opinion.

I have discovered many different forms of racism. As a black American, I thought that the most hurtful form of racism was violence against a person of color, but I have learned that bigots can do serious damage without casting one stone. Unfortunately, these bigots exist in our higher learning programs and institutions. Education does not eliminate or overcome genetic hatreds.

All Americans have the right in the First Amendment of the Constitution to say whatever they wish. This concept of freedom of speech responded to strict restrictions by the British government. In that age and time free speech was needed so the common man could have a voice. The press used it to get the word out on desirable and undesirable government policies. It enabled patriots to debate openly the issues of separation without fear of reprisal. I don't think Madison and the other framers of the Constitution realized that the free speech provision could be and would be used by America's own people to protect their slander of fellow Americans. However, perhaps the amendment on freedom of speech has lost its usefulness. The only time I hear about freedom of speech is when someone slanders someone else and then uses freedom of speech as a ticket to get out of trouble. This abuse of the amendment happens more and more today, especially on college campuses across America.

Waller introduces racism as a campus issue, and you, too, will need to make central issues relevant in the heart of your essay (see pages 260–268 on making a response to another person's idea and pages 279–295 on writing a rebuttal).

After reading Nat Hentoff's essay, "Free Speech on Campus," I felt grave disappointment. Hentoff cites instances of racial bigotry but focuses heavily on institutional punishment against those making racist remarks, which punishment he views as a violation of the Constitution's amendment on free speech. He argues that free speech must not be tempered by groups promoting "equality and justice." Thus, the conflict pits open expression against sensitivity and racial awareness. If universities all over the country cannot defend the rights of minorities and women against the rights of so-called free speakers, then America can add this problem onto the list with all the others. Whatever happened to the belief that we were all created equal? Obviously, this is not on the minds of college teachers. Hentoff quotes a professor by the name of Carol Teblen, who says that "administrators are getting confused when they are acting as censors and trying to protect students from bad ideas" (608). Teblen states that people who are being verbally abused should not be protected because they will not learn the skills to cope (608). This concept offends me, and I protest against it. If a white person slaps me, I can call the police and file a criminal complaint. But if the same person walks up to me and calls me the "n" word to my face, I should do nothing but learn to live with it? There has to be a better way and a better answer.

The racism exists on many campuses not with just words but with posters and fliers as well. In addition, some administrators are supporting it because they want to steer clear of constitutional lawsuits. People who use freedom of speech to support their racist acts are cowards hiding behind a misinterpreted law. The public should be protected from them. Blacks and other minorities who were born here in America should never have to cope with being called names. Many professors think the same as Teblen; some work in almost every university in the country. I have heard some of my professors using undesirable language in reference to certain ethnic groups or calling on black students to respond to black poetry, as though a white person could not comprehend the poem! Why single out a person of color! Maybe the problem does lie with the administration, but for sure, educated professors should know not to promote bad ideas or support unjust prejudice.

Waller reacts to the words of Hentoff, but she also makes reference to the Constitution in order to explain the reasons for the free speech amendment. One source may send you to other sources (see pages 302–334 about using multiple sources in your essay).

Note Waller's inclusion of a specific page number, indicating where Teblen's quote can be found in Hentoff's article (see Chapter 6).

Waller extends the constitutional issue to modern-day applications and shows how people abuse the amendment. You, too, will need to make the issues relevant to your readers (see pages 274-272).

Waller paraphrases and then cites the sources, and you will be doing the same (see Chapter 5).

Waller makes her appeal: The public should be protected from racists who hide behind the law (see pages 311–314 for more information on making assertions).

The major problem seems to be that no one knows the boundaries of the law. Where does free speech end and racism begin? If I may use an analogy, free speech should be treated like trash burning. If I burn some trash in my own back yard, it is called normal; however, if I burn an American flag in front of the White House, I can expect to go to jail. In like manner, Joe Bigot can curse me privately, but he better not slander me in public. A slap in the face and a racial curse are equal in my eyes. University administrators should use their powers for good, not evil. It would be comforting to know that when I awaken in the morning and come to school, I could be assured that the people taking thousands of dollars away from me every year in tuition fees will be there to defend my rights as a black American woman.

Waller provides evidence drawn from her personal life and combines it with evidence from the sources. See pages 180–184 on blending sources into your writing.

What are Waller's sources?
- The essay by Hentoff.
- The quotation from Tebben.
- The Constitution and its First Amendment.
- Her knowledge of history and law.
- Her personal experiences as a woman of color.

T I P   *Write from Personal Experience and from Other Sources*

WEB LINK
to Exercise
1.3
http://www.
ablongman.com/
lester

Waller writes a personal essay on one level, for she examines events from her life that touch upon racism, the subject at hand. She also writes an analysis of and evaluation of Hentoff's essay. Thus, Waller's writing differs from that of Zoya and Weed. Zoya depended on her personal experience as the only source. Weed analyzed and reported objectively on scientific findings. Waller combines these methods and does something more: She disagrees with the source, and that technique is also a focus of this textbook, as you will see in Chapter 8.

Chapter Review

A writer discovers a topic (or is assigned one), contemplates the issues involved, does some critical reading and thinking, finds a mission, and voilá, the paper progresses to completion. Of course, there will be obstacles along the way, but one lesson of this text is to persevere. Time is both your enemy and your friend. The deadline will loom over you and haunt you, but a week or so gives you plenty of time to absorb and contemplate an issue. Also, the best papers sometimes start with the worst initial drafts. Writing a good paper does not require a burst of brilliance. What it does require is (1) patience, (2) a willingness to draw upon yourself as a source, and (3) a determination to examine the ideas of others as fertile ground for your contemplation, your rejection, or your endorsement.

Composing a paper from a network of sources makes a few demands, whether you write for English Composition 101, Biology 101, or Introduction to Marketing 201:

- Draw upon your personal experience as a valuable source.
- Read sources with a comprehensive and critical eye.
- Summarize a source to put it in capsule form.
- Paraphrase and quote from the source with proper acknowledgement.
- Write with a mission.

Chapter 1 Assignment: Responding to a Brief Essay

To practice the lessons of this chapter, start by reading this brief essay, originally published in *Discover* magazine (November 2002).

The Art of, Um, Speaking Clearly

Josie Glausiusz

Sometimes when we aren't too sure what we, uh, intend to say, we, um, pepper our speech with all sorts of strange sounds. This is a universal habit: Americans say *uh* or *um*, the Spanish *eh*, and the Japanese *eeto* or *anoo*. A pair of psychologists now report that, far from distracting the listener, these seeming nonsense sounds improve the clarity of speech. Herbert Clark of Stanford University and Jean Fox Tree of the University of California at Santa Cruz find that conversation carries two simultaneous streams of information. The first is the actual content of the words. The second—the *uhs* and *ums*—signals the pace of the speaker's thoughts. After analyzing hours of recorded conversation, the two researchers discovered that *uh* tends to precede a minor pause in talk, and *um* a major one. More surprising, Clark finds that *um*-sprinkled talk is easier to comprehend, perhaps because the filler sound alerts the listener that an unusual word is on the way. But woe betide the politician who allows such terms to intrude. "When I say *uh* and *um* in conversation, I'm saying 'I'm not ready to go on.' If you're a public speaker, you don't want to be telling your audience that," Clark says. A case in point: Not a single *uh* or *um* appears in the recorded inaugural speeches of American presidents between 1940 and 1996.

1. Write a one-sentence summary that captures the essential idea of the passage.
2. Write a paragraph on the same subject. In doing so, use the following techniques:
   - Listen to your own speech and borrow from your own habits as a speaker.
   - Listen to others who talk with you and borrow from them.
   - Borrow from the passage above by summarizing or quoting Glausiusz or the two scientists cited in the passage. Remember to name the person you are quoting or summarizing.

Do not be concerned if you are not yet confident about the mechanics of quoting and summarizing. These are skills that you will develop as you read and work on the exercises in later chapters.

Tracing the Work of Two Students

Kaci Holtz and Haley Fishburn have volunteered to display their writing as examples of the work you will face during the semester. At the end of various chapters in the text, we will look at their efforts to frame a topic, find sources, summarize and quote from them, and eventually to put together a complete paper. Holtz decided to research a communication topic: the problems of cross-gender communication. Fishburn chose a political science topic: the constitutional issues of declaring war—who can do it, the president, Congress, or both acting in accord.

Kaci Holtz could draw upon her personal experiences in her successes and failures in talking with men. But she also wanted to read some of the experts on the topic. Here is Holtz's writing proposal.

Writing Proposal

Kaci Holtz

English 1010

I am interested, perhaps even concerned at times, by the manner in which men and women misinterpret each other. My experience has shown that men and women have different styles of communication that affect both intended meanings and perceived meanings. My research will gather input from sources to learn more about cross-gender communication. I hope to find scholarly studies that have tested how differences in gender have an effect on communication. My working title is "Cross-Gender Communication: How Men and Women Misinterpret Each Other."

Haley Fishburn observed the nature of the new fighting forces that the United States was placing in harm's way. Here is Fishburn's writing proposal:

Writing Proposal

Haley Fishburn

English 1010

I live near Fort Campbell, Kentucky, so I have contact quite often with the military personnel at convenience stores and on campus. Sometimes a military person disappears from class meetings, and I know what has happened—they've been called out for maneuvers or—worse—active duty in a war zone. But these are not GI Joe types; instead, the soldiers are women, many of them married and, most notably, mothers. Thus, when the president and Congress declare war, they are putting a new kind of fighting force into play. A declaration of war is a deadly document, and we must be sure that our leaders abide by the Constitution. Thus, this paper will examine the Constitution as well as the actions by Congress and our presidents. The working title is "Declarations of War: The Constitution, Congress, and the President."

Finding and Choosing Your Sources

Sometimes, when asking for an essay, your instructor will designate specific readings. Most of the time, however, the instructor will not assign the readings but make a general assignment: "Write an essay on tax fraud," "Investigate the possibility of life on other planets," or "What is *tragic* about the Greek drama *Oedipus Rex?*" In such cases, you are on your own, and you may need an assortment of material—books and articles from the library, Internet articles, and perhaps an interview with a knowledgeable person or a questionnaire distributed to your fellow students.

In this chapter we will consider the rich assortment of sources that are available:

- At the library
- On the Internet
- In the field

The chapter also addresses two questions:

- How do I determine the best sources?
- Are these sources authoritative?

The answers will come from your diligence in looking for certain kinds of information—the author's credentials, the sponsoring institution, the date, and the documentation. If a source does not give you enough information to frame a fairly full bibliography entry, you should avoid citing it in your paper. For example, see Figures 2.1 and 2.2, which include portions of two articles on "errors in writing." Figure 2.1 shows two pages from *College Composition and Communication,* a reputable journal. The marginal notes explain why it is reliable as a source.

The opening page provides the name of the author, the title, an abstract, and publication data–journal (CCC), volume and issue numbers (53.1), and the date (September 2001).

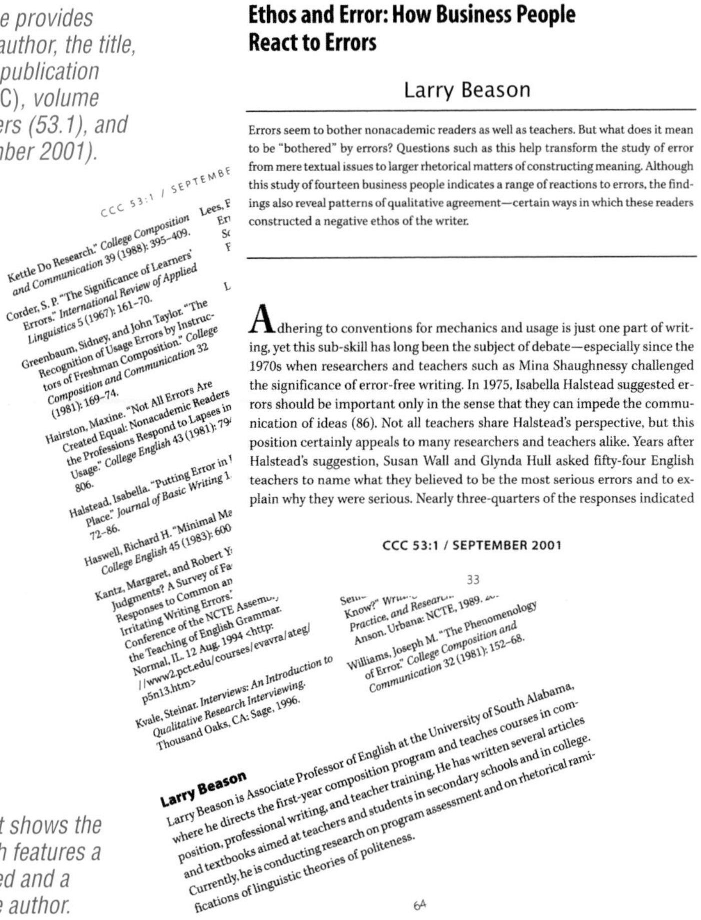

Ethos and Error: How Business People React to Errors

Larry Beason

Errors seem to bother nonacademic readers as well as teachers. But what does it mean to be "bothered" by errors? Questions such as this help transform the study of error from mere textual issues to larger rhetorical matters of constructing meaning. Although this study of fourteen business people indicates a range of reactions to errors, the findings also reveal patterns of qualitative agreement—certain ways in which these readers constructed a negative ethos of the writer.

Adhering to conventions for mechanics and usage is just one part of writing, yet this sub-skill has long been the subject of debate—especially since the 1970s when researchers and teachers such as Mina Shaughnessy challenged the significance of error-free writing. In 1975, Isabella Halstead suggested errors should be important only in the sense that they can impede the communication of ideas (86). Not all teachers share Halstead's perspective, but this position certainly appeals to many researchers and teachers alike. Years after Halstead's suggestion, Susan Wall and Glynda Hull asked fifty-four English teachers to name what they believed to be the most serious errors and to explain why they were serious. Nearly three-quarters of the responses indicated

CCC 53:1 / SEPTEMBER 2001

33

CCC 53:1 / SEPTEMBE

Kettle Do Research." College Composition and Communication 39 (1988): 395–409.

Corder, S. P. "The Significance of Learners' Errors." International Review of Applied Linguistics 5 (1967): 161–70.

Greenbaum, Sidney, and John Taylor. "The Recognition of Usage Errors by Instructors of Freshman Composition." College Composition and Communication 32 (1981): 169–74.

Hairston, Maxine. "Not All Errors Are Created Equal: Nonacademic Readers in the Professions Respond to Lapses in Usage." College English 43 (1981): 79

806.

Halstead, Isabella. "Putting Error in Place." Journal of Basic Writing 1. 72–86.

Haswell, Richard H. "Minimal Ma College English 45 (1983): 600

Kantz, Margaret, and Robert Y. Judgments? A Survey of Fa Responses to Common an Irritating Writing Errors." Conference of the NCTE Assem the Teaching of English Grammar. Normal, IL. 12 Aug. 1994 <http://www2.pct.edu/courses/evavra/ateg/p5n13.htm>

Kvale, Steinar. Interviews: An Introduction to Qualitative Research Interviewing. Thousand Oaks, CA: Sage, 1996.

Lees, E

Know?" Writ Practice, and Resear Anson. Urbana: NCTE, 1989.

Williams, Joseph M. "The Phenomenology of Error." College Composition and Communication 32 (1981): 152–68.

Larry Beason

Larry Beason is Associate Professor of English at the University of South Alabama, where he directs the first-year composition program and teaches courses in composition, professional writing, and teacher training. He has written several articles and textbooks aimed at teachers and students in secondary schools and in college. Currently, he is conducting research on program assessment and on rhetorical ramifications of linguistic theories of politeness.

64

The next excerpt shows the final page, which features a list of works cited and a biography of the author.

FIGURE 2.1 Excerpts from *College Composition and Communication.*

In summary, you are provided with significant information about Larry Beason and his essay. Now look at Figure 2.2, which is far less reliable.

The Internet material in Figure 2.2 is splashy with artwork and links to its various parts. Its advice is not unfounded, but certain things are missing: the name of the author, the author's credentials, a date, a sponsoring organization, and scholarly references.

WEB LINK to Audio-video 2.1
http://www.ablongman.com/lester

TIP ***Scrutinizing the Quality of Commercial (.com) Sites***

A commercial Internet site is intent on selling items, so the information that is offered is merely a byproduct to draw readers to the site and to the advertising. Thus, you will find academically excellent sources and you will find poor ones. Your task, with the help of this chapter, is to understand what to look for beyond the information itself, such as names of authors and sponsoring institutions as well as links to other reputable sites, not links to products for sale.

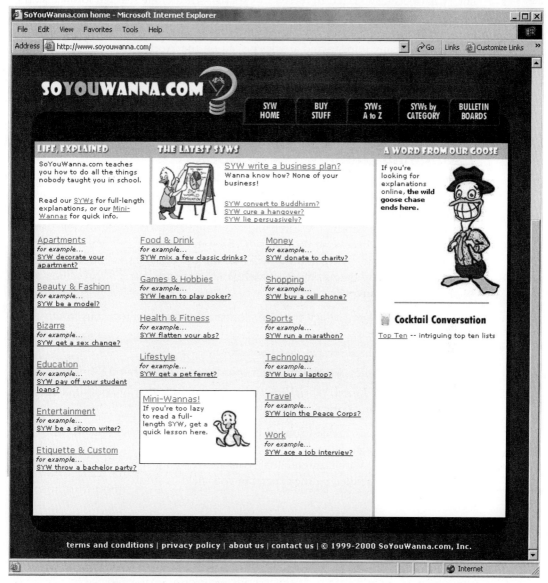

FIGURE 2.2 A nonacademic Internet site.

Searching the Library and Its Sources

WEB LINK
to Audio-
video 2.2
http://www.
ablongman.com/
lester

The library houses magazines, journals, books, and government documents in one convenient place with quiet cubicles for conducting your critical reading. Its computers can connect you to a wide array of reliable databases and scholarly Web sites. It thereby provides a safety net of reliable reading material. Most articles accessed in the library have been subjected to review by experts and carefully selected for inclusion in the library's holdings or within its computer sources. An article found on the library's academic databases, such as SilverPlatter or InfoTrac, has been screened for its scholarly value, unlike many unrestricted articles placed on the World Wide Web, where standards of excellence are sometimes absent.

In the library, begin your investigation for sources at the electronic catalog. Each library has its own system, with many windows, frames, and hyperlinks that direct you to different lists.

Examining the Indexes to Books

A college library is a repository for scholarly books, doctoral dissertations, publications of the university presses, reference works, and many textbooks. These books should be primary to your research; don't neglect them. Books cannot be as current as articles, but their depth of research and thoroughness make them valuable partners to any research project. Use the library's computer to make key word searches for books on your topic. The computer will indicate the call number and availability of each book. To locate the *best* book, consult your instructor, the reference librarian, or book reviews in sources such as:

> *Book Review Digest,* which features summaries and brief quotations from various review articles.
>
> *The Booklist,* which reviews new books for librarians.
>
> *Book Review Index,* which will direct you to reviews in about 225 magazines.
>
> *Contemporary Literary Criticism* (CLC), a database that provides full-text biographical and critical essays.

WEB LINK
to Chapter 2
Related Web
Destinations
http://www.
ablongman.com/
lester

You can find these book review sources in hardback form or, usually, online, using your university access code.

As not all books are created equal, your goal in your search should be the best authors, as recommended by the experts in your field of study.

Examining the Indexes to Articles

Scholarly articles on most topics can be accessed through the library's supply of general information databases, such as SilverPlatter, InfoTrac, EbscoHost, Electric Library, and others. State universities, or other academic groups, may be joined in a common database of sources. Just type in the key words of your subject (e.g., *depression* and *prozac*) and the database will give you citations to scholarly articles. You can click buttons to limit the search to:

- Full-text articles that you can print or save to a disk.
- Refereed scholarly articles, with popular magazines and newspapers eliminated from the search.
- Abstracts that summarize articles in about 100 words.

For example, a journal article about children and depression found in *Child Development* or in *Journal of Marriage and the Family* should be reliable, and you can read the abstract before requesting a printout of the entire essay.

In contrast, an article about depression in children found in a magazine or a Sunday newspaper supplement may be less reliable in its facts and opinions because these authors are not subjected to the rigorous standards of scholarly journals. Yet don't be deceived. Many magazines are noted for the quality of their essays—*Atlantic Monthly, Scientific Review, Psychology Today,* to name only three. The major newspapers—*New York Times, Atlanta Journal-Constitution, Wall Street Journal,* and others—hire the best writers and columnists, so many quality articles will be found in newspapers.

The Wilson indexes will also serve you well in hardbound or electronic form:

Readers' Guide to Periodical Literature

Social Sciences Index

Education Index

Humanities Index

These are comprehensive, interdisciplinary indexes, so your key word search will take you in many directions. In contrast, the discipline-specific databases, such as PsycInfo or Business Periodicals Index, direct you to works in their respective disciplines—for example, journals on psychology, business, astronomy, physics, or social work. The topic *depression and prozac* fits the health/medicine discipline, so you would make a key word search in medical journals, such as *PubMed, Health & Wellness,* and *CINAHL (Cumulative Index to Nursing & Allied Health Literature)*. You will find articles that address issues, like the one described in this database entry:

AUTHOR: Munro, R.
SOURCE: Nursing Times 2000 Jan 20-28; 96(3): 16
    ABSTRACT: With low-cost, generic Prozac on the cards, Robert Munro
      explores concerns that drugs are dominating treatment for depression at the
      expense of other therapies.
DOCUMENT TYPE: journal-article
DATABASE: CINAHL: Full Text: Available

EXERCISE 2.1

SEARCHING THE LIBRARY'S DATABASES

This exercise asks you to select a topic, choose from a list of citations, examine an abstract, and skim through the text of an article. At a computer linked to your library, look closely at the database sources it offers. Do you have general information databases, such as InfoTrac, SilverPlatter, Electric Library, or something similar? Do you have specialized databases, such as PsycInfo for psychology topics and MLA for literature topics? Enter the key words *depression* and *prozac* to see what sources the databases will supply. Find and print the opening page to one source, similar to that in Figure 2.3.

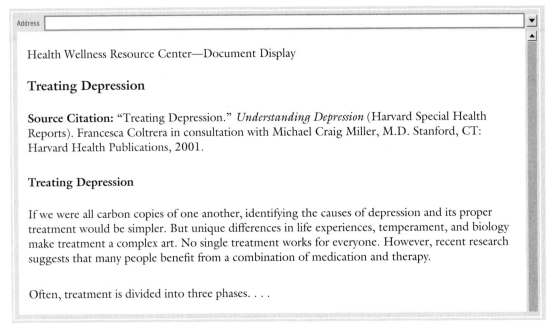

Address

Health Wellness Resource Center—Document Display

Treating Depression

Source Citation: "Treating Depression." *Understanding Depression* (Harvard Special Health Reports). Francesca Coltrera in consultation with Michael Craig Miller, M.D. Stanford, CT: Harvard Health Publications, 2001.

Treating Depression

If we were all carbon copies of one another, identifying the causes of depression and its proper treatment would be simpler. But unique differences in life experiences, temperament, and biology make treatment a complex art. No single treatment works for everyone. However, recent research suggests that many people benefit from a combination of medication and therapy.

Often, treatment is divided into three phases. . . .

FIGURE 2.3   Opening to an article on depression and Prozac found by a key word search.

Note: You may use a different key word search if you prefer.

Examining the Indexes to Biographies

WEB LINK to Audio-video 2.3
http://www.ablongman.com/lester

If your topic concerns a person, a biography can benefit your research. A biography will also inform you about the credentials of an author you wish to cite in your paper. Consult biographies for these reasons:

1. To verify the reputation of a person that you wish to cite in your paper.

2. To provide biographical details in your introduction. For example, the primary topic may be Carl Jung's psychological theories of the unconscious, but some information about Jung's life and career might be appropriate in the introduction.

WEB LINK
to Reading
2.2
http://www.
ablongman.com/
lester

3. To discuss a creative writer's life in relation to his or her work. For example, Joyce Carol Oates's personal life may shed light on your interpretation of her stories and novels.

The library's electronic resources will give you access to biographies in these databases:

Biography Index

Biography Reference Bank

Current Biography: 1940–Present

Current Biography Illustrated

Marquis Who's Who Online

Wilson Biographies Plus Illustrated

For example, in response to the key words *biographies* and *Winston Churchill*, the computer produced an article from *The Wilson Quarterly*, as shown in Figure 2.4 on page 28.

TIP   *Access to Electronic Files*

Many scholarly articles are located at sites that require a password. As a result, scholarly articles like those shown in Figures 2.3 and 2.4 must be accessed through your library's databases, *not* over the Internet via your browser.

Examining the Indexes to Newspaper Articles

WEB LINK
to Chapter 2
Related Web
Destinations
http://www.
ablongman.com/
lester

The standard bibliographic source for many years has been the *New York Times Index* in its printed form. Today, the best source is Newspapers.com. At this site you can research specific newspapers across the nation—for example, those in Denver, St. Louis, or Chicago. You can also access the archives of your local newspaper. Newspapers.com will help you search over 800 newspapers—from large ones such as the *Los Angeles Times* to small ones such as the *Aspen Times* or *Carbondale Valley Journal*, as demonstrated in Figure 2.5 on page 29.

Note: You can access Newspapers.com at the library or at any computer with Internet access.

TIP   *Using Hypertext Links*

At most Internet home pages, like the one for the *Larchmont Chronicle,* you have the opportunity to click on various hyperlinks not only for the feature stories but also for archives. Most archives have a search engine allowing key word searches of past issues. Magazine and journal sites also offer archival searches.

The Wilson Quarterly, Wntr 2002 v26 i1 p120(2)

Churchill: A Biography. (Current Books - History). (book review) *Jacob A. Stein.*

Full Text: COPYRIGHT 2002 Woodrow Wilson International Center for Scholars

Roy Jenkins. Farrar, Straus & Giroux. 1002 pp. $40

Winston Churchill had three contemporaries who he felt may, just may, have been up to his own standard as a world leader: David Lloyd George, Franklin D. Roosevelt, and Joseph Stalin. Each of the three has attracted many biographers, but few have been able to get behind the mask. Churchill's biographers do not have that problem. His psyche is exhaustingly documented in his own prodigious writings, Martin Gilbert's official biography of eight thick volumes, and countless other biographies.

Do we need another Churchill book? Jenkins answers by setting forth his unique qualifications. He has written well-received biographies of H. H. Asquith and William E. Gladstone. He has had wide parliamentary and ministerial experience. He served both as home secretary and Chancellor of the Exchequer, just as Churchill did. Both he and Churchill knew what is was like to wait for the call that didn't come, though Churchill's ultimately did come. Jenkins could have used in his defense Lord Chesterfield's words upon retiring: "I have been behind the scenes, both of pleasure and business. I have seen all the coarse pulleys and dirty ropes, which exhibit and move all the gaudy machines; and I have seen and smelt the tallow candles which illuminate the whole decoration to the astonishment and admiration of the ignorant audience."

Both he and Churchill knew what is was like to wait for the call that didn't come, though Churchill's

FIGURE 2.4   Full-text article accessed online.

Examining the Indexes to Government Documents

Your library's electronic database has made it much easier to search the gigantic files of the federal government. The Government Printing Office in Washington, D.C.,

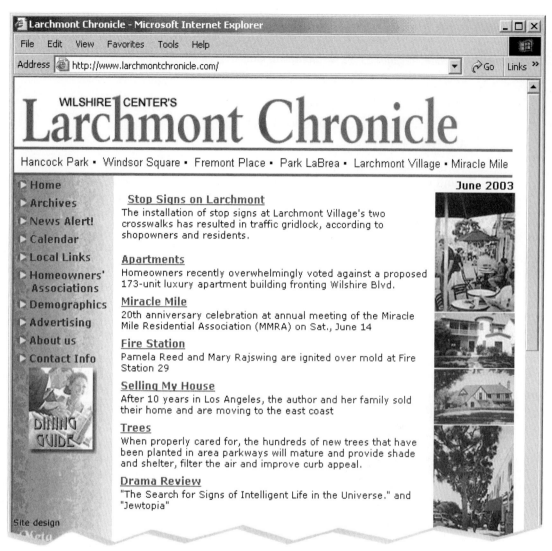

FIGURE 2.5   Home page of the *Larchmont Chronicle* as accessed by Newspapers.com.

WEB LINK
to Exercise
2.1
http://www.
ablongman.com/
lester

which produces well-written articles on almost any subject, can now be accessed at GPO on SilverPlatter in your library or at GPOAccess on the Web. Also available in print and/or electronic versions are:

Monthly Catalog of the United States Government Publications
Public Affairs Information Service Bulletin (PAIS)
The Congressional Record

Public Papers of the Presidents of the United States

The U.S. Code

Note: See pages 39–41 for additional guidelines on accessing government documents on the Web.

Examining the Indexes to Essays Within Books

You might find it helpful to search *Essay and General Literature Index,* either in a bound or electronic version. It identifies chapters or sections within books that you cannot locate in any other way. For example, a reference to R. A. Sherrill's *Religion and the Life of the Nation* would mean little to somebody researching the life of Martin Luther King Jr. Yet a key word search in *Essay and General Literature Index* produces this source:

King, Martin Luther, 1929–1968
Raboteau, A. J. Martin Luther King and the tradition of black religious protest. *In* Religion and the life of the nation; ed. R. A. Sherrill, pp. 46–65.

This article would be overlooked without *Essay and General Literature Index,* so make it a regular practice to use a key word search at this important database to locate thousands of essays buried within books as chapters and monographs.

GUIDELINES

Searching the Library

- Trust the library's computers to guide you to excellent works that have been edited and peer reviewed. There is no absolute test for scholarly excellence, but the academic databases maintain a high standard of integrity.
- Gather a mixture of library sources—books, magazine articles, journal articles, and photocopies of reference book entries.
- Document your notes to sources in case you must build a bibliography.
- Access the library's resources often. With your username and password, you can visit the library from the dorm room, your home, or while on spring break. Snowstorms are no longer an excuse.
- Don't let the richness of sources overwhelm you. Go for what you need right now; do not linger over odd or interesting articles by clicking on one link after another until you've lost your primary article or home page.

Searching the Internet and Its Sources

You will find many of the same sources on the Web as you have in the library, with some variations in presentation, but the tools for access are different. This section will review the variations in Web sites and how to access sites. Remember, as with print sources, some articles will be superior in quality to others. Your task is to find reliable, scholarly sources that will enhance the quality of your paper.

Consulting Home Pages

You can locate home pages for individuals, institutions, and organizations by using a search engine, such as Google or Yahoo! For example, go to **http://www.google.com**, type in the words *George W. Bush*, and you can find a link to the president's home page, **http://www.whitehouse.gov/president/** as shown in Figure 2.6 on pages 32–33.

Figure 2.6 shows how the technique differs between print and Internet searches. The home page itself has little value as a source of information, but clicking a hypertext link will transport you to information sites such as *Presidential Biography, President Bush's Cabinet, Oval Office History,* and so forth. Also, this home page, like many others, has an internal search engine in the upper right corner for entering your particular key words.

T I P   *The Speed of Hyperlinks*

The highlighted links to more specific information are what set the Internet apart from all former methods of research. With the click of the mouse you can find another piece of information relevant to your work, and then click right back to where you were. The speed of access dazzles older researchers, like your author, who recalls tedious step-by-step detective work in library archives.

Searching for Articles on the Internet

In general, you will find four types of articles on the Internet.

1. Articles first published on the Internet. They are originals and may or may not list a sponsoring organization.

2. Articles copied to the Internet from print sources. These will usually show the host publication, such as a magazine or scholarly journal.

3. Abridged or condensed articles. These are usually online versions of daily or weekly publications such as *USA Today.*

4. Articles on zines, or underground fringe sites, published privately by individuals.

FIGURE 2.6   Home page of the President of the United States.

A key word search in your browser will produce articles in all of these categories, although you might need to ask specifically for "zines" (e.g., "zines on health and fitness").

Approach with caution any article that has no author listed, no affiliation with an organization or institution, and no indication about the source of the work. That lack of information should send out warning signals to you. Remember that your documented research paper will require the following items in the bibliography entry for an electronic source:

Author

Title

Affiliation or organization

Date of the original posting

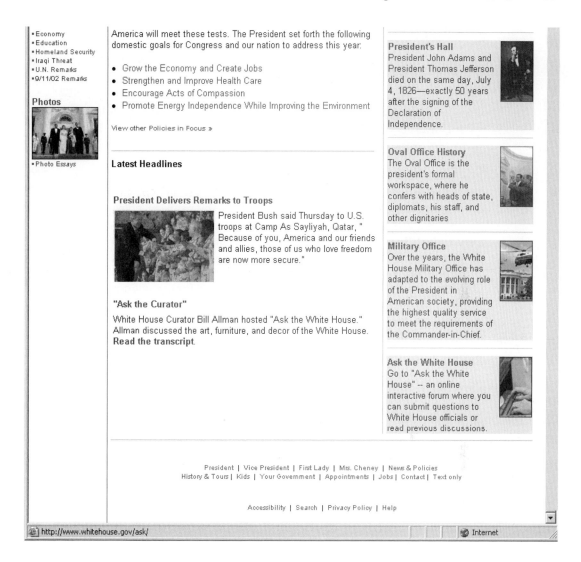

Date of your access

Address (the URL)

On occasion, one or even two of these items might be missing; however, you should avoid sources that contain only a title and the URL, as these cannot be properly documented. If an online article seems valuable but lacks information on the sponsor, go to the URL for more information. You may need to truncate the URL. For example, if you truncate

http://www.uark.edu/depts/physinfo/up2/k-12/magic2.html

you will get

http://www.uark.edu/depts/physinfo

which, you will discover, is the Web site for the Arkansas Precision Education Group at the University of Arkansas, a reputable site.

T I P   *Using Electronic Publications*

Online versions of articles offer several advantages, so don't let anybody discourage you from using the Web. You can view articles almost instantly, download files efficiently, and scan graphics and photographs into your text. Search engines and hyperlink buttons move you through the literature efficiently. Almost all the great works of literature are on the Web, as are classics in history, science, and other disciplines. Reading an online version of poem by Robert Frost accessed from your dorm room is just as effective intellectually as reading a print version accessed by walking to the library.

Finding Journal Articles on the Web

You can find the best online articles in several ways, but don't overlook number four below, the archival route to good material.

1. **Key word search.** A search for *online journals* and *women's studies* produces links to relevant journals such as *Feminist Collections, Resources for Feminist Research,* and *Differences.*

2. **Subject directory.** Selecting *Social Science* from the key directory accesses links to online journals such as *Edge: The E-Journal of Intercultural Relations* and *Sociological Research Online.*

WEB LINK
to Chapter 2
Related Web
Destinations
http://www.
ablongman.com/
lester

3. **Direct access.** A key word search for *Cognitive Therapy and Research, Speech Technology,* or *Journal of Sociology* leads to a link to the requested journal.

4. **Archives.** You can find non-current articles. A key word search to *archives* and *mental health articles* produces links to Archives of Women's Mental Health, Health Resource News Center Archives, and NCSU Libraries—Archives of Women's Mental Health.

The link provided by this text to journals on the Web (see the left margin) takes you to a site that shows you how to find scholarly journals on the general Web. You need not always go through your library's network of databases. Figure 2.7 shows a scholarly article located through a search at Google.

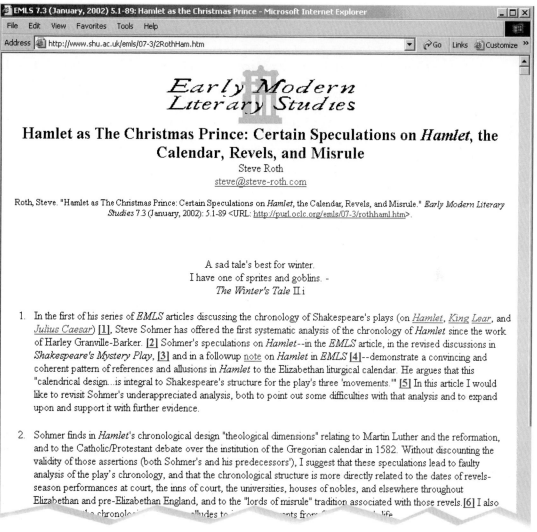

FIGURE 2.7   Article on *Hamlet* in *Early Modern Literary Studies*.

T I P   *Avoid Quoting from Abstracts*

Abstracts are summaries of an entire article, and they may not accurately represent the full article. In fact, many abstracts are not written by the author but by an editorial staff. Therefore, resist the desire to quote directly from the abstract. Instead, write a summary of your own to relay the ideas or, better, go in search of the full article. Chapters 4 and 5 will help you in writing summaries and paraphrases.

Finding Magazine Articles on the Web

Do not dismiss magazines as a good source of information. Magazines such as *Discovery* and *Scientific American* bring complex scientific theory to the lay reader. *The Atlantic Monthly* and *Harper's Magazine* go in search of the very best writers. In addition, magazine home pages on the Web will have links to more valuable information. Several directories exist for discovering magazine articles:

1. NewsDirectory.com at **http://www.ecola.com/new/** takes you to magazine home pages where you can begin your free search in a magazine's archives. Under "current events," for example, it will send you to *The Atlantic Monthly* at **http://www.theatlantic.com**, *Harper's* at **http://www.Harpers.org**, and *Newsweek* at **http://www.Newsweek.com**.

2. Electric Library at **http://www3.elibrary.com/** has a good search engine but requires membership, which is free for one month. Remember to cancel your membership after research is finished or charges will accrue.

3. Pathfinder at **http://pathfinder.com/** gives free access to *Time Magazine* and has a good search engine to thousands of archival articles.

4. ZD Net at **http://www.zdnet.com/** provides excellent access to industry-oriented articles on banking, electronics, computers, management, and so on. The site offers two weeks of free access before charges begin to accrue.

5. The subject directories at Alta Vista, Google, Yahoo!, and other search engines will take you to online magazines. For example, one student accessed Alta Vista, clicked on *Health and Fitness* in the directory on the home page, clicked on *publications*, then *magazines*. The result was a list of 40 magazines devoted to various aspects of health and fitness, such as *Healthology* and *Health Net*.

WEB LINK
to Chapter 2
Related Web
Destinations
http://www.
ablongman.com/
lester

EXERCISE   **2.2**

SEARCHING THE INTERNET FOR MAGAZINE ARTICLES

Most major magazines have online versions, and most provide free access to some of their articles. To see an example of what is available, go online to one of these sites:

http://www.theatlantic.com

http://www.discover.com

Find and click on the *Archive* button, as shown in Figure 2.8. Use the *Search* feature to find an article of interest. Print the abstract or a portion of the first page.

Accessing Online Newspapers and Other Media

Go to **http://www.newspapers.com** to locate almost any newspaper in the United States. You can find even small-town publications (see page 29 for an

FIGURE 2.8   Home page of *The Atlantic Online*.

example). In addition, most major news organizations maintain Internet sites. Consult one of these:

The Chronicle of Higher Education at **http://www.chronicle.com** requires a paid subscription but has great value for students in education.

CNN Interactive at **http://www.cnn.com** has a good search engine and takes you quickly without cost to transcripts.

C-SPAN Online at **http://www.c-span.org** emphasizes public affairs and offers both a directory and a search engine to transcripts. Good for research in public affairs, government, and political science.

Fox News at **http://www.foxnews.com** offers a mix of sources from Fox News, Reuters, and other news providers.

London Times at **http://www.the-times.co.uk/news/pages/Times/front page.html** provides directories and indexes but no search engine, so improve your search for articles in the *Times* with **http://www.searchuk.com**.

National Public Radio Online at **http://www.npr.org** provides audio articles, not print, so be prepared to listen closely and take careful notes.

The New York Times on the Web at http://www.nytimes.com offers recent articles for free. However, articles in the 365-day archive have a modest cost. After purchase, you can print and download them.

WEB LINK
to Chapter 2
Related Web
Destinations
http://www.
ablongman.com/
lester

USA Today DeskTopNews at http://www.usatoday.com has a fast search engine and will provide information about current events.

U.S. News Online at http://www.usnews.com has a fast search engine to help you find in-depth articles on current political and social issues.

Wall Street Journal at http://www.wsj.com has excellent business and investment information, but it requires a subscription.

The Washington Times at http://www.washingtontimes.com/ has up-to-the-minute political news and commentary.

The CQ Weekly at http://library.cq.com keeps tabs on congressional activities in Washington.

T I P   *Credit Internet Sources as Well as Print Sources*

If you borrow ideas or quotations from an Internet source, cite the Internet source to avoid giving the appearance that you are citing from the printed version. Internet texts often differ from the printed version. For example, major differences exist in the print version of *USA Today* and the online version of *USA Today DeskTopNews*. For a personal essay written in magazine style, identify the source in this manner: "'Congress must participate in any declaration of war,' says Robert Mitchum in *C-Span Online*," or "*Discover Magazine Online* reports that sonoluminescence might trigger nuclear fusion." In a research paper, supply a full reference to the source, including the URL.

EXERCISE 2.3

SEARCHING THE ONLINE MEDIA

Try your hand at finding a radio program of interest. Go to:

National Public Radio Online at http://www.npr.org.

WEB LINK
to Chapter 2
Related Web
Destinations
http://www.
ablongman.com/
lester

Select one program and listen to it, or click on *NPR Hourly News* and access it with *RealAudio* or *Windows Media*. As you listen, consider how you would take notes from the audio program. Remember, one advantage of the online version as opposed to listening on the radio is that you can replay the program to freshen your memory of what was said. Figure 2.9 shows a NPR home page. The link for NPR Hourly News is in the left column. However, keep in mind that these home pages frequently change their design.

FIGURE 2.9   Home page for National Public Radio Online.

WEB LINK
to Chapter 2
Related Web
Destinations

http://www.
ablongman.com/
lester

Finding Government Documents Online

GPOAccess on the Web gives you access to all government documents, including presidential papers, laws, and congressional bills and committee reports. At the Web site of the National Archives and Records Administration, **http://nara.gov,** you can click on one or more of these sites:

Research Room

Federal Register

Exhibit Hall

Digital Classroom

Records of Congress

Presidential Libraries

EXERCISE 2.4

ACCESSING GOVERNMENT DOCUMENTS

This exercise asks you to conduct a computer search using GPO on Silverplatter or GPOAccess on a Web browser. Figure 2.10 shows the home page of GPO Access, and Figure 2.11 shows the opening of a speech in the House of Representatives by Patsy T. Mink.

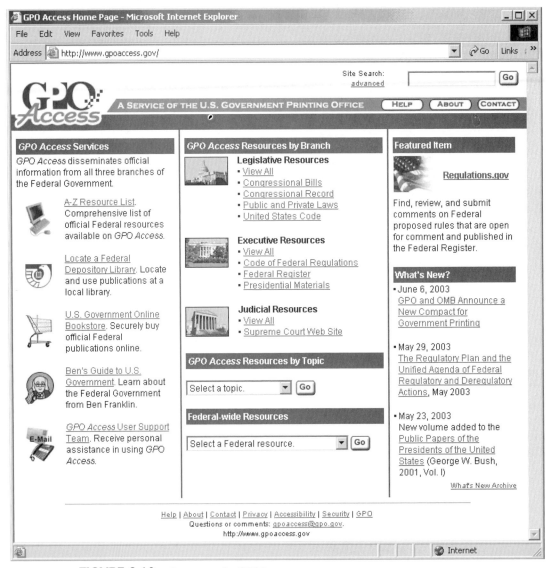

FIGURE 2.10   Home page for GPOAccess.

> ### ESTABLISHING FIXED INTEREST RATES FOR STUDENT AND PARENT BORROWERS
>
> SPEECH OF
> ## HON. PATSY T. MINK
> OF HAWAII
> ### IN THE HOUSE OF REPRESENTATIVES
> *Thursday, January 24, 2002*
>
> Mrs. MINK of Hawaii. Mr. Speaker, I rise today in support of S. 1762, which will provide students with low interest rates on Federal student loans, while preserving the health of the student loan industry by ensuring the current and future participation of lenders in this market. By helping lenders stay in the student loan markets, we are making sure that qualified students will have access to higher education, regardless of their financial background.
>
> S. 1762 represents a compromise between those representing students, and those representing the lending industry. This compromise essentially fixes a problem that would have arisen in 2003 in the student loan interest rate formula that, according to the lending community, would have dried up resources for students needing funds for college by potentially reducing returns for such loans below the cost of issuing such loans. S. 1762 preserves the current interest rate formula that determines how much lenders receive from the Federal

FIGURE 2.11   Opening paragraphs of a speech by Representative Patsy T. Mink of Hawaii.

WEB LINK
to
Government
Documents
http://www.
ablongman.com/
lester

Your assignment is to find similar documents for someone in your state's congressional delegation. Go to GPO on SilverPlatter (the library's database) or GPOAccess on the Web, click on *Congressional Record*, and at the *Search* window, type your local representative's name. Locate the text of a speech by your local representative. Print the article.

Accessing Entire Novels and Books Online

One of the best sources of full-text, electronic books is the Online Books Page at the University of Pennsylvania, **http://digital.library.upenn.edu/books/**, which

Address [   ]

The Picture of Dorian Gray

1890, 13-Chapter Version

Chapter 1

The studio was filled with the rich odor of roses, and when the light summer wind stirred amidst the trees of the garden there came through the open door the heavy scent of the lilac, or the more delicate perfume of the pink-flower thorn.

From the corner of the divan of Persian saddle-bags on which he was lying, smoking, as usual, innumerable cigarettes, Lord Henry Wotton could just catch the gleam of the honey-sweet and honey-colored blossoms of the laburnun, whose tremulous branches seemed hardly able to bear the burden of a beauty so flame-like as theirs. . . .

FIGURE 2.12   Opening of an electronic novel from the digital library at the University of Pennsylvania.

WEB LINK
to Reading
2.3
http://www.
ablongman.com/
lester

indexes books by author, title, and subject. It has a search engine that will take you quickly, for example, to the full text of Thomas Hardy's *A Pair of Blue Eyes* or to Linnea Hendrickson's *Children's Literature: A Guide to the Criticism*. Understand, however, that contemporary books, still under copyright protection, are not included; you can download an Oscar Wilde novel (see Figure2.12) but not one by John Updike.

Accessing E-mail News Groups

A *Listserv* is a program through which discussion groups correspond via e-mail on specific educational or technical subjects. For example, your literature professor might ask everybody in the class to join a Listserv group on Victorian literature. To participate, you would send an e-mail message to a Listserve address and subscribe to the group's mailing list. The Discussion Board for *Blackboard's* online system functions in similar fashion. To access a Listserv on your own, consult one of these sites:

L-Soft at http://www.lsoft.com/catalist.html where you can browse any of about 42,000 public Listserv lists on the Internet.

Egroups at http://www.egroups.com where you participate in such areas as Health and Fitness, Home, Recreation, Reference and Education, Science, and Sports.

Liszt at http://www.liszt.com to search a main directory of more than 90,000 mailing lists. Also click on a topic, such as Computers (250 lists), Health (271 lists), Humanities (254 lists), and many others.

Tile.Net at http://www.tile.net/ to access mailing lists, usenet newsgroups, and FTP sites.

T I P   *Using E-Mail, Discussion Boards, and Chat Groups*

Corresponding on the Internet is much like carrying on a conversation in the hallway. It is called "chatting." You might get an idea or two, but you cannot adequately document the sources, so as a general rule *do not use e-mail or chat in your research paper.* If by chance something is worthy, you will need to identify it in your text: for example, "Professor Carl Fisher has argued that history quite often plays a negative role in America's foreign policy (e-mail message, Nov. 3, 2003)."

Using Internet Access to Examine Library Holdings

Most public and government libraries now offer access to their collections via the Web, which will allow you to search their collections for books, videos, dissertations, audiotapes, special collections, and other items. You may sometimes order books through interlibrary loan online. Additionally, some libraries now post full-text documents, downloadable bibliographies, databases, and links to other sites.

> The Library of Congress at **http://www.loc.gov** allows you to search by word, phrase, name, title, series, and number. It provides special features, such as an American Memory Home Page, full-text legislative information, and exhibitions, such as the various drafts of Lincoln's Gettysburg Address.

> LIBCAT at **http://www.metronet.lib.mn.us/lc/lc1.html** gives you easy access to almost 3,000 online library catalogs.

> LIBWEB at **http://sunsite.berkeley.edu/libweb** takes you to home pages of academic, public, and state libraries. You will be prompted for a public-access login name, so follow directions for entering and exiting the programs.

> Carl UnCover at **http://www.carl.org.uncover/** provides a key word search of 17,000 journals by author, title, or subject. Copies of the articles will be faxed, usually within the hour, for a small fee.

Finding an Internet Bibliography

You can quickly build a bibliography on the Internet. At a search engine, such as Alta Vista, enter a descriptive phrase, for example, "child abuse bibliographies." You will receive a list of bibliographies, and you can click on a hyperlink, such as *Child Abuse* to get a citation and abstract, as shown here:

Child Sexual Abuse Bibliography—National Child Protection Clearinghouse Page 1 of 1

Goldman, J D G; Padayachi, U K. School counselors' attitudes and beliefs about child sexual abuse. Journal of Family Studies v.8 no.1 Apr 2002: 53-73, tables

School counselors are in a unique position to address child sexual abuse. However, little is known about their attitudes and beliefs on the issue. In order to examine these, all school counselors in Queensland were sent a questionnaire to ascertain their attitudes and beliefs about child sexual abuse. Results show that the 122 school counselors who responded, consisting of 52 males and 70 females, believe they have an important role in the detection of child sexual abuse. They believe they are the appropriate professionals to be part of programs aimed at preventing it. School counselors strongly object to sexual activities between adults and children, and overwhelmingly believe that sexual relationships education should not be left to parents. Most school counselors believe that children should help to legally prosecute adult perpetrators. Most school counselors also believe that child sexual abuse is a moderate or serious problem in Australia, but is less prevalent in their local community than in the country as a whole. (Journal abstract)

Available from: School of Public Health, La Trobe University, Bundoora Vic 3083. Email L.Morrison@latrobe.edu.au Hall, J.

Investigating Online Book Stores

WEB LINK to Chapter 2 Related Web Destinations http://www. ablongman.com/ lester

Use the search engines of Amazon.com and BarnesandNoble.com to gain a list of books currently in print. In most cases, the books on the list will be available in your library. For example, one student searched Amazon.com for books on "cross-gender communication." She found an entry for Charles Ess, *Culture, Technology, Communication: Toward an Intercultural Global Village,* 2001. She could order the book or search for it at the library.

Conducting Archival Research on the Internet

WEB LINK to Reading 2.4 http://www. ablongman.com/ lester

The Internet offers research into library and museum archives, where you will find online documents and records of historical interest. If you need these types of manuscripts for your project, consider several ways to conduct a search.

1. Ask your librarian about archival material on your topic. Even small libraries often have very valuable collections of local history. A topic such as "The Rise and Fall of Steamships" might invite you to make an archival study.

2. Search the library's electronic book catalog for "collections" and "archives." The Stanford University Library, for example, offers links to antiquarian books, manuscripts, and university archives. It also provides ways to find material by subject, by title, and by collection number. It carries the researcher to a link, such as *London (Jack) Papers, 1897–1916 (m0077) [html].*

3. Use a general search engine, such as Yahoo!, which may give you results quickly. For example, requesting "Baltimore archives" produced such links as *Special Collections at the University of Baltimore* and the Archive Index to *Baltimore CityPaperOnline.*

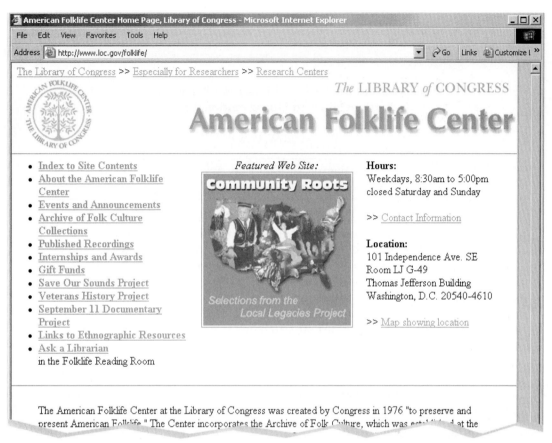

FIGURE 2.13   The Library of Congress American Folklife Center.

4. Use the directory and subdirectories of a search engine and let it take you deeper and deeper into the files. Remember, this tracing goes quickly. Here is an example:

Yahoo! ⟶ social science ⟶ anthropology and archeology ⟶ cultural anthropology ⟶ American Folklife Center ⟶ Archive of Folk Culture Collections

Figure 2.13 shows one of the stages of this search.

EXERCISE 2.5
JUDGING INTERNET ARTICLES

Shown in Figure 2.14 are the opening paragraphs of an online article. Study the material and then respond to the questions that follow.

Address | http://memory.loc.gov/ammem/mtjhtml/mtjprece.html

Thomas Jefferson Papers: America and the Barbary Pirates

America and the Barbary Pirates: An International Battle Against an Unconventional Foe

By Gerald W. Gawalt

Gerard W. Gawalt is the manuscript specialist for early American history in the Manuscript Division, Library of Congress

Ruthless, unconventional foes are not new to the United States of America. More than two hundred years ago the newly established United States made its first attempt to fight an overseas battle to protect its private citizens by building an international coalition against an unconventional enemy. Then the enemies were pirates and piracy. The focus of the United States and a proposed international coalition was the Barbary Pirates of North Africa.

Pirate ships and crews from the North African states of Tripoli, Tunis, Morocco, and Algiers (the Barbary Coast) were the scourge of the Mediterranean. Capturing merchant ships and holding their crews for ransom provided the rulers of these nations with wealth and naval power. In fact, the Roman Catholic Religious Order of Mathurins had operated from France for centuries with the special mission of collecting and disbursing funds for the relief and ransom of prisoners of Mediterranean pirates. . . .

FIGURE 2.14   "America and the Barbary Pirates," accessed at the Thomas Jefferson Papers, **http://memory.loc.gov/ammem/mtjhtml/mtjprece.html**.

1. Is the author identified?
2. What is the author's professional occupation?
3. Does the author write for a reputable organization?
4. What, exactly, is the sponsoring organization? To find it, truncate the URL to **http://memory.loc.gov/.**

Figure 2.15 shows the home page of the American Memory site at **http://memory.loc.gov/.** Study the material and then respond to the questions that follow:

1. Does this site give authenticity to the article by Gawalt?
2. Would this page serve as a launching pad for research into American history?
3. Would this be a good source to cite in a research paper?

FIGURE 2.15   American Memory home page, **http://memory.loc.gov/**.

WEB LINK
to Exercise
2.2
http://www.
ablongman.com/
lester

GUIDELINES

Accessing Internet Sources

- Use the hypertext links to carry you deeply and quickly to information, but don't get distracted from your central mission.
- Do take advantage of your ability to download articles, graphics, and photographs.
- Avoid using direct quotations from abstracts, which are often *not* written by the author.
- Use the internal search engines at home pages of journals, magazines, and newspapers, and remember to check out the archives.
- Identify Internet sources in your paper, just as you would identify a printed source.
- Be reluctant to cite in your paper information from e-mail or chat groups.
- Subject Internet articles to careful scrutiny by looking for the name of the author, the sponsoring organization, and links to other educational sites, and by carefully evaluating the general intellectual quality of the material.

Collecting Data Beyond the Library and the Internet

Field research refers to investigations by observation, survey, interview, archeological digging, questionnaire, and similar research on the street corner, in courthouses, at a riverbed, or in a wilderness area. Laboratory research refers to investigations made under designed conditions with controlled methods of procedure. Granted, in first-year courses a student is not likely to venture far into the field nor face complex lab problems; nevertheless, you should understand that research often goes beyond the library and the Internet. Talk with others by interview, letter, or e-mail. Administer a questionnaire if time permits. Watch the Discovery channel and television specials. Visit the courthouse archives. Do some observational research under the guidance of an instructor.

TIP   *Conducting Your Own Field Research*

Once you have a topic in mind, let's say it's *the impact of affirmative action*, gather the e-mail addresses of your classmates. Then conduct an e-mail survey that raises a few key questions that can be answered quickly. If your topic is a matter of history, perhaps *the role of women in the military during World War II*, you might write your grandparents for their insight. If your topic is *global warming*, you might go to your weather service to investigate the climatic shifts and changes locally over the past two decades. In truth, every topic will usually lend

(continues)

> *(continued from previous page)*
> itself to field research. Even literary and historical subjects can take you into the field to visit the home of Ernest Hemingway in Key West or to walk the fields where the Civil War's Battle of Gettysburg was fought.

Interviewing Knowledgeable People

Talk to people who have experience with your subject to elicit valuable in-depth information. For example, if you are writing on a folklore topic, you might contact the county historian, a senior citizens organization, or a local historical society. If necessary, post a notice soliciting help:

> I am writing a study of local folklore. Wanted: people with a knowledge of regional tales.

Be prepared when you conduct an interview. Gather information on the person's background and prepare a set of pertinent questions, with follow-ups. During the interview, keep your focus on the principal issue. If the person being interviewed drifts toward non-relevant ideas, bring him or her back to the central subject by asking an appropriate question. Also, maintain an ethical demeanor that honors with accuracy the statements of the subject. Use both handwritten notes and a tape recorder. It's not uncommon for researchers to use a video recorder. Finally, maintain accurate records in order to cite appropriately the source in your paper as well as to make a bibliography entry in a research paper:

Wathrop, Bernard A. Personal interview. 15 Dec. 2002.

T I P   *Using Interviews in Your Paper*

> You will probably want to give your readers several direct quotations from the person interviewed. Chapter 6 explains the techniques for that process. You will also want to paraphrase the source. Chapter 5 explains the techniques for translating into your own words what was said by another person. In fact, you should rephrase (paraphrase) to correct the rough edges of a person's informal conversation. To see an example of an interview and the paraphrased passage that resulted from it, see Chapter 5, pages 174–176.

Reading a Published Interview

WEB LINK
to Reading
2.5
http://www.
ablongman.com/
lester
Published interviews of notable persons give you a special insight into their ideas on various issues. Below is an excerpt from an interview with Annie Dillard by Peggy Langstaff from *BookPage*. Marginal notes show how one student marked certain passages, and the note at the end shows how the writer acquired information for use in a research paper on Annie Dillard, her works, and her themes.

When the West Was New: Annie Dillard's The Living

Interview by Peggy Langstaff

Pulitzer Prize–winning author Annie Dillard has been called a latter-day Thoreau, a mystic, a naturalist and a superior stylist of a difficult form of non-fiction, the familiar essay. Lauded for her debut work, *Pilgrim at Tinker Creek*, which appeared in the mid '70s and which is still considered her masterpiece, Dillard has tried her skills at a variety of forms—verse, criticism, and memoir among them—receiving rave reviews nearly every time out.

This month Dillard's first effort at yet another genre, the novel, is being published. *The Living* (HarperCollins, $22.50) is really quite a departure from her previous work. The publisher has ordered a major first printing, unusual for a work by an author who refuses to promote her works on TV and in other media.

Dillard admits that at this point in her life she had grown exceedingly tired of "the sound of my own voice," and wanted to try something entirely new. I spoke with Annie Dillard recently by phone at her home in Middletown, Conn., to hear what she had to say about this new chapter in her writing life. *She grew weary of hearing her own voice in her personal essays.*

PL: Tell us a little about the novel in general. What's it about? How would you describe it?

AD: *The Living* is a novel about the pioneer generation in Puget Sound in the 19th century. It takes place from 1855 to 1893 and concerns three men, the opening up of the Pacific Northwest, the settlement of that enormous forest, the distinctiveness of the region, the splendid landscape and the brave people who went out there. *She switches to history writing.*

PL: How accurate a portrayal is it of the times? Did you do a lot of research?

AD: I lived out there for five years. I spent part of that time on an island that had no amenities whatsoever. Not only did it have no electricity, but no telephone link with the mainland, no stores, no paved roads, no anything. It was very much a 19th-century life. We drew our water and heated it and so forth. And I also lived in town on Bellingham Bay in a restored old house that was built in the 1890s, and I became very interested in the history of the region which is sort of American history writ small.

The book tells the whole history of the region accurately. I did an enormous amount of research, all terrifically fun. It took three years altogether to write and I spent 16 months in just pure research. I decided early on to write it as if it were a 19th-century novel, as if Thomas Hardy wrote it. So it's a completely old-fashioned novel, and the language is old-fashioned.

I used a contemporary Webster's, an Oxford English Dictionary which gives the dates of first usage, and an enormous dictionary of American slang in two volumes. At the beginning I would read only 19th-century books so that I would be sure not to use any anachronistic language. After a while I got a feel for it.

The student wrote this note after reading the complete interview:

In her novel *The Living* Annie Dillard recreates the contrasts of light and dark, good and evil, because she fears America's optimism might turn to a negative collapse as the cycle of history unwinds. Hers is not an escapist novel of 1882 adventure on Puget Sound. She says, "This book is no agricultural idyll. I'm nowhere saying that the 19th century is a better time. Everything that characterizes the United States, its optimism and its greed, its sort of transcendental impulse and its piety, along with its deception and racism, it's all here."

WEB LINK to Interviews on the Web
http://www.ablongman.com/lester

This researcher's note on Dillard adds one thread to a comprehensive study of the writer. See Chapter 4 for detailed instructions on writing a summary, like the one above.

EXERCISE 2.6

DISCOVERING KEY INFORMATION FROM AN INTERVIEW

Many interviews are available on the Internet at *BookPage, Page One, Globebooks.com, BookBrowser, Interview Magazine*, or *Amazon.comInterviews*. Read carefully the interview with Alice Walker, which appeared on *BookPage*, and then answer the questions immediately following the interview.

The Same River Twice: Honoring the Difficult
Interview with Alice Walker by Ellen Kanner

"Anyone who is really alive in their own time will have to be a political writer. As we reveal different worlds to each other, we move us forward into being more compassionate people. Virginia Woolf said writing improves society and makes the writer a better person, too," says Alice Walker. For all the compassion in her life and work, Walker has never shied away from telling the world some things it might not want to hear.

For years she has decried the inhumane practice of female genital mutilation, a rite of passage in many countries. She has sided with Fidel Castro over the fate of Cuba. Her books have been banned and then restored to the shelves in public schools and libraries. She will not be silenced, she will not turn the other cheek. Walker's new memoir *The Same River Twice* is as brave as anything she's ever written.

Of the author's four novels, five books of poetry, two short story collections and numerous books of essays, the world knows and loves her best for *The Color Purple*, her 1982 novel about Celie, a young black woman struggling through pain and poverty to find dignity, love, and selfhood. It is a tale of healing which won Walker the Pulitzer Prize and the National Book Award. *The Same River Twice* chronicles the process of adapting *The Color Purple* to film in 1984. Steven Spielberg directed it, Quincy Jones wrote the music, Whoopi Goldberg and Oprah Winfrey starred. Walker hoped the film would be loving and true to her novel. She worried it might fall short. She hadn't expected the torrent of criticism the film unleashed.

"It was said that I hated men, black men in particular, that my work was injurious to black male and female relationships; that my ideas of equality and tolerance were harmful, even destructive to the black community," Walker writes. While critics hurled barbs at her, she suffered from Lyme disease, nursed her dying mother, and ended a long relationship with a partner. She wants the public to know of her hurt, subtitling her book *Honoring the Difficult*.

"I remember when I was little, my mother used to say the worst thing you could do is hurt someone's feelings," Walker says. "It's true. When you hurt someone's feelings, you really create a major transgression against the spirit. My heart felt waterlogged. My spirit lost its shine. My grief was kind enough to visit me only at night, in dreams; as I felt it wash over me, I didn't care that I might drown."

The author has articulated human suffering in her fiction and essays, but she has never allowed the public to come so close to her. Her daughter Rebecca questioned the wisdom of doing such a thing in print. Wouldn't it be better to keep silent, to never let people know the depths of her pain? That isn't Walker's way. "Daughters always have their ideas. You're their mom, they think they can tell you what to do." The author laughs then turns serious.

"I wanted to show the world," she says. "It was something I needed to do. It kept staying in the back of my mind, the whole experience of making a film from what was a very private book. I learned so much and it needed to be expressed. For those who are interested in film and in creativity, per se, I hope it will be a resource."

While *The Same River Twice* serves as a meditation on the assets and limitations of film, it is more than that. Incorporating correspondence, Walker's rejected screenplay of her own novel, and journal entries from before, during and after the filming of *The Color Purple*, it is a bold and often angry book which manages to be both personal and political.

What sustained Walker during this dark time was her family, her friends, and her writing. "Storytelling is how we survive," she says. "When there's no food, the story feeds something, it feeds the spirit, the imagination. I can't imagine life without stories, stories from my parents, my culture. Stories from other people's parents, their culture. That's how we learn from each other, it's the best way. That's why literature is so important, it connects us, heart to heart."

Compassion and rising above human frailty has been the touchstone of Walker's writing and her life. "As a child, I would reach out to people, wanting to be close, very trusting," says the author. "Even now, I find that no matter what has happened, I still have that trust. I have a lot of trust, that people can be better than they are. "

Speaking from her beloved farm outside Eureka, California, Walker's voice is light, musical. "I'm sitting in my bedroom and looking up a hill, a tall, tall, tall hill. I can't see the top of it." She has been sick in body and soul. She has been vilified and misunderstood, but her voice lets you know she's come through it and moved on. If she retreated from the world, it wasn't for long.

"I am a typical Aquarian, I need my periods of solitude, then going about the planet, stopping by friends in various countries, going back to Georgia, eating what's on the stove, on anyone's stove, really loving where I am. There are times of solitude, times when I want to be with people. I give very good parties."

Walker has learned to let go. "This period I was talking about, it was difficult being so sick, so attacked and betrayed, and at the same time, as with so many difficult situations, there became a lot of light, a lot of freedom and a lot of exhilaration," she says. "I wanted to go into that for myself, I wanted to share that.

"You just continue," the author concludes. "You just basically keep getting up and making your oatmeal, playing with your dog, doing your work, your life just goes on. And you learn not to accept what is unjust."

1. Based on your reading of the interview, which of the following statements are true?
   - Alice Walker campaigns against female genital mutilation.
   - She takes sides with Fidel Castro.
   - Her books have been banned from libraries.
   - The movie of her novel *The Color Purple* starred Whoopi Goldberg and Oprah Winfrey.

2. If you were writing a research paper on Alice Walker, which of the following statements by her would you consider worthy of quotation?
   - "Anyone who is really alive in their own time will have to be a political writer."
   - "When you hurt someone's feelings, you really create a major transgression against the spirit."
   - "I can't imagine life without stories, stories from my parents, my culture. Stories from other people's parents, their culture. That's how we learn from each other,

it's the best way. That's why literature is so important, it connects us, heart to heart."

- "You just basically keep getting up and making your oatmeal, playing with your dog, doing your work, your life just goes on. And you learn not to accept what is unjust."

Gathering Information by Letter or E-mail

Correspondence in the form of letters or e-mail provides a written record for research. As you would in a face-to-face interview, ask pointed questions so that correspondents will respond directly to your central issues. Tell the person who you are, what you are attempting to do, and why you have chosen to correspond. Usually, you will need to explain why you have chosen a particular topic. One student explained her project as follows:

> I am a college student conducting research into regional folklore. In particular, I am looking for information on the early schoolhouses in Montgomery County. Were they one-room schools? Were the teachers certified? How were schools funded? However, my primary focus is on the curriculum used in the primary grades. I am also surveying each elementary school principal in the county. I have contacted the central office also, but I wished to have perspectives from the historical records. What I would like from you is the opportunity to search any records that might be in your files. I have enclosed a self-addressed, stamped envelope for your convenience.

WEB LINK
to Tips and
Templates for
Writing Letters
http://www.
ablongman.com/
lester

This student makes a specific request for a minimum amount of information. She does not require an expansive reply.

Whether you are communicating by letter or e-mail, include your complete contact information—name, address, e-mail address, and a telephone number.

Reading Personal Papers

Search out letters, diaries, manuscripts, family histories, and other personal materials that might contribute to your study. Your city library may house private collections, and the city librarian can usually help you contact the county historian and other private citizens who have important documents. Obviously, handling private papers must be done with the utmost decorum and care. Keep careful records and sufficient material for a bibliography entry that will be needed for a research paper.

> Walthrop, Bernard A. "Notes on Early Schools of Montgomery County." Unpublished paper. Sango, TN, 1997.

Attending Lectures and Public Addresses

Watch bulletin boards and the newspaper for a featured speaker who might be giving a lecture at your campus or in your community. When you attend, take careful notes. You may also be able to request a copy of the lecture. Remember that many lectures, reproduced on video, are available in the library or in departmental files. Make a bibliography note if you anticipate using the words or ideas of the speaker.

> Petty-Rathbone, Virginia. "Folklore and Fact: Pioneer Schools in Tennessee." Lecture. Heard Library, Vanderbilt U., 2000.

Listening with a Critical Ear to Media Presentations

One of your fellow students might give a PowerPoint presentation that would serve your paper; by all means, use material from it. The same is true with a speech and a television program. All have great value in given instances. However, two rules apply: (1) be accurate in reporting what is said, and (2) provide documentation to the source in your text and in the bibliography.

Whenever possible, get a printed copy of a speech and use it as the basis for your citations rather than depending solely on your handwritten notes. With permission, make a tape recording and transcribe from the tape. Many television programs and some speeches are reproduced in digest form on the Internet, so it's likely that you could capture the key sections of a newscast and use it in your paper.

WEB LINK to Chapter 2 Related Web Destinations http://www. ablongman.com/ lester

You can download pictures, graphs, charts, and other material and place it directly into your report. Always provide proper documentation for the material. Remember, however, that you must get permission from the author if you publish your paper on the Internet. See pages 236–238 for more information on fair use of copyrighted material.

You can find important data in audiovisual materials: films, filmstrips, music, compact disc recordings, slides, audio cassettes, and video cassettes. You can access these sources both on and off campus. Consult such guides as *Educators Guide* (film, filmstrips, and tapes), *Media Review Digest* (nonprint materials), *Video Source Book* (video catalog), *The Film File*, or *International Index to Recorded Poetry.*

Television, with its many channels such as *The History Channel*, offers invaluable data. With a VCR you can record a program for detailed examination. Again, write bibliography entries for any source that contributes to your research paper.

> "Nutrition and AIDS." Narr. Carolyn O'Neil. CNN. 12 Jan. 1997.

G U I D E L I N E S

Using Media Sources

- Watch closely the opening and closing credits to capture the necessary data for your bibliography entry. The format is explained on pages 370–372.
- Your citations may refer to a performer, director, or narrator, depending upon the focus of your study.

(continues on next page)

(continued from previous page)

- As with a live interview, be scrupulously accurate in taking notes. It's best to write direct quotations because paraphrases of television commentary can unintentionally be distorted and colored by bias.

- Preplan the review of a media presentation, even to the point of preparing a set of criteria to help with your judgment, or prepare a list of questions in search of answers.

EXERCISE 2.7

ACCESSING AN AUDIO SOURCE

WEB LINK
to Reading
2.6
http://www.
ablongman.com/
lester

Go to your computer, connect to your browser, and enter *Bookworm* into your search engine or enter this URL: **http://kcrw.com/cgi-bin/db/kcrw.pl?tmplt_type = pro gram&show_code = bw.** Bookworm features online broadcasts, so you will find entries that look like the one below.

Susan Sontag [G2]
On *Summer in Baden Baden* by Leonid Tsypkin (New Directions)
Susan Sontag talks about the discovery of lost and forgotten masterpieces, in particular, the novel, never published in America, about an odd vacation in the life of Fyodor Dostoevski. She also discusses *Artemisia* by Anna Banti (University of Nebraska Press); *Fateless* by Imre Kertesz (Northwestern University Press); and *A Book of Memories* by Peter Nadas (Farrar, Straus and Giroux). Aired Thursday, February 14, 2002.

The *G2* after the name is a hyperlink that will take you to the audio recording. If you have *RealPlayer* on your computer, click the hyperlink, listen to the audio performance, and take notes as though you were planning to write about this person or about the topic being discussed.

Investigating Government Documents

Documents are available at three levels of government—county, state, and federal. As a constituent, you are entitled to examine many kinds of records on file at various agencies. If your topic demands it, you may contact the mayor's office, attend and take notes at a city council assembly, or search out printed documents.

TIP   *Find Government Documents*

For some research topics, you may need to go into the field to find evidence. In general, you have a right to access government papers, and you can enhance your paper by doing so. In addition, while visiting a government office, you may have the opportunity to interview an official. *Note:* For library sources to government documents, see pages 28–30. For Internet access to government documents, see pages 39–41.

County Government

Visit the courthouse or county clerk's office, where you can find facts on each election, census, marriage, birth, and death. These archives will include wills, tax rolls, military assignments, deeds to property, and much more. A trip to the local courthouse can be rewarding, for it can help you trace the history of the land and its people.

State Government

Contact by phone a state office that relates to your research, such as Consumer Affairs (general information), Public Service Commission (which regulates public utilities such as the telephone company), or the Department of Human Services (which administers social and welfare services). The agencies may vary by name in each state. Remember, too, that the state will have an archival storage building or library with records that will be available for your review.

Federal Government

WEB LINK
to Chapter 2
Related Web
Destinations
http://www.
ablongman.com/
lester

Write to your United States senator or representative, who can send you booklets printed by the Government Printing Office (GPO). A list of these materials can be found at GPOAccess. In addition, you can gain access to the National Archives Building in Washington, D.C., or to one of the regional branches in Atlanta, Boston, Chicago, Denver, Fort Worth, Kansas City, Los Angeles, New York, Philadelphia, or Seattle. A visit to Washington, D.C., will give you access to many government agencies and their specific libraries.

GUIDELINES

Securing Interviews, Letters, Private Papers, and Government Documents

- Set your appointments in advance.
- Consult with experienced persons. If possible, talk to several people in order to weigh different opinions. Telephone interviews are acceptable.
- Be courteous and on time for interviews and appointments.
- Be prepared in advance with a set of focused, pertinent questions for initiating and conducting the interview or the investigation of historic papers.
- Handle private and public papers with great care.
- For accuracy, record the interview with a tape recorder (with permission of the person interviewed, of course).
- Double-check direct quotations with your notes and the tape.
- Get permission before citing a person by name or quoting the person's exact words.
- Send interviewees a copy of your report along with a thank-you note.

WEB LINK
to Exercise
2.3
http://www.
ablongman.com/
lester

Conducting a Survey with a Questionnaire

Questionnaires can produce current, firsthand, and localized data that you can then tabulate and analyze. Of course, to achieve meaningful results, you must survey a random sample, one that is representative of the whole population or of a particular subgroup that is your focus. Various degrees of bias can creep into the questionnaire unless you remain objective. Thus, use the formal survey only when you are experienced with tests and measurements as well as with statistical analysis or when you have an instructor who will help you with the instrument. Be advised that most colleges and universities have a Human Subjects Committee that sets guidelines, draws up consent forms, and requires anonymity of participants for information gathering that might be intrusive. An informal survey gathered in the hallways of campus buildings lacks credibility for a research paper.

Those who conduct a survey will need to publish the results—usually in a chart—as part of the essay. A discussion to explore the implications of the results is mandatory. In turn, those who read the report must evaluate both the findings and the discussion. Let's examine the results and the discussion by a student researcher who conducted a survey on the controversial issue of campus parking spaces.

Mandatory Car Pooling and Shuttle-Bus Parking: A Survey

Parking spaces on campus are limited and cannot be expanded. The Student Government Association (SGA) is considering a proposal to limit campus parking to automobiles with multiple passengers (HOV entrances). Drivers of single-occupant automobiles will be required to park at off-campus lots and ride a shuttle bus. The SGA has said, "Students will support HOV entrances to control the parking problem." The survey tested that statement. It sought responses by Classification and Gender to this Question: Do you support HOV entrances to the campus parking lots?

	First Year	Second Year	Third Year	Fourth Year	Graduate	Female	Male
Yes	94	16	28	22	12	95	77
No	87	106	214	89	67	310	253

Discussion: The results show that 563 students do not endorse the plan. Only 172 favored the plan, and many of these are first-year students who are required to live on campus. If the SGA wants the support of the student body, it will need a strong educational campaign to win the support of the students. Comments by the students (Appendix A) indicate a preference for first come, first served. If a single driver arrives early, he/she should be allowed on the campus lots.

The chart shows that the student researcher questioned students from each grade, first year through graduate students, and recovered a balanced response from women and men. Keep in mind that surveys must be random and drawn from a fair sampling of each campus population. Distorting the survey were the first-year students, who are required to live on campus and therefore had a different perspective on commuting issues. However, the student researcher commented on that problem in the discussion.

GUIDELINES

Conducting a Survey

- Keep the questionnaire focused by understanding your purpose for posing the questions.
- Write unbiased questions. You may need your professor to examine the instrument before you release it.
- Design the survey to elicit a quick response to a scale (e.g., from 1 to 10), to a ranking (first choice, second choice, etc.), or to fill in blanks.
- Keep the survey as short as possible with each item bearing on one aspect of the topic.
- Make the survey easy to understand.
- Before starting, consult the Longman Web site and also consult with your instructor.
- Arrange for an easy return of the questionnaire, even to the point of providing a self-addressed, stamped envelope.
- Surveys by e-mail should be retained, even printed, until the project is complete.
- Provide a sample questionnaire and your tabulations as an appendix to your research paper.
- Tabulate the results objectively. Even negative results that deny your hypothesis have value.

EXERCISE 2.8

DISCOVERING KEY INFORMATION FROM A SURVEY

Shown below is a questionnaire submitted by the Department of Athletics of a prominent university to its season ticket holders. Included as a part of the questionnaire are the statistical results received by the department. Carefully study the questionnaire and the results and then do the assignment that follows immediately after them.

Department of Athletics XXX University

Dear Season Ticket Holder:

Students of the university have requested more access to basketball seats at the floor level. We have traditionally allowed season ticket holders to buy all seats in the first

25 rows. Please respond to the following questions on the postal card and drop it in the mail to us.

1. Are you willing to move to rows 26 or higher in order to accommodate the students?
   Yes   No

2. Should we retain one half of rows 1-25 for season ticket holders?
   Yes   No

3. Will you continue to buy season ticket(s) if your assignment is changed?
   Yes   No

Results

1. Are you willing to move to rows 26 or higher in order to accommodate the students?
   Yes   432
   No   2,190

2. Should we retain one half of rows 1-25 for season ticket holders?
   Yes   1,598
   No   1,024

3. Will you continue to buy season ticket(s) if your assignment is changed?
   Yes   897
   No   1,725

Assignment: Write a recommendation to the athletic director, based on these statistics.

Conducting Experiments, Tests, and Observation

Empirical research (practical experiments and not theory) is vital in the sciences. It requires testing and observation to arrive at answers that can be verified by others who duplicate the research. It often starts with a question: for example, "How stable is the oxygen level of the water in the River Bend area of Lake Barkley?" The question might provoke a period of testing and observation on site. Empirical research also begins with a *hypothesis,* which is a statement assumed to be true for the purpose of investigation. Here are two hypotheses:

Hummingbirds live as extended families governed by a patriarch.

The majority of people will not correct the poor grammar of a speaker.

Each hypothesis needs testing and observation to prove its validity. Sometimes performed in a laboratory, empirical research can determine why and how things exist, function, or interact with one another. The research gives us better drugs, clothing, tires, shampoo, and other products.

Observation occurs in the laboratory and in the field, which might be a child-care center, a movie theater, a parking lot, or the counter of a McDonald's restaurant. The field is anywhere you can observe, count, and record such elements as behavior, patterns, and systems. Observation might also include recording and testing the growth of certain wildflowers or recording the nesting patterns of a deer family. Retail merchandisers conduct studies on the buying habits of shoppers, and highway officials chart the flow of traffic and the number of auto accidents at certain intersections. Gathering data is a way of life for television networks, politicians, and thousands of marketing firms.

Such investigations are not out of the reach of students. The report on Mandatory Car Pooling on pages 58–59 is an example of empirical research by a first-year student. Some student assistants keep statistics for athletic teams, perhaps a shot chart for the basketball coach. The shot chart is one type of empirical research.

WEB LINK to the Form and Style for Reporting Empirical Research http://www. ablongman.com/ lester

Your paper, if you decide to conduct research, will need to describe your tools, subject, methods, and results. Not only will you report your findings, but you will also need to discuss how the findings answer the question or support the hypothesis that is the focus of your research. The survey on Mandatory Car Pooling was conducted in response to a statement by the Student Government Association, which asserted: "Students will support HOV entrances to control the parking problem." That statement was, in effect, the hypothesis tested.

GUIDELINES

Conducting an Experiment or Observation

- Have a clear understanding of your hypothesis. What is it that you want to prove, test, or investigate?
- Determine the best design for the study—lab experiment, observation, or the collection of raw data in the field.
- Bring into your introduction any literature on the subject for background evidence.
- Keep careful records and your corresponding responses to the data.
- Avoid bias so that your expectations do not affect the results.
- Maintain high respect for human and animal subjects.
- You may find it necessary to get approval for your research from a governing board.

Chapter Review

A writer chooses a working topic, as discussed in Chapter 1, and then must go in search of the sources, which are *everywhere*—at the library, on the Internet, and in the field. Explore all available avenues, even to conducting a survey or experiment. Some of your best ideas might come from an interview or from statistics gathered at the courthouse. The point is rather simple: Don't limit your search to the Internet or to the library. Branch out with an inquisitive mind, and remember another point from Chapter 1: Use your own personal experience as a source.

Chapter 2 Assignment: Gathering a Mix of Sources

Here's a chance to test your investigative skills. First, select one of the following subjects for research:

- grade inflation
- global warming
- online education

Next, assemble a variety of sources on the chosen topic:

1. A book on the subject.
2. A photocopy of an article from your library's databases (e.g., SilverPlatter).
3. A printout of an Internet article from the World Wide Web.
4. A typed version of an interview with one of your fellow students, or a typed discussion of the results to a questionnaire that surveyed the students in your class.

Tracing the Work of Two Students

Listing Sources

WEB LINK to Exercise 2.4
http://www.ablongman.com/lester

Here we continue to observe the work of two students as they pursue the development of their research papers. Kaci Holz is an English major researching gender communication issues. Halley Fishburn is a political science major searching for literature on the War Powers Act. Below, see how Holz has sought to balance a network of sources—books, articles, electronic material, and field research.

Library Books and Articles

Cohen, David. "Speaking across the Gender Gap." *New Scientist* 131 (1991): 36. 19

Sept. 2003. InfoTrac.

McCluskey, Karen Curnow. "Gender at Work." *Public Management* 79 (1997): 5–10.

Tannen, Deborah. *The Argument Culture: Moving from Debate to Dialogue*. New

York: Random House, 1998.

Multimedia Sources

Tannen, Deborah and Robert Bly. *Men and Women Talking Together*. New York Open
Center. Videocassette. Mystic Fire Video, 1993.

Weaver, Richard L. "Leadership for the Future: A New Set of Priorities." *Vital
Speeches of the Day* 61 (1995): 438–41.

Internet Articles

Green, Marlon. "Get Him to Listen." 2002 by When the Truth Knocks. 18 Jan. 2003
<http://www.httk.org/nourishment/gethimtolisten.htm>.

Sieger, Mike. Review of *Men Don't Listen* by Wayne L. Misner. 18 Jan. 2003
<http://www.mendontlisten.com>.

Field Research

I am conducting a survey of the members in my class for answers to two
questions:

Does your significant other listen to you?

Are you always honest when responding verbally to your significant
other?

Strategies for Critical Reading

After you find sources relevant to the subject of your paper, you should begin your critical reading. React to the material by doing something more than just reading—circle a word, highlight a phrase, make a note in the margin, jot something into your notebook. Pause often in your reading to contemplate what is being said. Reread some passages, remembering that you are looking for ideas and quotations for your essay. If the material is on a computer screen, print a hard copy so that you can make marginal notes. In this chapter we will examine several techniques that you can use to read with a critical eye.

Highlighting

You can highlight part of a text by underlining it, circling it, or using a colored marker. Highlighting words and phrases is a skill, and if you do it correctly it will serve you well. It requires restraint because you should mark only those items worthy of further consideration, especially those phrases that you might borrow to use in your essay as paraphrases or direct quotations.

TIP   *Evaluate Words, Sentences, Passages*

During your critical reading, you should estimate the value that a particular word, sentence, or passage might bring to your work. This textbook is designed to give you the skills and confidence necessary for blending the source material with your words.

Highlight certain words. Look for key words of the discipline or topic. For example, articles on the safety of automobile air bags will feature a common set of terms, such as *air bag technology, deployment force, belted occupants,* and *deactivate.* You should learn the relevant terminology and use it effectively in your paper. Some writers make a vocabulary list so that their paper will feature the appropriate language for the specific subject. In addition, highlight unfamiliar words that you probably need to know. The annotated excerpt by Caleb Carr on pages 66–67 demonstrates the techniques discussed here.

Highlight certain sentences. Search for sentences that you might quote in your paper; these sentences should make significant points in well-worded phrasing. Highlight sentences that establish the argument, that shift the argument to another level, and that provide proof and convincing conclusions.

Highlight examples. Mark any illustrations, graphs, charts, and text examples that will help you to analyze the passage or that you might use in your own paper.

Highlight comments that you might challenge. Many pieces that you read will be defending one side of an issue; make sure that you consider the other side. Waller's essay in Chapter 1, page 14, demonstrates how one student wrote a rebuttal to someone else's argument. A position might be questionable to you (see pages 71–73) or an argument might be unsupported (see pages 101–106). In such cases, circle the item and make an annotation in the margin, as explained in the next section. The circle can be your signal of an annotation.

Annotating with Marginal Notes

WEB LINK
to Chapter 2
Related Web
Destinations
http://www.
ablongman.com/
lester

To help you interpret, evaluate, define, and question a piece of writing, you should make notations on separate sheets of paper, on sticky notes, in the margins of your own books and magazines, and on photocopied materials and computer printouts. (Of course, don't write in library books.) If you keep a writing journal, fill it with your comments and ideas on the subject you are reading about.

Define words. When you encounter an unknown word, circle it and write a marginal notation that defines it (with the help of a dictionary), or put a question mark in the margin as a reminder to look up the word later.

Ask questions. Critical reading requires you to question a writer: *Is this true of all? Is this true in this situation? Why use this term? What does the writer really mean?* (See also "Questioning with a Critical Eye," page 70.)

Clarify. If you stumble over the meaning of a sentence, you may need to examine it carefully and rephrase it briefly in the margin. You may also want to reduce complex ideas to a brief phrase.

Interpret. You may need to interpret a writer's use of foreign words or highly technical terminology. Circle the term and define it in the margin, or put a question mark in the margin as a reminder for later.

Evaluate. Critical reading requires you to evaluate the piece of writing and respond with reasoned commentary. Make critical notations to challenge what is said: *This is*

WEB LINK
to Exercise
3.1
http://www.
ablongman.com/
lester

exaggerated. The writer is using clichés. This paragraph is full of general platitudes. This ignores the primary question. This can't be true in every case.

   Make notes about your ideas. As you read, you should be contemplating what *you* believe and how *you* feel about the issues. You can record these ideas in the margins or in your writing journal. Placing your thoughts in the margin puts the idea in proximity to words you might eventually quote or paraphrase. A note in your journal might introduce the quotation and record your response. The excerpt below has been highlighted and annotated to show how critical reading can examine passages with meticulous care—underlining important words and phrases, circling words to be defined, and making marginal notes.

From The Lessons of Terror

Caleb Carr

   Long before the deliberate military targeting of civilians as a method of affecting the political behavior of nations and leaders came to be called *terrorism*, the tactic had a host of other names. From the time of the Roman republic to the late eighteenth century, for example, the phrase that was most often used was *destructive war*. The Romans themselves often used the phrase *punitive war;* although strictly speaking punitive expeditions and raids were only a part of destructive war. For while many Roman <u>military campaigns were indeed undertaken as punishment for treachery or rebellion</u>, other destructive actions sprang out of the simple desire to impress newly conquered peoples with the fearsome might of Rome, and thereby (or so it was hoped) undercut any support for (indigenous) leaders. In addition, there was a pressing need to allow the famous Roman legions, who were infamously underpaid, to plunder and rape as a reward for their almost inhuman steadiness in the heat of battle. The example of Rome incorporates nearly every possible (permutation) of warfare against civilians: in this as in so many things, antiquity's greatest state provided a remarkably <u>complete, set of precedents for many later Western republics</u> and empires.

   The Romans knew only <u>one way to fight—with relentless yet disciplined ferocity</u>—but they eventually devised several ways to deal with the peace that ensued. The first and most successful was inclusive in nature: the peoples of conquered provinces could, if they agreed to abide by Roman authority and law, aspire to become citizens of the republic (and later the empire). Indeed, some new subjects, particularly merchants and other civic leaders, could achieve the status quite quickly. Even slaves could

terrorism has a far-ranging history

natives to the land

terrorism stifles local rebellion

transformation

Rome set the standards for terrorism

a telling description

possibilities for citizenship and freedom also stifle rebellion aspire to citizenship, for early on the Romans had devised a remarkable system of (manumission,) providing multiple avenues by which slaves could escape the hopelessness of unending bondage (and the tendency toward rebellion that hopelessness often breeds) by attempting to earn, buy, or be granted first freedom and then actual citizenship. Freedmen played an important part in Roman history (more than one emperor was saved by a loyal freedman); and on the whole, these complementary policies—granting citizenship to conquered peoples and offering slaves the hope of manumission—may safely be called the central domestic foundation on which the near millennium of Roman (hegemony) rested.

Perhaps a good passage to quote

War has always terrorized innocent people—children, women, the aged, and even the hospitalized.

domination of other nations

EXERCISE 3.1

ANNOTATING A PASSAGE

Quickly skim the following excerpt to catch its drift. Then read it critically to underline key passages, circle words needing definition, and write notes in the margins or in your journal. This excerpt by James Carville and Paul Begala, political strategists who were part of Bill Clinton's presidential campaign, is from their book *Buck Up, Suck Up, and Come Back When You Foul Up*, which gives advice on finding success in life as well as in political campaigns. Miz Nippy is Carville's mother, who helped raise her children in Louisiana by selling encyclopedias door to door.

Miz Nippy and the Bass Boat

James Carville and Paul Begala

While it's most noticeable in a political campaign or a war with the press, struggles over framing a decision take place in business every day. James's late mama, Miz Nippy Carville, was the queen of framing a debate. She put her eight children through college by selling encyclopedias door to door in and around her home of Carville, Louisiana.

Framing the decision was central to her sales pitch. She'd patrol a neighborhood looking for two telltale signs that a family was a good prospect: children's toys and a bass boat. Being perhaps the most Catholic state in the union, and calling itself "The Sportsmen's Paradise," Louisiana has an inordinate number of homes with both. She'd go to the door—preferably in the evening or on the weekend—and ask to see the man of the house. Now, conventional wisdom has it that women are a softer touch for children's books, but Miz Nippy knew more than the conventional wisdom. She knew how to frame the choice in a way that would shame the customer.

We wish you could've seen her. "You the father of these children?" she'd ask. When the daddy would grunt his assent, she'd start laying it on thick . "Such beautiful children," she'd gush. Then she'd exchange a word or two with one of the kids and, feigning shock the likes of which would have made Scarlett O'Hara proud, she'd say, "And so bright! My, sir, these children are indeed gifted. They have such potential. You must spend a lot of time with them, reading the encyclopedia. You *do* have a set of encyclopedias, don't you?"

When the guy said they didn't, his goose was cooked.

"Why, sir, how can that be? Such potential in these children, such God-given talent, and you're going to let it go to waste? Surely not. I am going to personally arrange for you to purchase one of the finest collections of children's educational materials ever published."

If the man said he didn't want it or, worse, couldn't afford it, Miz Nippy sprang the trap: "I see you can afford that beautiful bass boat, can't you? You can't tell me that chasing a bunch of pea-brained bass around a bayou is more important to you than the future of your children! You don't want them to grow up ignorant, do you? Trapped in a dead-end job, or unable to get a job at all, just because you and your beer buddies thought fishing was a more important thing to spend your money on than your children's education and their future?"

About that time the guy would look down sheepishly at the half-empty, now-warm bottle of beer in his hand. Then he'd gaze at his bass boat, which until that moment had been such a source of pride, such an unalloyed joy. Now, all of a sudden, it was a source of shame. And he was hooked better than any bass ever was.

The poor [man] never really stood a chance.

Once Miz Nippy framed the debate, the decision was a forgone conclusion. The battle was over before it had begun.

In every decision, that struggle takes place. Sometimes it's overt and sometimes it's unnoticed. Notice it. Engage it. Define the decision point and frame it in the light most favorable to you and you'll win more often than you'll lose.

GUIDELINES

Critical Reading

- Don't hurry, unless you want to make a quick, cursory reading to determine the source's relevance to your mission.
- Pause to contemplate key ideas and pause to reread a sentence now and then.
- Keep a pencil or pen and a supply of paper nearby for making notes if the book or periodical is not your own.
- Be prepared for physical as well as mental action—circle words, underline passages, write comments in margins or on note paper, frame questions in your notes, highlight in different colors.

Being Selective

Surrounded by several books and articles, many writers have trouble determining the value of the materials and the contributions each will make to the research paper. Be selective in choosing passages for quotation or paraphrase. To serve your reader, you need to cite material that is pertinent to your positioning of the topic. Avoid placing huge blocks of quotation in the paper—you will make your own voice disappear! In the following excerpt, James Campbell masterfully describes the British writer Robert Louis Stevenson. Note how Campbell has borrowed from Stevenson and merged quotations into his own prose. He has selected key passages that are short and to the point, not huge blocks of material that would mute the effects of his description. Campbell's full article on Stevenson appeared in *The Best American Essays, 2001.*

Travels with R.L.S.

James Campbell

WEB LINK
to Chapter 2
Related Web
Destinations
http://www.
ablongman.com/
lester

One evening in the spring of 1880, Robert Louis Stevenson dropped into the bar of the Magnolia Hotel in Calistoga, at the head of the Napa Valley. There was little more to the town than the springs, the railway station, and the enticement of a fortune to be made from mining gold or silver. The West was still pretty wild. Inside, someone asked Stevenson if he would like to speak to Mr. Foss, a stagecoach driver; Stevenson, always alert to the suggestion of travel, said yes: "Next moment, I had one instrument at my ear, another at my mouth, and found myself, with nothing in the world to say, conversing with a man several miles off among desolate hills."

It was "an odd thing," Stevenson reflected, that here, "on the very skirts of civilization," he should find himself talking on the telephone for the first time. Later, he adapted the incident for use in a novel. "May I use your telephone?" asks Mr. Pinkerton in *The Wrecker* (1892), one of the earliest occurrences in literature of that polite request.

Stevenson and his wife, Fanny, were in the middle of their honeymoon, spent mostly in an abandoned California silver mine. Throughout his life, Stevenson preferred to circumnavigate civilization, with its increasing reliance on contraptions, and steer toward the rougher fringes. Wherever we catch sight of him—tramping in the Highlands of Scotland or shivering in the Adirondacks or sailing in the South Seas, where he feasted with kings and cannibals—Stevenson is self-consciously turning his back on the Victorian idol, progress. In similar spirit, he chose the past more often than the present as a setting for fiction. His most popular novels—*Treasure Island, Kidnapped, The Master of Ballantrae*—are set in a semimythical realm, where the fire of adventure catches on every page. Stevenson loved the sound of clashing swords; he didn't want them getting tangled up in telephone wires overhead.

Just as Campbell has borrowed only a few selective items from Stevenson, so must a researcher borrow only selective items from Campbell. Some writers might be tempted to place this entire passage into their papers, but the better choice is to borrow only a pertinent phrase or two. The writer might focus on (1) Stevenson's desire to avoid civilization and its technology or (2) his interest in the past and semi-mythical settings. The student writer should then borrow only the passage that focuses on that one idea.

One might wonder about the great variety in the settings of Stevenson's novels, but we know his settings are authentic because he traveled the globe. James Campbell tells us that Stevenson traveled to many parts of the world to discover new and adventurous settings for his novels, "tramping in the Highlands of Scotland or shivering in the Adirondacks or sailing in the South Seas, where he feasted with kings and cannibals." Thus, we see the exotic locales pictured vividly in *Treasure Island* and his other great adventure stories.

This passage remains true to the student's voice; it is not overwhelmed or dominated by the voice of Campbell. What is the lesson? Pick and choose the best, most appropriate passage for citation in your work.

Questioning with a Critical Eye

Many of the questions you might note in the margins concern minor matters (a writer's use of italics, an unusual or unknown word, an odd phrase), but your critical reading should also include questions that challenge the writer and the meaning of the passage. Most pieces of writing are making an argument, and many writers don't defend their arguments with sound logic and convincing evidence. Therefore, you must at times question the content of a passage.

GUIDELINES

Questioning a Source

- Does this essay have a main idea—a thesis, a central assertion, a proposal or proposition?
- Where is the evidence for this statement?
- But did this first event actually cause the second event?
- What are the writer's premises that lead to this conclusion?
- Isn't this an exaggeration?
- Does this writer give evidence of research into the subject?
- Is the writer displaying bias? Is the bias justifiable?
- Is the writer being humorous or serious?

Ask in-depth questions as you read and develop your analysis. For now, let's apply critical reading skills to an article by Robert J. Samuelson that appeared in *Newsweek* (February 11, 2002). Read the passage and the critical questions in the margins, which demonstrate the types of questions you should be asking as you read. In addition, make your own marginal notes.

Remember that writers are seldom objective. They have agendas, and they use the power of words to promote their favorite ideas. Part of your task is to question the source as well as find support for your ideas.

A Sad Primer in Hypocrisy

Robert J. Samuelson

This being federal budget season, we'll hear stern lectures from the White House and congressional leaders of both parties about the need to return to surpluses and to maintain "fiscal discipline." You should greet these pronouncements skeptically for obvious reasons: pressures for new spending (defense, homeland security and a Medicare drug benefit) are intense; the willingness to raise taxes is slight, and the ability to cut existing spending—no matter how wasteful or unneeded—is virtually zilch. Government programs are, for all practical purposes, immortal.

Immortal, perhaps, and will he say also that some are immoral?

Anyone who doubts this last proposition should examine the farm-subsidy programs, which are the classic example of how unnecessary spending survives. It is a parable for our larger budget predicament. Every year the government sends out checks to about 700,000 to 900,000 farmers. Since 1978, federal outlays to support farmers' incomes have exceeded $300 billion. How large is that? Well, the publicly held federal debt (the result of past budget deficits) is about $3.3 trillion. The past two decades of farm subsidies equals almost 10 percent of the debt.

But wait: Congress is about to expand the subsidies. The Congressional Budget Office estimates that new farm legislation would increase costs by $65 billion over a 10-year period, on top of the $128.5 billion of existing programs. (And these figures exclude costs for agricultural research, trade and nutritional programs.) The Republican-controlled House has passed one version; the Democratic-controlled Senate is about to debate a slightly different version. And the Bush administration has supported what it calls the bill's "generous" funding levels. "Extravagant" would be more like it.

But did farm subsidies cause the debt? He calls farm subsidies a parable for the entire national budget; isn't that reaching toward a false analogy?

Government spending should reflect some "public interest." For farm subsidies, this is hard to find. Let's examine the possibilities.

Is his mission now clear: to arouse public sentiment and provoke efforts to block the new legislation? Isn't his bias and personal agenda exposed?

Do we need subsidies to ensure food production? No. The subsidies go mainly for wheat, corn, rice, cotton, soybean and dairy production, representing about a third of U.S. farm output. The rest (beef, pork, chicken, vegetables, fruits) receive no direct subsidies. Has anyone noticed shortages of chicken, lettuce, carrots or bacon? The idea that, without subsidies, America wouldn't produce ample wheat for bread, milk for ice cream or corn for animal feed is absurd. Before the 1930s no federal subsidies existed, yet annual wheat production rose 77 percent to 887 million bushels from 1880 to 1930.

Here is the first of three major questions, and doesn't he answer with the cause-effect fallacy "after this, therefore, because of this" (post hoc propter ergo hoc)?

Do subsidies "save the small family farm"? In the 1930s, or even 1950s, this argument might have been plausible. No more. Mechanization and better seed varieties have promoted farm consolidation. In 1935 there were 6.8 million farms. In 1997 there were 1.9 million and, of these, about 350,000 accounted for almost 90 percent of farm production. These farms had at least $100,000 in sales. About 42 percent of food production came from farms with $1 million or more in sales. Countless newspaper stories complain that subsidies go overwhelmingly to large, wealthy farmers. But given the distribution of food production, they must go to large farmers—unless government decides to subsidize farmers who essentially don't farm.

Where does Samuelson get his statistics? There seems to be more at work here than what he gives us; is he guilty of hasty generalization?

Do subsidies stabilize farm incomes, off-setting periods of low prices? Not much. There are two problems. First: when crop prices drop, the subsidies promote over-production, which prolongs and deepens the price decline. Second: the value of the subsidies increases the prices of agricultural land by about 20 percent, according to the Agriculture Department. This raises the purchase prices for new farmers or lease payments for farmers who rent their fields. About 45 percent of cropland is leased. And of course, there's this question: why should government stabilize farmers' incomes? It doesn't stabilize incomes of plumbers, print shops or most businesses.

Are we now getting the fallacy of false dilemma? We don't stabilize a print shop's income, so we shouldn't stabilize any income for any business?

Despite farm programs' nonexistent public benefits, Congress routinely extends the programs for political reasons. On the public-relations front, farmers are thought to be hardworking and, therefore, deserving. Somehow, it seems unfair to withdraw a government benefit they're accustomed to receiving. And if farm programs didn't exist, the congressional agriculture committees would be less powerful. So would various farm lobbies and interest groups. They all have an interest in perpetuating the subsidies. Finally, there's control of Congress.

Is he attacking the subsidies program or Congress and all the special interest groups that thrive on the program?

"The main factor is a concern among lawmakers of both parties that power in Congress could hinge on a few races in heavily subsidized agricultural regions," Sen. Richard Lugar, Republican of Indiana, bravely wrote in *The New York Times*. "If either party stands in the way of this largesse, they risk being labeled the 'anti-farm party' and targeted with sentimental imagery associated with farm failures."

Farm subsidies are huge political bribes. Though they're perfectly legal, the ethics are questionable. The trouble is that hardly anyone raises the questions. The silence defines Washington's self-serving and hypocritical "morality." Everyone in Congress is justifiably out-raged these days by Enron's collapse and the losses for workers and investors. But the same legislators will vote for massive giveaways of billions of dollars to farmers without any sense of shame or outrage. There is no inkling that they might be plundering the public purse and doing wrong. (The press is guilty of similar hypocrisy. Farm subsidies excite casual, intermittent curiosity. But despite billions of misspent money, they're hardly a "scandal.")

He says earlier that the program is immortal; is he now arguing that it is also immoral? Is he exaggerating with the phrase "huge political bribes"?

This brings us back to the overall budget. The recent surpluses had little to do with the spending restraint of the Clinton administration or the Republican-controlled Congress. They had everything to do with two strokes of good fortune: a decline in military spending after the cold war and a huge, unpredicted windfall of tax revenues from the economic boom. Both have now vanished, and, not surprisingly, budget deficits have reappeared. A resurgent economy and some other good fortune may restore surpluses. But we should not rely on the "fiscal discipline" of our leaders, because there's little evidence that it exists.

Is this conclusion another logical fallacy, the ad hominem (about the man), which attacks character, not issues? What is his target, the farm program or members of Congress?

WEB LINK to Reading 3.1
http://www. ablongman.com/ lester

As you can see, the penetrating questions in the margins assess the passage with a critical eye.

Consequently, the critical reader can begin to answer these valuable questions:

- What are the writer's basic premises? Can you grant assumptions without further proof?
- What evidence does the writer provide? Can you see any weaknesses, especially any points that are not defended with evidence?
- Do you see evidence of the writer manipulating the facts and the presentation to suit the argument being made?
- Can you find evidence of any negative bias or favorable leanings?
- Can you accept—based on the evidence provided—the conclusions drawn by the writer?

Outlining a Source to Discover Its Key Ideas

Outlining what you are reading is a method for assessment. The outline will show the hierarchy of issues, identify parallel parts, and locate supporting ideas.

WEB LINK
to Audio-
visual 3.1
http://www.
ablongman.com/
lester

T I P   *Outline Passages*

Your outline should correspond to the order of the passage you are examining. It may list only the main points of a long passage or, in the case of short passage, identify one main idea and the ideas supporting it.

An outline differs from marginal annotations. Marginal notes have little consistency, but the outline shows the progression of the writer's ideas to give an overview of the whole. Preparing an outline can help you write a summary, which is the subject of the next chapter.

G U I D E L I N E S

Outlining

You have choices when you decide to outline a passage:

- Describe the content of each paragraph with a phrase or sentence in sequential order.
- Capture each main point in a phrase or sentence and, under that heading, list the supporting ideas. *Note:* Each main point may have its support spread over several paragraphs.
- Write a formal outline using the traditional format:

  I. First Major Heading

      A. Subgroup Item

          1. Supporting element

          2. Supporting element

A formal outline is unnecessary for the assessment of a piece of writing unless the piece is long and complex. Let's consider a sentence outline of major ideas in the article by Robert J. Samuelson, "A Sad Primer in Hypocrisy." These sentences outline the ideas in Samuelson's paragraphs, one by one, in the order of presentation.

> It is the budget season in Washington, which means more spending by the government.
>
> Farm subsidies are an example of unnecessary spending.
>
> Now Congress plans to expand farm subsidies.

Farm subsidy programs reflect no "public interest."

Farm subsidies do not ensure food production.

Farm subsidies do not save the small farms.

Farm subsidies do not stabilize farm incomes.

Despite the failures, Congress extends farm subsidies for political reasons.

A political party does not wish to be labeled as an "anti-farm party."

Farm subsidies are "political bribes."

We cannot rely on the "fiscal discipline" of our elected officials.

If you were to use this outline of paragraphs to develop a summary, you would next construct a hierarchy in the list, similar to the following one:

During the budget season Congress spends unnecessarily, and the farm subsidy program is a classic example.

Farm subsidies have no "public interest."

They do not ensure food production.

They do not help the small farmer.

They do not stabilize farm incomes.

Nevertheless, farm subsidies continue because Congress has no "fiscal discipline" when it comes to the farm vote.

**WEB LINK
to Exercise
3.2**
http://www.
ablongman.com/
lester

By showing both the major ideas and supporting material, outlining gives you the best chance at assessing the value of a work and determining the contribution it can make to your paper. It also gives you a nice guideline for writing a summary.

Shown below are four paragraphs of the opening chapter of *The Birth of Pleasure* by Carol Gilligan. Here, she begins her search for the autonomy of the individual psyche, of sons breaking free from their fathers, of gays coming out, of women casting off patriarchy. Read this opening passage and study the outline that follows it. After that, you will be asked to read a few more paragraphs of Gilligan's book and, in the exercise that follows, write an outline for that portion of her book.

From The Birth of Pleasure

Carol Gilligan

I picked up the ancient road map of love at a time when relationships between women and men were changing. The waves of liberation that swept through American society in the second half of the twentieth century, freeing love from many constraints, set in motion a process of transformation. In a historic convergence, the civil rights movement, which galvanized a moral consensus against enslavement, was followed by the anti-war movement and the women's movement, initiating a conversation about freedom that included freedom from long-standing ideals of manhood and womanhood. For a man to be a man, did he have to be a soldier, or at least prepare himself for war? For a woman to be a woman, did she have to be a mother, or at least prepare herself to raise children? Soldiers and mothers were the sacrificial couple, honored by statues in the park, lauded for their willingness to give their lives to others. The gay liberation movement drew people's attention to men's love for men and women's for women and also men's love for women who were not the objects of their sexual desire and women's love for men who were not their economic protectors. In the 1990s, for the first time since suffrage, women's votes elected the president, more women were gaining an economic foothold, and wealth began shifting into the hands of young men who bypassed the usual channels of advancement. The tension between democracy and patriarchy was out in the open.

Democracy rests on an ideal of equality in which everyone has a voice. Patriarchy, although frequently misinterpreted to mean the oppression of women by men, literally means a hierarchy—a rule of priests—in which the priest, the hieros, is a father. It describes an order of living that elevates fathers, separating fathers from sons (the men from the boys) and placing both sons and women under a father's authority. With the renaissance of women's voices in the late twentieth century, with sons questioning the authority of fathers, especially with respect to war, with the revolution in technology reducing the need for a priesthood by providing direct access to knowledge, the foundations of patriarchy were eroding.

I was searching at the time for a washed-out road. Picking up the voice of pleasure in men's and women's stories about love and also among adolescent girls and young boys, I came to the places where this voice drops off and a tragic story takes over. The tragic story where love leads to loss and pleasure is associated with death was repeated over and over again, in operas, folk songs, the blues, and novels. We were in love with a tragic story of love. It was "our story."

If we have a map showing where pleasure is buried and where the seeds of tragedy are planted, then we can see an order of living that was presumed to be natural or inevitable as a road we have taken and trace alternative routes. Piecing together an ancient love story with the findings of contemporary research, I found myself led into the heart of a mystery and then to a new mapping of love. This book is a record of that journey.

Here is an outline of the passage above, showing:

- The hierarchy of major and minor points.
- Complete sentences rather than phrases.
- Items listed in the proper sequence

Outline of Gilligan's Passage

The second half of the twentieth century saw waves of change in our society.
> The civil right movement asserted black liberation.
> The anti-war movement pitted sons against their fathers.

The women's movement opened new doors for women of all races.

The gay liberation movement uncovered a man's love of men and a woman's love of women.

The tension arose in the conflict of democracy and patriarchy.

Democracy has the ideal of equality.

Patriarchy elevates the father's authority over wife, son, and daughter.

The century's close saw the erosion of patriarchy's basic foundations.

The voice of pleasure can be heard in the stories of love and tragedy.

Love stories often turn tragic.

Pleasure is often buried.

Nearby the seeds of tragedy are planted.

There is a need for a new mapping of love.

After considering the structure and content of the outline above, it is time for you to perform the same task. Read the next passage from Gilligan's book, then follow the directions in Exercise 3.2 for writing your outline.

From The Birth of Pleasure *(continued)*

In the mid-1980s, I began a study with women and men whose intimate relationships with one another had reached a point of crisis. People were asking new questions about love, finding their way alone and together across a shifting societal and psychic terrain. More women were speaking openly about their experiences of love, saying what they knew about pleasure. The double standard, or what Freud had called "a double morality," had led to "concealment of the truth, false optimism, self-deception and deception of others" on the part of both women and men. The poet Jorie Graham's questions became everyone's questions:

How far is true
enough?
How far into the
earth
can vision go and
still be
love?

A search for truth was uncovering a buried history, revealing the extent to which neither men nor women felt authentic. How had this happened? Where had they split with their souls, their desires, their connection to each other?

Led by an awareness of this disconnection, I began to explore the roots of what seemed a pervasive trauma. Trauma is the shock to the psyche that leads to dissociation: our ability to separate ourselves from parts of ourselves, to create a split within ourselves so that we can know and also not know what we know, feel and yet not feel our feelings. It is our ability, as Freud put it in *Studies on Hysteria,* to hold parts of our experience not as a secret from others but as a "foreign body" within ourselves.

The foundational stories we tell about Western civilization are stories of trauma. Oedipus is wounded and abandoned by his parents, who drive a stake through his feet (hence the name Oedipus, which means "swollen foot") and give him to a herdsman with instructions to leave the baby on a hillside to die. Saved by the herdsman, Oedipus is fated to kill his father, Laius, and marry his mother, Jocasta—a fate decreed by Apollo as retribution for Laius' having sexually violated a young boy.

The *Oresteia*, Aeschylus' trilogy about the founding of Athenian democracy, tells a story so horrible it is almost unspeakable. Atreus, the father of Agamemnon (the king who will lead the Greek army to Troy), had a brother Thyestes, who ran off with Atreus' wife. In response to this loss and the blow to male honor it carries, Atreus invites Thyestes to a banquet and serves him his children, cut up and cooked into a stew. Athenian democracy is the civic order created to contain the seemingly endless cycle of violence that follows in the wake of this trauma. The *Oresteia* links the establishment of democracy with the reinstatement of patriarchy, as Orestes, Agamemnon's son, is acquitted for the crime of killing his mother at the first recorded trial. Athena (born from the head of Zeus) casts the deciding vote in his favor, giving priority to fathers by saying: "The death of a wife who killed her husband is bad, but not so bad as the death of a father and king."

In the Book of Genesis, the trauma is the expulsion of Adam and Eve from the Garden of Eden; it too leaves a legacy of violence and betrayal. Cain, the son of Adam and Eve, murders his brother Abel. In the story of Noah, God brings a flood to wipe out this history and start over, but the residue of trauma returns in Noah's drunkenness and incestuous sexuality. Jacob, with the help of his mother, steals his brother Esau's birthright. And Jacob's son Joseph is sold into slavery by his brothers, who envy his relationship with his father.

In these foundational stories, a trauma occurs in a triangle composed of two men and a woman. When we focus more closely on what actually happens, we see that a father or a husband's authority is challenged. Oedipus is wounded by his father and mother because he is fated to kill his father; Atreus is betrayed by his wife and his brother; Adam and Eve disobey God. What follows has the cast of tragedy, as if what happens had to happen. The order of the triangle has been challenged (father over son, man over woman), and a man, wounded in his love, responds by unleashing a cycle of violence.

Perhaps patriarchy, by establishing hierarchy in the heart of intimacy, is inherently tragic, and like all trauma survivors, we keep telling the story we need to listen to and understand. At the same time, we look for ways to break what quickly becomes a vicious cycle, searching for "a new truth . . . [that would] establish the whole relation between man and woman on a surer ground of mutual happiness." The quotation is from *The Scarlet Letter*, where Nathaniel Hawthorne's narrator makes the observation that the new truth must be brought by a woman, echoing a thought that, once spoken, becomes inescapable: the presence of women in a democratic society contains the seeds of transformation—a second coming, a new beginning, a civilization that is not patriarchal. This is the radical geography of love, the wildflower seeded from generation to generation, the messiah perpetually in our midst.

EXERCISE 3.2
WRITING AN OUTLINE

On a separate sheet of paper write an outline of the above passage. Remember, the outline should maintain Gilligan's sequence, show major ideas with their support, and be written in complete sentences.

TIP   *Sentence Outlines*

Capture each main point in a sentence and under each one list the supporting ideas. The main point may spread over several paragraphs.

Discovering the Writer's Intentions

WEB LINK
to Chapter 3
Related Web
Destinations
http://www.
ablongman.com/
lester

Each writer has a unique agenda, and you will benefit from your critical reading and analysis by pausing now and then to determine the writer's intentions. In general, a line of reasoning meets one of three classifications:

- Inquiry
- Negotiation
- Persuasion

Inquiry is an exploratory approach to a problem in which the writer examines the issues without the insistence of persuasion. It is a truth-seeking adventure. For example, Thomas C. Harrison in "Keats's 'To Autumn,'" which follows, explores the poet's use of onomatopoeia (a technique in which the sound of the word echoes the meaning, as in *hiss* or *buzz*) to create scene and mood. Harrison's purpose is inquiry into the language choices of the poet which, while "intuitive and untutored," managed "to create the effects he wanted in verse." Harrison's article originally appeared in *The Explicator* (Spring 2001). For your reference, the entire poem by Keats follows the article.

Keats's "To Autumn"

Thomas C. Harrison

What John Keats's poem "To Autumn" is about has been much discussed. The reading that I usually give the poem in classes is that of a progression—the first stanza a depiction of the autumn harvest, the second an address to three personifications of autumn, and the third a confrontation with the end of the year, perhaps an acceptance of death. Hartman's ideological reading of the poem attempts to establish a place for it

WEB LINK to Reading 3.2

http://www.
ablongman.com/
lester

in poetic tradition. More recent readings have explored the interplay of speakers in the poem (Gaillard) and the influences of Shakespeare (Flesch) and Spenser (Scheil).

A more vexed issue, however, may be a more technical one involving the way Keats and other poets achieve their effects. Some critics dismiss the possibility of onomatopoeia, claiming that the "shape" of the sound is in the meaning of the word and has nothing to do with the sound at all (Barzun's position). This is a tempting position, because onomatopoetic words are supposed to make the sounds that they name: buzz, bop, bang, trickle, splash. But they obviously do not. The fly does not say "buzz" because he is not making speech sounds. The dog does not say "bow-wow," or even "woof" or "arf," for the same reason, and dogs are supposed to say quite different-sounding words in other languages.

Still, Walter Jackson Bate devotes considerable attention to the sounds Keats uses in his poetry, even stressing the dominance of "long" vowels in the first stanza of "To Autumn" (183). At least one other critic, Hugh Bredin, finds that onomatopoeia is indeed in the mind of the hearer and dependent on the context in which it occurs, but nonetheless real. Onomatopoeia "refers to a relation between the sound of a word and something else" (557). Bredin posits three kinds of onomatopoeia," "direct onomatopoeia," in which the word makes the sound it names (as in buzz), but in which the relation is at least partly determined by convention; "associative onomatopoeia" that occurs when the sound of the word resembles a sound associated with what the word denotes (as in cuckoo); and "exemplary onomatopoeia," which involves the amount of work expended in producing the sounds (so that nimble requires less effort to utter than slothful) and the sound echoes the sense, as Pope recommended.

The examples cited by Bredin are admittedly heavily influenced by the cultures and languages in which they occur. However, an example illustrating a broader principle, attributed to Otto Jespersen, is provocative. A professor drew the shapes in figures 1 and 2 on the board; he then named them (pronounced as in Italian or Spanish) umbulu and kikiriki. Which is which? he asked. Everyone agreed that the drawing with the round shapes was umbulu, and that the one with the points and angles kikiriki. Something about the sounds seems to suggest those shapes. [1]

Specifically, high front spread vowels like those in beet and bait, combined with the voiceless plosives p, t, and k (however they are spelled) seem to suggest angular, pointed shapes. They are cacophonous, harsh-sounding.

Rounded back vowels (so called because of the rounding of the lips) like those in pool, pole, and Paul combined with nasals (in, n, and the final consonant in sing), liquids (l and r), semivowels y and w, and even voiced stops like b, suggest soft, rounded, even heavy, shapes. They are euphonous.

In "To Autumn" Keats presents three kinds of images in the three sections of the poem. First, there are images of fruit ready to be harvested: "To bend with apples [. . .]" (5), "To swell the gourd, and plump the hazel shells" (7). The second stanza presents four personifications of the harvest: the granary keeper, the reaper, the gleaner, and the cider press operator, each with his sound effects, like the alliteration in "winnowing wind" (15). Finally, there are images of harvest done, stubble-plains, sunset, full-grown lambs, hedge crickets. And there are the many oblique allusions to death: "soft-dying day," "wailful choir," "small gnats mourn," "the light wind lives or dies" (25, 27, 29). All these images come with their appropriate sounds.

But Keats's sound effects are most remarkable in the first section. Reading through it, "Season of mists and mellow fruitfulness" (1), we are almost overwhelmed with ls, rs, nasals, and rounded back vowels. "Close bosom friend of the maturing sun" (2), "fill all fruit with ripeness to the core" (6), "swell the gourd, and plump the hazel shells / With a sweet kernel . . . " (7–8), all these lines are full of round, heavy images of the fruits of harvest so ripe they are ready to fall. And to back these images up, Keats gives us sounds that by themselves suggest the soft, round, and heavy.

In the progression of stanzas, the first stanzas gets the reader ready for the interplay between the speaker of the poem and the insecure deity of autumn (in Gaillard's reading) in the second stanza and the final, if gentle, confrontation of the last. "Where are the songs of spring?" (23). Perhaps, the implication is usually read, there will be no songs of spring, no spring. To start the progression, Keats does not warn us. He satisfies us with images and sounds that leave us full to bursting with the great abundance we already have. Before we reach the wailful choir mourning, as we turn from the feast to the sleepy, bemused images of the second stanza, we can feel so filled, so sated, metaphorically speaking, that we could almost belch.

Keats's phonetic knowledge was no doubt intuitive and untutored. He clearly knew how to create the effects he wanted in verse; however, our latter-day knowledge may help us better understand and appreciate his achievement.

To Autumn

John Keats

Season of mists and mellow fruitfulness,
    Close bosom-friend of the maturing sun;
Conspiring with him how to load and bless
    With fruit the vines that round the thatch-eaves run;
To bend with apples the mossed cottage-trees,
    And fill all fruit with ripeness to the core;
        To swell the gourd, and plump the hazel shells
    With a sweet kernel; to set budding more,
And still more, later flowers for the bees,
Until they think warm days will never cease,
    For Summer has o'er-brimmed their clammy cell.

Who hath not seen thee oft amid thy store?
    Sometimes whoever seeks abroad may find
Thee sitting careless on a granary floor,
    Thy hair soft-lifted by the winnowing wind;
Or on a half-reaped furrow sound asleep,
    Drowsed with the fume of poppies, while thy hook
        Spares the next swath and all its twined flowers;
And sometimes like a gleaner thou dost keep
    Steady thy laden head across a brook;
    Or by a cider-press, with patient look,
        Thou watchest the last oozings, hours by hours.

Where are the songs of Spring? Ay, where are they?
    Think not of them, thou hast thy music too,—

> While barred clouds bloom the soft-dying day,
>   And touch the stubble-plains with rosy hue;
> Then in a wailful choir, the small gnats mourn
>   Among the river sallows, borne aloft
>   Or sinking as the light wind lives or dies;
> And full-grown lambs loud bleat from hilly bourn;
>   Hedge-crickets sing; and now with treble soft
>   The redbreast whistles from a garden-croft,
>   And gathering swallows twitter in the skies.

As you can see, Harrison is making an inquiry into Keats's intuitive use of onomatopoeia, and he comments on current linguistic knowledge that helps to interpret the poem's progression toward an acceptance of the autumnal season and the death associated with it. In his chain of inductive reasoning, he examines onomatopoeia in its full context of forms. Using modern linguistic theory, Harrison reasons that Keats used effective images and sounds with profound effect on the readers' senses. Harrison's intention is inquiry, an intellectual pursuit.

Negotiation is a search for a solution. The writer attempts to resolve a conflict by inventing options that offer, perhaps, a mediated solution. John Gray's book *Men Are from Mars, Women Are from Venus,* while a bit dated since its publication in 1992, remains a classic example of negotiation. He balances the expectations and needs of the two sexes in an array of categories. The excerpt below demonstrates his negotiations with the two sides.

Good Intentions Are Not Enough

John Gray

Falling in love is always magical. It feels eternal, as if love will last forever. We naively believe that somehow we are exempt from the problems our parents had, free from the odds that love will die, assured that it is meant to be and that we are destined to live happily ever after.

But as the magic recedes and daily life takes over, it emerges that men continue to expect women to think and react like men, and women expect men to feel and behave like women. Without a clear awareness of our differences, we do not take the time to understand and react to each other. We become demanding, resentful, judgmental, and intolerant.

With the best and most loving intentions love continues to die. Somehow the problems creep in. The resentments build. Communication breaks down. Mistrust increases. Rejection and repression result. The magic of love is lost.

We ask ourselves:

How does it happen?

Why does it happen?

Why does it happen to us?

To answer these questions our greatest minds have developed brilliant and complex philosophical and psychological models. Yet still the old patterns return. Love dies. It happens to almost everyone.

Each day millions of individuals are searching for a partner to experience that special loving feeling. Each year, millions of couples join together in love and then painfully separate because they have lost that loving feeling. From those who are able to sustain love long enough to get married, only 50 percent stay married. Out of those who stay together, possibly another 50 percent are not fulfilled. They stay together out of loyalty and obligation or from the fear of starting over.

Very few people, indeed, are able to grow in love. Yet, it does happen. When men and women are able to respect and accept their differences then love has a chance to blossom.

Through understanding the hidden differences of the opposite sex we can more successfully give and receive the love that is in our hearts. By validating and accepting our differences, creative solutions can be discovered whereby we can succeed in getting what we want. And, more important, we can learn to best love and support the people we care about.

Love is magical, and it can last, if we remember our differences.

Gray negotiates a minefield of emotional entanglements as he traces the magic of love and its gradual, sometimes inevitable, decline. His chain of reasoning shows that love will diminish, and he cites statistics to support the theory. Yet, a few couples *do* grow in love, and they do so by "validating and accepting" the various differences in what it means to be male and female.

In using *persuasion* the writer wants, even strives, to convince readers that his or her position is valid, factual, and worthy of the reader's full and thoughtful consideration and approval. For example, CBS television reporter Bernard Goldberg published a book in 2001 under the title *Bias*. It exposes methods used by the various media in America to distort the news. The following passage shows the persuasive passion with which Goldberg pursues his target, the very media for whom he worked.

They Think You're a Traitor

Bernard Goldberg

I have it on good authority that my liberal friends in the news media, who account for about 98 percent of *all* my friends in the news media, are planning a big party to congratulate me for writing this book. As I understand it, media stars like Dan Rather and Tom Brokaw and Peter Jennings will make speeches thanking me for actually saying what they either can't or won't. They'll thank me for saying that they really do slant the news in a leftward direction. They'll thank me for pointing out that, when criticized, they reflexively deny their bias while at the same time saying their critics are the ones who are really biased. They'll thank me for observing that in their opinion liberalism on a whole range of issues from abortion and affirmative action to the death penalty and gay rights is not really liberal at all, but merely reasonable and civilized. Finally, they'll thank me for agreeing with Roger Ailes of Fox News that the media divide Americans into two groups—moderates and right-wing nuts.

My sources also tell me that Rather, Brokaw, or Jennings—no one is sure which one yet—will publicly applaud me for alerting the networks that one reason they're all losing viewers by the truckload is that fewer and fewer Americans trust them anymore. He'll applaud, too, when I say that the media need to be more introspective, keep an open mind when critics point to specific examples of liberal bias, and systematically work to end slanted reporting.

According to the information I've been able to gather, this wonderful event will take place at a fancy New York City hotel, at eight o'clock in the evening, on a Thursday, exactly three days after Hell freezes over.

Okay, maybe that's too harsh. Maybe, in a cheap attempt to be funny, I'm maligning and stereotyping the media elites as a bunch of powerful, arrogant, thin-skinned celebrity journalists who can dish it out, which they routinely do on their newscasts, but can't take it. Except I don't think so, for reasons I will come to shortly.

First let me say that this was a very difficult book to write. Not because I had trouble uncovering the evidence that there is in fact a tendency to slant the news in a liberal way. That part was easy. Just turn on your TV set and it's there. Not every night and not in every story, but it's there too often in too many stories, mostly about the big social and cultural issues of our time.

What made doing this book so hard was that I was writing about people I have known for many years, people who are, or once were, my friends. It's not easy telling you that Dan Rather, whom I have worked with and genuinely liked for most of my adult life, really is two very different people; and while one Dan is funny and generous, the other is ruthless and unforgiving. I would have preferred to write about strangers. It would have been a lot easier.

Nor is it easy to write about other friends at CBS News, including an important executive who told me that of course the networks tilt left—but also warned that if I ever shared that view with the outside world he would deny the conversation ever took place.

I think this is what they call a delicious irony. A news executive who can tell the truth about liberal bias in network news—*but only if he thinks he can deny ever saying it!* And these are the people who keep insisting that all they want to do is share the truth with the American people!

It wasn't easy naming names, but I have. I kept thinking of how my colleagues treat cigarette, tire, oil, and other company executives in the media glare. The news business deserves the same hard look because it is even more important.

Fortunately, I was on the inside as a news correspondent for twenty-eight years, from 1972, when I joined CBS News as a twenty-six-year-old, until I left in the summer of 2000. So I know the business, and I know what they don't want the public to see.

Many of the people I spoke to, as sources, would not let me use their names, which is understandable. They simply have too much to lose. You can talk freely about many things when you work for the big network news operations, but liberal bias is not one of them. Take it from me, the liberals in the newsroom tend to frown on such things.

And there are a few things that are not in this book—information I picked up and confirmed but left out because writing about it would cause too much damage to people, some powerful, some not, even if I didn't use any names.

But much of what I heard didn't come from Deep Throat sources in parking garages at three o'clock in the morning, but from what the big network stars said on their own newscasts and in other big public arenas, for the world to hear.

When Peter Jennings, for example, was asked about liberal bias, on *Larry King Live* on May 15, 2001, he said, "I think bias is very largely in the eye of the beholder." This might offend the two or three conservative friends I have, but I think Peter is right, except that instead of saying "*very largely*" he should have left it as "*sometimes* in the eye of the beholder." Because it's true that some people who complain about liberal bias think Al Roker the weatherman is out to get conservatives just because he forecasts rain on the Fourth of July. And some people who say they want the news without bias really mean they want it without *liberal* bias. *Conservative* bias would be just fine.

Some of Dan, Tom, and Peter's critics would think it fine if a story about affirmative action began, "Affirmative action, *the program that no right-thinking American could possibly support*, was taken up by the U.S. Supreme Court today." But I wouldn't. Bias is bias.

It's important to know, too, that there isn't a well-orchestraled, vast left-wing conspiracy in America's newsrooms. The bitter truth, as we'll see, is arguably worse.

Even though I attack liberal *bias*, not liberal *values*, I will be portrayed by some of my old friends as a right-wing ideologue. Indeed, I've already faced this accusation. When I wrote an op-ed for the *Wall Street Journal* in 1996 about liberal bias among the media elites, my professional life was turned upside down. I became radioactive. People I had known and worked with for years stopped talking to me. When a *New York Post* reporter asked Rather about my op-ed, Rather replied that he would not be pressured by "political activists" with a "political agenda" "inside or outside" of CBS News. The "inside" part, I think, would be me.

Sadly, too often it seems that Dan doesn't think that any critic who utters the words "liberal bias" can be legitimate, even if that critic worked with Dan himself for two decades. Such a critic could not possibly be well meaning. To Dan, such a critic is Spiro Agnew reincarnated, spouting off about those "nattering nabobs of negativism." Too bad. A little introspection could go a long way.

I know that no matter how many examples I give of liberal bias, no matter how carefully I try to explain how it happens, some will dismiss my book as the product of bad blood, of a "feud" between Dan Rather and me. How do I know this? Because that is exactly how Tom Brokaw characterized it when I wrote a second *Wall Street Journal* piece about liberal bias in May 2001.

In it, I said that as hard as it may be to believe, I'm convinced that Dan and Tom and Peter "don't even know what liberal bias is." "The problem," I wrote, "is that Mr. Rather and the other evening stars think that liberal bias means just one thing: going hard on Republicans and easy on Democrats. But real media bias comes not so much from what party they attack. Liberal bias is the result of how they see the world."

The very same morning the op-ed came out, Tom Brokaw was on C-SPAN promoting his new book. When Brian Lamb, the host, asked about my op-ed, Tom smiled and said he was "bemused" by the column, adding, "I know that he's [Goldberg's] had an ongoing feud with Dan; I wish he would confine it to that, frankly."

Here's a bulletin: In my entire life I have mentioned Dan Rather's name only once in a column, be it about liberal media bias or about anything else. Five years earlier, when I wrote my first and only other piece about liberal bias, I did, in fact, talk about the "media elites," of which Dan surely is one. So counting that (and before this book), I have written exactly two times about Dan Rather and liberal bias—or for that matter, about Dan Rather and any subject, period!

Two times! And that, to Tom Brokaw, constitutes a "feud," which strikes me as a convenient way to avoid an inconvenient subject that Tom and many of the other media stars don't especially like to talk about or, for that matter, think too deeply about.

I also suspect that, thanks to this book, I will hear my named linked to the words "disgruntled former employee" and "vindictive." While it's true I did leave CBS News when it became clear that Dan would "never" (his word) forgive me for writing about liberal bias in the news, let me state the following without any fear whatsoever that I might be wrong: *Anyone who writes a book to be vindictive is almost certainly insane and at any moment could find himself standing before a judge who, acting well within the law, might sign official papers that could result in that "vindictive" person being committed to a secure facility for people with mental defects.*

I don't know this from firsthand experience, but my guess is that it would be easier to give birth to triplets than to write a book, especially if you've never written one before. Staring at a blank page on a computer screen for hours and hours and hours is not the most efficient way to be vindictive. It seems to me that staring at the TV set for a couple of seconds and blowing a raspberry at the anchorman would take care of any vindictive feelings one might have.

So, does all of this lead to the inevitable conclusion that all the bigtime media stars bat from the left side of the plate? Does it mean that there are no places in the media where the bent is undeniably conservative? Of course not!

Talk radio in America is overwhelmingly right of center. And there are plenty of conservative syndicated newspaper columnists. There are "magazines of opinion" like *The Weekly Standard* and *National Review*. There's Fox News on cable TV, which isn't afraid to air intelligent conservative voices. And there's even John Stossel at ABC News, who routinely challenges the conventional liberal wisdom on all sorts of big issues. But, the best I can figure, John's just about the only one, which says a lot about the lack of diversity inside the network newsrooms.

On February 15, 1996, two days after my op-ed on liberal bias came out in the *Wall Street Journal*, Howard Kurtz of the *Washington Post* wrote about the firestorm it was creating. "The author was not some conservative media critic but Bernard Goldberg, the veteran CBS News correspondent. His poison-pen missive has angered longtime colleagues, from news division president Andrew Heyward and anchor Dan Rather on down."

Kurtz quoted several dumbfounded CBS News people, one of whom suggested I resign, and ended his story with something I told him, more out of sadness than anything else. Journalists, I said, "admire people on the outside who come forward with unpopular views, who want to make something better. But if you're on the inside and you raise a serious question about the news, they don't embrace you. They don't admire you. They think you're a traitor."

I am not a traitor, nor am I the enemy. And neither are the millions of Americans who agree with me. The enemy is arrogance. And I'm afraid it's on the other side of the camera.

There is little doubt that Goldberg has a persuasive agenda. His voice is so strident that it might cause you to back away. However, he doesn't care. He has an argument that he cannot repress, so he presents it with passion and deep belief that his cause is valid and just. He opens with irony, in which everybody, even each enemy, gathers to congratulate him. He admits that such congratulations will never happen. His chain of reasoning builds evidence against the liberal bias of Dan Rather and other network commentators. He emphasizes that his focus is directed at liberal "bias," not liberal "values." Ultimately, he says, the problem is one of arrogance by talk radio, which is too "right of center," and television news, which is far too liberal.

We have considered the three varieties of argument—inquiry, negotiation, and persuasion. Your task as a reader is to discover which one the writer is using and to introduce that mood into your notes:

- Harrison *inquires, queries, questions, examines*
- Gray *negotiates, explores, bargains, discusses, balances*
- Goldberg *argues, disputes, persuades, quarrels, bickers, attacks*

WEB LINK
to Methods
of Critical
Reading
http://www.
ablongman.com/
lester

In your paper, you might say something like this:

> Harrison investigates the word choices of John Keats in the poem
>
>   "To Autumn."
>
> Goldberg bickers repeatedly with his former colleague Dan Rather of
>
>   CBS News.

The descriptive verbs—*investigates* and *bicker*—display your slant on the writer's intentions.

EXERCISE 3.3

EVALUATING A WRITER'S INTENTIONS

Read critically the following essay by David L. Evans, senior admissions officer at Harvard University, which appeared in *Newsweek* (February 25, 2002). Evans argues for political activism by young African Americans. As you read, consider these questions:

- Is he *inquiring* about the issues, *negotiating* with the reader in search of answers, or *persuading* readers with a call to action?
- Does Evans offer sufficient evidence to make his case?
- Does his chain of reasoning give the essay validity?

If You're Tired of Jesse and Al, Get Involved
David L. Evans

Most of us can't name five young African-American activists. How will this affect the black community?

Last December a dispute between Harvard president Lawrence Summers and Prof. Comel West made headlines. As news of the disagreement over grade inflation and the caliber of West's academic work spread, leaders in the black community entered the fray. The Rev. Jesse Jackson arrived in Cambridge and called for a meeting with Summers, while the Rev. Al Sharpton threatened to sue the university's president. Several black graduates whom I've known since they were students e-mailed me asking: "Who invited Jesse and Al into this delicate situation? Isn't there anyone else who can look into this?"

I was surprised by the nearly unanimous responses from these liberal, moderate and conservative alums, and I wondered why none of them thought to "look into this" themselves. I also asked myself why Jackson would get into the middle of such a debate when he is in his 60s. Was he ego-tripping, or did he anticipate that younger folks like these former students would be reluctant to get involved?

I won't deny Jackson's sizable ego, but he would have a hard time finding a nationally recognized African-American political activist under 50 to take his place. Human rights advocate Martin Luther King III, litigator Constance Rice and Rep. J. C. Watts—but it would be difficult to name five more. By contrast, Martin Luther King Jr. was in his mid-20s when he organized the Montgomery bus boycott, and Julian Bond, Marian Wright Edelman and John Lewis have been activists since their college days.

I am not advocating the mass retirement of current leaders or a sudden inrush of disruptive know-it-alls. I am suggesting that some of the younger beneficiaries of the civil-rights movement use the pro bono policies of their law firms or businesses to take leaves of absence to work a year or two for civil—or human—rights groups. They could offer their legal expertise and fund-raising talents and, more important, gain the hands-on experience they have avoided.

Perhaps the responsibility for this younger generation's complacency lies with those of us who preceded them. We—their parents, teachers and clergy—may have kept them so far from the fires of political agitation that they never quite learned how to "cook." We shielded them from the brutal details of slavery, lynching and Jim Crow, but we also failed to show them how political activism helped to end these atrocities.

Consequently, few young people seem as willing to face controversy and make sacrifices as their forebears were. Maybe it is time to teach them that "controversy" is derived from Latin roots meaning, "to turn" and "against," and that to "sacrifice" originally meant to "make holy and worthy of the gods."

Young people who don't know the virtue of these words might be reluctant to "turn against" injustice, to fight problems like racial profiling. They will continue to focus on that one fleeting moment in Memphis on April 4, 1968, when King was assassinated, rather than the years of struggle against racism and oppression that made his life "worthy of the gods."

I don't wish to suggest that all African-Americans under 50 are uninformed, self-absorbed ingrates. Some of them are working hard for change at the local level and have legitimate questions about whether national organizations or one or two charismatic personalities can adequately address all black issues. But again and again we see—as we did in the 1990s, when a fast-food chain was caught refusing to serve blacks at restaurants across the country—that what initially appears to be a "local" problem is symptomatic of a much larger, national one.

National issues require centralized leadership. Admittedly, this can be a risky approach because it exposes a few individuals and organizations to constant scrutiny and makes them synonymous with the causes they advocate. If these high-profile leaders and organizations are involved in scandal or otherwise discredited, their constituencies are adversely affected, too. Regardless of these risks, it is difficult to imagine the anti-slavery movement without Frederick Douglass or the civil-rights movement without King and the NAACP.

Leadership shouldn't be the lifetime responsibility of just a handful of men and women. Even the most revered activists will want to retire at some point. I hope that members of the younger generation will step forward even before that happens. Then Jesse and Al won't have to carry the burden alone.

Now answer these questions about the essay:

1. In your opinion, what is the author's intention:

> To write *inquiry* that examines the issues?

> To *negotiate* with the reader in search of answers?

> To *persuade* readers with a call to action?

2. Does Evans offer sufficient evidence to make his case?

3. Does his chain of reasoning give the essay validity?

Testing the Validity of an Article or Essay

WEB LINK
to Audio-
visual 3.2
http://www.
ablongman.com/
lester

A chain of reasoning usually offers facts to support or refute a point. A piece of writing moves back and forth from assertion to evidence in the form of facts, observations, citation of authorities, and other data. The overall design will feature one of two types of development: (1) the writer begins with the answer and sets about defending it, or (2) the writer lays out the groundwork and evidence to build toward a conclusion. In each case, the evidence proves the point being made, so you should read with care to find the support and evidence for a writer's assertions. Here is a paragraph that presents a conclusion and the supporting rationale:

The Municipal Arts Council should receive no funding from taxes. First, art is a matter of individual taste in which governments should play no role. What one person considers valuable art, another person considers less than art. Second, the public should be taxed only to provide for the protection and well-being of citizens. Art is inessential to these concerns.

As a critical reader, you cannot accept the writer's conclusion in the first sentence if you find fault with the chain of reasoning in the remaining sentences. Here's an example, in which the conclusion follows a chain of evidence:

> Women consistently score below men on both the SAT and ACT. This fact is true as based on evidence from across the country. Reasons are unclear, but the performance by women affects the mix of most first-year classes. However, once they arrive on campus, women earn better grades than men, their retention rate is higher, and they are more likely to graduate within four years. Consequently, college admission boards should not use SAT and ACT as primary projections about a student's future success in the academic environment.

Again, you must be the judge. Is the evidence sufficient to warrant the conclusion drawn by the writer?

T I P   *Evaluating Assertions*

Always evaluate assertions against the evidence offered. Does the conclusion follow reasonably from the facts offered?

EXERCISE 3.4

JUDGING THE VALIDITY OF STATEMENTS

Which of the following assertions seem reasonable and thus worthy of citation in a paper as quotations or paraphrases?

1. Proposition 48 helps athletes. According to a survey by the *Atlanta Journal-Constitution,* the number of freshmen who did not qualify academically has dropped 42 percent in 24 Division 1 universities in the South. Of the 505 football players recruited, only 30 failed the standards of Proposition 48.

2. Quick and slow learners do not belong in the same classroom. Students need to learn at a pace comparable with that of their peers. Slow learners suffer undue pressure to perform, and quick learners gain a false sense of accomplishment by outperforming the slow learners. Slow learners also impede the pace of study, denying quick learners a wholesome academic experience.

3. This questionnaire, which represents a sizable cross-section of first-year college students, shows that 48 percent of college students know little about mononucleosis. Apparently, the health educational programs on mononucleosis are inadequate or nonexistent in high schools.

WEB LINK
to Methods
of Critical
Reading
http://www.
ablongman.com/
lester

4. Stem rust and leaf rust attack wheat just after the head appears, with devastating results, while smut strikes the kernel itself. Insects, especially the Hessian fly and periodically the grasshopper, cause great damage to wheat as it matures in the field. Therefore, farmers need an arsenal of weapons—fungicides, herbicides, and insecticides—to defend their crops.

Drawing Inferences

Your critical reading includes taking note of the writer's assertions and comparing these with your own positions. Writers make assertions, offer evidence, draw inferences, and make implications.

- *Assertion*—a statement, claim, declaration, affirmation, or denial. Writers make confident statements, backed by evidence, but they sometimes make assertions without adequate proof. Your task is often a search for proof or evidence to back up the assertion.

- *Evidence*—a writer's proof in the form of facts, data, support from experts on the topic, charts, and surveys. Evidence forms the basis for conclusions and claims.

- *Inference*—the writer's assumption, presumption, and interpretation of the evidence. Drawing inferences and making assumptions are acts of reasoning from factual knowledge, and they enable the writer to make implications.

- *Implication*—an insinuation, proposition, proposal, or suggestion. It usually occurs after the inference has been drawn from the evidence (e.g., *the implication of these findings . . .* or *the evidence suggests . . .*).

TIP   *Inference*

With inference, two windows open at once—the writer is making inferences about the evidence being supplied, and you, the reader, are making inferences about the same evidence and also about the writer's assertions about the evidence:

- The writer draws inferences from the evidence.
- The reader draws inferences from the evidence supplied in the essay.
- The reader draws inferences about the author and the author's intentions.

Let's see how inferences weave their way through an article. Here's an opening statement by Lindsey Tanner of the Associated Press from her article "Head Injuries in Young Adults Found to Raise Risk of Depression Years Later," which appeared in the *Nashville Tennessean* (January 15, 2002).

> Concussions and other head injuries in early adulthood may significantly raise the risk of depression decades later, a study of World War II veterans found.

Tanner gives an assertion based on unnamed evidence from her source. We wait to see if Tanner has proof, for in reading any essay we must determine if the writer is stating facts based on evidence and proof, drawing inferences, and making implications about the evidence. As critical readers, we must perform similar tasks; we ask for proof and make implications about the evidence offered. Tanner continues:

> The study has disturbing implications for football and hockey players, motor-cyclists, and others who have taken blows to the head.

Tanner uses one of the key words, *implications,* for she is implying that certain people are at risk as based on evidence that she has not yet provided. She continues:

> Other research has shown that head trauma patients may be prone to depression shortly after suffering their injuries. The new findings suggest that the risk persists even 50 years later.

Tanner implies (note the word *suggest*) that depression caused by head trauma to a teenager can extend into the person's later years.

T I P   *Implication*

When a writer uses implication, she or he suggests something to the reader without stating it outright. Inference, however, is an activity performed both by a writer and the reader in deriving conclusions about the evidence.

At this point, it is time for Tanner to offer *proof*:

> The study involved 1,718 veterans hospitalized for various ailments during the war and questioned 50 years later. About 11% who had experienced head injuries said they currently had major depression, compared with 8.5% of those hospitalized during the war for other reasons.
>
> Overall, the lifetime prevalence of major depression was 18.5% in the head injury group and 13.4% among the other veterans, Drs. Tracey Holsinger and Brenda Plassman of Duke University and colleagues reported in *Archives of General Psychiatry.*

Now we understand the source of Tanner's assertions; she provides explicit evidence and proof for her assertions: statistical data as gathered by professional psychiatrists and published in a scholarly journal. As readers we can now understand and perhaps accept the assertion, "Head injuries in young adults raise the risk of depression years later."

Perceptive readers, however, might question the differences between war-induced head injuries and those from civilian activities. Tanner anticipates this difference:

> The researchers found similar depression rates in veterans who had received their head injuries in combat and in those whose injuries occurred elsewhere. Thus, they said, it is unlikely that post-traumatic stress syndrome, which can include symptoms of depression, would explain the findings.

At this point, however, readers are forced to make an inference of their own, somewhat along these lines: *head injuries cause depression*. Tanner anticipates this problem and, at the end of the article, offers this evidence:

> While it is unclear how head injury is related to depression, Holsinger and colleagues offer some theories.
>
> Depression has been linked with dysfunction in the brain's frontal region, and research has suggested a strong link between depression and head trauma resulting in lesions in the frontal region, the researchers said.

The article ends with a chart (see Figure 3.1) to provide additional proof for the implications that Tanner reports from the study.

Finally, the reader must consider the conclusions that can be inferred:

"I've suffered a concussion so I'm at risk for depression."

"I'll not allow my son to play football or ride a motorcycle."

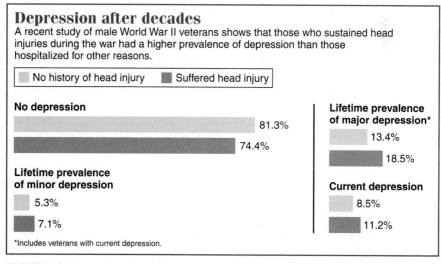

FIGURE 3.1   From Lindsey Tanner, "Head Injuries in Young Adults Found to Raise Risk of Depression Years Later," *Nashville Tennessean* 15 Jan. 2002, p. 10a. Chart reproduced by Tanner from *Archives of General Psychiatry*.

"This study fits the category of scare tactics like articles on smoking and drinking, so I will ignore it."

Note that readers may infer the very opposite of what the writer implies.

The lesson for you as a critical reader is fairly simple—be sure that writers make inferences based solidly on evidence. You then can draw your own inferences from the essay.

Read "But What's It Like?" by Margaret Loftus, an article accessed through http://www.usnews.com. Look for evidence and proof as well as ideas implied or inferred by Loftus on the basis of the evidence. After you have finished reading the essay, complete the exercise that follows, which will ask you to judge statements as assertion, evidence, or inference.

But What's It Like?

Margaret Loftus

Night is falling in Paris, and instead of heading out for dinner, Judy Rowe is in her hotel room, chatting online with her psychology classmates. As an international purser for American Airlines, Rowe, who lives in Davidsonville, Md., spends much of the week traveling. But her often frantic schedule hasn't kept her from pursuing a doctoral degree in psychology at the University of Maryland. She's fortunate, she says, that she doesn't have to "schlep" herself into a classroom each week. "If we didn't have online it would be nearly impossible for me to do my job and go to school at the same time."

Like Rowe, millions of people have rejected traditional education in favor of E-learning. In many ways, however, the two experiences aren't so different. As she would at a brick-and-mortar university, each semester Rowe peruses a course catalog and registers for classes. She reviews a syllabus. She studies textbooks, writes papers, takes exams, and engages in lively debates with other students, guided by her teachers. So how does her education differ from that of students enrolled in campus-based classes?

For starters, she sits in front of a keyboard for most of this activity, connected to the class via the Internet. Thanks to E-mail and threaded discussions—nonlive, electronic forums in which her classmates interact—Rowe never sets foot in a classroom, nor does she meet her colleagues face to face. But convenience doesn't mean such courses are a piece of cake, say E-students. "Don't think you [will] get off easy," says Steve Rauschkolb, a recent graduate of SetonWorldWide's online master's program in strategic communication and leadership. Rauschkolb, who took one course at a time, estimates he spent 10 hours a week—mostly evenings after dinner—reading, writing assignments, and participating in online discussions.

Equal time. His classmate, Michael Mahony, initially assumed that the course wouldn't be that tough but soon realized, he says, that "oh, my God, this is a lot to do." Mahony learned to slip in an hour of coursework every morning before work. He supplemented this time with additional hours in the evenings and on weekends. In general, says Nancy Stevenson, author of *Distance Learning Online for Dummies*, E-students can expect to spend as much time on their courses as they would on equivalent campus-based courses.

By contrast, the pacing of E-courses may be quite different. By the end of college, most students are all too familiar with the standard system for evaluating students each semester—a midterm, a final, and a couple of papers. Instead, online courses often require students to write papers each week and contribute regularly to class discussions. In Gina DeRossi's online poetry class at Syracuse University, for example, students were graded on the quality of their critiques of their colleagues' work. In a course called "Ethics in an E-global world," Lawrence Didsbury, an M.B.A. student at Jones International University (JIU), is required to submit two, two-to-three-page papers each week and to post contributions every day to the class's threaded discussion. All the writing, Didsbury says, requires students to "dig heavily into the content."

"Most people working full time find [the number of] 'deliverables' required each week to be taxing at first," warns Stevenson. If you're prone to procrastination, be prepared for many late nights. "When you have the freedom to do the work at your leisure, you invariably wait until the last possible moment before the deadline," says Tony Sellars, who is working on his M.B.A. at Oklahoma City University. He admits he sometimes ends up taking tests and submitting papers at 3 a.m. "or some other ungodly hour."

Working on some E-courses can feel more like playing a video game than joining in a discussion group. In his capital budgeting class at the strictly online Cardean University, M.B.A. student Jeremy Morrison was charged with figuring out which company his firm should acquire. For help in evaluating four prospects, Morrison could turn to video clips of a professor elaborating on important points and market projection spreadsheets. Other courses incorporate animation and PowerPoint presentations to help simulate business problems. Morrison says he likes the Cardean approach because it makes him feel like he's at work, doing a project for his boss.

For now, though, the majority of online courses—with the exception of corporate training, for which students typically have access to big company servers—are pretty low tech. Says Stevenson, "At this point universities are having to use technology that most people can access." And that usually means a 56-kbps dial-up modem, through which streaming video can look fragmented and jerky.

Even though most online courses don't employ electronic bells and whistles, students' most common complaints about E-learning revolve around technological snafus. Navigating a course's options and jargon—various folders, forums, study guides—can take practice and patience. After six futile attempts to file her first online paper, Rowe called her teacher in tears. Mike Burke, a classmate of Didsbury's who is taking his first online course, has had his share of misplaced assignments and says at times he feels "out of the loop." Then there was the time JIU's server went down: All Burke knew was that he suddenly couldn't access his course. "The ideas are great, the people are great, it's the technology that can be overwhelming if you don't have a background in it," he says.

Time out. A student's own Internet connection also can get cut off. "My biggest frustration was with my ISP," says Mark Plunkett, a Harvard M.B.A. student who, along with his classmates, took two online basic finance and accounting courses before starting Harvard's on-campus program. Besides getting knocked offline on several occasions while traveling, access was sometimes so slow that text-only was the sole real option. George Hutchison, who earned his master's in human resource management through Florida Institute of Technology while he was a naval officer stationed at the Sigonella air base in Sicily in the late '90s, recalls being in the middle of a timed online statistics test when his Internet connection crashed. A couple of anxious phone calls later, Hutchison was allowed to restart the test.

For some students, no amount of time spent in a chatroom can replace the feel of a classroom. "Sometimes people who are more outgoing find this sort of a lonely experience," says Stevenson. Dede Stabler took one online course toward an informational systems degree at the University of Maryland–University College before dropping out. She says she missed the social aspect of school, calling her venture into the world of E-learning "flat." People "who need a lot of face-to-face interaction," says Pamela Pease, president of JIU, "probably aren't going to do very well."

That said, there are individuals who actually prefer to interact with teachers and fellow students online. In a real classroom, a few students may dominate the discussions, and shy individuals don't stand a chance. By contrast, both the pushy and shy can easily speak up online. And because E-students tend to reflect more before participating, their viewpoints often contain more logic and coherence than those expressed in campus-based classrooms. Says Mahony, "People are extremely open; they're not overprotective of themselves." Just like anywhere else on the Web, says Syracuse's DeRossi, "the whole faceless thing helps people [reveal] problems that they wouldn't tell their best friend."

Although Mahony and Rauschkolb actually met their classmates three times in the course of their Seton Hall program, their relationships took root during their threaded discussions, many of which were about students' real-life professional problems. "We actually taught each other," says Mahony. "It was a lot of mentoring." Mahony graduated in the spring of 2000 but regularly keeps in touch with five of his 12 classmates. Hutchison was similarly enthusiastic about his E- experiences with education. "I only wish I could have met some of those folks face to face," he says. "They were great."

EXERCISE 3.5

JUDGING ASSERTIONS AND INFERENCES BY A WRITER

Judge the following sentences as:

a. An assertion made by the author

b. Evidence and factual information provided by the author

c. An inference drawn by the author from the evidence

1. Even though most online courses don't employ electronic bells and whistles, students' most common complaints about E-learning revolve around technological snafus.

2. Navigating a course's options and jargon—various folders, forums, study guides—can take practice and patience.

3. After six futile attempts to file her first online paper, Rowe called her teacher in tears. Mike Burke, a classmate of Didsbury's who is taking his first online

course, has had his share of misplaced assignments and says at times he feels "out of the loop." Then there was the time JIU's server went down: All Burke knew was that he suddenly couldn't access his course. "The ideas are great, the people are great, it's the technology that can be overwhelming if you don't have a background in it," he says.

4. That said, there are individuals who actually prefer to interact with teachers and fellow students online. In a real classroom, a few students may dominate the discussions, and shy individuals don't stand a chance. By contrast, both the pushy and shy can easily speak up online.

5. And because E-students tend to reflect more before participating, their viewpoints often contain more logic and coherence than those expressed in campus-based classrooms.

6. Says Mahony, "People are extremely open; they're not overprotective of themselves." Just like anywhere else on the Web, says Syracuse's DeRossi, "the whole faceless thing helps people [reveal] problems that they wouldn't tell their best friend."

EXERCISE 3.6

MAKING YOUR OWN INFERENCES

After having judged the article above by Margaret Loftus, what inferences can *you* draw about the following?

1. The merits of E-education.
2. The problems faced by online students.
3. The thoroughness of Loftus's examination of E-education.

GUIDELINES

Judging the Assertions of Others

- Search for any instance in which the writer seems to maneuver or contrive the evidence to defend his or her position.
- Consider any alternatives to the proposal that the writer ignores. Determine to your satisfaction that the writer provides sufficient and relevant evidence to support the theory.
- Examine the essay for a logical progression to the reasoning that builds judiciously toward the conclusion.
- Judge carefully the chain of reasoning upon which the writer builds the essay's conclusion and be prepared to accept or reject the conclusion.

Finding and Evaluating a Writer's Argument

WEB LINK
to Audio-
visual 3.3
http://www.
ablongman.com/
lester

Critical reading requires you, in most cases, to discover the writer's basic argument. Usually, it will be obvious that the writer has a special agenda, but you can use three processes to pinpoint the writer's approach to the topic.

1. Locate the writer's thesis.
2. Determine the reasons used to support the thesis.
3. Identify the supporting evidence.

These techniques will help you summarize the article and select portions that you wish to quote or paraphrase for your own paper.

Finding the Writer's Thesis

A thesis establishes an argument by asserting possibilities, probabilities, and interpretations that are subject to review in a rational presentation. A well-reasoned argument confronts a divided audience with an issue that has no easy answer. Thus, it is both a search for knowledge and a search for a common ground for purposes of discussion.

Keep in mind that some articles have no argument. Factual articles—a recipe for tomato soup, directions for building your own computer, or a description of the migratory patterns of Alaskan salmon—have no argument. You cannot argue against facts. In like manner, personal feelings have no argument. They are subjective and beyond reasonable measurement—"I don't like people who smoke." To become an argument, the writer's focus would need alteration: "A person who smokes cigarettes puts his or her children at risk for lung disease" or "Alaskan salmon race upstream against a current of water and government meddling."

A writer's thesis, the primary assertion, takes different forms, as we shall see below in examples from the articles in this chapter.

Call to Action

David L. Evans (page 87) challenges young African Americans to become political activists in "If You're Tired of Jesse and Al, Get Involved." He offers this thesis:

> I am suggesting that some of the younger beneficiaries of the civil-rights movement use the pro bono policies of their law firms or businesses to take leaves of absence to work a year or two for civil- or human-rights groups.

This kind of thesis asks readers to confront a problem, face up to a decision, cast their lot, and take action. You will find this type of thesis most often in articles on social, political, and religious issues.

Assertion of a Cause

Robert J. Samuelson (page 71) in "A Sad Primer in Hypocrisy" bemoans a losing cause, saying, "Government programs are, for all practical purposes, immortal." He

then describes the farm subsidy program as his prime example of programs that pro-
liferate without justification. John Gray (page 82) in "Good Intentions Are Not
Enough" promotes his program for accessing enduring love:

> Through understanding the hidden differences of the opposite sex, we can more
> successfully give and receive the love that is in our hearts. By validating and accept-
> ing our differences, creative solutions can be discovered whereby we can succeed in
> getting what we want.

You will find this type of thesis in papers advocating a cause, asking for reasonable
responses, pleading for proper behavior, or defending a social cause.

Interpretation

James Campbell (page 69) in "Travels with R.L.S." advances the thesis that Robert
Louis Stevenson turned his back on Victorian progress and preferred the past—"a
semimythical realm"—as the setting for *Treasure Island* and his other adventure tales.
This type of thesis is common for articles that require analysis of a text, a piece of music,
or a painting. Thomas C. Harrison (page 79) in "Keats's 'To Autumn'" develops an
interpretation of the poet's use of onomatopoeia (words that make the sounds that
they name, such as *buzz* or *splash*). In that light, he examines the images of the poem,
saying, "All these images come with their appropriate sounds."

Evaluation

Writers make judgments about products, social policies, government regulations,
airline travel, nursing homes—you name it and writers have evaluated it. Robert
Samuelson (page 71) says government officials have no "fiscal discipline" and the farm
aid bill demonstrates how immortal most government programs can be. Margaret Loftus (page 94) in "But What's It Like?" examines the merits and weaknesses of online
courses. Carol Gilligan (page 75) in *The Birth of Pleasure* evaluates the social role of
patriarchy (the male as the dominant force) and finds its weakness in the trauma and
tragedy of its love stories. She expresses this thesis:

> Perhaps patriarchy, by establishing hierarchy in the heart of intimacy, is inher-
> ently tragic, and like all trauma survivors, we keep telling the story we need to lis-
> ten to and understand.

Locating a thesis of evaluation requires some searching all the way to end of an article, for writers seldom announce their judgment until they've laid some groundwork
and rationale for it.

Search for Truth

"Let the truth be known" is the standard for writers who present this type of thesis.
They champion their opinion and defend it with reasons and evidence. Carol Gilligan

(page 75) in *The Birth of Pleasure* searches for an alternative to patriarchy's tragic love story—she delivers her thesis that the presence of women in modern society offers the "seeds of transformation" from the tragic nature of love that has existed under patriarchy. Bernard Goldberg (pages 83–87) in "They Think You're a Traitor" asserts that he forfeited his position with CBS News because he campaigned for truth in broadcasting and condemned the liberal bias of television newscasters.

EXERCISE 3.7

EVALUATING A THESIS

Which statements below could serve effectively as theses in an essay or article?

1. Title IX has built women's sports programs at the expense of men's minor sports.
2. Golf is a stupid sport on the level of lawn bowling.
3. A necessary ingredient for a championship team is teamwork.
4. The official language of the United States and the only language used in printed documents and public signs should be English.
5. A core curriculum of liberal arts courses is archaic and self-serving to the university.
6. Like men, women should be required to register for the draft.

Determining the Writer's Reasons

WEB LINK
to Exercise
3.3
http://www.
ablongman.com/
lester

As you read your sources, ask yourself *why* the writer makes an assertion, especially if it seems capricious or dogmatic. For example, why should women be required to register for the draft? Does the writer have valid reasons? Perhaps the reasons will be that women have gained equality, women have the expertise, and women have proved themselves in large numbers within current armed forces. These are reasons, and the writer should spell them out for you.

In another example, why should English be the official language of the United States? Does the writer have reasons that you can accept, such as saving money in printing, forcing immigrants to merge within the official language, eliminating bilingual teaching in the schools, or even mitigating the collective power of one culture. Be sharp, keep alert. Writers may bury their reasons under a cloud of self-serving evidence and unrelated examples. On that note, see this chapter's discussion of fallacies (pages 106–111).

In the articles and essays of this chapter, writers have demonstrated a variety of reasons for making their assertions. Caleb Carr (pages 66–67) wants us to examine the nature of terrorism by showing its consequences on the afflicted nations. James Campbell (pages 69–70) gives the reason for Robert Louis Stevenson's semi-mythical settings; the writer escaped from progressive London for quiet, remote colonies around the world. Robert Samuelson (pages 71–73) presents a clear reason why the federal budget is bloated—the lack of fiscal discipline by Congress and the president. Carol Gilligan (pages 75–78) wants to explain the reasons for the historical trauma of love stories, which she describes as a product of male dominance and jealousy.

Thus, your critical reading should include a note or two on a writer's purposes. For example, in a marginal note or a page of your writing journal, you might write:

David Evans wants young blacks to step forward as activists for human rights rather than remain in the shadows behind Jesse Jackson, Al Sharpton, and a few others.

News reporter Lindsay Tanner, citing a scientific study, wants to educate her audience about the relationship of head injuries and depression.

Bernard Goldberg wants to expose the liberal bias in television newscasters as well as the conservative bias of radio talk shows.

By making such notes, you make clear a writer's reasons, and that knowledge will serve you well as you summarize, paraphrase, or quote from the source.

Looking for Support to an Argument

WEB LINK
to Chapter 3
Related Web
Destinations
http://www.
ablongman.com/
lester

For support, writers use examples, statistics, the voices of authorities, comparisons, anecdotes, and textual evidence. Sometimes one type is sufficient, but usually a writer will merge several for support.

Examples

The use of examples is popular in all types of writing, but your critical reading should ascertain that the examples are representative, relevant, and truly supportive of the writer's thesis. For example, in *The Birth of Pleasure,* Carol Gilligan mentions several exemplary stories on the trauma of love as drawn from ancient literature. In like manner, Margaret Loftus in "But What's It Like?" provides examples of electronic courses that confound and confuse the students because of human error as well as technical malfunctions. Bernard Goldberg's "They Think You're a Traitor" presents a catalog of examples to prove his assertions about the liberal nature of prime-time newscasters.

Statistics

If the article is about social, economic, or medical issues, look for statistics in support of the thesis. Papers on education, for example, cite empirical data drawn from written tests and from classroom observation. A paper on the move of textile manufacturing to foreign countries would benefit by statistical data on the number of closed plants, lost jobs, shifts in the labor force, and the dollars lost in county and state taxes.

In the article on head injuries, Lindsey Tanner employs statistics by citing scientific studies and providing a chart from the *Archives of General Psychiatry*. Here's a sample of her statistics:

> The study involved 1,718 veterans hospitalized for various ailments during the war and questioned 50 years later. About 11% who had experienced head injuries said they currently had major depression, compared with 8.5% of those hospitalized during the war for other reasons.

Also in this chapter, Robert Samuelson uses statistics in his article on farm subsidies, but he neglects to reveal his source for the data.

Authorities

As you read, watch for writers who cite experts on the subject, especially authorities with credentials who truly support the writer's thesis and reasoning. The citation of experts gives credibility both to the article and to the writer who has done his or her research. Writers state the credentials of an expert either in the textual citation or in a bibliography entry at the end of the article. Notice how Lindsay Tanner identifies the credentials of her authorities on head injuries and depression:

> Overall, the lifetime prevalence of major depression was 18.5% in the head injury group and 13.4% among the other veterans, Drs. Tracey Holsinger and Brenda Plassman of Duke University and colleagues reported in *Archives of General Psychiatry*.

Other writers in this chapter who cite expert testimony are Thomas C. Harrison (page 79) and Margaret Loftus (page 94).

Comparisons

Writers often lay out two ideas, activities, or positions to compare and contrast. By showing two comparable items, the writer supports and clarifies the thesis of the article or essay. Caleb Carr in "Lessons of Terror" compares modern terrorism that targets civilians to the Roman terms *destructive war* and *punitive war*. Robert Samuelson compares the farm subsidy program to a "huge political bribe." Carol Gilligan compares modern love stories to the trauma and tragedy of ancient tales about Oedipus, Noah, and others. John Gray compares men to the planet Mars, named after the Roman god of war, and compares women to the planet Venus, named after the goddess of love.

In every case, the writers are using the comparisons to promote their thesis, for example:

- The tragic nature of love under a patriarchy must be measured against the "new truth" that "must be brought by a woman." (Gilligan)
- Farm subsidies are a poorly disguised quest for votes. (Samuelson)
- Terrorism is a destructive, punitive action against civilians. (Carr)
- Only by recognizing and accepting the contrasting natures of man and woman can the magic of love last. (Gray)

Anecdotes

A brief story about an experience or event can enliven and support an argument. Writers use short narratives to bring readers a vivid scene that will illustrate one aspect of the argument. Of course, the brief story must be true to life, believable, and a dramatic illustration of the writer's thesis. An anecdote often opens an article to make an issue realistic and vital to the human condition under discussion.

Campbell's passage about Robert Louis Stevenson (page 69) opens, as you will recall, with this anecdote:

> One evening in the spring of 1880, Robert Louis Stevenson dropped into the bar of the Magnolia Hotel in Calistoga, at the head of the Napa Valley. There was little more to the town than the springs, the railway station, and the enticement of a fortune to be made from mining gold or silver. The West was still pretty wild. Inside, someone asked Stevenson if he would like to speak to Mr. Foss, a stagecoach driver; Stevenson, always alert to the suggestion of travel, said yes: "Next moment, I had one instrument at my ear, another at my mouth, and found myself, with nothing in the world to say, conversing with a man several miles off among desolate hills."

Campbell uses this anecdote to introduce Stevenson as an eccentric writer and traveler who preferred to escape the trappings of civilization.

In like manner, David Evans (page 87) opens with an anecdote about academic turmoil at Harvard University to focus on civil rights activism. Bernard Goldberg (page 83) gives anecdotal narratives to support his attack on liberal bias in television newscasters. Margaret Loftus (page 94) opens her article with an anecdote about Judy Rowe, in Paris, France, connecting online with her class in the states.

Textual Evidence

Look for textual evidence from writers of interpretation because quotations, summaries, and paraphrases of the text provide the primary support for reading a play, novel, history book, song, and so forth. Each citation from the text should support the writer's thesis, but don't let a writer overwhelm you with too many citations. The selections drawn from a text should be highly selective and bear precisely on the issue under discussion.

The literary article by Thomas Harrison on Keats's poem "To Autumn" (page 69) demonstrates the use of textual evidence, for Harrison selectively cites relevant passages from the poem to defend his thesis, saying, for example:

> And there are the oblique allusions to death: "soft-dying day," wailful choir," "small gnats mourn," "the light wind lives or dies" (25, 27, 29). All these images come with their appropriate sounds.

Harrison's final sentence above connects the quotations to his thesis on the sound effects used by Keats in the poem.

Understanding Logic

This text cannot dwell in depth on the formal aspects of logic. As a critical reader, however, you should understand the ebb and flow of inductive and deductive reasoning. Most assertions you will encounter are based on inductive reasoning that reaches a conclusion based on gathered evidence, as with Samuelson's assertion that the farm subsidy program is a bribe by Congress for votes, or Tanner's assertion that head injuries can contribute to later depression. Sometimes the evidence is not conclusive:

WEB LINK
to Exercise
3.4
http://www.
ablongman.com/
lester

> Electronic classrooms via the Internet will continue to grow each year. The demand is greater than current offerings because student are enrolling in E-courses for a number of reasons: employment conflicts, children at home, distance from campus, and the convenience of working at home.

The writer should use the word *probably* in the first sentence because growth in electronic classrooms could slow at a semester's notice.

If the inductive evidence is inconclusive, the writer should use words that set a limit on the claim, such as *some, most, almost, probably, very likely,* and *almost certainly.* Note the use of *probably* in this passage:

> The use of microchips in ever smaller sizes to create miniature electronic equipment means that wrist watches of the future will probably have numerous functions, such as time, date, alarm, television, intercom, telephone, and many more.

At other times the inductive evidence may be conclusive. For example, a person has intense pain in the lower stomach. The doctor, based on years of inductive experience, suspects a kidney stone and orders a CT scan. Sure enough, the stone is located. The evidence established an absolute conclusion. In another case, a student has trouble reading. The teacher suspects that the student suffers from dyslexia. Tests prove the condition.

Inductive reasoning works in this pattern:

Observation of a condition or problem $\longrightarrow$

Search for a pattern $\longrightarrow$

Make a tentative hypothesis: This student's reading problems are caused by dyslexia.

Inductive reasoning moves from a specific observation toward a general conclusion. Deductive thinking, however, moves in the opposite direction, using this pattern:

A theory or idea is framed as a hypothesis: Dyslexia is caused by miscommunication between the hemispheres of the brain $\longrightarrow$

Observation and testing conducted to prove or disprove the hypothesis $\longrightarrow$

Hypothesis is confirmed or disproved by scientific testing.

Thus, by using deductive reasoning we try to prove a hypothesis. Once we confirm or disprove the hypothesis, we get factual statements:

A molecule of water always contains hydrogen and oxygen.

All persons with AIDS carry the HIV virus.

Concrete embedded with plastic fibers is stronger than regular cement.

Dyslexia is caused by miscommunication between the two hemispheres of the brain.

These conclusions feature indicator words such as *all, every, certainly, without fail, is, was,* and *always.*

Let us use one more illustration to understand the difference in the thinking process. A child has a toy glider that she flings into the sky, and she watches it glide to earth. She tries again with the same result. She says to her father, "I guess I can't make it fly. Every time it comes back down. Here, you throw it and I bet it comes back down for you too!" The father replies, "Yes, it will come back down. That's Newton's law of gravity, Sue. Everything that goes up will be pulled back down by the force of earth's gravity."

The child is thinking inductively; the father deductively. Newton has confirmed the hypothesis by careful observation. The child has observed the plane's pattern and arrived at a theory.

GUIDELINES

Identifying Inductive and Deductive Reasoning

- Does the writer base the conclusion on a set of premises, declarations, or propositions that have been confirmed by study and research? It's deductive.

- Does the writer reach a conclusion on the basis of observation and gathered evidence? It's inductive.

- Does the writer use words such as *all, every, certainly, without fail, always?* It's deductive.

- Does the writer use words such as *some, most, almost, probably, very likely?* It's inductive.

EXERCISE 3.8

INDUCTIVE AND DEDUCTIVE REASONING

Label each sentence below as inductive or deductive reasoning, based on how the statement is framed.

1. The coach said, "George, you've taken 88 shots in the first seven games—you made 80% of those inside the paint but only 25% of those outside the paint. What does that tell you, son?"

2. Gathering mail overnight in one central airport, sorting it, and redistributing it the same night is the basis for Fred Smith's MBA thesis and the foundation for his business—Federal Express.

3. Anybody who cruises the Mississippi River from Memphis to New Orleans will learn bits of history about the South.

4. Humans are the only animals in the northern hemisphere without natural protection from cold weather.

5. The questionnaire results show that 74 percent of the student population favors assigned parking spaces for mornings and open parking after 1:00 p.m. each day.

6. Four of a kind always beats a full house, and a pair of jacks has no chance against a straight.

7. Drinking eight glasses of water each day will keep you hydrated.

8. Muscles weigh more than fat.

9. If you exercise, stay on a low-carb diet, and avoid sugar products, you will probably lose weight.

10. Based on scientific evidence as gathered over the past 30 days, your home has dangerous levels of radon. Move out now!

Identifying Fallacies

When you find an article with specific passages that you wish to use in your own writing, pause for a moment to judge the overall stance of the writer. Look for bias and ineffective and even unsound arguments. The writer may not maintain a clear line of reasoning from one argument to another. The writer may even misrepresent the evidence or take quotations out of context.

WEB LINK
to Chapter 3
Related Web
Destinations
http://www.
ablongman.com/
lester

Every writer who launches an essay has an agenda, one that he or she wants to share. Some are pleasant personal narratives that carry a message about life's issues. Others are factual, informative essays presented in an objective manner. Still others give a pressing and hard-hitting argument to convince the reader that something must be done about an unjust situation. Your task, before you cite the source, is to judge the work for fairness to the issues and the evidence. It's not an easy task, because fallacies slip into a piece of writing like little gremlins (with or without the writer's realization), and they may influence readers who too readily accept the printed word.

A *fallacy* is a defective argument; it is an assertion that is either reasoned incorrectly or based on invalid premises. Here are a few of the most common fallacies, or errors in reasoning:

Argument Against the Person

Some writers attempt to discredit a person holding the opposing viewpoint rather than confront the opposing argument. The attack against the person's character or circumstances is usually irrelevant to the conclusion:

People who argue for gun control have no respect for the Constitution. Therefore, there should be no gun control.

Whether or not people respect the Constitution is irrelevant to the argument.

Naturally Mr. Jones favors early parole for nonviolent criminals. He is a defense attorney. Early parole is a terrible idea.

The attempt to discredit Jones does not address the primary issue.

Appeal to Authority

Citing an authority to support your argument is valid if the person is truly an expert, but writers sometimes promote a person as an expert who is not reputable, up to date, objective, or truly the final authority in the area of discussion. Is an athlete really qualified to judge the best deodorant or shave cream? Is the *National Enquirer* a good source of information about the future of oil prices? The example below provides authoritative evidence only if Jones, Barnes, and Lundlow have good credentials.

Although an isolated expert here and there might assert that steroid use for short periods of time will cause no permanent damage to an athlete's body (Jones 33–35), most authorities argue that steroid use by athletes produces lasting, harmful effects (see esp. Barnes 16–29 and Lundlow 177–214). Coaches and administrators should enact strict rules to prohibit steroid use by athletes and conduct frequent tests to enforce them.

Citing common sense or a consensus is one form of the appeal to authority. Watch out for "everybody knows (or agrees) that . . . " Remember that at one time everyone believed that the Earth was flat and also that the sun revolved around the Earth.

A First Event Caused a Second Event

Arguing that one event caused a succeeding event may be based on a false assumption.

Just days after the engine was tuned, it began to stall at intersections. Therefore, the mechanic did something wrong and caused the stalling.

The cause of the stalled motor might be a broken part that has nothing to do with the tune-up.

Circular Reasoning

Some arguments simply restate the conclusion as a premise. This next assertion assumes that every reader has a clear understanding of what constitutes a "master teacher":

Master teachers deserve higher salaries because they are the best teachers.

The writer should find a common ground with the reader:

If master teachers exist, and I believe we can identify them with clear criteria of education, performance in the classroom, and public service, they deserve higher salaries.

The next writer also begs the question by retreating into tradition, the very issue being questioned.

Sororities are for women and fraternities are for men, so we must not consider any sort of merger.

The writer should address the issue in a rational manner:

Historically, sororities and fraternities have been segregated by sex, yet today's new social climate suggests that we should re-evaluate their purposes and their membership requirements.

Hasty Generalization

A writer may draw a conclusion from inadequate evidence.

Of the ten women who were interviewed, seven preferred married life to being single. Therefore, it is safe to assume that most women prefer marriage.

This writer should not make a prediction about all women based on a sample of only ten. Yet some writers will make hasty generalizations based on a sample of only one, usually an eye-catching aberration that the writer knows of personally:

> Last Sunday Ted Jones, captain of the Lions football team, got in his car, buckled up, backed out of his driveway, and headed down Elm Street. Two blocks away he lost control of his car, ran off the road, turned over, and burned to death because he could not free himself from his seatbelt. I urge you to repeal the seatbelt law that brought about his ghastly death.

True, the writer can attribute this death, in part, to a faulty seatbelt. However, has the writer established that seatbelts kill more people than they save? What are the survival rates for people using seatbelts compared to those not using them?

The use of exit interviews of voters as a tool for predicting election results has come under fire as hasty generalization, especially when predictions are made while the polling booths are still open.

False Analogy

A false analogy is an illogical or flawed comparison.

> Like a ship at sea, the ship of state needs a strong captain, the president, whose orders are not subject to question at every turn. Congress should keep its nose out of the president's conduct of foreign affairs.

The government is not a ship at sea. It is a complex organization with its own precise rules, which give both Congress and the president separate roles to play.

Either–Or Argument

The use of either–or reasoning creates a false dilemma by arguing that a complicated issue has only two answers when, in truth, several options may be available. It reflects oversimplification by the writer.

> At this university either a first-year student joins a sorority or a fraternity to enter the mainstream of social activity or the student will remain an outsider, isolated and lonely.

This dilemma—join or be lonely—ignores other levels of social support on the campus.

False Emotional Appeal

False emotional appeals come in several well-disguised packages. *Flattery* uses insincere and excessive praise of the audience to disguise shallow reasoning. *Snob appeal* and the *bandwagon* encourage readers to join a cause or buy a product because the "best" people do it and because it will raise the readers' self-esteem. *Racial and sexist slurs* demean one class in a perverse appeal by one bigot to another.

> The enclosed bid offers you and a few other carefully screened freshmen an opportunity to join the most prestigious fraternity on campus, one that has produced more doctors, lawyers, and MBAs than all other local fraternities combined.

This sentence uses both flattery and snob appeal in its recruitment efforts.

Non Sequitur

A conclusion that does not follow from the premises is called a *non sequitur*. It is reached without valid evidence. This next statement is illogical.

> The math team cannot win this next competition because the University of Arizona has three wizards on their team and our Mark James is ill with hepatitis.

This conclusion does not follow from the premises. Neither the absence of James nor the presence of three wizards can automatically defeat the math team.

Avoiding the Issue

Avoidance of the real issue shifts the reader's attention to an unrelated issue. Deliberate use of this fallacy derives from an old technique by which a *straw man* or a *red herring* was used to divert attention from the real target.

> Although one administrator seems eager to examine the status of fraternities on campus, his time could be spent on more serious matters, such as the pathetic condition of library holdings. Did you know that the library has canceled its subscription to such important periodicals as *JAMA*, *Southern Review*, and the *Browning Newsletter*?

This writer waves a flag about library problems to divert attention from the administration's examination of fraternities.

WEB LINK
to Exercise
3.5
http://www.
ablongman.com/
lester

G U I D E L I N E S

Finding Fallacies in Logic

The reasoning and conclusions of an essay are suspect if:

- The writer bases an assertion on a premise or inference that is not convincing.
- The chain of reasoning breaks down with the result that the assertion does not follow logically from the evidence offered.

> - The writer manipulates or distorts the evidence in some way.
> - The writer misdirects the argument, appeals to a false authority, misinterprets the cause and effect, or jumps to hasty conclusions.

EXERCISE 3.9
IDENTIFYING FALLACIES

Identify the type of fallacy that you find in each of the following sentences.

1. Railroad companies had to build their own roadways, so trucking companies should do the same and stop crowding our interstate system.
2. People who support a large defense budget are contractors who benefit from the funding. Cut the defense budget.
3. Everybody knows that Russia's economy is weak and unstable, so we need have no fear of war.
4. Early in his term of office, President Reagan held firm and refused to negotiate with the Russians. Indeed, they soon capitulated and submitted to his terms.
5. George W. Bush became president in January 2001, and by 2003 America had declared war on two different countries.
6. War is the only answer for countries that abuse Americans.
7. A poll of 20 students reveals that 80 percent of the student body thinks that Rob Longstreet has performed well as president of the Student Government Association.
8. One student, Jennifer Lockwood, worked as an aide to a congressman last year, and now she has a government loan to pay her fees.
9. One congressman died in a private plane crash in Arizona and another died under similar circumstances in Mississippi. Congressmen should fly only by commercial airline.
10. Higher salaries for teachers will improve education because you get what you pay for.

Chapter Review

Chapter 3 encourages you to practice critical reading of the sources by using some basic techniques, such as highlighting phrases, making marginal notes, asking penetrating questions, and outlining.

The chapter then explores the methods for discovering a writer's intentions toward inquiry, negotiation, or persuasion. You are encouraged to look at an essay's chain of reasoning to determine its validity and to find the writer's use of evidence for making assertions, drawing inferences, and suggesting implications.

The chapter describes the best methods for finding and evaluating a writer's argument. These include finding the writer's thesis, checking out the writer's fundamental reasons for writing the article or essay, and then looking for the author's support in the form of examples, statistics, textual evidence, and the voices of authorities.

Finally, the chapter explores logic and the ebb and flow of inductive and deductive reasoning. It explains how each type affects not only the conclusions reached but also the structure of the article or essay, for inductive reasoning works from observation toward a reasonable answer or solution while deductive reasoning starts with a hypothesis that must be tested and proved. The section ends with a discussion of fallacies and examples that make clear how fallacies can disrupt the chain of reasoning and render an article less than reliable.

Chapter 3 Assignment:
Critical Reading to Find the Central Issues

Read with care the following essay by Robert Weinberg, a molecular biologist at the Massachusetts Institute of Technology, winner of the 1997 National Medal of Science, and author of several books. In this essay, originally published in *The Atlantic Monthly* (June 2002), Weinberg explains how serious scientific research is being handicapped and underfunded because of a media circus about the cloning issue. You will be asked to answer several questions at the end of your reading. Meanwhile, look for the following items:

- Passages that reveal the writer's chain of reasoning
- Passages in which the writer makes inferences from the evidence
- Passages in which the writer cites sources in defense of his assertions
- A fallacy anywhere in the line of reasoning
- The writer's primary claim
- The validity of the primary claim

Of Clones and Clowns

Robert Weinberg

Biologists have been rather silent on the subject of human cloning. Some others would accuse us, as they have with predictable regularity in the recent past, of insensitivity to the societal consequences of our research. If not insensitivity, then moral obtusensess, and if not that, then arrogance—an accusation that can never be disproved.

The truth is that most of us have remained quiet for quite another reason. Most of us regard reproductive cloning—a procedure used to produce an entire new organism from one cell of an adult—as a technology riddled with problems. Why should we waste time agonizing about something that is far removed from practical utility, and may forever remain so?

The nature and magnitude of the problems were suggested by the Scottish scientist Ian Wilmut's initial report, five years ago, on the cloning of Dolly the sheep. Dolly represented one success among 277 attempts to produce a viable, healthy newborn. Most attempts at cloning other animal species—to date cloning has succeeded with sheep, mice, cattle, goats, cats, and pigs—have not fared much better.

Even the successes come with problems. The placentas of cloned fetuses are routinely two or three times larger than normal. The offspring are usually larger than normal as well. Several months after birth one group of cloned mice weighed 72 percent more than mice created through normal reproduction. In many species cloned fetuses must be delivered by cesarean section because of their size. This abnormality, the reasons for which no one understands, is so common that it now has its own name—Large Offspring Syndrome. Dolly (who was of normal size at birth) was briefly overweight in her young years and suffers from early-onset arthritis of unknown cause. Two recent reports indicate that cloned mice suffer early-onset obesity and early death.

Arguably the most successful reproductive-cloning experiment was reported last year by Advanced Cell Technology, a small biotech company in Worcester, Massachusetts. Working with cows, ACT produced 496 embryos by injecting nuclei from adult cells into eggs that had been stripped of their own nuclei. Implanting the embryos into the uteruses of cows led to 110 established pregnancies, thirty of which went to term. Five of the newborns died shortly after birth, and a sixth died several months later. The twenty-four surviving calves developed into cows that were healthy by all criteria examined. But most, if not all, had enlarged placentas, and as newborns some of them suffered from the respiratory distress typical of Large Offspring Syndrome.

The success rate of the procedure, roughly five percent, was much higher than the rates achieved with other mammalian species, and the experiment was considered a great success. Some of the cows have grown up, been artificially inseminated, and given birth to normal offspring. Whether they are affected by any of the symptoms associated with Large Offspring Syndrome later in life is not apparent from the published data. No matter: for $20,000 ACT will clone your favorite cow.

Imagine the application of this technology to human beings. Suppose that 100 adult nuclei are obtained, each of which is injected into a human egg whose own nucleus has been removed. Imagine then that only five of the 100 embryos thus created result in well-formed, viable newborns; the other ninety-five spontaneously abort at various stages of development or, if cloning experiments with mammals other than cows are any guide, yield grossly malformed babies. The five viable babies have a reasonable likelihood of suffering from Large Offspring Syndrome. How they will develop, physically and cognitively, is anyone's guess. It seems unlikely that even the richest and most egomaniacal among us, intent on recreating themselves exactly, will swarm to this technology.

Biological systems are extraordinarily complex, and there are myriad ways in which experiments can go awry or their results can be misinterpreted. Still, perhaps 95 percent of what biologists read in this year's research journals will be considered valid (if perhaps not very interesting) a century from now. Much of scientists' trust in the existing knowledge base derives from the system constructed over the past century to validate new research findings and the conclusions derived from them. Research journals impose quality controls to ensure that scientific observations and conclusions are solid and credible. They sift the scientific wheat from the chaff.

The system works like this: A biologist sends a manuscript describing his experiment to a journal. The editor of the journal recruits several experts, who remain anonymous to the researcher, to vet the manuscript. A month or two later the researcher receives a thumbs-up, a thumbs-down, or a request for revisions and more data. The system works reasonably well, which is why many of us invest large amounts of time in serving as the anonymous reviewers of one another's work. Without such rigorously imposed quality control, our subfields of research would rapidly descend into chaos, because no publicly announced result would carry the imprimatur of having been critiqued by experts.

We participate in the peer-review process not only to create a sound edifice of ideas and results for ourselves; we do it for the outside world as well—for all those who are unfamiliar with the arcane details of our field. Without the trial-by-fire of peer review, how can journalists and the public possibly know which discoveries are credible, which are nothing more than acts of self-promotion by ambitious researchers, and which smack of the delusional?

The hype about cloning has made a shambles of this system, creating something of a circus. Many of us have the queasy feeling that our carefully constructed world of science is under siege. The clowns—those who think that making money, lots of it, is more important than doing serious science—have invaded our sanctuary.

The cloning circus opened soon after Wilmut, a careful and well-respected scientist, reported his success with Dolly. First in the ring was Richard Seed, an elderly Chicago physicist, who in late 1997 announced his intention of cloning a human being within two years. Soon members of an international religious cult, the Raëlians (followers of Claude Vorilhon, a French-born mystic who says that he was given the name Raël by four-foot-high extraterrestrials, and who preaches that human beings were originally created by these aliens), revealed an even more grandiose vision of human cloning. To the Raëlians, biomedical science is a sacrament to be used for achieving immortality: their ultimate goal is to use cloning to create empty shells into which people's souls can be transferred. As a sideline, the Raëlian-affiliated company Clonaid hopes to offer its services to couples who would like to create a child through reproductive cloning for $200,000 per child.

Neither Seed nor the Raëlians made any pretense of subjecting their plans to review by knowledgeable scientists; they went straight to the popular press. Still, this wasn't so bad. Few science journalists took them seriously (although they did oblige them with extensive coverage). Biologists were also unmoved. Wasn't it obvious that Seed and the

Raëlians were unqualified to undertake even the beginnings of the series of technical steps required for reproductive cloning? Why dignify them with a response?

The next wave of would-be cloners likewise went straight to the mainstream press—but they were not so easily dismissed. In March of last year, at a widely covered press conference in Rome, an Italian and a U.S. physician announced plans to undertake human reproductive cloning outside the United States. The Italian member of the team was Severino Antinori, a gynecologist notorious for having used donor eggs and *in vitro* fertilization to make a sixty-two-year-old woman pregnant in 1994. Now he was moving on. Why, he asked, did the desires of infertile couples (he claimed to have 600 on a waiting list) not outweigh the concerns about human cloning? He repeatedly shouted down reporters and visiting researchers who had the temerity to voice questions about the biological and ethical problems associated with reproductive cloning.

The American member of the team was Panayiotis Zavos, a reproductive physiologist and an *in vitro* fertilization expert at the Andrology Institute of America, in Lexington, Kentucky. "The genie is out of the bottle," he told reporters. "Dolly is here, and we are next." Antinori and Zavos announced their intention of starting a human cloning project in an undisclosed Mediterranean country. Next up was Avi Ben-Abraham, an Israeli-American biotechnologist with thwarted political ambitions (he ran unsuccessfully for the Knesset) and no reputable scientific credentials, who attempted to attach himself to the project. Ben-Abraham hinted that the work would be done either in Israel or in an Arab country, because "the climate is more [receptive to human cloning research] within Judaism and Islam." He told the German magazine *Der Spiegel*, "We were all created by the Almighty, but now we will become the creators."

Both Antinori and Zavos glossed over the large gap between expertise with established infertility procedures and the technical skills required for reproductive cloning. Confronted with the prospect of high rates of aborted or malformed cloned embryos, they claimed to be able to weed out any defective embryos at an early stage of gestation. "We have a great deal of knowledge," Zavos announced to the press. "We can grade embryos. We can do genetic screening. We can do [genetic] quality control." This was possible, he said, because of highly sensitive diagnostic tests that can determine whether or not development is proceeding normally.

The fact is that no such tests exist; they have eluded even the most expert biologists in the field, and there is no hope that they will be devised anytime soon—if ever. No one knows how to determine with precision whether the repertoire of genes expressed at various stages of embryonic development is being "read" properly in each cell type within an embryo. Without such information, no one can know whether the developmental program is proceeding normally in the womb. (The prenatal tests currently done for Down syndrome and several other genetic disorders can detect only a few of the thousands of things that can go wrong during embryonic development.)

Rudolf Jaenisch, a colleague of mine with extensive experience in mouse reproductive cloning, was sufficiently exercised to say to a reporter at the *Chicago Tribune*, "[Zavos and Antinori] will produce clones, and most of these will die in utero. . . . Those will be

the lucky ones. Many of those that survive will have [obvious or more subtle] abnormalities." The rest of us biologists remained quiet. To us, Antinori, Zavos, and Ben-
Abraham were so clearly inept that comment seemed gratuitous. In this instance we
have, as on other occasions, misjudged the situation: many people seem to take these
three and their plans very seriously indeed. And, in fact, this past April, Antinori
claimed, somewhat dubiously, that a woman under his care was eight weeks pregnant
with a cloned embryo.

In the meantime, the biotechnology industry, led by ACT, has been moving ahead
aggressively with human cloning, but of a different sort. The young companies in this sector have sensed, probably correctly, the enormous potential of therapeutic (rather than reproductive) cloning as a strategy for treating a host of common human degenerative diseases.

The initial steps of therapeutic cloning are identical to those of reproductive cloning:
cells are prepared from an adult tissue, their nuclei are extracted, and each nucleus is introduced into a human egg, which is allowed to develop. However, in therapeutic cloning
embryonic development is halted at a very early stage—when the embryo is a blastocyst,
consisting of perhaps 150 cells—and the inner cells are harvested and cultured. These
cells, often termed embryonic stem cells, are still very primitive and thus have retained
the ability to develop into any type of cell in the body (except those of the placenta).

Mouse and human embryonic stem cells can be propagated in a petri dish and
induced to form precursors of blood-forming cells, or of the insulin-producing cells of
the pancreas, or of cardiac muscle or nerve tissue. These precursor cells (tissue-specific
stem cells) might then be introduced into a tissue that has grown weak from the loss of
too many of its differentiated worker cells. When the ranks of the workers are replen-
ished, the course of disease may be dramatically reversed. At least, that is the current theory. In recent months one version of the technique has been successfully applied to mice.

Therapeutic cloning has the potential to revolutionize the treatment of a number of
currently untreatable degenerative diseases, but it is only a potential. Considerable
research will be required to determine the technology's possibilities and limitations for
treating human patients.

Some worry that therapeutic-cloning research will never get off the ground in this
country. Its proponents—and there are many among the community of biomedical
researchers—fear that the two very different kinds of cloning, therapeutic and reproductive, have merged in the public's mind. Three leaders of the community wrote a
broadside early this year in *Science*, titled "Please Don't Call It Cloning!" Call therapeutic cloning anything else—call it "nuclear transplantation," or "stem cell research." The
scientific community has finally awakened to the damage that the clowns have done.

This is where the newest acts of the circus begin. President George Bush and many
pro-life activists are in one ring. A number of disease-specific advocacy groups that view
therapeutic cloning as the only real prospect for treating long-resistant maladies are in
another. In a third ring are several biotech companies that are flogging their wares, often
in ways that make many biologists shudder.

Yielding to pressure from religious conservatives, Bush announced last August that
no new human embryonic stem cells could be produced from early human embryos that

had been created during the course of research sponsored by the federal government; any research on the potential applications of human embryonic stem cells, he said, would have to be conducted with the existing repertoire of sixty-odd lines. The number of available, usable cell lines actually appears to be closer to a dozen or two. And like all biological reagents, these cells tend to deteriorate with time in culture; new ones will have to be derived if research is to continue. What if experiments with the existing embryonic-stem-cell lines show enormous promise? Such an outcome would produce an almost irresistible pressure to move ahead with the derivation of new embryonic stem cells and to rapidly expand this avenue of research.

How will we learn whether human embryonic stem cells are truly useful for new types of therapy? This question brings us directly to another pitfall: much of the research on human embryonic stem cells is already being conducted by biotech companies, rather than in universities. Bush's edict will only exacerbate this situation. (In the 1970s a federal decision effectively banning government funding of *in vitro* fertilization had a similar effect, driving such research into private clinics.)

Evaluating the science coming from the labs of the biotech industry is often tricky. Those who run these companies are generally motivated more by a need to please stock analysts and venture capitalists than to convince scientific peers. For many biotech companies the peer-review process conducted by scientific journals is simply an inconvenient, time-wasting impediment. So some of the companies routinely bypass peer review and go straight to the mainstream press. Science journalists, always eager for scoops, don't necessarily feel compelled to consult experts about the credibility of industry press releases. And when experts are consulted about the contents of a press release, they are often hampered by spotty descriptions of the claimed breakthrough and thus limited to mumbling platitudes.

ACT, the company that conducted the successful cow-cloning experiment and has now taken the lead in researching human therapeutic cloning, has danced back and forth between publishing in respectable peer-reviewed journals and going directly to the popular press—and recently tried to find a middle ground. Last fall, with vast ambitions, ACT reported that it had conducted the first successful human-cloning experiment. In truth, however, embryonic development went only as far as six cells—far short of the 150-cell blastocyst that represents the first essential step of therapeutic cloning. Wishing to cloak its work in scientific respectability, ACT reported these results in a fledgling electronic research journal named *e-biomed: The Journal of Regenerative Medicine*, Perhaps ACT felt especially welcome in a journal that, according to its editor in chief, William A. Haseltine, a widely known biotech tycoon, "is prepared to publish work of a more preliminary nature." It may also have been encouraged by Haseltine's stance toward cloning, as revealed in his remarks when the journal was founded. "As we understand the body's repair process at the genetic level, we will be able to advance the goal of maintaining our bodies in normal function, perhaps perpetually," he said.

Electronic publishing is still in its infancy, and the publication of ACT's research report will do little to enhance its reputation. By the usual standards of scientific achievement, the experiments ACT published would be considered abject failures. Knowledgeable readers of the report were unable to tell whether the clump of six cells represented the beginning of a human embryo or simply an unformed aggregate of dying cells.

One prominent member of the *e-biomed* editorial board, a specialist in the type of embryology used in cloning, asked Haseltine how the ACT manuscript had been vetted before its publication. Haseltine assured his board member that the paper had been seen by two competent reviewers, but he refused to provide more details. The board member promptly resigned. Two others on the editorial board, also respected embryologists, soon followed suit. (Among the scientists left on the board are two representatives of ACT—indeed, both were authors of the paper.) Mary Ann Liebert, the publisher of the journal, interpreted this exodus as a sign that "clearly some noses were out of joint." The entire publication process subverted the potentially adversarial but necessary dynamic between journal-based peer review and the research scientist.

No one yet knows precisely how to make therapeutic cloning work, or which of its many claimed potential applications will pan out and which will not. And an obstacle other than experimental problems confronts those pushing therapeutic cloning. In the wake of the cloning revolution a second revolution has taken place—quieter but no less consequential. It, too, concerns tissue-specific stem cells—but ones found in the tissues of adults. These adult stem cells may one day prove to be at least as useful as those generated by therapeutic cloning.

Many of our tissues are continually jettisoning old, worn-out cells and replacing them with freshly minted ones. The process depends on a cadre of stem cells residing in each type of tissue and specific to that type of tissue. When an adult stem cell divides, one of its two daughters becomes a precursor of a specialized worker cell, able to help replenish the pool of worker cells that may have been damaged through injury or long-term use. The other remains a stem cell like its mother, thus ensuring that the population of stem cells in the tissue is never depleted.

Until two years ago the dogma among biologists was that stem cells in the bone marrow spawned only blood, those in the liver spawned only hepatocytes, and those in the brain spawned only neurons—in other words, each of our tissues had only its own cadre of stem cells for upkeep. Once again we appear to have been wrong. There is mounting evidence that the body contains some rather unspecialized stem cells, which wander around ready to help many sorts of tissue regenerate their worker cells.

Whether these newly discovered, multi-talented adult stem cells present a viable alternative to therapeutic cloning remains to be proved. Many of the claims about their capabilities have yet to be subjected to rigorous testing. Perhaps not surprisingly, some of these claims have also reached the public without careful vetting by peers. Senator Sam Brownback, of Kansas, an ardent foe of all kinds of cloning, has based much of his case in favor of adult stem cells (and against therapeutic cloning) on these essentially unsubstantiated scientific claims. Adult stem cells provide a convenient escape hatch for Brownback. Their use placates religious conservatives, who are against all cloning, while throwing a bone to groups lobbying for new stem-cell-based therapies to treat degenerative diseases.

Brownback would have biologists shut down therapeutic-cloning research and focus their energies exclusively on adult stem-cell research. But no one can know at present which of those two strategies is more likely to work. It will take a decade or more to find out. Many biologists are understandably reluctant to set aside therapeutic-cloning research in the meantime; they argue that the two technologies should be explored simultaneously.

Precisely this issue was debated recently by advisory committees in the United States and Germany. The U.S. committee was convened by Bruce Alberts, the president of the National Academy of Sciences and a highly accomplished cell biologist and scientific educator. Quite naturally, it included a number of experts who are actively involved in exploring the advantages and disadvantages of stem-cell therapies. The committee, which announced its findings in January, concluded that therapeutic cloning should be explored in parallel with alternative strategies.

For their trouble, the scientists were accused of financial self-interest by Steven Milloy of Fox News, who said, "Enron and Arthur Andersen have nothing over the National Academy of Sciences when it comes to deceiving the public. Enter Bruce Alberts, the Wizard of Oz–like president of the NAS. On his own initiative, Alberts put together a special panel, stacked with embryonic-stem-cell research proponents and researchers already on the taxpayer dole.... Breast-feeding off taxpayers is as natural to the NAS panel members as breathing."

The German committee, which reached a similar conclusion, was assembled by Ernst-Ludwig Winnacker, the head of his country's national science foundation. Winnacker and his colleagues were labeled "cannibals" by the Cardinal of Cologne. Remarks like the ones from Steven Milloy and the cardinal seem calculated to make public service at the interface between science and society as unappealing as possible.

President Bush, apparently anticipating the NAS panel's conclusion, has appointed an advisory committee all but guaranteed to produce a report much more to his liking. Its chairman, Leon Kass, has gone on record as being against all forms of cloning. (Earlier in his career Kass helped to launch an attack on *in vitro* fertilization.)

Meanwhile, a coalition of a hundred people and organizations recently sent a letter to Congress expressing their opposition to therapeutic cloning—among them Friends of the Earth, Greenpeace, the Sierra Club, the head of the National Latina Health Organization, and the perennial naysayer Jeremy Rifkin. "The problem with therapeutic cloning," Rifkin has said, "is that it introduces commercial eugenics from the get-go." Powerful words indeed. Few of those galvanized by Rifkin would know that therapeutic cloning has nothing whatsoever to do with eugenics.

Usually progress in biology is held back by experimental difficulties, inadequate instruments, poorly planned research protocols, inadequate funding, or plain sloppiness. But in this case the future of research may have little connection with these factors or with the scientific pros and cons being debated earnestly by members of the research community. The other, more public debates will surely be the decisive ones.

The clashes about human therapeutic cloning that have taken place in the media and in Congress are invariably built around weighty moral and ethical principles. But none of us needs a degree in bioethics to find the bottom line in the arguments. They all ultimately converge on a single question: When does human life begin? Some say it is when sperm and egg meet, others when the embryo implants in the womb, others when the fetus quickens, and yet others when the fetus can survive outside the womb. This is a question that we scientists are neither more nor less equipped to decide than the average man or woman in the street, than a senator from Kansas or a cardinal in Cologne. (Because Dolly and the other cloned animals show that a complete embryo can be produced from a single adult cell, some biologists have proposed, tongue in cheek, that a human life exists in each one of our cells.) Take your pick of the possible answers and erect your own moral scaffolding above your choice.

In the end, politics will settle the debate in this country about whether human therapeutic cloning is allowed to proceed. If the decision is yes, then we will continue to lead the world in a crucial, cutting-edge area of biomedical research. If it is no, U.S. bioloists will need to undertake hegiras [flight] to laboratories in Australia, Japan, Israel, and certain countries in Europe—an outcome that would leave American science greatly diminished.

WEB LINK to Exercise 3.6
http://www.ablongman.com/lester

Now, perform the following tasks:

1. Cite at least one passage that reveals the writer's careful development of a logical chain of reasoning.

2. Identify one passage in which the writer makes an inference on the basis of the evidence.

3. Identify a passage in which the writer cites a source in defense of various assertions.

4. Identify any fallacy in the author's reasoning.

5. Restate in your own words the writer's primary claim and discuss its validity.

Tracing the Work of Two Students

This section at the end of some chapters features the efforts of two students as they pursue the development of their papers. Kaci Holz is an English major researching gender communication issues. Halley Fishburn is a political science major researching the War Powers Act. Below, see how Holz has performed critical reading of a source by writing marginal annotations. Note that some annotations challenge the basic assumptions of the subject's work. She also drafted a set of questions, which follow the article, "Speaking across the Gender Gap." The article appeared in *New Scientist* (August 24, 1991). Holz accessed the article by using InfoTrac.

Speaking Across the Gender Gap

David Cohen

"Gimme That!"
"Let's do this."
"Get outta here!"
"How about doing that?"

Pre-school children spoke all these lines. According to Deborah Tannen, two utterances are typical of boys while two are typical of girls. Can you tell which sentence belongs to which sex?

Tannen is professor of linguistics of Georgetown University. For more than 40 weeks, her book *You Just Don't Understand* has been in the American best seller lists. It is a study, based on the analysis of conversations, of why men and women so often fail to understand each other. Virago has recently published the book in Britain. It will be interesting to see if it does as well in our less psychological culture.

Tannen argues that each sex does not just have its preferred topics—boys talk about things while girls talk about feelings— but its own conversational style. Provocatively, she suggests that talk between men and women ought to be studied as a form of cross-cultural communication. There is as much chance of men and women understanding each other automatically as there was of the Victorian British understanding the "darkest tribes of Africa."

Tannen claims that the examples of boys' and girls' speech quoted above show how styles of talking start very young. Women use conversations to establish intimacy and connection. The girls are always saying "Let's do something" which will include others. It is girls who use "maybe" often. The boys are more definite and suppress doubts. They use conversations to establish status. They like to stand alone so they give orders or take them. Tannen argues that men can show sympathy with one another and, indeed, with women, but they do it in a very different way.

All this sounds like the stuff of agony aunts. But Tannen insists that these mismatches of communication can be studied scientifically. She is careful to insist that while she is a feminist, she is not doing feminist linguistics. She does not blame men for having a different style of communicating. "Science is not about blaming," she says.

Cohen is reviewing a book by Deborah Tannen. The study is an analysis of conversations.

Men and women often misunderstand each other, so what else is new!

Each sex has its own conversational style.

Tannen uses the term "cross-cultural communication"

Women establish intimacy and connection, but men use conversation to establish status.

Tannen is too dogmatic for me, saying that women include others but men stand alone. I don't buy that idea.

Tannen has been analysing conversations, often her own, for a long time. She did her doctoral dissertation on a Thanksgiving dinner. Round the table were three New York Jews, two Californians and a Briton. They hailed from different linguistic universes. Tannen identified two distinct conversational styles. The first style she calls High Involvement and it is typical of the New York Jews. They speak with passion and enthusiasm. It is normal to talk personally. Diffidence is out. They can interrupt and ride roughshod over interruptions. They can argue and still be friends.

In her academic book *Conversational Styles* (published by Ablex) Tannen contrasted High Involvement with The High Considerateness style. No passion here, please. It would be considered embarrassing. It is normal (not to say polite) to listen to what other people say. You make sure someone has finished before you "venture" your own opinion. Stories should not be too personal. Rows are the end. You would never dream of imposing your point of view or intruding by asking personal questions. Interruptions are considered bad manners. Tannen's doctoral thesis found that the Briton at the dinner table was the most Highly Considerate of all. Should we be proud of this?

Tannen is a New York Jew. As a person, she feels more in sympathy with the High Involvement style. In her thesis, however, she stressed that one style was not better than the other. The styles reflected different cultures. To a Highly Considerate speaker, High Involvement speakers seem aggresive show-offs. But, then to the Highly Involved, the Highly Considerate don't seem very considerate at all but aloof, unfriendly and cold.

Tannen told me that she was always interested in making her findings accesible. On the basis of her thesis, she wrote a more popular book called *That's Not What I Meant*. She included a chapter on gender differences and got more letters about that chapter than about anything else. It convinced her that gender differences in conversation would be a rich area to study. She was also inspired by a colleague's videos of 7-year-old boys and girls talking to their best friends. "I looked and I was totally staggered by what I saw," Tannen says.

Tannen launched her book after noticing the dramatic differences in the talk of seven-year-old girls and boys.

She saw that these children were already speaking as if they belonged to different cultures. They were as far apart as the New York Jew and the stiff upper lipped Briton. She was seeing differences in these children that mirrored the classic differences between the way that men and women speak, differences that women frequently complain about. "I understand the female style instinctively but I couldn't say as a scientist that one way was better than another."

The psychology and politics of speech has been a growth area in the past few years. Feminist psychologists and sociologists, such as the Australian researcher Dale Spender, have argued that the ways men and women speak to each other show how men like to dominate. Men talk more and interrupt more. Men use talking to hog attention. Tannen has a number of nice anecdotes about how men often take centre stage in asking questions after she has given a lecture. The first question usually comes from a man; the question that really is an excuse to make a speech comes from a man. All too often men complain bitterly and interminably that women never give poor put-upon men the chance to speak. One man harped on this point until his audience started to fidget from annoyance.

Despite such persuasive anecdotes, Tannen is unwilling to dismiss men as selfish and self-centred. She argues that it is crucial that such scenes take place in public at a lecture. Men are comfortable with public speech. She calls this report-talk and contrasts it neatly with rapport-talk. Rapport-talk happens in private when two people either are or are trying to get close.

At least she does not diss men as selfish like so many feminists.

In private, women are not necessarily dominated. They often speak quite as much as men, but they use speech differently. For them, talk is a way of finding out how close and intimate they are. For men talk is a way of establishing who is in control and has the power. Tannen likes to give many examples of such mismatches. She asked me what I thought of this exchange:

By saying that men are comfortable giving a speech and women aren't, Tannen falls into the same sexist trap she's arguing against! Many women are comfortable speaking before a crowd.

Woman: How can you do this when it's hurting me?
Man: How can you try to limit my freedom?
Woman: But it makes me feel awful.
Man: You are trying to manipulate me.

Tannen argues that men often complain that their wives nag them because they feel that any attempt to give them advice is an attempt to put them at a disadvantage. Only the weak need advice. She claims that this is one reason why men hate asking questions. When you ask a question, you don't know the answer. To be ignorant is to admit that you are at a loss.

Boy, does she put men in her place! They can't take advice like a woman and they won't ask questions for fear of looking dumb. Is this extreme or what?

Tannen gives revealing examples of this male need for certainties. For instance, she tells of an instance in medical school where a female student who asked many questions that were received by the male instructor not as a sign of curiosity but as proof of the fact that she didn't know what she was supposed to know. Or consider the case of "Martha." Martha bought a computer and needed to learn to use it. The manual did not tell her all she needed to know so she returned to the shop where she had bought it. The man assigned to help her made her feel incredibly stupid. He deluged her with technical terms. His tone was patronising. Its "metamessage," as Tannen puts it, was that everything baffling her was obvious to him. A week later, still confused and "dreading the interaction," Martha returned to the shop. This time she talked to a woman assistant. The woman avoided using technical terms and often asked Martha if she understood what she was saying. Her tone never suggested that Martha was foolish for not understanding. Also, the woman often made Martha do things rather than demonstrating how an expert did it.

Here is an anecdote that fails. Just change Martha to George and put George in Victoria's Secret trying to buy a Valentine's gift.

These two experiences were utterly different. The man left Martha feeling humiliated; the woman "enabled" her. Tannen argues that her analysis of talk makes it possible to understand the context of these conversations. The man was showing that he had the knowledge and the upper hand. The woman was showing that she wanted to connect, to make it possible for Martha to share her problems. Tannen does not believe that women are altruists. It is just that they feel powerful when they can help.

Tannen argues that her training as a linguist is crucial. She snipes at some of the ways in which psychologists and sociologists study the use of language. They are too crude, even perhaps too political. Tannen records real conversations which she then analyses and interprets. She also plays back conversations to groups of men and women to see how they interpret them. Usually, the interpretations are very different.

"I feel that a lot of the people have been too unsophisticated in their analyses of conversation," she says. They count up the number of times the man interrupts, for example, "and leave it at that." Tannen claims that this is not enough. "Such an approach makes it easy to miss very subtle interactions."

Here, Tannen demonstrates that women often lean forward empathically and mumble to encourage their partner to speak more. This is not an interruption at all but a kind of prompt to encourage more talk and more intimacy. Unless you are subtle in your interpretations, you may score this wrongly as an interruption. The transcript shows the effect but not the intention. In Tannen's linguistics, it is the intention that matters.

She admits that some feminist scientists have criticised her because she does not blame men for having a different conversational style but, she adds, "this has been very much a minority response." Tannen's view is intriguing because she does not claim that men are more powerful. Instead, she says men talk and perceive relationships more in terms of power. The distinction is crucial because many men often feel themselves to be weak—only too aware of the power others have over them.

She sees some studies of language as invalid, but not hers.

Men are not more powerful, but they see things in terms of power.

Perhaps because she is aware that many men do not feel powerful, Tannen does not seem to want to change the sexes drastically. She sees no future, for example, in teaching men to be more like women. In the 1970s, liberal American psychologists preached the virtues of psychological androgyny. If you could teach men to behave more like women and women to behave more like men, we would soon reach unisexual bliss. Tannen rejects this view, but hopes that her analysis will help men and women to understand why they often feel so frustrated with one another. One of her teachers was John Gomperz, a linguist at the University of California at Berkeley, who studied the ways Indians and Britons failed to communicate across the colonial divide. She hopes to provide insights into why men and women often fail to understand one another.

Good for her. She does not wish to change conversational styles, or find androgyny. The key is understanding each other.

The reactions of British linguists and psycholinguists to Tannen's work is ambivalent. Few academics have actually read her latest book, but Tannen does not provoke the envy or outrage endured by many academics who get on the best seller lists. Yet my research (and not everyone wanted to be quoted) left me feeling that, in Britain at least, a slight air of disapproval surrounds her work.

Tannen has found popular success, but the linguistic scholars are less than impressed.

Nonetheless, several linguists and psychologists I talked to agreed that Tannen had done interesting work. The consensus is that her earlier, more academic book, *Conversational Style*, opened up useful areas.

Few quarrelled with her method of studying real-life conversations. Michael Garman, a linguist at the University of Reading and author of *Psycholinguistics* (published by Cambridge University Press), says that there had been a swing away from controlled, "perhaps artefactual" laboratory studies that scrutinise a tiny piece of text or speech. Garman was sympathetic to her work especially because he feels linguists have failed to establish "norms" for adult speech. "We know a good deal about how children develop their language skills but once they get to school, our knowledge becomes much less." Tannen's work has helped to show how, when, and by what stages, children come to speak like adults.

Despite welcoming Tannen's probing into an unprobed area, Garman was quite critical. "There isn't enough meat in Tannen's work." He prefaced this by saying, "It's a question of taste. I'm not particularly excited by analyses which are too global"—too all encompassing. Garman is not particularly curious about the kinds of problems that seem to excite the public, such as opening gambits in conversations or what sort of nonlinguistic signals are being sent. He is much more interested in the fact that people do not talk in sentences, although we are all meant to, yet we seem to think in something like sentences.

But whatever its scientific merits, Tannen's book has stirred the popular imagination. She has had scores of letters from women who say "now I understand" and also scores of letters from men. She judges her success partly through that.

There is one puzzle, though. Developmental psychology suggests that though the brain may be "wired" for language, children learn the patterns and rhythms of how to speak from their parents. Most infants and toddlers spend most time with their mothers, who repeat words and phrases, and pause to teach infants the art of taking turns to speak. Women teach the species how to speak. How and when, then, do boys learn to speak in the male style—and how is the influence of mothers erased? The answer may not yield a best seller but would be interesting to know.

Kaci Holz's Questions

Is this a pop culture book marketed to the mass audience rather than the scientific community? After all, it was on the best seller lists for 40 weeks.

Is she a linguistic scientist conducting careful research or a sociologist promoting her feminist agenda? I must find her book and read more, and find out more about her.

Well, does she use inductive or deductive reasoning to arrive at her findings? I think it's inductive because she observes, looks for patterns, and then arrives at her theories. And inductive findings are not as conclusive as deductive, so more work needs to be done.

Why make this such an issue? We all know the differences in the sexes. It's what makes life exciting. I don't want my husband talking like me, and I certainly don't want to assume his vocabulary and verbal mannerisms.

Should I read Tannen's book? Yes, I see her name everywhere in the literature, so I need to order it because the library doesn't have it.

Writing a Summary

WEB LINK
to Chapter 4
Related Web
Destinations
http://www.
ablongman.com/
lester

The summary represents a culmination of your critical reading, the topic of Chapter 3. Writing a summary is the logical follow-up to the techniques of highlighting, annotating, outlining, and evaluating a writer's chain of reasoning. In addition, writing a summary is one of the best ways to gain comprehension of a passage, article, or entire book. This chapter will prepare you to write effective summaries.

The term *summary*, as we shall use it here, mainly refers to a short passage that condenses the ideas of a work or a part of a work. It records your understanding of the information in an objective manner as you remain in the background. The purpose of the summary is to locate the primary ideas of a passage, the essential facts of an article or essay, the major points of a book—even the plot of a novel.

A summary should be an objective rendering of what's in the work, so you should not insert your opinion or interpretation unless you need to explain the unusual nature of the work—for example, the use of irony, discussed on page 132—or you will be using your summary as a review (see page 143).

T I P   *Writing a Summary*

You may want to use the summary in your own essay, so write it carefully in full sentences. As a part of your paper, your summaries of articles provide an effective overview of the literature on the topic, be it gambling, cloning, anorexia, or Edgar Allan Poe.

In most cases your summary should be comprehensive, one that gives a broad, sweeping understanding of the material. A summary of *Moby Dick*, for example, might include information about Melville's major characters and the principal events of the novel. The summary can, however, be very brief, as in "Melville's *Moby Dick* is the story of one man's obsession to confront the dark side of his soul." You are the judge about your summary's length.

GUIDELINES

Summaries

Keep in mind three reasons for writing a summary:

- The summary is the culmination of your critical reading.
- The summary highlights the principal issues in capsule form to confirm your reading and comprehension.
- The summary, used in your own paper, helps you explain to readers the relevance of the source to your subject.

When you have prepared five or six summaries from different sources, you will have formulated some clear ideas about the issues of your subject and the positions taken by various spokespersons.

Writing a Summary to Capture an Idea

In many instances you might want to borrow only one idea from a source, which you will rephrase into your own words (see Chapter 5 for details about paraphrasing a passage). Reproduced below is a brief excerpt from a book on the carnage of war as it relates to the culture behind the fighting forces. In a marginal note, a student focuses on one idea. Writing marginal notes is a good practice for critical reading. Following the selection is the student's summary note.

From Carnage and Culture

Victor Davis Hanson

Euphemism in battle narrative or the omission of graphic killing altogether is a near criminal offense of the military historian. It is no accident that gifted writers of war—from Homer, Thucydides, Caesar, Victor Hugo, and Leo Tolstoy to Stephen Runciman, James Jones, and Stephen Ambrose—equate tactics with blood, and strategy with corpses. How can we write of larger cultural issues that surround war without describing the way in which young men kill and die, without remembering how many thousands are robbed of their youth, their robust physiques turned into goo in a few minutes on the battlefield?

We owe it to the dead to discover at all costs how the practice of government, science, law, and religion instantaneously determines the fate of thousands on the battlefield—and why. During the Gulf War (1990–91) the designer of an American smart bomb, the assembler in its plant of fabrication, and logistician who ordered, received, stockpiled, and loaded it onto a jet, all functioned in a manner not unlike their Iraqi opposites—if there were such exact counterparts—and so ensured that an innocent conscript in Saddam Hussein's army would find himself blown to pieces with little chance to escape the attack, display heroism in his demise, or kill the pilot who killed him. Why Iraqi adolescents were targets in the flashing video consoles of sophisticated American helicopters, and not vice versa, or why GIs from icy Minnesota were better equipped to fight in the desert than recruits from nearby sweltering Baghdad, is mostly a result of cultural heritage, not military courage, much less an accident of geography or genes. War is ultimately killings. Its story becomes absurd when the wages of death are ignored by the historian.

People die in war, not by military success but by cultural heritage. Who you are determines in large measure whether you live or die.

Rather than copy an entire paragraph or two into her paper, the researcher first read the excerpt, related the reading to her thesis and her outline, and then wrote this summary. She had found what she needed from the article.

Young people *die* in war, and Victor Hanson is one of the few historians to acknowledge that a nation's culture dictates the terms of the fighting. He says that military success is almost always the "result of cultural heritage" and not merely an "accident of geography or genes." The more advanced culture with its sophisticated smart bombs has the edge down through the centuries from Roman times to America's current army.

Writing a Summary of a Paragraph

Your first task in writing a summary of a paragraph is to read it carefully, making marginal annotations and examining the writer's argument, as we discussed in Chapter 3. Only then will you begin to see the comprehensive relationship of all the sentences.

Sometimes the opening or closing sentence will give you the summary statement that you need. Notice the final sentence, italicized for emphasis, in this passage:

It will be asked, how does the historian know when Decadence sets in? By the open confessions of malaise, by the search in all directions for a new faith or faiths. Dozens of cults have latterly arisen in the Christian West: Buddhism, Islam, Yoga, Transcendental Meditation, Dr. Moon's Unification Church, and a large collection of others, some dedicated to group suicide. To secular minds, the old ideals look outworn or hopeless and practical aims are made into creeds sustained by violent acts: fighting nuclear power, global warming, and abortion; saving from use the environment with its fauna and flora ("Bring back the wolf!"); promoting organic against processed foods, and proclaiming disaffection from science and technology. *The impulse to PRIMI-TIVISM animates all these negatives.*

—Jacques Barzun, *From Dawn to Decadence*

The final sentence of the paragraph provides its own summary; however, you might want to frame your own summary, perhaps in this way:

Barzun describes historic "decadence" as the time when new cults emerge that revert to primitive, negative impulses, such as mass suicide and rejection of new technology.

In the next example, Napoleon Bonaparte, the defeated emperor of France, addresses his troops for the last time. They have lost their last battle, and he prepares for his exile at the island of Helena.

Farewell to the Old Guard

Soldiers of my Old Guard: I bid you farewell. For twenty years I have constantly accompanied you on the road to honor and glory. In these latter times, as in the days of our prosperity, you have invariably been models of courage and fidelity. With men such as you our cause could not be lost; but the war would have been interminable; it would have been civil war, and that would have entailed deeper misfortunes on France.

I have sacrificed all my interests to those of the country.

I go, but you, my friends, will continue to serve France. Her happiness was my only thought. It will still be the object of my wishes. Do not regret my fate; if I have consented to survive, it is to serve your glory. I intend to write the history of the great achievements we have performed together. Adieu, my friends. Would I could press you all to my heart.

The summary below captures the essence of Napoleon's words:

WEB LINK
to Exercise
4.1
http://www.
ablongman.com/
lester

Napoleon refers to their past glories and recognizes the soldiers' faithfulness and willingness to continue the fight. Yet he asks them, for the sake of France, to avoid civil war. Meanwhile, he will write the memoirs of their exploits.

Keep this idea in mind: even when a topic sentence or closing sentence adequately summarizes the passage, you should write a summary in your own words. The alternative is to quote the source, for example:

Quotation:

Deborah Tannen says, "Conversation is a ritual" that affects male/female relations, according to her essay "But What Do You Mean?"

Summary:

> The rituals of everyday conversation are rich in connotations regarding male/ female relations, according to Deborah Tannen in her essay "But What Do You Mean?"

Summarizing a Paragraph That Contains Irony

WEB LINK
to Exercise
4.2
http://www.
ablongman.com/
lester

Summarizing irony presents a special challenge. Your summary must not only objectively describe the paragraph's content, but it must also interpret for the reader the special tone being employed. *Otherwise, the reader will misunderstand.* Note this next paragraph:

> I have been studying the traits and dispositions of the "lower animals" (so-called), and contrasting them with the traits and dispositions of man. I find the result humiliating to me. For it obliges me to renounce my allegiance to the Darwinian theory of the Ascent of Man from the Lower Animals; since it now seems plain to me that the theory ought to be vacated in favor a new and truer one, this new and truer one to be named the Descent of Man from the Higher Animals.
>
> —Mark Twain, "The Damned Human Race"

This paragraph is taken from one of Mark Twain's essay's in which he compares humans with animals to arrive at his perverse view that humans, with their moral sense, think they are superior when, in truth, they are not. This kind of writing requires a summary that is not purely objective:

> With a voice dripping his brand of bitter irony, Mark Twain rejects scientific theory to argue that humans, when compared to the animals, are descending and, quite clearly, not ascending to higher levels.

Only by desciding the author's irony can the writer of the summary gain distance from Twain's unusual and contrary view of the human race.

GUIDELINES

Summarizing a Paragraph

- Mention the author being summarized to make clear that the ideas are not your own.
- Write the summary in your own words but place any borrowed phrase within quotation marks.
- Make the summary comprehensive, and use more than one sentence, if necessary, to cover each major idea if more than one exists.
- The summary of irony must objectively describe content but must also interpret the tone.
- For purposes of clarity, you can rearrange the sequence of ideas.

EXERCISE 4.1

WRITING A SUMMARY OF A PARAGRAPH

Write a one- or two-sentence summary of each of the following paragraphs after reading each one carefully and highlighting any sentences that contain major ideas. Marginal annotations may also prove helpful.

Paragraph 1

Culture—what a word! Up to a few years ago it meant two or three related things easy to grasp and keep apart. Now it is a piece of all-purpose jargon that covers a hodge-podge of overlapping things. People speak and write about the culture of almost any segment of society: the counterculture, to begin with, and the many subcultures: ethnic cultures, corporate cultures, teenage cultures, and popular cultures. An editorial in the *New York Times* discusses the culture of the city's police department, and an article in the travel section distinguishes the culture of plane travel from the bus culture. On a par with these, recall the split between the "two cultures" of science and the humanities, which is to be deplored—like the man-and-wife "culture clash," which causes divorce. Artists feel the lure—no, the duty—of joining an adversary culture; for the artist is by nature "the enemy of his culture," just as he is "a product of his culture." In education, the latest fad is multiculturalism, and in entertainment the highest praise goes to a "cross-cultural event." On the world scene, the experts warn of the culture wars that are brewing. At the bottom of the pile, "culture," meaning the well-furnished mind, barely survives.

—Jacques Barzun, *From Dawn to Decadence*

Paragraph 2

Everything which is in any way beautiful is beautiful in itself, and terminates in itself, not having praise as part of itself. Neither worse then nor better is a thing made by being praised. I affirm this also of the things which are called beautiful by the vulgar, for example, material things and works of art. That which is really beautiful has no need of anything; not more than law, not more than truth, not more than benevolence or modesty. Which of these things is beautiful because it is praised, or spoiled by being blamed? Is such a thing as an emerald made worse than it was if it is not praised? Or gold, ivory, purple, a lyre, a little knife, a flower, a shrub?

—Marcus Aurelius, *Thoughts of Marcus Aurelius Antoninus*

Paragraph 3

For now, cloning should rightly be confined to animals. But as the technology evolves to invite human experimentation, it would be better to watch and regulate rather than prohibit. Outlaw the exploration of human cloning and it will surely go offshore, only to turn into bootleg science that will find its way back to our borders simply because people want it.

—Daniel Kevles, "Study Cloning, Don't Ban It," *New York Times*
(February 16, 1997)

Paragraph 4

As millions of people had discovered before me, e-mail was fast. Sixteenth-century correspondents used to write "Haste, haste, haste, for lyfe, for lyfe, haste!" on their most urgent letters; my "server," a word that conjured up a delicious syco-phancy, treated *every* message as if someone's life depended on it. Not only did it get there instantly, caromed in a series of analog cyberpackets along the nodes of the Internet and reconverted to digital form via its recipient's modem. (I do not understand a word of what I just wrote, but that is immaterial. Could the average Victorian have diagrammed the mail coach route from Swansea to Tunbridge Wells?) More important, I answered e-mail fast—almost always on the day it arrived. No more guilt! I used to think I did not like to write letters. I now realize that what I didn't like was folding the paper, sealing the envelope, looking up the address, licking the stamp, getting in the elevator, crossing the street, and drop-ping the letter in the postbox.

—Anne Fadiman, "Mail," *The American Scholar*

Paragraph 5

If one considers that Napoleon revealed his powers in 1796 at the age of twenty-seven, it is plain that nature endowed him extraordinarily. These talents he applied unceasingly through the whole length of his prodigious career.

Through them he marks out his way along a resplendent path in the military annals of humanity. He carries his victorious eagles from the Alps to the Pyramids, and from the banks of the Tagus to those of the Moskova, surpassing in their flight the conquests of Alexander, of Hannibal and of Caesar. Thus he remains the great leader, superior to all others in his prodigious genius, his need of activity, his nature, ardent to excess, which is always favorable to the profits of war but dangerous to the equilibrium of peace.

—Marshal Ferdinand Foch, "Napoleon," on the one hundredth anniversary of Napoleon's death, 1921.

Writing a Summary of an Article, Essay, or Book

By writing a brief summary—50 to 100 words—you can describe an entire arti-cle, essay, or book. The summary should capture, in comprehensive fashion, the major ideas of the work. Generally, it should be objective, so if you decide to interject your opinions, you must clearly identify them. Here's a summary of the Samuelson article that appears on pages 71–73.

Robert Samuelson speaks with a critical voice about the hypocrisy of Congress in its lavish support of the farm-subsidy programs. He calls farm subsidies a "huge political bribe," says they do not serve the best interests of the public, and argues that the programs are "plundering the public purse and doing wrong."

The writer of the summary has condensed the original article into a digest of 52 words. In addition, this writer has captured the tone and mood of the original and retained a few phrases of Samuelson within quotation marks.

GUIDELINES

Summarizing a Complete Work

- Perform a critical reading to capture the major ideas of the piece.
- Identify the writer's central thesis, which will appear throughout the work in various guises.
- Understand the writer's purpose—inquiry, negotiation, or persuasion (see pages 79–89). You may need to explore the general nature or agenda of the magazine, journal, Web site, or organization that published the work.
- Write a summary in your own words while incorporating, if appropriate, some phrasing of the original, placed within quotation marks, of course.
- Make the summary a comprehensive view of the whole.
- Maintain an objective tone that you will break only to give the reader insight into the writer's irony or bias (see page 132) or to make an evaluation in a brief review (see page 143).

Now let us look at a lengthy essay and apply the techniques for summarizing it. We have read Robert J. Samuelson's argument against farm subsidies. This next excerpt offers a rebuttal. Willie Nelson, the country music singer, brings his passionate views into print. Read the excerpt from *The Facts of Life* and consider any ideas that should go into a summary in order to capture the essence of Nelson's message. He has been an advocate for family farms for many years, and he serves as host for Farm Aid festivals to raise awareness as well as funds. His essay includes his agenda for saving the family farm as a viable institution. In marginal annotations, you will see student Andrea Bone's reactions. At the end of the essay you will see Bone's summary of Nelson's essay.

From The Facts of Life

Willie Nelson

Farm Aid will happen in Indiana on September 29, 2001. I hope it all goes well. I'm sure it will. It's in the middle of the farm belt and John Mellencamp's home state. It will be possible to show the Capitol Hill crowd that there are still some of us who believe in the small family farmer, the first rung on the economic ladder. When you see things going wrong in a country, the first thing you should do is look at how family farmers are treated. How are we treating the first rung on our ladder? Because when the backbone of our country is broken and the first rung on the ladder is weakened, everything collapses. We all come crashing down. You can cut taxes all you want. You can do everything in this world for every other rung on the ladder. But when the family farmer goes under, it's just a matter of time before everyone else follows.

He still believes in the family farmer.

Farmers are the basis of our economy, and a vital prop like the bottom rung on a ladder.

We had well over eight million small family farmers, and now we're down to two million, losing three hundred to five hundred a week. If we don't get a farm bill, a good one, there will be no more small family farmers left. Farm Aid will help all we can, because someone has to repair that bottom rung of the ladder, and time is of the essence. The reason every civilization has gone under in the past was because of an inability to feed its people. We are running out of time. . . .

A good farm bill will stop the demise of the family farm.

Both Democrats and Republicans are going to have to agree in order to pass a new farm bill. The factory farms are the worst possible things we can do to the people, the environment, and the general health of everyone. We have already seen the dangers of disease in our livestock. Mad cow disease, foot-and-mouth disease—there are all kinds of diseases which, according to government reports, "may or may not be harmful to humans." Either way, it's easier for small family farmers to insure a healthier climate on the farm, because there are a few pigs on a few acres of ground, or a variety of products spread over several hundred acres—not a hundred thousand pigs in one big pig-pen outside your retirement home in the country. The flies and smell from the waste is unbearable for miles. Just ask any of the people who live there. I daresay that there are no politicians living in those areas, or they would be screaming at the top of their lungs.

Both Republicans and Democrats must join in a crusade to restore the family farm.

Big corporate farms are not the answer because massive feedlots generate health dangers.

I hear politicians from both parties debating various issues on TV or radio talk shows—tax breaks for the wealthy, health benefits for the poor, social security benefits for the old, medicine and drug costs. *No one* mentions the family farmer. This is because there are millions and millions of dollars spent each year by big food conglomerates who want to keep things just the way they are. Hopefully someone with balls will come out against the money that keeps the farmer down. So far, the brave guys have been beaten back. Keep fighting! There are a lot of farmers and ranchers who need your help.

Five Point Agenda for Saving Family Farmers and Reclaiming Rural America

1. Pass a farm bill that will restore a fair price for farmers.
   - Establish price supports to ensure that farm income comes from the marketplace and not from taxpayers.
   - Create a farmer-owned reserve to ensure food security in times of scarcity and price stability in times of plenty.
   - Avoid wasteful overproduction through inventory management.
   - Maintain planting flexibility.
   - Establish national dairy policy to ensure a farmer's cost of production plus a return on investment.

2. Restore competition through strict enforcement of antitrust law.
   - Place a moratorium on mergers and acquisitions in agribusiness, transportation, food processing, manufacturing, and retail companies.
   - Require strict enforcement of the Packers and Stockyards Act to end price discrimination.
   - Enact a ban on packer ownership of livestock.

3. Protect consumers and the environment.
   - Require labeling of meat and other foods imported into the U.S. to give consumers the right to know and choose the country of origin of their food.
   - Stop the expansion of large-scale factory farms.
   - Protect environmentally fragile lands and habitats.

4. Eliminate industry subsidies paid by independent producers.
   - Hold referenda on the mandatory pork and beef check offs as petitioned by independent producers to break up corporate control of livestock.
   - Oppose governmental nominations that represent the interests of corporate agriculture.

5. Negotiate fair trade agreements.
   - Ensure that all countries retain the right to develop farm programs that respond to the needs of their farmers and consumers.
   - Put an end to export dumping (the sale of commodities below the cost of production), which undermines our domestic economy.

His five-point program would restore competition, protect consumers, stop corporate control of livestock, and assure fair trade agreements.

WEB LINK
to Exercise
4.3
http://www.
ablongman.com/
lester

• Ensure that environmental protection, fair wages, and workers rights are part of every trade agreement.

Andrea has succinctly and appropriately summarized Nelson's essay as follows:

Willie Nelson believes in the family farmer, and he sees the small farm as the "backbone" of America's economy. He fears that dependence on corporate farming will pollute our meat and the environment. Thus, he asks for a new farm bill that would restore competition, protect consumers, stop corporate control of livestock, and assure fair trade agreements. Every individual who cares should become a political activist for this cause.

EXERCISE 4.2

WRITING A SUMMARY OF AN ESSAY

Choose one of the two pieces of writing that appear below and read it critically, highlighting phrases, making marginal notes, and using other techniques as explained in Chapter 3. Then perform the exercises listed at the end of the essay. The first essay—"What Does It Mean to Be Good?"—is an excerpt from the first of twelve sermons delivered by Albert Schweitzer in 1919 in Strasbourg, France. In this writing, he first defined his well-known phrase "reverence for life." The second article—"From the Heart"—examines the masks worn by physicians to gain distance from the reality of their work and from the pain and fear of their patients. As a physician with years of experience, Rachel Naomi Remen explains how she abandoned a mask to cultivate the heart.

What Does It Mean to Be Good?

Desire for knowledge! You may seek to explore everything around you, you may push to the farthest limits of human knowledge, but in the end you will always strike upon something that is unfathomable. It is called life. And this mystery is so inexplicable that it renders the difference between knowledge and ignorance completely relative.

What difference is there between the scholar who observes the smallest and least expected signs of life under a microscope and the old peasant, who can scarcely read and write, when he stands in his garden in the spring and contemplates the blossoms bursting open on the branches of his tree? Both are confronted with the riddle of life! The one can describe it more thoroughly than the other, but for both it is equally inscrutable. All knowledge is finally knowledge of life. All realization is astonishment at this riddle of life—reverence for life in its infinite, yet ever new, manifestations. For what does it mean for something to come into being, live, and pass away? How amazing that it renews itself in other existences, passes away again, comes into being once more, and so on and so forth, from infinity to infinity? We can do all things and we can do nothing, for in all our wisdom we are not able to create life. Rather, what we create is death!

Life means strength, will coming from the abyss and sinking into it again. Life means feeling, sensitivity, suffering. And if you are absorbed in life, if you see with perceptive eyes into this enormous animated chaos of creation, it suddenly seizes you with vertigo. In everything you recognize yourself again. The beetle that lies dead in your path—it was something that lived, that struggled for its existence like you, that rejoiced in the sun like you, that knew anxiety and pain like you. And now it is nothing more than decomposing material—as you, too, shall be sooner or later.

You walk outside and it is snowing. Carelessly you shake the snow from your sleeves. It attracts your attention: a snowflake glistens on your hand. You cannot help looking at it, whether you wish to or not. It glistens in its wonderful design; then it quivers, and the delicate needles of which it consists contract. It is no more; it has melted, dead in your hand. The flake, which fell upon your hand from infinite space, which glistened there, quivered, and died—that is you. Wherever you see life—that is you!

What is this recognition, this knowledge apprehended by the most learned and the most childlike alike? It is reverence for life, reverence for the impenetrable mystery that meets us in our universe, as existence different from ourselves in external appearance, yet inwardly of the same character with us, terribly similar, awesomely related. The dissimilarity, the strangeness, between us and other creatures is here removed.

Reverence before the infinity of life means the removal of the strangeness, the restoration of shared experiences and of compassion and sympathy. And thus the final result of knowledge is the same, in principle, as that which the commandment to love requires of us. Heart and reason agree together when we desire and dare to be men who attempt to fathom the depths of things.

—Albert Schweitzer, *Sermons on Reverence for Life*

1. Read again your marginal notes and highlighted passages.
2. Create an outline that lists in order the major idea of each paragraph.
3. Write out Schweitzer's central message in a nutshell.
4. List any key words or phrases that you might carry into your summary.
5. Using the critical reading tools of items 1 through 4, write a summary of the sermon.

From the Heart

Almost fifty-eight years ago, I attended preschool in the little park around the corner from our apartment in upper Manhattan. As the shy and timid only child of older parents it had taken me a long time to feel safe in the company of other children, and my mother or my nana often sat on a bench within eyesight to give me the courage to remain in the group.

Eventually I was able to stay there alone. One day close to Halloween, my nana left me at the park, and I spent the morning with the other four-year-olds making masks. Close to noon the teachers threaded string through our creations and helped us to put them on. I had never worn a mask and I was entranced. About this time, mothers began arriving to pick up their children, and as soon as I saw my own mother walking toward the class I stood and waved to her. She did not respond in any way. She stopped just inside the door, her eyes searching the room. Suddenly I realized that she did not know who I was and I began to cry, terrified. All her efforts to soothe me and explain why she had not recognized me failed to comfort me. I simply could not understand why she had not known me. I knew who I was with my mask on. Why didn't she? I never went back to the nursery school again. I felt too invisible, too alone, too vulnerable.

Most of us wear masks. We may have worn them so long that we have forgotten we have put them on. Sometimes our culture may even demand we wear them.

A young woman named La Vera told me of something that happened when she was a first-year medical student. Those were anxious times, and it was not uncommon for people to work and study eighteen hours a day for weeks on end. In the evening, members of her class were in the habit of releasing the day's tension by playing basketball on the court in the basement of the medical students' residence. No one kept score, and people would drop in and out of the game for fifteen minutes or a half hour—however long it was before their anxiety about needing to study took them back upstairs to their desks. Often the game went on for hours, and the two teams that called it quits had no players in common with the teams that had started the game.

About four months into the year, in the midst of one of these games, one of her classmates had suddenly collapsed and died surrounded by other freshman students who had no idea how to help him. He was twenty-one years old.

Although many of the students were deeply shaken by the event, nothing further was said about the matter. The school made no opportunity to acknowledge either the tragedy of the death or the feelings of the class. The young man's belongings had been packed up and sent to his parents who lived in another state. No one from his class or from the school had attended his funeral, which was held near his home.

The pace of the first year was intense and the competition fierce. Despite their shock and distress, the members of the class simply went on. Few talked about their classmate even at first, and by the spring of the year, the incident seemed almost forgotten.

At the beginning of their second year, the class began the study of pathology. In one of the laboratory sessions on congenital anomalies the instructor began passing around trays, each holding a preserved human specimen that demonstrated a specific birth defect. Wearing gloves, the students examined each specimen and then passed it on.

One of these specimens was a heart with a congenitally malformed anterior coronary artery. As it was being passed hand to hand through the class, the instructor commented in a casual way that it was the heart of the young man who had died the year before.

Without lifting her head, La Vera looked out of the corner of her eye. No one around her seemed to react. All her classmates wore expressions of detached scientific interest. A wave of panic rose up in her until she realized that she, too, was wearing a mask of professional detachment. No one could possibly know the terrible distress she was feeling. She was flooded with relief. She remembers thinking that she was going to be able to DO this. She was going to be able to become a real physician.

La Vera closed her eyes as she finished her story and sat in silence for a moment. She rocked back and forth slightly and began to cry.

After more than thirty-five years as a physician, I have found at last that it is possible to be a professional and live from the heart. This was not something that I learned in medical school.

Medical training instills a certain scientific objectivity or distance. Other perspectives may become suspect. In particular, the perspective of the heart is seen as unprofessional or even dangerous. The heart with its capacity to connect us to others may somehow mar our judgment and make us incompetent. Such training changes us. We may need to heal from it. It has taken me years to realize that being a human being is not unprofessional.

My training encouraged me to give away vital parts of myself in the belief that this would make me of greater service to others. In the end I found that abandoning my humanity in order to become of service made me vulnerable to burnout, cynicism, numbness, loneliness, and depression. Abandoning the heart weakens us.

The heart has the power to transform experience. No matter what we do, finding fulfillment may require learning to cultivate the heart and its capacity for meaning in the same way that we are now taught to pursue knowledge or expertise. We will need to connect intimately to the life around us. Knowledge alone will not help us to live well or serve well. We will need to take off our masks in order to do that.

—Rachel Naomi Remen, *My Grandfather's Blessings*

1. Read again your marginal notes and highlighted passages.
2. Create an outline that lists in order the major idea of each paragraph.
3. Write out Remen's central message in a nutshell.
4. List any key words or phrases that you might carry into your summary.
5. Using the critical reading tools of items 1 through 4, write a summary of the essay.

Writing the Specialized Summary

You may be asked to write one or more of these specialized summaries:

- A review of an article, essay, story, book, software, or other product.
- Annotations for a bibliography.
- A plot summary or book summary.
- An abstract.

WEB LINK
to Chapter 4
Related Web
Destinations
http://www.
ablongman.com/
lester

Each of these summaries has a particular purpose and serves the reader in a different way. The review describes, evaluates, and makes a recommendation on the quality of a new product, such as a computer software program, DVD, movie, or novel. It might be positive or negative, even to the point of telling readers to save their money.

An annotated bibliography expands each entry to include commentary on the work. Writing the annotation serves the student, who grasps the essence of the article or book, and serves other researchers who get a digest of each work on the list.

The plot summary and the book summary are tools that serve both you and your reader. By writing the summary, you grasp the essential ideas of one writer, and by reading the summary, your audience gets a quick overview of the work.

The abstract is a tool for academic papers and dissertations. Placed at the front of an article, it provides a summary of the contents, usually as written by the author. Abstracts are sometimes collected and published as a service to the academic discipline, as are *Abstracts of English Studies, Psychological Abstracts,* or *Historical Abstracts.* Abstracts provide you with the means to quickly assess which works you should study in depth.

G U I D E L I N E S

Writing Specialized Summaries

- Condense the original with precision and directness. In just a few words you can describe an article or an entire book.

- Preserve the tone of the original. If the original is serious, suggest that tone in the summary. In the same way, indicate moods of doubt, irony, skepticism, optimism, and so forth.

- Write the summary in your own words. Because summaries are very short, you do not have space to quote many phrases from the original.

- Provide documentation that conforms to one of the professional styles, if appropriate, as with the annotation of a bibliography entry. These bibliographic conventions are described in Chapters 10–12 and an example of one appears in Kaci Holz's bibliography at the end of this chapter.

Writing the Brief Review

A review is an evaluation of a work. It advises the reader in a succinct fashion, helping to shape attitudes and spending habits. It is *not* objective because it evaluates as well as summarizes.

Here's how *Smithsonian Magazine* described a new children's book in their review section:

WEB LINK
to Reading
4.1
http://www.
ablongman.com/
lester

> *Hoot* by Carl Hiaasen (Knopf, $15.95). In the best-selling author's first novel for kids, Hiaasen turns his gift for twisted comedy to the tale of a 13-year-old ecoguerrilla who pits himself against developers about to mow down a patch of Florida Wilderness. The young saboteur's campaign is on behalf of tiny burrowing owls who inhabit that contested landscape of sandy scrub.

The next example, a short review of a Web site, was written by a student doing research on heart transplants.

> The National Foundation for Transplants has a website devoted to its initiatives. This website has merit, and it's receiving good response. Its goal is to communicate a key problem—the tremendous need for donors; for example, more than 55,000 people are on the waiting lists. The organization seeks a greater participation from the public.
>
> http://www.transplants.org

Here's how **SlantMagazine.com** reviewed a new CD by Justin Timberlake:

Justin Timberlake

Justified

Jive, 2002

> 'NSync's golden boy has finally struck out on his own, and the results are, ahem, golden. Though Timberlake had a hand in the creation of every one of its songs, *Justified* is very much a producer-driven record. The album can be divided into three unequal parts: tracks helmed by the Neptunes, tracks produced by Timbaland and two comparably drab slow jams ("Still on My Brain" and "Never Again," produced by The Underdogs and Brian McKnight, respectively). Timberlake meshes with the Neptunes so well he virtually relinquishes his personality to the super-duo—he could very well be the third member of N.E.R.D. But that's not to say their tracks don't glide along like any other well-oiled Neptunes production. The robust instrumentation of "Senorita" is far from the slinky "I'm a Slave 4 U," while the acoustic guitar loops and snap-crackle-pop percussion of "Like I Love You" pick up where 'NSync's hit "Girlfriend" left off. Pharrell Williams' typical Jacko-esque falsetto

bridges—the ones that have provoked comparisons between Timberlake and the former king of pop—are littered throughout songs like "Last Night." Timberlake gets a
bit less lost in the ultra-distinct fabric of Timbaland's beats. *Justified*'s standout track
is the string-laden "Cry Me a River," a stinging farewell (to Britney, perhaps?) featuring beatbox and vocal arrangement courtesy of Timberlake himself. Other Timbo productions like "(And She Said) Take Me Now," featuring Janet Jackson, and "(Oh No)
What You Got" might seem a bit racy for those expecting more boy-band fare. He
sings cockily, "I could think of a couple positions for you" on the surprisingly organic
"Right for Me." The album is also surprisingly cogent and distinctive, Jacko be
damned. In many ways, *Justified* is what last year's *Invincible* shoulda/coulda been.

—Sal Cinquemani, **SlantMagazine.com**, 2002

WEB LINK
to Exercise
4.4
http://www.
ablongman.com/
lester

As shown in these examples, a review identifies the target work—be it book, DVD,
movie, Web site, magazine, or other product. It judges the work on a set of criteria
without much interpretation. It gives a quick overview for the reader, and its purpose
is apparent—buy this DVD, don't go to this movie, visit this Web site, read this book.
To prepare for writing a review, you can list the criteria by which you will judge
the work and use those criteria to build your review. For example, the review of Justin
Timberlake has criteria on (1) his ability to mesh with other groups, (2) the instrumentation, (3) his use of falsetto bridges, and (4) the arrangements by Timberlake and
the production companies. It's a review about production, but it could just as easily
focus on other criteria, such as the beauty of the songs and their meaning.

EXERCISE 4.3
WRITING A BRIEF REVIEW

1. Visit the Internet, using your favorite search engine, and find a brief review of
   your favorite CD or DVD movie. Your task? Print the review and bring it to class
   as an example of the *summary* used as a review.

2. Visit the Internet to find a place where *you* might write a review. Many exist, but
   you should obviously know the work before offering a review. For example,
   Amazon.com always asks visitors to their site to review a book, CD, game, camera, and so forth. Your assignment is to write a review for one of the products
   on Amazon.com or some other site and bring a notation of the URL to class so
   that your peers can check out your work.

Writing an Annotated Bibliography

An annotation within a bibliography is a sentence or short paragraph that offers
explanatory commentary on an article, book, or any other type of entry. The bibliography entry indicates the author, work, publisher, date, and other information essential for finding the work. The annotation appears as an extension of the entry. Thus,
the term *annotated bibliography* means a formal citation to a book or article followed

immediately by a summary, usually of three to six sentences. The goal in writing this kind of summary is to capture the main idea of the source in only a few sentences, as shown here in two examples:

> Standiford, Les. *Last Train to Paradise: Henry Flagler and the Spectacular Rise and Fall of the Railroad That Crossed an Ocean.* New York: Crown, 2002. This book is not a biography of Flagler but a sweeping tale about Flagler's ingenuity in building a railroad from Miami to Key West on a collision course with nature's worst hurricanes. Along the way, Standiford uncovers the treacherous world in which thousands of workers laid track through infested swamps. It reads like a novel.
>
> Top Ten Myths about Donation and Transplantation. (2000). Retrieved October 10, 2000, from http://www.transweb.org/myths/myths.htm. This Web site dispels the many myths surrounding organ donation, showing that selling organs is illegal, that matching donor and recipient is highly complicated, and that secret backroom operations are almost impossible.

A fully annotated bibliography is one that gives citations and annotations to all the works used in a paper. See pages 163–165 at the end of this chapter for Kaci Holz's working bibliography. (Chapters 10–12 discuss in detail the methods for writing a bibliography to meet the demands of various disciplines.)

EXERCISE 4.4

WRITING AN ENTRY FOR AN ANNOTATED BIBLIOGRAPHY

Using the examples above as models, write an annotated bibliography entry on your favorite music CD, a movie, or a book.

Writing a Plot Summary or a Book Summary

In just a few sentences a summary can condense an entire book or the plot of a novel, drama, narrative poem, or similar work, as shown by this next example:

> *Great Expectations* by Charles Dickens describes young Pip, who inherits money and can live the life of a gentleman. But he discovers that his "great expectations" have come from a criminal. With that knowledge his attitude changes from one of vanity to one of compassion.

The plot summary does not retell the whole plot, yet it gives the reader a quick overview of the principal events of the work.

EXERCISE 4.5

WRITING A PLOT SUMMARY AND BOOK SUMMARY

1. Watch one of your favorite television programs and make careful notes about the plot. Then write a brief plot summary, similar to the one shown above.

2. Write a brief plot summary of a book or short story that you have read recently.

Writing an Abstract

The term *abstract* refers to a summary that appears at the beginning of an article to summarize the contents. It helps readers make decisions about reading or skipping the article. Usually, the author writes the abstract for his or her own work, but professional abstracting services also write abstracts anonymously. Abstracts are so important in this age of mass distribution of knowledge that abstracting services publish thousands of abstracts yearly for most academic disciplines, such as *Physics Abstracts*. The sample below indicates both the author of the article and the author of the abstract.

Type: Article
Author: Stanton, Lucia.
Title: LOOKING FOR LIBERTY: THOMAS JEFFERSON AND THE BRITISH LIONS.
Citation: Eighteenth-Century Studies 199326(4): 649–668.
Abstract: British writers and reformers held a variety of opinions about Thomas Jefferson and his ideas. Thomas Moore visited the United States in 1803 and was so horrified by the lack of social decorum that he recanted his republican sentiments. In 1814 Frances Wright visited Monticello and was so inspired by democratic ideals that she began designing schemes to liberate slaves and later joined Robert Owen in his cooperative village projects. In an 1837 book English writer Harriet Martineau avoided either extreme in describing the democratic features of American society, based partly on a visit with Jefferson's daughter.
Documentation: Based on published correspondence and other personal papers and secondary sources; 32 notes.
Abstracter: M. A. Miller
Language: English
Period: 19c.
Subject: <u>Attitudes.</u>
    <u>Great Britain.</u>
    <u>Jefferson. Thomas.</u>
    <u>Martineau. Harriet.</u>
    <u>Moore, Thomas.</u>
    <u>Wright, Frances.</u>
ISSN: 0013-2586
Entry: 47 A: 1906

In fewer than one hundred words, the abstract gives full information on the article, identifies both the author and the person who wrote the abstract, and offers related subjects as hypertext links.

Writers in the social and natural sciences, especially, are required to write abstracts and place them at the front of their articles. Here is a student's abstract for his paper on "functional foods":

Abstract

The functional food revolution has begun! Functional foods are products, especially herbs, to provide benefits beyond basic nutrition. They are adding billions to the nation's economy each year. Nutrition stores are now common sights at most shopping malls. Herbs are advertised as a form of preventive medicine, and this news has made the public swarm and food nutritionists crank out the products. Many researchers believe that functional foods may be the answer to lower health care costs. This paper attempts to identify certain functional foods, locate the components, and explain the role that each plays on the body.

TIP *Avoid Quoting from an Abstract*

WEB LINK
to Reading
4.2
http://www.
ablongman.com/
lester

Avoid drawing any direct quotations from an abstract. Instead, paraphrase a key sentence or two. You cannot assume that the words of the abstract are the words of the listed author for the scholarly article.

EXERCISE 4.6
FINDING AND READING ABSTRACTS

Go to the Web at **http://serials.abc-clio.com/** and search out *Historical Abstracts*, which is part of ABC-CLIO History Online. Locate a sample abstract and print it out to bring to class.

EXERCISE 4.7
WRITING AN ABSTRACT

Read "Health Is Membership," by Wendell Berry, reproduced below from his book *Another Turn of the Crank.* Then write an abstract that describes its contents in about 50 words. Berry's essay examines the cold, impersonal atmosphere of a hospital in contrast with the warm, congenial environment of a home. Remember, the abstract is a very brief summary of a work's content, devoid of personal opinion or subjective response. In that sense, it differs from the review, which usually evaluates and makes a recommendation to the reader. Be sure you capture the essential nature of the work and identify the source.

Health Is Membership

Wendell Berry

On January 3, 1994, my brother John had a severe heart attack while he was out by himself on his farm, moving a feed trough. He managed to get to the house and telephone a friend, who sent the emergency rescue squad. The rescue squad and the emergency room staff at a local hospital certainly saved my brother's life. He was later moved to a hospital in Louisville, where a surgeon performed a double-bypass operation on his heart. After three weeks John returned home. He still has a life to live and work to do. He has been restored to himself and to the world.

He and those who love him have a considerable debt to the medical industry, as represented by two hospitals, several doctors and nurses, many drugs and many machines. This is a debt that I cheerfully acknowledge. But I am obliged to say also that my experience of the hospital during John's stay was troubled by much conflict of feeling and a good many unresolved questions, and I know that I am not alone in this.

In the hospital what I will call the world of love meets the world of efficiency—the world, that is, of specialization, machinery, and abstract procedure. Or, rather, I should say that these two worlds come together in the hospital but do not meet. During those weeks when John was in the hospital, it seemed to me that he had come from the world of love and that the family members, neighbors, and friends who at various times were there with him came there to represent that world and to preserve his connection with it. It seemed to me that the hospital was another kind of world altogether. . . .

Like divine love, earthly love seeks plenitude; it longs for the full membership to be present and to be joined. Unlike divine love, earthly love does not have the power, the knowledge, or the will to achieve what it longs for. The story of human love on this earth is a story by which this love reveals and even validates itself by its failures to be complete and comprehensive and effective enough. When this love enters a hospital, it brings with it a terrifying history of defeat, but it comes nevertheless confident of itself, for its existence and the power of its longing have been proved over and over again even by its defeat. In the face of illness, the threat of death, and death itself, it insists unabashedly on its own presence, understanding by its persistence through defeat that it is superior to whatever happens.

The world of efficiency ignores both loves, earthly and divine, because by definition it must reduce experience to computation, particularity to abstraction, and mystery to a small comprehensibility. Efficiency, in our present sense of the word, allies itself inevitably with machinery, as Neil Postman demonstrates in his useful book, *Technopoly*. "Machines," he says, "eliminate complexity, doubt, and ambiguity. They work swiftly, they are standardized, and they provide us with numbers that you can see and calculate with." To reason, the advantages are obvious, and probably no reasonable person would wish to reject them out of hand.

And yet love obstinately answers that no loved one is standardized. A body, love insists, is neither a spirit nor a machine; it is not a picture, a diagram, a chart, a graph, an anatomy; it is not an explanation; it is not a law. It is precisely and uniquely what it is. It belongs to the world of love, which is a world of living creatures, natural orders and cycles, many small, fragile lights in the dark.

In dealing with problems of agriculture, I had thought much about the difference between creatures and machines. But I had never so clearly understood and felt that difference as when John was in recovery after his heart surgery, when he was attached to many machines and was dependent for breath on a respirator. It was impossible then not to see that the breathing of a machine, like all machine work, is unvarying, an oblivious regularity, whereas the breathing of a creature is ever changing, exquisitely responsive to events both inside and outside the body, to thoughts and emotions. A machine makes breaths as a machine makes buttons, all the same, but every breath of a creature is itself a creature, like no other, inestimably precious.

Logically, in plenitude some things ought to be expendable. Industrial economics has always believed this: abundance justifies waste. This is one of the dominant superstitions of American history—and of the history of colonialism everywhere. Expendability is also an assumption of the world of efficiency, which is why that world deals so compulsively in percentages of efficacy and safety.

But this sort of logic is absolutely alien to the world of love. To the claim that a certain drug or procedure would save 99 percent of all cancer patients or that a certain pollutant would be safe for 99 percent of a population, love, unembarrassed, would respond, "What about the one percent?"

There is nothing rational or perhaps even defensible about this, but it is nonetheless one of the strongest strands of our religious tradition—it is probably the most essential strand—according to which a shepherd, owning a hundred sheep and having lost one, does not say, "I have saved 99 percent of my sheep," but rather, "I have lost one," and he goes and searches for the one. And if the sheep in that parable may seem to be only a metaphor, then go on to the Gospel of Luke, where the principle is flatly set forth again and where the sparrows stand not for human beings but for all creatures: "Are not five sparrows sold for two farthings, and not one of them is forgotten before God?" And John Donne had in mind a sort of equation and not a mere metaphor when he wrote, "If a clod be washed away by the sea, Europe is the less, as well as if a promontory were, as well as if a manor of thy friend's or if thine own were. Any man's death diminishes me."

It is reassuring to see ecology moving toward a similar idea of the order of things. If an ecosystem loses one of its native species, we now know that we cannot speak of it as itself minus one species. An ecosystem minus one species is a different ecosystem. Just so, each of us is made by—or, one might better say, made as—a set of unique associations with unique persons, places, and things. The world of love does not admit the principle of the interchangeability of parts.

When John was in intensive care after his surgery, his wife, Carol, was standing by his bed, grieving and afraid. Wanting to reassure her, the nurse said, "Nothing is happening to him that doesn't happen to everybody."

And Carol replied, "I'm not everybody's wife."

In the world of love, things separated by efficiency and specialization strive to come back together. And yet love must confront death, and accept it, and learn from it. Only in confronting death can earthly love learn its true extent, its immortality. Any definition of health that is not silly must include death. The world of love includes death, suffers it, and triumphs over it. The world of efficiency is defeated by death; at death, all its instruments and procedures stop. The world of love continues, and of this grief is the proof.

In the hospital, love cannot forget death. But like love, death is in the hospital but not of it. Like love, fear and grief feel out of place in the hospital. How could they be included in its efficient procedures and mechanisms? Where a clear, small order is fervently maintained, fear and grief bring the threat of large disorder.

And so these two incompatible worlds might also be designated by the terms "amateur" and "professional"—amateur, in the literal sense of lover, one who participates for love; and professional in the modern sense of one who performs highly specialized or technical procedures for pay. The amateur is excluded from the professional "field." For the amateur, in the hospital or in almost any other encounter with the medical industry, the overriding experience is that of being excluded from knowledge—of being unable, in other words, to make or participate in anything resembling an "informed decision." Of course, whether doctors make informed decisions in the hospital is a matter of debate. For in the hospital even the professionals are involved in experience; experimentation has been left far behind. Experience, as all amateurs know, is not predictable, and in experience there are no replications or "controls"; there is nothing with which to compare the result. Once one decision has been made, we have destroyed the opportunity to know what would have happened if another decision had been made. That is to say that medicine is an exact science until applied; application involves intuition, a sense of probability, "gut feeling," guesswork, and error.

In medicine, as in many modern disciplines, the amateur is divided from the professional by perhaps unbridgeable differences of knowledge and of language. An "informed decision" is really not even imaginable for most medical patients and their families, who have no competent understanding of either the patient's illness or the recommended medical or surgical procedure. Moreover, patients and their families are not likely to know the doctor, the surgeon, or any of the other people on whom the patient's life will depend. In the hospital, amateurs are more than likely to be proceeding entirely upon faith—and this is a peculiar and scary faith, for it must be placed not in a god but in mere people, mere procedures, mere chemicals, and mere machines.

It was only after my brother had been taken into surgery, I think, that the family understood the extremity of this deed of faith. We had decided—or John had decided and we had concurred—on the basis of the best advice available. But once he was separated from us, we felt the burden of our ignorance. We had not known what we were doing, and one of our difficulties now was the feeling that we had utterly given him up to what we did not know. John himself spoke out of this sense of abandonment and helplessness in the intensive care unit, when he said, "I don't know what they're going to do to me or for me or with me." As we waited and reports came at long intervals from the operating room, other realizations followed. We realized that under the circumstances, we could not be told the truth. We would not know, ever, the worries and surprises that came to the surgeon during his work. We would not know the critical moments or the fears. If the surgeon did any part of his work ineptly or made a mistake, we would not know it. We realized, moreover, that if we were told the truth, we would have no way of knowing that the truth was what it was.

We realized that when the emissaries from the operating room assured us that everything was "normal" or "routine," they were referring to the procedure and not the patient. Even as amateurs—perhaps because we were amateurs—we knew that what was happening was not normal or routine for John or for us.

That these two worlds are so radically divided does not mean that people cannot cross between them. I do not know how an amateur can cross over into the professional world; that does not seem very probable. But that professional people can cross back into the amateur world, I know from much evidence. During John's stay in the hospital there were many moments in which doctors and nurses—especially nurses!—allowed or caused the professional relationship to become a meeting between two human beings, and these moments were invariably moving.

The most moving, to me, happened in the waiting room during John's surgery. From time to time a nurse from the operating room would come in to tell Carol what was happening. Carol, from politeness or bravery or both, always stood to receive the news, which always left us somewhat encouraged and somewhat doubtful. Carol's difficulty was that she had to suffer the ordeal not only as a wife but as one who had been a trained nurse. She knew, from her own education and experience, in how limited a sense open-heart surgery could be said to be normal or routine.

Finally, toward the end of our wait, two nurses came in. The operation, they said, had been a success. They explained again what had been done. And then they said that after the completion of the bypasses, the surgeon had found it necessary to insert a "balloon pump" into the aorta to assist the heart. This possibility had never been mentioned, nobody was prepared for it, and Carol was sorely disappointed and upset. The two young women attempted to reassure her, mainly by repeating things they had already said. And then there was a long moment when they just looked at her. It was such a look as parents sometimes give to a sick or suffering child, when they themselves have begun to need the comfort they are trying to give.

And then one of the nurses said, "Do you need a hug?"

"Yes," Carol said.

And the nurse gave her a hug.

Which brings us to a starting place.

Did you write your summary of Berry's article in about 50 words? Does it capture the essential nature of the article? Did you provide identification or documentation to the source? If you did these things, review your abstract once more and submit it to your instructor.

Writing a Detailed Summary of a Lengthy Work

Writing a detailed summary of a lengthy essay or book necessitates more preparation than does writing a brief summary of a short essay like the one by Willie Nelson.

**WEB LINK
to Reading
4.3**
http://www.
ablongman.com/
lester

For a summary of a longer work, you should carefully make a note of each major point in the work.

Reproduced next is a lengthy essay by Robert K. Goldman, a professor at Washington University College of Law. The piece appeared in the journal *Human Rights* (Fall 2001). In it Goldman discusses the legal consequences flowing from the 9/11 terrorist attacks on the World Trade Center and the Pentagon. At the time, President George W. Bush acted with prudence and did not rush into action, and by reading Goldman's essay we can see the complicated legal debate about action against the nation of Afghanistan. Read the essay and then study the three items at the end that one student developed in response to Goldman's essay:

- A set of numbered notes that identify the major issues raised by Goldman.
- An interpretation of Goldman's hypothesis.
- A summary of the essay.

Spend some time with the essay and the student's work in order to understand how the student crafted her summary from miscellaneous notes she took as she read through the quasi-legal document.

Certain Legal Questions and Issues Raised by the September 11th Attacks

Robert K. Goldman

In trying to analyze the legal implications of the events of September 11th, international lawyers and government officials are finding themselves in somewhat uncharted territory. Because the attacks on the Pentagon and the World Trade Center complex were apparently carried out by non-state actors who may have planned, organized and financed key aspects of their illicit activities in other states, it is not easy to frame U.S. responses within familiar categories recognized by international law. Normally, a state goes to war against another state or internal enemies. Although the war that the U.S. has pledged to wage against the perpetrators of these horrific acts and the state(s) that harbor them does not fit neatly within existing paradigms, any ensuing hostilities will nonetheless be largely based on or extrapolated from preexisting international law rules and principles.

In analyzing these events, it is important to distinguish two separate, but interrelated branches of international law: the law governing the resort to armed force, and the law applicable to the conduct of hostilities. The former is found in the United Nations Charter (Charter) and state practice, and the latter in the law of armed conflict, also known as International Humanitarian Law (IHL).

Historically, states recognized a right to resort to war between or among themselves as a lawful means to settle political disputes. Hostilities were frequently triggered by formal declarations of war, armed attacks followed by such a declaration, or other acts indicating an intention to engage in warfare. With the adoption of the UN Charter in the wake of World War II, the legal rules changed in this regard. By virtue of Articles 2(3) and 2(4) of the UN Charter, states renounced the use of force as a means of settling disputes and effectively outlawed aggressive war. However, Article 51 of the Charter recognizes that a state that is the victim of an armed attack (presumably by another state) can lawfully resort to force in exercise of the inherent right of individual or collective self-defense against aggression.

The term "war" has a particular meaning in U.S. law, which involves complex constitutional issues of separation of powers. Under the federal Constitution, only Congress can declare war and it has not done so since World War II. However, the U.S., without such a declaration, but under the President's express and implied powers, has been involved in numerous armed conflicts, including Korea, Vietnam, Kosovo, Grenada, and Panama. Like his father in the Gulf war, President Bush has received from Congress, not a declaration of war as such, but a joint resolution authorizing him to use military force against nations, organizations and persons involved in these attacks and those states which harbor such organizations and persons. Various actions on the international level also have significantly strengthened the President's hand to undertake, consistent with international law, hostile acts against these persons, groups and/or states.

Certainly, if a state had launched these attacks, the U.S., as the victim of aggression, could under Article 51 of the Charter legitimately take military action against that state and call on other states to assist it. Significantly, the NATO Treaty—which declares an attack on one member an attack on all members of the alliance—has been invoked for the first time, and may well result in unprecedented joint military operations under that treaty. A claim by NATO members to be acting in accordance with Article 51 and the Charter's purposes would carry great weight and contribute to the interpretation of Charter norms. Most importantly, the United Nations Security Council, on September 12, 2001, unanimously approved Resolution 1368 (2001), stating that any act of international terrorism was a threat to international peace and security. While calling on all states to bring to justice "the perpetrators, organizers and sponsors" of these terrorist acts, it stressed that "those responsible for aiding, supporting or harboring them would be held accountable," and pointedly recognized the right to individual and collective self-defense under the Charter. This measure, while not expressly authorizing the use of force, is sufficiently broad that it will unquestionably be relied on by the U.S. if it decides to employ force against any or all of these parties.

Can the U.S. be at "war" and engage in hostilities against non-state actors? Historical precedents suggest that it can. For example, the U.S. in 1805 sent an expeditionary force to Tripoli to destroy the Barbary Pirates. In 1916, the U.S. military was sent into Mexico to capture or kill Pancho Villa and his band after they attacked U.S. nationals in New Mexico. It is well settled that non-state actors who engage in hostile acts during an armed conflict may be lawfully killed or wounded. IHL permits governments engaged in civil wars and lesser internal hostilities to attack members of dissident armed groups, as well as the targeting of individual civilians who directly participate in internal or interstate hostilities. All such persons are effectively non-state actors. One might anticipate that the U.S., by analogy to interstate armed conflict rules, will treat Osama bin Laden and his associates as constituting a paramilitary organization whose members do not comply with the most basic rules and customs of warfare. As such, the U.S. could treat them as unprivileged combatants subject to direct attack and, if captured, not entitled to prisoner of war status. Accordingly, they would be liable for trial in a U.S. court and punishment for all their hostile acts, as well as pre-capture offenses. These offenses entail multiple crimes under U.S. and international law associated with the attacks on the Pentagon and the World Trade Center complex, and the bombings of the U.S. embassies in Kenya and Tanzania in 1998, for which bin Laden has already been indicted.

Had a state launched these attacks, that state would clearly be responsible for having initiated an aggressive war in violation of the UN Charter. It is unclear whether non-state actors can be charged with and tried for this particular offense. However, if their attacks are treated as acts of war, those acts would constitute serious violations of the laws and customs of war. In this regard, IHL categorically prohibits launching intentional attacks against the civilian population, individual civilians, as well as civilian objects. Moreover in 1977, states by treaty (Protocol Additional to the Geneva Conventions of 12 August, 1949, and Relating to Protection of Victims of International Armed Conflicts—Protocols I & II) prohibited in all armed conflicts acts or threats of violence whose primary purpose is to terrorize the civilian population. The World Trade Center complex was a civilian object dedicated to ordinary civilian purposes and inhabited by peaceable civilians. Thus, these buildings were immune from direct attack. Their deliberate destruction with the clear intent to kill or wound civilians within those structures constituted an illegal indiscriminate attack. Another clear and illicit purpose of the attacks was to terrorize and attack the morale of the civilian population. So great was the intended and actual number of civilian deaths attending these attacks that they also might well qualify as a crime against humanity. The attack against the Pentagon arguably was also illegal. Although the Pentagon does qualify under IHL as a military objective, and is thus a lawful target of attack during an armed conflict, it was attacked by perfidious or treacherous means—a hijacked civilian jetliner.

Other international crimes, punishable under U.S. law and the laws of other nations, were committed by the perpetrators of these attacks and their confederates. The seizure and destruction of the jetliners violated the 1970 Hague anti-hijacking convention, as well as 18 U.S.C. § 32, which imposes criminal liability for, *inter alia*, willfully destroying an aircraft and assaulting its passengers and crew. Further, the effect on the passengers of these hijacked planes might well amount to hostage taking in violation of the Convention against the Taking of Hostages and 18 U.S.C. § 1203, which contains a similar proscription. Most of these crimes are already within the subject matter jurisdiction of U.S. courts. War crimes, crimes against humanity, hijacking, hostage taking, and other serious violations of the laws and customs of war are international crimes of universal jurisdiction, making the perpetrators subject to criminal prosecution by other states. At present, there is no international court with jurisdiction to try the perpetrators and their accomplices. However, the UN Security Council, or perhaps a group of states which are parties to these treaties, such as NATO members, could establish an ad hoc tribunal for this purpose, based on the Yugoslav and Rwanda models.

President Bush has stated that the U.S. will make no distinction between the perpetrators and those, presumably states, who harbor them. Can the U.S. invoke Article

51 of the UN Charter to justify taking military action against a state that did not perpetrate the attacks of September 11, but merely harbors the intellectual authors of and other accomplices in these events? It is legally plausible that the U.S. and its allies might impute these acts of terrorism, constituting an armed attack, to such a state, thereby holding it responsible for these crimes. International law recognizes that the acts of non-state actors may be attributed under certain circumstances to a state. The U.S. may argue that Afghanistan, for example, is guilty of both omission and commission in connection with these and previously realized or foiled attacks by Osama bin Laden and his associates. That argument might posit that the Taliban's failure to take action against bin Laden effectively amounts to a pattern of state tolerance of and acquiescence in these illicit acts sufficient to impute and thus attribute the conduct to the state itself. International human rights bodies have used such reasoning in finding states responsible for the conduct of non-state actors. For example, in 2000, the Inter-American Commission on Human Rights (Commission) in the Massacre of Rio Frio case found Colombia responsible for atrocities committed by the *Autodefensas Unidas de Colombia*, a paramilitary group. The Commission found that, even though the state had declared such groups to be illegal, it tolerated their presence and had acquiesced in their depredations and killings in the particular circumstances of that case.

If the United States takes military action against Afghanistan or any other state, it will be involved in an international armed conflict with that state within the meaning of Article 2 common to the 1949 Geneva Conventions. As such, the U.S., its allies, if any, and the target state will be legally bound to conduct hostilities in accordance with IHL, most particularly, the Geneva Conventions and the laws and customs of warfare contained in the Hague Regulations. Unlike UN law, modern IHL is not concerned with the legality of the resort to force. Rather, its fundamental rules are designed to regulate and restrain the conduct of hostilities in order to spare the victims of armed conflicts. Foremost among these rules are those designed to ensure the immunity of the civilian population and civilian objects, such as houses and schools, etc., from direct attack by requiring the belligerents to distinguish at all times such protected persons and objects from military objectives and to direct their attacks solely against the latter. The warring parties, moreover, cannot attack military targets with impunity. When so doing, they must take the necessary precautions to avoid or at least minimize expected civilian casualties, i.e., collateral damage. In other words, the U.S. cannot fight terror with terror. Apart from being unlawful, attacks against civilians and their morale are totally counterproductive, as the reaction of the American people demonstrates, and wasteful of military assets.

Can the U.S., without violating U.S. and international law directly, target bin Laden in connection with such an attack? The answer is yes. Executive Order 12333 (Order) effectively renounces the use of assassination as an instrument of U.S. policy. While so doing, the Order does not define the term "assassination," but it should be understood as meaning an act of murder undertaken for political purposes. The ostensible purpose of the Order at the time of its adoption was to preclude the U.S. from killing, for example, a foreign leader of a state with whom the U.S. was not at war. The Order not only prohibits this, but also the willful killing of a private person for political purposes. This prohibition is consistent with international human rights law, which prohibits a state from engaging in arbitrary deprivations of life.

The legal situation is different during situations of armed conflict. Combatants may lawfully target and kill enemy combatants, as well as civilians who directly participate in the hostilities. As these persons are legitimate targets of attack, their deaths are treated as justifiable homicide for which the attacker incurs no liability under domestic or international law. Such killings do not constitute assassinations within the meaning of the Executive Order or IHL, nor would they violate, in principle, the prohibition against arbitrary deprivation of life in human rights law.

As previously noted, the U.S. is justified in treating bin Laden and the members of his organization as a paramilitary force which engages in the illegal use of force. Whether they be regarded as paramilitary or merely civilians who have assumed a combatant's role, they are in the context of interstate hostilities unprivileged combatants who are subject, individually and collectively, to direct attack. So long as they are not attacked in a "treacherous" manner, which does not include by commando raid, their deaths would be lawful acts of war.

WEB LINK
to Exercise
4.5

http://www.
ablongman.com/
lester

Student Notes and Summary of a Long Article

Student Margaret Bibb has taken extensive notes on the Goldman document. She has methodically registered these ideas in her writing journal in order to understand each major point made by Goldman. She could have chosen instead to write the notes in the margins.

1. Agents without countries who perform illegal activities fall outside most regulations and might escape regular international law.

2. Two laws apply: the law applicable to the conduct of hostilities and the law governing the resort to armed force.

3. After World War II aggressive war was outlawed, but a nation can resort to forceful self-defense against aggression.

4. War has peculiar meanings and can be enacted only by Congress, so since World War II we have had "armed conflicts" initiated by presidents. President George W. Bush has a congressional joint resolution authorizing his use of military force.

5. NATO has a resolution for uniting Europe behind "collective self-defense" against terrorists and those who harbor the terrorists.

6. The attack on the World Trade Center—a civilian center—was an illegal attack as well as a "crime against humanity." The attack on the Pentagon—a lawful target for attack—was also illegal because the terrorists used a hijacked civilian jetliner.

7. The seizure and destruction of the jetliners violated the 1970 Hague anti-hijacking convention and violated the Convention against the Taking of

Hostages. President Bush will make no distinction between those who committed the acts and those who harbor them because the "acts of non-state actors may be attributed . . . to a state." The Taliban can be held accountable.

8. If the United States attacks Afghanistan, it will be held accountable under the 1949 Geneva Convention to ensure the immunity of civilians and civilian targets.
9. Can the U.S. target Osama bin Laden? Yes. The U.S. cannot assassinate for political purposes, but armed conflict permits the killing of a foreign leader.
10. The United States may treat bin Laden and his organization as a paramilitary force subject to immediate retaliatory attacks, and the destruction would be lawful.

Next, Bibb has framed in her own words the general principle or hypothesis that Goldman explores and defends.

Hypothesis:

The United States has a legal basis for an assault on military targets in Afghanistan that harbor terrorists and on the compounds of Osama bin Laden.

Armed now with plenty of notes and her understanding of the general legal position of the president, Bibb is ready to write her summary. You will see how she has drawn from the information in her writing journal.

Summary

Robert Goldman, a professor at the Washington University College of Law in Washington, D.C., has laid out the legal grounds upon which President George W. Bush and the United States attacked both the Taliban and Osama bin Laden in Afghanistan in retribution for the terrorist attacks on the World Trade Center and the Pentagon. In "Certain Legal Questions and Issues Raised by the September 11th Attacks," Goldman explains international law as it applies in this case. By citing precedent, national law, and international conventions, Goldman provides the legal casework for America's attack with the clear understanding that the innocent civilians of Afghanistan must be protected from the military attacks. Crimes against humanity, hijacking, hostage taking, and mass murder are international crimes worthy of drawing the censure and retaliation by the affected nations. Goldman classifies terrorists as "unprivileged combatants" subject to "direct attack," and "their deaths would be lawful acts of war."

The detailed summary of an entire book is similar to that of a lengthy article except that you will be dealing with chapters, sections, or a collection of articles. Thus, your summary should explain both the arrangement of the book and summarize its contents.

Consider this summary of an entire book, *The Majesty of the Law: Reflections of a Supreme Court Justice* by Sandra Day O'Connor. The summary was written by a student, Wanda Martin-Winchell, who was researching the roles of women in the legal profession.

Supreme Court Justice Sandra Day O'Connor has written a new book that looks at many aspects of her life in the court. It is not an autobiography in any sense of the word, although her Preface touches on the appointment in 1981 by President Ronald Reagan of the first woman justice, and the Epilogue explores her optimism for her granddaughter and the children of America. In between, she examines six aspects of America's legal history from her perspective. "Life on the Court," explains a few things about the justices, policies, and procedures in hearing oral arguments and writing the majority and minority opinions.

In Part Two, "A Bit of History," O'Connor reviews the prevailing power of the Rule of Law as established by the Constitution, the Bill of Rights, and the Writ of Habeas Corpus. The next section, "People Who Have Helped Shape the Court," provides a historical portrait of Oliver Wendell Holmes and his concern for the power of the states; William Howard Taft, who organized the court more efficiently; Charles Evans Hughes; who prevented President Franklin Roosevelt from increasing the size of the court; Thurgood Marshall, who became the first black justice and who elevated the court's examination of legal rules that affect human lives; Warren Burger, who administered the court to fine tune it for efficiency; and Lewis Powell, who provided wisdom and "equity at the bottomline."

In Part Four, "Women and the Law," Justice O'Connor comments on the role of women in government, from Belva Lockwood, Elizabeth Cody Stanton, and Susan B. Anthony to Indira Gandhi, Golda Meir, and Margaret Thatcher. She explores the history of suffrage and brings us forward to contemporary issues of the "glass ceiling" and "gender equity." In Part Five, "The Legal Profession and the Courts," she examines the basic organization of the federal and state courts since the original Judiciary Act of 1789. She also touches on the jury system and the professionalism of attorney behavior—both the good and the bad.

In her final part, "The Rule of Law in the Twenty-first Century," O'Connor argues that the Rule of Law "offers the best approach to securing freedom and equality for all people," despite the events of 9/11 and after. She affirms her faith in a future that will be secure as long as we maintain an independent judiciary that protects and enforces individual rights and liberties.

EXERCISE 4.8
WRITING THE LENGTHY SUMMARY

As an exercise in developing a lengthy summary, select a work of nonfiction—perhaps a biography or autobiography—that you have read recently or have studied in the past. Secure a copy of the work, review it, and write a summary similar to the one that appears above about Justice O'Connor's book *The Majesty of the Law: Reflections of a Supreme Court Justice.*

Chapter Review

WEB LINK
to Chapter 4
Related Web
Destinations
http://www.
ablongman.com/
lester

Chapter 4 has introduced you to the various techniques for writing a basic summary, several specialized summaries, and the more detailed summary for a lengthy work. Primarily, writing a summary is a tool for your own understanding of an article or essay. It serves as the culmination of your critical reading.

A summary itemizes the key points of a paragraph, an article, or an entire book. Once it is written, you can insert it into your own essay if you wish to make reference to a particular idea or writer or both.

The chapter has also introduced you to several kinds of specialized summaries. The brief review lets you evaluate a work and make recommendations about it. The plot summary and book summary help you retain the essence of a work. The annotated bibliography and the abstract are academic tools that will serve you well when you write a full-blown research paper. Searching out and reading abstracts and annotated bibliographies are a prelude to in-depth critical reading of complete articles and books.

Finally, the chapter has offered guidelines for writing more detailed summaries of a lengthy essay or an entire book.

Chapter 4 Assignment:
Writing a Summary

Read William Safire's essay "Four Score and Seven" on Lincoln's Gettysburg Address. The essay originally appeared in the *New York Times* (February 9, 2003). Accompanying the piece are the two transcripts that Safire discusses, the "Nicolay Draft" and the "Hay Draft." You may wish to refer to them as you study Safire's argument.

The assignment asks you to accomplish three tasks:

1. As you read the essay, take plenty of notes in the margins or in a writing journal.

2. Frame a thesis or hypothesis that governs Safire's essay.

3. Write a summary of Safire's essay.

Four Score and Seven

William Safire

Six years from this Wednesday will be the 200th anniversary of the birth of Abraham Lincoln, and I'm glad that Congress is making plans for that bicentennial. It will be a big day for celebration of emancipation, of majority rule and, at a lesser degree of magnitude, of memorable political phrases.

How do these phrases come to be? Some are "in the air," attributed to nobody, and are made famous by a powerful leader or when spoken on a great occasion. (Few in the crowd at a Boston antislavery convention in 1850 paid attention to the definition of democracy given by the Rev. Theodore Parker: "a government of all the people, by all the people, for all the people.") Others are worked out in a speaker's mind or tried out in front of a crowd before being committed to paper. Consider a phrase that was tossed out to begin remarks at a historic moment.

President Lincoln had not participated in the Independence Day celebrations of the Union victory at Gettysburg in July 1863 because he was worried about the outcome of the Battle of Vicksburg, half a nation away. Instead, he issued a formal, third-person prayerful statement concluding, "The President . . . . desires that on this day, He whose will, not ours, should ever be done, be everywhere remembered and reverenced with profoundest gratification."

Then on July 7 came the news that the Confederate bastion at Vicksburg had fallen to General Grant and Admiral Porter and that the Mississippi River was open to traffic clear down to the port of New Orleans. "The Father of Waters," as Lincoln later put it in a letter, "flows unvexed to the sea." (*Unvexed*, an unfamiliar synonym for "untroubled, unimpeded" used by the poets Shakespeare, Donne and Dryden, shows the Illinois lawyer's literary bent.)

"At 8 P.M., a crowd assembled in front of the National Hotel," went a dispatch to the *New York Times*, "and marched up Pennsylvania Avenue, headed by the Marine Band, to the executive Mansion, and serenaded and enthusiastically cheered." Lincoln appeared at a window and gave an impromptu response. A few newspaper reporters made notes, and a semiofficial copy was later handed out and used in various forms by editors. All agreed that after thanking God for the occasion, Lincoln reportedly opened with these words:

"How long ago is it? Eighty-odd years since, on the Fourth of July, for the first time in the world, a union body of representatives was assembled and declared as self-evident that all men were created equal."

Four months later, at the dedication of the Gettysburg cemetery, in what became the speech at the apex of American oratory, Lincoln took his ad-libbed question and answer—"How long ago is it? Eighty-odd years since . . ."—and gave his dedicatory opening a biblical gravity: "*Four score and seven years ago.*"

I recall a cartoon of Lincoln, pencil in hand, thinking aloud something like "Eighty seven? Three score and twenty-seven? Five score less thirteen?" In fact, Lincoln must have gone through that thought process in coming to that sonorous, rhythmic count—one, two, one-two-three, with the words *Four score and seven*—more memorable than his earlier, offhand "Eighty-odd."

Recalling the root of the ringing Gettysburg opening in the casual ad-lib response to the post-Vicksburg serenade, the novelist and biographer Thomas Keneally, in his short Lincoln biography in the "Penguin Lives" series, takes the text as produced in the *New York Times*, which differs in many passages from that in the *Washington Star*. Did Lincoln, recalling for the crowd the near-simultaneous death on the Fourth of July, 1826, of both Thomas Jefferson and John Adams, say, as the *Star* recorded, "This extraordinary coincidence we can understand to be a dispensation of the Almighty Ruler of Events"? Or did he say only, as the *Times* reported, "This was indeed an extraordinary and remarkable event in our history"? (Editors in those prerecording days had a lot of leeway to fix up presidential prose.)

But in a deeper sense, as he would say, Lincoln also knew how to rewrite. To the serenaders, he said, "This is a glorious theme and the occasion for a speech, but I am not prepared to make one worthy of the occasion." After he had four months to prepare, that well-balanced, self-deprecating sentence was rebalanced to "The world will little note, nor long remember, what we say here, but it can never forget what they did here."

Did he edit the Gettysburg Address after he wrote it out the first time? That's a mystery, but we have a few clues. Five copies of the speech exist in his handwriting. Set aside the last three, which he made later as souvenir gifts, and focus on comparing the two that went to his two secretaries. The "Nicolay draft" may well have been his reading copy that eyewitnesses said he took from his coat pocket, while the "Hay draft" contains interesting improvements that indicate to me the way he wanted the speech to be remembered.

If I'm right, he changed "for those who died here" to the more active "for those who here gave their lives." Lincoln strengthened "This we may, in all propriety do" to "It is altogether fitting and proper that we should do this." He sharpened the contrast of "while it can never forget what they did here" by substituting *but* for *while*.

And then there is the editing that still has political reverberations. In 1954, Congress added the phrase *under God* to the Pledge of Allegiance after the phrase "one nation." That was recently challenged by some who feel that an official evocation of the deity breaches the constitutional wall of separation between church and state.

Neither the Nicolay copy nor the Hay copy has that phrase in it. But all three copies he later made for gifts did read "that this nation *under God* shall have a new birth of freedom." So did the speech as transcribed by different reporters on the scene at Gettysburg that was published contemporaneously. Did he ad-lib those two words? "He wouldn't have improvised," says David Donald, this generation's leading Lincoln biographer. "That would have been highly uncharacteristic. That would be unlike Lincoln. But I would say he did, in fact, say it during the speech."

That suggests to me that Lincoln inserted *under God* into his reading copy, which has vanished. (If you find it in your attic, call the Library of Congress.) Forget the "back-of-the-envelope" myth; that final addition shows he was polishing that speech right until the time came to deliver it.

Two Transcripts of the Gettysburg Address

Differences between the texts of the two drafts are indicated by **emphasis** type. Please note that the Nicolay and Hay versions of the Gettysburg Address differ somewhat from the generally printed Bliss version.

The "Nicolay Draft"

Four score and seven years ago our fathers brought forth, upon this continent, a new nation, conceived in liberty, and dedicated to the proposition that "all men are created equal."

Now we are engaged in a great civil war, testing whether that nation, or any nation so conceived, and so dedicated, can long endure. We are met on a great **battle field** of that war. We come to dedicate a portion of it, as a final resting place for those who **died here, that the** nation might live. **This we may, in all propriety do.** But, in a larger sense, we can not dedicate—we can not consecrate—we can not hallow, this ground—The brave men, living and dead, who struggled here, have **hallowed** it, far above our poor power to add or detract. The world will little note, nor long remember what we say here; **while it** can never forget what they **did** here.

It is rather for us, **the living, we here be** dedicated to the great task remaining before us—that, from these honored dead we take increased devotion to that cause for which they here, gave the last full measure of devotion—that we here highly resolve these dead shall not have died in vain; that **the** nation, shall have a new birth of freedom, and that government of the people by the people for the people, shall not perish from the earth.

The "Hay Draft"

Four score and seven years ago our fathers brought forth, upon this continent, a new nation, conceived in Liberty, and dedicated to the proposition that all men are created equal.

Now we are engaged in a great civil war, testing whether that nation, or any nation so conceived, and so dedicated, can long endure. We are met **here** on a great **battlefield** of that war. We have come to dedicate a portion of it as a final resting place for those who **here gave their lives that that** nation might live. **It is altogether fitting and proper that we should do this.**

But in a larger sense we can not dedicate—we can not consecrate—we can not hallow this ground. The brave men, living and dead, who struggled, here, have **consecrated** it far above our poor power to add or detract. The world will little note, nor long remember, what we say here, **but** can never forget what they **did** here. **It is for us, the living, rather to be dedicated here to the unfinished work which they have, thus far, so nobly carried on.** It is rather for us **to be here** dedicated to the great task remaining before us—that from these honored dead we take increased devotion to that cause for which they here gave the last full measure of devotion—that we here highly resolve **that** these dead shall not have died in vain; that **this** nation shall have a new birth of freedom; and that **this** government of the people, by the people, for the people, shall not perish from the earth.

Tracing the Work of Two Students
Annotated Bibliography

This section at the end of some chapters features the work of two students in the development of their papers. Kaci Holz is an English major researching gender communication issues. Halley Fishburn is a political science major searching for literature on the War Powers Act. Kaci Holz has written an annotated bibliography to guide her research, and six of her nineteen entries are shown below. They demonstrate how the summary functions as an annotation to each entry in a working bibliography. By writing the summaries, Holz has captured in her mind and on paper the essential characteristics of each work.

Annotated Bibliography

Armstrong, Colleen, "Deborah Tannen Comes to Class: Implications of Gender and

Conversation in the Classroom." *English Journal* 85.2 (1996): 15. In a

conversation with a male student, Armstrong thought she was "helpful" and

"supportive" when she "nodded vigorously" and punctuated his words with

"yes." The male thought she was "rude" and "intrusive." Concerned at the

failure of conversation, Armstrong read Deborah Tannen's *You Just Don't*

Understand, which helped Armstrong understand the ways men and women

interrupt each other. Men see interruptions as "conversational bullying." Women

see them as "cooperative overlapping." What Armstrong thought was support

and involvement the male student saw as manipulation.

"Bill and coo." *The Economist* 321 (1991): 107. The author of this article is not given.

He/she describes a debate held at the Cooper Union in New York between

Deborah Tannen and John Bly, two authors "whose work has discussed the

female and male perspectives on understanding between the sexes." Many people

expected this debate to be "a battle of the sexes," but instead it was "a high

minded debate between two earnest intellectuals before a large and attentive

audience." Both authors praised each other's ideas and research in the field. Bly claimed Tannen's book to be "a lively but serious examination of the different conversational styles of men and women." Tannen also complimented Bly's book *Iron John,* "which, unusually, puts the blame for the failure of boys to grow up on their fathers, not their mothers."

Deborah Tannen and Robert Bly: Men and Women Talking Together. New York Cooper Union. Videocassette. Mystic Fire Video, 1993. This video presents two of the most popular and exciting people at the forefront of men's and women's issues, talking to each other about gender styles. Each brings an informed perspective on how men and women approach each other and conversation itself. Bly and Tannen agree that "it is crucial to describe both the differences and similarities, so that men and women can respect each other, and in the process, present a model of how that is done" (back cover of the videocassette).

Gergen, Mary. Rev. of *Talking Difference: On Gender and Language*, by Mary Crawford. *Archives of Sexual Behavior* 30.3 (2001): 338- . *InfoTrac.* Woodward Lib., Clarksville, TN. 28 Sept. 2002 <http://web1.infotrac.galegroup.com>. In her review of Crawford's book, Gergen suggests that the "differences between the ways men and women talk suggest that we might as well have come from different planets." Today, some view it as necessary to take a quick course in conversational translations. Gergen says Crawford made in-depth inquiries into issues of how conversation affects relations, power, and discrimination.

Glass, Lillian. *He Says, She Says: Closing the Communication Gap between the Sexes.* New York: Putnam, 1992. Glass's book begins with the author's interest in gender communication. The first chapter is a Sex Talk Quiz that the reader can take to check his or her responses. The second chapter addresses "the evolution of sex differences in communication." Glass addresses the issue that different hormones found in men's and women's bodies make them act differently and therefore communicate differently. In later chapters Glass discusses brain development, environmental factors, and treatment of infants, and ends with recommendations for improving communication and thus the relationships with the other sex.

Tannen, Deborah. "Boys Will Be Boys." *The Argument Culture: Moving from Debate to Dialogue.* New York: Random House, 1998. In Chapter 6 of *The Argument Culture* Tannen addresses the issue that boys or men "are more likely to take an oppositional stance toward other people and the world" and "are more likely to find opposition entertaining—to enjoy watching a good fight, or having one." She says girls try to avoid fights. She also claims that a girl tries to offer a view that would benefit the opponent. A boy, on the other hand, just argues for what is best for him. She concludes that patterns of opposition and conflict result from both biology and culture.

Writing a Paraphrase

U sing a well-written paraphrase allows you to interpret in your own words, point by point, another person's ideas. The use of a paraphrase improves the style of your paper because the writer listens to your voice, not various voices in a string of multiple quotations. The paraphrase also acts as an intellectual bridge between your source on one side and the reader on the other. You will carry the wisdom of the source to the reader in approximately the same number of words.

WEB LINK
to Chapter 5
Related Web
Destinations
http://www.
ablongman.com/
lester

Writing paraphrases is a bit more difficult than sprinkling quotations here and there in your paper. Paraphrasing a source, however, will give you a comprehensive under-standing of the work because you must interpret in your own words the thought, meaning, and attitude of someone else. Use the paraphrase for these reasons:

- To maintain your own voice in your paper.
- To sustain your own writing style.
- To avoid an endless string of direct quotations.
- To interpret the source as you rewrite it.
- To gain a comprehensive understanding of a passage.

Let's see how these elements come into play by watching one student create a paraphrase. Student Ramon Magrans has gone in search of information on the topic "Voting and Ballot Design." He has found this next passage, which is a bit formal and cumbersome. Rather than placing it in his paper as a long quotation, which would slow the flow of his own writing, Magrans has decided to rewrite it both to understand the concept and to share it with his readers.

Perceived obligations of citizen duty may compel some people to cast votes in democratic elections even when they lack sufficient information to make informed choices. Psychological theories of choice suggest that, under such circumstances, voters may be influenced by the order in which candidates' names appear on the ballot, biasing people toward candidates listed early (when voters can generate reasons to vote for the candidates) or late (when voters can only generate reasons to vote against the candidates).

> —Joanne Miller and Jon Krosnick, "The Impact of Candidate Name Order on Election Outcomes," *Public Opinion Quarterly*

Magrans's paraphrase, below, captures the essence of the original in about the same number of words, and it demonstrates his grasp of the people's behavior in a voting booth.

Voters who enter election booths without knowing the candidates are likely to vote for the candidate listed first on the ballot. In a recent study, Joanne Miller and Jon Krosnick determined that the ballots influence people to vote for candidates listed early and neglect candidates listed late. One might think voters would merely skip that part of the ballot, but a sense of civic duty makes them pull a lever for every contest whether they know the people or not.

This paraphrase of a portion of the passage shows how a student has worked out his own interpretation of the issue of ballot design. Whether he uses the paraphrase in his paper or not, the student has gained a better understanding of voting habits.

When you interpret information and express it in your own words, you must (1) understand what has been said, (2) capture the wisdom, humor, anger, or pessimism of the writer, and (3) express it in a new way. You will be enlightened by your effort.

T I P   *Writing a Paraphrase*

Writing a paraphrase is similar to writing a summary, with a significant difference. A summary can reduce an entire article to a sentence or two, but a paraphrase will rewrite a passage in about the same number of words. Like writing a summary, writing a paraphrase can be an end in itself, as one way for you to understand a passage and a writer's argument.

Writing an Effective Paraphrase in Two Steps

If you are unsure about how to write a paraphrase, as a first step you can begin by writing a *literal paraphrase*. A literal paraphrase duplicates the original as closely as possible, retaining the basic grammatical structure; it merely uses different words. It maintains the length, the meaning, and the tone of the original. Let's look at a passage from an article and one student's interpretation of it.

Original

WEB LINK
to Exercise
5.1
http://www.
ablongman.com/
lester

Skin cell to embryo—it's one of the most remarkable quick-change scenarios modern biology has to offer. It's also one of the most controversial. Since the announcement, in 1997, of the cloning of Dolly the sheep, attempts to use human cells for cloning have provoked heated debate in the United States, separating those who have faith in the promise of the new technology from those who envision its dark side and unintended consequences.

—Kyla Dunn, "Cloning Trevor," *The Atlantic Monthly*

Here is the student's literal paraphrase:

Kyla Dunn, in an article for *The Atlantic Monthly*, says transforming a human cell into an embryo seems to be a shining new scientific moment. However, Dunn explains that cloning a human being remains highly divisive. Ever since Dolly the sheep was cloned in 1997, arguments have raged on both sides, with some advocates expressing confidence in the scientific accomplishments to be gained and others forecasting shadowy results.

Above, *controversial* becomes *divisive* and *heated debate* becomes *arguments*. Likewise, *those who have faith in the promise of the new technology* is replaced by *some advocates expressing confidence in the scientific accomplishments to be gained*.

However, a literal paraphrase is often insufficient because it "clones" the original too much. Thus, the literal paraphrase should launch a free paraphrase, one that is not a slave to the original and that removes any hint that you have copied too much of the original. Chapter 7, Practicing Academic Integrity, will discuss this matter in detail.

A *free version paraphrase* displays more of your own voice. In the example that follows the student blends the free version paraphrase into the middle of a paragraph, rather than beginning with the source and staying with it throughout the paragraph. She has created her own topic sentence and moved smoothly into the paraphrase.

Cloning has produced division, especially between medical scientists on one side and the lay community on the other. Scientists, searching for new procedures of cell transfer to cure a multitude of ills, would endorse limited cloning in the laboratory. However, transforming a human cell into an embryo, according to Kyla Dunn, writing in *The Atlantic Monthly*, might be a shining new scientific moment but it also provokes heated opposition from a large group who forecast dark and shadowy results. Many people do not want scientists reducing the mystery of human birth to a petri dish. Yet everybody wants medical science to keep them alive, perhaps forever, or frozen to await the final cure. We can't have long life if we stifle medical experimentation.

Look carefully and you will see that the free paraphrase features the student's voice in the first sentence and again in the final three. Thus, the paraphrased material is absorbed into the paragraph, where it serves as an extension of her thinking on this matter. Such blending of a source, whether a summary, paraphrase, or quotation, requires you to keep the focus on *your* voice and *your* message, not to make the source the single focus.

T I P   *Free Paraphrasing*

A free paraphrasing of a source allows you to take liberties in your translation while remaining true to the meaning and mood of the original. You have the option of quoting key words and phrases within your version. However, you are not a slave to the structure and phrasing of the original—you can bend it and twist it to fit your style and your message.

Let's look at another example as this same student again paraphrases a second passage from the Kyla Dunn article, which discusses the two types of scientific cloning, the reproductive and the therapeutic.

Original

Crucial to the debate is the fact that human cloning research falls into two distinct categories: reproductive cloning, a widely frowned-on effort that aims to produce a fully formed child, and therapeutic cloning, a scientifically reputable procedure that takes place entirely at the microscopic level and is designed to advance medical therapies and cure human ailments. The two start out the same way—with a new embryo in a Petri dish. But the scientists I was observing in the lab had no intention of creating a person.

—Kyla Dunn, "Cloning Trevor," *The Atlantic Monthly*

Here is the student's paragraph that incorporates her free version paraphrase:

WEB LINK
to Exercise
5.2
http://www.
ablongman.com/
lester

Education of the public—that's what we need in medical research. Right now the word *cloning* produces all sorts of negative vibes, protest marches, and even violence. It need not be that way. According to Kyla Dunn, those persons concerned about cloning should understand that research in human cloning has two separate purposes. Some researchers want to create an actual child. Other researchers wish to conduct therapeutic cloning to cure various illnesses and birth defects by laboratory investigations. Both groups begin with the same Petri dish containing a human embryo, but there the gap widens considerably. The public weighs in strongly against reproducing a child, and the scientific community looks for medical cures and answers to biological questions. Somehow, the public's trust in the integrity of medical science has eroded. We have malpractice suits in abundance, flights by patients to foreign countries for medical care, heavy dependence on alternative herbal medicines, and now this, cloning, as yet another reflection of the loss of trust.

The student writer has established her position in the opening and closing, yet she has effectively woven the ideas of Kyla Dunn into the paragraph. Her paraphrase is not a slave to the original, yet it remains true to the ideas of the original author.

GUIDELINES

Paraphrasing a Source

- Do not be a slave to the original. Establish your position, express your ideas, and blend the paraphrase into your intellectual context.
- Avoid paragraphs devoted entirely to paraphrase; instead, establish your own topic sentence, offer the paraphrase, and then wrap the paraphrase into your thinking and your comprehension of the issues.
- Rewrite the original in about the same number of words.
- Identify the source.
- Retain exceptional words and phrases from the original by enclosing them within quotation marks.
- Preserve the tone of the original by suggesting moods of satire, anger, humor, doubt, and so on. Show the author's attitude with appropriate verbs: "Edward Zigler condemns . . . defends . . . argues . . . explains . . . observes . . . defines . . ."
- Put the original aside while paraphrasing to avoid copying word for word. Compare the finished paraphrase with the original source to be certain that the paraphrase truly rewrites the original and that it uses quotation marks with any phrasing or key words retained from the original.

TIP *Paraphrasing vs. Quoting*

When instructors see an in-text citation but no quotation marks, they will assume that you are paraphrasing, not quoting. Be sure that their assumption is true.

Paraphrasing Cumbersome, Archaic, or Technical Passages

In your first-year courses you have an obligation to make your papers readable, so write your papers in everyday terminology. For now, interpret complex passages of technical language with paraphrases. Later, in advanced, upper-division courses, you will need to use, with precision, the scientific and specialized wording of the discipline. Your vocabulary will broaden and grow with each course you attend.

The writing in some of your sources will be complex, technical, cumbersome, or simply dull. As you write your paper using these sources, you have an obligation to:

- Paraphrase a cumbersome style.
- Paraphrase passages written in archaic language.
- Paraphrase a highly technical style.
- Paraphrase spoken words and fragments from an interview.

Paraphrasing Cumbersome Passages

Let's suppose that you are writing a paper on textile manufacturing, emphasizing the way in which factories have left the United States only to reappear in foreign countries where labor is cheaper. You come across this passage:

> Critical discourse today locates an antagonism between globalization and citizenship. The deepening of globalizing processes strips citizens of power, this position maintains. As economic processes become globalized, the nation-state loses its ability to protect its population. Citizens lose their ability to elect a leadership that effectively pursues their interests. When production facilities are dispersed beyond the nation, jobs are lost to foreigners, labor markets are affected by conditions in countries with diverse living standards, and capital flows, at the speed of light, to places of optimum return.
>
> —Mark Poster, "Digital Networks and Citizenship," *PMLA*

Rather than quote the passage and burden your paper with such cumbersome writing, you need to paraphrase the passage to fit the design of your paper:

> The massive manufacturing base of the United States has gradually diminished. Mark Poster has commented that the global marketplace is coming into conflict with the lives of citizens and affecting the population of small towns and cities across America. When textile factories are closed in the United States, jobs and paychecks go to workers in foreign countries, and our money flows to foreign workers. Gradually, the United States will lose its ability to provide for its citizens, says Poster, and the citizens will find it difficult to elect local politicians who will protect the industrial base of their cities.

The paraphrase above makes the ideas more accessible to a reader, and it conforms to the flow of the student's style.

WEB LINK
to Exercise
5.3
http://www.
ablongman.com/
lester

Paraphrasing Archaic Language

Consider the following lines by the fourteenth-century poet Geoffrey Chaucer from the prologue to *The Canterbury Tales*:

> A Knight ther was, and that a worthy man,
> That fro the time that he first bigan
> To ridden out, he loved chivalrie,
> Trouthe and honour, freedom and curteisie. (ll. 43–46)

This passage of poetry might need paraphrasing, depending on the knowledge of your reader.

Chaucer, in introducing his knight, described him as a worthy man who, throughout his life, loved chivalry, integrity (*trouthe*), honor, generosity of spirit (*freedom*), and courtesy.

T I P   *Writing for Instructors and Others*

In writing for your instructor as well as other readers, you walk a delicate line. On one side are knowledgeable readers who might be offended that you have translated language that they know; on the other are readers who will need your interpretation and clarification of complex terminology. Thus, keep your audience in mind and write accordingly.

Paraphrasing Technical Wording

Depending on the expertise of your audience, you might paraphrase technical passages like this one:

> This issue is concerned with clinical pharmacology of the tumescent technique for local anesthesia using large volumes of very dilute lidocaine and epinephrine. The tumescent technique produces profound local anesthesia of the skin and subcutaneous fat that lasts for many hours.
>
> —http://www.liposuction.com

WEB LINK
to Exercise
5.4
http://www.
ablongman.com/
lester

In the paraphrase below, notice how the writer uses everyday terms and places the technical words within parentheses: "the use of a local anesthesia (lidocaine)." As an alternative, you can reverse this style "the use of lidocaine (a local anesthesia)."

The tumescent technique for liposuction is the use of a local anesthesia (lidocaine) and a constrictor of blood vessels (epinephrine). Injected into fatty tissue, the two drugs provide a local anesthesia for both the patient's skin and the underlying tissue to be withdrawn (www.liposuction.com).

This paraphrase shows how to recognize the source in a parenthetical citation, a technique that works well when you are citing from a work that does not identify the author.

EXERCISE 5.1

PARAPHRASING CUMBERSOME, ARCHAIC, AND TECHNICAL PASSAGES

This exercise has three parts. In each you are asked to write a paraphrase. (*Note:* Keep a dictionary handy.)

1. Read the following rather cumbersome passage and in your writing journal or on a separate sheet write a paraphrase.

   > I've just had my genome scanned, and unfortunately I have common mutations that give me a mildly increased risk for dangerous blood clots, schizophrenia and type 2 diabetes. Worst of all, my ApoE gene indicates I have three times the average risk for getting Alzheimer's. On the other hand, I don't have plenty of common nasty mutations, such as those associated with colon cancer and melanoma. All in all, the analysis of 130 of my genetic markers, coupled with more traditional medical data, suggests that I'm subsidizing my life insurance company—which is the way I like it. This kind of genetic screening may be the Next Big Thing. It offers a glimpse of how genetics will transform human life in this century.
   >
   > —Nicholas D. Kristof, "Staying Alive, Staying Human," *New York Times*

2. Read the following passage from Shakespeare's *Hamlet* and in your writing journal or on a separate sheet write a paraphrase. (*Note*: Hamlet is lamenting the death of his father.)

   > O, that this too too sullied flesh would melt,
   > Thaw and resolve itself into a dew!
   > Or that the Everlasting had not fixed
   > His canon 'gainst self-slaughter—O God! God!
   > How weary, stale, flat and unprofitable
   > Seem to me all the uses of this world!
   > Fie on't! ah fie! 'tis an unweeded garden,
   > That grows to seed; things rank and gross in nature
   > Possess it merely. That it should come to this!
   > But two months dead! Nay, not so much, not two:
   > So excellent a king; that was, to this,
   > Hyperion to a satyr.
   >
   > —William Shakespeare, *Hamlet*, I.ii.129–140

3. Read the following technical passage and in your writing journal or on a separate sheet write a paraphrase.

   > Elimination and eradication of human disease have been the subject of numerous conferences, symposia, workshops, planning sessions, and public health initiatives for more than a century. Although the malaria, yellow fever, and yaws eradication programmes of earlier years were unsuccessful, they contributed greatly to a better understanding of the biological, social, political, and economic complexities of achieving the ultimate goal in disease control. Smallpox has now been eradicated and programmes are currently under way to eradicate poliomyelitis and guinea-worm disease. In 1993, the International Task Force

for Disease Eradication evaluated over 80 potential infectious disease candidates and concluded that six were eradicable (1). In 1997, the World Health Assembly passed a resolution calling for the "elimination of lymphatic filariasis as a public health problem". Also in early 1997, WHO listed leprosy, onchocerciasis, and Chagas disease as being candidates for elimination "as public health problems within ten years". With this background, the Dahlem Workshop on the Eradication of Infectious Diseases was held in March 1997 (2). The Workshop was unique in that it focused on the science of eradication, with the understanding that the present Atlanta Conference would address specific candidate diseases for elimination or eradication in the context of global health strategies. The Workshop addressed four questions: 1) How is eradication to be defined and what are the biological criteria? 2) What are the criteria for estimating the cost and benefits of disease eradication? 3) What are the societal and political criteria for eradication? and 4) When and how should eradication programmes be implemented?

—Walter R. Dowdle, from *The Principles of—Disease Elimination and Eradication*

Paraphrasing Spoken Words and Fragments from an Interview

For some assignments you might be required to conduct an interview and transcribe some of that source material into your paper. The paraphrase is a great tool for conveying to your readers the oral comments of an interviewee. Here's the transcript of one student's interview with Margent Landers, a sixty-seven-year-old Briton, followed by the student's paraphrased version.

WEB LINK
to Exercise
5.5
http://www.
ablongman.com/
lester

Student: Do you remember going into London bomb shelters during the war with Nazi Germany?

Margaret Landers: Oh my, yes. We had a bomb shelter. Just down the back alley, uh, about 25 yards away. But I promise you one thing—uh—seemed like 500 yards what with sirens blaring and bombs starting to explode over by the quay. Terrible. Too many people crowded together. Smelly. People messing in their clothes cause they couldn't move or cause of fear. More than one time I wet my panties when a bomb would explode near the bunker. I was a terrified little child.

Student: Did you understand why you were being bombed?

Landers: Certainly. The Germans were going to invade us. Uh, kill the Jews. Slaves, yes, make us slaves and haul us in cattle cars to Bavaria.

Student: Did the experiences affect you as you grew older?

Landers: Hah! I still have nightmares. My best friend was a Jewish girl who lived in the next flat. We still talk by phone, and, and, well, the scars never heal. No, not ever. She's my rock, though, and I'm her guardian.

Rather than a verbatim reproduction of Margaret Lander's comments, the student interviewer chose to write a paraphrase, which, as shown, may include direct quotation.

In Europe, the aggression of Nazi Germany caused far-reaching trauma that haunts survivors to this day. Margaret Landers was an eight-year-old during

Germany's siege of London, and she recalls blaring sirens, a frantic race down the alley, and the swarm of too many people in the bunker. Her fear was intensified by her youthful knowledge that the Germans would invade England, kill her best friend who was a Jewish girl, and carry her and her parents by train deep into Germany. That trauma still haunts her and her friend, who still keeps in touch with her. Landers says, "She's my rock, though, and I'm her guardian."

This paraphrase will enhance the student's paper, which was designed to explore the effects of war on innocent citizens, especially children.

EXERCISE 5.2

PARAPHRASING AN INTERVIEW

Shown below are four question-and-answer passages from an interview in which John S. Rhodes questions Steve Krug, author of *Don't Make Me Think*, a book on Web design. The interview, "True Simplicity: Krug-o-rama," was published on the Web at the Web word.com site. Your task is to (1) read the questions and answers, (2) select one set, **a, b, c,** or **d,** and (3) write a paraphrase of it.

a. Rhodes: Many Internet businesses are dying. What is your best advice for companies that are sinking fast? Is this the same advice you would give to a profitable company?

Krug: For companies that are sinking fast, I suppose I'd suggest that they figure out what's wrong with their basic premise. I've been amazed in the last five years how often I've listened to a company's business model and said to myself, "Who would ever pay for that?" A lot of them just didn't make any sense. Of course, most companies in that position have already disappeared, or at least revamped their business model.

For companies that are profitable, I'd probably suggest that they focus on improving their conversion rate. Even on successful sites, there are almost always a few glaring problems that are either (a) keeping people from concluding a purchase (if it's an e-commerce site), or (b) sending them bouncing off your site before they've even had a chance to experience what you have to offer. These problems tend to show up right away if you just drag in a few people and watch them try to use the site. (As my corporate motto says, "It's not rocket surgery.")

b. Rhodes: Don't users want rich content? Don't they want exciting colors, flashy animations, and really cool web applications? Why should a web site be simple?

Krug: The whole notion that users are dying for "rich content" has always struck me as a strange one. I think it's based on the idea that the Web is going to be TV when it grows up, and the only thing that's keeping it from growing up is a lack of bandwidth. For me, it's like saying that movies will be better when they're all holographic, or even that they got better when they made the transition from black and white to color.

When was the last time you heard someone say that they spent a few hours surfing the Web? Most of the time, we just want to get things done: buy airplane tickets, read movie reviews, or learn how to fix the leak in the shower. Personally, I tend to think that settling bar bets ("Name the seven dwarves") and answering nagging questions ("What's the part number for the glass shelf I just broke in my refrigerator?") are the real killer app of the Internet, and that we really haven't figured out how to do them well enough yet.

There are some specific kinds of rich content that work, like games, sports highlights, and movie trailers, for example. But good rich content is surprisingly hard to create, as anyone who's ever produced even a short film or video knows. And even though powerful tools like Flash make it much easier, our appetite for bouncing letters probably has its limits. And mediocre rich content, well.... Once the initial novelty wears off, it's pretty much the same as any other mediocre content.

c. Rhodes: Humans are basically smart and flexible, but if I understand your ideas correctly, you believe that web sites shouldn't make people think. That sort of seems counterintuitive. Can you tell me why people shouldn't need to think when they are using a web site?

Krug: I'd say rather that humans are incredibly smart and flexible. My point isn't that they're incapable of figuring things out. It's that they're smart enough to know that it's usually not worth their time and effort to bother figuring things out. If a site's navigation is confusing, they generally won't try to figure it out; they'll just poke around and see if they can get to what they want. Poking around can work, and it can even be fun, but it's inefficient and it doesn't have a very high success rate. So if it's your site and it's important to you (economically or personally) that people find things there, it's incumbent on you to make it dead-easy for them to find them.

d. Rhodes: Web sites lose people all of the time. They get lost, they get frustrated, and they leave if they are not satisfied. Give us your help. What should designers and developers do to stop people from leaving?

Krug: For starters, don't try to stop them from leaving. The whole notion of adopting "stickiness" as a goal seems pretty misguided to me for most sites. It always makes me think of those posters from the sixties that said "If you love something, let it go. If it comes back, then it's yours forever. If it doesn't, then it was never meant to be." (Or, as Mike Myers put it in *Wayne's World*: "I say hurl. If you blow chunks and she comes back, she's yours.") I think users are smart enough to sense when you're trying to keep them corralled, and—by contrast—when you're confident enough in your site that you're not afraid to let them go.

The real way to keep people on your site is to (a) have things that they want, whether it's products, information, or useful tools, and (b) make sure that it's easy for them to get to these things and use them. And the only way to know that you're succeeding at (a) and (b) is by doing some testing.

Paraphrasing Passages That Require Your Subjective Response

Many times, you will need to consider passages that are not worthy of quotation but that require your response to their ideas or your argument against the positions they take. In other cases, you will need to respond to a writer's irony, sarcasm, unspoken agenda, and other devices that might deceive a reader. Paraphrase such passages in order to:

- Use the ideas but maintain your narrative flow.
- Explain and interpret the ideas.
- Disagree with the ideas.
- Expose a writer's irony or concealed intentions.

Paraphrasing to Maintain Your Narrative Flow

Here's a passage that a student has read on marriage laws, the topic of her paper.

> Geoffrey Chaucer had negative views about many social programs, and marriage was one that received his acute denigration. In the "Prologue" to the *Wife of Bath's Tale,* we observe the wife's failures to follow neither the "biheste" (promise) of marriage or the "dette" (obligation). The Wife of Bath flaunts the marriage bonds because she has property of her own by manipulating settlements with five husbands. She maneuvered "biheste" and "dette" to her own advantage, for England's marital statutes often precipitated repugnant and even shocking arguments of infidelity on both sides of "biheste" and "dette."
>
> —Gregory Marshall

The student realizes that this passage has a narrow focus on Chaucer and uses terminology unnecessary for her paper. Yet, although her focus is contemporary marriage laws, she wants to borrow the idea that marital disputes have existed far into the past. Accordingly, she paraphrases a portion of the passage rather than quoting the long passage, which would be disruptive to her textual flow. Here's her paragraph incorporating the paraphrase:

> Discord and anger over marriage laws might appear as contemporary reactions, yet judges have a rich set of precedents as they try to sort out hundreds of divorce proceedings every month. The problem with the marriage laws is not a new one at all. Gregory Marshall, a scholar of the British poet Geoffrey Chaucer (1343–1400), has noted Chaucer's negative feelings about almost every aspect of marriage, indicating that marriage laws in medieval England often entangled husband and wife in fierce competitive battles, which neither could win. We might recall, for example, that Chaucer's Wife of Bath had five husbands. So marital disputes and courtroom wrangling have existed since Chaucer's time, certainly, and further into the past than the 1300s.

In the example above, the student connects the issues of her thesis to ancient sources by using the paraphrase of Gregory Marshall's thoughts about Chaucer.

Exploring a Writer's Irony or Concealed Intentions

Let's now examine a paraphrase that another student uses as a springboard to her own ideas, which disagree with the source. The paraphrase launches a discussion to be developed fully in the student's paper. You will find the Twain quote on page 132.

In his essay "The Damned Human Race," Mark Twain dismisses Darwin's theory on the gradual ascent of human beings from the lower animals to argue for a new theory of his own in which humans are descending downwards. Granted, his irony is obvious because he focuses on the frailty and infirmity of human beings. Physically, the opposite is most certainly true. Humans beings have never been taller, stronger, or physically and mentally healthy as they are now. This study will launch an investigation into the *ascent* of men and women, for adolescents are reaching puberty early; teenagers are taller, stronger, and—in many cases—more intelligent than their parents; and athletes are quicker and bigger than Mark Twain in his time could have ever imagined.

As shown above, the student identifies Twain's irony and then advances her own ideas.

Paraphrasing to Respond to or Rebut an Idea or Position

WEB LINK
to Reading
5.1
http://www.
ablongman.com/
lester

If you wish to write a rebuttal to an idea or position, you may present the other position as a direct quotation or as a paraphrase—the choice is yours. If the quotation is cumbersome or technical, as we have discussed above, paraphrase it. If the quotation is long and you prefer to use your own voice, paraphrase it. Otherwise, a quotation will work well (see Chapter 6).

Let's look at a passage about the collection of state sales taxes from the purchases of online sales of products and services. We can then see how one student blended the ideas into his paper. Here is the original source:

Efforts to impose an eventual Internet sales tax reached the end of the beginning phase Tuesday when representatives from 32 states approved model legislation designed to create a system to tax Web sales.

Spearheaded by the National Governors Association (NGA), the Streamlined Sales Tax Project (SSTP) would require participating states to have only one tax rate for personal property or services effective by the end of 2005. Included in those services would be online sales.

Currently, sales and use taxes are owed on all online transactions, but states are prohibited from requiring remote sellers to collect and remit those levies. A 1992 U.S. Supreme Court decision said states can only require sellers that have a physical presence or "nexus" in the same state as the consumer to collect so-called use taxes.

The court ruled that the current patchwork of roughly 7,500 taxing jurisdictions across the country is too complex and burdensome for online retailers to charge and collect sales taxes. In order to collect the taxes, the court ruled, states would need to first simplify the existing system.

—Roy Mark, "End of the Beginning: Internet Sales Tax," *InternetNews: Ecommerce*

This passage is long, not strong stylistically, and would interrupt the student's own tone of voice. In addition, the student wishes to insert his own opinion at appropriate places. Thus, paraphrase is the proper choice, as shown below. The student's personal disapprovals and rebuttals are sprinkled throughout the paraphrased passage.

Roy Mark, in a recent article published at InternetNews.com, addresses a complex issue, one that has no easy answer. The National Governors Association (NGA) has endorsed a plan that Mark calls the "end of the beginning," for after years of inaction thirty-two states have given their stamp of approval for a tax collection system on Internet sales. However, thirty-two states do not control fifty.

Here's the catch. The Streamlined Sales Tax Project imposes a uniform sales tax on all states in the program effective at the close of 2005. Note that all states will have the same sales tax rate with online sales included. It sounds so simple that it might work, but how can states with no income tax and high sales tax find a middle ground with states that have an income tax and thus a low sales tax? The intrastate wrangling will be fierce.

This entire mess developed from a ruling by the 1992 U.S. Supreme Court, which declared that a state can collect sales taxes if the Internet company has a physical facility within the state where the consumer makes the order. So Texas online companies collect Texas sales taxes on sales to Texans—but not on sales to consumers in Hawaii, Michigan, or any other state. The court saw a pandora's box of 7,500 taxing jurisdictions spread across the land, so "poof," online sales started climbing so that now, twelve years later, the states are crying foul. "We are losing billions," the NGA cries in alarm.

The answer, a uniform sales tax for participating states, forecasts a disservice to nonparticipants and predicts a veritable cat fight in the legislative halls of our state capitol buildings. Roy Mark, the article's author, offers no solution, and he, too, elsewhere in the article wonders if the new system "will be unworkable without employing an army of accountants."

As shown in the above example, the paraphrase offers you an important option that is not available when you write a summary or insert a direct quotation. You can insert personal opinion within the paraphrase as you work your way through the ideas and issues. The reader hears your voice as well as your interpretation of the source.

Blending Several Paraphrases into Your Passage

WEB LINK to Reading 5.2
http://www. ablongman.com/ lester

As you conduct research on a topic, you will collect an array of passages containing information that you wish to bring into your paper, but citing one sizable quotation after another is not advised. Rather, weave the material into your own piece of writing by paraphrasing some passages, summarizing a concept, and incorporating direct quotations. Let us join one student, Jeffery Ray Wallace, as he works with several original passages from different sources. His topic, business engagement, took him to comments by business executives such as Bill Gates of Microsoft and observers of business communications such as motivational speakers Jim Loehr and Tony Schwartz. First, read the passages that Jeff Wallace has collected, shown below, and afterward read his composition to see how he managed to blend the material from several sources into his own piece of writing.

To function in the digital age, we have developed a new digital infrastructure. It's like the human nervous system. The biological nervous system triggers your reflexes so that you can react quickly to danger or need. It gives you the information you need as you ponder issues and make choices. You're alert to the most important things, and your nervous system blocks out the information that isn't important to you. Companies need to have that same kind of nervous system—the ability to run smoothly and efficiently, to respond quickly to emergencies and opportunities, to quickly get valuable information to the people in the company who need it, the ability to quickly make decisions and interact with customers.

—Bill Gates with Collins Hemingway, *Business @ the Speed of Thought: Using a Digital Nervous System*

We live in digital time. Our rhythms are rushed, rapid fire and relentless, our days carved up into bits and bytes. We celebrate breadth rather than depth, quick reaction more than considered reflection. We skim across the surface, alighting for brief moments at dozens of destinations but rarely remaining for long at any one. We race through our lives without pausing to consider who we really want to be or where we really want to go. We're wired up but we're melting down.

—Jim Loehr and Tony Schwartz, *The Power of Full Engagement*

A few years ago I came to understand that when we all enter this world we do so with two wings. One wing is the wing of grace, and whether you know it or not, that wing is flapping by your side, supporting you, twenty-four hours a day, 365 days a year, from now through eternity. The other wing, which you have to consciously activate, is the wing of self-effort. This wing has got to flap as equally as hard as the wing of grace. When it does, you will have flight, flight into the world of unlimited possibilities, where anything and everything is possible for you. Then and only then will you understand how truly powerful you are, and that you have all that it takes within you to keep what you have and to create what you deserve.

—Suze Orman, *The Laws of Money, the Lessons of Life*

Bill Hewlett was the friendly, zesty inventor: the genius who could see a little farther into the future than anyone else. He was endlessly curious about everything: the way a lock worked, the history of sixteenth-century Mexico, the business goals of HP's best customers. Even after he became an enormously powerful executive, some of Hewlett's favorite moments involved sitting with young engineers, brainstorming about what their sketches and prototypes could become. "Hewlett allowed you to dream with him," onetime protégé Bruce Woolpert recalled. "He would become a twenty-year-old, asking, 'What do you think: Could we do that?'" A few weeks later, Hewlett might bombard the project's champion with all the tough questions that top executives should ask, but he never lost track of the young inventor's passion that fuels any great company's growth. Even as a middle-aged executive, Hewlett wanted to stay in the game, and he would tiptoe into HP's labs at night to run his own experiments. By the end of his career, Hewlett had won thirteen patents for everything from oscillators to distance-measuring devices. The last one came in 1971, when he was nearly sixty years old.

—George Anders, *Perfect Enough*

Engaging in creative work is another way to nourish the soul, and business is one of the most creative acts a person can engage in. Every day in business, products are being imagined, designed, and produced. Lives and careers are made and lost; companies are born, die, and are reborn. Money is an object of vast creative handling, and business relationships demand the utmost in personal character and imagination. A person entering business is stepping into an infinite potential for creative work. Then why does business so often feel uncreative?

Misconceptions about creativity keep it at a distance from many people, especially those in business. We tend to think of creativity as extraordinary self-expression, the work of the artist who is frequently inspired and who comes up with unceasing novel ideas and productions. But creativity could be imagined in less spirited terms.

—Thomas Moore, "Caring for the Soul in Business"

Jeff faces a task similar to ones that await you. He has a group of quotations roughly related, and he needs to blend them into his essay. He had gone in search of information about "business engagement," but soon found himself focusing on the creative side of business endeavors, and his collected passages reflected that interest.

First, it is vital that he establish his voice and his thesis at the beginning.

For all their focus on the bottom line, business executives need a touch of creativity, for genius lies in design, not just production.

Next, Jeff can introduce the issue that his wishes to examine.

Men and woman in the board rooms of America's corporations might take a lesson from persons like Bill Gates, the guru of empire building in our computer world, and Bill Hewlett, the co-founder of Hewlett–Packard Corporation. Both built companies founded on creative genius, not just management skills.

Then he gets more specific.

For example, Bill Gates makes clear his vision for the successful person who must plug into his or her own special digital nervous system, which is like the human nervous system. He says we need a "new digital infrastructure." His comparison places biology next to technology. Just as our nerves signal reactions to various stimuli, so do the digital grooves in our modern system help us in business. Gates explains that the nervous system warns us of danger, keeps us aware, helps us make wise decisions, and even smothers or buries nonessential matters. In like manner, Gates emphasizes that the best companies have a similar nervous system created out of the digital age. If accessed, the company can "run smoothly and efficiently" and respond to opportunities as well as problems. In truth, Gates is demonstrating his cutting-edge wisdom. Some business people are high tech without genius. Others are high tech without management skills. But people like Gates have both and rise above the crowd.

Jeff can then transfer his attention to another figure in the computer industry, as found in his recorded passages.

George Anders in his book *Perfect Enough* describes another creative genius of the business world, Bill Hewlett, one of the founders of Hewlett-Packard Corporation, one of giants in the computer industry. It's worth noting that Anders describes Hewlett as a "friendly, zesty inventor: the genius who could see a little farther into the future than anyone else." It proves again that the successful business requires creativity, and Hewlett often sat with his engineers to brainstorm with them on their drawings and models and technical prototypes. Anders reports that Hewlett wanted to stay in the game, and he would tiptoe into HP's labs at night to run his own experiments." Hewlett's partner, David Packard, was a great manager, but it was Hewlett who had a history of patents for his inventions.

Next, Jeff drifts away from the sources to explore his own thoughts.

Creativity, however, is not often appreciated in the workplace. For example, I worked for a brief time one summer at a fast food outlet. After a few weeks, I considered the drive-through system inadequate, and I made the mistake of telling that news to the manager. He said, "Just do your job as assigned and get out if you can't do it." Well, so much for my ideas, and I suspect that scene repeats itself many times in businesses every day all over the world.

Jeff continues to draw upon his sources with paraphrase and direct quotation.

Thomas Moore observes, "Engaging in creative work is another way to nourish the soul, and business is one of the most creative acts a person can engage in." There—that's the essential point. Many people do not or cannot perceive a business as a creative act, yet products must be created, manufacturing tools must be created, and distribution methods must be created. Moore adds, "A person entering business is stepping into an infinite potential for creative work." Granted, a business person is not an artist in the traditional sense, yet the right-brain creative side must be allowed to function.

Next, Jeff liked a passage so much that he decided to quote it rather than paraphrase it.

In their book, *The Power of Full Engagement*, Jim Loehr and Tony Schwartz stress the values of this new age:

> We live in digital time. Our rhythms are rushed, rapid fire and relentless, our days carved up into bits and bytes. We celebrate breadth rather than depth, quick reaction more than considered reflection. We skim across the surface, alighting for brief moments at dozens of destinations but rarely remaining for long at any one. We race through our lives without pausing to consider who we really want to be or where we really want to go. We're wired up but we're melting down.

Perhaps an effective closing to this discourse would be a metaphor as advanced by Suze Orman in her book, *The Laws of Money, the Lessons of Life*. She explains that we all have a pair of wings. One she calls the "wing of grace," and it constantly flaps to support us now and perhaps into the everlasting. It sustains us. The other is the "wing of self-effort." We must "consciously activate" it and flap it as hard as the wing of grace if we wish to attain any sort of flight where "anything and everything is possible for you." At that point we will have creative power. Both wings are necessary—the gifted one and the self-motivated one.

Right now, in my college courses, I better be flapping away. I see too many students with one wing hanging lifeless.

XERCISE 5.3
BLENDING SEVERAL PARAGRAPHS

In Appendix C you will find three selections on the topic of the rise of tuberculosis in the past decade, pages 520–524. Your task is to read a portion of each essay, find a passage from each, and blend them into a brief essay in the manner of Jeffery Ray Wallace, as shown immediately above. That is, record the passages that relate to a central theme and draw them into your own paper with paraphrase, mainly, but with some quotations on key phrases or striking passages.

Acknowledging the Source of a Paraphrase

EB LINK
to Reading
5.3
http://www.
ablongman.com/
lester

Your paraphrase should always recognize the source, as with "According to Kyla Dunn, those with. . . . " However, you must also signal the end of the paraphrase. For example, you would need to start a new paragraph or shift the focus to another source or to yourself, saying something like this:

> Another study by Wallace Simpson confirms this divided focus on cloning research.
>
> My investigation has confirmed this divisive atmosphere surrounding the cloning topic.
>
> Others have weighed in on this issue.

Let's look again at the paraphrase of Kyla Dunn (page 168) and note how the student, continuing to write, shifts the focus from Dunn to another source and then to herself with the lines "Dunn's perceptions have been confirmed by other scientists" and "My study . . . ":

> According to Kyla Dunn, those observing the debate about cloning should understand that research in human cloning has two separate purposes. Some researchers want to create an actual child. Other researchers wish to conduct therapeutic cloning to cure various illnesses and birth defects by laboratory investigations. Both groups begin with the same Petri dish containing a human embryo, but there the gap widens considerably. The public weighs in strongly against reproducing a child, and the scientific community looks for medical cures and answers to biological questions. Dunn's perceptions have been confirmed by other scientists. For example, Richard Ashcroft weighs in on the conflict between human dignity proponents and the scientific community and says that "we have no good ethical reasons to prevent research on both reproductive and therapeutic cloning." My study will attempt to confirm Ashcroft's position.

WEB LINK
to Chapter 5
Related Web
Destinations
http://www.
ablongman.com/
lester

The methods for citing a source vary from discipline to discipline. For example, some academic styles require a parenthetical citation at the end of a paraphrase. We shall consider academic styles more completely in Chapters 10–12. The three most commonly used styles that you should be familiar with are:

Modern Language Association (MLA) for papers in literature, composition, language, and many humanities disciplines. (See Chapter 10.)

Chicago Manual of Style (CMS) for papers in history, the arts, humanities, and some disciplines in the social and physical sciences. (See Chapter 11.)

American Psychological Association (APA) for papers in the social sciences, business, and some natural sciences. (See Chapter 12.)

For now, you should know that MLA style requires a page number as part of the citation. The CMS note system requires a superscript note number that corresponds with a bibliography entry. APA style does not require a page number as part of the citation for a paraphrase but advises including it.

T I P *End a Paraphrase with a Source Citation*

Inserting a citation or note symbol at the end of a paraphrase accomplishes one very important thing—it identifies when the paraphrase has ended. It also gives other researchers a specific location for the paraphrased information.

The three most commonly used citation styles will be explained in detail later in the text. Here, let's look at a limited number of examples of paraphrases and their source citations in the different styles.

MLA Style:

According to Kyla Dunn, those observing the debate about cloning should understand that research in human cloning has two separate purposes: reproductive cloning to create a child and therapeutic cloning to investigate and cure a variety of illnesses (31). Also, Richard Ashcroft defends both types as highly beneficial to cell research (34). My study will attempt to confirm Ashcroft's position.

CMS Note Style:

According to Kyla Dunn, those observing the debate about cloning should understand that research in human cloning has two separate purposes: reproductive cloning to create a child and therapeutic cloning to investigate and cure a variety of illnesses.[1] Also, Richard Ashcroft defends both types as highly beneficial to cell research.[2] My study will attempt to confirm Ashcroft's position.

MLA Style:

Fred Hein explains that heredity is special and distinct for each of us, unless a person is one of identical twins (294).

APA Style:

Hein (2002) has explained that heredity is special and distinct for each of us, unless a person is one of identical twins.

APA style identifies a source by using the author's last name and the year of publication. It does not require the page number with a paraphrase, only with a quotation. The next example shows how to include a page number in APA style.

APA Style:

Hein (2002) has specified that twins have identical chromosomes because they grow from one egg that divides after it has been fertilized. He affirmed that most brothers and sisters differ because of the "chance selection" of chromosomes transmitted by each parent (p. 294).

CMS Note Style:

Fred Hein explains that heredity is special and distinct for each of us, unless a person is one of identical twins.[1]

EXERCISE 5.4
EVALUATING PARAPHRASES

In this exercise, first read the original source material, an excerpt from an article used by a student who is studying right-brain, left-brain theory. Then judge each of the paraphrases that follow the passage and evaluate its effectiveness based on these criteria:

- It is rewritten in the student's voice in about the same number of words as the original.
- It captures the mood and tone of the original.
- It identifies the source.

> The findings on hemispheric specialization tell us that our education system, and modern society generally, with its very heavy emphasis on communication and on early training in the three R's, discriminate against one whole half of the brain. I refer, of course, to the non-verbal, non-mathematical, minor hemi-

sphere, which we find has its own perceptual, mechanical and spatial mode of apprehension and reasoning. In our present school system, the minor hemisphere of the brain gets only the barest minimum of formal training, essentially nothing compared to the things that we do to train the left hemisphere.

—Roger Sperry, 1973, qtd. in Mike Bourcier, "The Right-Brain Way to Manage Change"

Paraphrase 1:

Our public schools are shortchanging students by offering a limited curriculum that addresses the left side of the brain and not the more imaginative right side.

Your rating: Good   Poor

Reason for rating: _____

Paraphrase 2

According to Roger Sperry, our school systems have discriminated against training for the non-verbal right side of the brain (as cited in Bourcier). The heavy training is focused on the left hemisphere of the brain for reading, writing, mathematics, and other courses grounded in logic. The more artistic, emotional side lies almost dormant in the classroom.

Your rating: Good   Poor

Reason for rating: _____

Paraphrase 3

The right hemisphere of the brain has its own modes of learning and reasoning, but it tends to be non-verbal and non-analytical, according to psychologist Roger Sperry, as quoted in Bourcier's article on using the right hemisphere of the brain to manage things. Sperry argues that society and its educational system discriminates against the right hemisphere by its emphasis on mathematics, reading, and writing, the primary functions of the left hemisphere.

Your rating: Good   Poor

Reason for rating: _____

Paraphrase 4

Schools should offer more courses in creative writing, art, music, and non-cognitive activities.

Your rating: Good   Poor

Reason for rating: _____

Chapter Review

WEB LINK
to Chapter 5
Related Web
Destinations
http://www.
ablongman.com/
lester

Chapter 5 has introduced you to paraphrase, the technique for rewriting the words of another person in order to blend that information into your own passage. Paraphrase plays an important role in your work with the sources. Unlike the summary, which is usually an objective digest, and unlike the direct quotation, which gives the precise wording of the source, a paraphrase allows you the freedom of interpretation and lets you wrap the ideas of others into your own style of writing. The flow of your writing continues unabated by the interruption of numerous quotations.

The paraphrase also allows you to serve the reader by your rewriting of cumbersome and technical passages. It allows you to absorb the bits and pieces of an interview into a rounded whole. In addition, the paraphrase enables you to make subjective responses to the source material, interjecting your contrasting ideas or reacting to another writer's satiric voice.

The chapter has also demonstrated how you can and should blend several paraphrases from different sources into one passage. Finally, it has introduced you briefly to the proper forms of acknowledging the source according to academic standards.

Chapter 5 Assignment:
Writing an Effective Paraphrase

1. Read this next sentence carefully and write, first, a literal paraphrase of it and, second, a free paraphrase that wraps the material into your voice and style.

   In a perfectly functioning democracy, both candidates will appear equally imperfect, elections' voter turnout will often be low, and all elections will end in near ties.

   —W. Daniel Hillis, "How Democracy Works," **http://www.edge.org**

   In your literal paraphrase, did you remain true to the grammatical structure of the original yet change the wording? In the free paraphrase, did you write your own passage, perhaps with an opening sentence of your own, then the paraphrase, and then a closing sentence of your own? In each paraphrase, did you identify the source?

2. Read the following paragraph carefully, digest what it says, put it aside, and write a free version paraphrase of it. Remember: with the free version paraphrase you are not a slave to the structure and phrasing of the original; you can bend it and twist it to fit your style and your message. Afterward, compare what you have written with the original.

   Many people believe that democracy works by giving voters a chance to elect a candidate whose views match their own. Actually, this isn't true. In a perfectly functioning democracy, both candidates will appear equally imperfect, elections' voter turnout will often be low, and all elections will end in near ties [and] a two-party system is better than a many-party system. Voters are more likely to like their choice of candidates in a many-party system, but they are less likely to like the winner of the election.

— W. Daniel Hillis, "How Democracy Works," http://www.edge.org

Have you used any exact wording of the original, and if so, did you place it within quotation marks? Did you identify the source?

Tracing the Work of Two Students

Preliminary Paraphrases

We have been tracking the work of two students, Kaci Holz and Halley Fishburn. Here we shall look at the work of Fishburn, a political science major searching for literature on the War Powers Act. Below are two items: (1) a portion of an article on her topic, and (2) her preliminary paraphrases to show how she blended them into her own passage. In 2003, as she prepared her paper, Fishburn observed the conflict of the War Powers Act firsthand. President George W. Bush was aggressively building his armed forces to attack Iraq, using Congress's "use of force" resolution passed after September 11, 2002. Members of Congress questioned the president's extension of that resolution to include his right to declare war on Iraq. Here's the original wording of several paragraphs from the article that Fishburn decided to use, not as a long direct quotation but as a series of paraphrases with an occasional quotation:

> Senator Russell Feingold [Democrat of Wisconsin] made a critical distinction in saying that Congress's "use of force" joint resolution after Sept. 11 was very limited in that it approved only actions clearly responsive to those attacks. Congressional sources say the administration at first sought an open-end resolution in the nature of the 1964 Gulf of Tonkin resolution that then-President Lyndon Johnson took as a blank check for whatever military action he chose to initiate in Vietnam.
>
> It was to undo this legislative mistake that Congress in 1973 enacted the War Powers Act. It requires regular consultation with Capitol Hill in contemplating military action, written notification within 48 hours of such action and its "estimated scope or duration" and congressional consent through either a declaration of war or "specific statutory authorization." If such approval is not granted in 60 days, the president is supposed to withdraw U.S. forces within 30 days.
>
> The details of the War Powers Act, however, have usually been honored in the breach. But in this latest case, Congress wrote the empowering resolution specifically confining military action against "nations, organizations or persons [the president] determines planned, authorized, committed or aided the terrorists . . . or harbored such organizations or persons, in order to prevent any future acts of international terrorism" by them.

Such language, as Mr. Feingold noted in response to the *Times* story, makes it imperative that unless the administration can establish Iraqi complicity in the events of Sept. 11, the administration will be obliged to go back to Congress for new authorization of any invasion or other assault on that country.

An administration spokesman at Mr. Feingold's earlier hearings, Deputy Assistant Attorney General John Yoo, insisted, however, that the president is not bound by the War Powers Act requiring specific congressional approval because of his constitutional powers as commander in chief.

—Jules Witcover, "What about the War Powers Act?" *Baltimore Sun*

This contemporary debate goes to the heart of Fishburn's history paper, which is tracing the War Powers Act from James Madison's suggestion in 1781 that the Articles of Confederation be changed to give Congress more control over the use of the American army. She felt that it would contribute to her paper by bringing the issues home to her contemporary audience. Thus, she has framed the following passage, which paraphrases and quotes the article by Jules Witcover.

The War Powers Act is not a relic of history; it is a vibrant and throbbing document that rattles down the halls of the Capitol building and the White House on a regular basis. James Madison in 1781 was well intentioned in the desire to have the army answerable to the government, but he established a never-ending conflict between the commander in chief, who orders the forces into battle, and Congress, who must approve the action.

This discord surfaced again in 2003 when Senator Russell Feingold questioned President George W. Bush's power to declare war on Iraq. Writer Jules Witcover of the *Baltimore Sun* said the debate centered on the so-called "use of force" joint resolution that both Houses of Congress passed after the September 11 terrorist attacks at the World Trade Center and the Pentagon. Feingold and others said the resolution empowered the president to a limited action against "nations, organizations or persons [the president] determines planned, authorized, committed or aided the terrorist . . . or harbored such organizations or persons, in order to prevent any future acts of international terrorism."

In his article, Witcover explained how Feingold argued that Congress set limits in accordance with the War Powers Act of 1973. That Act addressed the aggressive war against Vietnam by former president Lyndon Johnson, who had used a resolution by Congress on a Gulf of Tonkin incident in 1964 like "a blank check for whatever military action he chose to initiate in Vietnam."

So now Congress did it again in 2003; that is, it provided the president a resolution subject to interpretation. Feingold argued that the resolution was clear and made it "imperative" that the Bush administration "establish Iraqi complicity in the events of Sept. 11"; otherwise, Bush needed to go back to Congress for approval to act against Iraq.

Meanwhile, the deputy assistant attorney general insisted that President Bush, because he is commander in chief, was not required by the War Powers Act to seek further approval of Congress.

Here's the question: Should Congress go back and create a new War Powers Act or should Congress learn to write joint resolutions in which the wording is absolutely clear in its authorization to the commander in chief?

Probably, history will continue to repeat itself.

Using Quotations

WEB LINK
to Chapter 6
Related Web
Destinations

http://www.
ablongman.com/
lester

Examining evidence is the heart of research. Scientists do it with testing in the laboratory and observation in the field. Humanists do it by poring over the words and artwork of the centuries. Examining evidence will be a part of your life also. In first-year college writing classes especially, you will be expected to read and write on a wide range of topics. Your essays will draw from informed sources through your use of summaries, paraphrases, and quotations. Chapters 4 and 5 have addressed the former; now this chapter will address the latter.

Some of your best evidence will be the exact words of an expert on the subject. That is, a piece of writing will be so exact, so precise, and so well expressed that it deserves quotation rather than paraphrase.

Using Quotations for a Variety of Reasons

Quotations that you transcribe into your draft provide a number of valuable services.

Authority

The voices of experts will lend authority to your paper. Note this passage from a student's paper on the music of Bruce Springsteen:

Bruce Springsteen in both music and words is the voice of the working people of America, as described by Greg Smith, an authority on the songwriter: "Springsteen is actually the working-class rock poet supreme, laying out in uncompromising terms and detail the shattered lives and broken countenances that make up the dark side of

American existence as it is experienced by working people for whom the American Dream is a taunting, cruel, and ungraspable abstraction." Furthermore, Springsteen's song "Cadillac Ranch" encapsulates much of his message. This paper will examine the one song to show Springsteen's vision of the bitter irony inherent in the lives of the working class everywhere.

This passage gives authority to the student's intended work; that is, the student will explore one song, "Cadillac Ranch," in light of Greg Smith's interpretation of the rock artist's primary motif. In addition, because the sentence by Smith has style in its phrasing, it is worthy of quotation. Paraphrasing Smith's words would mute his message and destroy wording that is effective.

Dialogue

Using the voices of others in your paper will reveal the dialogue that exists in the literature. You are not alone in this adventure; others have traveled this path in investigating the singer, and you will share some of that literature with your readers. For example, the writer includes this paragraph later in the paper:

Springsteen recognizes his role as prophet and visionary, like one of the ancient minstrels of Europe carrying his message from castle to castle. He roams the world and makes himself accessible. He has his own web site, Backstreets.com, his own magazine, *Backstreets Magazine,* and has welcomed interviews rather than shunned them like some rock stars. He has been interviewed by James Petersen for *Playboy,* by Karen Schoemer for *Newsweek,* by Mike Greenblatt for *The Aquarian,* and by many others. With each appearance and each interview he enhances his image to the point that Karen Schoemer says, "If Springsteen was once the savior of rock and roll, right now he's its Puritan minister, taking America to task for its sins."

This paragraph features one quotation but hints at other works the student will bring into the paper, especially the words of Springsteen as found in the interviews. Using these sources will also establish conflicting points of view about the rock star.

Distance

You might use a quotation to distance yourself from an idea or opinion—for example, you might not want to embrace the descriptions of some writers. By putting key words within quotation marks, you establish a disassociation:

One critic called Springsteen America's "Puritan minister" and another referred to him as a "nice boy" who faced the bitter world with "naivete." That's not the Springsteen that emerges from "Cadillac Ranch."

By putting the words of the critics within quotation marks, the writer distances himself from those ideas and offers a rebuttal.

Scholarly Demeanor

By citing sources from various authorities and from the principal person—in this case Springsteen—the writer develops a scholarly demeanor that signals several things to the reader. The writer researched in depth. The writer respects the sources and uses them effectively and appropriately in the paper. The writer understands how to avoid plagiarism—the unacknowledged use of someone else's words. Thus, the writer appears ethical and can be trusted.

GUIDELINES

Reasons for Bringing Quotations into Your Paper

- To capture the authoritative voices of the experts who will give support to your paper with essential, well-expressed statements.
- To show the dialogue and the breadth of the literature that exists for the topic.
- To distance yourself from some statements and comments or to offer rebuttal to others.
- To establish your ethical posture by proving that you know how to cite the sources correctly.

Selecting Effective Sources and Blending Them into the Paper

Before we consider the technical aspects of using quotations, such as correct punctuation and citation forms, we should learn something about selecting the best phrases, sentences, and passages for quotation. Sometimes we get lured into the use of a telling phrase or well-worded passage even though it contributes little to our purpose. Worse, we might select burdensome passages that have little relevance to our paper.

Let us look at a typical situation. Megan Thompson has selected this topic:

Water Conservation

Her working hypothesis is:

Water conservation programs have enriched lives but impoverished the environment.

She has gone in search of literature to defend her position and has copied into her writing journal some passages from an article by Mark W. T. Harvey, "Humans and the Environment in America's Past," which appeared in *OAH Magazine of History* in 1996. Megan must decide which passages to use and how to cite them effectively. Here is the first passage she recorded in her notebook:

Passage 1

What seemed most remarkable to colonists about North America was its abundance of resources. None had ever seen such vast quantities of animals, expansive forests, or sizeable parcels of land. More than any other factor, abundance shaped American environmental history from the colonial era until well into the nineteenth century.

The passage offers a key idea, the abundance of resources in America, which would include the abundance of fresh water, but the passage need not be quoted. The best strategy is to borrow the thought with a summary (see pages 129–130 of Chapter 4 for details). Here's Megan's statement based on passage 1, using APA style, which will be discussed in brief later in this chapter and explained more fully in Chapter 12:

Harvey (1996) has noted that early Americans found an abundance of natural resources, and this would include plentiful supplies of fresh water.

Passage 2

In Chicago, cattle became sides of beef, logs from northern Michigan became board feet, and grain from the Great Plains helped establish the Chicago Board of Trade. This commodification of nature was critical not only to the economy but also in shaping Americans' relationship with nature. As grain, lumber, and beef were commodified, Americans—city dwellers especially—gradually lost sight of the prairies, forests, and grasslands—of nature itself. Together then, abundance and the production of raw materials distanced people from nature. They took nature's wealth for granted; then they forgot it existed.

Passage 2 also offers a significant point—that city life slowly removed many people from farms and other rural areas, so the populace lost sight of how natural resources were being devoured to satisfy their needs in the cities and towns. Thus, the writer might borrow part of the passage, but not necessarily all of it. Here's Megan's use of the passage:

Chicago removed city dwellers from the land. "As grain, lumber, and beef were commodified, Americans—city dwellers especially—gradually lost sight of the prairies, forests, and grasslands—of nature itself," Harvey (1996) has argued. The result is that people distanced themselves from the natural surrounding, they "took nature's wealth for granted," and, Harvey asserted, "they forgot it existed" (p. 6).

Passage 3

Flowing water uncontrolled by dams went to waste, it was thought, so a flurry of dam construction began in the 1930s to control floods, supply irrigation water, and generate hydroelectric power. In 1933, Congress created the Tennessee Valley Authority. This agency produced and marketed power that elevated living standards for one of the nation's poorest regions. In the West, a similar faith in the power of hydroelectricity underpinned construction of the Boulder Dam on the Colorado River and Grand Coulee Dam on the Columbia River.

Passage 3 offers a clear focus on Megan's hypothesis: *Water conservation programs have enriched lives but impoverished the environment.* She could quote the entire passage as a block, so let's look at that version with a block quotation before we consider ways to weave pieces of it into Megan's prose.

In his article "Humans and the Environment in America's Past," historian Mark Harvey (1996) has chronicled the fateful decisions by Congress and government regulators:

> Flowing water uncontrolled by dams went to waste, it was thought, so a flurry of dam construction began in the 1930s to control floods, supply irrigation water, and generate hydroelectric power. In 1933, Congress created the Tennessee Valley Authority. This agency produced and marketed power that elevated living standards for one of the nation's poorest regions. In the West, a similar faith in the power of hydroelectricity underpinned construction of the Boulder Dam on the Colorado River and Grand Coulee Dam on the Columbia River. (p. 7)

Here we see the 1930s setting the stage for environmental disasters to follow for decades afterwards. Well-intentioned programs provided much good for the American people, but the dams could not harness the majestic power of nature.

However, the long block of quoted material interferes with Megan's own prose Therefore, blending her ideas with Harvey's will give a more fluid reading, as shown here:

In the early 1930s, during the Depression, Congress saw our natural resources as a way to invigorate America's economy. "Flowing water uncontrolled by dams went to waste, it was thought, so a flurry of dam construction began in the 1930s to control floods, supply irrigation water, and generate hydroelectric power" (Harvey, 1996, p. 7). Thus, the Tennessee River, the Colorado River, the Columbia River, and others became pawns in the grasp of giant government agencies like the Tennessee Valley Authority and the Bureau of Reclamation. The agencies, according to Harvey, "elevated living standards for one of the nation's poorest regions," but the agencies soon found themselves at war with the environment. Nature did not bow down willingly to the dams and other restrictions, so today we have entire subdivisions, built on various floodplains, being washed away in flash floods. As the television commercial states, "It's not nice to fool Mother Nature."

WEB LINK to Reading 6.1
http://www.
ablongman.com/
lester

In this version, you hear Megan's voice while she blends the comments by Harvey into the paragraph. Megan controls the passage with her style because the passage is no longer dominated by the Harvey quotation. Many readers will enjoy the blended paragraph more than the one with a long block quotation.

Passage 4

Environmental history is not only a chronicle of government management of natural resources. It is also the story of energetic individuals and or organizations dedicated to protecting wildlife or to safeguarding particular landscapes. Besides the Sierra Club, which John Muir helped found in 1892, major organizations include the Audubon Society, which fought for legislation to prohibit hunting of non-game birds, and the Izaak Walton League, which supported the interest of fishermen and various outdoor recreationists. Another key organization, founded in 1935, was the Wilderness Society.

In passage 4, the cited article mentions several valuable organizations that have affected environmental history. Again, the question emerges: How much of this passage is relevant to Megan's essay? Her listing of the organizations will suffice.

Helping to guard the water and other natural wonders of the environment have been several organizations: the Sierra Club, which is dedicated to protecting parklands; the Audubon Society, which focuses on protection of birds and wildlife; the Izaak Walton League, which has supported the interests of fishermen and various outdoor recreationists; and the Wilderness Society, which has a "dedication to maintaining roadless areas in national forests and parks" (Harvey, 1996, p. 8). Now we need a powerful, national lobby to protect the nation's water supply. There is the River Management Society and the National Fish and Wildlife Foundation, but most organizations are local (e.g., People's Alliance in Durham, North Carolina), narrowly focused (e.g., Bass Anglers' Sportsman Society), or regional (e.g., Blue Ridge Environmental Defense League).

In this example, Megan has gone well beyond the quoted material to mention organizations not found in the Harvey article but that she has found independently in other research.

DETERMINING RELEVANCE

Reproduced below is an article by Bob Berman from *Astronomy* magazine, which student Benni Jones has used in her research paper. Following the essay, in Exercise 2, you will find several passages from the student's paper. Your task is to judge the relevance of the student's citations from the essay—some are effective but some are not. Her citations conform to the MLA style, which will be discussed briefly later in this chapter and explained in detail in Chapter 10.

Wrong Time, No Bang
Bob Berman

Astronomers generally regard the Steady State theory as a lovely idea that is as dead as the passenger pigeon. Older than science itself, the notion of an eternally existing universe is widely associated with Sir Fred Hoyle who, until his death last August, crusaded for its acceptance since the 1940s. Certainly it carries great philosophical appeal.

After all, its rival, the Big Bang (a name Hoyle himself disdainfully coined), promises only a cosmos that will either someday crush itself down to the size of a pea, or else—much more likely—blow itself apart into isolated icy islands of frozen death.

Neither sounds particularly attractive.

Tough luck, say astrophysicists. The universe will perform its drama on its own terms; our sensibilities are irrelevant. And because we trust science, most of us are pretty much resigned to the Big Bang's dreary denouement, and are consoled perhaps by the fact that humans will no longer be seated in the audience.

Yet many harbor a hopeful feeling that the same cosmos that came up with Beethoven and beagles will not utterly self-destruct. Optimists argue that any sort of permanent turn-off-the-lights nothingness seems out of character with the universe's leitmotif.

Wishful thinking? Perhaps. A lot of impressive evidence supports the Big Bang. Why else do we observe a 2.7° K back-ground radiation, a specific ratio of hydrogen to helium to lithium, and redshifts that indicate an expanding universe? Is there any plausible escape clause without resorting to wacky stuff unworthy of science and logic?

Surprisingly—yes. And rather than being a "stretch," it's looking more and more like something not to be dismissed out of hand. It all comes about if we entertain the possibility that time gradually changes its rate of flow.

This is hardly a new notion, nor was its chief advocate any sort of crank. No less a physicist than Paul Dirac, who first predicted antimatter in 1928 and later won the Nobel Prize, argued periodically that there's no reason time should flow at a steady rate forever.

Time is strange to begin with. On many levels—and perhaps even on the most fundamental planes—it may not exist at all. Until interactions between kaons and their antiparticles showed a slight asymmetry a couple of years ago, it was hard to find any solid evidence that time really existed, though the Second Law of Thermodynamics was sometimes controversially invoked for its support. (Our minds' ability to link experiences with remembered or anticipated occurrences is not the same thing as time. Thoughts of the past or future are, after all, neuro-electrical events that occur strictly in the present moment.)

But let's not make this unnecessarily mysterious. Rather than invoke other dimensions, we can simply deal with time's everyday guise as a sort of synchronicity between events. While half of a carbon-14 sample decays, Earth performs 5,730 orbits of the sun and Saturn circles our sky 196 times. Those three events and trillions of others will continue to occur in sync. Dirac's question: What if the whole shebang gradually slows down in unison and on every level? We wouldn't notice a thing, but it would have enormous cosmological implications.

If time ran differently long ago, we could now observe a cosmic background radiation that pointed to a Big Bang that would seem to have happened 14 billion years ago. In reality, said Dirac, the universe would be infinitely old. There would not be a natal instant of creation. It would all revert to some variation of Hoyle's Steady State theory.

Variable time seems more likely now than it did a year ago. Physicists recently uncovered evidence that the universe's physical constants do indeed change. Specifically, the strength of the electromagnetic force ("Alpha") was apparently a tiny bit smaller eight billion years ago. Astrophysicists reached this conclusion after observing photons interact with distant nebulae on their way to Earth. Indeed, the value for the Planck Constant, which in turn derives its stability from the supposedly unchanging nature of three other constants, seems to have been slightly different back then. That astronomers measured this alteration to be exactly the same in many separate places gives the discovery far more credibility than if the effect derived from a single observation.

If some "constants" can change over the eons then why not time? Dirac directed particular suspicion toward the stability of the gravitational constant, finding no reason its force, among others, has to forever remain the same. In fact, if time alone has changed, then other things can seem to alter but actually be constant.

Tricky business. Even if it were happening, we would not expect to see any difference in the flow of time when we observe far off galaxies. Their images have long been traveling to us, and during that vast en route interval their incoming photons have also been caught up in the new rate of time passage. When we finally observe distant images, frames of that movie run through the projector of today's temporal pace, so that it appears no time mutations have occurred at all. How, then, can we know one way or the other about the rate of time's passage?

Evidence on Earth might reveal it, except that our measurements of the way time passed here a million years ago are not remotely precise enough to detect a minute alteration from the way it flows today. Dirac himself could offer no decisive way to determine whether or not time is stable.

What do we do with all of this information? Armed with credible evidence that one or more of the universe's constants may not be constant, but lacking any knowledge that time could also mutate, our conclusions are limited. Still, those of us who teach science may well wonder whether we should really present the Big Bang as a done deal.

It's probably safest to tell students current evidence points strongly to a Big Bang that happened 14 billion years ago. Further, the cosmos appears to be increasing its rate of expansion and therefore seems unlikely to ever come back together into a crunch that offers rebound possibilities. This means that right now, we don't seem to be mailing our letters in an oscillating universe that eternally inflates and deflates like a balloon.

But the case is far from airtight. A little intellectual humility never hurts, especially when the prospect persists that the universe is infinitely old and never had any sort of birth at all. Our impatience notwithstanding, it's still too early to know for certain whether or not the Game is played "according to Hoyle."

Face it: We've only begun to decipher the rulebook.

EXERCISE 6.2

DETERMINING RELEVANCE

Choosing relevant passages for citation in a paper is not always easy. Judge the following passages for their effectiveness and relevance to Benni Jones's topic:

"Fickle Finger of Fate: The Life of the Universe"

and her thesis:

Perhaps the universe originated with a big bang, but it need not end that way.

Passage 1

Two theories of universal order have been embraced but also condemned in recent history—the big bang theory and the steady state theory. Bob Berman argues that the steady state theory "is as dead as the passenger pigeon" (88), so that leaves us with the big bang theory. Yet the big bang theory suggests the ultimate death of the universe when the cosmos "will either someday crush itself down to the size of a pea, or else—much more likely—blow itself apart into isolated icy islands of frozen death" (Berman 88).

Rate passage 1 by Benni Jones in its understanding and presentation of Berman's ideas, and explain your rating.

Excellent   Acceptable   Poor

Why? _____

Passage 2

One astronomer (Bob Berman 88) has called for a new investigation of time and the possibility that time gradually changes its rate of flow. After all, time is rather strange to begin with, and it may not exist at all.

Rate passage 2 by Benni Jones in its understanding and presentation of Berman's ideas, and explain your rating.

Excellent   Acceptable   Poor

Why? _____

Passage 3

If universal time can change, as scientists now assert, the big bang theory might not carry the dire consequences of a final Armageddon of fiery explosions. Astronomer Bob Berman asks, "If some 'constants' can change over the eons then why not time?" (88). If some sort of "variable time" exists, we might want to revise our forecasts about the earth's demise. Berman suggests that "the cosmos appears to be increasing its rate of expansion and therefore seems unlikely to ever come back together into a crunch that offers rebound possibilities" (89).

Rate passage 3 by Benni Jones in its understanding and presentation of Berman's ideas, and explain your rating.

Excellent   Acceptable   Poor

Why? _____

Passage 4

Do we accept the Steady State theory of the universe, the Big Bang theory, or something in between? Astronomer Bob Berman examines the element of "time" in cosmic terms to suggest the "possibility that time gradually changes its rate of flow" (p. 89). If time can change, the inevitable thrust toward a second big bang of cosmic destruction could be slowed. So, have we found a way to combine the two theories—a big bang to start things and a steady state to keep the flow? Berman seems to think along these same lines, saying that the cosmos might "all revert to some variation of Doyle's Steady State theory" (88).

Rate passage 4 by Benni Jones in its understanding and presentation of Berman's ideas, and explain your rating.

Excellent   Acceptable   Poor

Why? _____

GUIDELINES

Using Quotations

- *Do not overuse quotations.*
  The effective use of quotations requires careful selection of the most telling and graceful sentences and phrases that you can find relative to your specific topic. Gone are the cut and paste days of middle school when you could use huge blocks of material to flesh out a report. Sophisticated readers expect your quotations to serve a purpose in support of your commentary. You should not provide quotations in order to comment on them; the quotations should be commenting on your ideas and opinions.

(continues on next page)

(continued from previous page)

- *Truncate the quoted material as much as possible.*
  Avoid using a block quotation unless it is necessary for a major contribution to your essay. Instead, try to find the very best sentence that fits your paragraph; then blend it with your commentary. Be willing to cut a passage down to a key phrase or two. In that way, you will not allow quoted matter to exceed 20% of your text.

- *Keep quotations away from the beginning of your paragraphs.*
  The openings of all your paragraphs should establish your point of view on the subject. Make the topic sentence establish one aspect of your study that will support your thesis or hypothesis. Only then should you begin bringing quotations into the paragraph. In like manner, try to close your paragraphs with personal summation. Thus, quoted matter, as a general rule, belongs in the body of the paragraph. That said, there will always be exceptions.

- *Don't reiterate the quotation.*
  Let the quotation stand on its own. You do not need to rephrase it or tell again what it has said. If you have selected wisely, the grace and style of the quotation does not require repetition. Let the quotation support your writing. However, this restriction does not dismiss your interpretation. That is, give your reader the lines of a Sylvia Plath poem, for example, in order to interpret the meaning, the imagery, and the context. Here are the lines of a poem:

Love set you going like a fat gold watch.	1
The midwife slapped your footsoles, and your bald cry	2
Took its place among the elements.	3

Do not say: *Plath says the baby starts out like a fat gold watch when the midwife slaps its footsoles.*
Do say: *Plath brings a surprising image into the birth of a child—a ticking watch running out the time of a new life.*

Following the Conventions for Quoting Others in Your Text

Before venturing further, let us review the rules for quoting sources in your paper. You must follow a number of basic conventions.

Quote Only Items That Have Significance

Select quoted material that is important, well phrased, and in context, not something that is trivial, is common knowledge, or is poorly expressed.

One writer said, "Eleanor Roosevelt married her fifth cousin, Franklin Delano Roosevelt, the future governor of New York State and, ultimately, president of the United States."

This quotation is somewhat trivial because the information is common knowledge or it can be found in any encyclopedia.

While her husband FDR guided the nation toward war with Nazi Germany, Eleanor Roosevelt whispered, "The clouds of uncertainty and anxiety have been hanging over us for a long time. Now we know where we are." She knew the nation could not maintain its isolationism from Europe in the face of the reports of unspeakable cruelty.

This second quotation allows us to hear the voice of the principal person, and the quotation is set within a context to make it meaningful. It wraps the quotation into the narration of the passage.

EXERCISE 6.3
SELECTING QUOTABLE MATERIAL

Study this next passage and select by underlining or a marginal note the sentence(s) that you think are most quotable. At this point you do not need to write a passage; rather just identify worthy passages. The passage is written by Sandra Day O'Connor and appeared in her book *The Majesty of the Law: Reflections of a Supreme Court Justice.* It describes in part her nomination by President Ronald Reagan to the Supreme Court in 1981.

The person making the nomination—the President—doubtless pays special attention to these appointments. From the President's point of view, I suppose it's a little like trying to rear children. The President only gets to control the process for a brief period—in choosing a particular nominee—and then the Justice, like an eighteen-year-old, is free to ignore the President's views. And Justices are usually walking around in their judicial chambers long after the President who appointed them has departed the Oval Office. Parenting and nominating Justices have both been common activities among Presidents; all of our Presidents except seven had children, and all except three—Harrison, Taylor, and Carter—nominated at least one Supreme Court Justice. Like fathers in an earlier day, the President makes the proposal and escorts the new Justice down the aisle in the marriage between the Justice and the Court, which, barring impeachment, lasts until death does them part.

As I suspect has been the case with most Justices, my nomination to the Court was a great surprise to the nation but an even greater surprise to me. My former colleague Justice Lewis Powell once said that being appointed to the Court was a little like being struck by lightning in both the suddenness and the improbability of the event. I certainly never expected to be on the Court. Rather,

I looked forward to continuing my career as a state court judge, having served happily as a trial judge and then, with equal contentment, on the Arizona Court of Appeals, for whose members I had deep affection and great professional respect. I had anticipated that I would live the balance of my life in our adobe house in the desert, where John and I had many friends and a pleasant way of life, and where we expected our sons to settle.

My situation changed dramatically on June 25, 1981, when then–Attorney General William French Smith called my home and said he wanted to talk to me about the Potter Stewart vacancy on the Supreme Court. The metaphorical lightning bolt suddenly seemed as if it might head in my direction, and I was about as astonished, though slightly less frightened, as if I had seen a real bolt of lightning making its way straight for me.

The attorney general asked me to come to Washington to visit with him, with some of President Reagan's staff and close advisors, and with the President himself. I did so, and on July 6, twelve days after Attorney General Smith first phoned me, the President called to ask if he could announce his intention to nominate me to the Court. I said I would be honored if he did.

Provide a Citation to Identify the Source of Quoted Material

WEB LINK
to Exercise
6.1
http://www.
ablongman.com/
lester

Do not copy the words of a source into your paper in such a way that readers will think *you* wrote the material. Your passage will have two parts, the citation that identifies the speaker and the quotation itself:

> Addressing the Democratic Presidential Convention in 1940, a time when world war hovered over the nation, Eleanor Roosevelt cautioned the delegates, "No man who is candidate or who is President can carry this situation alone. This is only carried by a united people who love their country."

Use the person's full name the first time you cite that person; thereafter, use the last name only, not "Mrs. Roosevelt said" and not "Eleanor said." Exception: If you refer to both Eleanor Roosevelt and Franklin Delano Roosevelt, you will need to distinguish between them after a first mention to use, perhaps, "FDR" and "Eleanor Roosevelt."

EXERCISE 6.4

PROVIDING CITATIONS TO QUOTATIONS

Look above to Exercise 6.3, select a phrase, a sentence, or several sentences from the O'Connor passage. Write a passage of your own that incorporates the words of O'Connor, cited clearly with an effective verb, not *said*, for the introduction (e.g., "O'Connor reveals"). See page 205 for examples.

Use an Appropriate Verb to Introduce the Quotation

WEB LINK
to Exercise
6.2
http://www.
ablongman.com/
lester

The verb *said* gets overused and shows little about the speaker's attitude. Verbs like the ones shown in the following list enable you to set the context and signal something about the speaker's attitude. These verbs add punch to your citation:

argues	complains	insists	calls for	emphasizes
declares	maintains	explains	proposes	compares
quarrels	observes	suggests	offers	opens with
adds	indicates	proves	provides	believes

Again, you should introduce many of your quotations with something other than the word *said*.

> Zigler calls for an increase in child care services and "a reexamination of our commitment to doing what is in the best interest of every child in America."

> Sylvia Plath opens the poem with "Love set you going like a fat gold watch."

> *Note: As you will see in Chapter 12, these present tense verbs will change when you use the APA style, which requires the past tense or the present perfect tense for citing a source—for example: "Zigler (2003) called for. . . ."*

Vary the Citation/Quotation Sequence

Vary the form of the introductions. Avoid a monotonous series of sentence beginnings, such as "Smith said that . . . " and "Walters questioned. . . . " For example, place the citation in the middle, or at the end of the quotation:

> "Success in marriage depends on being able, when you get over being in love, to really love," advised Eleanor Roosevelt, who added, "You never know anyone until you marry them."

> "You will have to rise above considerations which are narrow and partisan," warned Eleanor Roosevelt.

Use different grammatical forms. Change the quotation from a direct object to a subordinate clause:

> As Eleanor Roosevelt warned, "You will have to rise above considerations which are narrow and partisan."

Reduce the quotation by using only a key phrase with your comments wrapped around it.

> If you wish to "gain strength, courage, and confidence" in your activities, says Eleanor Roosevelt, "you must find the strength to "do the thing you think you cannot do."

T I P   *Using Separated and Integrated Quotations*

There are two ways of presenting direct quotations—separated and integrated. When *separated,* the citation ends in a comma or colon, and there is a complete separation of your ideas and the source.

> Sylvia Plath opens her poem with this line: "Love set you going like a fat gold watch."

When *integrated,* no punctuation separates the citation and the quotation, and the quotation is wrapped into your phrasing and presentation:

> Sylvia Plath says love starts a ticking in the heart "like a fat gold watch."

EXERCISE 6.5
VARYING THE CITATIONS

Rewrite the following citation to put it in the middle of the quotation and to give it a better introductory verb:

Commenting on her first days on the bench, Sandra Day O'Connor in 2003 said, "The press constantly accompanied me in huge flocks; everywhere that Sandra went, the press was sure to go."

Alter Some Capital Letters and Lowercase Letters

Change Some Initial Capital Letters to Small Letters. If you change the quotation to a subordinate clause or a phrase, as discussed above, you will often integrate the quotation. *The Chicago Manual of Style* decrees that when a quotation is integrated, the first letter of the quotation should be small *even it was a capital letter in the original:*

> Eleanor Roosevelt warned her audience that "you will have to rise above considerations which are narrow and partisan."

Compare to "Eleanor Roosevelt warned, "You will. . . . "

Sylvia Plath surprises her readers with unusual similes as in "love set you going like a fat gold watch."

The original line reads: "Love set you going like a gold watch."

Change Some Small Letters to Capitals. The *Chicago Manual of Style* also permits changing a small letter to a capital with a separated citation. That is, if a quotation, which is only part of a sentence in the original, forms a complete sentence as quoted, the initial lowercase letter may be changed to a capital where your introductory structure permits it. Your citation will need to end in a comma or colon. For example, in this next quotation note that the word *the* is in lower case.

"Men can never lead if they are afraid, for the leader who is afraid will never be followed."

—Eleanor Roosevelt

Notice how the word *the* may be changed to a capital letter:

Eleanor Roosevelt wisely observed, "The leader who is afraid will never be followed."

EXERCISE 6.6
ALTERING INITIAL CAPITAL LETTERS

Change the following quotation to a phrase or subordinate clause introduced by the word *that* and change the initial capital to lowercase:

Justice O'Connor explains, "The concept of the Rule of Law—that laws should be enacted by democratically elected bodies and enforced by independent judiciaries—is fundamental to a free society."

Avoid Needless Repetition of the Citation

Unless confusion might result, introduce the speaker once, not repeatedly.

Eleanor Roosevelt reached out to serve the downtrodden, especially "the plight of a single person whom I have seen with my own eyes." The individual who suffered helped her focus on issues worldwide. "Out of my response to an individual develops an awareness of a problem to the community, then to the country, and finally to the world." She insisted that all people are equal and should be treated equally, but "the tragedy of hunger" seemed ever present around the globe.

WEB LINK
to Reading
6.2
http://www.
ablongman.com/
lester

Place Long Quotations in an Indented Block

For longer quotations, usually 40 words or more, give a formal introduction ending in a colon and provide the quotation, indented one tab space—or ten character spaces if using MLA style. Do not use quotation marks around an indented block quotation.

Facing the convention delegates, the president's wife laid down a challenge:

> So each and every one of you who give him this responsibility, in giving it to him assume for yourselves a very grave responsibility because you will make the campaign. You will have to rise above considerations which are narrow and partisan. This is a time when it is the United States we fight for.

Her frail yet strong voice brought petty bickering and rivalries to an end, and her husband moved toward his third presidency.

EXERCISE 6.7
BLENDING QUOTATIONS

Write a passage that quotes from the following passage by Justice O'Connor. Quote with a clause or phrase run on into your sentence and also quote a block of the passage (four lines or more).

> We live in a world that is constantly shrinking. Cellular phones, fax machines, beepers, e-mail—all of these new forms of communications have made it much easier for us to talk to one another, no matter where we are. We need, however, more than technology to communicate with people from other nations. We need language skills. We need deeper understanding of foreign cultures. We need to know how to survive in an increasingly multinational environment.

Quote Accurately

Be diligent in copying quotations to your notes and then into your text. You cannot alter the original words. Therefore, precisely transcribe the words as spelled in the original with the original punctuation in place. In this next example, the student has carefully cited with precision an indented block, two phrases, and a sentence. There can be no doubt which are the student's words and those of the poet T. S. Eliot:

Images of frustration are sprinkled throughout T. S. Eliot's poetry, as when J. Alfred Prufrock states:

> For I have known them all already, known them all:—
> Have known the evenings, mornings, afternoons,
> I have measured out my life with coffee spoons;

I know the voices dying with a dying fall
Beneath the music of a farther room.
So how should I presume? (lines 49-54)

Prufrock, Eliot's persona, says he has "known the eyes already" and also has "known the arms" (lines 55 and 62). He moves eventually to despair: "I should have been a pair of ragged claws / Scuttling across the floors of silent seas" (lines 73-74).

The first quotation is separated from the student's text as a block quotation, introduced with a colon, indented without quotation marks, and documented to the specific lines. Note that the student writer uses double spacing for the six quoted lines of verse. The second and third quotations are phrases integrated into the flow of the student's words without punctuation and *with* quotation marks. The fourth quotation is separated from the student's words with a colon and *with* quotations marks. A virgule (slash) is used with a space before and a space after to separate two consecutive lines of poetry.

Be Aware of Your Verb Tense

The *historical present tense* has universal popularity because ideas, statements, and literature remain vital long after the writers have died. Convention dictates that you refer to these items in the present tense.

WEB LINK
to Exercise
6.3
http://www.
ablongman.com/
lester

In T. S. Eliot's poem the primary character and narrator, J. Alfred Prufrock, **laments,** "I have measured out my life with coffee spoons." While the poet Eliot **says** little externally about Prufrock, the poem itself **reveals** all we need to know.

This writer appropriately uses the present tense *laments, says,* and *reveals.*
References to historical and political documents should appear in the present tense:

Title IX **promises** every woman that the equivalent of every athletic dollar spent on men's programs will be spent on women's programs.

History should be written in the past tense.

Eleanor Roosevelt **warned** her audience that "you will have to rise above considerations which are narrow and partisan."

Scientific writing requires the past tense (*proved*) or the present perfect (*has proved*) for references to scientific findings:

Morganthal **demonstrated** the effect of certain pesticides on the bee population of Warren County.

EXERCISE 6.8

USING THE APPROPRIATE VERB TENSE

Explain the use of verb tense in the next three passages. Why do they differ from one another?

1. The appointment of a woman to the Supreme Court opened many doors to young women all across the country.—Sandra Day O'Connor

2. In her new book Justice O'Connor proudly comments, "The appointment of a woman to the Supreme Court opened many doors to young women all across the country."

3. One justice, Sandra Day O'Connor, observed that "the appointment of a woman to the Supreme Court opened many doors to young women all across the country."

Note: See Chapter 12 for a full discussion on tense for papers written in the APA style.

Punctuating by the Rules

WEB LINK
to Chapter 6
Related Web
Destinations
http://www.
ablongman.com/
lester

Punctuate carefully, setting off an integrated quotation with a comma or a colon after your introduction. At the end of the quotation, periods and commas go inside the closing quotation marks. Semicolons and colons go outside the closing quotation marks.

Eleanor Roosevelt observed, "You gain strength, courage, and confidence by every experience in which you really look fear in the face"; then she added, "You must do the thing you think you cannot."

Exclamation marks and question marks may go inside or outside the quotation mark. If the quotation itself is a question or exclamation, the mark goes inside; if the sentence that contains the quotation is a question or exclamation, the mark goes outside.

Was it Eleanor Roosevelt who said, "You must do the thing you think you cannot"?

FDR asked, "Where is Eleanor?"

"We face hostility at home and abroad!" shouted the president.

Using Single Quotation Marks

When a quotation appears within another quotation, use single quotation marks with the interior one.

George Thompson confirms that "the death wish of Hamlet cannot be ignored in light of the prince's cry, 'O, that this too too sullied flesh would melt, / Thaw and resolve itself into a dew!' "

Periods and other terminal marks go inside both the single quotation mark and the double quotation mark.

Editing a Quotation with *sic*, Ellipsis Points, and Brackets

You are permitted to invade a quotation under certain circumstances. You must use brackets around material you insert, and you must use ellipsis points if you delete part of a quotation.

Use [sic] to Signal a Mistake in a Quotation

When a quotation has a questionable spelling or word usage, let your reader know that you are quoting exactly and that the structure is not your error. The word *sic* ("thus," "so," "in this manner") is placed in brackets immediately after the word in question. In the next example the student writer makes clear that the year *1964* was the error of Lovell. The assassination occurred in 1963.

Lovell says, "John F. Kennedy, assassinated in November of 1964 [*sic*], became overnight an immortal figure of courage and dignity in the hearts of most Americans."

The word *sic* is not an abbreviation and therefore takes no period. Because it is a Latin word, it is usually set in italics. Do not overuse the device. In a language or literature study, for example, it is unnecessary to call attention to every variant, as in the lines from Chaucer:

Whan that Aprille with his shoures sote
The droghte of Marche hath perced to the rote.

Use Brackets to Enclose Interpolation, Corrections, Explanations, Translations, or Comments within Quoted Matter

Use square brackets, not parentheses, to clarify a statement:

Eleanor Roosevelt warned her audience [the Democratic delegates] that "you will have to rise above considerations which are narrow and partisan."

Use the brackets, without ellipsis, to correct or adjust the grammar within an abridged quotation:

ORIGINAL: "Eleanor Roosevelt, who served in the United Nations after FDR's death, gained international attention, especially as a champion of the impoverished people around the globe."—Orin Roberts

ABRIDGED: "Eleanor Roosevelt [became] a champion of the impoverished people," one historian notes.

Use brackets to note any addition or change that you make in the quotation:

Eleanor Roosevelt observed, "You gain strength, courage, and confidence by every experience in which you really *look fear in the face* [my emphasis]"; then she added, "You must do the thing you think you cannot."

Use brackets to substitute a proper name for a pronoun. The pronoun *she* is replaced in the following example.

Railford added, "We all know [Roosevelt] implored us into action by saying 'look fear in the face.' "

Use Ellipsis Points to Omit Portions of a Quotation

An ellipsis is an omission of a word, phrase, line, paragraph, or more from a quoted passage. The ellipsis is marked with points, not asterisks, printed as spaced periods. Three points indicate an omission within a quoted sentence.

ORIGINAL: Success in marriage depends on being able, when you get over being in love, to really love.

ELLIPSIS: "Success in marriage depends on being able . . . to really love," advised Eleanor Roosevelt.

The three ellipsis points are separated from each other and from the text by a space. When the ellipsis occurs at the end of a sentence and what remains is still grammatically complete, use a period followed by three spaced points.

ORIGINAL: Osburn observed, "The final years of Eleanor Roosevelt's life were filled with public service to the needy and the private love of her family in travels around the world that always brought her back to the New York mansion."

ELLIPSIS: Osburn observed, "The final years of Eleanor Roosevelt's life were filled with public service to the needy and the private love of her family. . . . "

Three spaced dots are also used to show that a quoted sentence is purposely and grammatically incomplete:

Everybody knows that the "Gettysburg Address" begins with the line, "Four score and seven years ago . . . " But who can recite the entire speech?

Note: Because style guides and handbooks vary somewhat on the rules of ellipsis, consult one as described on page 220 if you have issues beyond those discussed here.

EXERCISE 6.9
USING ELLIPSIS POINTS AND SQUARE BRACKETS

1. Several quotations are provided below. Select one, incorporate it into a sentence of your own, but use ellipsis to shorten it so that it fits your context.

2. Select a second quotation from the list below. Incorporate the quotation into a sentence of your own, but use brackets to insert an interpolation or clarification into the quotation.

   a. In the future days, which we seek to make secure, we look forward to a world founded upon four essential human freedoms. The first is freedom of speech and expression—everywhere in the world. The second is freedom of every person to worship God in his own way—everywhere in the world. The third is freedom from want—which, translated into world terms, means economic understandings which will secure to every nation a healthy peacetime life for its inhabitants—everywhere in the world. The fourth is freedom from fear—which, translated into world terms, means a world-wide reduction of armaments to such a point and in such a thorough fashion that no nation will be in a position to commit an act of physical aggression against any neighbor—anywhere in the world. (Franklin W. Roosevelt)

   b. I think, at a child's birth, if a mother could ask a fairy godmother to endow it with the most useful gift, that gift would be curiosity. (Eleanor Roosevelt)

   c. Twenty years from now you will be more disappointed by the things that you didn't do than by the ones you did do. So throw off the bowlines. Sail away from the safe harbor. Catch the trade winds in your sails. Explore. Dream. Discover. (Mark Twain)

   d. To those people in the huts and villages of half the globe struggling to break the bonds of mass misery, we pledge our best efforts to help them help themselves, for whatever period is required, not because the Communists may be doing it, not because we seek their votes, but because it is right. If a free society cannot help the many who are poor, it cannot save the few who are rich. (John F. Kennedy)

   e. I've surpassed any goal I set for myself as far as my body, my career, and getting married. (Ricki Lake)

Using a Quotation to Open the Paper

WEB LINK
to Reading
6.3
http://www.
ablongman.com/
lester
If relevant, you may place a quotation as a separate block preceding your first line of text. This method is effective because it highlights a well-phrased passage and introduces another writer who has addressed the subject and found it worthy of discussion. Shown below is a quotation on the opening page to a section of Carol Gilligan's book *The Birth of Pleasure*.

Regions of Light

Love merely as the best
There is, and one would make the best of that
By saying how it grows and in what climates . . .
To say at the end, however we find it, good,
Bad, or indifferent, it helps us, and the air
Is sweetest there. The air is very sweet.
—James Merrill

It is eight o'clock on Thursday morning, and I am sitting on a small chair in a sunny pre-kindergarten room. Next to me, an Egyptian spiny mouse runs, spinning its wheel against the wall of its glass cage. The four-year-old boys begin to drift in. Gabe comes in, carried by his father, his face buried in his father's neck. Slowly, this large man lowers himself onto the floor with his son, takes out a plastic container of toys, and begins to arrange the small figures of people and horses into a scene. Curious, Gabe unwraps his arms from around his father's neck, turning to see, his face flushed, his blond hair tousled. Soon, father and son are playing together, quietly absorbed. After a time, when Gabe has settled, his father gently takes his leave.

EXERCISE 6.10

AVOIDING PLAGIARISM

Plagiarism is discussed in detail in Chapter 7, but it is valuable to take just a moment in this chapter on using quotations to remind you that copying material into your paper without citing it properly is a serious offense. The only way you can avoid plagiarism when borrowing actual words of another person is with a citation and quotation marks or an indented block quotation. To see how easily others can detect plagiarism, read the following passage, watching for the dramatic shift in style as the writer copies from a source. Underline the sentence that has been borrowed without citation and quotation marks.

We know that Newton explained the lunar tides many years ago with the Law of Gravitation. And the tides are fascinating. Standing on the beach at 8:00 a.m. is a totally different experience from that at 2:00 p.m. Somehow, the Moon exerts a gravitational force on every object on Earth. Tides occur because the Earth is a body of finite extent and these forces are not uniform: some parts of the Earth are closer to the Moon than other parts, and since the gravitational force drops off at the inverse square distance, those parts experience a larger gravitational tug from the Moon than parts that are farther away. In plain language, water is fluid and more easily affected by gravity, so this leads to the tidal effects where one's feet are dry at 8:00 a.m. and wet in the same place at 2:00 p.m.

Using Quotations in a Nonacademic Article

WEB LINK
to Reading
6.4
http://www.
ablongman.com/
lester

"Dinosaurs, the Media and Andy Warhol," an article published in 2002 in *American Scientist*, demonstrates a nonacademic style for identifying quotations, as the marginal notations will explain. Academic styles, to be discussed in the next section of this chapter, require a more conscientious, even meticulous citation and documentation.

Dinosaurs, the Media and Andy Warhol

Keith S. Thomson

History will no doubt record Andy Warhol as a major 20th century artist. One of Warhol's "gifts" was to make everything with which he was associated—his work, his friends, his life—appear cheap and shallow. If he set out to irritate and confuse, then he certainly succeeded. In the process he mocked us and, above all, himself. Warhol will also be famous for his pronouncement, now nothing less than a curse, that in the future everyone will have the chance to be famous for 15 minutes.

All successful artists have to be showmen, it seems. Mozart and Chopin were no shrinking violets. They would have adored television unless, like those fabled old silent-screen movie stars, they had been betrayed by squeaky voices or uncouth accents. Today, although technical virtuosity is still a necessary condition for success as a solo musician, charisma is almost equally

Here Thomson gives an indirect quotation to something that Warhol said. The exact source is not provided, but a diligent researcher could find information on Warhol quickly.

important; hence all the CD covers featuring female classical violinists in revealing clothing, or little at all. All the more reason, then, to admire the steadily nonglamorous types, such as the pianist Alfred Brendel, who let their music talk for them.

Perhaps, in a modern-day version of *Faustus*, those 15 minutes of fame form a contract with the devil, granted through the agency of the media, who are a fickle-enough ally in the best of times. At a recent London film premiere, the Hollywood stars wandered unnoticed into the theater while journalists gathered like flies around two recent participants in a television program called "Big Brother." Well, a plague on both their houses, we might say. Except that the rot is spreading. Getting oneself noticed by the press and especially by television, if only for 15 minutes, has infected the one field where, in a perfect world, people would be immune to cheap blandishments and hew strictly to a line of puritan truth and detachment. Fat chance, of course, when we are talking about science!

The "boffins" of World War II made science glamorous, as did the late Christian Barnard, pioneer heart surgeon. German naturalist and explorer Alexander von Humboldt and English biologist Thomas Henry Huxley had already perfected the art a century earlier, however, and I have no doubt that Charles Darwin worked long and diligently, if quietly, at his "Saint Charles" image. But perhaps nowhere have scientists pursued an often too-transient fame further than in paleontology, and particularly with respect to dinosaurs. Dinosaurs are God's gift to television and the newspapers, just as science fiction is the lifeblood of the supermarket tabloids. Tyrannosaurs and little green men—sure winners, both.

In these two paragraphs, Thomson makes quick references to several men of prominence without citing exactly how to find a source, but today they can be researched quickly on the Web.

Dino-stories

Just why dinosaurs have always been so prominent in the public imagination, and why they fascinate a particular age class of (mostly male) children, has long perplexed scholars. An old Philadelphia museum guard gave me a good answer. "They're half real, and half not real." When Richard Owen, who coined the term *dinosaur* in 1842, and Waterhouse Hawkins erected the first life-size reconstructions of dinosaures—half real, half wrong, as it happened—for the Crystal Palace exhibition of 1854, they were openly courting the sort of public mania that has persisted ever since. In the first half of the following century, the fictional Professor Challenger of Conan Doyle's *The Lost World* was echoed in real life by people like Roy Chapman Andrews and his

American Museum of Natural History expeditions to the Gobi Desert, and a host of lesser but equally colorful characters.

For today's hungry media, a cornucopia of new dinosaur science and new-style paleontologists, some marketing themselves as a cross between Indiana Jones and the mountain men of the Old West—with beards, boots, silly hats, unwashed shirts and unedited opinions—have been a gift from heaven. One is forced to ask, however, whether some of those who have leapt onto the back of this particular tiger might not be finding the ride uncomfortable and whether more sober paleontologists might feel that their work suffers something of a taint by association. If one had a truly sensational discovery, one might in fact feel like hushing it up, lest the media convert it into something quite appalling in order to sell another day's newspapers, only to drop the subject equally abruptly. On the other hand, in this media-driven world, grant funding may require publicity.

The whole dinosaur publicity business got a boost from the famous discovery of the iridium spike in the Earth's crust and its evidence for an asteroid impact at the end of the Cretaceous. Here was something whose fame could last more than 15 minutes. But once again, the public-relations aspect was dreadfully overblown. The public was given the impression that at one moment there were millions of dinosaurs, in their full diversity, doing their Mesozoic thing, and then at the next moment all were extinct. The reality seems to be that any dinosaurs made extinct by the impact were the stragglers of an already dwindling group, whereas the real extinction story was in less glamorous taxa.

In a neat example of journalistic excess, the London *Times* of October 30, 1998, carried a story headlined: "Rock solid proof that comet killed dinosaurs." The facts of the case, which the article blithely laid out, were quite different. Two scientists from the Scripps Institution of Oceanography had discovered a chromium spike at the Cretaceous-Tertiary boundary, the isotopic signature of which suggested an extraterrestrial origin. Their work simply confirmed that there had been an asteroid impact, and nowhere did they use the word "dinosaur." Apparently the newspaper could not resist adding that the scientists had proved that the asteroid killed the dinosaurs. They hadn't. But it made a better story.

Here the writer provides a quotation from the London Times *and gives the specific date for anybody who wishes to find the full article.*

How *Tyrannosaurus* Got Its Feathers

The chief thing we know about *Tyrannosaurus rex*, the fabled king of the Late Cretaceous, is that we still have much to learn about it, which should be a signal for caution, although it is also a license for speculation. There are only 25 or so specimens of *T. rex,* most incomplete, even though the species may have survived for several million years and tens of thousands of them, if not more, must have lived at one time or another.

In popular imagination, *T. rex* started out as a ferocious tyrant. How are the mighty fallen, however! In 2001, Warhol's curse struck *T. rex* and ushered in a drastic makeover for the *capo di capo* of dinosaurs. (How easy it is to fall into the style!) It had already been noised about that the thing was really only a scavenger of something else's kills, more a hyena than a lion. By May 2001, *T. rex* had become cuddly and possibly even covered with feathers. By October, it had become the "Woody Allen of dinosaurs," even neurotic.

This may turn out to be a just-not-so story. *T. rex* is a member of a large group of dinosaurs called theropods. The idea that theropod dinosaurs and birds are related is very old, dating back at least to T. H. Huxley and now having much modern support. So far, so good. But how did *T. rex* get feathers? In 1999, *National Geographic* magazine published a story under the title "Feathers for *T. rex*" in which an amazing new find from China, intermediate between a bird and a dromaeosaur, was described. Amazing indeed; it was a fake. In April 2001 in *Nature,* Qiang Ji *et al.* published an account of a new Chinese theropod that had evidence of a kind of proto-feathers. Once again the media homed in on *Tyrannosaurus*: "Maybe even mighty *Tyrannosaurus rex* had feathers," and "Maybe baby tyrannosaurus looked something like a cute, fuzzy baby chick," said ABCNEWS.com. Perhaps the best line went to science writer Deborah Smith of the Sydney (Australia) *Morning Herald,* April 27, 2001: "T-Rex in a feather boa turns heads among fossil hunters." (T-rex instead of *T. rex* seems very popular with journalists.)

Here Thomson cites from National Geographic, Nature, ABCnews.com, *and the* Sydney Morning Herald. *All sources could be accessed by a researcher.*

Next, Jim Kirkland of the Utah Geological Survey and Doug Wolfe of Mesa Southwest Museum released an account of a new North American theropod—*Nothronychus*—at a Discovery Channel press conference. *Nothronychus* was evidently a vegetarian but with "bird-like characters and . . . probably covered with feathers, said the scientists" (Reuters, June 19, 2001), to the newspapers' delight. But was there any evidence? At the press conference it was stated that no feathers were found with *Nothronychus.* Certainly none have been found with *Tyrannosaurus.* So far the sequence is as follows: *T. rex* is related (but not closely) to *Nothronychus,* where there is no evidence of feathers; *Nothronychus*

Here Thomson cites the Discovery Channel.

is more closely related to the Chinese dinosaur *Beipaosaurus,* where there is disputed evidence of proto-feathers. Score: feathers 3, logic 0.

From Cuddly to Sad

This past October, as the date for the annual meeting of the Society of Vertebrate Paleontology drew near, the world waited for the inevitable sensational announcement that would hog the headlines while a great deal of excellent work was ignored. Predictably, sensation once again found our poor, put-upon friend *Tyrannosaurus rex;* but this one was a classic. As the London *Times* trumpeted: "Neurotic T-rex cast in a Woody Allen role." On the web, the Associated Press had spread the news: "T-rex wasn't happy . . . T-rex was probably T-wrecks." Obviously someone was getting his 15 minutes of fame!

What happened had started out with good straightforward science. Elizabeth Rega at Western University of Health Sciences in Pomona and Chris Brochu at the University of Iowa had read a paper concerning skeletal abnormalities in *T. rex,* especially the Chicago specimen known as Sue. There was evidence of osteomyelitis of the left fibula, healed rib fractures and healed jaw lesions. They concluded: "While the number of these pathologies indicate that Sue was not healthy during life, the maturity of the specimen and the clear evidence of healing indicate that Sue was a robust individual who successfully survived many insults. . . . No evidence of cause or manner of death is apparent." So far, so sober. No drama there and no headlines, either.

In this paragraph Thomson provides a paraphrase of and a quotation from Elizabeth Rega and Chris Brochu, and he provides the affiliation of the writers in case somebody needs more information.

Then the Associated Press interviewed Robert Bakker, who was not an author of the paper but who announced the meaning in Rega and Brochu's study that everyone else had missed: "If we did Jurassic Park 4, T-rex would be portrayed in an angst-ridden role—sort of a large Woody Allen character. . . . They were beat up, limping, had oozing sores, were dripping pus and disease ridden, and had to worry about their children starving and other T-rexs coming in and kicking them out." And worse, the London *Times* article wrongly claimed that "Mr Bakker's view, is endorsed by Elizabeth Rega," thus adding injury to insult.

Thomson quotes Robert Bakker with only a passing reference to the Associated Press interview.

Here the gap between the science and the hyperbole is truly staggering. Perhaps it is only some paleontologists, not the dinosaurs, who are like Woody Allen—sometimes combative, sometimes cuddly, bearing the scars of old battles and confused? Perhaps this sort of thing is perfectly harmless or even positive for paleontology, on the grounds that all publicity is good, especially if it remains divided into 15-minute chunks. But the creationists certainly had a field day with the faked "feathered dinosaur."

Admittedly, all progress in science involves the breaking of old stereotypes, and mistakes will be made all along the way. Who knows, maybe even a *Tyrannosaurus* with true feathers will someday be found; that is what makes science a real adventure. And, as Robert Browning famously wrote, "Ah, but a man's reach should exceed his grasp" ("Andrea del Sario," 1855). Perhaps, though, both the scientists and the public deserve to travel a less jolting path toward enlightenment.

Thomson quotes the poet Robert Browning and gives the name of the poem and the date.

—Keith Stewart Thomson is Professor and Director of the Oxford University Museum of Natural History.

Bibliography

Ji, Q., M. A. Norell, K. Gao, S. Ji and D. Ren. 2001. The distribution of integumentary structures in a feathered dinosaur. *Nature* 410:1084–1088.

Shulolyukov, A., and G. W. Lugmair. 1998. Isotopic evidence for the Cretaceous-Tertiary impactor and its type. *Science* 282:927–929.

Thomson provides a bibliography that lists two sources for additional reading.

Citing Quotations in One of the Academic Styles

Because serious researchers wish to confirm and sometimes even replicate the findings of their colleagues, several scholarly associations have established rules and guidelines for citing quotations. In particular, some academic styles require a parenthetical citation for any material drawn from a source. We shall consider these parenthetical references more completely in later chapters, but you should learn the three basic styles most frequently used for academic writing.

Modern Language Association (MLA) for papers in literature, composition, language, and many humanities disciplines. MLA style uses parenthetical citations. See Chapter 10 for complete details.

Chicago Manual of Style (CMS) for papers in history, the arts, humanities, and some disciplines in the social and physical sciences. CMS style uses either endnotes, footnotes, or parenthetical citations. See Chapter 11 for complete details.

American Psychological Association (APA) for papers in the social sciences, business, and some natural sciences. APA style uses parenthetical citations. See Chapter 12 for complete details.

For now, here are the basic guidelines with an example of each, but go to the appropriate chapter for complete explanations.

MLA Style

WEB LINK
to Chapter 6
Related Web
Destinations
http://www.
ablongman.com/
lester

Quotations in MLA style should be introduced with the full name of the author on first appearance and thereafter with last name only. Use the historical present tense to introduce quotations. The citation is not complete without a page number at the end of the quotation unless the work has none, as in the case of an interview or an Internet article without pagination. Do not use *p.* or *pp.* before the page number.

> Margaret Leech reports, "The new President [Abraham Lincoln] had formed an inflexible determination to entertain no compromise on the extension of slavery, and to defend the Constitution, as his oath of office required" (45).

This citation would then require a bibliography entry in a Works Cited list at the end of the article:

> Leech, Margaret. <u>Reveille in Washington: 1860-1865</u>. New York: Harper and Row, 1969.

CMS Note Style

Quotations in CMS style should be introduced with the full name of the author on first appearance and thereafter with last name only. Use the historical present tense to introduce quotations. The citation is not complete without a superscript number at the end of the quotation if you are using the note style instead of parenthetical references.

> Margaret Leech reports, "The new President [Abraham Lincoln] had formed an inflexible determination to entertain no compromise on the extension of slavery, and to defend the Constitution, as his oath of office required."[3]

This citation would then require either an endnote entry in a Notes section at the end of the article or a footnote at the bottom of the page to identify the source, including the page number.

> 3. Margaret Leech, *Reveille in Washington: 1860-1865* (New York: Harper and Row, 1969), 45.

APA Style

Quotations in APA style should be introduced with the last name only of the author on first and all other appearances. The name should be followed immediately by the year of publication, set within parentheses. Use the past tense (*reported*) or present perfect tense (*has reported*) to introduce quotations, but use the present tense when you discuss results (*the findings indicate*) and when you mention established knowledge (*salt contributes to hypertension*). The citation is not complete without a page number at the end of the quotation unless the work has none, as in the case of an interview or an Internet article without pagination. Use *p.* or *pp.* before the page number(s).

Leech (1969) reported, "The new President [Abraham Lincoln] had formed an inflexible determination to entertain no compromise on the extension of slavery, and to defend the Constitution, as his oath of office required" (p. 45).

This citation would then require a bibliography entry in a References section at the end of the article:

Leech, M. (1969). *Reveille in Washington: 1860-1865*. New York: Harper and Row.

GUIDELINES

Use of Primary and Secondary Sources

- A primary source is an original work—poem, essay, drama, test results, presidential speech, movie, interview. Use quotations from primary sources to draw upon the wisdom of the source and display the grace and style of the original work.

- A secondary source is a paper after the fact—about a public figure's speech, a writer's short story, a biography, a history article, a Broadway show. Use quotations from these sources to draw upon the body of literature that attaches itself to a work of art, an important event, or a person's life. Comments exist on almost every topic imaginable. Your task is to find the best comments for quotation.

Using Citations in a Scholarly Article

Reproduced below is the opening section of an essay on Edgar Allan Poe by Roger Platizky as published in *The Explicator*, a literary journal devoted to short analyses of poetry and fiction. The marginal notes will identify and explain various aspects of Platizky's quotations from Poe's story, which is the primary source. The marginal notes will also identify quotations from various critics—the secondary sources—who have commented on the story. As you read, examine the citations by Platizky, which meet the standards of the MLA style.

"Poe's 'The Cask of Amontillado'"

Roger Platizky

WEB LINK
to Reading
6.5
http://www.
ablongman.com/
lester

"There came forth in return only a jingling of the bells. My heart grew sick; it was the dampness of the catacombs that made it so." ("Cask" 1263)

Platizky opens with an indented quotation from the story.

The threat of being buried alive is both a psychological fear and a historical reality that Edgar Allan Poe capitalizes on, ambiguously, in his famous short story of revenge, "The Cask of Amontillado" (1846). Written just two years after "The Premature Burial" (1843–44), "The Cask" is Poe's last and best known short story dealing with what J. Gerald Kennedy calls Poe's "obsessive nightmare" (33), his fixation on living interment. To a significant degree, Poe's fear of live burial had a cultural counterpart. Kennedy and others have shown that premature burial was a preoccupation in eighteenth- and nineteenth-century America and Europe largely because death was more often in the hands of the medical community and funerals had become secularized.

Platizky quotes J. Gerald Kennedy, a scholar on Poe's works.

Here Platizky paraphrases the source.

In an attempt to keep living entombments from occurring, coffins and vaults—especially for the wealthier classes—were equipped with special springs and sounding devices to give the person mistakenly buried alive a chance to be rescued (Michael Crichton 326–28). One of the most pragmatic of these devices, which involved the "placing of bells on the limbs of the recently dead," was exhibited at Brooklyn's Greenwood Cemetery in 1845, just a year before Poe published his short story. "Mr. Eisenbrandt's life-preserving coffin" boasted a death-defying device, "a mechanism whereby a cord attached to the hand of a corpse would at the slightest movement activate an external bell" (Kennedy 38). Although a creative variation of this device—the jingling bells on Fortunato's fool's cap—is placed and ironically deployed at the end of "The Cask of Amontillado," the bells do not assist in the resurrection of the entombed jester except, perhaps, in the living memory of Montresor's revenge.

Here the author paraphrases and quotes the critic Crichton.

Kennedy is again quoted.

Since Montresor is costumed as an executioner ("Cask" 1258) when he walls up Fortunato, it is worth recalling that live burial was once a practiced form of capital punishment, a "rite of

The author makes a reference to the story.

social purification," in Europe. Especially in the sixteenth cen- *Here he both quotes and* tury, being buried alive was the severe punishment for sexual *paraphrases the critic van* offenses and grand larceny (Richard van Dulmen 6). Although *Dulmen.* there is no concrete evidence of Fortunato's having committed either of these offenses, Montresor implies that his rival, a member of the Freemasons, is responsible for his loss of status, hap- *Here the quotation comes* piness, love, and respect: "You are rich, respected, admired, *from the story itself.* beloved; you are happy, as once I was" (1259). Sardonically twisting justice, for what he mockingly tells Fortunato is "the love of God!" (1263), Montresor uses Fortunato's pride in being a Mason and a wine connoisseur to entrap his adversary. The device however of entombing an enemy behind a brick wall is neither Montresor's nor Poe's invention. . . .

Chapter Review

WEB LINK to Chapter 6 Related Web Destinations http://www. ablongman.com/ lester

Chapter 6 has encouraged you to use quotations in your papers, and to do so responsibly. You cannot cut and paste huge pieces of material into the paper and twist and dodge among them with your own text. Each quotation should have a specific purpose in the support of *your* ideas. The essay is yours and the quotations and paraphrases are there to lend substance, expertise, and even grace and style in composition.

Each quotation in your paper should be as brief as possible, pared down to a phrase or sentence. Seldom should you reproduce a block of material unless your purpose is the examination of a text, as might be required in a study of Hemingway's prose style in *The Old Man and the Sea*. In that case, you would need numerous passages to make your point.

The use of quotations in your paper will give it authority, will show the dialogue that exists on the subject, and will allow you to distance yourself, identify your ideas, and even differ with opinions of others.

The chapter has also discussed in detail the methods for blending the quotations into your prose. Knowing these techniques and understanding the conventions for citations will serve you well in your general essays for different courses as well as in your scholarly papers that must conform to an academic style.

Chapter 6 Assignment: Using Quotations

In Chapters 4, 5, and 6 we have discussed the various methods for using source material, condensing it with summary, rewriting it with paraphrase, or quoting it. Anytime you begin to borrow from the sources, these techniques come into play repeatedly and in a mixture as you transfer from personal commentary to borrowing from the sources. Reproduced below is an essay by Krista West originally published in *Scientific American* (May 2002). In it, she shifts from one technique to another as she weaves the sources into her commentary on the status of mountain lions and bighorn sheep. Marginal annotations will signal her use of (1) summary, (2) paraphrase, and (3) quotation. Your task is to read the essay, note the techniques at work, and answer the questions posed in the exercise at the end of the essay.

Lion Versus Lamb

Krista West

What do you do when one rare, protected species threatens the livelihood of another, even more endangered species? In New Mexico shrinking ecological niches and fragmenting habitats have put two species on a collision course—and set state administrators and wildlife managers against one another in the courts. Here the state-protected mountain lion (*Puma concolor*) preys on the endangered desert bighorn sheep (*Ovis canadensis*). New Mexico officials recently voted for a plan to kill more mountain lions in an effort to protect more sheep.

There is good reason to worry about the state's sheep population. It has been steadily declining for decades and is one of the smallest in the Southwest, according to the U.S. Geological Survey. Only about 130 bighorns exist in the state, says the New Mexico Department of Game and Fish (NMDGF), which since the mid-1990s has tracked sheep populations using radio collars. Of the 40 sheep deaths the agency recorded during the study, 30 were caused by mountain lions. Richard Beausoleil, a biologist for the NMDGF, remarks that "the department was left with a choice: do nothing and watch populations of very limited species decline to extinction or control the dominant source of mortality."

She summarizes a report by the NMDGF.

She quotes a biologist.

According to the new regulation passed by the New Mexico Game Commission, which oversees the NMDGF, hunters will be allowed to kill 234 mountain lions (up from 176) when the season begins in October. They will also be allowed to kill unlimited numbers on private lands, and each hunter will be allowed to take two lions (instead of the usual limit of one) in designated bighorn habitats. This extra removal of mountain lions, officials believe, will relieve predation pressures on the endangered sheep.

She paraphrases from a new regulation.

Opponents of the plan, including the non-profit group Animal Protection of New Mexico, have filed a lawsuit to stop the hunts. The group acknowledges that something needs to be done to save the sheep but is concerned that the new kill quotas threaten

She paraphrases an animal group.

WEB LINK
to Exercise
6.4
http://www.
ablongman.com/
lester

the long-term survival of the predatory cats. Kenneth A. Logan, head of the NMDGF's 10-year study of lions, determined that no more than 11 percent of the state's lion population should be harvested each year. Animal Protection and others, however, estimate that the 234 kills could amount to 33 percent of the population, in contrast to the NMDGF's estimate of 10 percent. The problem is that because the cats are elusive, no one really knows how many of them there are—both estimates are based on mathematical models.

She paraphrases Kenneth Logan.

Ecologist Howard Passell of Sandia National Laboratories calls this management plan a "Band-Aid" fix. The real issue for New Mexico and other Western states, he argues, is how to manage these predator-prey relationships in the long run. Indeed, Logan suggests that culling those lions with a preference for sheep would be better than random removal by hunters. Logan's study, the most comprehensive of its kind, found that only a few cats developed a taste for bighorns. In the study, mule deer made up the bulk of the mountain lion's diet (up to 91 percent), whereas sheep constituted just 2 percent. But selective removal of the sheep-loving mountain lions is a difficult and expensive proposition.

She paraphrases and quotes from Howard Passell.

Again, she paraphrases Logan.

D. J. Schubert, an independent wildlife biologist who is studying lion management policies in four Western states, says he does not "believe that a single Western state has the evidence necessary to justify its current mountain lion management practices." Many ecologists feel that the rules stem from an antiquated antipredator attitude. Schubert adds that "all Western states except California are allowing an unsustainable level of sport hunting." (California prohibits such hunting.)

She paraphrases and quotes from D. J. Schubert.

What's needed to balance the interests of lions, sheep and humans is further research. Large, long-term studies of these complicated relationships are under way in California and Arizona, and the NMDGF is just beginning a DNA study of the state's lions to better estimate the size and range of the population. All hope that more information will lead to more effective management policies.

License to Kill

Critics suggest that one reason New Mexico adopted the new regulations to raise kill quotas of mountain lions was to please the growing number of hunters. Permits have been steadily increasing over the past two decades. Most hunts are led by guides or outfitters that charge up to $3,000 a hunt. The hunting season runs from October through March.

She provides a statistical table for the years 1989–2000 that shows the increase in hunting licenses.

Hunt Year	Licenses Issued	Total Harvest
1989–90	482	112
1990–91	781	108
1991–92	765	119
1992–93	826	105
1993–94	926	127
1994–95	1,145	150
1995–96	842	119
1996–97	980	177
1997–98	974	168
1998–99	1,485	153
1999–2000	1,702	156

Source: The Status of the Mountain Lion in New Mexico, 1971–2000, by Richard Beoulolel, New Mexico Department of Game and Fish, 2000.

Assignment: Read the essay by Krista West, including the table that she supplied and the marginal annotations about her citations. Then write a passage of about 200 words in which you discuss West's use of summary, paraphrase, and quotation. Consider answering these questions in your analysis:

1. What role does summary play in the essay?
2. Does West make enough commentary of her own to establish her position clearly?
3. Are the quotations effective and worthy of that treatment?
4. Does she blend the paraphrases effectively into the essay?
5. Does she make a clear distinction between her own commentary and the paraphrased passages?

Practicing Academic Integrity

WEB LINK
to Chapter 7
Related Web
Destinations
http://www.
ablongman.com/
lester

omposing from sources exercises your critical thinking and prompts you toward conscientious writing. It requires you to cross an intellectual bridge as you walk from the sources on one side of your journey over to an audience of interested readers on the other side. The ideas borrowed from the sources must blend effortlessly into your prose, but the identity of the sources cannot disappear—for several reasons.

Let's first consider the positive benefits of using sources before we examine the dangers. Using one or more sources correctly in your paper will reveal your ability to collect ideas, digest them, rework them into your prose, and share them with the reader. In blunt terms, it allows you to show off just a little and to display your reading on the topic. You don't need to write a paper in which everything you express is your original idea.

Bringing sources into the paper proves your ethical nature. As your readers see how effectively you handle quotations and paraphrases, they will recognize your sense of responsibility. Thus, they will likely accept your theories, opinions, and conclusions. Be willing to say something like this: "My idea is an extension of Peterson's comments on college basketball's role as a training ground for the professional leagues" or "Lofton confirms this paper's contention that school lunch programs have sold out to children by giving them what they want to eat and not what they need to eat."

Bringing sources into the paper displays the breadth and depth of your investigations on the subject. Sometimes it will be a penetration into the ideas of only one source to show how you and another person approached the issues. For example, you might respond to a magazine article on a topic of interest by expanding upon the ideas found there or by disagreeing with the ideas. At other times your work will be an extensive display of eight, fifteen, even twenty authors that you bring into play, with all their voices joining yours in the discussion. Can you imagine the vast number of articles on "women in the military" or "sports medicine" or "automobile safety"? There's no way you could present a topic in those subjects without extensive reading and the subsequent sharing of numerous quotations and paraphrases.

WEB LINK
to Audio-
visual 7.1
http://www.
ablongman.com/
lester

Bringing the sources into the paper enables you to share with readers the rich literature surrounding the topic. Until they see your paper, some readers may not realize that an extensive list of articles exists for, let's say, the diets of school children in lunch programs. Your readers will enjoy having a collection of opinions, which can come from authorities, certainly, but also from parents, teachers, and the children themselves. The voices of the children who ask for pizza, French fries, and hot dogs can be set in opposition to nutritionists advocating vegetables, fruit, and chicken. Let the debate rage in your paper, and you can accomplish that only if you bring in multiple sources.

Bringing the sources into the paper also gives it authority. Your readers may not know you, but they will recognize the credentials and even the names of your sources. If your topic is "term limits for politicians," for example, why not bring in the top guns and let them speak—Tom Daschle, Bill Frist, Dennis Hastert, Hillary Clinton, and other figures serving in Washington? Of course, with a topic such as "sports medicine" you will need to go in search of the best, most reliable figures, who might be obscure. We have talked in detail about how to find the best quotations from the best sources on your limited topic (see pages 194–202).

The purpose of this chapter is to make you comfortable with and knowledgeable about the ethics of research, especially about these matters:

- Explaining and sharing the literature on a subject.
- Placing sources into a proper context.
- Honoring property rights.
- Avoiding plagiarism.
- Understanding the methods for scholarly citations.
- Seeking permission to publish material on your Web site.

Explaining and Sharing the Literature on a Subject

By clearly announcing a source, you reveal the scope of your reading on a subject and thus your credibility as a researcher. Only by bringing expert testimony into your paper can you establish yourself as a scholar who is knowledgeable about the literature. Read this next passage to witness one student's engagement with planetary scientist David Kring. Student Linda Rawls wrote this passage for an essay on catastrophes that have threatened or will threaten the earth:

> The planet Earth is resilient. It has endured a number of catastrophic events, from the mythic flood of Noah to massive earthquakes and volcanic eruptions. About 65 million years ago, an asteroid or comet smashed into the Earth on the Yucatan Peninsula of Mexico. It precipitated the death of the dinosaurs. David Kring, a

planetary scientist at the University of Arizona, said the catastrophic event marked "the transition between the age of reptiles and the age of mammals." In theory, the crash released poisonous gases that, along with dust and smoke, blotted the sun and reduced temperatures. Kring, the director of the research team on Mexico's Yucatan Peninsula, added this thought: "Mammals were able to develop because the impact caused a complete change in the biological landscape of Earth." After that, mused Kring, "Evolution took advantage of the change." Theories of all sorts have been advanced to explain the disappearance of the dinosaurs, and this one adds to the evidence. Yet it seems to stretch credulity that one incident in Mexico could have such far-reaching consequences. It makes one fear the consequences of a nuclear bomb explosion. The atomic bomb destroyed a city; could a nuclear explosion destroy human and animal life as we know it? Would the Earth endure?

There is much to praise in this student's paragraph. First, Linda Rawls identifies Kring, not just by name but also by his professional status and his role as director of the Yucatan project. She uses his words within quotation marks twice and paraphrases his information once. Moreover, she uses Kring's comments on the dinosaurs to launch her own discussion on catastrophic events that damage the Earth and its environment.

The passage gives clear evidence of the writer's investigation into the subject. It also enhances the student's image as a researcher.

T I P   *Talk to Your Instructor*

Your writing instructor wants you to employ sources correctly and will, in almost every case, give you advice if you seek it, or make suggestions on first drafts if you submit them. Take advantage of this resource. Do not hide your paper until the final manuscript is due.

Quoting and Paraphrasing with Precision

The next examples show one student's struggle to get it right—that is, to bring a source into her paper with a citation to the source and with accuracy in the use of quotation and paraphrase. First, read the original reference material; next, examine her four versions as she worked to meet the requests of the instructor.

Canada's Cyber-Snooping Plans Raise Ire

Rina Chandarana

Laws Must Be Updated

Canada's solicitor-general, Lawrence MacAulay, has said law enforcement agencies need updated tools to deal with increasing use of the Internet by terrorists and criminals. The original laws to allow police to wiretap telephone conversations was passed in 1974, when rotary phones were used.

The United States passed the U.S.A. Patriot Act last October to give the government access to Web activity without having to get a warrant. To do this, the FBI is creating new technology called "Magic Lantern" to install over the Internet to enable investigators to monitor Web and computer activity without users' knowledge by sending a virus through the Internet.

At the moment, the FBI uses a less-sophisticated technology called Carnivore that also allows them to intercept e-mail and online activities of suspected criminals. But this can be done only by first gaining physical access to the computer.

The United Kingdom already requires ISPs [Internet Service Providers] to keep records of e-mail, Web site and text messaging of their clients under the Regulation of Investigatory Powers Act, enacted after Sept. 11.

—Rina Chandarana, "Canada's Cyber-Snooping Plans Raise Ire," Reuters New Service, Friday, September 27, 2002.

Student's First Note:

So now the FBI can use federal law to snoop into our e-mail and even send out a virus, and it's legal because of the U.S.A. Patriot Act passed in October in the frenzy to stop terrorism. The FBI's "Carnivore" program can intercept our e-mail and their new "Magic Lantern" system will soon invade our homes via an electronic virus and other clandestine gadgets.

The instructor praised the student for finding an issue that gets her emotionally charged and motivated to write. However, the instructor explained that she failed to identify the authority consulted for the information. Challenged to show her source, the student produced this version:

An article by Rina Chandarana explains that privacy experts and Internet service providers are worried by proposed amendments to Canadian laws that provide police updated tools to deal with increasing use of the Internet by terrorists and criminals. Writing for Reuters online Internet service, Chandarana also exposes how the U.S.A. Patriot Act last October gave the government access to Web activity without having to get a warrant.

The instructor found this version somewhat better because it provides a reference to the author of the online article; however, the instructor cautioned her that the paraphrasing contained far too much of Chandarana's language—words that should be enclosed within quotation marks or rewritten. Challenged again by the instructor, the student wrote:

An Internet article for Reuters news service by Rina Chandarana has raised a warning flag for all citizens who value their privacy, especially the privacy of their e-mail communications. It now seems that, in the name of the fight against terrorism, governments in Canada, the United Kingdom, and the United States have created new legal documents that give them broad powers. The United Kingdom has forced Internet service providers to maintain secret records of all messages by their clients. The United States has given the FBI broad powers to snoop with new technology called Carnivore and Magic Lantern. Chandarana is probably the vanguard to others who will issue warning signals about the invasion of privacy. My report will examine how much access the various agencies have to our Web activity as we work in the dormitory. Let's find out who can snoop on us—Campus police? State agencies? The Feds?

"Okay," said her instructor, "but why not let us hear the voices of the experts?" In response, the student added some direct quotation of her source:

WEB LINK
to Exercise
7.1
http://www.
ablongman.com/
lester

> An article by Rina Chandarana explains that privacy experts and Internet service providers are worried by proposed amendments to Canadian laws that invade privacy. She quotes Canada's solicitor-general, Lawrence MacAuley, who argues that "law enforcement agencies need updated tools to deal with increasing use of the Internet by terrorists and criminals." Writing for Reuters online Internet service, Chandarana also exposes how the U.S.A. Patriot Act last October "gave the government access to Web activity without having to get a warrant." Chandarana is probably the vanguard to others who will issue warning signals about the invasion of privacy. This report will examine how much access the various agencies have to our Web activity as we work in the dormitory. Let's find out who can snoop on us— Campus police? State agencies? The Feds?

This version represents a satisfactory handling of the source material. The writer has provided a clear citation to the source of the information, has used direct quotation effectively, and has paraphrased accurately. In addition, and this is an important point, her passage is not merely a summary of Chandarana's article. She uses the citation to launch her own investigation.

Placing a Source in Its Proper Context

Your sources will reflect all kinds of special interests, even biases, as we discussed in Chapter 3. Now, as you begin to use the sources in your paper, you will need to place them in the proper context. For example, this next citation signals that the expert is knowledgeable, sponsored by a reputable organization or institution, and, most likely, objective in tone and attitude:

> David Kring, the director of the research team on Mexico's Yucatan Peninsula, added this thought: "Mammals were able to develop because the impact caused a complete change in the biological landscape of Earth."

Now consider another citation in which the authority's position suggests a special interest:

> Rina Chandarana quotes Canada's solicitor-general, Lawrence MacAuley, who argues that "law enforcement agencies need updated tools to deal with increasing use of the Internet by terrorists and criminals."

WEB LINK
to Exercise
7.1
http://www.
ablongman.com/
lester

MacAuley has a special interest in upholding the law and wishes to broaden the powers for eavesdropping on the Internet. Only by mentioning MacAuley's role as a solicitor-general can the writer keep the readers informed about possible bias.

Thus, if you cite from a biased or questionable source, tell your reader up front. Some magazines are conservative, some liberal; some newspapers pursue a national focus, while others give preference to local matters and put a local slant even on national news. *You have an obligation to your reader to identify a source's bias, special interest, or slanted positions.* For example, if you are writing about the dangers of a diet program, you will find many different opinions in health and fitness magazines, medical journals, pharmaceutical advertisements, and online sites. No matter what your topic might be, always examine a source for:

- *Any special interest that might color the report.* A farm magazine will favor government projects not just for farm aid but also for water conservation, an open season on predators, and farm to city highway projects. In like manner, a nursing magazine, a newspaper column, or a television news broadcast will promote special agendas (see the excerpt from *Bias* by Bernard Goldstein, pages 83–87).

- *A lack of credentials,* which is not to say that you cannot quote your peers and laypersons who respond to an interview. Just inform your reader with an appropriate citation (*Three classmates were unanimous in their endorsement* NOT *Three different sources were unanimous in their endorsement*). Also, Internet articles are notorious for the absence of credentials for authors. As a general rule, avoid unidentified writers on the Internet; however, if an article is well written and makes a valid point, you *should* use it in your paper with an appropriate citation (*An anonymous commentator* at **http://www.ablongman.com/lester** *offers an interesting alternative to ever-increasing gasoline prices*).

- *A Web site that lists no sponsoring organization.* If an article looks promising to you but does not list a sponsor, you may need to truncate the address. Reducing **http://www.loc.gov/access/visitor.html#metro** to **http://www.loc.gov** will take you to the home page of the Library of Congress, certainly a reputable organization. Be suspicious of sites using the *.com* suffix; they are commercial in nature, not educational. Do consult sites with the suffixes *edu, gov, org, mil,* and the more recently added *biz, museum, pro, coop,* and *info.*

- *An opinionated speculation,* especially that found in chat rooms. Surely you know not to cite somebody with an anonymous username. The Internet discussion groups are best avoided during your research, even though some have the suffixes *humanities, sci,* or *soc* to designate discussions of literature, music, science issues, and social problems.

- *An overtly liberal or conservative position,* unless your goal is to display the extremity of debate on an issue. Inform your audience by lines such as: *Jason Marshall, spokesman for the Conservative Coalition in Alabama, has argued for a Supreme Court reversal on women's abortion rights.* Such a citation places the source in its correct context.

Let us now read a passage that exposes the split between conservatives and liberals, and then see how one student positions the source for the reader. In an article for the *New York Times,* one journalist confronts the Christian conservatives who complained about a course of study at the University of North Carolina. Here are his opening paragraphs:

Cuckoo in Carolina

Thomas L. Friedman

The ruckus being raised by conservative Christians over the University of North Carolina's decision to ask incoming students to read a book about the Koran—to stimulate a campus debate—surely has to be one of the most embarrassing moments for America since Sept. 11.

Why? Because it exhibits such profound lack of understanding of what America is about, and it exhibits such a chilling mimicry of what the most repressive Arab Muslim states are about. Ask yourself this question: What would Osama bin Laden do if he found out that the University of Riyadh had asked incoming freshmen to read the New and Old Testaments?

He would do exactly what the book-burning opponents of this U.N.C. directive are doing right now—try to shut it down, only bin Laden wouldn't bother with the courts. It's against the law to build a church or synagogue or Buddhist temple or Hindu shrine in public in Saudi Arabia. Is that what we're trying to mimic?

As a recent letter to the *Times* observed, the problem with the world today is not that American students are being asked to read the Koran, it is that students in Saudi Arabia and many other Muslim lands are still not being asked to read the sacred texts of other civilizations—let alone the foundational texts of American democracy, like the Bill of Rights, the Constitution or the Federalist Papers.

A student introduced a quotation from Friedman by putting it into the context of the dispute:

The University of North Carolina is under attack by conservative Christians for asking students to read the Koran as a vehicle for stimulating debate across the campus. Thomas Friedman, in an article in the *New York Times,* takes a liberal stance that attacks the conservative complaint as "one of the most embarrassing moments for America since Sept. 11." He adds:

> Why? Because it exhibits such profound lack of understanding of what America is about, and it exhibits such a chilling mimicry of what the most repressive Arab Muslim states are about. Ask yourself this question: What would Osama bin Laden do if he found out that the University of Riyadh had asked incoming freshmen to read the New and Old Testaments?

Friedman confronts the conservatives to make a valid point. America is about freedom; it allows debate and expressions of protest. A few years ago a girl basketball player turned her back to the flag before games. She was expressing a political protest in public, and some people foolishly condemned her for it. Friedman therefore raises an important point for us: we must protect our rights, whether it's reading the Koran, speaking against the majority opinion, marching for a cause with banner held high, or standing with our backs to the flag. Above all, we must *never* punish anybody just because they take a different point of view on a subject.

By establishing the context of the argument, this writer helps the reader understand the points of contention. More importantly, she extends the topic to embrace the American concept of freedom. Along the way, she provides an effective and informative citation and places the longer quotation in a block without quotations marks, as is appropriate (see page 208).

EXERCISE 7.1
EXPLAINING THE SPECIAL INTEREST OR BIAS OF A SOURCE

Examine the following two passages. Remember, most writers have an agenda, and they use their prose to promote that bias. Your task is twofold. First, on a sheet of paper identify the passage that does the best job of identifying the sources and pinpointing any special bias that might affect the response of the reader. Second, explain in specific detail why the chosen passage is more effective in its citation and its use of quotation or paraphrase.

Example 1

Robert Woodson reminds us that libraries have changed in the past few years. He says, "You will now find rows of computer terminals networked with various printers. Gone are the old oak card catalogs. Instead you can find cases loaded with videos and DVDs. Perhaps an espresso counter occupies one corner." Woodson, of course, has a vested interest in libraries, having served for 23 years as editor of

Library Magazine. He continues, "More importantly, the librarian has changed." He then describes the new librarian, who is part of a group that is now diverse in gender, age, ethnicity, and personality. In addition, the new librarian is an information expert on Internet research and a technology wizard. Indeed, Woodson is right, the new librarian is the heart of the new library and can help you burn a CD, find ancient printed archives, or plug you into an electronic database. He or she can be your best resource, especially in time of need.

Example 2

Experts are warning us that our precious Florida peninsula is swollen with millions of newcomers every year, and we are entering a period of untold urban crime, crowded and crumbling schools, water shortages, pollution, and—worst of all—the rape of the environment. The wetlands are disappearing. Encroaching subdivisions and their accompanying strip malls and schools are pushing relentlessly into the Everglades and other natural reserves. One source said, "Unless Florida acts decisively in this first decade of the new century, Florida as we have known and loved it will be gone forever, lost under the trampling feet of humanity."

Honoring Property Rights

Trademarks and patents protect a person's invention, whether it is new software, a gadget for the kitchen, or a child's toy. In like manner, copyrights protect writers, composers, and other creative artists who produce stories, songs, or children's picture books.

WEB LINK
to Reading
7.2
http://www.
ablongman.com/
lester

That's good news for you if someday you create a chapbook of poetry and compose a song. You own the booklet and the song, and the copyright law protects you from theft. Other people who quote from your poems or song should give you recognition with a proper citation. If somebody wishes to publish the chapbook or make a CD of the song, they should seek your permission before they print the booklet or go into a recording studio. You may even receive royalty payments for a percentage of the sales.

The principle behind the copyright law is relatively simple. Copyright begins at the time a creative work is recorded in some tangible form—a written document, a drawing, a compact disc burned with your songs. It does not depend upon a legal registration with the Copyright Office in Washington, D.C., although published works are usually registered. Thus, a creation on paper, canvas, or floppy disc is intellectual property. For that reason, songwriters, cartoonists, fiction writers, and other artists guard their work and do not want it disseminated without credit and, in many cases, without compensation.

WEB LINK
to Chapter 7
Related Web
Destinations
http://www.
ablongman.com/
lester

That said, however, the copyright law gives students like you the right to reproduce material in your papers without permission of the artists and without compensation to them. This doctrine of *fair use* is recorded in the U.S. Code, which says:

> The fair use of a copyrighted work . . . for purposes such as criticism, comment, news reporting, teaching (including multiple copies for classroom use), scholarship, or research is not an infringement of copyright.

However, you have the obligation to recognize sources with citations and proper quotation and paraphrase. Thus, as long as you borrow for educational purposes, such as quoting a source in a paper to be read by your instructor, you should not be concerned. However, if you decide to *publish* your report or article on a Web site, and you have reproduced substantial portions of another person's work, such as twelve cartoon strips of *Doonesbury,* then new considerations may come into play (see "Seeking Permission to Publish Material on Your Web Site," page 251).

EXERCISE 7.2
HONORING AN AUTHOR'S COPYRIGHT

Reproduced below is a passage from Edwin Dobb's article "What Wiped Out the Dinosaurs?" originally published in *Discover* (June 2002), from which three students have drawn ideas on the destruction of the early forms of life, creatures that may have lived a tranquil life but died a violent one. Your task is (1) name which student passage or passages fairly credit the author's work, and (2) explain why.

Original

All that changed drastically and violently 64.5 million years ago when a giant asteroid slammed into the planet north of the Yucatan Peninsula, apparently creating a worldwide pall of dust, ash, and debris. During the next three to six months—some have postulated an aftermath that lasted up to a year—of darkness, freezing cold, and perpetual acid rain, a catastrophic die-out occurred, affecting both marine and terrestrial organisms. Among the many casualties were dinosaurs.

Student Passage 1

The dinosaurs were probably wiped out by the fallout from a giant asteroid that crashed into the earth 65.5 years ago near the Yucatan Peninsula. It affected both marine and terrestrial organisms.

Student Passage 2

One theory, mentioned by expert Edwin Dobb of *Discover Magazine,* is that the dinosaurs were destroyed 64.5 millions ago when a giant asteroid slammed into the planet north of the Yucatan Peninsula, causing a pall of dust, ash, and debris to choke the life out of the terrestrial beings.

Student Passage 3

One theory on the death of the dinosaurs goes back 64.5 million years ago. Edwin Dobb, writing for *Discover Magazine,* explains that a huge asteroid crashed with horrible consequences near the Yucatan Peninsula. Dobb says the asteroid created "a worldwide pall of dust, ash, and debris." The sun was blocked, the air became icy, and acid rain pelted the surface to cause "a catastrophic die-out" that killed many species, perhaps even the dinosaurs.

Avoiding Plagiarism

We have discussed in detail the benefit of proper citations for your sources and the reward of carefully crafted paraphrases and properly marked quotations. Nevertheless, let's look carefully at the conventions your instructors will want you to follow.

You will commit plagiarism if you offer the words or ideas of another person as your own.

Some dishonest students will knowingly copy whole passages into their work without documentation. Others will buy an entire research paper from an Internet source or borrow one from a friend. Unacknowledged use of another person's sentences, phrases, and special terminology is plagiarism, so *provide a citation and employ quotation marks!* Also, unacknowledged use of another person's ideas, research, and special approaches is plagiarism, so *write careful paraphrases!*

G U I D E L I N E S

Documenting Your Sources

- *Citation.* Let a reader know when you begin borrowing from a source by introducing the quotation or paraphrase with the name of the authority.
- *Quotation marks and indented blocks.* Enclose within quotation marks all quoted key words, phrases, or sentences. Long quotations should be set as indented blocks without quotation marks. See Chapter 6.
- *Paraphrase.* Provide a citation to a paraphrase just as you do for quoted matter. Make certain that paraphrased material has been rewritten into your own style and language. The simple rearrangement of words or sentence patterns is unacceptable. See Chapter 5.
- *Parenthetical citations and notes.* In a scholarly research paper that must conform to one of the academic models of documentation (MLA, CMS, or APA), provide specific in-text documentation for each borrowed item according to the rules of the discipline. These standards are discussed briefly below and in depth in Chapters 10–12. The CBE style is explained in Appendix B.

(continues)

(continued from previous page)

- *Works Cited or References Sections.* For scholarly research papers, provide a bibliography entry at the end of the paper for every source cited, conforming to MLA, CMS, APA or CBE standards.

TIP   *Adapting to Changes in Academic Standards*

You should learn to adapt to changes in academic standards, which differ from field to field; that is, literary papers conform to the style set by the Modern Language Association, whereas papers in the social sciences conform to the style established by the American Psychological Association. You will find that standards set by your instructors will shift considerably as you move from class to class and from discipline to discipline. Thus, this text carefully walks you through the differences. These styles are discussed below (see pages 242–246) and in detail in Chapters 10–12.

Understanding the Common Knowledge Exceptions

WEB LINK to Reading 7.3
http://www. ablongman.com/ lester

Common knowledge items need no citation. These exceptions exist because you and your readers will share some knowledge on a subject—for example, that Michael Jordan raised the standard for professional basketball players, Thomas Jefferson designed his home in Virginia and named it Monticello, Illinois is known as the "Land of Lincoln," the Mall in Washington, D.C., has the Lincoln Memorial at one end and the U.S. Capitol Building at the other end. Information of this sort requires *no* in-text citation because almost all readers will know these facts.

Nevertheless, it's best to put a personal limit on the extent of your knowledge: *Did you know this information before you began your research?* For example, many readers probably know about Henry Winkler and his leading role as "Fonzie" on the sitcom *Happy Days*. They would also know that Ronnie Howard was a co-star with Winkler and later became a director of several successful movies. With that in mind, read the following passage to determine if everything not given a citation is common knowledge:

Henry Winkler burst into fame as a co-star with Ronnie Howard on the sitcom *Happy Days*. While portraying "Fonzie," Winkler established his thumbs up tribute to the good life in small-town America. Recently, in a *Newsweek Magazine* column, Winkler reflected on his influence:

I hear a lot of stories along the lines of this one: a spastic child in a hospital, a boy who could not move his hands, learned to lift his thumbs in the air so he could imitate Fonzie's most famous gesture. He found strength enough in what I did on the TV screen to make himself a more complete person, to be able to begin to use his own body. I find that very moving. And very scary.

Winkler, who studied acting at Emerson College and the Yale School of Drama, personifies Lord Byron's image, "I awoke one morning to find myself famous."

WEB LINK
to Exercise
7.2
http://www.
ablongman.com/
lester

Did you catch it? The passage was going so well until the last sentence! Where did the student writer learn about Winkler's training as an actor? Also, where did the student find the quotation from Lord Byron? The last sentence of the passage needs this sort of revision:

Newsweek notes that Winkler was no overnight surprise before his role as Fonzie. He studied acting at Emerson College and the Yale School of Drama, worked in repertory theater, and appeared in the film *The Lords of Flatbush*. In the *Newsweek* article, Winkler compares himself to Lord Byron by adopting Byron's line, "I awoke to find myself famous."

T I P   *Spotting Borrowed Material*

Your instructors know about the paper mill Web sites. They know how easily you can cut and paste information from the Web into your text file. They understand your writing style and can spot almost instantly the intrusion of borrowed material. On that note, look at Exercise 6.10 on pages 214–215 and notice how quickly you can spot the borrowed material in one student's passage.

Remember this test: Did I know this information before I began writing the paper? For example, in an art history class, where you have been studying the master artists for many weeks, you will acquire common knowledge with your peers. Thus, you need not cite a source for basic information as displayed in this passage:

The museums of Florence, Italy, feature an amazing array of artistic masterpieces. Michelangelo's magnificent sculpture *David* attracts millions of visitors to Florence's Academy of Art. Botticelli's painting *The Birth of Venus* decorates the walls of the Uffizi Gallery; nearby at the Pitti Palace, art lovers can see Raphael's painting of John the Baptist. Indeed, Florence is home to many Renaissance masterpieces.

This basic information learned over a semester need not be cited. However, as you gather more specific information about the painters who are the subject of your report, citations become mandatory because the information goes beyond common knowledge:

Louder explains how Botticelli's *The Birth of Venus* dared to render the image of the Virgin Mary in the mythic guise of the Greek goddess of love, showing clearly "the attempts by the Renaissance artists to merge mythic Greek and Roman themes with Christianity."

GUIDELINES

Common Knowledge

- If in doubt, cite the source. If you are writing with a book or article in front of you, you will likely borrow ideas from it. Why not gain credit for your research while being correct in your citations?

- Do not document the source if an informed person would and should know this information, given the context of both writer and audience. Thus, do not document a source for basic information that your peers know as well as you, such as basic facts in a history class for a history paper, or the fundamental descriptions for forms of mental illness for a paper in a psychology class. That is, a common knowledge will develop within an intellectual group.

- Do not document information that has become general knowledge by being reported repeatedly in many different sources (e.g., Michael Jordan holds several NBA scoring records).

- If you are writing a passage today based on something you read the day before, go search it out and cite it properly. Ideas gathered over the past few days of research are not common knowledge.

EXERCISE 7.3

IDENTIFYING PASSAGES THAT REQUIRE CITATION

Shown below are ten items about Henry Winkler, Ronnie Howard, and the television show *Happy Days.* Read each one and circle the number for those statements that need a citation.

1. Henry Winkler played the role of Fonzie, who was a counterpart to the clean-cut role of Ronnie Howard as Richie Cunningham.

2. A sense of focus is mandatory to succeed as an actor, and I suspect also to succeed at anything. It releases the imagination, which heightens your perception of what you're doing, on or off the screen. It makes me, I'd like to think, a little more humane, and it makes Fonzie more human, and ultimately more magnetic.

3. Winkler stands 5 feet 6 $1/2$ inches tall.

4. Winkler studied acting at Emerson College and the Yale School of Drama.

5. Winkler appeared in repertory theater and in the film *The Lords of Flatbush* before starring in *Happy Days.*

6. *Happy Days* currently airs on TVLand every day at 4:00 P.M., 8:30 P.M., and 1:30 A.M.

7. Former child star Ron Howard won the Academy Award as best director for his work on *A Beautiful Mind,* an exploration of the fine line between genius and

insanity. The film, based on Sylvia Nasar's 1998 book about Nobel Prize–winning mathematician John Nash and his lifelong struggle with schizophrenia, earned Howard his first Oscar nomination. The movie, for which Howard shares producer credits, also won best picture.

8. A longtime Hollywood favorite who has built a nice guy reputation in an industry known for bad boys, Howard's victory with *A Beautiful Mind* marks a new high for a director many critics felt was overlooked when he did not score an Oscar nomination for *Apollo 13* in 1995.

9. Howard's filmmaking credits include *Cocoon, Backdraft, Apollo 13,* and *Dr. Seuss's How the Grinch Stole Christmas.*

10. *Happy Days* changed dramatically from the series that premiered on January 15, 1974. Originally it was the story of two high school kids, Richie Cunningham and his pal Warren "Potsie" Weber, at Jefferson High in Milwaukee, Wisconsin. Howard Cunningham, Richie's father, ran a hardware store while Chuck was Richie's college-bound older brother and Joanie his 12-year-old kid sister. Richie and most of his friends hung out at Arnold's Drive-In, a malt shop near the school. Richie was supposed to be the innocent teenager and Potsie his more worldly pal. The producers decided to add a greasy-haired motorcycle kid, Arthur "Fonzie" Fonzarelli, to give the show a bit of an edge. That was the move that would soon make the show a hit with viewers. Instead of the fairly hackneyed Richie-Potsie relationship, the show came to center on the relationship between the "cool" dropout Fonzie, and the "straight" kids represented by Richie Cunningham. Henry Winkler made the character of Fonzie three-dimensional, vulnerable as well as hip. As Fonzie's popularity spread (his thumbs-up gesture, "aaayyh!" and leather jacket would soon become trademarks), the show became a bigger and bigger hit.

Using Scholarly Citations

WEB LINK
to Chapter 7
Related Web
Destinations
http://www.
ablongman.com/
lester

Writing a scholarly paper, as opposed to a personal essay, transports your writing to another level, one that requires precise documentation of each source, even down to the page number for every quotation. A casual introduction of the speaker and quotation marks around words will not suffice in a research paper. Instead, you will need to follow the dictates of one of several models that set the standards for scholars in their respective disciplines. The three most frequently used systems are explained briefly below and in greater detail in Chapters 10–12.

Modern Language Association (MLA) Style

First, let's look at three citations in MLA style and then we will consider the distinguishing features of this style.

With a touch of humor, Bruce Cameron writes, "One of the most endearing traits of children is their utter trust that their parents will provide them with all of life's necessities, meaning food, shelter, and a weekend at a theme park" (591).

"While classroom time alone doesn't produce a well-educated child," says Ellen Goodman, "learning takes time and more learning takes more time." She adds, "The long summers of forgetting take a toll" (584).

Michael Barrett, a state senator in Massachusetts, wants to extend the state's school calendar from 180 days to 220 days. He argues that American children, when compared with children in Asia and Europe, do poorly in their school work, and they do less of it as well (Barrett 585–586).

The above examples show several distinguishing characteristics of MLA style:

- Use the full name of the author on first mention and last name thereafter.
- Use the present tense to introduce quotations and paraphrases.
- Identify a specific page or pages within parentheses but do not use *p.* or *pp.*
- Even paraphrases require a page citation.

A Works Cited entry should provide full publication information for each source so that other scholars can investigate it if they so desire:

Goodman, Ellen. "U.S. Kids Need More School Time." Steps to Writing Well. Ed.
   Jean Wyrick. New York: Thompson Learning, 2002: 583-84.

To avoid plagiarism in a scholarly paper that you write in MLA style, you must conform to these standards. Chapter 10 will explain the standards more fully.

The Chicago Manual of Style (CMS style)

Let us look again at the three examples, this time written in the CMS documentation style that uses notes.

With a touch of humor, Bruce Cameron writes, "One of the most endearing traits of children is their utter trust that their parents will provide them with all of life's necessities, meaning food, shelter, and a weekend at a theme park."[1]

"While classroom time alone doesn't produce a well-educated child," says Ellen Goodman, "learning takes time and more learning takes more time." She adds, "The long summers of forgetting take a toll."[2]

Michael Barrett, a state senator in Massachusetts, wants to extend the state's school calendar from 180 days to 220 days.[3] He argues that American children, when compared with children in Asia and Europe, do poorly in their schoolwork, and they do less of it as well.[4]

The above examples show several distinguishing characteristics of CMS note style:

- Use the full name of the author on first mention and last name thereafter.
- Use the present tense to introduce quotations and paraphrases.
- Identify a source citation with a superscript numeral that matches a footnote or endnote.
- Even paraphrases require a superscript numeral.

A footnote or endnote will provide full publication information to the source so that other scholars can investigate it if they so desire:

1. Ellen Goodman, "U.S. Kids Need More School Time," in *Steps to Writing Well,* ed. Jean Wyrick (New York: Thompson Learning, 2002), 583–84.

To avoid plagiarism in a scholarly paper that you write in CMS note style, you must conform to these standards. Chapter 11 will explain the standards more fully.

American Psychological Association (APA) Style

Again, let's look at the three citations, this time in APA style.

With a touch of humor, Cameron (1999) has written, "One of the most endearing traits of children is their utter trust that their parents will provide them with all of life's necessities, meaning food, shelter, and a weekend at a theme park" (p. 591).

"While classroom time alone doesn't produce a well-educated child," said Goodman (1990, p. 584), "learning takes time and more learning takes more time." She added, "The long summers of forgetting take a toll."

Barrett (1989) wanted to extend the state's school calendar from 180 days to 220 days. A state senator of Massachusetts, he argued that American children, when compared with children in Asia and Europe, do poorly in their school work, and they do less of it as well.

The above examples show several distinguishing characteristics:

- Use only the last name of the author.
- Use the past tense or the present perfect tense to introduce quotations and paraphrases.
- Provide a page number or numbers within parentheses for each quotation, but not for a paraphrase.
- Use *p.* with the page number and *pp.* for more than one page.

A References section at the end of the paper should provide full publication information for each source so that other scholars can investigate it if they so desire:

> Goodman, E. (2002). U.S. kids need more school time. In J. Wyrick (Ed.), *Steps to writing well* (pp. 583–584). New York: Thompson Learning.

To avoid plagiarism in a scholarly paper that you write in APA style, you must conform to these standards. Chapter 12 will explain the standards more fully.

WEB LINK
to Exercise
7.3
http://www.
ablongman.com/
lester

GUIDELINES

When to Cite a Source

A source citation is required for any of the following material. Examples are shown in MLA Style.

1. An original idea derived from a source, whether quoted or paraphrased. This next sentence requires an in-text citation and quotation marks around a key phrase.

   > Genetic engineering, by which a child's body shape and intellectual ability are predetermined, raises for one source "memories of Nazi attempts in eugenics" (Riddell 19).

2. Your summary of original ideas by a source.

   > Genetic engineering has been described as the rearrangement of the genetic structure in animals or in plants, which is a technique that takes a section of DNA and reattaches it to another section (Rosenthal 19–20).

3. Factual information that is not common knowledge.

   > Robert Madigan explains that genetic engineering has its risks: a nonpathogenic organism might be converted into a pathogenic one or an undesirable trait might develop as a result of a mistake (51).

(continues on next page)

(continued from previous page)

4. Any exact wording copied from a source.

> Kenneth Woodward asserts that genetic engineering is "a high stakes moral gamble that involves billions of dollars and affects the future" (68).

EXERCISE 7.4

BLENDING PARAPHRASE AND QUOTATION INTO YOUR OWN PARAGRAPH

An essay by Nanci Hellmich follows. Read it carefully, digest its essential message, and look for a key quotation or two that captures the central ideas in well-worded sentences.

Caught in the Catty Corner
Nanci Hellmich

Katy Montague's seventh-grade year was a girl's worst nightmare.

She was excluded from parties, lunch table groups, conversations and cliques. She was teased and taunted about her looks and her glasses. She was treated this way by "the meanest people I ever met, and they were all girls," says Montague, of St. Louis.

"There was a lot of plotting and scheming behind people's backs. It was horrible. I don't remember anything I learned that year."

But there was a silver lining: She met her best friend during that trying time. "We do almost everything together. She's always there for me," says Montague, now 17.

Montague's experience mirrors that of millions of girls across the country as they make their way through the often painful passage of adolescence. Out of this pain often comes strength of character and genuine friendships, but while it's happening, a girl's life can be total misery. Now, some behavior experts are doing research to try to understand this phenomenon. And while they realize they may not be able to—and perhaps shouldn't—totally change it, there may be ways to help girls get through it with fewer scars.

Experts use the term "relational aggression" to describe the cattiness, meanness and nastiness that happens between some people but especially among girls.

Girls may gossip, spread malicious rumors, write nasty e-mails, give the silent treatment, exclude people from social events, betray secrets or snicker about people's clothes and mannerisms behind their backs. They may tell a girl that they're not going to be friends with her unless she does what they want.

"We all get angry. We all have the need to control others and our environment, and boys and girls have tendencies to do those things in different ways," says Nicki Crick, a professor of child development at the University of Minnesota–Minneapolis. She has studied relational aggression in thousands of people, from preschoolers to adults.

Boys and girls are equally capable of being kind or unkind, she says. "But where boys might use physical intimidation, girls will say, 'I won't be your friend anymore,' or 'I'm not going to talk to you.'"

Several researchers, including Crick, are trying to figure out why this happens so frequently, especially among girls from third grade to seniors in high school, when they really value close friendships.

This spring, several books are coming out to help parents understand the phenomenon, including *The Secret Lives of Girls; The Friendship Factor: Trust Me, Mom — Everyone Else Is Going!; Queen Bees & Wannabes: Odd Girl Out.*

Psychologists believe there are several explanations for some of this behavior. One may be that girls are under enormous pressure to be nice and sweet. Unlike boys, girls have few opportunities to openly express their aggression or anger, so they strike out at other girls in covert ways, says Sharon Lamb, author of *The Secret Lives of Girls* and a psychology professor at Saint Michael's College in Colchester, Vt.

Some girls today work out their aggression in sports, but even there they can't be as aggressive as boys without risking criticism, she says.

And teen girls don't dare express their anger or aggression at boys their own age because the guys wield too much power, Lamb says. "Boys don't have a problem retaliating. They might spread a rumor that the girl's a slut."

Plus, boys are becoming more important to girls during adolescence. Girls evaluate each other by boys' standards, Lamb says. That makes them turn against each other and compete for boys' attention. So for these reasons, girls go after other girls, "It's like the weak fighting the weak."

They often tell each other their secrets, and those secrets can be used against them, Lamb says. Boys keep their secrets close to their chest.

Girls value relationships very highly, and when they want to hurt someone, they do it in a way that is most hurtful, says Nicole Werner, a researcher at the University of Idaho in Moscow.

Rachel Simmons, who interviewed 300 kids for her book, *Odd Girl Out,* says many girls say they'd rather be hit or screamed at than cut out of a clique with no warning or have a rumor started about them.

Friendships Come and Go

There are a couple of types of girls who frequently use relational aggression. One is a socially incompetent child who doesn't get along with her peers.

Another is the "Queen Bee," a nickname for the leader of cliques, Crick says. "If you ask girls if they like this person, they say, 'No, I hate her.'"

These are girls who are popular because they are dominant. They have looks, possessions and status, says Kenneth Rubin, author of *The Friendship Factor* with Andrea Thompson.

Queen Bees have friends because others would rather have them on their side than have them against them, he says. But their friends don't feel secure, and their friendships come and go. On the other hand, some girls are popular and have many friends because they are really decent people, he says. These are the people other kids truly want to be friends with.

Montague, a member of *USA Today*'s Teen Panel, says the Queen Bees consider themselves above other people and spread gossip and ruin reputations.

"I'm definitely afraid if I say the wrong thing with them, it'll get around," she says.

But there are other girls who are really involved in the community and school, and they really try to reach out and give back, she says. "They are popular because everyone knows them, and they know them for good reasons."

Children Can Figure It Out

As director of the Laboratory for Child and Family Relationships at the University of Maryland. Rubin has examined the importance of the friendships for hundreds of children as they make the stressful transition from elementary school to middle school.

In their friendships, children figure out how to get along with people, how to initiate friendships, how to walk away from relationships, and how to maintain the ones that are enjoyable and valuable, he says.

They learn about trust, intimacy and security. They learn they can tell their friends about things they wouldn't want anyone else to know, which is called intimate disclosure, Rubin says. They learn how they can make others feel good and secure, and they learn how others can make them feel good and secure, he says.

"Friendship is about having fun, enjoying each other. It's about helping, sharing and being kind. It's through friendship that you can learn to be decent." Rubin says. People who are good friends as kids become good romantic partners and good friends as adults, he says.

Montague says friends are crucial. "They are someone you can go to when you have a crush on a boy, and there is no one else you can tell. If you're having a bad day with your parents or at school, there is someone you can lean on."

Because friends are so important, it makes having trouble with them even more traumatic, experts say.

Lamb believes girls would have less relational aggression with other girls if they learned to be more straightforward and honest about their feelings. "In all relationships, if you get angry with people, you talk it out," she says.

Parents Can Help

She recommends that parents teach their girls how to handle confrontation with dignity. They need to teach them to stand up against injustice for other people and for themselves.

Parents can help by giving their daughter the words to express her feelings. For example, if their daughter is teased about her clothes, the parents might suggest she say, "What you are doing is hurtful, and there is no good reason to treat me this way because clothes really don't matter."

Even if the daughter doesn't say the words to her tormenter, she can rehearse them in her mind and find comfort in them, Lamb says.

Parents also need to be good listeners and guide their children without telling them what to do, Rubin says. Parents should be a big ear, not a commandant, he says.

For example, if a girl says she wants to be friends with a girl who is shunning her, then the parent might ask: "Why do you want to be friends with her? What would you get out of the relationship? Is there anybody else in school whom you might be interested in being friends with?"

Clinical psychologist Roni Cohen-Sandler, author of *Trust Me, Mom—Everyone Else is Going!*, says kids can learn lifelong lessons in these experiences.

They need to know there is meanness in the world, and they need to figure out how they are going to deal with it, she says. This prepares them for jobs where they'll confront people who are "nice and collaborative, and people who are mean and jockey for power."

When Montague was suffering through friendship traumas, her parents were always there for her and willing to listen, she says. One of the most valuable lessons she has learned from her experiences is the hurtfulness of gossiping and meanness. "I catch myself when I want to say something mean, and I stop because I know what it feels like to be on the other side."

Assignment: After reading Hellmich's essay, write a full paragraph that includes a combination of these ingredients:

1. A thesis sentence for your paragraph to express your personal commentary on the issues and problems associated with the passage of adolescence.

2. A one-sentence summary that digests the essential message of Hellmich's article.

3. A direct quotation from the article, one that is effective in its analysis of the problem.

4. Appropriate in-text citations in MLA style to acknowledge the source.

EXERCISE 7.5

REVIEWING THE USE OF SOURCES IN ACADEMIC WRITING

Examine the following three student passages. Each one serves as the opening paragraph to an essay. Your task is twofold. First, identify the scholarly style used—MLA, APA, or CMS. Second, grade the passage (good – fair – poor) on its use of sources, and explain your rating.

Opening 1

Kimberly Sipsy

English Composition 1020

Organ Donation: A Vitally Important Matter

Technology has aided medicine by advancing it to the point of successful organ transplants. Unfortunately, many of those waiting will never receive a transplant due to a shortage of organ donors. According to DePalma and Townsend (2002), there were 39,082 patients on the national waiting list for organ transplantation, but one source has added a tragic note by saying "about one-third of the patients who are on the list for heart, liver, and lung transplants die while waiting because of a lack of available organs" (LaMaster, 2002, p. 8). It is estimated that "each year at least 5,000 human organs deemed medically suitable for transplantation are not donated" (DePalma and Townsend, 2002, p. 3). The deaths of patients awaiting transplants have become hard to accept because of the success rate of transplants. Organ transplantation is a remarkable medical success story, and many more people could be given the gift of a second chance at life if more people would become donors.

Opening 2

Michael Hook

English 1020

The Exploration of Natural Beauty in Three Poems by John Keats

What is beauty? Where do its boundaries lie? Of what does beauty consist? In an age of standards and qualifications these and other related questions remain partially or completely unanswered even today. Beauty, a concept often used and rarely fully understood, stands as one of the most enigmatic and subjective ideas known. It is a thing so hopelessly abstract that one may ask 1,000 people what is beautiful and receive many different replies.

One artist is particular, Romantic poet John Keats, delves deeply into the mystery. Keats was especially interested in the concept of beauty, both in the natural and in the deeper, more metaphysical sense.[1] Keats had the talent of exploring the themes of beauty in an intellectual fashion, while simultaneously creating something suffused with its own distinct beauty through his masterful manipulation of imagery and his attention to detail.[2] Keats's work is "heady and sensual,"[3] providing the reader with a complete sensory experience while providing insight into the author's own imagination and philosophy.

Example Opening #3

Michael Stancil

October 1998

Isolation of the Lyme Disease Spirochete

from Small Mammals at Land between the Lake Natural Area

Lyme disease is an arthropod-borne zoonosis caused by the spirochete *Borrelia burgdorferi* and is transmitted by various ixodid ticks (Burgdorfer et al., 1993; Burgdorfer, 1994; Johnson et al., 1994). Various mammals and birds have been implicated as reservoir hosts (Anderson et al., 1993, 1997a, 1996b). However, *Peromyuscus leucopus* (the white-footed mouse) appears to be one of the most important hosts in maintaining the bacterium in nature (Levine et al., 1995). In endemic areas of the United States, particularly the New England region, evidence suggests that there may be a natural transmission cycle between the tick *Ixodes dammini* and the white-footed mouse (Anderson et al., 1993; Bosler et al., 1993; Levine et al., 1995).

Seeking Permission to Publish Material on Your Web Site

If you decide to place your papers on the Web, you are, in effect, publishing to everybody all over the world. If your paper includes extensive use of borrowed images, text, music, or artwork, you may need permission to reproduce those materials on the Web. The courts are still refining the law, but the borrowing cannot affect the market value of the original work and you cannot misrepresent it in any manner. So what represents usage that might require permission?

- The reproduction in your paper of twelve Doonesbury cartoons
- The color reproduction of five paintings by Thomas Kinkade
- The use of six cartoons from the *New Yorker*
- The reprinting in your report of all song lyrics in Michael Jackson's *Invincible* album

A significant borrowing like one of the above probably requires permission.

GUIDELINES

Publishing Your Paper on the Web

- Seek permission for reproducing significant portions of copyrighted material within your Web article. Most owners will grant free permission to students. The problem is tracking down the copyright holder.

- If you make the attempt to get permission and if your motive for using the material is *not for profit,* it's unlikely you will have any problem with the copyright owner. Your use of the image or text must not cause the owner financial harm.

- You may publish without permission works that are in the public domain, such as a section of Hawthorne's *The Scarlet Letter* or a speech by the president from the White House.

- Document any and all sources that you feature on your Web site.

- You may provide hypertext links to other sites. Right now the Internet rules on access are being freely interpreted, but at some time we may need permission to provide hypertext links to other sites.

- Be prepared for other persons to visit your Web site and even borrow from it. Decide beforehand how you will handle requests for use of your work, especially if your site includes your creative efforts in poetry, art, music, or graphic design.

EXERCISE 7.6

ANALYZING AN ESSAY'S USE OF REFERENCE CITATIONS

WEB LINK to Reading 7.4
http://www. ablongman.com/ lester

The article by Laura Madson and Robert M. Hessling that follows appeared in a professional journal and therefore cites its sources with the utmost accuracy. Using APA style, the writers report on their original, investigative research. They first provide a quick review of the literature on the topic. They then explain their hypothesis in paragraph two. They next set out their method for conducting the study, followed by the results. The writers finish with a discussion of their findings. They complete their article with a list of references used in the study. This form and order provide the classic model for scientific reports. Read the article and add marginal notes to identify the writers' in-text citations that honor their sources.

Readers' Perceptions of Four Alternatives to Masculine Generic Pronouns
Laura Madson and Robert M. Hessling

Style guides suggest a number of ways to avoid using masculine pronouns in reference to mixed-gender groups: (a) using paired pronouns such as "he or she" (American Psychological Association, 1994; Miller & Swift, 1988; Schwartz, 1995), (b) alternating between masculine and feminine pronouns (Addison Wesley Longman, 1998; Frank & Treichler, 1989), or (c) using the pronoun "they" in singular contexts (American Heritage Dictionary, 1992; Chicago Manual of Style,

1993). Unfortunately, some of those strategies have disadvantages that may not be intuitively obvious. For example, Madson and Hessling (1999) found that readers overestimated the frequency of feminine pronouns in alternating text, perceiving it to be lower in overall quality and more biased in favor of women in comparison with text containing the paired pronouns "he or she."

We designed the present study to replicate and extend those findings (Madson & Hessling, 1999) by using different stimulus material and additional conditions. Specifically, we wanted to determine (a) whether readers would perceive the singular "they" as a good alternative to generic masculine pronouns and (b) whether readers would perceive the paired pronouns "she or he" as essentially equivalent to "he or she."

A total of 231 introductory psychology students (113 men, 118 women; 43% Hispanic, 39% Caucasian; M age = 19 years, SD = 2.66) participated in partial ful-fillment of a course requirement. The participants read one of four versions of an essay describing techniques for improving study skills. Two versions contained paired pronouns beginning with the masculine pronoun (i.e., "he or she") or with the feminine pronoun (i.e., "she or he"). The third version contained the plural pronoun "they," and the fourth alternated between masculine and feminine pro-nouns (i.e., "he" in one paragraph, "she" in the next). Dependent variables were the perceived frequency of masculine and feminine pronouns, perceived gender bias in the text, the perceived effectiveness of pronoun usage in eliminating gen-der bias, and the overall quality of the passage.

The participants estimated pronoun frequency on a Likert-type scale (1 = never 5 = all the time) and on a percentage scale—that is, they estimated what per-centage of all the pronouns in the article were masculine or feminine. In the alter-nating condition, the readers indicated on both measures that feminine pronouns were used significantly more often than masculine pronouns, despite the fact that masculine and feminine pronouns actually occurred with equal frequency. For the Likert-type measure, mean scores were 2.43 and 1.67 (SDs = .98 and .99) for fem-inine and masculine pronouns, respectively; paired t(45) = 3.46, p = .001. For the percentage measure, Ms = 40% and 18% (SDs = 16% and 6%) for feminine and masculine pronouns, respectively; paired t(45) = 4.13, p [<] .001. Perceived fre-quency did not differ significantly in the other three conditions. With the forego-ing finding as an informal manipulation check, it appears that students attended to the pronouns used in the text and accurately perceived no difference in the fre-quency of masculine and feminine pronouns in the "he or she," "she or he," and "they" versions.

On a Likert-type scale (1 = not at all gender biased, 7 = very gender biased), the readers also rated the alternating text as more gender biased than the other three conditions. For the alternating text, "he or she," "she or he," and "they," Ms = 2.34 (SD = 1.05), .66 (SD = 1.20), 1.33 (SD = 1.99), and .57 (SD = 1.17), respec-tively; F(3, 160) = 10.71, p [less than] .001; Bonferroni post hoc contrast, p [less than] .05.

More specifically, the readers indicated on a Likert-type scale (1 = favored women, 7 = favored men) that the alternating text was biased in favor of women. For the alternating text, "he or she," "she or he," and "they," Ms = 2.34 (SD = 1.34),

3.12 (SD = .55), 2.86 (SD = .54), and 2.95 (SD = .55), respectively; $F(3, 161) =$ 6.98, p [less than] .001; Bonferroni post hoc contrast, p [less than] .05.

Furthermore, on a Likert-type scale (1 = very poor use of pronouns, 7 = very good use of pronouns), the readers rated the alternating text as least effective in eliminating gender bias through the use of pronouns. For the alternating text, "he or she," "she or he," and "they," Ms = 2.36 (SD = 2.03), 4.52 (SD = 1.52), 4.61 (SD = 1.38), and 4.55 (SD = 1.40), respectively; $F(3, 161) = 20.48$, p [less than] .001, Bonferroni post hoc contrast, p [less than] .001.

Interestingly, according to their ratings on a Likert-type scale (1 = very poor quality, 7 = very high quality), the readers thought that the "they" version was lowest in overall quality. For "they," alternating text, "he or she," and "she or he," Ms = 3.33 (SD = 1.58), 3.89 (SD = 1.20), 4.05 (SD = 1.17), and 4.03 (SD = 98), respectively; $F(3, 161) = 3.01$, p = .03; Student-Newman-Keuls post hoc contrast, p [less than] .05.

Text that alternates between masculine and feminine pronouns may not be a nonbiased alternative to generic masculine pronouns. Consistent with the results of Madson and Hessling (1999), the present readers overestimated the frequency of feminine pronouns in alternating text and perceived it to be biased in favor of women. In addition, the use of "they" in singular contexts may not be ideal because the readers perceived this strategy as low in overall quality. Interestingly, the readers' perceptions of paired pronouns did not differ depending on which pronoun appeared first in the pair (i.e., "he or she" vs. "she or he").

References

Addison Wesley Longman Higher Education Publishing Group. (1998). *Author's guide.* Reading, MA: Author.

American Heritage dictionary of the English language (3rd ed.). (1996). New York: Houghton Mifflin.

American Psychological Association. (1994). *Publication manual of the American Psychological Association* (4th ed.). Washington, DC: Author.

Chicago manual of style (14th ed.). (1993). Chicago: University of Chicago Press.

Frank, F. W., & Treichler, P. A. (1989). Guidelines for nonsexist usage. In F. W. Frank & P. A. Treichler (Eds.), *Language, gender, and professional writing: Theoretical approaches and guidelines for nonsexist usage* (pp. 137–280). New York: The Modern Language Association of America.

Madson, L., & Hessling, R. M. (1999). Does alternating between masculine and feminine pronouns eliminate perceived gender bias in text? *Sex Roles, 41,* 559–575.

Miller, C., & Swift, K. (1988). *The handbook of nonsexist writing.* New York: Harper & Row.

Schwartz, M., & Task Force on Bias-Free Language of the Association of American University Presses. (1995). Guidelines for bias-free writing (pp. 8–29). Bloomington: Indiana University Press.

EXERCISE 7.7

READING YOUR COLLEGE BULLETIN AND STUDENT HANDBOOK

Examine your college bulletin and the student handbook. Do those publications say any-thing about plagiarism? If so, write a sentence or two that describes the school's posi-tion on plagiarism. Do the publications address the matter of copyright protection? If so, write a sentence or two that describes the school's position on copyright protection.

Chapter Review

WEB LINK
to Chapter 7
Related Web
Destinations
http://www.
ablongman.com/
lester

Chapter 7 has emphasized the value of bringing sources into your papers and has carefully explained how displaying the sources properly will display your integrity as a writer. By providing a clear citation to the source and handling the mechanics of quo-tation and paraphrase, you will demonstrate your reading and research abilities, espe-cially your talent for delving into works for the very best quotations and paraphrases. As your readers see you weaving and blending the sources, they will more likely accept your theories, which you will have built on solid evidence, not whimsy or personal opinion. In addition, you will be sharing the literature on a topic, enabling the read-ers to enjoy a collection of opinions. Ultimately, composing from sources in an ethi-cal manner gives your paper authority and brings strength to your conclusions.

At the same time, this chapter insists that you conform to the basic conventions of scholarship. You must incorporate the sources with precision, show the material in its proper context, and honor the property rights of others, especially if you publish your papers on the Web. Avoiding plagiarism is a must, but if you have accomplished the positive actions described in the paragraph above, plagiarism should not be a fac-tor in your writing. At the same time, you will need to keep abreast of the latest guide-lines regarding technology and Internet access.

Finally, the chapter reminds you that research papers demand additional citation beyond that required in personal essays and general articles. When assigned a research paper, you must determine quickly the style required by your instructor, whether MLA, CMS, or APA style. Each makes different demands, and because your courses carry you across the campus from discipline to discipline, you need to know all three forms.

Chapter 7 Assignment:
Practicing Academic Integrity

Shown below are several annotated bibliographies to articles commenting on a relatively new type of self-mutilation. This problem has been dramatized by the situ-ation of Elizabeth Franas, a "cutter" who uses everything from staples, razor blades, her fingernails, and broken glass to draw blood from her left arm and left hip. She has said, "We [cutters] don't know how to verbalize our pain, so we write it on our bod-ies." She added, "I bleed it out instead of talking it out." Franas was featured in an Associated Press article by Martha Irvine in 2002.

Your assignment: Using the information above on Franas, and drawing citations from at least three of the summaries below, draft an introduction to a hypothetical research paper on "cutters." Let your introduction primarily be an introduction to the literature on the subject, and it may be more than one paragraph in length. Use the APA style for your in-text citations. You do not need to write a complete paper nor prepare a bibliography for this assignment.

9809120 JA
Self-mutilation in clinical and general population samples: prevalence, correlates, and functions
Of almost 1000 randomly selected, stratified US adults, the prevalence of self-injury in the general population, male and female, was 4%, and was 21% in a psychiatric clinic group. There was a strong correlation with childhood sexual or physical abuse. The practice reportedly reduced anger at self and others, fear, emptiness, hurt, loneliness and sadness.
1998 Am J Orthopsychiatry 68;4:609–20
Briere, J. and Gil, E.

9612442 RT
The coming of age of self-mutilation
Review of diagnosis, symptoms, etiology and treatment. Self-mutilation refers to the "deliberate, direct destruction or alteration of body tissue without conscious suicidal intent", and is a "self-help effort providing rapid but temporary relief from feelings of depersonalization, guilt, rejection, boredom, hallucinations, sexual preoccupations, and chaotic thoughts."
1998 J Nerv Ment Dis 186;5:259–68
Favazza, A. R.

9172240 RT
The identification and management of self-mutilating patients in primary care
Self-cutters describe a period of depersonalization leading to painless cutting, followed by relaxation and repersonalization after bleeding. Complications include social rejection due to the behavior as well as the resulting disfigurement. Primary care providers can identify and intervene by establishing a trusting relationship.
1997 Nurse Pract 22;5:151-3, 159–65
Dallam, S. J.

2711856 JA
Female habitual self-mutilators
"Data are presented on 240 female habitual self-mutilators. The typical subject is a 28-year-old Caucasian who first deliberately harmed herself at age 14. Skin cutting is her usual practice, but she has used other methods such as skin burning and self-hitting, and she has injured herself on at least 50 occasions. Her decision to self-mutilate is impulsive and results in temporary relief from symptoms such as racing thoughts, depersonalization, and marked anxiety. She now has or has had an eating disorder, and may be concerned about her drinking. She has been a heavy utilizer of medical and mental health services, although treatment generally has been unsatisfactory. In desperation over her inability to control her self-mutilative behavior this typical subject has attempted suicide by a drug overdose."
1989 Acta Psychiatr Scand 79;3:283–9
Favazza, A. R. and Conterio, K.

11901779 RT
Reducing repeated deliberate self-harm
Deliberate self-harm may be seen as a temporary escape from an intolerable situation or psychic or physical pain, a way of communicating distress or anger, or a way to try to influence the behavior of others. Many DSH patients have decreased problem-solving skills, so they can't think of an alternative solution. 60–70% are significantly depressed, and 20% have an alcohol dependency. 25% of suicide victims presented with an episode of DSH in the previous year.
2002 Practitioner 246;1632:164–6, 169–72
Sinclair, J. M. and Hawton, K.

9245269 JA
"Why don't you do it properly?" Young women who self-injure
Interviews with four female teens who self-injure reveal that they consider this an adaptive alternative to suicide. Issues of communication and control are discussed.
1996 J Adolesc 19;2:111-9
Solomon, Y. and Farrand, J.

11452679 R
Self-mutilation: review and case study
Severe self-mutilation may occur when a person is under the delusional belief that a part of the body is causing trouble, is deformed, or needs to be sacrificed. Causes may include guilt, religious guilt, self-punishment, and gender dissatisfaction. An abrupt change in appearance (ie shaved head) may precede the injurious act.
2001 Int J Clin Pract 55;5:317–9
Parrott, H. J. and Murray, B. J.

10972574 JA
Self-injurious behavior in anorexia nervosa
Of 236 patients with anorexia, over 60% reported some form of self-injurious behavior, including skin cutting/burning, hair pulling or severe nail biting, classified as either impulsive or compulsive. Childhood sexual abuse or anxiety significantly predicted impulsive self-injury, whereas obsessionality and younger age were associated with compulsive self-injury. Those with both impulsive and compulsive components had a 72% drop-out rate in treatment.
2000 J Nerv Ment Dis 188;8:537–42
Favaro, A. and Santonastaso, P.

7894450 JA
Self-mutilation, anorexia, and dysmenorrhea in obsessive compulsive disorder
Article describes 19 female patients with a similar biphasic pattern, consisting of anorexia/amenorrhea followed by return of menses over time with subsequent bulimia, obsessive-compulsive disorder and self-mutilation. 70% reported childhood sexual abuse.
1995 Int J Eat Disord 17;1:33–8
Yaryura-Tobias, J. A., Neziroglu, F. A., and Kaplan, S.

Note: The annotated bibliographies were drawn from "Women's Center for Mind-Body Health" at http://womensmindbodyhealth.info/self-cutting528.htm.

Tracing the Work of Two Students

Kaci Holz: Introduction to "Gender Communication"

Over several chapters we have seen Kaci Holz and Halley Fishburn develop their papers. Let's look now at a portion of Kaci Holz's introduction to her paper entitled "Gender Communication," which she wrote using MLA style. Introducing the literature on a topic should be a part of every introduction to a research paper, for it establishes your integrity as a student writer. A willingness to share what various experts are saying quickly displays your agility at composing from sources. Below, the marginal notes will explain the citations made by Holz.

Let us examine several theories about different male and female communication styles. Deborah Tannen, Ph.D., is a professor of sociolinguistics at Georgetown University. In her books *You Just Don't Understand* and *The Argument Culture,* she addresses many issues surrounding the patterns of conversation styles between men and women. While she stresses that not all men and not all women communicate in the same ways, she claims there are basic gender patterns or stereotypes that can be found. Tannen says that men participate in conversations to establish "a hierarchical social order" (*Don't* 24), while women most often participate in conversations to establish a "network of connections" (*Don't* 25). She distinguishes the way women most often converse as "rapport-talk" and the way men most often converse as "report-talk" (*Don't* 74).

Holz provides a clear citation to Tannen.

Note here her summary (see Chapter 4).

Holz adds an abbreviated title to identify which book she cites.

Tannen continues to differentiate between the male communication style and the female communication style by describing each one's purpose for communicating. She explains that women often communicate to gain sympathy or understanding for a particular problem. However, men often respond to such communication with their typical "report-

In this paragraph Holz uses summary to establish Tannen's basic position. Holz makes it very clear that the ideas are Tannen's, not hers, and she cites the pages used.

talk" by trying to offer solutions to a woman's problems. Those opposing communication styles often conflict and cause problems. The miscommunication is caused by different purposes for communicating. The woman wants sympathy, while the man thinks she wants him to solve her problems (*Don't* 49-53).

Other theorists agree with Tannen. For example, Phillip Yancey's article in *Marriage Partnership* also asserts that men and women "use conversation for quite different purposes" (71). He claims that women converse to develop and maintain connections, while men converse to claim their position in the hierarchy they see around them. Yancey asserts that women are less likely to speak publicly than are men because women often perceive such speaking as putting oneself on display. A man, on the other hand, is usually comfortable with speaking publicly because that is how he establishes his status among others (Yancey 71).

Holz wisely brings additional experts into the introduction to display the literature, not give a one-sided display of Tannen's work.

For clarity, Holz repeats the source's name in the closing citation.

Many more differences in communication patterns of men and women can be found. Richard L. Weaver II, a public speaker, points out another author who identifies different communication styles for men and women. In his speech "Leadership for the Future: A New Set of Priorities," Weaver references Dr. Julia T. Wood's book, *Gendered Lives*. According to Weaver, Wood claims that "male communication is characterized by assertion, independence, competitiveness, and confidence [while] female communication is characterized by deference, inclusivity, collaboration, and cooperation" (qtd. in Weaver 440). This list of differences describes why men and women have such opposing communication styles.

Now Holz adds another authority.

Holz indicates that the source of the Wood quotation is Weaver's speech.

Writing the Single-Source Essay

At times, you will be asked to write a paper based on a single source, such as one article, a performance, an event, a song, a book, or a report. This type of assignment will ask you to accomplish these things:

WEB LINK
to Chapter 8
Related Web
Destinations
http://www.
ablongman.com/
lester

- Read one piece of writing, or attend one event or performance.
- Think about your reaction to it.
- Write a paper that gives your response.
- Cite the work in your paper and refer to it often.

This chapter will introduce four basic essay types: the personal response, the interpretation, the rebuttal, and the evaluation or review.

1. In a personal response essay, you write subjectively about a work to express your own ideas and positions on some aspect of the work's contents.

2. In an interpretation, you give an objective treatment of a work, which requires you to stay focused, analyze the work to find its basic parts, summarize the parts, and write the interpretation with a non-personal point of view.

3. In a rebuttal, you disagree with a work, but you respond only after critical study. You write an intelligent response that probes deeply into the motivations of the writer or artist and examines the basic principles that underlie the writer's argument. Until you understand the original source, you cannot effectively frame a rebuttal.

4. In an evaluation or review, you establish the criteria by which you will judge a work. The criteria will differ for a music CD, live performance, movie, speech, and so forth. You are expected to judge the overall quality of the work and, in some instances, make a recommendation to the reader.

Writing a Personal Response Essay

WEB LINK
to Reading
8.1
http://www.
ablongman.com/
lester
One way to generate an effective essay is by responding to ideas found in another source. The comments by the writer of an essay or magazine article might provoke your curiosity, or your visit to a PGA golf tournament might provide a gateway to your own ideas. Thus, your response to a work or event or experience will inspire you into critical thinking that will culminate in the creation of your own essay.

For this type of writing, you will use a work or experience as a springboard to launch your concepts. To get started, do not analyze, interpret, or offer rebuttal. Just let the source provoke your ideas. Follow these steps:

1. Read the material with a critical eye, or think critically about the experience.

2. Make notes on any issue that interests you.

3. Write a thesis of your own that grows out of one or more of your notes.

4. Write a draft to develop *your* ideas, not to describe or analyze the other work or experience. Yet *do* mention the work or event that provoked your interest in the topic.

Let us begin by reading a brief essay and observing how one student responds with notes and her own essay. Here's an essay that originally appeared in *Discover* magazine (June 2002). Note the marginal notes by Ramona Parke.

Chaotic Warnings from the Last Ice Age

Fenella Saunders

The last ice age, from 120,000 to 10,000 years ago, was not in fact always cold: During 20 brief interludes, temperatures shot up 10 to 18 degrees within a decade. Andrey Ganopolski and Stefan Rahmstorf, climatologists at the Potsdam Institute for Climate Impact Research in Germany, think they have figured out why. Chaotic weather variations occasionally triggered a cascade of changes that switched temperatures from cold to warm.

Changes in global temps are often triggered by chaotic forces.

Ganopolski and Rahmstorf developed a computer model showing how the change could have happened. During the glacial era, the Gulf Stream current in the Atlantic normally turned before reaching Iceland. But every 1,500 years or so, the circulation abruptly changed, sending warm waters all the way to Europe. The researchers found that random fluctuations would sometimes produce times of cool weather, when relatively little freshwater melt flowed into the ocean. If these cool spells happened to coincide with an additional chilling factor—say, a periodic episode when the sun was slightly dimmer than usual—the reduction in freshwater would cause saltier, denser ocean water

The Gulf Stream plays a vital role in global stability, but it can be pulled north by dense, sinking water in the north Atlantic

to sink. This effect would destabilize the Gulf Stream and pull the surface waters northward, leading to a brief European warm spell. Ganopolski is unsure what triggered the 1,500-year pattern. But the existence of these wild swings suggests that it doesn't take a lot to switch the oceans from one mode to another. "Strong changes in the system may not necessarily be triggered by strong external perturbation," he says. In other words, pollution and other environmental damage wrought by humans could spawn huge, unpredictable climate changes.

"Pertubation" means agitation of a physical system.

The small things can cause enormous upheavals; that's what the essay is saying.

—from *Discover*, June 2002, p. 14.

The marginal notes above show a few reactions by student Ramona Parker. Her next step was to write a few notes and questions about the topic.

1. We may not face a new Ice Age, but a global warming could be far worse.
2. If the sun can be "slightly dimmer than usual," can it also be slightly warmer than usual, thereby causing the global warming?
3. We have no control over the sun, but we can, perhaps, control conditions on earth that allow overheating.
4. If nature exhibits these "wild swings," should we merely wait for the swing to cooler climates?
5. A "perturbation" is a change in a physical system. The fragile balance of earth and sun could endure a serious "perturbation" as a result of human pollution and blatant damage to the environment.
6. The question that comes to my mind is this: Can humans affect climate changes or does nature vacillate from warm to cold in a chaotic fashion?

Ramona has made some intellectual responses to the source. Now she needs to frame her own thesis:

The crushing demands of the human population may, indeed, affect the cycles of nature, but alarmists should base their positions on reason, not speculation.

Next, Ramona could begin drafting her essay, but first, she might consider a few writing strategies for this kind of essay.

- **Definition** will play a role if Ramona wishes to explore the word *perturbation*. She could also explore the meanings of *chaos, global warming, chilling factor,* and perhaps the *glacial era.*
- **Process** might help Ramona explain what the normal process might be and how it might differ from the "chaotic" process. In another example, she

might explain the role of the Gulf Stream and its process of carrying warm water into the north Atlantic.

- **Cause and effect** analysis would serve the essay in a manner similar to *process*. Ramona might explore the consequences of gasoline emissions, coal-fired generators, or chemical herbicides and insecticides spread on farm fields. She might explore how one act—the dismantling of the rain forests—has affected global weather patterns.

- **Comparison** could enable Ramona to drive home a point or two. Global weather patterns could be compared to the daily fluctuations of fair skies to cloudy skies and warm breezes to snowy conditions. The perturbations of the weather could be compared to a marriage in which the small things—failing to pick up the dirty laundry, or drinking one beer too many—can cause a tempest.

Ultimately, Ramona Parker must settle on a specific problem or issue and offer her discussion. She should now:

1. Revise her thesis.
2. Sketch an outline.
3. Draft the essay.

After some further thought, Ramona abandoned her original thesis as unworkable because of her limited insight into the issues. Instead, she developed a thesis that seemed within her reach:

Small things can cause enormous upheavals on many levels.

Her rough outline then took shape.

Don't ignore the small stuff:
    domestic settings
    national politics
    global warming

Although brief, the items on the list set a pattern for Ramona's rough draft, which is reproduced below.

Don't Ignore the Small Stuff

Ramona Parker

I read an article recently on global warming that caused me to contemplate human behavior as a factor in the vast and magnificent realms of universal order. Fenella Sauders, in a short article in *Discover* magazine, makes the observation that the small things, like "environmental damage by humans," might disrupt universal order. For the average citizen, who needs gasoline for his car, lumber for his new home, and electricity from coal-fired generators, the bountiful riches of our land provide the good life. Besides, the universal forces seem so magnificent in their splendor that human behavior is microscopic and irrelevant. Not so! We need to confront and control the small things in life.

My marriage was a big thing in my life, yet I let the little things destroy it. I confess. I bitched about his dirty clothes, his manners in public, his flirtations with other women (but no real affairs that I know about), and his infrequent but totally freaky binge drinking that not only made him crazy but also violently ill for three or four days. I really didn't do anything to make modifications in his behavior. He loved me, and I think we could have worked out solutions, but I complained with a temper tantrum once too often and he walked out the door, never to return. Saw him in court; end of marriage. Zap! The small stuff got me.

The Federal Bureau of Investigation announced recently that it will totally reorganize the way it conducts its business. This comes in the wake of a whistleblower who said she had sent a notice to the Washington office about foreigners on visas who were taking flying lessons but who only wanted to learn to fly the big commercial jets, not learn to take off or land. A small memo in a huge bureaucracy, the small stuff, got buried. Now, in the wake of the tragedies of 9/11, the bureau has begun a massive overhaul in procedures and operations. But the damage is done; the public's confidence in the FBI is shattered, perhaps beyond repair.

Then we come to matters of the environment. The big organizations promote environmental wisdom with dollars and publications—the Sierra Club, Greenpeace, the Audubon Society, and others. They constantly send out warnings about "greenhouse gases" caused especially by the burning of "fossil fuels." But like the average cow in the pasture emitting her methane gases, the average Joe drives his automobile, sitting there alone, thirty miles to work each day and thirty miles back home. Carpooling? Saving on the emissions of fossil fuels? Not on your life. I drove through Atlanta recently with my friend Gloria on the way to Florida. We drove in the HOV lane, and Gloria remarked on the thousands of cars bottled in the six other lanes of traffic, "They all have only one driver in the car!" Mass transit is the answer, but the HOV lane was practically empty for us, and a MARTA commuter train that passed nearby looked half empty.

I suspect that we're arriving at the stage of environmental damage at which we should, as individual citizens, begin to contribute in a serious way to a cleaner environment in a multitude of little ways—emission controls, recycling, cleaner fuels, thermostat adjustments, and mass transit. Meanwhile, the people with power—the politicians and corporate giants—need to establish regulations to enforce environmental controls for the big industries. We can't wait until rolling blackouts on electricity sweep nationwide for months on end with thermal conditions pushing temperatures into the 100s regularly, incessantly, and catastrophically.

Let's address the little stuff today, not next year.

WEB LINK
to Exercise
8.1
http://www.
ablongman.com/
lester
Ramona Parker has developed her own essay out of the one source. She has acknowledged the source, quoted briefly from it, but moved beyond it. Her focus on addressing "the small stuff" moves from her personal, domestic matters to national political policies and to the impact of global warming. It's not an in-depth research paper, but Ramona responds to the one source with some critical thinking and then creates an effective personal essay. Her work could easily launch a longer study of the issues or even a research paper.

EXERCISE 8.1
RESPONDING TO A SOURCE WITH YOUR SPIN

Read critically one of the following essays: William Raspberry's "Our Problems vs. Enemies" or Dave Barry's "Farm Security: The Mohair of the Dog That Bites You." As you read, write notes that raise issues of interest to you. Look for one phrase or sentence that might launch a brief essay of your own. Write a thesis that establishes your perspective. Write a rough outline to plan the paper. Finally, write your draft.

Our Problems vs. Enemies

William Raspberry

"Our Problems vs. Enemies," by William Raspberry. Copyright © 2002, The Washington Post Writers Group. Reprinted by Permission.

Learn the difference between problems and enemies. It's the best and simplest advice I can offer newly minted graduates facing uncertain job prospects. It is in particular the best advice I can give those who would change—who would improve—our world.

We will find the world a more tractable, more perfectible place if we could learn the difference between problems and enemies. The distinction might bring us nearer solutions to some of our more vexing social and political difficulties.

And yet we refuse to make the distinction. We have been taught not to make it—if not by our instructors at least by our political and social activists. Give us a problem, and we'll find an enemy.

Let me give you a recent example. I recently wrote a piece, based on a book by Sylvia Ann Hewlett, in which I talked about the growing trend of childlessness among successful women. Many of the women Hewlett talked to for her book, including many who were happily married, didn't plan to be childless, as they made poignantly clear. It was almost as though childlessness caught them by surprise while they were focused on their successful careers.

I thought it was an excellent springboard for discussing something too few of us talk about among ourselves or with our own children: the differential sacrifices women make in comparison to men, the need to think about those sacrifices and to plan around them, even the need to think about the whole issue of blending family and career life.

Quite predictably, much of the reader response was from people who read the column as a chastisement of women for having careers (and by implication of going to college to prepare for careers). Hewlett and I were cast as their enemies, and discussion of the problem became impossible.

Something very similar happened when I wrote a piece supporting experimenting with boys-only classes, preferably headed by male teachers, as a way of dealing with some of the issues confronting inner-city schools. Among the responses were several accusing me of wanting to discriminate against girls—even blaming them for the ills of the inner-city schools. How did they get there? If boys-only classes are the solution, then girls must be the problem.

I can't tell you how often I've seen it happen, or how sad it makes me. Look at what happens on our campuses, where a lack of community is a serious problem. Seldom, however, do we discuss the problem. Each subgroup on campus—women, Asians, blacks, gays, Hispanics—will organize itself to fight the perceived prejudice against it. Most often, the grievances they present are real. But their implied analysis is false. They proceed on the assumption that if each group does its best to ameliorate its own grievances, the result will be peace and equity on campus.

We know better, of course. Political movements that come into being to fight grievances, and leaders whose political power is grievance-based, tend not to acknowledge progress, even when it happens. They need the grievance to justify their existence. And the result, often, is not greater equity and peace but greater upheaval, as more and more subgroups create (and magnify) their own grievances, chargeable to their special enemies, in the quest for a greater share of power for themselves.

I don't say that groups with grievances shouldn't try to get those grievances resolved. But doesn't it strike you how few groups are making it their priority to knit the campus into a community? Doesn't it strike you that many of the grievances would be much easier to resolve if the campus did become more of a community? And doesn't it strike you that, at the end of the day, community is what most of us in fact want?

Unfortunately, we can't get to community unless we first learn the difference between problems and enemies.

Enemies have to be fought—and even then they go on being enemies. Problems, on the other hand, can be worked out, often with the participation of those who caused them.

Surprisingly often, I have discovered, a focus on the problem rather than on enemies could disclose common interests and lead to innovative solutions.

The distinction I'm urging won't eliminate enemies. But it just might keep their numbers down to manageable size and free us to deal mutually with our mutual problems.

Farm Security: The Mohair of the Dog That Bites You

Dave Barry

If you're like most American taxpayers, you often wake up in the middle of the night in a cold sweat and ask yourself, "Am I doing enough to support mohair producers?"

I am pleased to report that you are, thanks to bold action taken recently by the United States Congress (motto: "Hey, It's not OUR money!"). I am referring to the 2002 Farm Security Act, which recently emerged from the legislative process very much the way a steaming wad of processed vegetation emerges from the digestive tract of a cow. The purpose of the Farm Security act is to provide farmers with "price stability." What do we mean by "price stability?" We mean: your money. You have already been very generous about this: Last year alone, you gave more than $20 billion worth of price stability to farmers. Since 1996, you've given more than a million dollars apiece to more than 1,000 lucky recipients, many of which are actually big agribusinesses. Some of the "farmers" you've sent your money to are billionaires, such as Ted Turner and Charles Schwab, as well as major corporations, such as Chevron, DuPont and John Hancock Mutual Life Insurance.

But that is NOTHING compared with how generous you're about to get, taxpayers! Thanks to the Farm Security Act, over the next 10 years, you'll be providing farmers with 70 percent MORE stability, for a total of $180 billion. At this rate, in a few years farmers will be so stable that they'll have to huddle in their root cellars for fear of being struck by bales of taxpayer-supplied cash raining down on the Heartland states from Air Force bombers. Perhaps you are asking yourself, "Wait a minute! Isn't this kind of like, I don't know . . . welfare?"

No, it is not. Welfare is when the government gives money to people who produce nothing. Whereas the farm-money recipients produce something that is critical to our nation: votes. Powerful congresspersons from both parties, as well as President Bush, believe that if they dump enough of your money on farm states, the farm states will re-elect them, thus enabling them to continue the vital work of dumping your money on the farm states. So as we see, it's not welfare at all! It's bribery.

But let us not forget the element of National Security. This is where your mohair comes in. As you know, "mohair" is the hair of any animal whose name begins with "mo," such as moose, mouse, mongoose or moray eel. No, wait, sorry. "Mohair" is actually wool made from the hair of a goat. During WWII, mohair was used to make military uniforms, so it was considered to be a strategic material, and Congress decided that you, the taxpayer, should pay people to produce it! But of course today mohair has no vital military purpose, and so . . . you are STILL paying people to produce it! And thanks to the Farm Security Act, you will continue to pay millions and millions of dollars, every year, to mohair producers!

As I say, this is for National Security. If terrorists, God forbid, ever manage to construct a giant time machine and transport the United States back to 1941, and we have fight World War II again, WE WILL BE READY. You will also be thrilled, as a taxpayer, to learn that the Farm Security Act provides new *subsidies* for producers of lentils and chickpeas. And not a moment too soon. This nation has become far too dependent on imported lentils and chickpeas. Try to picture the horror of living in a world in which foreigners, in foreign countries, suddenly cut off our lentil and chickpea supply. Imagine how you would feel if you had to look your small child in the eye and say. "I'm sorry, little Billy or Suzy as the case may be, but there will be no lentils or chickpeas tonight, and all because we taxpayers were too shortsighted to fork over millions of dollars in support for domestic lentil and chickpea producers, who thus were forced to compete in the market like everybody else, and . . . HEY, COME BACK HERE!"

Yes, that would be a horrible world, all right. And that is why I totally support the Farm Security Act. I hope you agree with me, though I realize that some of you may not; in fact, some of you may be so angry about this column that you've decided to never read anything by me again.

Well, guess what: I don't care! Thanks to the Humor Security Act recently passed by Congress, I'll be getting huge sums of money from the federal government to continue grinding out these columns, year after year, even if nobody wants to read them!

No, that would be stupid.

Interpreting a Work, Performance, or Event

WEB LINK to Reading 8.2 http://www. ablongman.com/ lester

Interpretation requires analysis that examines in depth the meaning and significance of a movie, a NASCAR race, a reality television program, or an exhibit at a museum. In other words, any single item or collective body of items is subject to your analysis. For an interpretation you should not wander off into your own opinions, nor should you attempt a rebuttal. Keep the focus on the work or event that you are interpreting. The task will require these actions on your part:

1. Preview the subject to form your expectations.
2. Read or experience the work or event in question.
3. Identify the parts, issues, and ideas in a reasonable classification.
4. Analyze the issues, parts, events.
5. Write your interpretation of each part.
6. Synthesize your pieces of interpretation into a unified whole.

If you remember the discussion of the term *inductive reasoning* (Chapter 3), then you will understand the task at hand. Interpretation uses inductive reasoning to identify and understand the basic facts about a subject in order to reach some believable conclusions about the issues being discussed. Let's join student Ralph Conover as he advances through each step.

Previewing the Work, Performance, or Event

First-year student Ralph Conover has been asked to write an interpretation of a speech, one that has historic fame—John F. Kennedy's inaugural address, which the newly elected president presented at the U.S. Capitol in 1961. In his preview work on the speech, Conover should consider the following elements:

- *Length.* Determining the length of the work or event to be interpreted can help set the time needed for the initial critical reading, marginal annotations, or notes. Kennedy's speech is reasonably short and can be read in one sitting.

- *Presentation or publication facts.* What is the date of the publication or performance? Does that timeframe bear significance? Would it help to know more about the publisher of a work or the Web site where it was accessed? In Conover's case, the timeframe could be significant, for Kennedy faced a world crisis with Cuba and the Soviet Union during his tenure.

- *Author, speaker,* or *creator.* What biographical information can you gather about the creator or performer of the work? Does that information bear directly on the work? Conover, of course, will have access to many biographical studies of Kennedy.

- *Content.* What is the work about? What can you learn from the title and general design or presentation of the material? Is the work accompanied by art, photographs, or other elements? Is there an abstract, summary, or bibliography? Conover will probably need to study the historical context and political background of the speech to grasp the reasoning behind some of Kennedy's assertions.

Reading or Experiencing the Work That You Will Interpret

Before writing your interpretive essay, you will have to do some critical reading if you are responding to a written work, or critical thinking if you are responding to an event or other experience. As you know from reading Chapter 3, critical reading involves several steps. First comes the initial reading to grasp the general nature of the work. Then comes the serious reading that will result in marginal annotations, notes in a research journal, and questions about the definitions of words and phrases. Shown below is Kennedy's address with Ralph Conover's margin annotations and a quickly written summary at the end.

Inaugural Address

John F. Kennedy

We observe today not a victory of party but a celebration of freedom, symbolizing an end as well as a beginning, signifying renewal as well as change. For I have sworn before you and Almighty God the same solemn oath our forebears prescribed nearly a century and three-quarters ago.

His inauguration is a "celebration of freedom"

The world is very different now. For man holds in his mortal hands the power to abolish all forms of human poverty and all forms of human life. And yet the same revolutionary belief for which our forebears fought is still at issue around the globe, the belief that the rights of man come not from the generosity of the state but from the hand of God.

Religious freedom

We dare not forget today that we are the heirs of that first revolution. Let the word go forth from this time and place, to friend and foe alike, that the torch has been passed to a new generation of Americans, born in this century, tempered by war, disciplined by a hard and bitter peace, proud of our ancient heritage, and unwilling to witness or permit the slow undoing of those human rights to which this nation has always been committed, and to which we are committed today at home and around the world.

Human rights is a freedom to be defended

Let every nation know, whether it wishes us well or ill, that we shall pay any price, bear any burden, meet any hardship, support any friend, oppose any foe to assure the survival and the success of liberty.

Freedom is worth all these things

This much we pledge—and more.

To those old allies whose cultural and spiritual origins we share, we pledge the loyalty of faithful friends. United, there is little we cannot do in a host of cooperative ventures. Divided, there is little we can do, for we dare not meet a powerful challenge at odds and split asunder.

To those new states whom we welcome to the ranks of the free, we pledge our word that one form of colonial control shall not have passed away merely to be replaced by a far more iron tyranny. We shall not always expect to find them supporting our view. But we shall always hope to find them strongly supporting their own freedom, and to remember that, in the past, those who foolishly sought power by riding the back of the tiger ended up inside.

He welcomes third world nations to freedom

To those peoples in the huts and villages of half the globe struggling to break the bonds of mass misery, we pledge our best

He would help the poor to help themselves & thus find freedom

efforts to help them help themselves, for whatever period is required, not because the Communists may be doing it, not because we seek their votes, but because it is right. If a free society cannot help the many who are poor, it cannot save the few who are rich. *maybe use this as a quote*

To our sister republics south of our border, we offer a special pledge: to convert our good words into good deeds, in a new alliance for progress, to assist free men and free governments in casting off the chains of poverty. But this peaceful revolution of hope cannot become the prey of hostile powers. Let all our neighbors know that we shall join with them to oppose aggression or subversion anywhere in the Americas. And let every other power know that this hemisphere intends to remain the master of its own house. *His "alliance for progress" will "assist free men and free governments" to escape poverty*

To that world assembly of sovereign states, the United Nations, our last best hope in an age where the instruments of war have far outpaced the instruments of peace, we renew our pledge of support to prevent it from becoming merely a forum for invective, to strengthen its shield of the new and the weak, and to enlarge the area in which its writ may run. *offers support to the United Nations*

Finally, to those nations who would make themselves our adversary, we offer not a pledge but a request: that both sides begin anew the quest for peace, before the dark powers of destruction unleashed by science engulf all humanity in planned or accidental self-destruction. *He argues for freedom by strength of arms and military power, but he is willing to search for peace & to negotiate*

We dare not tempt them with weakness. For only when our arms are sufficient beyond doubt can we be certain beyond doubt that they will never be employed.

But neither can two great and powerful groups of nations take comfort from our present course—both sides overburdened by the cost of modern weapons, both rightly alarmed by the steady spread of the deadly atom, yet both racing to alter that uncertain balance of terror that stays the hand of mankind's final war.

So let us begin anew, remembering on both sides that civility is not a sign of weakness, and sincerity is always subject to proof. Let us never negotiate out of fear, but let us never fear to negotiate.

Let both sides explore what problems unite us instead of belaboring those problems which divide us.

Let both sides, for the first time, formulate serious and precise proposals for the inspection and control of arms, and bring the absolute power to destroy other nations under the absolute control of all nations.

Let both sides seek to invoke the wonders of science instead of its terrors. Together let us explore the stars, conquer the deserts, eradicate disease, tap the ocean depths and encourage the arts and commerce.

Let both sides unite to heed in all corners of the earth the command of Isaiah to "undo the heavy burdens . . . [and] let the oppressed go free."

And if a beachhead of cooperation may push back the jungle of suspicion, let both sides join in creating a new endeavor, not a new balance of power, but a new world of law, where the strong are just and the weak secure and the peace preserved. *a "new world of law" would preserve peace & assure freedom*

All this will not be finished in the first one hundred days. Nor will it be finished in the first one thousand days, nor in the life of this Administration, nor even perhaps in our lifetime on this planet. But let us begin.

In your hands, my fellow citizens, more than mine, will rest the final success or failure of our course. Since this country was founded, each generation of Americans has been summoned to give testimony to its national loyalty. The graves of young Americans who answered the call to service surround the globe.

Now the trumpet summons us again—not as a call to bear arms, though arms we need; not as a call to battle, though embattled we are; but a call to bear the burden of a long twilight struggle, year in and year out, "rejoicing in hope, patient in tribulation," a struggle against the common enemies of men: tyranny, poverty, disease and war itself. *His will be "a long twilight struggle" against forces that might destroy freedom*

Can we forge against these enemies a grand and global alliance, North and South, East and West, that can assure a more fruitful life for all mankind? Will you join in that historic effort?

In the long history of the world, only a few generations have been granted the role of defending freedom in its hour of maximum danger. I do not shrink from this responsibility; I welcome it. I do not believe that any of us would exchange places with any other people or any other generation. The energy, the faith, the devotion which we bring to this endeavor will light our country and all who serve it, and the glow from that fire can truly light the world. *He will defend freedom in "its hour of maximum danger."*

And so, my fellow Americans, ask not what your country can do for you; ask what you can do for your country.

My fellow citizens of the world, ask not what America will do for you, but what together we can do for the freedom of man.

Finally, whether you are citizens of America or citizens of the world, ask of us here the same high standards of strength and sacrifice which we ask of you. With a good conscience our only *Citizens of all nations must work for the freedom of all people.*

sure reward, with history that final judge of our deeds, let us go forth to lead the land we love, asking His blessing and His help, but knowing that here on earth God's work must truly be our own.

Initial Summary: Kennedy says the torch of freedom has passed to a new generation that must struggle against the enemies. He welcomes the challenge and asks Americans and citizens of the world to join his quest for freedom.

Writing a Summary of the Work, Performance, or Event

Chapter 4 introduced you to the methods and reasons for writing a detailed summary, and that's usually a good next step toward interpretation. In your own words you will create a digest of the work or event under study. In Conover's case, he needs to work through the speech once again to identify key sections that can be reduced to summary. He will probably need five, six, maybe seven sentences for a speech the length of Kennedy's length. If well drafted, they can become part of his interpretive essay.

Kennedy begins by recalling that he and America now benefit from the revolutionary spirit of the past and also must carry the "torch" of human rights that is so ingrained into our being as a nation. Next, he issues his pledge that America will fight vigilantly for this freedom and work closely with its allies and the United Nations in that cause across the world. He then extends his hand of "civility" and asks both sides in the Cold War conflict to find areas of cooperation. Last, he turns to the American people and allies to join him in the struggle to defend freedom at home and across the oceans.

With this summary, Conover has identified the basic issues in a reasonable classification of Kennedy's speech: the pledge to fight for freedom, the willingness to work in harmony with America's enemies, and the call to the people of the United States and the free world to meet the challenges lying ahead.

Analyzing the Work, Performance, or Event

WEB LINK
to Exercise
8.2
http://www.
ablongman.com/
lester

Once you have classified the basic parts of a work, you can begin a systematic analysis to discover the significance of each part and to interpret its contribution to the whole. For example, if you were writing an interpretation of a thirty-minute infomercial on television, you would examine the product, its value, the testimonials, and the pitch by the announcer. In Ralph Conover's case, he has identified four basic sections of Kennedy's speech for analysis and interpretation: the opening, the pledge, the olive branch offer, and the summons. Here is Conover's interpretation of the third section, on Kennedy's willingness to negotiate with the enemy.

Addressing the Soviet Union and its allies, Kennedy makes a request rather than a pledge. He requests a search for peace before the world powers destroy not just each other but the entire globe. He asks for a new set of negotiations so that world powers might embrace themes of unity, sign agreements on disarming nuclear weapons, and build, perhaps, a "new world of law" to preserve peace. He admits such cooperation might not be possible during his administration nor even during his lifetime, but it must start on his watch as president.

With four such interpretations in hand, Conover will be well on his way to a complete interpretation of Kennedy's inaugural address.

Synthesizing Your Various Notes and Interpretations

The final task of interpretation requires you to fold all your summaries and interpretations into a finished product, one with an effective opening, the interpretations of the different sections, and a conclusion. Your synthesis will make the necessary connections among the various parts.

Let us look at Ralph Conover's interpretation.

Ralph Conover

May 2003

Dr. Roberts

John F. Kennedy: The Inaugural Address

In 1961 President John F. Kennedy swore the oath of office and launched a speech that has gained almost as much respect as Lincoln's Gettysburg Address. The speech seems notable to this writer because Kennedy did not boast about the accomplishments to come under his administration, nor did he promise a land of milk and honey. Instead, he hit hard at a reality—America faced a struggle for its liberty that was as astounding and frightful as that first fight for freedom 175 years ago.

Kennedy begins by recalling that he and America now benefit from the revolutionary spirit of the past, and he with a "new generation of Americans" must carry the "torch" of human rights that is so ingrained into our being as a nation. He reminds the audience that the American heritage will not allow an unraveling or outright destruction of human rights. He makes clear that America will pay the necessary price and face any adversity to preserve the liberty of the United States.

Next, he extends his pledge that America will fight vigilantly for the liberty of all free nations, from the poor in huts around the globe to nations in our hemisphere, and to the sovereign states of the United Nations. He builds a coalition of free countries that will fight in united fashion against "aggression and subversion."

He then extends his hand of "civility" and asks both sides in the Cold War conflict to find areas of cooperation. Addressing the Soviet Union and its allies, Kennedy makes a request rather than a pledge. He requests a search for peace before the world powers destroy not just each other but the entire globe. He asks for a new set of negotiations so that world powers might embrace themes of unity, sign agreements on disarming nuclear weapons, and build, perhaps, a "new world of law" to preserve peace. He admits such cooperation might not be possible during his administration, nor even during his lifetime, but it must start on his watch as president.

Last, he turns to the American people to join him in the struggle to defend freedom at home and across the oceans. His will be "a long twilight struggle" against forces that might destroy freedom. He calls on Americans to join him in the fight against "the common enemies of men: tyranny, poverty, disease and war itself."

He does not mince his words or put the best possible spin on world affairs. The freedom of America faces "its hour of maximum danger." Then he issues his powerful, rhetorical challenge:

> And so, my fellow Americans, ask not what your country can do for you; ask what you can do for your country.

> My fellow citizens of the world, ask not what America will do for you, but what together we can do for the freedom of man.

The second half of the challenge is often omitted, but it has great relevance. Kennedy did not intend for America alone to carry the torch. Free men everywhere would need to march in unison against Soviet aggression.

In effect, Kennedy assumed the office and moved toward his new home, the White House, knowing full well the dangers of the Cold War and forecasting with his address the reality of hostilities to come. He saw violence on the horizon, not knowing it would destroy his life and presidency in just three short years.

Conover's interpretation of Kennedy's inaugural address demonstrates the essence of a good interpretation. It maintains its focus on the speech and the ideas of the president. Conover does not extend the essay to his personal opinion, he does not judge the speech or evaluate it, and he certainly does not offer any rebuttal. The essay represents well the category of interpretation.

EXERCISE 8.2

WRITING AN INTERPRETATION

Reproduced below is the inaugural address of George W. Bush as delivered at the U.S. Capitol on January 20, 2001. Read it critically while keeping in mind both the turmoil of Bush's election victory over Al Gore and also subsequent events in his presidency. The writing assignments follow the speech.

Inaugural Address
George W. Bush

President Clinton, distinguished guests and my fellow citizens, the peaceful transfer of authority is rare in history, yet common in our country. With a simple oath, we affirm old traditions and make new beginnings.

As I begin, I thank President Clinton for his service to our nation.

And I thank Vice President Gore for a contest conducted with spirit and ended with grace.

I am honored and humbled to stand here, where so many of America's leaders have come before me, and so many will follow.

We have a place, all of us, in a long story—a story we continue, but whose end we will not see. It is the story of a new world that became a friend and liberator of the old, a story of a slave-holding society that became a servant of freedom, the story of a power that went into the world to protect but not possess, to defend but not to conquer.

It is the American story—a story of flawed and fallible people, united across the generations by grand and enduring ideals.

The grandest of these ideals is an unfolding American promise that everyone belongs, that everyone deserves a chance, that no insignificant person was ever born.

Americans are called to enact this promise in our lives and in our laws. And though our nation has sometimes halted, and sometimes delayed, we must follow no other course.

Through much of the last century, America's faith in freedom and democracy was a rock in a raging sea. Now it is a seed upon the wind, taking root in many nations.

Our democratic faith is more than the creed of our country, it is the inborn hope of our humanity, an ideal we carry but do not own, a trust we bear and pass along. And even after nearly 225 years, we have a long way yet to travel.

While many of our citizens prosper, others doubt the promise, even the justice, of our own country. The ambitions of some Americans are limited by failing schools and hidden prejudice and the circumstances of their birth. And sometimes our differences run so deep, it seems we share a continent, but not a country.

We do not accept this, and we will not allow it. Our unity, our union, is the serious work of leaders and citizens in every generation. And this is my solemn pledge: I will work to build a single nation of justice and opportunity.

I know this is in our reach because we are guided by a power larger than ourselves who creates us equal in His image.

And we are confident in principles that unite and lead us onward.

America has never been united by blood or birth or soil. We are bound by ideals that move us beyond our backgrounds, lift us above our interests and teach us what it means to be citizens. Every child must be taught these principles. Every citizen must uphold them. And every immigrant, by embracing these ideals, makes our country more, not less, American.

Today, we affirm a new commitment to live out our nation's promise through civility, courage, compassion and character.

America, at its best, matches a commitment to principle with a concern for civility. A civil society demands from each of us good will and respect, fair dealing and forgiveness.

Some seem to believe that our politics can afford to be petty because, in a time of peace, the stakes of our debates appear small.

But the stakes for America are never small. If our country does not lead the cause of freedom, it will not be led. If we do not turn the hearts of children toward knowledge and character, we will lose their gifts and undermine their idealism. If we permit our economy to drift and decline, the vulnerable will suffer most.

Together, we will reclaim America's schools, before ignorance and apathy claim more young lives.

We will reform Social Security and Medicare, sparing our children from struggles we have the power to prevent. And we will reduce taxes, to recover the momentum of our economy and reward the effort and enterprise of working Americans.

We will build our defenses beyond challenge, lest weakness invite challenge.

We will confront weapons of mass destruction, so that a new century is spared new horrors. The enemies of liberty and our country should make no mistake: America remains engaged in the world by history and by choice, shaping a balance of power that favors freedom. We will defend our allies and our interests. We will show purpose without arrogance. We will meet aggression and bad faith with resolve and strength. And to all nations, we will speak for the values that gave our nation birth.

America, at its best, is compassionate. In the quiet of American conscience, we know that deep, persistent poverty is unworthy of our nation's promise.

And whatever our views of its cause, we can agree that children at risk are not at fault. Abandonment and abuse are not acts of God, they are failures of love.

And the proliferation of prisons, however necessary, is no substitute for hope and order in our souls.

Where there is suffering, there is duty. Americans in need are not strangers, they are citizens, not problems, but priorities. And all of us are diminished when any are hopeless.

Government has great responsibilities for public safety and public health, for civil rights and common schools. Yet compassion is the work of a nation, not just a government.

And some needs and hurts are so deep they will only respond to a mentor's touch or a pastor's prayer. Church and charity, synagogue and mosque lend our communities their humanity, and they will have an honored place in our plans and in our laws.

Many in our country do not know the pain of poverty, but we can listen to those who do.

And I can pledge our nation to a goal: When we see that wounded traveler on the road to Jericho, we will not pass to the other side.

America, at its best, is a place where personal responsibility is valued and expected.

Encouraging responsibility is not a search for scapegoats, it is a call to conscience. And though it requires sacrifice, it brings a deeper fulfillment. We find the fullness of life not only in options, but in commitments. And we find that children and community are the commitments that set us free.

Our public interest depends on private character, on civic duty and family bonds and basic fairness, on uncounted, unhonored acts of decency which give direction to our freedom.

Sometimes in life we are called to do great things. But as a saint of our times has said, every day we are called to do small things with great love. The most important tasks of a democracy are done by everyone.

I will live and lead by these principles: to advance my convictions with civility, to pursue the public interest with courage, to speak for greater justice and compassion, to call for responsibility and try to live it as well.

In all these ways, I will bring the values of our history to the care of our times.

What you do is as important as anything government does. I ask you to seek a common good beyond your comfort; to defend needed reforms against easy attacks; to serve your nation, beginning with your neighbor. I ask you to be citizens: citizens, not spectators; citizens, not subjects; responsible citizens, building communities of service and a nation of character.

Americans are generous and strong and decent, not because we believe in ourselves, but because we hold beliefs beyond ourselves. When this spirit of citizenship is missing, no government program can replace it. When this spirit is present, no wrong can stand against it.

After the Declaration of Independence was signed, Virginia statesman John Page wrote to Thomas Jefferson: "We know the race is not to the swift nor the battle to the strong. Do you not think an angel rides in the whirlwind and directs this storm?"

Much time has passed since Jefferson arrived for his inauguration. The years and changes accumulate. But the themes of this day he would know: our nation's grand story of courage and its simple dream of dignity.

We are not this story's author, who fills time and eternity with his purpose. Yet his purpose is achieved in our duty, and our duty is fulfilled in service to one another.

Never tiring, never yielding, never finishing, we renew that purpose today, to make our country more just and generous, to affirm the dignity of our lives and every life.

This work continues. This story goes on. And an angel still rides in the whirlwind and directs this storm.

God bless you all, and God bless America.

Assignments

Write an interpretive essay of George W. Bush's inaugural address. To prepare your interpretation, do the following:

1. Preview Bush's speech and do a careful reading that considers both the content and context.
2. Write a summary of the speech in which you identify its major sections.
3. Analyze each major section with your interpretation.
4. Put it all together in a complete interpretation of Bush's inaugural address.

Writing a Rebuttal

WEB LINK
to Reading
8.3
http://www.
ablongman.com/
lester

Students sometimes find themselves disagreeing with the ideas expressed in a written work or speech or song. If you disagree with someone's ideas, you might want to write a rebuttal.

The next two articles debate an English-only work rule in Georgia, as reported in the *Atlanta Journal-Constitution*. The first is an editorial by the staff of the newspaper, and the second is a response by Jim Boulet Jr., who is executive director of English First, a national organization that argues for English as America's official language.

English-Only Work Rule Is Dumb in Any Language

Atlanta Journal-Constitution

Adios to the Hall County Health Department's shortsighted, divisive and unconstitutional order to bilingual employees to speak only English—or risk being fired. The rule was quashed by the Georgia Department of Human Resources, which oversees county health departments.

The dumb English-only policy had been in effect in Hall County since last week and would have spread to 12 more counties in northeast Georgia if DHR had not interceded.

Melody Stancil, health director for the 13-county health district, had cited a concern about the dangers of communicating in a language other than English. "In any business, but particularly in a medical setting, it is extremely important for communication to be clear and correct," she said in a statement that explained (and rescinded) her directive. "Failure to ensure this may jeopardize patient care."

She was right, of course, about needing clear communications. But how is medical care impeded when, say, two Spanish-speaking people communicate in Spanish? What was she thinking?

Aside from the constitutional and legal minefield, Stancil's draconian directive was offensive. The discomfort level soared among department employees in a county that is at least 20 percent Latino.

According to the American Civil Liberties Union, at least 20 employees complained that the policy "violates their constitutional rights and threatens their jobs." Had the policy remained in effect, it would have increased hostility, hindering the very communications Stancil sought to improve.

Stancil's new policy reflects a healthier attitude toward cultural diversity in Georgia, which has one of the fastest-growing Latino populations in the nation. From now on, there will be other measures to improve communication and provide "opportunities for staff to be educated regarding multicultural issues, to participate in Spanish language classes and to understand the importance of showing mutual respect and behaving in a professional manner."

Expect Host of Problems When Languages Collide

Jim Boulet, Jr.

The Georgia Department of Human Resources was wrong to strike down the Hall County Health Department's English-only policy for its employees. The Hall County Health Department, and thus Georgia's taxpayers, will end up footing the bill for the state's political correctness.

Employers impose English-only rules primarily to protect themselves from costly discrimination lawsuits. In the case of Garcia v. Spun Steak (1993), Spanish-speaking employees were insulting African-American employees in Spanish. This created what is known as a "hostile working environment" once the other employees figured out that they were being ridiculed.

Spun Steak decided to require that its employees speak only English during the day shift. The Ninth Circuit Court of Appeals agreed that the company had done the right thing.

The Hall County Health Department was merely trying to obey the same civil rights laws. There is also the issue of potential malpractice litigation involving any conversation which occurs on Hall County Health Department property. Medical translations into other languages remain subject to malpractice claims. Linguists agree that there are tremendous variations in the spoken versions of languages like Spanish and Arabic.

Thus, the most careful translation may still not be properly understood by a patient. A supervisor, doctor or nurse may suffer legal consequences for simply being present while a conversation with a patient is conducted in a language he does not understand.

A doctor or a nurse may easily end up on a witness stand someday as a malpractice lawyer intones, "Didn't you know that the translation into Mandarin Chinese was not properly understood by my client because he speaks Cantonese?"

There is also the issue of patient safety, given that two heads are generally better than one when it comes to solving a problem. An English-speaking nurse may need to give a warning to a busy doctor. But she would not realize that a mistake had been made if the doctor-patient conversation were conducted in a language other than English.

Opponents of English-only policies suggest the solution is to hire medical personnel who speak both languages. But Spanish and English aren't the only languages spoken here.

What is the Hall health department supposed to do when employees speak a third language, such as Tagalog? Hire a new supervisor who speaks that same tongue to follow those employees around during their shift?

Etiquette experts used to agree that it was rude for people to speak in a language not understood by everyone else present at the time. Whether intentional or not, such a conversation sends the message that "the rest of you are not supposed to understand what we are talking about." Encouraging this kind of exclusionary behavior is not likely to enhance workplace teamwork, especially essential in a medical setting.

The Georgia Department of Human Resources was wrong to kowtow to the ACLU. The Hall health department deserved better from the folks in Atlanta.

WEB LINK to Exercise 8.3 http://www.ablongman.com/lester

On one side, the *Atlanta Journal-Constitution* takes a liberal view to defend freedom of speech. On the other side, Jim Boulet offers the conservative view as upheld by English First, an organization for which he serves as executive director. Both writers make valid points, and you probably agree with one more than the other. However, to write an intelligent rebuttal, you need to probe deeply, not for the surface issues, but for the basic principles that underlie the arguments.

The real issue here is not the directive by the health director of Hall County, Georgia. The real issue is a view of American society in the twenty-first century. Some would encourage an open policy for the expression of ethnic identity and language usage. Others would embrace tighter controls. This conflict rolls over into other matters just as volatile, such as police profiling, bilingual education, integration, and religious beliefs.

GUIDELINES

Writing a Rebuttal

Before you launch any rebuttal to someone else's views, you will need to discover that person's fundamental philosophy and examine how that

(continues on next page)

(continued from previous page)

underlying foundation has colored the content of the article, speech, song, or other work that you are responding to. Here are the steps you must take.

1. Subject the work to critical reading or analysis, as described in Chapter 3.

2. Write a summary of the work or build a set of notes that will present honestly and without any bias on your part the position taken by the source. Try to discover and lay out for your readers the premises upon which the other person has built the argument. Specify, if possible, the basic principle that seems to underlie the source's position.

3. React to the source by looking at the issue holistically; that is, summarize the issues and the principles at work here. Look at the big picture. Ask yourself: What basic truths are being challenged or changed or endorsed by the source? Now is the time to give the source the benefit of the doubt by giving credit for positive points.

4. Draft a set of notes that gives your reasons for disagreeing with the position taken by the source.

5. Clarify in your own mind what your position is on the issue.

6. Identify a fundamental principle that you wish to defend. It may not be mentioned in the work that you are rebutting, but it should be a foundation for your argument.

Read the essay "Family Counterculture" by Ellen Goodman, below, which originally appeared in the *Boston Globe* (August 16, 1991). Following the essay, we shall consider the manner in which one student responded with his own essay.

Family Counterculture

Ellen Goodman

Sooner or later, most Americans become card-carrying members of the counterculture. This is not an underground holdout of hippies. No beads are required. All you need to join is a child.

The latest evidence of this frustrating piece of the parenting job description came from pediatricians. This summer, the American Academy of Pediatrics called for a ban on television food ads. Their plea was hard on the heels of a study showing that one Saturday morning of TV cartoons contained 202 junk-food ads.

The kids see, want, and nag. That is, after all, the theory behind advertising to children, since few six-year-olds have their own trust funds. The end result, said the pediatricians, is obesity and high cholesterol.

Their call for a ban was predictably attacked by the grocers' association. But it was also attacked by people assembled under the umbrella marked "parental responsibility." We don't need bans, said these "PR" people, we need parents who know how to say "no."

Well, I bow to no one in my capacity for nay saying. I agree that it's a well-honed skill of child raising. By the time my daughter was seven, she qualified as a media critic.

But it occurs to me now that the call for "parental responsibility" is increasing in direct proportion to the irresponsibility of the marketplace. Parents are expected to protect their children from an increasingly hostile environment.

Are the kids being sold junk food? Just say no. Is TV bad? Turn it off. Are there messages about sex, drugs, violence all around? Counter the culture.

Mothers and fathers are expected to screen virtually every aspect of their children's lives. To check the ratings on the movies, to read the labels on the CDs, to find out if there's MTV in the house next door. All the while keeping in touch with school and, in their free time, earning a living.

In real life, most parents do a great deal of this monitoring and just-say-no-ing. Any trip to the supermarket produces at least one scene of a child grabbing for something only to have it returned to the shelf by a frazzled parent. An extraordinary number of the family arguments are over the goodies—sneakers, clothes, games—that the young know only because of ads.

But at times it seems that the media have become the mainstream culture in children's lives. Parents have become the alternative.

Barbara Dafoe Whitehead, a research associate at the Institute for American Values, found this out in interviews with middle-class parents. "A common complaint I heard from parents was their sense of being overwhelmed by the culture. They felt their voice was a lot weaker. And they felt relatively more helpless than their parents."

"Parents," she notes, "see themselves in a struggle for the hearts and minds of their own children." It isn't that they can't say no. It's that there's so much more to say no to.

Without wallowing in false nostalgia, there has been a fundamental shift. Americans once expected parents to raise their children in accordance with the dominant cultural messages. Today they are expected to raise their children in opposition.

Once the chorus of cultural values was full of ministers, teachers, neighbors, leaders. They demanded more conformity, but offered more support. Now the messengers are Ninja Turtles, Madonna, rap groups, and celebrities pushing sneakers. Parents are considered "responsible" only if they are successful in their resistance.

It's what makes child raising hard. It's why parents feel more isolated. It's not just that American families have less time with their kids. It's that we have to spend more of the time doing battle with our own culture.

It's rather like trying to get your kids to eat their green beans after they've been told all day about the wonders of Milky Way. Come to think of it, it's exactly like that.

Summarizing the Key Ideas of the Source

The writer who reacts to Goodman's essay must first summarize the essay's content to focus on the issue under question. One student, Lamar Clift, wrote this summary:

Ellen Goodman laments the role parents must play in today's media circus. A columnist for the *Boston Globe*, Goodman suggests that children are bombarded by attractive but negative information that sets them at opposition with parental control. She makes this observation: "Americans once expected parents to raise their children in accordance with the dominant cultural messages. Today they are expected to raise their children in opposition." Her argument evolves in this manner: Parents should raise healthy children who respect and honor others. The media in their various forms negatively affect the physical and mental health of the children. Therefore, popular culture affects the children and forces the parent into a rebuttal counterculture.

The summary should be objective and provide a fair, unbiased view of the writer's position. The summary by Lamar Clift gives a fair summary of Goodman's position, and it includes a quotation to highlight Goodman's argument.

In like manner, any essay of rebuttal should open with a fair representation of the source's fundamental positions. Only then would the rebuttal begin. As a writer, you must appear objective in the initial treatment of the source. Gradually, then, you can lay out your premises and conclusion that differ (for an example, see the draft of Lamar Clift's essay, pages 286–288).

Listing the Principles That Underlie a Position

After writing a summary of the ideas you will be rebutting, you will need to identify the foundation for the source's position.

What fundamental principles are at work?

What value does the writer treasure the most?

Here's how Lamar Clift identified Goodman's basic principles.

Today's parents represent a counterculture against modern media forces that corrupt the children.

Parental control has been sabotaged by a modern culture that destroys the morals and the physical health of today's children.

In the first statement, Clift recognizes that Goodman considers herself a victim of outside forces assailing her family. In the second, he interprets Goodman as saying that parental control has been lost, an issue that is vitally important to Goodman. Control of her life is what Goodman wants, says Clift, and her dismay stems from an apparent loss of control.

Asserting Your Position

The next task for the writer who wishes to challenge the ideas of another person will be the assertion of the writer's own position. Here are Lamar Clift's notes:

> One of Goodman's assumptions is that popular culture has a corrupting influence on children. That idea is not entirely true, nor does she support it with evidence.

In opposition to Goodman, Clift says:

> Today's culture is a training ground. True, it differs remarkably from the culture of 20 years ago or 30 or 40. Every generation creates its own way of life and ethnicity. Every generation is a counterculture to the previous one.

Implied here is Clift's idea and rebuttal, that each new generation creates its own culture that works as the counterculture to the previous one. The new generation will always rebel against the standards of the old.

> Goodman has it wrong. Her generation is the culture; the children offer the counterculture.

In clear and simple terms, Clift identifies the difference in his views and Goodman's. Goodman claims to represent a counterculture, but Clift explains that she represents the establishment and the children represent the new wave, the counterculture.

> Since the children provide the counterculture, and since the media cater to the whims of the children, who have more money than most people suspect, then it only follows that the media will feed the counterculture, which is the new generation, not the old one.

Clift has a ready answer about the role of the media, which Goodman condemns. According to Clift, the media will meet and respond to the marketplace. The children control an enormous amount of capital, directly and indirectly, so of course the advertising dollars will flow in that direction. The result may be good or bad; that's a judgment call by the observer of the pop culture. Clift's position is that a parent might not be the best judge because of natural fears and prejudices.

> Goodman is just a complaining parent. Like all parents, she wants little milksops who conform to her every wish. But if they did, she would hate them for their lack of imagination and their loss of a spirit of adventure.

Here Clift attacks Goodman more directly, seeing her as an interfering parent who wishes to force the children into a conformity created by the adults. Clift also argues that children who meekly obey parents on every occasion are weak and less than inspiring or exciting.

Drafting an Essay of Rebuttal

The paradigm for a rebuttal essay is as follows:

1. Explain that the source establishes a position that has merit.
2. Mention that certain issues need clarification.
3. Argue that some issues are not addressed adequately, or not addressed at all.
4. Offer a more valid position.

Here is Lamar Clift's draft in response to Ellen Goodman's essay on parents and their roles in this new century.

The Children Are the Counterculture

Lamar Clift

Ellen Goodman in her essay "Family Counterculture," which was first published in the *Boston Globe*, laments the role parents must play in today's media circus. She explains that children are bombarded by attractive but negative information that sets them in opposition with parental control. She makes this observation: "Americans once expected parents to raise their children in accordance with the dominant cultural messages. Today they are expected to raise their children in opposition." Her argument evolves in this manner: Parents should raise healthy children who respect and honor others. The media in their various forms negatively affect the physical and mental health of the children. Therefore, popular culture affects the children and forces the parent into a rebuttal counterculture. That is, parental control has been sabotaged by a modern culture that destroys the morals and the physical health of today's children.

Goodman makes a valid point. Children are bombarded by false, deceptive, and downright wicked information at movies, on television, at ball parks and playgrounds, on the Internet, and in classrooms. The parent must be on guard but not become a prison warden. But that's how Goodman sounds, a warden saying "no" all day long.

One of Goodman's assumptions is that popular culture has a corrupting influence on children. That idea is not entirely true, nor does she support it with evidence. I can go to the magazine racks and find many good publications that endorse the best of behavior. I can flip through the channels on television and be rewarded with outstanding programming. I have a choice of radio stations, movies, and clubs.

Granted, sex and appeals to sex are a given in today's society, but that doesn't make it evil. The openness is more honest and healthful than having sex buried or hidden from the view of children. Knowing and understanding does not translate into doing it! Responsible children can handle information on drugs, sex, crime, violence, and marital discord. They live with it daily and weekly.

Today's culture is a training ground. True, it differs remarkably from the culture of 20 years ago or 30 or 40. Every generation creates its own way of life and ethnic identities. Every generation is a counterculture to the previous one.

In truth, Goodman has it wrong. Her generation is the culture; the children offer the counterculture. It is the nature of the child to rebel, to find new ways, new music, and new entertainment. The teen years prepare the child for breaking free and leaving the home, and no parent can stop that process. Surely Goodman does not want little milksops who conform to her every wish. If they did, she would hate them for their lack of imagination and spirit of adventure. She would be pushing them out the door, saying, "Go do something!" Of course, the way children perform seldom matches mature logic or "the way we did it in the old days."

Invention and innovation come from the young, such as Bill Gates—that foolish child—playing around with little computers in the garage, or Marion Frank Rudy— that crazy kid—putting gas in a tennis shoe to create Nike's successful sneakers. The young have curiosity. Would Goodman say "no" to that?

Finally, it only follows that the media will feed this youthful counterculture composed of children and teens. There will be vulgarity, nudity, sexual displays, piercings, tattoos, wicked dancing, and more—all in the name of innovation for the new culture. Every generation revolts against the older one, and the older generation finds it revolting, as does Goodman. Mom and Dad, you can't stop the momentum of a new age, and you shouldn't blame the media, which only cater to the whims of the children.

This student has responded to the Goodman essay by affirming the positive aspects of children and teens, seeing them as responsible youngsters able to handle the vulgar as well as the beauty in today's society. He places no blame, neither on the media nor the youth of America. Each side feeds off the other, and, according to Lamar Clift, that's not a bad thing.

EXERCISE 8.3

WRITING A REBUTTAL TO THE IDEAS OF A SOURCE

First, skim the following two essays by Kay Hawes and Jay Walljasper. Next, select one for critical reading and rebuttal. Finally, write an essay that features these basic parts:

1. Explain that the source establishes a position that has merit.
2. Mention that certain issues need clarification.
3. Argue that some issues are not addressed adequately, or not addressed at all.
4. Offer a more valid position.

In responding to Hawes's essay, "Gender Research Shows Mixed Results for Women," you would react to the issues generated by Title IX, which mandated a balanced funding for women's and men's athletic programs. In responding to Walljasper's "Why Johnny and Jana Can't Walk to School," you would react to the issues generated by large central schools, requiring busing, as opposed to small neighborhood schools.

Gender Research Shows Mixed Results for Women
Kay Hawes

Women's participation and scholarship dollars show slow but steady gains on the gender-equity front, while salaries for the coaches of women's teams continue to lag behind those of men's teams, according to the recently released 1999–2000 NCAA Gender-Equity Study.

The biannual report shows that in Division I overall, women's athletics participation crept to 41 percent from 40 percent in the 1997–98 study. The study also showed incremental gains in scholarship dollars for women, from 41 percent to 43 percent of the scholarship funds in Division I overall.

Significant gaps remain between women's and men's coaches' salaries, however. According to the study, assistant coaches of Division I-A men's teams receive 74 percent of the dollars spent on assistant coaches and 62 percent of the funds spent on head coaches.

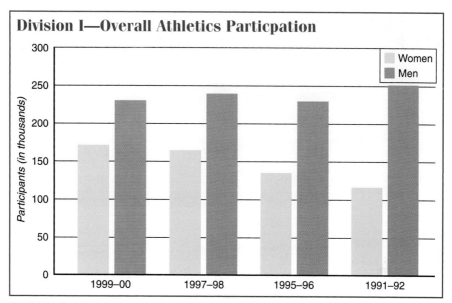

FIGURE 8.1

Operating expenses have remained largely unchanged, with some divisions reporting a slight increase in the percentage allotted to women's sports and Division II reporting a 4 percent decrease.

"Overall, the progress is slow but steady in some areas and stagnant in others," said Rosie Stallman, NCAA director of education outreach, "but the study is important because it can help athletic administrators see where the challenges are and develop a gender-equity plan to address some of those areas. By doing the study, the NCAA can provide information and groundwork for progress, but the actual planning and numbers for each institution are in the hands of those administrators on campus.

"We should commend those institutions that have gender-equity plans and are working on their goals. Those are the institutions that can serve as models for others."

The Gender-Equity Study provides summary information concerning personnel, revenues, expenses and other comparative variables of men's and women's intercollegiate athletics programs at NCAA member institutions for the 1999–2000 fiscal year. This report is the result of a survey conducted during the fall of 2000. Similar studies have been conducted by the NCAA since 1991, with resulting reports published in 1991–92, 1995–96 and 1997–98.

Participation and Scholarships

The survey reports on the average number of student-athlete participants at each institution and also the proportion of athletes by gender. Since the 1991–92

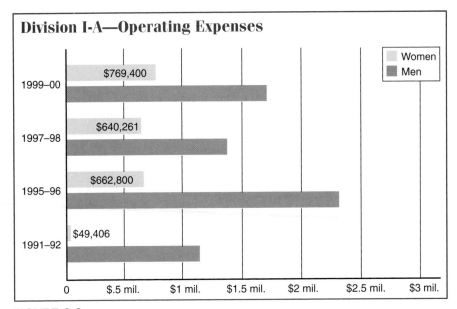

FIGURE 8.2

study, most divisions and subdivisions have reported a 10 percent gain in women's participation, though it has come in small increments over the years.

In Division I overall, women's participation stands at 41 percent, with an average of 163 student-athletes per institution. That figure is up 10 percent from the first study in 1991–92. This year's report also showed that in Division I overall, the average number of male participants decreased, from 241 in the last study to 233. In Division I-A, men's participation numbers decreased from 310 to 296, while the female participation numbers remained the same. Women's participation in I-A proportionally increased by one percent, from 38 percent in the previous study to 39 percent in this study. Again, that represents an overall gain of 10 percent since the 1991–92 study.

Men's and women's participation both increased in Division I-AA, which reported an average of eight more male participants per institution and 14 more female participants per institution, bringing the proportional numbers to 60 percent for the men and 40 percent from the women. The previous study had reported male participation at 62 percent and female participation at 38 percent, while the 1991–92 study reported 70 percent male participation and 30 percent female participation.

In Division I-AAA, which experienced a large loss in male participants from 1992 to 1996, the average number of male student-athletes rebounded by 11 per institution in 1998 and decreased by four in 2000. Females now compose 48 percent of the participants at this level, up from 47 percent in the last study and 36 percent in the 1991–92 study.

The 1-percent shift continued in Division II, which reported an average of 38 percent for female participation, up one percent from the last study and up from 32 percent in the 1991–92 study.

In Division III, women's participation decreased by an average of nine student-athletes per institution. Men's participation also decreased by an average of 15 student-athletes per institution, the same number they had increased by in the previous report. Because male and female participation decreased at the same rate, the proportion of female student-athletes remained at 40 percent, where it had been for the previous study, up from the 35 percent reported in the 1991–92 study.

In terms of women's team sponsorship, which can be an indicator of the potential for future participants, Division I overall saw gains in women's soccer, up from 182 teams reported in the previous study to 244 teams; women's lacrosse, up to 63 teams from 46; and women's ice hockey, up from 6 teams to 16. (Many more ice hockey teams have been added since then that will appear on the next report.) Also, rowing sponsorship went from 48 reported in the previous study to 73, while water polo went from 13 reported to 21 reported in this study.

"As institutions add more women's teams, we should see the number of female participants increase," Stallman said. "I'm surprised, with the increase of interest in women's sports over the last 10 years, that the participation numbers aren't higher than they are. Now that the groundwork is in place and many of these sports—such as ice hockey and water polo—are championships for women, we may see changes in participation over the next few years."

When it comes to scholarship dollars, there was an average of a 2 percent increase overall in money awarded to female student-athletes. Interestingly, the participation numbers in Division I-A have not kept up with the scholarship dollars. Division I-A reported that 40 percent of its scholarship dollars go to female student-athletes, up from 38 percent in the previous study and from 28 percent in the 1991–92 study. Division I-AAA remains the only subdivision or division that averages more scholarship money for women, with female student-athletes receiving an average of 52 percent of the funds.

Coaching Salaries

The gap in coaching salaries is most clearly seen in Division I-A assistant coaches, where the coaches of men's teams receive 74 percent of the dollars and the coaches of women's teams receive 26 percent. That's a one percent increase from the previous study, in which the women's teams received 25 percent, and a 10 percent increase from the 1991–92 study.

Though the funding in Division I-A for assistant coaches of women's teams has risen from the $118,897 reported in 1991–92 to the overall average sum of $374,500, the average amount spent on assistant coaches for men's teams has increased in that same period from $624,312 to $1,063,900, resulting in the 74–26 ratio.

Even in Division III, which it could be argued would likely have fewer assistant coaches for such sports as football, men's teams receive 69 percent of the funds

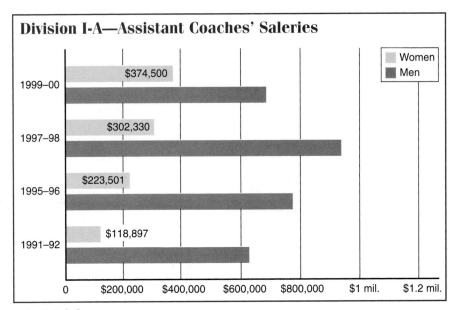

FIGURE 8.3

used for assistant coaches, down one point from the 70 percent reported in the last study, and women's teams receive 31 percent. Again, Division I-AAA reports the smallest gap, with the coaches of men's teams receiving 55 percent of the funds and the coaches of women's teams receiving 45 percent.

The proportion for head coaches' salaries remained unchanged in Division I-A, with 62 percent of the funds devoted to the coaches of men's teams and 38 percent to women's teams. That's only a four-point shift from 1991–92, when 66 percent of the funds went to men's teams and 34 percent to women's teams.

"When you raise the level of pay for a coaching position that's underfunded, you raise the level of experience you bring to the student-athlete," Stallman said.

Operating, Recruiting Expenses

In both operating and recruiting expenses, women gained slightly, though they lost ground in Division II operating expenses. In Division I-A, men receive an average of 67 percent of the operating expenses and 71 percent of the recruiting expenses, down from 69 and 72 percent from the previous study.

Recruiting also continues to be an area where women's teams lag behind. In 1991–92, Division I-A institutions spent 84 percent of their recruiting dollars on men's teams. Though 71 percent of the recruiting dollars were reportedly spent on men's teams in this most recent report, that remains a significant difference.

Division I-AAA and Division III reported the largest proportional gains for women's recruiting, with I-AAA increasing from 39 percent to 45 percent and Division III increasing from 31 percent to 35 percent.

This year's study also showed that institutions in Division II increased the proportion of money spent on men's operating expenses to 66 percent, up from 62 percent in the previous study.

When it comes to operating expenses in Division I-A, women have gained more than half a million dollars since 1991–92, but the men's expenses also increased by more than a half million. The study in 1991–92 showed that an average of $1,049,020 was devoted to men's operating expenses and $262,570 to women's operating expenses. The most current study shows that women's operating expenses have risen to an average of $769,400, while men's expenses have risen to $1,583,000.

Division III reported a 1 percent increase in funds devoted to women's operating expenses, from 40 percent in the previous study to 41 percent, while Division I-AAA reported a 2 percent gain, up to 45 percent.

Hard copies of the 1999–2000 NCAA Gender-Equity study should arrive at all NCAA member institutions by the end of the month. It also is available online at **www.ncaa.org/library/research.html#gender_equity.**

Why Johnny and Jana Can't Walk to School
Jay Walljasper

As autumn rolls around again, we're resuming a favorite ritual at our house. My son, Soren, starts first grade, and so each morning he, his mother Julle, and I will stroll a few blocks to the Clara Barton public school in Minneapolis, built in 1911 and recently renovated to add a gym. Along the way we'll note the falling leaves, the steadily later sunrise, the morning frost, and so on through the school year until tulips bloom and the scent of lilacs hang in the breeze.

Walking to school is a special childhood rite of initiation, but, sadly, it is disappearing from the life of many American communities. And not for the reasons many people think. Racial integration plans and fear of abduction drive fewer kids into school buses and parents' minivans than other, less recognized factors: the closing of small neighborhood schools and speeding traffic that imperils pint-sized pedestrians.

"Communities are abandoning historic neighborhood schools that students can walk to in favor of new schools the size of shopping malls built in far-flung locations," writes Edward T. McMahon, director of the American Greenways Program, in a dispatch for the Elm Street Writers Group, an online news service covering environmental and community issues (**www.mlui.org**). "Schools serve as community anchors," McMahon notes. Many events, from Little League games to fitness classes to public meetings, happen after-hours at the local school. The fact that many of these threatened schools are in inner-city neighborhoods or struggling small towns means that their closing cuts deep into the heart of places that already have been battered.

Alarmed by what's happening all across the country, the National Trust for Historic Preservation included neighborhood schools in its 2000 list of America's Most Endangered Historic Places. But this is a bigger issue than simply architectural heritage. Communities that have lost their school feel different without kids laughing and clowning along the sidewalks. It's more difficult for parents (especially low-income families) to participate in activities at distant schools, and they must shoulder more responsibility for chauffeuring their kids home from after-school programs.

Bigger, far-flung schools add to the already rising costs of education. A study in Maine found that while school enrollment in the state dropped by 27,000 between 1970 and 1995, the annual costs for busing jumped from $8.7 million to $54 million, due in large part to the consolidation of local schools.

The trend toward larger, out-of-the-way schools defies a tide of recent evidence showing that small schools serve students better than large ones do (see *Utne Reader,* Jan./Feb. 2001, p. 26). Kathleen Cotton, an educational research specialist at the Northwest Regional Educational Laboratory in Portland, Oregon, notes that "a large body of research in the affective and social realms [of child development] overwhelmingly affirms the superiority of small schools."

"Although it is often assumed that large schools are cheaper to operate and provide richer curricula than small schools," Cotton is quoted in *Planning Commissioners Journal* (Summer 2000), "studies show that neither of these things [is] necessarily true."

Low-income kids, especially, feel the effects of big schools, according to the *Atlanta Journal-Constitution,* which reported "the gap in academic achievement between rich schools and poor schools is greatly reduced when school are smaller."

The trend toward demolishing existing schools in favor of big, new ones represents something more than just shifting population and the obsolescence of old buildings. McMahon explains that state and national educational policies greatly favor building new schools over renovating existing ones. He notes that the Council of Educational Facility Planners International, a professional organization, established a formula governing the size of school grounds that is completely blind about land use patterns in urban areas. As McMahon explains, "A 2,000-student high school requires at least fifty acres, or more than almost any city, big or small, has available near its residential neighborhoods." (The National Trust for Historical Preservation is now working with the Council to develop a new formula that takes urban land use into account, reports *Preservation* magazine [July/Aug. 2001].) An even bigger obstacle are regulations in most states that forbid funding of school renovations if the costs are half or two-thirds the price of building a new one. And the *New York Times* reports that school renovation costs are sometimes grossly inflated. The price tag for fixing up the 1914 Kokomo (Indiana) High School, for example, was figured at $20 million to $25 million, but the work was eventually done for $4 million.

Innovative efforts underway in Maryland show that a shift in policies can make a dramatic difference in preserving neighborhood schools. As part of Governor Parris Glendening's campaign to curb sprawl, the state has evened the playing field in funding between school renovation and new construction. In 1995, just 34 percent of state funding went to improvements on existing schools; in 1998, it was 84 percent.

Another reason fewer kids are strolling to school these days is fear about them crossing busy streets. But a growing national movement of pedestrian activists are successfully lobbying for new measures to make streets safer for walkers of all ages, reports *Governing* magazine (May 2001). San José, California, for instance, has tripled to $5 million its spending on traffic calming—road design features that induce motorists to slow down. Portland, Oregon, is implementing a comprehensive plan that takes pedestrian concerns into account in the planning of many projects throughout the city. And the state of California is spending $20 million a year to identify "safe routes to school" aimed at giving kids an option to walk or bike.

It may seem a trifling concern whether children (and their parents) have the pleasure of walking to school in the morning, but it's not. The state of our society—and health of our environment—is built upon a foundation of small, everyday events. When the school is miles away, it means more vehicles flood the streets, more kids learn that all mobility begins with the turn of an ignition, more students are funneled through large institutions, and more neighborhoods see a decline in their sense of community. These conditions, in turn, start us down the road to further sprawl, alienation, and a coming generation that accepts those things as perfectly natural. That's why this renewal of interest across America in preserving kids' chance to stroll to and from school delights me. And if you're ever in Minneapolis, out on the sidewalks in the vicinity of Barton School anytime around 7:30 am, please come over and say "hi."

Writing an Evaluation or Review

WEB LINK to Reading 8.4
http://www. ablongman.com/ lester

You may need to write an evaluation or review of a story, a poetry chapbook, a musical or dramatic performance, an art display, a film, or some other work. Any of these will require you to accomplish several tasks.

- Summarize the work if you think it might be obscure to your reader or unknown (see Chapter 4 for details about writing the summary).
- Explain the nature of the work and the context within which it is presented.
- Determine the work's quality on the basis of several criteria of judgment.
- Relate the work to the larger issues it addresses.
- Make a judgment on the work's overall quality.
- Provide, usually, a recommendation to the reader.

These can all be accomplished rather quickly. Here is a brief review of a musical production.

Oklahoma!

There are stupendous pleasures in the Royal National Theatre's award-winning version of Rodgers and Hammerstein's 1943 American classic. Many of them are due to the high-spirited, humorous choreography of Susan Stroman, and to Anthony Ward's picturesque set, which immediately submerges us in a gorgeous world of folk innocence. But technique, which can make a show work, is not enough to make it wonderful.

—From *The New Yorker,* May 13, 2002.

This writer identifies the virtues of good choreography and set design but laments the absence of great acting, singing, and other criteria appropriate to musical comedies.

Here's another example, which quickly reviews a book about American novels after World War II.

Leopards in the Temple, by Morris Dickstein (Harvard; $15.95). In this sharply sketched history of American fiction in the postwar years, Dickstein upends prevailing caricatures, showing that the culture of the fifties was "highly self-critical . . . and alive with change at the margins," and that the new American novel epitomized the era. Writers who once would have been considered "outsiders"—Ellison, Baldwin, Bellow, Roth, and Mailer—became central, producing works that fused the novel's traditional emphasis on the social with a newfound fascination with the psychological. Kerouac and Salinger reinvigorated first-person narrative while writers like Updike and Yates explored spiritual doubt in suburbia. Dickstein's criticism is pointed without being harsh, and he is alive to the pleasures that even flawed works can provide. Most impressively, he uses history to illuminate fiction, and vice versa, but never forgets to keep the two realms separate.

—From "Briefly Noted," *The New Yorker,* May 13, 2002.

Although the review is brief, this writer considers several issues—the quality of the writing, originality, tradition, new issues, and the roles of history and literature.

Drafting the Review

Some college writing assignments will ask you to review a local drama production, a current movie, a poem, or an art exhibit. Roland Stamps was asked to review a Doonesbury comic strip, which we have reproduced here. Several steps are required by Stamps in the writing of an evaluation.

Step 1

Examine and experience the work in order to write a general impression.

Source: DOONESBURY © 2002 G. B. Trudeau. Reprinted with permission of Universal Press Syndicate. All rights reserved.

Stamps made this note:

This cartoon by G. B. Trudeau satirizes corporate America, especially the CEOs who fleece company funds and leave shareholders and employees with a bankrupt company.

Step 2

Write down as many details of your overall judgment as possible.

Note: You will need a set of criteria with which to judge the work. For example, I will consider this comic strip a good one if it is humorous, makes a valid point about the human condition, and features interesting fictional characters. *A novel or an art display would require different criteria.*

Stamps wrote:

Trudeau attacks the greed of corporate executives who pay themselves huge salaries, manipulate the value of the stock, create false accounts, give themselves golden parachutes for retirement, and practice insider trading.

A quick trip to the Internet with a search under the key words *corporate greed* produced several names: Ken Lay at Enron, Dennis Kozlowski of Tyco, Carleton S. Fiorina at Hewlett-Packard, and even Martha Stewart, the guru to homemakers, for her suspected insider trading of ImClone stock. They are all caught in a web of greed, profit taking, and total disregard for the welfare of the corporation, its workers, and its stockholders.

Arthur Anderson, a national accounting firm, now lies in ruins because it, too, participated in Enron's secret accounts and then shredded paperwork to hide the duplicity.

Trudeau, in his subtle way, shows his distaste by having the daughter Alex refer to the newspaper's business section as the crime page.

Step 3

WEB LINK
to Exercise
8.4
http://www.
ablongman.com/
lester

Write the review, using a fairly standard paradigm:

1. Identify the work being reviewed with name, genre, title, location, price, publisher, and so forth.
2. Give a quick evaluation.
3. Provide any background information that is necessary to place the work in its context.
4. Give a very short summary of the work.
5. Provide the details of judgment to defend your positive or negative evaluation.
6. Restate your general evaluation and make some sort of recommendation to the reader. If necessary, note and identify the level of audience for the work.

Here is the review by Roland Stamps.

Roland Stamps

English 1010

Professor Martinez

May 7, 2003

Doonesbury on Corporate Greed

The comic strip artist who creates *Doonesbury,* G. B. Trudeau, manages his cartoons with a satiric whip that cuts across the backsides of those persons who abuse their power or ignore common decency and the rule of law. In his strip of June 24, 2002, Trudeau attacks the CEOs of the business world for their corporate greed.

The cartoon uses an ironic play on a newspaper's "crime page" that, in truth, is the newspaper's "business page."

The daughter Alex, speaking for Trudeau, observes that business CEOs are involved in trials and scandals but "no one ever goes to jail." The satire cuts to the bone.

Trudeau attacks the greed of corporate executives who pay themselves huge salaries, manipulate the value of the stock, create false accounts, give themselves golden parachutes for retirement, and practice insider trading.

A quick trip to the Internet with a search under the key words *corporate greed* produced several names: Ken Lay at Enron, Dennis Kozlowski of Tyco, Carleton S. Fiorina at Hewlett-Packard, and even Martha Stewart, the guru to homemakers, for her suspected insider trading of ImClone stock. They are all caught in a web of greed, profit taking, and total disregard for the welfare of the corporation, its workers, and its stockholders.

Arthur Anderson, a national accounting firm, now lies in ruins because it, too, participated in Enron's secret accounts and then shredded paperwork to hide the duplicity.

Thus, Trudeau must get high marks for his penetrating analysis and criticism of the corrupt business dealings that leave stockholders destitute while CEOs walk away as millionaires.

EXERCISE 8.4

WRITING A REVIEW

Following the directions of your instructor, write a review of a movie, a music CD, a video game, one of your textbooks, or a product such as new computer software, new jogging shoes, a brand of microwave popcorn, or the latest Harley motorcycle.

Chapter Review

WEB LINK
to Chapter 8
Related Web
Destinations
http://www.
ablongman.com/
lester

This chapter has encouraged you to respond to a single source both to discover the ideas of others but also to find your own position on an issue. It shows students finding ideas but also reacting and even refuting the ideas of others. It demonstrated the four basic types of single-source essays: personal response, interpretation, rebuttal, and evaluation or review.

In the first, you are asked to respond to an essay by finding your own ideas and positions on some aspect of the essay's contents. This subjective response allows you to drift away from the primary source to develop a personal essay that explores ideas not necessarily present in the source.

In the second, you are asked to interpret the source without inserting your personal opinion and without disagreeing with the source. This objective treatment of the text requires you to stay focused, analyze the work to find its basic parts, summarize the parts, and write an interpretation.

In the third type of single-source essay, you are asked to disagree with a source and write a rebuttal. You probe deeply into the motivations of the creator of a work and find the basic principles that underlie the person's argument. Until you understand the original source, you cannot effectively frame a rebuttal. Your rebuttal will probably defend a fundamental principle.

In the fourth type, an evaluation or review, you are required to establish the criteria by which you will judge the work. Criteria will differ for a performance, movie, speech, and so forth. A good practice is to write a list of the criteria that pertain to the work *before* you begin to write. Ultimately, you must judge the overall quality of the work and, in some instances, make a recommendation to the reader.

Chapter 8 Assignment: Writing the Single-Source Essay

This assignment has two parts, each requiring you to write a one-page paper.

1. Write an interpretation. Study the cartoon from *The New Yorker* magazine reproduced below. Then write a one-page interpretation of it. TIP: If you don't know the myth of Sisyphus, look up the myth before writing the paper.

2. Study the cartoon by John McPherson reproduced at the right, especially noting the victim and the clerks behind the counter. Then write a one-page personal essay in response to the cartoon.

"Can't you ever relax?"

Source: "Can't you ever relax?" by C. Weyant. Copyright © The New Yorker collection 2002 Christopher Weyant from cartoonbank.com. All Rights Reserved.

**Department of Motor Vehicles employee
Charlene Rumpf celebrates after sending a
customer back for a record ninth form.**

Source: CLOSE TO HOME © by John McPherson. Reprinted with permision of UNIVERSAL
PRESS SYNDICATE. All rights reserved.

Tracing the Work of Two Students

Here's a brief example showing how Kaci Holz, in developing her research
paper, interpreted the work of one expert on the topic of gender communication.
In this passage, Holz has written a basic interpretation. She does not spin off into
her own ideas, she does not argue against the source, and she does not review the
book by Glass.

What are the causes for the differences in the communication styles of men and
women? Lillian Glass, a linguistics researcher, provides some answers in her book *He
Says, She Says: Closing the Communication Gap Between the Sexes.* The third chapter
of her book addresses "the evolution of sex differences in communication" (61). Glass
addresses the issue that different hormones found in men's and women's bodies make
them act differently and therefore communicate differently. She also discusses how
brain development has been found to relate to sex differences. She writes extensively
in this chapter and others about the manner in which environmental factors,
specifically the way we treat boy and girl infants, directly affect the ways children
learn to communicate (64-73).

Writing the Multi-Source Essay

Composing from multiple sources requires a delicate balance of your ideas and words and those of several other people. The task is not easy, but other voices and opinions—blended effectively within your content—will reinforce your essay and may even challenge you and your readers to confront new and perhaps unusual views of the topic.

Choosing Your Sources

WEB LINK
to Chapter 9
Related Web
Destinations
http://www.
ablongman.com/
lester

Drawing several different sources into your paper broadens its scope, enriches the content, offers contrasting ideas, and signals your sophistication as a writer. The multi-source essay allows you to show how a variety of opinions enhances the discussion of the topic. Consider the following topics:

- The redevelopment of the World Trade Center is enriched by a variety of architectural designs.
- The debate on abortion must embrace divergent views that seem irreconcilable.
- The state lottery benefits many students by funding scholarships, but many people forfeit their paychecks and savings in the delusion of "hitting the jackpot."

Your topic, like the ones above, needs to be significant and current so that you will find outside sources discussing various aspects of the issue. (See Chapters 1 and 2) for specific guidelines on selecting a subject.) In addition to finding a suitable topic, you will need to establish your own position on the issue, which can then be augmented by the sources. Your opinion is the anchor for the essay, and all outside sources must form a chain so that each source is linked to your position.

T I P   *Multiple Sources in Your Essay Exams*

You have already created multi-source writing in your essay exams. For example, consider this question: *Even though he won the war, General Grant of the Union Army never won the respect given General Lee of the Confederate Army; why not?* An essay answer will usually require the student to bring in some ideas from the text, from the instructor's lectures, and, perhaps, another source or two. However, the essay answer must not mimic the instructor nor the text.

Developing methods for synthesizing the sources and blending them into your prose style is the focus of this chapter. Therefore, before we go any further, let's look at a short essay that does two things: it identifies a topic of significance and it synthesizes a number of sources. Thereby, we can launch a discussion on the values as well as the dangers of the multi-source essay.

As you read Shirley I. Wilcher's essay, originally published in the *Nashville Tennessean* (January 17, 2003), identify the times that the author draws a source into her work. The marginal notes provide clues.

Racism Is Still Alive Throughout the United States

Shirley J. Wilcher

In the federal courts, we are facing the most concerted effort in recent history to destroy equal-opportunity programs, including affirmative action. When the U.S. Supreme Court hears the cases brought against the University of Michigan, wherein 5 white students say they were denied admission because race was factored into the admission of minority students, we could lose the rights we gained with such difficulty. The number of college minority students could plummet.

Her first source is a Supreme Court case.

Those of us who entered college in the late 1960s and beyond understand what is at stake.

She uses personal experience as a source.

The recent Trent Lott affair and the nationwide debate it sparked reminded me why affirmative action is still desperately needed. Discrimination in America is alive and well.

She references Senator Trent Lott's discriminating remarks in 2002.

While serving as deputy assistant secretary at the Labor Department in the 1990s, I traveled to meet the CEO of a company that repaired equipment for the federal government. I wanted to *Again, she uses personal* know how the company could have tolerated the raffle of a Ku Klux *experience as a source.* Klan knife by members of its repair shop. Compliance officers discovered this behavior during a routine review of the company's affirmative-action program. The contractor had signed an agreement to run the program in exchange for the privilege of doing business with the government.

In addition to the Klan raffle, we found racist and sexist graffiti on the walls of the lavatories. Blacks said the N-word was used profusely. Women had resigned rather than tolerate the sexual harassment.

When I asked the CEO for an explanation, he attempted to *She paraphrases the CEO.* minimize the problem and even suggested there were very few Klan members among the staff.

This is only one of a dozen egregious discrimination cases we posted on our Web site during the Newt Gingrich years to remind America that equal opportunity was not yet a reality. The Lott affair clearly underscores this point and unfortunately brings it into this century.

Affirmative action constitutes steps employers, colleges and *She paraphrases the* procurement officers take to promote equal opportunity and to *nature of affirmative* remedy or prevent discrimination. It means recruitment and out- *action laws.* reach, adding diversity to the pool of qualified candidates. It means eliminating barriers and providing equal pay. It is not quotas or preferences, it does not require hiring, promoting or admitting the unqualified, and it is not reverse discrimination.

Critics argue that race should not be considered in awarding contracts, making hiring decisions or admitting students to col- *She uses a direct* lege. However, as Kathleen Kennedy Townsend, recent candi- *quotation from Kathleen* date for Maryland's governorship, declared: "Slavery was based *Townsend.* on race. Lynching was based on race. Discrimination was based on race. Jim Crow was based on race. And affirmative action should be based on race." I think she's got it.

Wilcher uses six sources in this brief essay, and she blends them effectively into her argument. As the marginal notes explain, she summarizes the Supreme Court case, draws on her knowledge of affirmative action laws, paraphrases a company CEO, provides a direct quotation from Townsend, and recalls her own personal experience.

Wilcher's piece is a good example of a multi-source essay, for several reasons.

- Wilcher identifies the source, whether she is quoting, paraphrasing, or merely making a reference, as in the case of Trent Lott.

- Wilcher keeps the central issue alive in each paragraph and draws the source into the paragraph as a natural extension of her ideas. That is, the sources do not drive the essay forward, Wilcher does.

- The use of multiple sources suggests that Wilcher has carefully researched the topic. By her references, she gives the strong impression that she knows her subject well.

Of course, there can be drawbacks to writing a multi-source essay. As a writer adds more and more sources to the paper, the danger of losing the controlling voice grows. Drifting from one source to the next can obliterate the writer's voice and the central message. Merely collecting a group of opinions on the topic, one after the other, in a patchwork fashion, will mute your voice and obscure your ideas.

This chapter, therefore, will provide you with the necessary techniques for these important tasks:

- Discovering your own point of view on a significant subject.
- Reading critically to discover shades of meaning in various sources.
- Explaining how a source speaks to the issue.
- Synthesizing the sources into your own work.
- Comparing sources to keep each source distinctive from others and explaining how they disagree but still fit your purpose.

EXERCISE 9.1

JUDGING A WRITER'S USE OF SOURCES

By way of introduction to the process of using sources, let's get our feet wet by examining one writer's multi-source article. Read critically the essay below by Suzanne Fields, underlining, highlighting, and making marginal annotations about the writer's references to singers and sources. Answer the questions at the end of the essay.

Bad Raps: Music Rebels Revel in Their Thug Life
Suzanne Fields

WEB LINK
to Reading
9.1
http://www.
ablongman.com/
lester

Nothing in the culture wars makes a stronger argument for the defense of conservative values than rap music. Rap expresses the worst kind of images emanating from a postmodern society that has consigned a generation of young men and women to the darkest dramas of the desperately lost.

The megastars of this genre are not about to sing of "you and me and baby makes three." Their lyrics come from a world of broken families, absent fathers, illegitimate children and matriarchal dominance, often subsidized by welfare.

For the men who denigrate women as "bitches" and "ho's," this is not merely misogyny (though it is that), but alienation from common humanity and community. The lyrics employ vulgar street idioms because both the language and experience of poetry or romance are absent from the lives of the rappers and their audience as well.

Frank Sinatra grew up on the mean streets of New Jersey and he knew the Mafia well, but when he sang "You're the top, You're the Tower of Pisa. . . . You're the Mona Lisa" he aspired to sophistication and wanted others to see him as debonair. (Is there a rapper alive who knows the difference between the Tower of Pisa and a towering pizza?) When Frankie was bad, literally, he didn't want his fans to hear about it. He wasn't as innocent as his lyrics, but he cultivated that impression.

Rappers Sean "Puffy" Combs and Eminem, by contrast, must live like they sing. They're rich, but their attraction resides in perverse behavior on and off stage. When as adults they tap into adolescent rebellion, they dumb down both their emotions and their economic success.

Shelby Steele, a black scholar, has their number when he writes that to keep their audience they can't just sing about alienation—they had better experience it as well, either with the audience or for the audience.

"The rappers and promoters themselves are pressured toward a thug life, simply to stay credible," Steele writes in the *Wall Street Journal*. "A rap promoter without an arrest record can start to look a lot like Dick Clark."

A rapper such as Eminem, who revels in affecting a white-trash identity, has defenders, too. They find irony, satire and poetic metaphor in his lyrics, but it's difficult to see how most of his fans take those lyrics as anything but straight. Lurking in them is a cruel depravity that seeks ways to go over the line by singing of macho brutality—of raping women, holding gay men with a knife at their throats and helping a group of friends to take a little sister's virginity.

These lyrics are powerful, but the power resides in psychological defensiveness that provides a perverse rationalization for brutality: If you don't love you can't be rejected, so you might as well hate and rape.

Every generation since Elvis has driven through adolescence on popular music—looking for the new sound and sensibility that rejects what their parents liked. Elvis was the cutting edge of the sexual revolution; innovative then, but tame and hardly even titillating today. It's hard to believe that for his first appearance on the Ed Sullivan Show, the maestro wouldn't allow the cameras to focus below the singer's waist.

Elvis brilliantly combined the black, blues and sex rhythms of the honky-tonks of the backroads South of his time, liberating teen-age rebels in dance and song. But nearly every music hero and heroine after him has had to push the envelope or raise the ante to be a big winner. For some teenagers the explicit meanness may provide an imaginary escape, the permission to act in a dark, forbidden drama of their imaginations. For these young men and women, the incentives to "act out" may be no more aggressive than dyeing hair purple or wearing ugly clothes. For others, "acting out" as in "men behaving badly," may be the preferred response in human relationships.

Rappers, rollers and rockers who tap into the big time with bite and bitterness draw millions to their records and concerts for different reasons. The teenage and young-adult zeitgeist is made up of rebels with and without causes. It didn't hurt Eminem that his mother sued him for $10 million for using lyrics such as "my mom smokes more dope than I do." (It might have been Eminem's press agent's idea.) That's on the same track in which he ponders which Spice Girl he would prefer to "impregnate."

There are lots of other popular singers who get less notice by being less bizarre. They make up a popular lifestyle that eventually will morph into a healthy nostalgia. The pity is that the nasty stuff of violent rap may never reach the nostalgic mode but congeal into a brutal life perspective.

In one of Eminem's hits he sings of a deranged fan. Eminem suggests the fan get counseling, but the fan doesn't. Instead he kills himself and his pregnant girlfriend. Fantasy or reality?

Answer these questions about the essay by Suzanne Fields:

1. How many sources does Field bring into the essay?
2. Fields cites from which scholar?
3. How does Fields set Frank Sinatra and Elvis Presley in opposition to the rap singers?
4. How does Fields show Elvis as a forefather to the modern rappers?
5. Which two rappers does Fields use as her source for the nature of rap music?
6. What is Fields's attitude toward modern rap music?
7. Could you write an essay that defends rap music? What sources would you use? Which singers? Can you find any scholars to support rap music?

Establishing Your Own Point of View

WEB LINK
to Audio-
videos 9.1
and 9.2

http://www.
ablongman.com/
lester

At the very beginning of any writing project that involves outside sources, you must determine your personal position on the issues or problems. If you don't, you will drift unanchored from the strength of one source to another, or—perhaps worse—you will fall under the shadow of one source that will dominate your essay. Another danger also looms: getting caught in a vacuum with no position of your own, which might occur if you remain neutral in an attempt to be fair to all the sources. In consequence, you would produce a meaningless paper without a heart. To help you avoid these dangers—drifting from source to source, letting one source dominate, and remaining neutral—let's look at four techniques that will help you develop a point of view:

1. Summarizing the facts of the issue
2. Framing an initial statement of opinion.
3. Reading critically for principles that lie behind another person's statement to see how that position affects yours.
4. Grouping sources into categories based on their reasoning and positions to find a synthesis or to locate a disagreement that might affect your position.

Summarizing the Facts of the Issue

WEB LINK
to Exercise
9.1
http://www.
ablongman.com/
lester

In Chapter 4 you were introduced to guidelines for writing a summary to capture the central idea of a source. Those guidelines apply here with a different perspective; rather than summarizing a paragraph or an article, you will identify and summarize the basic issues. Thus, the term *summary* in this context means a short passage that condenses the ideas of a topic. You can find these ideas in the literature, and you will see that the positions of different writers often conflict with each another. Your task is to sort through the various sources to put things into perspective.

One student, George LaBaron, found several pieces of literature on the topic of human cloning.

Source 1

Normal human development depends on precise genomic imprinting. This chemical reprogramming of the DNA, which takes place in adult reproductive tissue, takes months for sperm, and years for eggs. During cloning, by contrast, the reprogramming of the donor DNA must occur within a few minutes. . . . Cloning fails because there is simply not enough time in these few minutes to get the reprogramming job done properly.

—Dr. George Johnson

Source 2

One web site—**www.globalchange.com**—offers three reasons against cloning: health risks from mutation of genes, emotional risks, and abuse of the technology. This site raises the specters of monsters, incest, and Hitler.

Source 3

Correctly to understand why cloning is such a perverse mode of generating human life it is necessary to reflect on (1) the truth that human life is a human person's concrete reality and is hence of incomparable dignity and sanctity, and (2) the bond uniting marriage, the marital act, and the generation of human life. We can then (3) see how grotesquely cloning perverts the beginning of human life. . . . All forms of artificial reproduction are depersonalizing because they treat human life as a product and not as something of incomparable worth. But of all these forms cloning is the most perverse because it more radically tears the origin of human life from the bodily union of man and woman, from their one-flesh unity.

—William E. May, PhD

Source 4

Within the last year, a great deal of evidence has emerged that indicates that stem cells can be obtained from a variety of sources. You don't have to create an embryo, or destroy one, to obtain such cells. Not long before the British gave their support to embryo cloning, studies conducted in England and the United States and published in a range of leading journals including *Science, Nature,* and *Hepatology* found that stem cells can be obtained from adult humans, using sources such as bone marrow cells. These cells would still have the all-important pluripotentiality of stem cells—the ability to develop into heart, lung, or brain cells, or any cells that you desire, with the proper manipulation. Why make or destroy embryos to obtain stem cells when we don't have to?

—Edmund Pellegrino, MD

Source 5

Human genes are not sacred, people are.

—Ronald Bailey in Reasononline

Source 6

Crucial to the debate is the fact that human cloning research falls into two distinct categories: reproductive cloning, a widely frowned-on effort that aims to produce a fully formed child; and therapeutic cloning, a scientifically reputable procedure that takes place entirely at the microscopic level and is designed to advance medical therapies and cure human ailments.

—Kyla Dunn

Using just these six passages, LaBaron wrote this summary of the issue:

The cloning debate seems to pivot on the issue of human life with (1) the church and humanitarians arguing for the sanctity of the embryo and (2) the scientists arguing the inestimable value of therapeutic cloning. Thus, as long as an embryo remains central to either type of cloning—reproductive or therapeutic—the two sides will never meet on common ground. The scientific community faces an almost impossible task in its attempts to conduct stem cell research against a massive tide of protest from the conservative right and the church organizations.

This student has identified the sides in conflict; accordingly, he can move forward with his research, and his organization of the essay can move forward also. In particular, the student will need to express soon, in his own words, the position he will take on the issue.

EXERCISE 9.2

SUMMARIZING THE ISSUES

Reproduced below are five statements on the topic "Education and State Lotteries." Read each critically, taking notes as you go, and then write a summary of the issues, similar to the one written by George LaBaron, above, on the issue of cloning.

Several [online] companies have started trying to attract visitors to their sites by giving away money. The most well-known of these is iWon.com, which gives away $10,000 a day, $1 million a month, and $10 million a year. Similarly well known is the Publisher's Clearinghouse; Jackpot.com has a top prize of $2 million. There are also trivia sites, such as GoldPocket.com, that let users compete online for cash prizes. Other sites give away free scholarships. Your odds of winning a free scholarship in these lotteries are low, since the sites expect the lure of free scholarship to attract millions of visitors. The sites hope the visitors will click on advertisements and buy products from their stores. Yet, so long as the sites do not charge you a fee to enter, there doesn't seem to be much harm in it.

—FinAid: The SmartStudent Guide to Financial Aid

Thirty-seven states, as well as Puerto Rico and Washington, DC, use lotteries to raise funds, often for education. Debates are ongoing now in several other states about whether or not to institute a lottery. As Christians participate in these discussions, there are several critical questions we should ask. First, are lotteries immoral? If so, why? Second, do state education lotteries provide the benefits to education that are commonly advertised? Can private education be harmed by a lottery? Third, can we justify setting the state up in the entertainment business as a competitor with the private sector?

—Timothy D. Terrell, "Lotteries and the State," The Chalcedon Foundation
22 Apr. 2004

Less easily quantifiable, but no less important, are the social costs of lotteries, which include problem gambling, underage participation, misleading or false advertising, and discouragement of the work ethic. Problem and pathological gamblers behave in ways that are harmful to themselves and their families, and this behavior can contribute to depression, domestic abuse, divorce, homelessness, and suicide.

—Erinn Staley, "Gambling in America: Politics and Policy," 23 Apr. 2001

Any debate on a state education lottery may appear to reduce to a contest between those concerned with morality questions and gambling addiction on one hand, and promoters of education on the other. Yet this may oversimplify the discussion. Without downplaying the importance of moral issues or the social consequences of habitual gambling, we should recognize that a state lottery may produce significant negative economic effects. A brief review of some of the evidence suggests that state education lotteries may harm some businesses while failing to produce the advertised benefits for education. A lottery sets the state government up as a competitor to private businesses, and encourages a misallocation of valuable resources. At the same time, projections of lottery profits are unrealistic, if the results obtained by lotteries in neighboring states are any guide. Lottery proponents have indicated that $300 million in net profits can be anticipated, while a figure 60 percent smaller would be more reasonable. Studies have shown, too, that much of this money would be raised from low-income households. Certainly, before Oklahoma decides on a lottery, voters should become aware of these concerns.

—Timothy D. Terrell, "If an Education Lottery Right for Oklahoma?"
Oklahoma Council of Public Affairs

Florida Lottery

Education Enhancement Trust Fund $12.05 billion

Georgia Lottery Corporation

HOPE Scholarships $2.1 billion

Pre-Kindergarten Program $1.8 billion

Capital Outlay and Technology for Primary and Secondary Schools $1.8 billion

Idaho Lottery

    Public Schools (K–12) $105.5 million

    Public Buildings $105.5 million

Illinois Lottery

    Illinois Common School Fund (K–12) $11.06 billion

Kentucky Lottery

    Education $214 million

    Vietnam Veterans $32 million

    General Fund $1.3 billion

    Post-Secondary and College Scholarships $203 million

    Affordable Housing Trust Fund $17 million

    Literacy Programs and Early Childhood Reading $9 million

        —North American Association of State and Provincial Lotteries (NASPL),
        30 June 2002

Assignment: Write a summary of the issues raised by the five passages above.

Framing an Initial Statement of Opinion

When writing on a controversial issue, such as cloning, you will need to find your own comfort zone as to your position. It need not be one side or the other, although usually that's the case. Student George LaBaron, mentioned above, expressed this position on cloning:

    Medical necessity and scientific ingenuity will need to produce new methods for stem cell research; otherwise, the gulf will widen and the medical community might lose its support and respect.

With this position, the student has a mission—to search out articles offering new methods of stem cell research and, thus, new hope for those persons who might benefit.

The Thesis Sentence

In many cases, the position is evident in the writer's thesis sentence:

    We must protect the Everglades from industrial encroachment.
    Rave parties offer a false and very dangerous ecstasy.

From the start, these two thesis sentences have a point of view and a built-in plan to focus the research. One will borrow from sources that advocate methods for healing the wilderness in Florida. The other will consult sources on the dangers of drugs mixed with dance parties. Each of these writers has a thesis statement that he or she must prove with the evidence gathered in research.

However, these obvious positions will produce one-sided arguments. Who would want to trash the Everglades? Who believes that rave parties build moral character? In addition, rushing into a thesis might lock your position and limit your search to sources that support it. Contrary views may not receive consideration. Note how these next two positions lock the writer to one point of view:

> Nutritional foods can become an economic weapon in the battle against
>   rising health care expenses.
> The exorbitant tuition at America's colleges is forcing out the poor and
>   promoting an elitist class.

Both positions offer conclusions that seem to shut off debate. Will the writer merely search out evidence to support the thesis? In truth, both positions need nonbiased research. For example, can nutritional foods prevent disease? Is tuition exorbitant? Does college promote an elitist class? Has tuition affected enrollment of any economic class?

The Hypothesis

WEB LINK
to Exercise
9.2
http://www.
ablongman.com/
lester

An excellent approach as you begin your work is to frame a hypothesis that you can test, modify, and even discard as you consult sources and conduct your investigations. A hypothesis is a theory that requires testing to prove its validity. Put another way, it's an assumption taken to be true for the purpose of investigation. Here are two hypotheses that correspond to the thesis statements above:

> Certain nutritional foods can prevent disease.
> High tuition is affecting the enrollment of some economic classes.

Both statements have the ring of truth, but they need evidence that may or may not support the supposition.

Sometimes the hypothesis will be conditional:

> Our campus has a higher crime rate than other campuses in the city.
> Poverty, not greed, forces many young people into a life of crime.

These assertions on a state of being could be tested by statistical comparison (in the first) and by interviews and surveys (in the second). The evidence might also be found in the literature on the topics.

Sometimes the hypothesis will be relational:

> Class size affects the number of writing assignments by instructors.
> Dense population in some urban housing projects contributes to a high
> crime rate.

This type of hypothesis claims that as one variable changes, so does another, or that something is more or less than another. Will statistics show that instructors change their assignments on the basis of class size? Only research can prove it. As population swells in a neighborhood, does crime? The writer must investigate and defend the statement.

Sometimes you will have a causal hypothesis:

> Industrial pollution has made most well water in Rutherford County
> unsafe for drinking.
> A child's choice of a toy is determined by television commercials.

This kind of hypothesis assumes the mutual occurrence of two factors and asserts that one factor is responsible for the other. Obviously, the writer must consult sources to prove or disprove the supposition.

T I P   *The Advantages of the Hypothesis*

The great thing about a hypothesis is that you are not locked into defending a position. You are merely establishing a statement that needs investigation. What's more, the research may *disprove* the hypothesis, and that's perfectly fine. Negative results have value and deserve discussion as the researcher admits, perhaps, that little evidence exists to blame industrial pollution for the poisoning of well water in Rutherford County. The hypothesis invites open research; the thesis statement pushes you toward a more focused reading.

Another difficulty in finding a point of view comes with neutral topics—for example, *patriotism, computers, shopping malls, child care*—as opposed to topics with clearly divided sides—*Title IX, gambling, grade inflation, cell research, abortion, cloning*. In either case, frame a hypothesis that you can test, modify, and even discard as you consult the sources.

> Parents use shopping malls for child care.
> Title IX has brought women's sports into the national spotlight.
> Gambling is an addiction.
> Student evaluation of faculty has had a direct effect on grade inflation.

Each of these hypotheses requires investigative research of several sources, not just one or two.

EXERCISE 9.3
FRAMING AN INITIAL STATEMENT OF OPINION

Listed below are four topics. For each topic, first write a thesis sentence (one that has a built-in conclusion) and, second, write a hypothesis (one that expresses a theory to be tested and researched).

1. Binge drinking by college students
2. The psychological aspects of spring break frolics
3. Access on campus for the handicapped
4. Tap water and bottled water

Reading Critically to Discover Shades of Meaning in Various Sources

When you examine several sources commenting on the same general subject, you will need to examine them in several ways:

- What is the context of the presentation?
- What is implied by the writer or speaker? What can I infer from the words of this source?
- How do the various speakers differ in their implications?

Discovering Context

WEB LINK
to Reading
9.2
http://www.
ablongman.com/
lester

Try to discover where, when, and how the sources were published. For example, George LaBaron, who researched cloning (see pages 308–309), discovered a wide divergence in the origins of his sources, everything from the Web sites http://www.christianity.com, http://www.newscientist.com, and http://www.reason.com to the magazine *Atlantic Monthly*. LaBaron's investigation showed that the Christianity site is sponsored by the Culture of Life Foundation and Institute, a group devoted to the fight against cloning. The *New Scientist* site, devoted to medical advances, offers such articles as "Stem Cells Can Mend Human Hearts" and "MS Damage Repaired by Stem Cells." LaBaron found that Reason.com is a Libertarian site with this self-description: "*Reason* provides a refreshing alternative to right-wing and left-wing opinion magazines by making a principled case for liberty and individual choice in all areas of human activity." Despite this disclaimer, LaBaron found Reason.com more liberal than middle of the road. The fourth source, the *Atlantic Monthly*, is a mainstream, intellectually upscale magazine with a fine reputation for carefully crafted and well-researched articles.

Thus, LaBaron found himself with two liberal views on cloning, one conservative view, and one more scholarly work in the *Atlantic Monthly*. He turned to the latter as his most reliable source.

A journal article will usually surpass the quality of a magazine article in its scholarly base. A sponsored Web site has greater legitimacy than a personal home page. You should make a judgment about each source. Let's look at excerpts from two sources that discuss the same topic and then examine the context of each source.

Comment 1

Ecstasy—The drug we can thank for making "clubbing" what it is today—a multi-million pound industry supported by a multi-million pound underground industry of criminal drug producers and distributors. "E" first appeared in London during the early 1980's and became a popular social group drug. It wasn't really until the early 90's that the ecstasy-driven dance music storm arrived bringing with it the now commercial house and techno sound which had its origins in "Acid House."

—**www.aromadome.com**

The context and framework of this source are commercial. The webmaster wants to sell you something. It will not offer much scholarly information, although it does offer information on taking the drug and provides an e-shop for ordering it.

Comment 2

A few years ago it was heroin. Before that, everyone was talking about cocaine. Today, the drug of the moment is ecstasy, otherwise known as "E" or MDMA. The man-made psychotropic tablets—like LSD, a product of the lab rather than the poppy field—have experienced a stunning surge of popularity in the last 10 months, demand that has led to a surge of trafficking from the drug's main source, Europe. Stepped-up vigilance at American airports since January has yielded 4 million doses. That's compared to 3 million in all of 1999 and 750,000 in 1998, according to U.S. Customs officials.

The rapid growth in demand for ecstasy can be directly linked to its insidiously cuddly reputation. Since users only have to pop a pill—rather than snort a line or inject a dose—ecstasy isn't perceived as being nearly as dangerous as cocaine or heroin. It has also gained a reputation as being a "safe" drug that brings few side effects. But the little pills, which are sold for up to $40 each, can have a devastating impact: although users often experience feelings of extreme joy and contentment, they can suffer from dizziness, severe dehydration and even brain damage. "There's a notion that ecstasy makes you feel good, that there's no downside," said U.S. customs commissioner Raymond Kelly. "But there's plenty of horror stories."

That it is safe is only the first misconception surrounding the new "it" drug. While still popular with black-clad, street-smart city kids dancing to techno music at all-night "raves," ecstasy has now begun to infiltrate the suburbs as well as college frat houses and dorm parties from Oregon to Virginia. "A lot more people are doing E these days," says *Time* senior writer John Cloud. "So law enforcement agencies are cracking down." Unfortunately for anti-ecstasy forces, adds Cloud, the same characteristics that make ecstasy so popular among pushers and party-goers—it's easy to hide, disguise and consume—also make it very difficult to track down the culprits.

—From *Time*, April 3, 2000

Time is a reputable weekly news magazine targeted to an educated general public. Its articles are well researched by noted writers. In this article, the writer has carefully researched the subject and offers insightful information for its readers. For example, he says, "tablets—like LSD, a product of the lab rather than the poppy field—have experienced a stunning surge of popularity in the last 10 months, demand that has led to a surge of trafficking from the drug's main source, Europe. Stepped-up vigilance at American airports since January [a three-month period] has yielded 4 million doses. That's compared to 3 million in all of 1999 and 750,000 in 1998." Thus, the *Time* article should provide useful and dependable information for somebody researching the topic "ecstasy."

Source 2

Abstract: The authors discuss recreational use and potential physiological effects of the amphetamine analogue MDA (3, 4-methylenedioxymethamphetamine), commonly referred to as "Ecstasy." There have been some deaths from hypothermia and individual reactions, but these have been rare, and more users regard it as a safe drug. Since there is no ethical or legal way to do a controlled study with first time users, the authors rely on animal tests and or reports. The studies suggest that MDMA can be neurotoxic with those who use two or more doses of MDMA at a time, who inject it, or use it frequently. Brendon P. Boot, Iain S. McGregor, Wayne Hall, "MDMA (Ecstasy) Neurotoxicity: Assessing and Communicating the Risks."

—Brendon P. Boot, Iain S. McGregor, Wayne Hall, "MDMA (Ecstasy) Neurotoxicity: Assessing and Communicating the Risks." *The Lancet* 355 (2000): 1818.

Abstracts are rare for magazine and newspaper articles; they are reserved for scholarly articles. Thus, the environment of this comment is scholarly. *The Lancet* is a reputable medical journal, so the researcher should examine the complete article where the authors examine in much greater detail the various risks associated with rave parties and the consumption of Ecstasy. This source will give greater credibility to the student's text than a Web site or a magazine.

EXERCISE 9.4
DISCOVERING CONTEXT

Shown below are statements from markedly different sources. Write a brief paragraph that discusses the context of the following sources on the novels of John Saul. Discuss in your paragraph the sources that would be valuable for citation in a research paper.

1. In Guardian, the forces of nature and the forces of evil combine chillingly in a complexly woven novel of psychological suspense, as a peaceful haven becomes a prison

where, along in the howling winter whiteness, MaryAnne Carpenter must guard her children against an unseen, ever more insatiable killer—a killer who is closer than she thinks.

—Dust jacket comments by Ballantine Books

2. The fans who have met me pretty much know that I'm not your standard brands horror writer. There was a guy years ago who did a book—a series of interviews with all the so-called horror novelists; there were around 25 people he interviewed—and when I saw the book, the piece [on me] began, "John Saul is the only person in this group who does not fit the mold at all. There is nothing dark about him, nothing forbidding about him. He doesn't seem to take this very seriously at all, and he seems to be having a great deal of fun writing scary books while not being twisted. He seems to have had a normal childhood. His mind is not all bent." So every now and then, if I'm being interviewed on television where I'm supposed to do the scary writer persona, I can do it a bit. I'm not very successful at it, because my sense of humor always gets the best of me—I start giggling.

—Interview with John Saul, http://www.advocate.com

3. *New York Times:* Mr. Saul is a skillful writer.

4. *Atlanta Journal:* Another thriller by one of the masters of the genre.

5. *Tulsa World:* Normally I don't read this kind of book, but I'm glad I did. John Saul kept me spellbound to the horror with exquisite details that rallied primeval fears from darkness that dwells below the subconscious in us all.

6. *Kirkus Reviews:* Saul is . . . creepily compelling. A skillful manipulation of primal fears about the natural world and the corruption of innocence.

7. *Providence Journal:* Reading Saul is like being buried alive in a nightmare . . . he haunts his shadowy realm ingeniously and persistently, and I think that *Nightshade* may be his masterpiece!

Assignment: Write a paragraph that evaluates briefly the sources above.

Discovering Implications and Making Inferences

WEB LINK to Reading 9.3
http://www.ablongman.com/lester

In Chapter 3, on critical reading, we discussed the importance of a writer or speaker's implications and a reader's inferences. For example, a member of Congress might say, "Small businesses will get an average tax break of $2,000." The speaker implies that *all* small business persons will benefit on a somewhat equal basis. However, a careful reader might infer something far different because of the word *average*. Some businesses might get $100,000 in tax benefits and others only $10. The total dollar amount divided by the number of businesses produces the average. A better representation of the information might be worded in this way: "Each small business will receive a 2 percent cut in taxes on its net income." Now each business person can figure the individual gain. Therefore, read carefully for the spin that a writer or speaker might put into a statement.

T I P *Implications vs. Inferences*

Writers imply or make implications; readers infer or make inferences about the piece of writing. You task is to identify the writer's position and make judicious inferences about that position.

All of us are aware of the recent U.S.–Iraqi conflict in 2003 and perhaps even the Persian Gulf War of 1991. However, you may not know that in 1983 President Ronald Reagan sent the U.S. military onto the island of Grenada in the Caribbean (1) to oust a Cuban and Soviet-backed government in order (2) to rescue 600 American medical students. The first reason was the primary one; the second was the reason presented to the public. The intervention received a variety of responses. One resident of Grenada writes:

> The INTERVENTION (as Grenadians prefer to refer to it) was quite out of the ordinary quiet life that we lived. Locals were at look-out points and on the beaches with boom-boxes and picnic boxes, cheering the helicopters and other aircraft dropping bombs, and yelling things like "Give em' in de bum!" The Grenadians were "liming," which is an expression that means observing, hanging out, and, believe you me, the locals limed. They said, "America, what took you so long?" Reagan is to most Grenadians a great hero. There are T-shirts with slogans, "God Bless America," and a wall painted with the same slogan.
>
> —Paul Balfour, a native of Grenada

Implication: Balfour implies that Reagan's actions benefited Grenada and won great praise from the people of the island. He wants us to think kindly toward President Reagan and his actions.

Inference: As a reader you can make inferences from Balfour's statement; that is, the Granadians have an affection for the U.S. president who saved them from the clutches of a communist regime.

Here is how one historian described the same event and the reactions in America to Ronald Reagan's actions.

> America had won [control of Grenada]. What would be the reaction? From the Democrats, it was one of outrage. They ridiculed the notion that Grenada was part of the Soviet bloc, dismissed the idea that the Cubans on the island were mercenaries, and were openly skeptical that any American lives were in danger. The thrust of the criticism was that the United States was simply throwing its weight around in the traditional manner of the neighborhood bully. Some said the United States even intended to occupy Grenada and establish a form of colonial rule. How did such aspirations and behavior, the Democrats asked, make America any different from the Soviet Union?
>
> There were calls for Reagan to resign, and a handful of congressmen . . . submitted a resolution that called for the president to be impeached for violating international law. The reaction abroad was equally strident. The United Nations voted to condemn the U.S. action. Even Reagan's closest ally, Margaret Thatcher, sternly protested that Grenada was a commonwealth country and the United States had no right to intervene.
>
> —Dinesh D'Souza, *Ronald Reagan: How an Ordinary Man Became an Extraordinary Leader*

Implication: D'Souza implies that Reagan received great criticism for his actions, which were questioned and challenged by many people in the United States and around the world.

Inference: Reagan may have been wrong by charging into another country, even though he was rescuing the American medical students.

A biographer had this to say:

> "Operation Urgent Fury" was an embarrassingly clumsy success. The world's ranking superpower, hampered by old tourist maps and incompatible radio frequencies, needed two full days to overcome the resistance of an island not much bigger than Washington, D.C. State-of-the-art helicopters were brought down by World War II vintage ack-ack guns. Democracy was restored, and some damp Cuban documents impounded, along with 24,768 signal flares—clear evidence of incendiary Red activity. Nineteen U.S. servicemen were killed, but all the students were rescued, and [they] returned to kiss home soil. American television viewers, Reagan included, wept at the sight. Margaret Thatcher and her compatriots were less moved. "Sodding Yanks," Philip Larkins complained, "breaking and entering British territory."
>
> —Edmund Morris, *Dutch: a Memoir of Ronald Reagan*

Implications: The operation in Grenada was awkward but successful, and the medical students were overjoyed to escape the great dangers they faced on the island.

Inferences: Although Operation Urgent Fury was clumsy and offensive to Margaret Thatcher and other Britons, it did successfully bring home the students who kissed their home soil.

EXERCISE 9.5

DISCOVERING IMPLICATIONS AND MAKING INFERENCES

This exercise asks you to search carefully for the "spin" that a writer might make in order to advance a position. At the same time, you can make your own inferences about the circumstances. Examine the following document, submitted by Memphis representative Harold E. Ford, Jr., and then answer the questions following the document.

108th CONGRESS
1st Session
HOUSE CONCURRENT RESOLUTION 13

Recognizing the importance of blues music, and for other purposes.

Whereas blues music is the most influential form of music indigenous to the United States, providing the roots for contemporary music heard around the world such as rock and roll, jazz, rhythm and blues, and country, and even influencing classical music;

Whereas the blues is a national historic treasure, which needs to be preserved and studied for the benefit of future generations;

Whereas blues music documents twentieth-century United States history, especially during the Great Depression and in the areas of race relations and pop culture;

Whereas the various forms of blues music trace the transformation of the United States from a rural, agricultural society to an urban, industrialized country;

Whereas the blues is an important facet of African-American culture in the twentieth century;

Whereas every year, people in the United States hold hundreds of blues festivals, and millions of new or reissued blues albums are released;

Whereas blues musicians from the United States, whether old or new, male or female, are recognized and revered worldwide as unique and important ambassadors of the United States and its music;

Whereas it is important to educate the young people of the United States so that they understand that the music they listen to today has its roots and traditions in the blues;

Whereas there are many living legends of blues music in the United States who should be recognized and have their stories captured and preserved for future generations; and

Whereas the year 2003 would be an appropriate time to recognize the importance of blues music since it is the centennial anniversary of when W.C. Handy composed the first blues music to be released throughout the United States: Now, therefore, be it

Resolved by the House of Representatives (the Senate concurring), That the Congress—

(1) recognizes the importance of blues music with respect to many cultural developments in United States history;

(2) calls on the people of the United States to take the opportunity to study, reflect on, and celebrate the importance of the blues; and

(3) requests that the President issue a proclamation calling on the people of the United States and interested organizations to observe the importance of the blues with appropriate ceremonies, activities, and educational programs.

It behooves all congressional representatives to promote features and activities in their home states, as shown here by the congressman from Tennessee. Your task, after examining the document, is to answer the following questions.

1. What are the implications made by the writer of the document?
2. What inferences can you draw from the material?
3. What, in your opinion, is the primary goal of the document? What is a secondary goal, if any?

Grouping Multiple Sources for Analysis and Synthesis

As you gather a variety of sources on your topic, you need to search for common ideas. Analyze each piece to find its key idea. Look for common threads in the sources so that you can synthesize them for a central idea. To accomplish this task, you need to establish *your* thesis so that the materials will merge with the position you have selected. In particular, provide an opening topic sentence:

Year-round school is the present-day answer to crowded classrooms and the shortage of teachers.

Then give a few preliminary remarks on the subject.

Why should teachers have three months of vacation in the summer? Why do the students need such vacation time? They no longer work in the fields during the summer.

Next, begin to bring the sources into the passage.

Robin Morgan argues that summer vacation is an "absurd waste of money by school boards all across the country" (23). In a similar vein, Margaret Baker-Jones compares school buildings with a factory to argue that an industry would never close its factory for three months, yet the public gives little thought to idle school buildings throughout the summer months (243-44). In similar fashion, Walter Bronkowski laments the fact that every fall teachers "must re-teach basic information that the students have forgotten during the summer break" (91).

The next step is to bring a focus to the citations by relating them to the central thesis of the paper.

Thus, several reasons exist for the conversion to year-round schools. The buildings sit empty, the students abandon their learning, and teachers either get an absurd vacation or get paid extra for teaching summer school. We need to examine each of these issues in more depth.

The writer, having crafted this opening paragraph, can now build the essay in full, dwelling sequentially on each of the three issues.

As your papers get longer, you cannot roll the quotations into one paragraph; they will be spread throughout the work. At the same time, they must conform to your outline or general plan. Therefore, it is vital that you identify the essence of each quotation and chart where it will appear in your essay. Thus, you should label each of your passages so that you may appoint it to its special place in relation to other ideas and quotations. Let's watch one student at work.

Student Robert Sanders likes to climb. Sometimes he climbs a cliff and other times a mountain. What sustains him is the exhilaration of conquering heights. For a college writing assignment, Sanders turned his interest and motivations into an article on climbing. However, the assignment demanded a multi-source essay, so he went in search of articles by and about mountain climbers. In order to synthesize the various responses, he performed these tasks:

1. Collected quotations on the topic.
2. Wrote a brief summary to describe each passage's general message.
3. Charted the summaries.
4. Assigned passages to his outline, synthesizing them with each other and with his own commentary.

Let's look at a few of the passages Robert Sanders collected. The first is by Maurice Herzog, who climbed and conquered Mount Annapurna in the Himalayan Mountains for the first time in 1950 as the leader of a French group of climbers. He writes:

The summit was a corniced crest of ice, and the precipices on the far side, which plunged vertically down beneath us, were terrifying, unfathomable. There could be few other mountains in the world like this. Clouds floated half way down, concealing the gentle, fertile valley of Pokhara, 23,000 feet below. Above us there was nothing!

Our mission was accomplished. But at the same time we had accomplished something infinitely greater. How wonderful life could now become! What an inconceivable experience it is to attain one's ideal and, at the very same moment, to fulfill oneself. I was stirred to the depths of my being. Never had I felt happiness like this—so intense and yet so pure. That brown rock, the highest of them all, that ridge of ice—were these the goals of a lifetime? Or were they, rather, the limits of man's pride?

Summary: The focus by Herzog is on fulfillment of one's ideals and goals.

The next passage is written by Edmund Hillary of New Zealand who, with his Sherpa guide Norgay Tenzing, became in 1953 the first human to scale Mount Everest. This passage by Hillary is part of his introduction to *Challenge of the Unknown:*

Modern developments in machinery and equipment have produced major changes in the technique of exploration. Aircraft and vehicles are in many cases replacing the human legs; oxygen bottles are giving new strength to air-starved lungs in the thin air that clothes the giants of the Himalayas; and radio communication has removed the loneliness from the most desolate land. But despite all this I firmly believe that in the end it is man himself that counts. When the going gets tough and things go wrong the same qualities are needed to win through as they were in the past—qualities of courage, resourcefulness, the ability to put up with discomfort and hardship, and the enthusiasm to hold tight to an ideal and to see it through with doggedness and determination.

The explorers of the past were great men and we should honour them. But let us not forget that their spirit still lives on. It is still not hard to find a man who will adventure for the sake of a dream or one who will search, for the pleasure of searching, and not for what he may find.

Summary: Modern technology makes climbing easier but it's the climber's inner core of courage and determination that counts.

Edmund Hillary also included the following statement in his book:

It is not the mountain we conquer but ourselves.

Summary: Climbers must conquer themselves—their fears and careless feet—rather than conquer a mountain.

The next passage is by Leslie Stephen in *The Playground of Europe,* which recounts his adventures in the Alps. Stephen, a nineteenth-century writer, was the first mountaineer to conquer the Schreckhorn.

> The mountains are exquisitely beautiful, indeed, from whatever points of view we contemplate them; and the mountaineer would love much if he never saw the beauties of the lower valleys, or pasturages deep in flowers, and dark-pine-forests with the summits shining from far off between the stems. Only, as it seems to me, he has the exclusive prerogative of thoroughly enjoying one, and that the most characteristic, though by no means the only element, of the scenery. There may be a very good dinner spread before twenty people; but if nineteen of them were teetotalers, and the twentiest drank his wine like a man, he would be the only one to do it full justice; the others might praise the meat or the fruits, but he would alone enjoy the champagne; and in the great feast which Nature spreads before us (a stock metaphor, which emboldens me to make the comparison) the high mountain scenery acts the part of the champagne. Unluckily too, the teetotalers are very apt, in this case also, to sit in judgment upon their more adventurous neighbours. Especially are they pleased to carp at the view from the high summits. I have been constantly asked, with a covert sneer, "Did it repay you?"—a question which involves the assumption that one wants to be repaid, as though the labour were not itself part of the pleasure, and which implies a doubt that the view is really enjoyable. People are always demonstrating that the lower views are the most beautiful; and at the same time complaining that the mountaineers frequently turn back without looking at the view from the top, as though that would necessarily imply that they cared nothing for scenery. In opposition to which I must first remark that, as a rule, every step of an ascent has a beauty of its own, which one is quietly absorbing even when one is not directly making it a subject of contemplation, and that the view from the top is generally the crowning glory of the whole.

Summary: The goal of the climber is not merely to reach the top but to enjoy the grandeur of every step of the ascent. The entire mountain is beautiful, not just the view from the top.

Francis Kilvert, a village vicar in Wales in the nineteenth century, was a great walker. He made this remark in *On the Black Mountain:*

> It is a fine thing to be out on the hills alone. A man can hardly be a beast or a fool alone on a great mountain.

Summary: Climbing elevates the human being to another level.

John Muir was an explorer, naturalist, and conservationist. He is known for his campaign that culminated with an act of Congress establishing Yosemite and Sequoia National Parks in 1890.

> Thousands of tired, nerve-shaken, over-civilized people are beginning to find out that going to the mountains is going home; that wildness is a necessity; and

that mountain parks and reservations are useful not only as fountains of timber and irrigating rivers but as the fountain of life.

Summary: Mountains are a necessary "fountain of life" for the spirit of humans as well as the source of water and timber.

William O. Douglas was a Supreme Court justice and also a writer. Drawing on his travels, he wrote many books on nature and conservation, including *Of Men and Mountains,* published in 1950:

> A people who climb the ridges and sleep under the stars in high mountain meadows, who enter the forest and scale the peaks, who explore glaciers and walk ridges buried deep in snow—these people will give their country some of the indomitable spirit of the mountains.

Summary: Climbers bring back with them the "indomitable spirit of the mountains."

The next quotation is by William Blake, the pre-Romantic poet, painter, engraver, and mystic. Blake is well known for his poems *Songs of Innocence* and *Songs of Experience.*

> Great things are done when men and mountains meet.

Summary: This line would make a good title for my paper because something special happens when I climb a mountain.

Claudia Baumier and Hartmut Bielefeldt wrote a diary that described their expedition to the Tibetan side of Mount Everest. They reached the summit on May 17, 2002.

> On the right side behind the edge, there is a horizontal traverse. Coming from the snow, we enter scree-covered bands of limestone, completely free of snow. Looks like "at home" in the Alps; I feel reminded of Sulzfluh. But here, at 8800 meters, it is the wind that removes the snow rather than a warming sun.
>
> A short zigzag through the bands, and a little further up it becomes snowy again. Another few little hilltops and I finally can see the summit where Claudia and a couple of other people are standing. Twenty minutes for twenty height meters, and I am standing on the small ridge, maybe twenty meters long. On the other side a gentle slope leads down to the southeast ridge.
>
> It is 13:50; it is cold, but there is almost no wind. And still the weather is beautiful. 8850 meters—all the world's mountains are below us. Lhotse looks so unspectacular from here, we had almost overlooked it. We easily recognize some prominent mounts like Makalu, Kangchenjunga, and Cho Oyu; around these, there is a vast sea of smaller summits. There are five or six people on the summit. In total, about twenty mountaineers were on the north route today. We see nobody come from the south. At half past two we begin our way back.

Summary: The arrival at the summit seems to be an anticlimax, as though Claudia and Hartmut say, "Here we are, we did it, now let's start back." The challenge of the climb was the test, not crossing to the top.

Charting and Synthesizing Your Sources

The next task for Robert Sanders is to chart the major ideas he has expressed in his summaries, and to decide on an effective sequence. Here are the major ideas:

WEB LINK
to Exercise
9.3
http://www.
ablongman.com/
lester

Fulfillment

Identity with nature

Conquering

The spirit of life

The grandeur and beauty

Here is the sequence that Sanders chose as his outline:

1. We set out to conquer the mountain.
2. During the climb we identify with nature.
3. We find the spirit of life in the grandeur and beauty of the mountain.
4. Ultimately, we find fulfillment in who we are, not what we have conquered.

Sanders can now select a title and assign the paraphrases and quotations from his sources, gaining synthesis for separate sources while maintaining his common mission.

Mountain Climbing: It's Not Just a Sport

"Great things are done when men and

mountains meet"—William Blake

I. We set out to conquer the mountain.

      Hillary: Climbers must conquer themselves—their fears and careless feet—rather than conquer a mountain.

      Hillary: Modern technology makes climbing easier but it's the climber's inner core of courage and determination that counts.

II. During the climb we identify with nature.

      Stephen: The goal of the climber is not merely to reach the top but to enjoy the grandeur of every step of the ascent. The entire mountain is beautiful, not just the view from the top.

III. We find the spirit of life in the grandeur and beauty of the mountain.

      Douglas: Climbers bring back with them the "indomitable spirit of the mountains."

      Muir: Mountains are a necessary "fountain of life" for the spirit of humans as well as the source of water and timber.

IV. Ultimately, we find fulfillment in who we are, not what we have conquered.

> Herzog: The focus by Herzog is on fulfillment of one's ideals and goals.
>
> Kilvert: Climbing elevates the human being to another level.
>
> Claudia Baumier and Hartmut Bielefeldt: The arrival at the summit seems to be an anticlimax, as though to say, "Here we are, we did it, now let's start back." The challenge of the climb was the test, not crossing to the top.

Sanders is now ready to write the entire paper. He will develop his own ideas and use the material from his sources at appropriate places. As you can see, charting the sources to help frame his outline helped Sanders arrange the essay, which follows:

Sanders 1

Robert Sanders

English 1020

Professor Beach

April 22, 2003

Mountain Climbing: It's Not Just a Sport

"Great things are done when men and mountains meet"

—William Blake

Climbing, like hiking or running, is an addictive sport. Hiking to the top of a local mountain can be exhausting but stimulating and invigorating. Climbing goes a step beyond hiking because of the challenge and exertion it demands. Joggers and runners don't conquer the roadway, but climbers conquer the mountain. And, like the runner, the climber must conquer herself or himself—find that inner strength and determination to reach the top.

In a very real sense, it's a test of will and physical fitness. Edmund Hillary says it best, "It is not the mountain we conquer but ourselves." Hillary in 1953 with his Sherpa guide Norgay Tenzing became the first human to scale Mount Everest, the highest mountain in the world. So that is the challenge for us lesser mortals who climb local cliffs: we must conquer ourselves—our fears and our careless feet—rather than conquer a mountain. Here's how Hillary describes it:

> I firmly believe that in the end it is man himself that counts. When the going gets tough and things go wrong the same qualities are needed to

win through as they were in the past—qualities of courage,

resourcefulness, the ability to put up with discomfort and hardship,

and the enthusiasm to hold tight to an ideal and to see it through with

doggedness and determination.

Those lines could be the credo for all climbers.

Modern technology has made climbing easier with better equipment, high-tech boots, and communications networks. We're not up there alone and can contact the base camp immediately. Help is only a helicopter away! Yet, as Hillary points out, human resourcefulness is mandatory. And that finally is the thesis: a climber may have the best physique and conditioning possible, but he or she must "hold tight to an ideal and to see it through."

Inspiring a climber is the beauty of the natural surroundings. The goal of the climber is not merely to reach the top but to enjoy the grandeur of every step of the ascent. The entire mountain is beautiful, not just the view from the top. Leslie Stephen touches on this idea in recounting his adventures in the Alps:

People are always demonstrating that the lower views are the

most beautiful; and at the same time complaining that the

mountaineers frequently turn back without looking at the view

from the top, as though that would necessarily imply that they

cared nothing for scenery. In opposition to which I must first

remark that, as a rule, every step of an ascent has a beauty of its

own, which one is quietly absorbing even when one is not directly

making it a subject of contemplation, and that the view from the

top is generally the crowning glory of the whole.

The key line here is this, "Every step of an ascent has a beauty of its own." That captures the essence of climbing, and it's not just the beauty but also the suspense, the challenge, the danger, and the frequent adrenaline rush.

In truth, we find the spirit of life in the grandeur and beauty of the mountain. William O. Douglas, a Supreme Court justice and mountaineer, says that climbers bring back with them the "indomitable spirit of the mountains," and John Muir, an explorer, naturalist, and conservationist, argues that mountains are a necessary "fountain of life" for the spirit of humans as well as the source of water and timber. Here are Muir's words:

> Thousands of tired, nerve-shaken, over-civilized people are beginning to find out that going to the mountains is going home; that wildness is a necessity; and that mountain parks and reservations are useful not only as fountains of timber and irrigating rivers but as the fountain of life.

Muir lived his words; his campaign in 1890 convinced Congress to establish Yosemite and Sequoia National Parks, thereby initiating a park system that has protected thousands of acres of land.

Ultimately, as climbers, we find fulfillment in who we are, not what we have conquered. Maurice Herzog, who was the first to conquer Mount Annapurna in the Himalayans, writes, "Our mission was accomplished," and adds this statement: "What an inconceivable experience it is to attain one's ideal and, at the very same moment, to fulfill oneself." Herzog adds:

> I was stirred to the depths of my being. Never had I felt happiness like this—so intense and yet so pure. That brown rock, the highest of them all, that ridge of ice—were these the goals of a lifetime? Or were they, rather, the limits of man's pride?

Climbing may be irrational, but it builds the imagination and grows personal values. Francis Kilvert has argued that climbing elevates the human being to another level.

In 2002 Claudia Baumier and Hartmut Bielefeldt described their arrival at the summit of Everest as an anticlimax, as though to say, "Here we are, we did it, now let's start back." The challenge of the climb was the test, not crossing to the top.

Thus, in my climbing and my research on climbing I have come to understand my obsession. It's not strapping on the equipment (you probably noticed I haven't talked about belay, rappel, and camming devices, or harnesses and the best boots). It's not reaching the top and standing like Rocky with arms outstretched (although I have assumed that pose). It is, instead, the step by step wonder of fulfilling oneself in nature's rich environment. As William Blake says, "Great things are done when men [and women] and mountains meet."

GUIDELINES

Charting and Synthesizing Your Sources

- Establish your own point of view early in the project by framing an initial statement of your position in a thesis statement or by framing a hypothesis to be researched and proven true or false.

- Discover what the sources say and let them establish most of the issues. You can do this by summarizing each source to identify the key issues, source by source.

- List the issues, apply each source to one (or more) of the issues, and begin to build an outline for the paper. This will group sources under the various headings.

- As you begin to write from the outline, synthesize the various sources that fall under each category. Build paragraphs with several citations in defense of the paragraph's topic sentence.

- When sources speak to the same issue, use your summaries to combine two or more authors: "Winchell, Thompson, and Manchester all endorse a school lunch menu that features what appears to be junk food to the children but that in truth has wholesome value because of its carefully designed nutritional content."

- Try to make the topic sentence of each paragraph your own general concept, usually derived from your outline. If several sources speak to the issue, mention them in general after the topic sentence and then begin to cite each in turn as necessary. Sometimes only one or two sources will need citation.

- When you have opposing and complementary viewpoints, use appropriate transitions to slide from one to the other—for example: *in contrast, with a contrary view, similarly, likewise.*

EXERCISE 9.6

CHARTING AND SYNTHESIZING SOURCES

Reproduced below are several statements on a common subject—school lunch programs. These statements appear in random order and may not even apply to your concern. However, here is your assignment: Chart the statements into reasonable groupings that you can then synthesize into an outline. You need not write a paper—just build an outline.

1. Sue Locke, nutritionist, says, "Fast food is not nutritionally sound on a regular basis."

2. On the menu of burgers, fries, and fajitas for the children, Marilyn Holloman, head of food services, says, "That's what they come to school asking for."

3. Fresh fruit and vegetables are not on the radar.

4. A full lunch has an estimated 697 calories, 22 fat grams and 1,813 milligrams of sodium.

5. One lunchroom, one day: 750 orders of French fries, 200 orders of pizza, 254 chocolate chip cookies, and 10 apples.

6. Karen E. Stout, a professor at Lehigh University in Pennsylvania, who has observed more than 2,000 school cafeterias: "We've got an epidemic of childhood obesity, and the schools are feeding into it."

7. Given a choice of a turkey sandwich, an apple, and a corn dog, the children will choose the corn dog. But if you took away the option and served only the sandwich and apple, many children would choose not to eat.

8. One side advocates serving children food they *will* eat; the other would serve what children *should* eat.

9. One lunchroom, one day: 618 slices of pizza, 700 orders of crinkle-cut fries, 50 children ate at the fresh salad bar.

10. "We have to listen to our customers," says Marilyn Holloman. "We are into our children ingesting their food and milk rather than taking it to the garbage can."

11. Holloman adds, "What looks like junk food, isn't. The pizza is made from a wheat crust. It has a high fiber content. The tacos are made with turkey. Much of the fruit is canned, but they are in their own juice, not syrup. The hot dogs are made from turkey—but don't tell the kids that."

12. Karen Stout: "We capitulate to the fast-food mentality of the kids. It's a mistake. We are supposed to be the adults. We are supposed to know what is good for them."

13. One reason schools serve food that could have come from a drive-through lane is simple. It sells. Since offering pizza, the number of students eating at one school has gone up 7 percent.

14. Jerry Jones, 16, eats lunch every day. "I eat normal things," he said. "Like fries, school pizza, burgers, or chicken patties. I don't see French fries as being that bad for you."

Assignment: Chart the issues and write an outline.

Chapter Review

Chapter 9 has introduced you to the task of blending several sources into your essay, suggesting the following:

WEB LINK
to Chapter 9
Related Web
Destinations
http://www.
ablongman.com/
lester

- Rather than searching for a quotation or something to paraphrase during the composition stage, you are encouraged to examine a number of likely sources and summarize each one for its central issue.

- Once you have a fairly complete set of summaries, you can chart them into categories, which in effect build or help to build the design of the paper. That is, several issues will emerge, and each will demand its share of space in your essay.

- In addition, you can copy and insert material from both your summaries and direct quotations that you have identified as vital to your paper.

Chapter 9 Assignment: Writing the Multi-Source Essay

WEB LINK
to Exercise
9.4
http://www.
ablongman.com/
lester

This assignment asks you to chart the key issues in the debate on affirmative action and then write your own essay on this topic, citing from the two articles reprinted below. For now, read the two articles that follow. Then complete the four tasks explained at the end of the two articles. The two articles appeared under one banner headline in the *Nashville Tennessean* newspaper (January 7, 2003).

Should the United States End Affirmative Action?

NO: Racism Is Still Alive Throughout the United States

Shirley J. Wilcher, Executive Director of Americans for a Fair Chance

In the federal courts we are facing the most concerted effort in recent history to destroy equal-opportunity programs, including affirmative action. When the U.S. Supreme Court hears the cases brought against the University of Michigan, wherein 5 white students say they were denied admission because race was factored into the admission of minority students, we could lose the rights we gained with such difficulty. The number of college minority students could plummet.

Those of us who entered college in the late 1960s and beyond understand what is at stake.

The recent Trent Lott affair and the nationwide debate it sparked reminded me why affirmative action is still desperately needed. Discrimination in America is alive and well.

While serving as deputy assistant secretary at the Labor Department in the 1990s, I traveled to meet the CEO of a company that repaired equipment for the federal government. I wanted to know how the company could have tolerated the raffle of a Ku Klux Klan knife by members of its repair shop. Compliance officers discovered this behavior during a routine review of the company's affirmative-action program. The contractor had signed an agreement to run the program in exchange for the privilege of doing business with the government.

In addition to the Klan raffle, we found racist and sexist graffiti on the walls of the lavatories. Blacks said the N-word was used profusely. Women had resigned rather than tolerate the sexual harassment.

When I asked the CEO for an explanation, he attempted to minimize the problem and even suggested there were very few Klan members among the staff.

This is only one of a dozen egregious discrimination cases we posted on our Web site during the Newt Gingrich years to remind America that equal opportunity was not yet a reality. The Lott affair clearly underscores this point and unfortunately brings it into this century.

Affirmative action constitutes steps employers, colleges and procurement officers take to promote equal opportunity and to remedy or prevent discrimination. It means recruitment and outreach, adding diversity to the pool of qualified candidates. It means eliminating barriers and providing equal pay. It is not quotas or preferences, it does not require hiring, promoting or admitting the unqualified, and it is not reverse discrimination.

Critics argue that race should not be considered in awarding contracts, making hiring decisions or admitting students to college. However, as Kathleen Kennedy Townsend, recent candidate for Maryland's governorship, declared: "Slavery was based on race. Lynching was based on race. Discrimination was based on race. Jim Crow was based on race. And affirmative action should be based on race." I think she's got it.

YES: Double Standards Don't Fix Racial Inequality

Abigail Thernstrom, Member of the U.S. Civil Rights Commission and author of *America in Black and White*

Do you believe in judging people by the color of their skin? Or do you think that precisely such judgments have been at the heart of America's ugly racial past and should play no role in our nation's life today? That is the question that the affirmative-action case involving the University of Michigan's undergraduate college and law school has placed squarely before the Supreme Court.

A black or Hispanic applicant to the college gets a lot of extra points just for being, well, black or Hispanic. In competitive college admissions, members of certain racial or ethnic groups are privileged. Asian Americans are not among them though. Asians are a race, according to the U.S. census, but when it comes to admission to highly selective colleges like Michigan, they're white. Or, rather, they're treated like whites by admissions offices. Neither Asian nor white applicants are eligible for automatic extra points whatever disadvantages they may have experienced.

The white or Asian-American teenager whose single parent works a minimum-wage job is not considered disadvantaged. But competitive colleges drop their admissions standards significantly for black and Hispanic students—even those who live in Scarsdale and whose parents are wealthy lawyers.

The system makes no sense, yet it survives. And in the name of racial and ethnic equality, it is passionately defended. Look at all the discrimination and racial inequality around us, these defenders will say. We need to do something. But they exaggerate the level of discrimination. And racial double standards (aka affirmative action) are no fix for inequality.

It's true that blacks' and Hispanics' earnings are typically lower than those of whites and Asians. But income inequality today is mainly the result of educational differences. At the end of high school the typical black student is reading at a junior high school level. The Hispanic picture is not much better.

Black and Hispanic underperformance in the K–12 years is a national catastrophe. Racial preferences in college admission, by seeming to level the playing field, are just fool's gold. They do nothing for students who need not a pass—a waiver—but a basic education.

Real equality will come only when black and Hispanic youngsters learn as much as whites and Asians before they get to college.

The civil rights groups should be taking to the streets once again. But not in defense of racial preferences—privilege based on skin color.

Good schools for all children should be their cause. They're make or break for America's non-Asian minority kids.

1. After your critical reading of both articles, go back through them and select what you consider to be key passages.

2. Write a brief summary to describe each passage's general message.

3. Chart and synthesize the summaries in the manner of Robert Sanders on pages 322–324 by outlining the major issues and placing each of your summaries under the appropriate issue. Note: You should have both positive and negative positions.

4. Using your outline as your guide, write an essay to express your position on affirmative action and, at the same time, use the quoted passages and summaries within the essay. Some items you will use for support; others you will attack, dismiss, or deny *unless you can find a middle ground that somehow embraces both sides of the debate.*

Tracing the Work of Two Students

Halley Fishburn: Developing Research Paper

Periodically throughout the text, we have displayed the work of two students—Kaci Holz and Halley Fishburn—as they develop their papers. A brief analysis of just one portion of Fishburn's paper will demonstrate her careful selection of passages, her charting them to fit the design of her paper, and the synthesis she achieves.

The separation of powers has been a hotly debated subject since the Lincoln administration. The fact that most of the War Powers are bestowed upon Congress does not override the fact that Congress is explicitly given authority to "declare" war not "conduct" war. That is reserved for the commander in chief, the president.[14]

Fishburn charts authority as bestowed on Congress and the president using information from one source: Timothy Boylan.

---

14. Timothy Boylan, "War Powers, Constitutional Balance, and the Imperial Presidency Idea at Century's End," *Presidential Studies Quarterly* 29 (June 1999): 232.

The Constitution also assures that individual states have no War Powers. Article 1, Section 10, asserts that states shall not keep troops or ships of war or engage in war without the consent of Congress. Furthermore, Article 4, Section 4, assures that the United States as a nation will defend individual states, giving them no need to employ means of defending themselves. Madison writes, "Protection against invasion is due from every society to the parts composing it. The latitude of the expression here used seems to secure each state, not only against foreign hostility, but against ambitious or vindictive enterprises of its more powerful neighbors.[15] He also writes to reassure those supporters of states rights:

Fishburn cites from the War Powers Act.

She cites James Madison from The Federalist Papers.

> The operations of the federal government will be most extensive and important in times of war and danger; those of the state governments in times of peace and security. As the former periods will probably bear a small proportion to the latter, the state governments will here enjoy another advantage over the federal government. The more adequate, indeed, the federal powers may be rendered to the national defense, the less frequent will be those scenes of danger which might favor their ascendancy over the governments of the particular states.[16]

Again, Fishburn's charting and synthesis brings more words from The Federalist Papers.

---

15. James Madison, Alexander Hamilton, John Jay, and Edward Mead Earle, *The Federalist* (New York: Modern Library, 1941), No. 43, 312.

16. Madison, No. 45, 328-29.

In this brief passage from her paper (see pages 411–417), Fishburn has blended three major sources—an article from the *Presidential Studies Quarterly,* the Constitution (Articles 1 and 4), and *The Federalist Papers,* numbers 43 and 45.

Writing a Paper Using MLA Style

WEB LINK
to Chapter 10
Related Web
Destinations
http://www.
ablongman.com/
lester

Writing with sources requires a delicate balance of your words and ideas, the language of the discipline itself, and the words of the sources. How you handle this balancing act determines, in large part, your success as a writer—whether you are a student or a professional. In this chapter we address MLA style, established by the Modern Language Association. You will need to use this style in language, literature, and rhetoric courses, and especially in a first-year composition course.

Academic writing style in the English department is different from academic writing style in the social or the physical sciences. In addition, your approach to the subject matter will differ according to your discipline. So before we discuss the technical aspects of the citation forms, we need to understand a number of things about style.

Style is the distinctive feature of expression or performance, and it characterizes a particular person as well as a group, school, or era. Yet blind adherence to a style diminishes one's personality and flair—we must seek a balance of convention and individuality. The academic conventions of writing have evolved over the years, and you cannot ignore them. Instructors expect your papers to have a certain format and style of writing. Thus, in your English courses you will become a part of the academic world by conforming to certain conventions. You may need to abandon some of your personal style, but you should not allow the MLA standards to smother or swallow completely your special handling of the language. In summary, you are encouraged to keep your originality while embracing the academic style.

Considering an Academic Approach to the Subject Matter

Humanists and scientists approach subject matter in different ways; consequently, they do different things within their writing. At the start, and this is a vast generalization, humanists tend to be preoccupied with the quality of life, of art, of ideas, and of large ethical standards. They use the present tense to indicate that issues and problems are enduring and affect humans of past ages as well as the present and into the future. Thus, most of their papers are theoretical. Scientists, again as a broad generalization, are more objective in their approach to a topic and avoid signs of personal commitment. The scientist tends to focus on one bit of data, test it, prove it true or false, and go then to the next problem. The scientist prefers empirical research to explore a hypothesis, which enables him or her to say, "Thompson (2003) has shown the effects of laser technology on cornea treatment." It's been done; now let's go forward to more tests and experiments.

That being said, it is entirely appropriate for a composition student to engage in empirical research by conducting, perhaps, a survey to test a hypothesis on keyboarding techniques as a component of successful writing, or performing a scientific interview of 100 subjects to discover gender bias in the classroom. In like manner, a biology student might conduct a theoretical study. Thus, these descriptions are simplified, but they give you a clue to the mindset of writers in the different disciplines. We will discuss scientific writing in detail in Chapter 12.

With the above points in mind, your selection of a topic for an MLA style paper in a first-year composition course should, in general, reflect these impressions:

- An interest in ethical standards.
- A concern for the quality of life, art, and humanistic ideas.
- A love of history, art, myth, and literature.
- A preference for theoretical studies over empirical research.

EXERCISE 10.1

SUBJECT MATTER AND ACADEMIC STYLE

Shown below, side by side, are two versions of the same subject: organ and tissue donation. Examine them closely and then write a paragraph that describes in your own words the differences in the approach to the subject and the writing style.

Organ and tissue donation is the gift of life. Each year many people confront health problems due to diseases or congenital birth defects. Tom Taddonia explains that tissues such as skin, veins, and valves can be used to correct congenital defects, blindness, visual impairment, trauma, burns, dental defects, arthritis, cancer, vascular and heart disease (8). Steve Barnill says, "More than 400 people each month receive the gift of sight through yet another type of tissue donation—corneal transplants. In many cases, donors unsuitable for organ donation are eligible for tissue donation" (324). Barnill notes that tissues are now used in orthopedic surgery, cardiovascular surgery, plastic surgery, dentistry, and podiatry (325). Even so, not enough people are willing to donate organs and tissues.

Organ and tissue donation has been identified as a social as well as medical problem in the United States. On one side, people have confronted serious problems in securing organs and tissue to correct health problems; on the other, people have demonstrated a reluctance to donate their organs. This need has been identified by Taddonia (2001), Barnill (1999), Ruskin (2000), and others. This hypothesis remains: People are reluctant to sign the donor cards. Consequently, this study will survey a random set of 1000 persons who have driver's licenses. The tabulations will indicate reasons for signing or not signing for donation. Further investigation can then be conducted to determine ways of increasing participation by potential donors.

Selecting an Appropriate Design for Your Paper

In most cases, the design of your study should match an appropriate organizational model, called a *paradigm*, which is a universal format, one that governs most papers of a given type. It provides a basic academic pattern for all papers with a certain purpose. In contrast, a traditional outline, because it is content specific, is useful for only one paper. For now, start with a paradigm that fits your project. Discussed below are the paradigms used most often in MLA-type papers. The first is a general model that fits the demands of most instructors. The second provides a plan for a persuasive paper. The third will serve you well in an assignment in which you must examine differing positions about a topic.

All-Purpose Model

If you are uncertain about your assignment, start with this basic model and expand it with your material. Readers, including your instructor, are accustomed to this sequence for research papers. It offers plenty of leeway.

Introduction

The introduction should identify the subject, offer some background information, perhaps a review of the literature on this topic, followed by your thesis sentence or hypothesis. You can also include a quotation, an anecdote, a definition, or comments from your source materials.

Identify the subject (Introduction):

- Explain the problem.
- Provide background information.
- Frame a thesis statement.

Body

In the body of the paper you will classify the major issues and spend time with an analysis of each one. Here you will write several paragraphs to develop each of the major issues with definition, interpretation, evidence and evaluation, cause and effect, comparison, and other techniques of development.

Analyze the subject (Body):

- Examine the first major issue.
- Examine the second major issue.
- Examine the third major issue.

Conclusion

The conclusion of your paper should be more than mere summary. If you have introduced a problem and analyzed the issues in depth, you owe it to your audience to discuss and interpret your findings and ultimately to provide a proposal toward a solution or at the very least an opinion about the implications of your study. Here you can challenge an assumption, take exception to a prevailing point of view, and reaffirm your thesis.

Discuss your findings (Conclusion):

- Restate your thesis or hypothesis and point beyond it.
- Interpret the findings.
- Provide answers, solutions, a final opinion, a proposal, or a discussion of the findings.

Model for Persuasion Papers

WEB LINK
to Reading
10.1
http://www.
ablongman.com/
lester

If you write persuasively or argue from a set position, your paper should conform in general to this next plan. Select the elements that fit your design.

Introduction

The introduction should establish the nature of your paper to make it clear to readers that your paper is (1) an exploratory and truth-seeking adventure, (2) a negotiation at resolving a conflict by your presentation of options, or a mediated solution, and (3) a persuasion to convince your reader that your position on the issue is valid. The introduction will also need to identify the major issues, explain any complex terminology, review the literature, and make any necessary concessions on key points.

Introduction:

- Establish clearly the problem or controversy that your paper will examine.
- Summarize the issues.

- Define key terminology.
- Make concessions on some points of the argument.
- Use quotations and paraphrases to explore the controversy.
- Provide background information.
- Write a thesis to establish the direction you will take: persuasion, inquiry, negotiation.

Body

The body of a persuasive paper requires you to lay out the evidence clearly and in a well-organized sequence. The evidence provided here must win the support of your reader. Issue by issue, you must present your case while recognizing, as necessary, the opposing viewpoints. The strength of support from authorities is vital, as is your presentation of quotations and paraphrases.

Body:

- Develop arguments to defend one side of the subject.
- Analyze the issues, both pro and con.
- Give evidence from the sources, including quotations from the scholarly sources as appropriate.

Conclusion

Keep in mind one important aspect of a good conclusion: It does not need to win the argument. It does need to prove that your position is valid, has merit, and cannot be dismissed even by readers who take another position. You want to win respect for being reasonable and not win everybody to your viewpoint.

Conclusion:

- Restate your thesis.
- Demonstrate that your position has been formulated logically through careful analysis and discussion of the issues.

Model for Comparative Essays

WEB LINK
to Reading
10.2
http://www.
ablongman.com/
lester

The comparative study requires you to examine two schools of thought, two issues, two pieces of writing, two songs, and so forth. Thus, you might examine the differing positions taken by two people on a topic of interest, perhaps the debate to relieve traffic congestion by building more highways or switching to mass transit systems.

Introduction

Your introduction should establish early on the two sides to be compared and contrasted, so mention both, usually in an objective manner without indicating your preference for one side or the other. It is vital that you introduce the subject clearly and give the central issues that govern the problem. You might offer a quotation from each of the principal figures in the dispute or provide quotations from authorities on each side. Then you should give your thesis, hypothesis, or general purpose: *This paper will explore this hypothesis: Mass transit systems, not highways, will preserve effective transportation in major cities.*

Introduction:
- Introduce the central issues.
- Cite from the sources, briefly.
- Present your thesis.

Body

For the body of a comparison paper, you have choices. The first method will give you three or four sections to the body, each examining one of several issues. Discuss each issue in turn while moving back and forth from side A to side B, showing how A addresses the issue and how B addresses it. Then go on to the second issue and then the third issue. Another method has two basic parts. First, show similarities in the two sides, giving a detailed comparison and, second, show differences by building elements of contrast. A third method allows you to explore in depth side A before devoting your attention to side B; thereafter you would develop your comparison/contrast of the two.

Plan 1: Discuss each of the topic's major issues from both sides.

Plan 2: Discuss similarities of both sides and then discuss the differences.

Plan 3: Examine side A, examine side B, and then compare and contrast them.

Conclusion

In your closing discuss again the significant issues, rate the two sides under debate, discuss the implications of both sides, and arrive at a conclusion that might prefer one side over the other but might also recognize the merits of both.

Conclusion:
- Identify again the issues.
- Rate how each side addresses or reflects the issues.
- Rank one over the other or recognize the merits of both side A and side B.

Other Useful Models

Many papers written in MLA style feature theoretical inquiry. If yours fits that pattern, see pages 421–422 for a complete discussion. Other papers written in MLA style feature interpretation. If yours fits this pattern, see pages 392–393.

Writing an Outline

An outline differs from the overall paradigms discussed on the previous pages. The outline is specific to one paper only, while the general model for a persuasion paper can be used for many papers. Keep in mind also that not all papers require a complete, formal outline, nor do all researchers need one. A short research paper can be created from key words, a list of issues, a rough outline, and a first draft. However, an outline sometimes becomes important, for it classifies the issues of your study into clear, logical categories with main headings and one or more levels of subheadings. An outline will change miscellaneous notes, computer drafts, and photocopied materials into an ordered progression of ideas. In addition, the outline is the natural fulfillment of the all-purpose model, as discussed on pages 337–338.

T I P   *Using an Outline*

A formal outline is not rigid and inflexible; you may, and should, modify it while writing and revising. In every case, treat an outline or organizational chart as a tool. Like an architect's blueprint, it should contribute to, not inhibit, the construction of a finished product.

WEB LINK
to Audio-
video 10.1
http://www.
ablongman.com/
lester

You may wish to experiment with the "outline" feature of your word processing software, which will allow you to view the paper at various levels of detail and to try out different organization patterns.

If you think it will help you control the organization of the paper, build a topic outline of balanced phrases. You can use noun phrases ("the rods of the retina"), gerund phrases ("sensing dim light with retina rods"), or infinitive phrases ("to sense dim light with retina rods"). No matter which grammatical format you choose, follow it consistently throughout the outline. Student Sarah Bemis used noun phrases to outline her scientific analysis:

I. Diabetes defined

    A. A disease without control

        1. A disorder of the metabolism

        2. The search for a cure

    B. Types of diabetes

        1. Type 1, juvenile diabetes

        2. Type 2, adult onset diabetes

II. Health complications

    A. The problem of hyperglycemia

        1. Signs and symptoms of the problem

        2. Lack of insulin

> B. The conflict of the kidneys and the liver
>
>   1. Effects of ketoacidosis
>
>   2. Effects of arteriosclerosis
>
> III. Proper care and control
>
>   A. Blood sugar monitoring
>
>   1. Daily monitoring at home
>
>   2. Hemoglobin test at a laboratory
>
>   B. Medication for diabetes
>
>   1. Insulin injections
>
>   2. Hypoglycemia agents
>
>   C. Exercise programs
>
>   1. Walking
>
>   2. Swimming
>
>   3. Aerobic workouts
>
>   D. Diet and meal planning
>
>   1. Exchange plan
>
>   2. Carbohydrate counting
>
> IV. Conclusion: Balance of all the factors

In contrast to the phrases above, you may use full sentences for each heading and sub-heading. The sentence outline has two advantages over the topic outline:

1. Many entries in a sentence outline can serve as topic sentences for paragraphs, thereby accelerating the writing process.

WEB LINK to Exercise 10.1 http://www. ablongman.com/ lester

2. The subject/verb pattern establishes the logical direction of your thinking (for example, the phrase "Vocabulary development" becomes "Television viewing can improve a child's vocabulary"). Consequently, the sentence outline brings into the open any possible organizational problems.

The time devoted to writing a complete sentence outline, like writing complete, well-synthesized notes (see pages 320–329), will serve you well when you write the rough draft and revise it. Here is a brief portion of one student's sentence outline:

> I. Organ and tissue donation is the gift of life.
>
>   A. Organs that can be successfully transplanted include the heart, lungs, liver, kidneys, and pancreas.
>
>   B. Tissues that can be transplanted successfully include bone, corneas, skin, heart valves, veins, cartilage, and other connective tissues.
>
>   C. The process of becoming a donor is easy.
>
>   D. Many people receive organ and tissue transplants each year, but still many people die because they did not receive the needed transplant.

EXERCISE 10.2

RECOGNIZING THE DESIGN OF AN ARTICLE

Shown below are three abstracts to articles on the subject of communication. Read each one to determine the writer's basic design for the full article: a general all-purpose design, persuasion, comparison, or some other design.

Abstract 1

This study examined communication behaviors and perceptions of Black and White communicators. Seventeen behaviors were identified in the literature as representing either "Black" or "White" communication. Black and White university students (N = 525) were asked to recall a past conversation with a Black or White communicator and to complete a questionnaire regarding their overall impressions of the racial other's communication behaviors. Factor analyses were conducted to create stereotype clusters for Black and White participants. The findings suggest three strong second-order stereotypic impressions for each sample. Multiple regression analysis revealed that certain behaviors are associated with each stereotypical impression. Results suggest that there is a diversity of communication styles among a single ethnic group and various stereotypic impressions are associated with particular communication behaviors.

Abstract 2

Scholars increasingly theorize about the power of communication to organize and structure social collectives. However, two factors threaten to impede research on these theories: limitations in the scope and range of existing methods for studying complex systems of communication and the large volume of communication produced by even small collectives. Centering resonance analysis (CRA) is a new text analysis method that has broad scope and range and can be applied to large quantities of written text and transcribed conversation. It identifies discursively important words and represents these as a network, then uses structural properties of the network to index word importance. CRA networks can be directly visualized and can be scored for resonance with other networks to support a number of spatial analysis methods. Following a critique of existing methodologies, this paper describes the theoretical basis and operational details of CRA, describes its advantages relative to other techniques, demonstrates its face validity and representational validity, and demonstrates its utility in modeling organizational knowledge. The conclusion argues for its applicability in several organizational research contexts before describing its potential for use in a broader range of applications, including media content analysis, conversation analysis, computer simulations, and models of communication systems.

Abstract 3

The authors explore the heuristic implications of chaos theory for the study of the process of communicating. Chaos theory's application to the study of communication is delineated from a socio-cultural perspective. The basic tenets of chaos theory are outlined and some of the parallels between chaos theory, as developed for the physical sciences, and the process of communicating are described. Theoretical foundations for a chaos theory of communicating are laid, and suggestions are made for future evolution and testing of these foundations.

Handling Text Citations in MLA Style

Citing sources in the text of your paper requires that you use the verb tense appropriate for MLA style, and that you effectively blend the source information into your text.

Using the Correct Tense

As strange as it may seem, your use of verb tense will signal your sophistication as a scholarly writer. In MLA style, you use the historical present tense to introduce the words of writers whether they are dead or alive. Note these citations:

> William Shakespeare **wants** the ghost of Hamlet's father to evoke the medieval world of magic and superstition, as well as the Catholic doctrine of Purgatory.
>
> Michelangelo **depicts** both the salvation of humans and their eternal damnation in his Last Judgment on the Sistine Chapel wall.
>
> In his Declaration of Independence, Thomas Jefferson **says,** "We hold these truths to be self-evident: that all men are created equal."

These men are dead, which might suggest the use of *designed, depicted,* and *said,* yet their works live today, reverberating with force because they reflect human values and human concerns of this age. The use of the present tense indicates that a problem, issue, or concern is an enduring one. This verb usage differs from that of the scientific community, as explained in Chapter 12.

Of course, use the past tense when writing about events of the past:

> Shakespeare **lived** his adult life in London after a childhood in Stratford-on-Avon.
>
> Michelangelo **painted** the entire ceiling himself because he could not trust his assistants to conform to his standards.

When introducing your sources, use the present tense, as shown in these examples:

> March McGruder **explains** the nature of fat cells and their effects on diets. He **says,** "The fat cells generated during binge eating never die, so they're just waiting for another moment of weakness and another binge (321).

This style will be true for an authority that you know is dead. Notice this blend of past and present tenses:

William O. Douglas (1898-1980) **served** many years as a Supreme Court justice, but he **loved** mountain climbing. In his book *Of Men and Mountains*, he **says** mountaineers "give their country some of the indomitable spirit of the mountains" (34).

EXERCISE 10.3
IDENTIFYING VERB TENSE IN SCHOLARLY WRITING

Read the following passage, circle or underline the verbs, and make a notation in the margin on the tense being used: historical present tense or past tense.

Along with her explanation on the different purposes for communication, Deborah Tannen also addresses different ways men and women communicate. In the lecture that Tannen and Robert Bly gave in New York in 1993, Tannen notes the different ways men and women handle communication throughout the day. She explains that a man talks during the workday to establish his status in the office, but a woman guards what she says to avoid confrontation.

Blending Sources Effectively in MLA Style

WEB LINK
to Chapter 10
Related Web
Destinations
http://www.
ablongman.com/
lester

The MLA style, as established by the Modern Language Association, governs papers in literature, languages, and other humanities disciplines. The MLA style puts great emphasis upon identifying the writer of source material that is being used in a paper. It requires you to list the full name of the scholar on first mention but last name only thereafter and last name only in parenthetical citations.

Quotations, paraphrases, and summaries support your paragraph's topic sentence, and they contribute coherence as well as support if the references are introduced as a logical extension of the paragraph's argument. Make certain that you mention the name of the source. Add other information as necessary, while keeping in mind that the works cited entry will contain full information to the source. Add specific page numbers where appropriate, and give identifying information when necessary to verify the credentials of the source. Let us look at one paragraph to note the general style, and then we'll look at specific elements.

Men and women have different communication styles because of biological and environmental differences. A close examination can uncover possible causes, some results, and perhaps some solutions to communication failures between men and women. **Deborah Tannen, a professor of sociolinguistics at Georgetown**

University, addresses many issues surrounding the patterns of conversation styles. In her text *You Just Don't Understand,* Tannen **claims** there are basic gender patterns or stereotypes to be found. She **says** that men participate in conversations to establish "a hierarchical social order" **(24)**, while women most often participate in conversations to establish "a network of connections" **(25)**. Tannen **distinguishes** the way women most often converse as "rapport-talk" and the way men most often converse as "report-talk" **(74)**.

Writing in MLA style, as shown above, displays these citation characteristics:

WEB LINK
to Exercise
10.2
http://www.
ablongman.com/
lester

- Use of the present tense to indicate that the issue under discussion is enduring—relevant for humans of past ages as well as those of the present and the future.
- Use of the authority's full name on first usage and last name thereafter.
- Identification of the authority's professional affiliation (not required).
- Identification of specific page numbers for quotations, paraphrases, and summaries, without a "p." or "pp."

Making a General Reference without a Page Number

When you refer to the entire work, you need mention only the name of the source, as highlighted here in boldface:

Mitchel's article addresses medical ethics.

Beginning with the Author and Ending with a Page Number

Use this standard citation to inform the reader of the beginning and the end of borrowed materials:

Robert Randolph states that the use of video games by children improves their hand and eye coordination **(45)**. An authority on motor skills, **Randolph adds,** "The mental gymnastics of video games and the competition with fellow players are important to young children and their physical, social, and mental development" **(47)**

Several sources address this aspect of gang warfare as a fight for survival, not just for control of the local turf **(Robertson 98-134; Rollins 34; Templass 561-65).**

Putting the Page Number Immediately after the Name

Sometimes, notes at the end of a quotation make it expeditious to place the page number immediately after the name:

Boughman (46) urges car makers to "direct the force of automotive airbags <u>upward</u> against the windshield" (emphasis added).

Putting the Name and Page Number at the End of Borrowed Material

You can, if you like, put the entire citation at the end of a quotation or paraphrase.

"Post-colonial outrage against the plundering of a country's rich resources has fueled rebellion against foreign occupation" **(Justice, Moody, and Graves 462)**.

In the case of a paraphrase, you should give your reader a signal to show when the borrowing begins and ends:

The Horse Whisperer won rave reviews in 1995 for Nicholas Evans. **One source describes** its redemptive and healing qualities as the main characters share an emotional quest in a world of lost hopes and reaffirmed dreams **(Wilson 186)**. Wilson says it "explores our ancient bonds with earth and sky and hearts untamed" **(187)**.

T I P   *Author and Page Number*

In MLA style do not place a comma between the author's name and the page number, and do not use "p." or "pp." before page numbers.

Citing a Source When No Author Is Listed

When no author is shown on a title page, use instead the title of the article or book. Shorten titles to a key word or phrase for the parenthetical citation, but provide the complete title in the bibliography entry.

At various foundations of their homes, Americans are threatened by chemistry and its attacks on the human system. The dangers of Chlordane and the problems with Dursban are explored in one article (**"Termites"**), but termites just grab the headlines. There are many more dangers lurking in the crevices of the average home.

The Works Cited entry will read:

"Terminating Termites." *Southern Living* July 2000: 110.

Citing a Corporate Body as Author

Some publications are the work of a corporation, institute, or government body, which are cited as the author:

The report by the school board endorsed the use of Channel One in the school system and said that "students will benefit by the news reports more than they will be adversely affected by advertising" **(Clarion County School Board 3-4).**

Identifying Nonprint Sources That Have No Page Number

In your citation, identify that a source is a speech, song lyric, compact disc, interview, or lecture. No page citation is necessary, for obvious reasons.

Marshall's lecture defined *impulse* as "an action triggered by the nerves without thought for the consequences."

Identifying Internet Sources

Internet articles usually lack pagination and consequently are usually cited without page numbers.

Hershel Winthop interprets Hawthorne's stories as the search for holiness in a corrupt Puritan society.

One Web site claims that any diet that avoids carbohydrates will avoid some sugars that are essential for the body **("Fad Diets").**

T I P *Scholarly Value*

Indicate in the citation your best estimate of the scholarly value of a source. If you are not certain that the Web site has a valid sponsor (university, organization, agency), consider omitting the material from your paper.

However, some sites, such as JSTOR, give reproduced images of the original with page numbers embedded, like this **[end of page 312]**. Do include these numbers in your citation. And include paragraph numbers if the document displays them.

The most common type of diabetes is non-insulin-dependent diabetes mellitus (NIDDM), which "affects 90 percent of those with diabetes and usually appears after age 40" **[Larson 312]**.

One source advises against making the television industry the "scapegoat for violence" **[par. 16]**.

WEB LINK
to Chapter 10
Related Web
Destinations
http://www.
ablongman.com/
lester

T I P   *When to Summarize, Paraphrase, or Quote*

As you select items for your paper, look for material that is pertinent and relevant. Then decide how you want to handle it—as a summary, paraphrase, or direct quotation. Reserve direct quotation for comments that are well phrased and therefore deserving. Use paraphrase or summary to maintain the sound of your voice in the paper. When working with one person's theory or an author's creative work, cite that primary source often.

Citing Indirect Sources

Sometimes the writer of a book or article will quote another person. Your citation should open with the name of the person making the statement and close with a parenthetical reference to where the material was found.

Martin Greenburg says, "The interventions can be construed by the adolescent as negative, overburdening and interfering with the child's ability to care for himself" **(qtd. in Peterson 9A)**.

Without the reference to Peterson, nobody could find the article. Without the reference to Greenburg, readers would assume that Peterson spoke the words.

Citing Material from Textbooks and Large Anthologies

If you quote lines of a poem, story, novel, or drama that is part of a collection or anthology, cite the author of the piece and page of the anthology.

For **William Carlos Williams,** "so much depends" on the red wheel barrow as it sits "glazed with rain water beside the white chickens" **(1,926)**.

Your works cited entry will make clear that you are citing from an anthology:

Williams, William Carlos. "The Red Wheelbarrow." The Norton Anthology of
    American Literature. Ed. Nina Baym et al. 1926–27. Vol. 1. New York: Norton,
    1999. 1,926-27.

Adding Extra Information to In-text Citations

As a courtesy to your reader, add extra information within the citation. Show parts of books or plays, or different titles if you cite several works by the same writer. For example, your reader may have a different anthology from yours, so a clear reference to *Great Expectations* such as "(681; ch. 4)" will enable the reader to locate the passage. For plays, include act, scene, and line numbers, as needed: "(*Rom.* 2.3.65-68)." The reader of this citation, for example, will find the passage in any edition of Shakespeare's *Romeo and Juliet.* Note these other sample entries:

> **Joseph Campbell suggests** that man is a slave yet also the master of all the gods (*Masks* **1: 472**).

The Campbell work cited here, *The Masks of God*, is a four-volume work. The next citation refers to two novels by Hardy.

> **Thomas Hardy reminds** readers in his prefaces that "a novel is an impression, not an argument" and that a novel should be read as "a study of man's deeds and character" (*Tess* **xxii;** *Mayor* **1**).

> Because he stresses the nobility of man, **Joseph Campbell suggests** that the mythic hero is symbolic of the "divine creative and redemptive image which is hidden within us all . . . " (*Hero* **39**). The hero elevates the human mind to an "ultimate mythogenetic zone—the creator and destroyer, the slave and yet the master, of all the gods" (*Masks* **1: 472**).

NOTE: The complete titles of the two works by Campbell that are referenced *The Hero with a Thousand Faces* and *The Masks of God*, a four-volume work.

This next example includes a reference to a note number and also a citation that calls attention to one page for special notice.

> **Horton (22, n. 3)** suggests that Melville forced the symbolism, but **Welston (199-248, esp. 234)** reaches an opposite conclusion.

Indenting Long Quotations

In MLA style, set off long prose quotations of four lines or more as a block quotation. Double space the quotation, the same as for your regular text, but indent the block quotation one inch, two clicks of the tab key, or ten character spaces from the left margin. Do not use quotation marks with the indented material. If you quote only one paragraph or the beginning of one, do *not* indent the first line an extra five spaces. Place the parenthetical citation *after* the final mark of punctuation.

If you quote more than one paragraph, indent all paragraphs after the first paragraph an extra three character spaces, or a quarter inch. However, if the first sentence of a subsequent paragraph does not begin a paragraph in the original source, do not indent it an extra three spaces.

Zigler makes this observation:

> With many others, I am nevertheless optimistic that our nation will eventually display its inherent greatness and successfully correct the many ills that I have touched upon here.
>
> Of course, much remains that could and should be done, including increased efforts in the area of family planning, the widespread implementation of Education for Parenthood programs, an increase in the availability of homemaker and child care services, and a reexamination of our commitment to doing what is in the best interest of every child in America. (42)

Zigler's position on parenthood programs has not met a wide or spontaneous welcome.

Citing Poetry

Incorporate short quotations of poetry (one or two lines) into your text, and include a line number rather than page number in the paranthetical citation.

In Part 3 of Eliot's "The Waste Land" (1922) we see a springtime search for nourishing water: "Sweet Thames, run softly, for I speak not loud or long" says the speaker in "The Fire Sermon" (3.12) while in Part 5 the speaker of "What the Thunder Said" yearns for "a damp gust / Bringing rain" (5.73-74).

Observe these guidelines for short quotations of poetry:

1. Set off the short quotation of poetry with quotation marks.
2. Indicate separate lines of a poem by using a virgule or slash mark (/) with a space before and after the slash mark.
3. Place line documentation within parentheses immediately following the final quotation mark and before the sentence period. Do not use the abbreviation *l.* or *ll.*
4. Use arabic numerals for volumes, chapters, acts, scenes, cantos, stanzas, and other part designations.

When quoting three lines or more of a poem, set off the lines by indenting ten character spaces or one inch (usually two tabs). Use double-spaced lines. A parenthetical citation to the lines of indented verse follows the last line of the quotation. If the parenthetical citation will not fit on the last line, place it on the next line, flush with the right margin of the poetry text. Abbreviate the name of the work, in this case Shakespeare's Henry IV, Part I.

> The king cautions Prince Henry:
>> Thy place in council thou has rudely lost,
>>
>> Which by thy younger brother is supplied,
>>
>> And art almost an alien to the hearts
>>
>> Of all the court and princes of my blood.
>>
>>   (*1H4*.1.1.15-18)

Handling Quotations from a Play

Set off from your text any dialogue of two or more characters. Begin with the character's name, indented one inch and written in all capital letters. Follow the name with a period, and then start the character's lines of dialogue. Indent subsequent lines of dialogue an additional quarter inch or three spaces.

At the end of *Oedipus the King*, Creon chastises Oedipus, reminding him that he no longer has control over his own life nor that of his children.

> CREON: Come along, let go of the children.
>
> OEDIPUS: No—
>
> Don't take them away from me, not now! No, no, no!
>
> KREON: Still the king, the master of all things?
>
> No more: here your power ends.
>
> None of your power follows you through life. (1673–78)

GUIDELINES

Providing a Sufficient Assortment of Sources

- Books are always a valuable addition to any bibliography. They represent thorough and exhaustive work on a subject.

- Periodicals will enhance your paper, but understand the types. Journal articles give your paper a scholarly touch. Magazine articles vary in quality, so examine them carefully. Newspapers, especially the major ones, like the *New York Times*, can add substance to your essay. Articles from Web sites may be good; again, judge them critically, and use the guidelines in Chapter 2 to judge them.

- Librarians and instructors can offer advice on the best sources to enrich your list.
- A citation search enables you to find those writers important to the discipline. These are writers who are cited by other writers. You will find them by looking at four or five bibliographies on your topic, watching for names that resurface time and again.
- Remember that your instructor or reader can look at your bibliography and determine almost immediately the substance of your work and your dedication to finding relevant sources.

Using Commas and Periods

Place ending commas and periods inside quotation marks unless the page citation intervenes.

"Modern advertising," says Rachel Murphy (192), "not only creates a marketplace, it determines **values**." She adds, "I resist the advertiser's argument that they 'awaken, not create **desires**.'"

Using Semicolons and Colons

Both semicolons and colons go outside the closing quotation marks.

Brian Sutton-Smith (64) says, "Adults don't worry whether *their* toys are **educational**"; nevertheless, parents want to keep their children in a learning mode.

Using Question Marks and Exclamation Marks

When a question mark or an exclamation mark is part of the quotation, keep it inside the closing quotation mark.

Thompson (16) passionately shouted to union members, "We can bring order into our lives even though we face hostility from every **quarter!**"

"Does scientific cloning pose a threat to the human **species?**" wonders Mark Durham (546).

If you are asking the question or doing the exclaiming, not the source, then the question mark or exclamation mark is placed outside the closing quotation mark.

The philosopher Brackenridge (16) asks, "How should we order our **lives?**"

Did Brackenridge (16) say that we might encounter "hostility from every **quarter**"?

Using Single Quotation Marks

Use single quotation marks around a quotation that appears within another quotation.

George Loffler (32) confirms that "the unconscious carries the best of human thought and gives man great dignity, but it also has the dark side so that we cry, in the words of Shakespeare's Macbeth, **'Hence, horrible shadow! Unreal mockery, hence.'** "

Using Ellipsis Points

Use three spaced ellipsis points (periods) to signal material omitted from *within* a sentence:

Phil Withim objects to the idea that "such episodes are intended to demonstrate that **Vere . . . has** the intelligence and insight to perceive the deeper issue" (118).

Note that ellipsis points are not used at the beginning of the quoted material. If an omission occurs at the end of a sentence, use four spaced ellipsis points.

R. W. B. Lewis (62) declares that "if Hester has sinned, she has done so as an affirmation of life, and her sin is the source of **life. . . .**"

If a page citation also appears at the end with the ellipsis, use three spaced ellipsis points followed by the closing quotation mark, the page citation within parentheses, and the period.

R. W. B. Lewis declares that "if Hester has sinned, she has done so as an affirmation of life, and her sin is the source of **life . . ." (62).**

If you omit one or more sentences within a quotation, your ellipsis points indicate the omission.

Zigler reminds us that "child abuse is found more frequently in a single (female) parent home in which the mother is **working. . . . The** unavailability of quality day care can only make this situation more stressful" (42).

If you omit a word or phrase in a quotation of poetry, indicate the omission with three or four ellipsis points just as you would with omissions in a prose passage. However, if you omit a complete line or more from the poem, indicate the omission by a line of spaced periods that equals the average length of the lines.

> They are leaning their young heads against their mothers,
>
> And *that* cannot stop their tears.
>
> . . . .
>
> They are weeping in the playtime of the others,
>
> In the country of the free. (Browning 382)

Using Parentheses and Brackets

Use parentheses to enclose your comments or explanations that stand outside any quotation, as shown in this example:

> Boughman (46) urges car makers to "direct the force of automotive airbags *upward* against the windshield" **(emphasis added).**

Use brackets to enclose your comments or explanations that stand within a quotation.

Use brackets to clarify:

> This same critic indicates that "we must avoid the temptation to read **it** [The Scarlet Letter] heretically" (118).

Use brackets to establish correct grammar:

> He observes that "many students [have] developed computer skills superior to their classroom teachers" (34).

Use brackets to note the addition of italics or underlining:

> He says, for instance, that the "extended family is now rare in contemporary society, and with its demise the new parent has lost the wisdom **[my emphasis]** and daily support of older, more experienced family members" (Zigler 42).

Use brackets to substitute a proper name for a pronoun:

> "As we all know, **he [Kennedy]** implored us to serve the country, not take from it" (Jones 432).

Use brackets with *sic* to indicate errors in the original:

Lovell says, "John F. Kennedy, assassinated in November of **1964 [sic]**, became overnight an immortal figure of courage and dignity in the hearts of most Americans" (62).

Note: The assassination occurred in 1963.

EXERCISE 10.4

INTRODUCING CITATIONS IN MLA STYLE

Shown below are four statements. Transform each of them into proper citations in MLA style.

1. Carol Gilligan, page 8 on the word *psyche.* "This ancient word carries the wisdom that we are more than our genetic makeup, more than our life histories, more than our cultural lineage."

2. Anne Mallory, page 225: "As an emergent concept, boredom encompasses indolence but connotes something else as well: while an indolent person may enjoy periods of inactivity, a bored person finds them all but impossible to endure."

3. Lewis Thomas, page 119: "The evolution of language can be compared to the biological evolution of species, depending on how far you are willing to stretch analogies."

4. Jerome Lowenstein, page. 25: "If it be granted that it is possible and necessary to teach compassion, where is the time and where is the place?"

Formatting the MLA Paper

WEB LINK
to Audio-
video 10.2
http://www.
ablongman.com/
lester

A research paper that is prepared using MLA style consists of the following parts (items 1, 3, and 6 are required):

1. Opening page with author's name and address and the title of the paper
2. Outline (if required)
3. The text of the paper
4. Content notes
5. Appendix
6. Works Cited or other bibliographic list

Opening Page

A research paper in MLA style does not need a separate title page. Number your pages, and include your last name before the page number in the upper right corner of each page. Place your full name and other identification in the upper left corner of your opening page. For college papers, instead of your address, include information that identifies your course.

WEB LINK
to Chapter 10
Related Web
Destinations
http://www.
ablongman.com/
lester

Holz 1

Kaci Holz

English 102c, U of A

Professor England

May 17, 2003

Gender Communication

Men and women differ. Obvious enough, right? Not so obvious, however, are the different communication styles that the two sexes employ and the reasons behind the styles. For only about the first four weeks of existence is the human embryo neither male nor female (Starr and Taggart 190).

Outline

Include your outline with the finished manuscript only if your instructor requires it. Place the pages of your outline after a separate title page, and number the outline pages with lowercase roman numerals, beginning with ii (for example, ii, iii, iv, v).

The Text of the Paper

Double space throughout the paper and use one-inch margins for your text, excluding page number lines. In general, you should *not* use subtitles or numbered divisions for your paper, even if it is more than twenty pages long. Instead, use continuous paragraphing without subdivisions or headings. If the closing page of your text runs short, leave the remainder of the page blank. Do not write "The End" or provide artwork as a closing signal. Do not start "Notes" or "Works Cited" on this final page of text; begin each of those sections on a new page.

Content Endnotes

You may have used content notes in your paper in addition to parenthetical source citations. In that case you will add a Notes section after the last text page. Label the opening page of this section with the word "Notes" centered at the top, at least one double space below your page numbering sequence in the upper right corner. Number the notes in sequence with raised superscript numerals to match those within your text. Double space these pages, just as you did for your text pages.

Appendix

Place additional material, if necessary, in an appendix that precedes the Works Cited page. This is the logical location for computer data, questionnaire results, complicated statistics, mathematical proofs, or detailed descriptions of special equipment. Double space appendixes and begin each appendix on a new page. Continue your page numbering sequence in the upper right corner. Label the opening page "Appendix," centered at the top. If you have more than one appendix, use "Appendix A," "Appendix B," and so forth.

Works Cited or Other Bibliographic List

Start the list of works cited on a new page, and center the heading "Works Cited" one inch from the top. Continue your page numbering sequence in the upper right corner. Double space throughout. Your paper might also include another type of bibliographic section, so select a heading that indicates the nature of your list.

Works Cited for a list of printed works, films, recordings, Internet sources, etc.

Annotated Bibliography for a list that includes a description of the contents of each source (see pages 144–145).

Bibliography for a complete listing of *all* works related to the subject, an unlikely prospect for most research papers unless the topic is very narrow indeed.

Works Consulted for a list that is not confined to the works cited in the paper.

Selected Bibliography for a list of readings on the subject.

Works pertinent to the paper but not quoted or paraphrased, such as an article on related matters, can be mentioned in a content note (see page 402) and then listed in the Works Cited. See pages 411–417 for examples.

Writing Entries for the Works Cited Section

WEB LINK to Reading 10.3
http://www.ablongman.com/lester

Begin the Works Cited section on a new page. Use the hanging indention format for your Works Cited or other bibliographic list; that is, set the first line of each entry one inch from the edge of the page and indent subsequent lines five spaces or one-half inch. Alphabetize entries by the last name of the author. Always give authors' names in the fullest possible form, for example, "Cosbey, Robert C." rather than "Cosbey, R. C." unless, as indicated on the title page of the book, the author prefers initials. Double space throughout.

For details about the format and information to include for different types of works, such as books, articles, government documents, and electronic sources, see the sections that follow.

Books

Enter information as shown in the sample entries below. Author, title, and publication data form the basic three parts. Use either italics or underlining for titles of books, periodicals, films, and other major works. Whichever formatting you choose, be consistent throughout your paper.

WEB LINK
to Exercise
10.3
http://www.
ablongman.com/
lester

Author

Reamer, Frederic G. Social Work Values and Ethics. New York: Columbia UP, 1999.

Author, Anonymous

Begin with the title. Do not use "Anonymous" or "Anon." unless the title page lists *Anonymous* in place of the author's name.

The Song of Roland. Trans. Glyn Burgess. New York: Penguin, 1990.

Authors, Two or Three

Mickelson, James S., Karen S. Haynes, and Barbara Mikulski. Affecting Change: Social Workers in the Political Arena. 4th ed. Boston: Allyn, 2000.

Authors, More Than Three

After the first author's name, use "et al.," which means "and others," or list all the authors.

Balzer, LeVon, et al. Life Science. Glenview, IL: Scott, 1990.

Author, Corporation or Institution

A corporate author can be an association, a committee, or any group or institution when the title page does not identify the names of the members. List a committee or council as the author even when the organization is also the publisher, as in the first example below:

American Council on Education. Annual Report 1999. Washington: ACE, 2000.

American Medical Society. Guide to Prescription and Over-the-Counter Drugs. Ed. Charles B. Clayman. New York: Random, 1988.

Author, Two or More Books by the Same Author

Do not repeat the author's name with each entry. Rather, for subsequent entries insert a continuous three-hyphen line flush with the left margin, followed by a period. Also, list the works alphabetically by the title (ignoring *a, an,* and *the*), not by the year of publication.

Rowling, J. K. Harry Potter and the Chamber of Secrets. New York: Scholastic, 1999.

---. <u>Harry Potter and the Goblet of Fire</u>. New York: Scholastic, 2000.

---. <u>Harry Potter and the Sorcerer's Stone</u>. New York: Scholastic, 1998.

Alphabetized Works, Encyclopedias, and Biographical Dictionaries

If no author is listed, begin with the title of the article. Well-known works need only the edition and the year of publication after the title of the book.

"Astronaut." <u>The American Heritage Dictionary of the English Language</u>. 3rd ed.
1992.

Anthology, Component Part

Provide the inclusive page numbers for the piece used.

Warshow, Robert. "The Gangster as Tragic Hero." <u>The Oxford Book of Essays</u>.
Ed. John Gross. 2nd ed. New York: Oxford UP, 1998. 581–86.

The Bible

Do not underscore or italicize the word Bible or the books of the Bible, but underscore or italicize special editions of the Bible.

<u>The New Open Bible</u>. New Living Translation. Nashville: Nelson, 1998.

Classical Works

You are likely to find a classical work in an anthology, which would require this citation:

Homer. <u>The Odyssey</u>. Trans. Robert Fitzgerald. <u>The Norton Anthology of</u>
<u>World Masterpieces.</u> Ed. Maynard Mack et al. New York: Norton, 1997.
96–336.

Cross-References to Works in a Collection

If you cite several different selections from one anthology, use an abbreviated reference to the anthology in the entries for the individual selections, and add a separate full entry for the anthology itself.

Behrens, Laurence, and Leonard J. Rosen. <u>Writing and Reading across the</u>
<u>Curriculum</u>. New York: Longman, 2000.
Bettelheim, Bruno. " 'Cinderella': A Story of Sibling Rivalry and Oedipal
Conflicts." Behrens and Rosen 638–45.

Kelley, Karol. "Pretty Woman: A Modern Cinderella." Behrens and Rosen 646–55.

Morrison, Toni. "Cinderella's Stepsisters." Behrens and Rosen, 657–59.

T I P   *Prepositions in Titles*

A convention of MLA style is to use lowercase prepositions in titles of books, articles, and other words, no matter how long the prepositions are. Thus, use the lowercase for such words as *across, through, between,* and other prepositions.

Edition

Indicate the edition number for any edition beyond the first.

Orfali, Robert, Dan Harkey, and Jeri Edward. Client/Server Survival Guide. 3rd ed. New York: Wiley, 1999.

Editor, Translator, Illustrator, or Compiler

List the editor first only if your in-text citation refers to the work of the editor (for example, the editor's introduction or notes).

Toibin, Colm, ed. Foreword. Irish Fiction. London: Penguin, 1999. iii–vi.

Introduction, Preface, Foreword, or Afterword

Lowell, Robert. Foreword. Ariel. By Sylvia Plath. New York: Harper, 1966. vii–ix.

If the author has written the prefatory matter, use only the author's last name after the word *By.*

Vonnegut, Kurt. Prologue. Jailbird. By Vonnegut. New York: Delacorte, 1979. 32–40. 1-7.

Title of a Book in Another Language

In general, use lowercase letters for foreign titles except for the first major word and proper names. Provide a translation in brackets if you think it necessary (e.g., *Etranger* [*The Stranger*] or Praha [Prague]).

Castex, P. G. Le rouge et le noir de Stendhal. Paris: Sedes, 1967.

Note: Le rouge et le noir *is a book title within a book title, thus it does not receive italics or underscoring.*

Volume Numbers

> Seale, William. The President's House: A History. Vol. 1. Washington: White
> House Historical Assn., 1986.

> *Note: If you use all volumes, write "2 vols.".*

Journals and Magazines

For journal and magazine articles, the Works Cited entry should include author, title, name of the periodical, date of publication, and inclusive page numbers.

Author

> Mallory, Anne. "Burke, Boredom, and the Theater of Counterrevolution." PMLA
> 118 (2003): 224-38.

Journal, with All Issues for a Year Paged Continuously

> Bartley, William. "Imagining the Future in The Awakening." College English 62
> (2000): 719-46.

Journal, with Each Issue Paged Anew

Add the issue number after the volume number or add the month or quarter.

> Naffziger, Douglas W., Jeffrey S. Hornsby, and Donald F. Kuralko. "A Proposed
> Research Model of Entrepreneurial Motivation." Entrepreneurship: Theory
> and Practice 18.3 (Spring 1994): 29-42.

Loose-Leaf Collection

If the article is reprinted by an information service that gathers together several articles on a common topic, as part of a series, use the form shown in the following example.

> Cox, Rachel S. "Protecting the National Parks." The Environment. CQ Researcher
> ser. 23 (2000): 523+.

If the service reprints articles from other sources, use this next form, which shows original publication data and then information on the SIRS booklet—title, editor, and volume number.

> Hodge, Paul. "The Adromeda Galaxy." Mercury July/Aug. 1993: 98+. Physical
> Science. Ed. Eleanor Goldstein. Vol. 2. Boca Raton: SIRS, 1994. Art. 24.

Magazine

For a weekly magazine, include the day and month as well as the year. For a monthly or quarterly, include the month or quarter with the year. Do not list volume and issue numbers.

> Levingston, Steven. "Steer Clear of These Dangerous Drivers." <u>Reader's Digest</u>
> July 1997: 50-55.

> Nash, J. Madeleine. "The New Science of Alzheimer's." <u>Time</u> 17 July 2000: 51-57.

For discontinuous pages, write only the first page number and a plus sign with no intervening space:

> Cannon, Lou. "Reagan Radiated Happiness and Hope." <u>George</u> Aug. 2000: 58+.

Notes, Editorials, Queries, Reports, Comments, Letters

Identify the type of pieces that are not full-fledged articles.

> Trainor, Jennifer Seibel, and Deborah Klein. Comment and Response. <u>College</u>
> <u>English</u> 62 (2000): 767-72.

Reprint of a Journal Article

> Simonds, Robert L. "The Religious Right Explains the Religious Right." <u>School</u>
> <u>Administrator</u> 9 (Oct. 1993): 19–22. Rpt. in <u>Education Digest</u> Mar. 1994:
> 19-22.

Review Article

> Seymour, Jim. "Push Back." Rev. of <u>Pointcast</u> and <u>Backweb</u> [computer software].
> <u>PC Magazine</u> Aug. 1997: 93-94.

If the review is neither signed nor titled, begin the entry with "Rev. of" and alphabetize the entry under the title of the work reviewed.

> Rev. of <u>Anthology of Danish Literature</u>, ed. F. J. Billeskov Jansen and P. M.
> Mitchell. <u>Times Literary Supplement</u> 7 July 1972: 785.

Title, Quotation within the Article's Title

> Danald, Margaret Loftus. " 'As Marriage Binds, and Blood Breaks': English
> Marriage and Shakespeare." <u>Shakespeare Quarterly</u> 30 (1979): 68-81.

Title, within the Article's Title

Dundes, Alan. " 'To Love My Father All': A Psychoanalytic Study of the Folktale Source of <u>King Lear</u>." <u>Southern Folklore Quarterly</u> 40 (1976): 353-66.

Title, Foreign

Rebois, Charles. "Les effets du 12 juin." <u>Le Figaro Magazine</u> 2 July 1994: 42-43.

Newspapers

Jonsson, Patrik. "New Racial Climate in Suburban South." <u>The Christian Science Monitor</u> 28 July 2000: 1+ .

Morrison, Blake. "Sierra Fire Continues Rampage." <u>USA Today</u> 31 July 2000: 10A.

Jones, Tim. "New Media May Excite, While Old Media Attract." <u>Chicago Tribune</u> 28 July 1997, sec. 4: 2.

Add the city in square brackets if necessary to locate the publication.

"Legislative Endorsement." Editorial. <u>Tennessean</u> [Nashville] 31 July 2000: 12A.

Add a description to explain the special nature of the citation.

Fisher, Marc. "A Memorial, Yes, But What about the Message." Column. <u>Washington Post</u> 22 July 2000: B1.

Government Documents

As a general rule, place information in the work cited entry in this order: government, body or agency, subsidiary body, title of document, identifying numbers, publication facts. When you cite two or more works by the same government, in subsequent entries substitute three hyphens for the name of each government or body that repeats.

United States. Cong. House.

---. ---. Senate.

---. Dept. of Justice.

Begin with the author's name if known, especially if you cited the name in your text.

Poore, Benjamin Perley, comp. <u>A Descriptive Catalogue of the Government Publications of the United States, September 5, 1774-March 4, 1881</u>. US 48th Cong., 2nd sess. Misc. Doc. 67. Washington: GPO, 1885.

Abbreviate the *Congressional Record* and provide only the date and page numbers.

> Cong. Rec. 27 July 2000: S7839-41.

> United States. Dept. of State. Foreign Relations of the United States: Diplomatic Papers, 1943. 5 vols. Washington: GPO, 1943-44.

> ---. President. Health Security: The President's Report to the American People. Pr Ex 1.2:H34/4. Washington: GPO, 1993.

Legal Citations and Public Statutes

These are easily cited in full in your text, negating any reason to cite them in the bibliography, for example:

> One source resorted to the state law to defend the environment (California. Constitution. Art. 2, sec. 4). In contrast, another source used court precedent (Environmental Protection Agency et al. v. Mink et al.).

Electronic Sources (Internet, E-mail, Databases, CD-ROMs)

MLA style places angle brackets around Web site addresses. Include any publication date for the material as well as the date you accessed it.

T I P *Internet Articles*

Do not include page numbers unless the Internet article shows original page numbers from the printed version of the journal or magazine. Do not include the total number of paragraphs or specific paragraph numbers unless the original Internet article has provided them.

Abstract

> Ladouceur, Robert, et al. "Strategies Used with Intrusive Thoughts: A Comparison of OCD Patients with Anxious and Community Controls." Journal of Abnormal Psychology 109 (2000). Abstract. 10 May 2000 <http://www.apa.org/journals/abn/500ab.html>.

Anonymous Article

> "People: Your Greatest Asset." Human Resources 15 July 1999. 11 Sept. 2000 <http://netscape/business/humanresources/>.

Archive or Scholarly Project

Give the location or name of the database (e.g., *JSTOR*).

British Poetry Archive. Ed. Jerome McGann and David Seaman. 1999. U of
  Virginia Lib. 19 Aug. 2000 <http://etext.lib.virginia.edu/britpo.html>.

Coleridge, Samuel Taylor. "Kubla Khan." The Samuel Taylor Coleridge Archive.
  Ed. Marjorie A. Tiefert. 10 May 1999. U of Virginia Lib. 10 June 2001
  <http://etext.lib.virginia.edu/stc/Coleridge/poems/Kubla_Khan.html>.

Dorson, Richard M. "The Eclipse of Solar Mythology." Journal of American
  Folklore 68 (1955): 393-416. JSTOR. 7 Apr. 2003
  <http//www.jstor.org/search>.

Article, Reproduced from a Scholarly Journal

Schwyzer, Philip. "A Map of Greater Cambria." Early Modern Literary Studies.
  Spec. Issue 4.2 (1998) 4-13. Apr. 2003 <http://pul.oclc.org/emls/
  04-2/schwamap.htm>.

T I P   *Long URLs*

MLA style permits you to shorten long and complicated URLs if typing them
becomes onerous or mistake prone. List the primary site followed by the word
search, as with **<http://memory.loc.gov/search>**. If a URL does not all fit on
one line, divide the URL only after a slash, and do not introduce a hyphen at
the end of the first line.

Article at a Library's Online Service with a Listed URL

Most libraries have converted their computer searches to online databases provided by services such as Lexis-Nexis, ProQuest Direct, EBSCOhost, Electric Library,
InfoTrac, and others. If the source provides the URL, omit the identifying numbers
for the database or the key word used in the search and include the URL.

Lee, Catherine C.. "The South in Toni Morrison's Song of Solomon: Initiation,
  Healing, and Home." Studies in the Literary Imagination 31 (1998): 109-23.
  Abstract. InfoTrac. U of Tennessee, Hodges Lib. 19 Sept. 2001
  <http://firstsearch.oclc.org/next = NEXTCMD>.

Article from an Online Service to Which You Personally Subscribe

You may research topics from your home, apartment, or dormitory room, where you use such services as America Online or Netscape. List the database, underlined, and the service. If the URL is provided, use the form of this next example.

> "Nutrition and Cancer." Discovery Health 1 May 2000. MEDLINEplus. America
>
> Online. 3 Aug. 2000. Keyword: Nutrition.

> *Note: You may also supply the path, as in* Path: Health; Diseases and Conditions;
> Cancer, *or you may provide a URL, as in* <http://www.discoveryhealth.com/search>.

Article from an Online Service with an Unlisted or Scrambled URL

Three possible forms are available to you when the online service provides no URL: key word, path, and server.

If you access the site by using a key word, provide a citation that gives the name of the service, the date of access, and the key word:

> Esslin, Martin. "Theater of the Absurd." Grolier Multimedia Encyclopedia. 1995
>
> ed. Netscape. 3 Aug. 2000. Key word: Theater of the Absurd.

If you follow a series of topic labels to reach the article, and there is no URL provided, write "Path" followed by the sequence of topic labels that you followed to obtain the article. Use a semicolon to separate each topic.

> "Kate Chopin: A Re-Awakening." 23 June 1999. PBS. College Webivore. Netscape.
>
> 4 Aug. 2000. Path: US Literature; 19th Century; Women Authors; Chopin,
>
> Kate (1850-1904).

Make a citation to the source, then give the name of the database, underlined (if known), the name of the service, the library, and the date of access. If you can easily locate the URL of the service's home page, provide it in angle brackets after your date of access.

> Brezina, Timothy. "Teenage Violence toward Parents as an Adaptation to Family
>
> Strain: Evidence from a National Survey of Male Adolescents." Youth and
>
> Society 30 (1999): 416–44. MasterFILE Elite. EBSCOhost. Clarksville
>
> Montgomery County Lib., Clarksville, TN. 3 Aug. 2000
>
> <http://www.ebsco.com>.

Article from an Online Magazine

Carney, Dan, Mike France, and Spencer E. Ante. "Web Access Is Becoming a
Dicey Issue for Industry and Regulators." <u>BusinessWeek Online</u> 31 July
2000. 2 Aug. 2000 <http://www.businessweek.com/2000/00_31>.

Article from a CD-ROM

Some articles will be found on a library's database rather than the Web. Italicize
the database and name the server used.

Figueredo, Aurelio J., and Laura Ann McCloskey. "Sex, Money, and Paternity:
The Evolutionary Psychology of Domestic Violence." <u>Ethnology and
Sociobiology</u> 14 (1993): 353-79. Abstract. PsycINFO. CD-ROM. SilverPlatter.
12 Jan. 1999.

Some compact discs have articles, stories, and other data that you can cite:

Poe, Edgar Allan. "Fall of the House of Usher." <u>Electronic Classical Library</u>.
CD-ROM. Garden Grove, CA: World Library, 1999.

"Abolitionist Movement." <u>Compton's Interactive Encyclopedia</u>. CD-ROM. The
Learning Company, 1999.

Cartoon Found Online

Adams, Scott. "The Pointy-Haired Boss Wants to See You." Cartoon. <u>Dilbert</u>.
15 Aug. 1999. 24 Aug. 2000 <http://umweb2.unitedmedia.com/
comics/dilbert/archive/cal-35.html>.

Chapter or Portion of a Book

Place chapter title after the author's name:

Whiting, William. "Introduction." <u>The War Powers of the President, and the
Legislative Powers of Congress in Relation to Rebellion, Treason and
Slavery</u>. Boston: Shorey, 1862. 3-16. 18 Sept. 2003 <http://www.hti.
umich.edu/cgi/t/text/text-idx?c=moa;idno=AEW5618>.

E-mail

Clemmer, Jim. "Writing Lab." E-mail to the author. 24 Aug. 2001.

Encyclopedia Article Online

"Coleridge, Samuel Taylor." Encyclopaedia Britannica Online. Vers. 99.1.
1994–99. Encyclopaedia Britannica. 19 Aug. 2001 <http://www.eb.com/
bol/topic?eu=25136&sctn=1>.

Film, Video, or Film Clip Online

"A Light Still Bright: Video on the Ecumenical Patriarchate of Constantinople."
The History of the Orthodox Christian Church. 1996. GoTelecom Online.
24 Aug. 2001 <http://www.goarch.org/goa/departments/gotel/
online_videos.html#LIGHT>.

Home Page for a Web Site

Dawe, James. Jane Austen Page. 1996-2000. 15 May 2000
<http://www.jamesdawe.com>.

Interview from an Online Radio

Hamill, Pete. "Is Journalism Dead?" Interview with Marc Strassman. Strassman
Files. BookRadio 1998. 24 Aug. 2000 <http://www.bookradio.com/>.

Newsgroup, Listserv, Usenet news, Forum, MOO, MUD

Link, Richard. "Territorial Fish." Online Posting. 11 Jan. 1997. Environment
Newsgroup. 11 Mar. 2000 <http://www.rec.aquaria.freshwater.misc>.

Newspaper Article, Column, Editorial

Firestone, David. "Anonymous Louisiana Slaves Regain Identity." New York
Times on the Web 30 July 2000. 30 July 2000
<http://www.nytimes.com/library/national/073000la-slaves.html>.

Novel at an Online Database

Lawrence, D. H. "Chapter 1." Lady Chatterly's Lover. 1928. Bibliomania. 26 Sept.
2001 <http://bibliomania.com/fiction/dhl/chat/chat1.html>.

Online Posting for E-mail Discussion Group

Chapman, David. "Reforming the Tax and Benefit System to Reduce
Unemployment." Online Posting. 25 Feb. 1998. Democracy Design Forum.
27 May 2000 <http://www.democdesignforum.demon.co.uk/
unemp.nexus.html>.

Sound Clip or Recording

Nader, Ralph. "Live Webcast with Ralph Nader." Press Club. NPR Online.
18 July 2000. Audio transcript. 27 July 2000 <http://www.npr.org/
programs/npc/000718.rnader.html>.

University Posting, Online Article

Siewers, Alf. "Issues Online." Online Posting. July/Aug. 2000. U of Illinois at
Springfield. 28 July 2000 <http://www.uis.edu/~ilissues//owl.htm>.

Artistic Works and Performances
Art Work or Exhibit

Remington, Frederic. <u>Mountain Man</u>. Metropolitan Museum of Art, New York.

"Gertrude Vanderbilt Whitney: Printmakers' Patron." Whitney Museum of
American Art, New York. 22 Feb. 1995.

Use this next form to cite reproductions in books and journals.

Raphael. <u>School of Athens</u>. 1510-1511. The Vatican, Rome. <u>World Book</u>
<u>Encyclopedia</u>. 1976 ed.

Broadcast on Radio or Television

Cooper, John. "Woodrow Wilson." Interview. <u>American Presidents</u>. C-SPAN2.
13 Sept. 1999.

Film, Videocassette, or DVD

Cite the title of a film, the director, the distributor, and the year of release. Include
other information if relevant—for example, the major performers or the writer.

<u>Shakespeare in Love</u>. Dir. John Madden. Universal Pictures, 1998.

<u>Little Women</u>. Dir. Gillian Armstrong. Screenplay by Robin Swicord. Columbia
Pictures, 1993.

<u>There's Something about Mary</u>. Dir. Bobby Farraley and Peter Farraley. DVD.
20th Century Fox, 1999.

Musical Composition

For a musical composition, begin with the composer's name, followed by a period. Underline the title of an opera, ballet, or work of music identified by name, but do not underline or enclose within quotation marks the form, number, and key when these are used to identify an instrumental composition.

> Mozart, Wolfgang A. <u>Jupiter</u>. Symphony no. 41.

Treat a published score as you would a book.

> Legrenzi, Giovanni. <u>La Buscha</u>. Sonata for Instruments. <u>Historical Anthology of Music</u>. Ed. Archibald T. Davison and Willi Apel. Cambridge, MA: Harvard UP, 1950. 70-76.

Performance

Cite a play, opera, ballet, or concert performance as you would a film, but include the location (normally the theater and city) and the date of the performance.

> <u>Asylum Night</u>. Transit Dance Company. Studio 210, San Francisco. 28 Oct. 2000.

> <u>Hairspray</u>. By John Waters. Dir. Jack O'Brien. Perf. Harvey Fierstein, Marissa Janet Winokur, and Dick Latessa. Neil Simon Theater, New York. 2003.

If your text emphasizes the work of a particular individual, begin with the appropriate name.

> Kurt Masur, cond. Opening Night Performance. Boston Symphony Orchestra. Tanglewood, MA. 5 July 2003.

Public Address or Lecture

Identify the speaker and the nature of the address (e.g., Lecture, Reading), include the location (normally the lecture hall and city), and the date of the performance.

> Leonard, Elmore. Lecture. Wharton Center Great Hall, Michigan State U Celebrity Lecture Series. East Lansing, MI. 17 Apr. 2003.

Recording, Tape, or Disk

Indicate the medium: e.g., audiocassette, audiotape (reel-to-reel tape), CD, or LP (long-playing record).

Tchaikovsky. <u>Romeo and Juliet</u>. Fantasy-Overture after Shakespeare. New
Philharmonia Orchestra London. Cond. Lawrence Siegel. DVD. Classical
Masters, 2000.

Reproductions and Photographs

Snowden, Mary. <u>Jersey Pears</u>. 1982. <u>American Realism: Twentieth Century
Drawings and Watercolors</u>. New York: Abrams, 1986. 159.

Television or Radio Program

Give the title of the episode in quotation marks; the narrator, performer, actor,
director (if relevant); the title of the series in italics or underscored; the host or anchor
(if relevant); name of the network, call letters and city of the local station; the broadcast date.

"Women and Fibroids." Narr. Jovita Moore. <u>Action News</u>. WATC, Atlanta.
8 Aug. 2000.

"Frankenstein: The Making of the Monster." <u>Great Books</u>. Narr. Donald
Sutherland. Writ. Eugenie Vink. Dir. Jonathan Ward. Learning Channel. 8
Sept. 2003.

Other Miscellaneous Sources

When you have an unusual source, label it in the bibliography entry with such
words as *advertisement, letter, map, transparency,* or *voice mail.* Here are a few examples of this form.

Datek Online. Advertisement. <u>CNBC</u>. NBC. 16 Nov. 2000.

French, Earl. <u>Personal Problems in Industrial Research and Development</u>.
Bulletin No. 51. Ithaca: New York State School of Industrial and Labor
Relations, 2001.

Miller, Wilma J., ed. <u>Writing across the Curriculum</u>. Proceedings of the Fifth
Annual Conference on Writing across the Curriculum. Feb. 1995. U of
Kentucky. Lexington: U of Kentucky P, 1995.

Shore, Zandra Lesley. "Girls Reading Culture: Autobiography as Inquiry into
Teaching the Body, the Romance, and the Economy of Love." Diss. U of
Toronto, 1999.

Thompson, Paul. "W. B. Yeats." Lecture. Videocassette. Memphis U, 2003.

"The Human Genetic Code." Illustration. <u>Facts on File</u> 29 June 2003: 437-38.

"Earth Day." Poster. Louisville. 23 Mar. 1998.

"Gospel Arts Day." Program. Nashville: Fisk U. 18 June 2000.

Sharp, La Vaughn, and William E. Loeche. The Patient and Circulatory Disorders: A Guide for Instructors. 54 transparencies, 99 overlays. Philadelphia: Lorrenzo, 2001.

Warren, Vernon. Voice mail to the author. 6 Jan. 2001.

G U I D E L I N E S

Writing the Works Cited Section

A sample Works Cited list is shown on pages 384–385. Study it for style and form. Meanwhile, keep in mind a few guidelines:

- Start the Works Cited or other bibliography section on a new page.
- Double space throughout.
- Begin each entry with the last name of the author and place the entries in alphabetical order. If no author is listed, begin with the title of the article or book, ignoring any "a" or "the" that begins the title. Begin with "Anonymous" only if that is written on the title page of the source.

Each entry will usually have three parts: author, title, and publication data. The MLA conventions of form and punctuation may seem irrelevant or busy work, but your instructors take the conventions seriously and so should you.

Chapter Review

WEB LINK to Chapter 10 Related Web Destinations http://www. ablongman.com/ lester

This chapter has taken you on a journey into academic scholarship, which requires special conventions in style and form. Don't dismiss them lightly; they bring uniformity to the academy, just as inventory control serves a business or regimentation serves the army.

Research papers in literature, languages, and other humanities disciplines follow standards set by the Modern Language Association (MLA).

For many years the Modern Language Association conformed to the footnote style, but the cumbersome burden of keeping footnotes and footnote numerals on the same page became a problem. In addition, printing costs skyrocketed for the use of special fonts, different sizes, superscript numerals, etc. Remember, there was an age before the computer! In 1951 William Riley Parker, executive secretary of the Modern Language Association, compiled *The MLA Style Sheet*. It was a little booklet of only 30 pages, but it launched the tradition of scholarly associations as the authority on publication standards within the discipline. Over time, MLA moved from footnotes to in-text citations, and today the standards embrace Internet citations as well as those of CD-ROM and Web-based publications. This chapter has demonstrated those standards, as established most recently by the sixth edition of the *MLA Handbook for Writers of Research Papers* (2003). Thus, you are expected to perform certain skills if writing in MLA style:

- Use the historical present tense for presenting your citations.
- Choose subject matter that lends itself to theoretical study of topics concerning quality of life, art, ideas, ethics, and other enduring issues.
- Select a design or layout paradigm for your paper that fits the discipline.
- Adopt a plan that works for you and your subject.

Then, you will need to conscientiously blend your source material into your text, following the guidelines in this chapter.

- Mention the authority and provide a page number, if appropriate.
- Because other scholars can use your Works Cited list to investigate any source of interest, your Works Cited entries are of vital importance. Give all pertinent data on each of your sources so that others can investigate if they so desire.
- Internet sites often present a problem because URLs shift and change at a day's notice. Nevertheless, give the information that you used to gather the information.

Chapter 10 Assignment: Evaluating Use of MLA Style

A research paper on gender communication, written by Kaci Holz, appears below. In it, she has attempted to follow the guidelines for the MLA style, as described in this chapter. Your task is to examine the paper to make marginal comments on her precision in using MLA style but also to note any failures. Read carefully and critically the Holz essay and then make detailed marginal comments on Holt's in-text citations and other matters of documentation. Be prepared to discuss the style and content of her paper in class.

Tracing the Work of Two Students

Research Paper in MLA Style

Shown next is the paper of Kaci Holz, whose developing work we have seen displayed at the ends of various chapters. Here, in MLA style, she develops a comprehensive description of a communication issue: the differences in the ways men and women communicate with one another. She pinpoints several key issues, and along the way she visits the literature and shares it with her readers.

Note: MLA style permits underlining or italics for books and emphasis on a word. Kaci Holz chose to use italics, and you may also do so.

Kaci Holz

Dr. Bekus

April 23, 2003

English 1010

Gender Communication

Men and women are different. Obvious enough, right? Not so obviously, men and women have different communication styles. For only about the first four weeks of existence the human embryo is neither male nor female (Starr and Taggart 190). During this time (if human embryos could talk) gender communication is not an issue. However, after the first four weeks the human embryo starts to develop either male or female reproductive organs (Starr and Taggart 190). With these male or female developments come other differences. Men and women develop different communication styles because of biological and environmental differences.

First, let us examine several theories about different male and female communication styles. Deborah Tannen, Ph.D., is a professor of sociolinguistics at Georgetown University. In her book *You Just Don't Understand*, she addresses many issues surrounding the patterns of conversation styles between men and women. While she stresses that not all men and not all women communicate in the same ways, she claims there are basic gender patterns or stereotypes that can be found. Tannen says that men participate in conversations to establish "a hierarchical social order" (Tannen, *Don't Understand* 24), while women most often participate in conversations to establish "a network of connections" (25). She distinguishes the way women most often converse as "rapport-talk" and the way men most often converse as "report-talk" (74).

Tannen continues to differentiate between the male communication style and the female communication style by describing each one's purpose for communicating. She explains that women often communicate to gain sympathy or understanding for a particular problem. However, men often respond to such communication with their typical "report-talk" by trying to offer solutions to a woman's problems. These opposing communication styles often conflict and cause problems. The miscommunication is caused by different purposes for communicating. The woman wants sympathy, while the man thinks she wants him to solve her problems (Tannen, *Don't Understand* 49-53).

Other theorists agree with Tannen. Susan Basow and Kimberly Rubenfeld notice that "women may engage in 'troubles talk' to enhance communication; men may avoid such talk to enhance autonomy and dominance" (186). In addition, Phillip Yancey's article in *Marriage Partnership* also asserts that men and women "use conversation for quite different purposes" (71). He claims that women converse to develop and maintain connections, while men converse to claim their position in the hierarchy they see around them. Yancey asserts that women are less likely to speak publicly than are men because women often perceive such speaking as putting oneself on display. A man, on the other hand, is usually comfortable with speaking publicly because that is how he establishes his status among others (Yancey 71). Similarly, men are "less likely than androgynous individuals to feel grateful for advice" (Basow and Rubenfeld 186).

Many more differences in communication patterns of men and women can be found. Richard L. Weaver II, a public speaker, pointed out another author who identifies different communication styles for men and women. In his speech "Leadership for the Future: A New Set of Priorities," Weaver references Dr. Julia T. Wood's book *Gendered Lives*. According to Weaver, Wood claims that "male communication is characterized by assertion, independence, competitiveness, and confidence [while] female communication is characterized by deference, inclusivity, collaboration, and cooperation" (qtd. In Weaver 440). This list of differences describes why men and women have such opposing communication styles.

In another book, Deborah Tannen also discusses opposition in communication among men and women. Chapter six of Tannen's *The Argument Culture* is titled "Boys Will be Boys: Gender and Opposition." In this chapter, Tannen addresses the issue that boys, or men, "are more likely to take an oppositional stance toward other people and the world" and "are more likely to find opposition entertaining—to enjoy watching a good fight, or having one" (Tannen, *Argument* 166). Tannen goes into detail by giving examples from real life and research studies of how boys and girls play and fight differently. She claims that boys tend to cause fights, while girls try to avoid fights. A girl often tries to convince her opponent that her view would benefit the opponent. A boy, on the other hand, just argues for what is best for him (Tannen, *Argument* 170-174). Tannen addresses other gender opposition factors such as how men and women insult differently, men's negotiating status and women's forging bonds, the paradox of male and female fighting, conflict on the job, watching fights for fun, and talking in public (184-205).

Now that we have mentioned several differences in the communication styles of men and women, let us look at some possible causes for these differences. Two different theories involve biological factors and/or environmental factors. Lillian Glass, another linguistics researcher, wrote a book called *He Says, She Says: Closing the Communication Gap Between the Sexes*. The third chapter of her book examines "the evolution of sex differences in communication" (61). Glass addresses the issue that different hormones found in men and women's bodies make them act differently and therefore communicate differently. She also discusses how brain development has been found to relate to sex differences. Glass writes extensively, in this chapter and others, about how environmental factors, specifically the way we treat boy and girl infants, directly affect the ways we learn to communicate (64-73). One source states: "The way men and women are raised contributes to differences in conversation and communication . . . " (James and Cinelli 41).

Another author, Susan Witt, in "Parental Influence on Children's Socialization to Gender Roles," discusses the various findings that support the idea that parents have a great influence on their children during the development of their self-concept. She states, "Children learn at a very early age what it means to be a boy or a girl in our society" (253). Things that affect a child's idea of self-concept are the things they encounter early and throughout life such as: "parent-child interactions, role modeling, reinforcement for desired behaviors, parental approval or disapproval, friends, school, those around them, media, television" (Witt 253). Witt sums her theory up by saying, "Through all these socialization agents, children learn gender stereotyped behavior. As children develop, these stereotypes become firmly entrenched beliefs and thus, are a part of the child's self-concept" (253).

To further demonstrate the environmental factor that influences learned gender characteristics, Witt discusses how parents treat sons and daughters differently from the time they are babies. She says that parents "[dress] infants in gender-specific colors, [give] gender-differentiated toys, and [expect] different behavior from boys and girls" (Witt 254). At play and in chores, parents tend to "encourage their sons and daughters to participate in sex-typed activities" (Witt 254). Witt claims that women have even admitted a preference to having male children over female children in order to "please their husbands, to carry on the family name, and to be a companion to the husband" (254). On the other hand, Witt found that women want daughters to have a companion for themselves and to have fun dressing a girl and doing her hair" (254). These choices affect a child's learned patterns of communication. The environmental factors around a child help determine how a child will act and how he/she will communicate with others.

Phillip Yancey discusses the environmental factor. He explores the differences between men and women by discussing the fact that many times a communication difference between genders exists simply because of their different roots (69). Two people that come from two different families often have different ideas of how men and women should communicate. Different families have different conversation styles, different fighting styles, different communication styles overall. Yancey addresses the communication problems between genders as a cultural gap, defining culture as "shared meaning" (68). He says, "Some problems come about because one spouse enters marriage with a different set of 'shared meanings' than the other" (69).

Yancey goes into detail about the issue "that boys and girls grow up learning different styles of communicating" (70). So not only does the cultural gap between families sometimes pose a problem, the gender gap between the way boys and girls are raised can also impair efficient communication. Yancey points out:

> Boys tend to play in large groups that are hierarchically
>
> structured, with a leader who tells the others what to do and how to
>
> do it. Boys reinforce status by giving orders and enforcing them;

their games have winners and losers and are run by elaborate rules.
In contrast, girls play in small groups or in pairs, with 'best friends.'
They strive for intimacy, not status. These gender patterns continue
into adulthood. (70) The different ways that boys and girls play help
help to explain different ways that boys and girls, or men and
women, communicate.

Yancey also talks about the "Battle of the Sexes" as seen in conflict between men
and women. Reverting back to his 'childhood gender pattern' theory, Yancey claims,
"Men, who grew up in a hierarchical environment, are accustomed to conflict.
Women, concerned more with relationship and connection, prefer the role of
peacemaker" (71). Men often use and value criticism, but women avoid and dislike
outright criticism for fear of offending (Yancey 71-72).

Like Yancey, Deborah Tannen also addresses the fact that men and women often
come from different worlds, or from different influences anyway. Men are taught to be
masculine and women are taught to be feminine. She says, "Even if they grow up in
the same neighborhood, on the same block, or in the same house, girls and boys grow
up in different worlds of words" (Tannen, *Don't Understand* 43). Tannen distinguishes
between the way boys are talked to and the way girls are talked to, and she addresses
the differences between the way boys play and the way girls play (43-47).

Though Tannen often addresses the nurture, or environmental, issue in much of
her research, she also looked at the nature, or biological issue in her book *The
Argument Culture*. Tannen states, "Surely a biological component plays a part in the
greater use of antagonism among men, but cultural influence can override biological
inheritance" (Tannen, *Argument* 205). She sums up the nature versus nurture issue
by saying, "the patterns that typify women' s and men' s styles of opposition and
conflict are the result of both biology and culture" (207).

Karen McCluskey is another author whose research backs up Tannen's ideas about
the nature versus nurture issue. In her article published in *Public Management*, she
comments on other studies that have been done about gender differences. One author
that she mentions is Judy Mann, who commented that "Most experts now believe that

what happens to boys and girls is a complex interaction between slight biological differences and tremendously powerful social forces that begin to manifest themselves the minute the parents find out whether they are going to have a boy or a girl" (qtd. In McCluskey 6). Another author mentioned in her article, Dr. Patricia Heim, "agrees that societal pressures have a strong impact on male and female behaviors and perceptions" (qtd. in McCluskey 7). Heim even goes as far to say "men and women behave and communicate differently because they are raised in two separate gender cultures" (7).

We see there are some that say the causes of different styles of gender communication are biological, while others attribute causes to environmental factors. Still more people contend that men and women have different communication styles because of a combination of biological and environmental factors. Now that we have looked at different styles of gender communication and possible causes of gender communication, let us look at the possible results. Michelle Weiner-Davis is a marriage and family therapist who wrote the best seller *Divorce Busting*. She says, "Ignorance about the difference in gender communication has been a major contributor to divorce" (qtd. In Warren 106).

Let us look briefly at a hypothetical situation that will demonstrate different gender communication styles. We will examine the results of this situation to grasp an understanding of possible results in life. Consider the following scenario. A husband and wife have just arrived home after a long day of work in the business world. The wife asks her husband, "How was your day?" And the husband replies, "Fine." The wife is offended by this simplistic response and expresses her hurt by saying, "That's it? 'Fine'? Why don't you ever talk to me?" In confusion as to where this statement has come from, the husband defends himself declaring, "What are you talking about? I do talk to you. I'm talking to you right now!" They both blow each other off and refuse to talk to each other for the rest of the night. What went wrong in this conversation? The resulting failure of communication happened because men and women have different communication styles that directly affect intentional and perceived meaning from one to the other. Perhaps the communication failure above can be explained when backed by an understanding of the differences between the purposes and the ways that men and women communicate. Let us take this specific example and examine the results as compared to theories about gender communication.

In my opening scenario, the husband and wife are exhibiting different communication styles that directly relate to their own gender. Through various studies, Tannen has concluded that men and women have different *purposes* for engaging in communication. In *You Just Don't Understand*, Tannen states, "For girls, talk is the glue that holds relationships together" (85). Boys, on the other hand, use language when "they feel the need to impress, [or when they are] in situations where their status is in question" (85).

In the open forum that Deborah Tannen and Robert Bly gave in New York in 1993, Tannen (on videotape) explains the different ways men and women handle communication throughout the day. She explains that a man constantly talks during his workday in order to impress those around him and to establish his status in the office. When a man comes home from work, he is tired of talking. He expects to be able to be silent in his home where he does not have to impress anyone or establish his status.

On the other hand, a woman is constantly cautious and guarded about what she says during her workday. Women try hard to avoid confrontation and avoid offending anyone with their language. So when a woman comes home from work she expects to be able to talk freely without having to guard her words. Can we see the controversy that the man's expectation to be silent and the woman's expectation to talk can cause?

With Tannen's input, hopefully we can begin to see the differences in the communication styles of the wife and the husband? When the wife asked, "How was your day?" she expected a detailed response because her purpose of communication was to strengthen her relationship with her husband. She honestly wanted to know what specific things happened during her husband's workday so that she would be able to sympathize with what he was feeling and become closer to him. She wanted to talk freely because she had been busy guarding her words all day.

The husband's response of "fine" was direct and to the point because he felt no need to communicate further. At home with his wife, he wasn't in a situation in which he needed to impress anyone or establish status. He simply answered the question

Holz 8

that was asked of him and was willing to leave it at that. He wanted to be silent because he had been working hard at communication all day.

Though the intentions of both husband and wife seem innocent enough when looking at them with the thought of different communication styles in mind, the husband and wife obviously didn't see the other's response as innocent. Because the wife didn't receive the in-depth description she was expecting, she was disappointed. Tannen says that "when a woman who expects her partner to talk to her is disappointed that he doesn't, she perceives his behavior as a failure of intimacy: He's keeping things from her; he's lost interest in her; he's pulling away" (*Understand* 83). Can we imagine the wife's pain now?

The husband did not sense her pain. When his wife came back with "That's it? Fine? Why don't you ever talk to me?" this just triggered anger and defense. Because the wife and the husband had different purposes for and different ways of communicating, they misinterpreted each other. This misinterpretation led to anger, and the anger led to frustration and the abandonment of communication.

As we can see, the results of gender communication can look bleak. But, what can we do about this apparent gap in communication between genders? Some researchers have offered several solutions. In his article published in *Leadership*, Jeffrey Arthurs has the suggestion that women should make an attempt to understand the male model of communication and that men should make an attempt to understand the female model of communication. Having men that can better understand women and having women that can better understand men cannot be a bad thing. Even a general study of the different communication styles could benefit men and women by helping them understand possible misinterpretations before cross-gender communication is abandoned.

In his article "Speaking Across the Gender Gap," David Cohen mentions that experts didn't think it would be helpful to teach men to communicate more like women and women to communicate more like men. This attempt would prove unproductive because it would go against what men and women have been taught since birth. Rather than change the genders to be more like one another, we could simply try to understand each other better. By doing a little research and a little thoughtful consideration about the differences in gender communication styles, men and women would be able to communicate more successfully.

In his speech, Weaver makes this observation, "The idea that women should translate their experiences into the male code in order to express themselves effectively . . . is an outmoded, inconsistent, subservient notion that should no longer be given credibility in modern society" (439). He suggests three things we can change: 1.) Change the norm by which leadership success is judged, 2.) Redefine what we mean by power, and 3.) Become more sensitive to the places and times when inequity and inequality occur (Weaver 439). Warren tells us that Michelle Weiner-Davis gives wives some tips on how to better communicate with their husbands. She lists them as "1.) Establish a time for talking, 2.) Eliminate distractions when talking, and 3.) Compliment him when he listens" (qtd. in Warren 106). Phillip Yancey also offers his advice to help combat "cross-cultural" fights. He suggests: 1.) Identify your fighting style, 2.) Agree on rules of engagement, and 3.) Identify the real issue behind the conflict (Yancey 71). In her article, McCluskey claims that "men and women must understand one another, communicate honestly and respectfully, and manage conflict in a way that maintains the relationship and gets the job done" (5). She asserts, "To improve relationships and interactions between men and women, we must acknowledge the differences that do exist, understand how they develop, and discard dogma about what are the "right" roles of women and men" (5).

Now that we can see there are differences between the way men and women communicate, whether caused by biological and/or environmental factors, we can be on the watch for circumstances that might lead to miscommunications. We can consider the possible causes, results, and solutions discussed previously. Using this knowledge, we should be able to more accurately interpret communication between genders. The next cross-gendered misinterpretation we face, we should stop for a second and consider the differing gender patterns before we make things worse or abandon communication all together.

Works Cited

Arthurs, Jeffrey. "He Said, She heard: Any Time You Speak to Both Men and Women,
You're Facing Cross-Cultural Communication. *Leadership* 23.1 (Winter 2002):
49. Expanded Academic. Austin Peay State U, Woodward Lib. 22 Sept, 2003
<http://www.web5.infotrac.galegroup.com/search>.

Basow, Susan A., and Kimberly Rubenfeld. " 'Troubles Talk': Effects of Gender and
Gender Typing." *Sex Roles: A Journal of Research* (2003): 183–. *Expanded
Academic.* Austin Peay State U., Woodward Lib. 24 Apr. 2003
<http://www.web5.infotrac.galegroup.com/search>.

Cohen, David. "Speaking across the Gender Gap." *New Scientist* 131.1783 (1991): 36.
Expanded Academic. Austin Peay State U, Woodward Lib. 28 Sept 2003
<http://www.galegroup.com>.

Deborah Tannen and Robert Bly Men and Women: Talking Together. New York Open
Center. Videocassette. Mystic Fire Video, 1993.

Glass, Lillian. *He Says, She Says: Closing the Communication Gap between the Sexes.*
New York: G.P. Putnam's Sons, 1992.

James, Tammy, and Bethann Cinelli. "Exploring Gender-Based Communication
Styles." *Journal of School Health* 73 (2003): 41-41.

McCluskey, Karen Curnow. "Gender at Work." *Public Management* 79.5 (1997):
5-10.

Staff, Cecie, and Ralph Taggart. *Biology: The Unity and Diversity of Life.* 7th ed. New
York: Wadsworth, 1995.

Tannen, Deborah. *The Argument Culture: Moving from Debate to Dialogue.* New
York: Random House, 1998.

---. *You Just Don't Understand: Women and Men in Conversation.* New York:
Ballantine, 1990.

Warren, Andrea. "How to Get Him to Listen." *Ladies' Home Journal* 113 (Mar.
1996): 106.

Weaver, Richard L. "Leadership for the Future: A New Set of Priorities." *Vital Speeches of the Day* 61 (1995): 438-41.

Witt, Susan D. "Parental Influence on Children's Socialization to Gender Roles." *Adolescence* 32 (1997): 253.

Yancey, Phillip. "Do Men and Women Speak the Same Language?" *Marriage Partnership* 10 (1993): 68-73.

Writing a Paper Using CMS Note Style

T he *Chicago Manual of Style* (CMS) numbered note system for documentation has been a standard for many decades, and it governed scholarly writing in all fields at one time. It is a creature of book publishing and the printing industry. Years ago, only printers could create the fonts, sizes, and special characters that are common with today's computer software. So historically, scholars drafted their manuscripts by pen, and printers transformed the copy to a typset version as shown below, which is an article published almost 100 years ago, in 1909:

WEB LINK
to Chapter 11
Related Web
Destinations
http://www.
ablongman.com/
lester

The Dhudhuroa Language of Victoria

By R. H. Mathews

The Dhudhuroa was spoken by the Dyinningmiddhang tribe on the Mitta Mitta and Kiewa rivers, and along the Murray valley from Albury to Jingellic. Minyambuta, a dialect of the Dhudhuroa, was the speech of the tribes occupying the Buffalo, King, Ovens, and Broken rivers, with the tributaries of all these streams. From Jingellic eastward was the country of the Walgalu tribe, whose speech resembled partly the Dhudhuroa and partly the Dyirringan, a tongue spoken from about Nimmittabel to Bega. In 1902 I published a short grammar of the Dyirringan language.[1]

The *Wanggoa* ceremony of initiation, which was in force among the Dyinningmiddhang and Minyambuta tribes, was described by me in 1904.[2] The initiation ceremony of the Kyirringan is fully set forth in an article communicated to the Anthropological Society of Washington, U. S. A., in 1896.[3]

North of the Dyinningmiddhang, on the opposite side of the Murray, the country was occupied by the outskirts of the Wiradjuri nation. As a consequence of this,

---

[1] *Journal Royal Society New South Wales*, XXXVI, 160–167.
[2] Ibid., XXXVIII, 306–322.
[3] *American Anthropologist*, IX, 1896, 327–344, with plate.

we find that the Wiranjuri system of marriage and descent[4] overlapped some distance southerly from the Murray among the Dhudhuroa speaking people. For example, along a narrow strip of country on the southern bank of Murray from Albury to Jingellic, the descent of the children is through the mother. Among the Minyambuta the descent was paternal, the same as among the tribes to the west and south of them, particulars of which I have given elsewhere.[5]

[4] *American Anthropologist*, IX, 1896, 411–416; Ibid., X, 345–347.
[5] *Journal of Royal Society New South Wales*, XXXVIII, 2977–305.

Source: www.jstor.org, a reproduction of the *American Anthropologist*, New Series, Vol. 11, No. 2, Apr.–Jun., 1909.

As you can see in the example, printers were able to provide superscript numerals, small caps, italics, full justification on lines, and other features—all unavailable to the average writer at that time, yet so very common today.

In the middle of the 20th century, scholarly societies were having to pay printers a high price for all the special fonts and superscripts, and different type sizes, so they began to look toward in-text citation, e.g., "(Jones 345)," to save expense. Had they only known how computers would emerge, we would probably still have footnotes as the standard for scholarly citation.

Nevertheless, the footnote system has a rich history, and it remains a staple of documentation in many areas of the humanities. Today's software can provide you with all the mechanisms you need for writing in this style. As you probably know, when you ask the computer to insert a footnote or endnote, it automatically adds a superscript numeral and then sends you to the bottom of the screen to insert the text of the note.

This chapter prepares you for writing papers in certain courses in the humanities, such as history, music, art, communication, philosophy, religion, theology, and theater. However, a different note system is used in many physical and applied science courses, such as chemistry, computer science, engineering, physics, health, medicine, nursing, and biomedicine. Those disciplines usually follow the guidelines of the Council of Science Editors (CSE). For the details of CSE note style, see Appendix B. Once again, as you move about campus from course to course, you will encounter instructors who expect you to use one particular note system rather than others.

Considering an Academic Approach to the Subject Matter

Almost any subject is available to you, but as a humanist or a scientist you must approach it in a distinctive manner. For example, as we discussed in Chapter 10, *cloning* and *abortion* are scientific in their origins, but they are certainly available to the humanist as topics worthy of discussion. Here's an example of a scientific topic written from a humanist's point of view in the CMS note style:

Organ and tissue donation is the gift of life. Each year many people confront health problems due to diseases or congenital birth defects. Tom Taddonia explains that tissues such as skin, veins, and valves can be used to correct congenital defects, blindness, visual impairment, trauma, burns, dental defects, arthritis, cancer, vascular and heart disease.[8] Steve Barnill says, "More than 400 people each month receive the gift of sight through yet another type of tissue donation—corneal transplants. In many cases, donors unsuitable for organ donation are eligible for tissue donation."[9] Barnill notes that tissues are now used in orthopedic surgery, cardiovascular surgery, plastic surgery, dentistry, and podiatry.[10] Even so, not enough people are willing to donate organs and tissues.

This passage demonstrates the mindset of the humanist, who in general has a preoccupation with the quality of life, with art and ideas, and with other enduring issues, as shown above in the very first sentence and as echoed in the last sentence. Writing as a humanist in courses of philosophy, religion, or history, you will probably be drawn to topics such as these:

> Alzheimer's disease and its effects on human conditions in nursing homes.
>
> Harry S. Truman's decision to drop the atomic bomb on Japan.
>
> Adapting existentialism to one's religion.
>
> The morality of Beethoven's music.
>
> The underlying philosophy within Picasso's paintings of the blue period.

As you can see, the topics suggest an involvement in ethical standards—the condition of nursing homes, the moral implications of using a dreadfully destructive bomb, the complexities of religion, the underlying contexts of great music and paintings.

Thus, you will most likely be writing from a theoretical posture—that is, you will operate from a system of assumptions and accepted principles to analyze and explain the nature of the human condition. That may sound like a mouthful! But what it means is this: you are grounded in fundamental principles that govern your life. College professors are notorious for challenging those principles, which you hold precious. As a result, you will find yourself defending or arguing thesis statements like these:

> A government of the people cannot work, and it has *not* been the backbone of America's democracy.
>
> One cannot embrace existentialism and also be a Christian, Muslim, or Jew.
>
> The theater of the absurd is far from absurd and has more reality than standard theater.
>
> The gift of life begins at birth.
>
> The gift of life begins at conception.

With these thesis sentences, you cannot launch your work as a scientist would, objectively examining the data. Instead, you must consult your heart and the literature. It is the literature that will inform your research. Your opinions, as based on what your heart tells you, are important, but your instructors will expect more—a recitation of evidence from informed sources.

Thus, you walk a delicate balance in the humanities. Choose your subjects with care.

EXERCISE 11.1
CHOOSING AN ACADEMIC APPROACH

Listed below are several topics. For each one, write both a thesis sentence to reflect the humanist approach and a hypothesis to reflect the scientific approach. If you don't understand the word *hypothesis*, see pages 312–314.

For example, if the topic is *church steeples*, you might write:

Humanist approach: Church steeples symbolize since ancient times the ascension of the human soul toward heaven.

Scientific approach: The physical properties of the steeple or spire enable architects to design structures that reach upward while tapering to a point.

1. marijuana
2. hospitals
3. water
4. bread
5. weapons of mass destruction

Many rich topics exist for such an exercise. As a humanist, you can discuss Thomas Jefferson for his statesmanship but as a scientist you might look at his architectural designs at Monticello. With a topic like the Wall of China, the scientist might examine the mechanical engineering of the wall while the humanist would consider the wall's history or symbolism. Thus, this exercise should help you distinguish approaches to a subject based on the discipline from which you are working.

Selecting an Appropriate Design for Your Paper

Because research papers in the humanities can take a variety of forms, the models provided in this chapter are presented to help you find a working pattern. Your own outline will be subject specific, but knowing what to include in your introduction, body, and conclusion can help you organize and, perhaps, strengthen the content of the paper. For a general, all-purpose model, see Chapter 10, pages 337–338.

Writing an Analysis of History

If you are writing a historical paper that analyzes events and their causes and consequences, your paper should conform in general to the following plan.

Introduction

WEB LINK
to Reading
11.1
http://www.
ablongman.com/
lester

In the opening of your paper you should identify the event of history, describing
it briefly but saving in-depth discussion for the body of the paper. You may need to
provide the background leading up to the event in order to set the stage for what happened. For example, if your focus is on the fall of the Berlin Wall, you will need to
explain a few things about the collapse of the Soviet economy and the efforts of Premier Gorbachev to salvage the union. Mention of President Reagan's pressure on the
Soviet Union would also be in order.

In the opening you may also offer quotations and paraphrases from experts found
in the literature. These should be brief and relevant to your thesis sentence, which
should probably end the introduction. The thesis sentence, as you know by now, offers
a conclusion that you will defend with evidence from your research. It might read like
this: *The fall of the Berlin Wall gave Germany the grandeur of reunification but the
nightmare of economic crisis.*

Body

In the body of your paper you should describe and analyze fully the background
leading up to the event, if that is your primary focus. Otherwise, you should describe
the event itself and then analyze the consequences, both short term and long term.
Citing the literature will serve your purposes here.

For longer periods of history, you might offer a chronological sequence that
explains how one event relates directly to the next. For example, you might explore
the history of the American Civil War by moving from one key battle to another. In
another situation, you might trace events from one historic episode to another—for
example, commenting on America's wars, from the Revolution to the War of 1812,
Civil War, Spanish-American War, and so forth. Again, you will be citing authorities
who have also investigated these events in history.

Conclusion

In your closing you need to reaffirm your thesis and discuss the implications of
your finding. You might focus here on the causes, the consequences, or a little of both.
Finally, in almost every case, you will want to comment on the implications of these
events for the world today, showing how they set in motion conditions that exist today
or provide a model that we can use as a lesson. For an example, see the conclusion to
Halley Fishburn's essay on page 416.

Writing about Philosophy or Religion

For papers analyzing or arguing philosophical or religious ideas, use this next design, but adjust it as necessary.

Introduction

WEB LINK
to Reading
11.2
http://www.
ablongman.com/
lester

In the opening, establish the idea or question that is your subject and, as necessary, trace its history briefly. You should also discuss its significance to the world of ideas and introduce one or two experts who have addressed the idea. This material will indicate the significance of the topic to the academic community. Provide a thesis sentence that presents your approach to the issue, and from a fresh perspective if at all possible. For example, a fairly obvious position statement would be: *The conservative movement of the far right has won a strong political base in the southern states.* Instead, say something a bit provocative or off center: *Whether Republicans will admit it or not, their conservative positions have created a white wave of converts to the party.* Now you have a thesis needing detailed research and heavy support from the literature.

Body

In the body of your paper you will evaluate the issues surrounding the concept, giving perhaps an exhaustive history and analysis of the growth of the idea. Your evaluation will usually involve past-to-present examination of theories as shown in the literature. The body is also a place for you to analyze the major and minor issues. As you trace the various issues, you will need a variety of development—definition, example, comparison, cause, effect, and others.

Conclusion

Your closing will advance and defend your thesis as it grows out of evidence about the idea and your analysis. It might relate the idea to contemporary life, showing how the concept is still active in the modern age. Closing with a quotation from a noted person can be effective in this type of paper.

Reviewing a Performance

In the arts you will be asked on occasion to review a musical, artistic, or literary performance, such as an opera, a poetry reading, or a theatrical performance. Adjust this next design to your subject and purpose by letting it grow into a content-specific outline. Keep in mind that a review differs from an interpretation (see immediately below) by its focus on evaluation rather than analysis.

Introduction

Identify the work that you will review, usually giving details of time and place of the performance and the principal participants: *The poetry reading by Gary Snyder was*

held in the Clement Auditorium on April 24, 2003, with about 450 people in attendance.
That brief summary can be followed by background information, history of the work,
or a brief biographical description of the artist that relates to the specific performance
under review. A quotation from the principal or one from an authority is often appropriate in the introduction. End the opening with an initial assessment or judgment of
the performance: *Snyder did not disappoint his audience, providing telling anecdotes
from his association with other well-known poets and reading from some of his classic poems,
many of which have been read by the students in their literature anthologies.*

Body

Offer an evaluation based upon a predetermined set of criteria. That is, a drama
instructor will expect your assignment to evaluate such matters as staging and acting. A
music instructor will expect you to examine and discuss musical themes, quality of voice
and instruments, narration, and other items. Write the review by moving from one cri-
terion to another, judging in sequence the role of image, symbol, theme, and so forth.

Conclusion

In your closing keep a fundamental focus on the performance, the performers, and
the artist of the work. Offer a final judgment based on the criteria given in the body:
*With his humor mixed wickedly with his assessment of the human treatment of his beloved
environment, Snyder won many new converts last night and confirmed the adulation of
his long-time readers.*

Interpreting Creative Works

If you are asked to interpret a musical performance, work of art or art display, or
literary work, use the following design, adjusted to fit an opera, a set of sculptures, a
piece of architecture, a movie, or other work.

Introduction

Identify the work in question with specific details as to the nature of the work.
You need not be specific about the time and place because yours is an interpretation,
not a review to entice others to the performance. Provide whatever background information might be appropriate about the work, and give pertinent biographical information about the creative artist, who might be a sculptor, movie director, or
song stylist.

You may give a brief summary, but keep it short. Don't get caught giving a long
plot summary of an opera, not here in the opening nor even in the body. Make this
your only summary.

As with other openings, quote and paraphrase from authorities to establish the
scholarly traditions that you might explore in the work. Finally, close the introduction
with your thesis sentence that establishes your particular view of the creative work: *The*

persistent image of the fallen angel, as displayed in the facial features, halos, and broken wings of myriad statues and oil paintings, marks this show by Nadia Whitehall as an analysis of a begrudged fall from grace.

Body

In the body of the paper you will move step by step through your interpretive analysis. You might use several paragraphs to analyze each part of the work in question:

- each aspect of design
- the various uses of color
- the variations on a theme
- the various shades of symbolism
- the handling of characterization
- the musical motifs

Thus, the body is a systematic journey through the creative work to defend your thesis and explore the meaning of the work. Along the way, you may use quotations and paraphrases from the sources to embellish and strengthen your comments.

Conclusion

Now that you have examined in great detail the work in question, you need to shift your focus to the artist. Explore here the contributions of the artist both to the world of art and to the subject of your thesis. This might be a good time to close, if possible, with the words of the artist.

EXERCISE 11.2
SELECTING AN APPROPRIATE DESIGN

This chapter has introduced you to four basic designs for building a paper in the humanities. Other models that you could adopt for your paper are described in Chapter 10, pages 337–340, and Chapter 12, pages 420–424. Your assignment in this exercise is to choose a design that you think might be appropriate for each topic listed below. There are no right or wrong answers, but you should be prepared to explain your rationale for selecting a particular design. Choose from the four designs described in this chapter: analysis of an event in history, discussion of a philosophical or religious idea, review of a work, and interpretation of a work.

1. The opening of a new chapel on campus that has been designed by one of the school's professors of architecture.
2. The death penalty.

3. The Iraq War of 2003.

4. Elton John's songs of the year 2002.

5. Standardized testing in the elementary grades.

6. A current movie playing in local theaters.

7. The portrayal of Confederate soldiers in the movie *Gone with the Wind*.

8. The historical traditions of television soap operas.

9. The design of shopping malls.

10. Homophobia.

Handling Text Citations in CMS Note Style

WEB LINK
to Reading
11.3
http://www.
ablongman.com/
lester

Citing sources in the text of your paper requires that you use the verb tense appropriate for CMS style, and that you effectively blend the source information into your text.

Using the Correct Tense

Like the MLA style (see Chapter 10), the CMS note style in the humanities requires that you use the historical present tense for your citation to sources.

In one of his most moving speeches, Franklin D. Roosevelt **cries** out, "We have nothing to fear but fear itself."[1]

The work of Morton and Scroggins **shows** the results of the expanding frontier on the Native Americans of the Mississippi Valley.[2]

In Luke 2, verse 19, the writer **says**: "But Mary kept all these things and pondered them in her heart."

Of course, if the context of the passage, not a reference citation, refers to a historical moment, use the past tense:

Franklin D. Roosevelt **died** while in the White House, and Harry S. Truman **replaced** him during the middle of a world war.

According to Luke and other gospels, Jesus Christ **was born** in Bethlehem, the city of David.

EXERCISE 11.3

VERB TENSE

Correct any problems with verb tense in the following citations. Remember, CMS style prefers the historical present tense unless the context is clearly in the past.

1. Hershel Marshall, professor of anthropology at Chicago University, **has said** that existentialism grew out of ancient mythology.[5]

2. Beethoven **worked out** his compositions with great care, sometimes over a period of several years. This painstaking workmanship **appeared** clearly in the first movement of the fifth symphony, according to Paul Chihara.[8]

3. Warren Lathan **said** the terrorist attack on the World Trade Center in 2001 set in motion "a new world order of strike and counterstrike, aggression and anti-aggression."[9]

4. Blindness **was** an important social problem. It has **existed** all through human history, and thousands of people still **suffered** from many intermediate stages of blindness.[9]

Blending Sources Effectively in CMS Note Style

With the note system advocated by the *Chicago Manual of Style*, you will need to employ superscript numerals within the text (like this[15]) and include corresponding endnote or footnote entries. Ask your instructor which type of note to use in your assignments. Endnotes appear together at the end of the paper; footnotes appear at the bottom of individual pages.

If available, use the footnote or endnote feature of your software. It will not only insert the raised superscript number but also keep your notes arranged properly at the bottom of each page or together at the end of your paper. In most instances, the software will first insert the superscript numeral and then skip to the bottom of the screen so that you can write the text of the note. You must type in the essential data in the correct style.

Using Superscript Numerals

For the note numbers in the text, use arabic numerals typed slightly above the line (like this[12]). Place this superscript numeral at the end of quotations or paraphrases, with the number following immediately without a space after the final word or mark of punctuation, as in this sample:

"Unlike Wallis Warfield, Edward Albert Christian George Andrew Patrick David, the future King Edward VIII, had never known anything but the material security that goes with wealth and birth at the apex."[7] In this way J. Bryan and Charles Murphy introduce the gulf of social distance between the man who would be king but for his infatuation with a married woman. As Thomas Hardy writes in "The Famous Tragedy of the Queen of Cornwall":

> Judge them not harshly in a love
>
> Whose hold was strong;
>
> Sorrow therein they tasted of,
>
> And deeply, and too long.[8]

Thus, it was only a matter of time, with no higher authority to perform the act,[9] that Edward presented to Parliament his "royal assent" to his own Act of Abdication.[10] And a shudder shook the commonwealth.

Introducing the Sources

Introduce your sources with the full name of the author at first mention and with last name thereafter:

James C. Curtis describes Andrew Jackson as "more than a symbol; he was a vital force." Curtis adds, "As the force was rarely at rest, so the man was rarely at peace."[4]

Providing Extra Details with the Numeral

Thomas C. Thomas sides with President Clinton on the matter of Supreme Court appointments.[5, item 7] Thomas adds a cautionary note about the Senate's role in the appointments. . . .

Listing a Series of Footnotes

Several sources comment on this question,[7–9] but Jay Sugartree offers the definitive definition.[10]

Omitting The Author's Name

Since the author's name is readily available in the endnote or footnote, you can omit the name in the text. This technique is more common in disciplines of the applied sciences than in those of the humanities, as shown in this next example.

Three possible causes for autism have been identified: behavioral syndrome, organic brain disorder, or a range of biological and psychosocial factors.[11]

Nevertheless, mentioning the full name in your text is the most common way to introduce a source citation in history, philosophy, and other disciplines in the humanities.

Shaun Barbetti comments on the devastating effects of autism on the family unit. He finds that "the child suffering with autism shakes the family to its core in economic, spiritual, and familial terms."[12]

Placing Superscript Numerals

Place the superscript numeral after any punctuation mark except the dash, which it precedes.

Martin Luther King Jr. had planned a new campaign to help all poor people, white and black. (He never launched it.)[13]

This theme was obvious in the first novel[14]—and it would not reappear until her final one.

Superscript numerals should, in general, come at the end of a clause or the end of a quotation. Avoid placing the numeral between the subject and the verb (*not*, Smith[15] stipulates).

Smith stipulates that an entire family suffers depression when "autism spreads its effects."[16]

TIP   *Notes in Tables or Figures*

If a table or figure in your paper contains notes, those notes are considered part of the table or figure. Instead of numbers, use lowercase superscript letters (a, b, c) or an asterisk if there is only one note. Place the corresponding note entry at the bottom of the table or figure.

Citing Several Sources with One Note Reference

If you have several sources lumped into one paragraph speaking on the same general issue, you can use one superscript numeral and combine the sources into one note.

When we gather the work of the Miami suspense writers—James W. Hall's *Gone Wild*, Carl Hiaasen's *Tourist Season*, and Les Standiford's *Bone Key*—we have the legacy of the late John D. MacDonald and his Travis McGee series.[17]

Note 17 will then need to cite, in order, information on each source mentioned.

17. These contemporary recipients of MacDonald's tradition all work in the Miami area: James W. Hall, *Gone Wild* (New York: Delacorte Press, 1995); Carl Hiaasen, *Tourist Season* (New York: Warner Books, 1986); Les Standiford, *Bone Key* (New York: G. P. Putnam, 2002).

WEB LINK
to Exercise
11.1
http://www.
ablongman.com/
lester

Writing a Collective Footnote

If your paper involves numerous quotations from the same work, provide a note at the first instance to signal the source of all quotations. Therefore, use in-text page references, not footnotes.

> 18. All quotations in the text are to Hall's novel *Gone Wild* (New York: Delacorte Press, 1995).

Writing Full or Abbreviated Notes

Many instructors will permit you to omit a bibliography page as long as you give full data to the sources in each of your first footnotes.

> 1. James W. Hall, *Rough Draft* (New York: St. Martin's Press, 2000), 49.

However, if you have a comprehensive bibliography to each source, you may abbreviate all footnote entries since full data will be found in the bibliography.

> 1. Hall, *Rough Draft*, 49.

The bibliography will read this way:

> Hall, James W. *Rough Draft*. New York: St. Martin's Press, 2000.

T I P   ***Content Notes and Documentation Notes***

Some of your notes will be "content" notes rather than "documentation" notes (see page 402 for details).

Writing the Note Entries

WEB LINK
to Reading
11.4
http://www.
ablongman.com/
lester

Place footnotes at the bottom of pages to correspond with the superscript numerals on a page. For college papers, single space each footnote. Indent the first line of each note five spaces.

Endnotes appear all together in a separate Notes section at the end of a paper. For details about formatting a Notes section, see pages 402–403.

Books or Parts of Books

> 3. Carl Hiaasen, *Tourist Season* (New York: Warner Books, 1986), 128.
>
> 4. Zora Neale Hurston, "How It Feels to Be Colored Me," in *The Best American Essays of the Century*, ed. Joyce Carol Oates and Robert Atwan (Boston: Houghton Mifflin, 2000), 115.

T I P   *Italics vs. Underscore*

Use either italics or underscoring for titles of books, films, magazines, and other major works. Whichever format you choose, use it consistently throughout your paper.

Periodicals
Journal Article

5. John R. Sutton, "Imprisonment and Social Classification in Five Common-Law Democracies, 1955-1985," *American Journal of Sociology* 106 (2000): 351.

When the reference includes a volume number, use a colon after the date, and then give the page number or the page numbers without *p.* or *pp.* Compare that style to the next three entries below that uses a comma before the page numbers.

Magazine Article

6. T. Edward Nickens, "Sherlock of Spuds," *Smithsonian*, December 2002, 30.

Newspaper Article

7. Nell Irvin Painter, "Black Studies, Black Professors, and the Struggles of Perception," *Chronicle of Higher Education*, December 15, 2000, B7.

Review Article

8. Barry Seltzer, "Windows Code Unites," review of *Microsoft Whistler Beta 1* (computer software), *PC Magazine*, January 2001, 46.

Electronic Sources

Include a publication date but not the date accessed, and give an electronic address.

Book Online

9. D. H. Lawrence, *Lady Chatterly's Lover*, 1928, http://bibliomania.com/fiction/dhl/chat.html.

Journal Article Online

10. B. A. Miller, N. J. Smyth, and P. J. Mudar, "Mothers' Alcohol and Other Drug Problems and Their Punitiveness toward Their Children," *Journal of Studies on Alcohol* 60 (1999), http://www.ncbi.nlm.hih.gov.htbin.

Scholarly Project Online

11. *British Poetry Archive*, ed. Jerome McGann and David Seaman (Univ. of Virginia Library, 1999), http://etext.lib.virginia.edu/britpo.html.

WEB LINK
to Exercise
11.2
http://www.
ablongman.com/
lester

Government Document Online

12. United States, Congress, Senate, *Superfund Cleanup Acceleration Act of 1997* (105th Cong., Senate Bill 8, January 21, 1997), http.thomas.loc.gov/egi-bin/query/2?C105:S.8:.

Article from an Online Service

13. "Nutrition and Cancer," *Discovery Health,* May 1, 2000, http://www.discoveryhealth.com/search.html.

Database from an Academic Library

14. Carolyn J. Sachs and Michael A. Rodriguez, "Should Physicians Be Required to Report Domestic Violence to the Police?" *Western Journal of Medicine,* 173 (2002), http://web4.infotrac.galegroup.com.

Electronic Mailing List, Archived

15. Warren Watts, e-mail to Victorian Association for Library Automation mailing list, September 23, 2003, http://www.vala.org.au/conf2004.htm.

E-Mail

Because personal e-mail is not retrievable, do not document with a note or bibliography entry. Instead, mention the nature of the source within your text by saying something like this:

Walter Wallace argues that teen violence stems mainly from the breakup of the traditional family (E-mail to the author).

Note: Footnote numbers may appear as raised numerals if you use a computer program, as shown in the Fishburn paper, pages 411–417.

Notes for Other Sources
Biblical Reference

16. Matt. 10:5.

17. 1 Pet. 5:1-3.

Nonprint Source: Lecture, Sermon, Speech, Oral Report

18. Dick Weber, "The Facts about Preparing Teens to Drive" (lecture, Morrow High School, Morrow, Ga., 2001).

Encyclopedia

19. *The World Book Encyclopedia*, 2000 ed., s.v. "Raphael."

Note: "s.v." means sub verbo, *"under the word"*

Government Document

20. U.S. Dept. of the Treasury, "Financial Operations of Government Agencies and Funds," *Treasury Bulletin* (Washington, DC: GPO, June 1974), 134-41.

21. U.S. *Constitution*, art. 1, sec. 4.

22. United Kingdom, *Coroner's Act, 1954*, 2 & 3 Eliz. 2, ch. 31.

23. State v. Lane, Minnesota 263 N.W. 608 (1935).

Interview

24. George Stephanopoulos, interview by George Will, April 4, 2003, *This Week*, ABC News.

Television Program

25. Dan Rather, *CBS News*, CBS-TV, April 4, 2003.

Film, DVD

26. *Merlin*, DVD, directed by Steven Barron (1998; Los Angeles, CA: Hallmark Home Entertainment, 2001.)

Musical Work

27. Wolfgang A. Mozart, *Jupiter*, Symphony No. 41.

Subsequent References to a Source

After a first full reference, subsequent notes should be shortened to the author's last name and a page number. When an author has two works mentioned, also employ a shortened version of the title, such as "Jones, *Paine*, 25." See the sample "Notes" on the next page for examples. In general, avoid Latinate abbreviations such as *loc. cit.* or *op. cit.*; however, whenever a note refers to the source in the immediately preceding note, you may use "Ibid." to refer to the same page number of the preceding entry or use "Ibid." with a new page number as shown below:

28. Julie Shively, *American Civil War Places* (Nashville: Ideals Publications, 1999), 174.

29. Ibid., 175.

Formatting the Notes Section

WEB LINK
to Audio-
video 11.1
http://www.
ablongman.com/
lester
When you put all your notes together as a single group of endnotes, you lessen the burden of typing the paper. Most computer software programs offer features that help you with this task.

Begin the Notes section on a new page at the end of the text. Center the title "Notes" two inches from the top of the page. For the rest of the Notes section, use one-inch margins.

Indent the first line of each note five spaces. Use double-spacing throughout the Notes section.

Notes

1. Elizabeth Larsen, "Bossy's Lament," *UTNE Reader*, July/August 2000, 18.

2. Ibid., 19.

3. Robert Cohen and Jane Heimlich, *Milk: The Deadly Poison* (Chicago: Argus, 1998), 121.

4. P. F. Fox and Paul L. H. McSweeney, *Dairy Chemistry and Biochemistry* (Philadelphia: Chapman and Hall, 1998), 48.

5. Cohen and Heimlich, 130.

6. "Milk Allergy and Lactose Intolerance," *Medinix,* May 6, 2000, http://www. adelade.net.au/~ndk/> no_milk.htm.

7. Larsen, 19.

8. Ibid.

9. Fox and McSweeney, 51-52.

Content Notes

Another type of footnote or endnote, as opposed to the documentation note, is the content note, which offers additional commentary to something in the text. Use a content note to explain research problems, to resolve or report conflicts in the testimony of the critics, to provide interesting tidbits, and to credit people and sources not mentioned in the text. Content notes should be intermingled with your documentation notes.

3. The initial study in 2002 examined only Shakespeare's tragedies, but the 2003 study included the comedies and the histories.

See the notes to the Jager essay, pages 405–410 for examples.

EXERCISE 11.4
WRITING NOTES IN CMS STYLE

Write a set of notes, in the correct CMS form, for the following sources.

1. "Qualified Low-Income Students Locked Out of Higher Education, Says Report." *Black Issues in Higher Education*. March 15, 2001. Volume 18. Page 28. No author mentioned.

2. Kristin W. Davis. "You May Not Be Out of Luck." *Kiplinger's Personal Finance Magazine*. May 2001. Vol. 55. Page 94.

3. No Author. "Is Financial Aid Meeting Its Goals?" *USA Today (Magazine)*. August 1999, Vol. 128. Page 6.

4. Nicholas Lemann. "Open the Doors to College." *Washington Monthly*. January-February 1996, vol. 28, page 38.

5. Lisa C. Jones. "The $42 Billion College Cash Bonanza." *Ebony*. May 1995, vol. 50, pages 60–66.

6. Ben Kaplen. *How to Go to College almost Free*. HarperCollins publ of New York, 2001, page 23.

Writing a References List or Bibliography

WEB LINK
to Chapter 11
Related Web
Destinations
http://www.
ablongman.com/
lester

In addition to footnotes or endnotes, you may need to supply a separate Bibliography or References section that lists your sources in developing the paper. Center the title "References" or "Bibliography" at the top of the page. Use the hanging indention; that is, type the first line of each entry flush left; indent subsequent lines five spaces. Alphabetize the list by last names of authors, and double space throughout. List alphabetically by title two or more works by the same author. See page 417 for an example.

T I P   *References List*

A References or Bibliography section is somewhat redundant since your endnotes or footnotes will contain all pertinent information for finding the source. Of course, a References page does give all sources, arranged alphabetically, in one list. Check with your instructor to be sure a references page is required for your paper before spending time on preparing it. If so, you can use a shortened form for all of your footnotes. See page 398].

Writing Reference List Entries
Book

WEB LINK
to Exercise
11.3
http://www.
ablongman.com/
lester

Hiaasen, Carl. *Tourist Season*. New York: Warner Books, 1986.

Journal Article

Parker, Arthur C. "Secret Medicine Society of the Senaca." *American Anthropologist* 11 (1999): 161-85.

Newspaper Article

Davey, Monica, and David Leonhardt. "Jobless and Hopeless, Many Quit the
Labor Force." *New York Times*, April 26, 2003, B5.

Some of the notes from the sections above would appear like this in a References
section:

References

Cohen, Robert, and Jane Heimlich. *Milk: The Deadly Poison*. Chicago: Argus,
1998.

Fox, P. F., and Paul L. H. McSweeney. *Dairy Chemistry and Biochemistry*.
Philadelphia: Chapman and Hall, 1998.

Larsen, Elizabeth. "Bossy's Lament." *UTNE Reader*, July/August, 2000, 18-20.

"Milk Allergy and Lactose Intolerance." *Medinix,* May 6, 2000, http://www.
adelade.net.au/~ndk/>no_milk.htm.

Shively, Julie. *American Civil War Places*. Nashville: Ideals Publications,
1999.

U.S. Dept. of the Treasury. "Financial Operations of Government Agencies and
Funds." *Treasury Bulletin*. Washington, DC: GPO, June 1974.

G U I D E L I N E S

Writing in the CMS Style

1. Write using the historical present tense in your citations but use the past tense for historic events.

2. As a humanist, approach your subject in a distinctive manner and with a preoccupation with the quality of life, with art and ideas, and with other enduring issues.

3. Design your paper to fit the traditions of the disciplines, such as the analysis of history or the interpretation of creative works.

4. Blend sources into your paper using the note system standardized by *The Chicago Manual of Style*.

5. Add a References section or Bibliography that will list your sources alphabetically if required by your instructor.

Chapter Review

WEB LINK
to Chapter 11
Related Web
Destinations
http://www.
ablongman.com/
lester

This chapter has discussed the nature of writing in the humanities to distinguish it from writing in the sciences. In particular, the chapter discusses the subject matter of papers in the humanities, where the quality of life, art, and ideas carry great import. Thus, the disciplines of history, art, music, philosophy, religion, communication, and others will demand papers that conform to the note style standardized by *The Chicago Manual of Style* (CMS).

The chapter demonstrates the basic style for writing endnotes or footnotes and a References list or Bibliography. Beyond that it explains how to design your papers for advancing philosophical ideas, writing about history, reviewing a performance, and writing an interpretation.

Chapter 11 Assignment: Evaluating Writing in the Humanities

Having completed this chapter, you should understand the basic rationale of writing in the humanities. Therefore, read the following excerpts from a scholarly paper and then write a paragraph that completes this thought: "This essay represents humanistic writing because it . . ."

Tool and Symbol: The Success of the Double-Bitted Axe in North America

Ronald Jager

Hurrah for the axe, the brave, sharp axe,
Hurrah for its notes that sing,
Through the valley wide, up the mountain side,
When it sweeps like a falcon's wing.
And down crashes the pine, with its lordly crest,
For the axe hath cleaved through its knotted breast.
Let others sing of the sword and flash
Of a forest of dancing spears;
But their path is red with the blood of the dead,
Whilst behind them a sea of tears.
And the maiden shall wait for her lover in vain,
For he sleeps where the moon glances cold on the stain.
Not such thy triumph, my brave, sharp axe,
On your blade are no stains of sin,
With a sweep and a blow, you strike your foe,

And up from his grave doth spring
The yellow grain, the broad-leaved corn,
And my children bless you at early morn.
—Dillon O'Brien, "Song of the Western Pioneers"[1]

The encounter between humankind and forest is an underlying theme of history, and until very recently the axe typically mediated that encounter. Few hand tools have been so fundamental to human endeavor. A simple woodworking tool, created within a technological world not dependent upon science, the axe evolved into an exotic weapon and a potent symbol, even for those pioneers who wished only to slay trees and raise corn. But today the axe is fast fading to memory and museum piece: the chain saw has nearly swept it from the scene, and the forests of the industrialized world are now populated with skilled loggers who rarely swing an axe.

Some historians of technology and students of material culture have begun to focus sharply on things as objects of historical interpretation.[2] However, they have rarely dwelled on ordinary hand tools to the extent that might be hoped; certainly few have fastened their attention on the axe, despite (because of?) the fact that this lowly tool participates in a large compass of symbolic meanings and myths: precision work, violence, conquest, pioneering, triumphant glamour, craftsmanship, harvest, heroic strength, and more. Some may yet suppose there is just too little for serious historical picking among the saws, shovels, picks, rakes, axes, pruning hooks, hammers, and the rest of the grab-bag rural arsenal of hand tools, that we need to wait only upon implements more resonant with historical drama, such as the sword, the plow, or the musket. If so, it will be unsurprising that crucial events in axe history have remained unnoticed or garnered little attention, even among historians of logging and the lumber trades.[3] Perhaps the trick is to ask the right question. In the heyday of the axe, a hundred years ago, the rapid switch by American loggers from the single-bitted to the double-bitted felling axe came as a small revolution in timber-harvesting technology. Within a single generation after the Civil War, tens of thousands of loggers reversed hundreds of years of practice in the New World and more than a thousand years of practice in Europe before that. The double-bitted axe entered the forest by stealth, without even the passport of a patent. The swift success of this tool, limited though it was to the United States and Canada, was a transition largely unheralded at the time, and it has not been analyzed or even described since. Doing so requires that we position ourselves to look carefully over the shoulder, as it were, of the frontier farmer, the pioneer, the blacksmith, the professional logger, the factory craftsman—those who knew their axe with a daily intimacy, and knew very well its potential and its limits. It is difficult now to appreciate fully how patently ridiculous—not to mention dangerous—a double-bitted axe must have looked to experienced axemen when they faced it for the very first time near the middle of the last century. It came from nowhere and arrived without pedigree. It was weird and exotic. To some it must have seemed stupid, like a hammer with two heads; or monstrous, like a horse with two tails; or quite unsafe, like a knife sharp on two edges. No way! would have been a natural response. For a thousand years we have known what an axe looks like; and it doesn't look like that! Yet it prevailed in less than a generation, and "by the end of the century, most choppers used the double-bitted axe."[4] The history of the double-bitted axe in America lies at an intersection of disciplines: of lumbering and logging, of technology history, of toolmaking and design, of economic history; and it lies within a framework of larger national values and cultural pressures that mold the technologies of a people. At that crossroads, simple questions still await excavation: Why did this axe triumph at just this time and place? Why not in another country or another century? Deborah Fitzgerald has recently written: "The question of why people adopt technological innovations, and why they do not, has had a sturdy but unresolved life among historians of technology. It has never been easy to explain the ultimate success or failure of technologies."[5]

[Note: A large portion of the essay has been omitted.]

The mythos of the double-bitted axe in North America persists today, irrespective of its withdrawal from the woods, and sometimes it recapitulates the entire romance of the axe in America. Many states and provinces have anonymous statues honoring loggers, and if these include an axe it will inevitably be a double-bitted axe. Recreated logging camps are named for Paul Bunyan, mythical American logger, he of the great blue ox and the prodigious double-bitted axe, who consolidated the logger as one kind of raw American hero. Once an emblem of the American pioneer, the double-bitted axe is now even a symbol of masculinity for the advertising industry: a two-page advertisement shows a pile of logs and a husky lumberjack with the advertised cigarette ("when your taste grows up") and a double-bitted axe at hand—we are to make the desired associations. Not long ago President Clinton was sketched in the *Washington Post* negotiating with loggers in the Pacific Northwest, the President flannel-shirted and leaning upon—what else?—a double-bitted axe. St. Olaf's College in Minnesota has a double-bitted axe in its logo, even though the axe that felled its patron, St. Olaf of Norway, in the eleventh century was a single-bitted axe. (All Viking axes were single-bitted, although they are now often erroneously upgraded to double-bitted axes.) Years ago the University of Northern Arizona adopted the double-bitted axe as the university symbol—its athletic teams are (Lumber)Jacks and Jills—and has an all-copper double-bitted axe on permanent display. The former lumber town of Nackawic, New Brunswick, erected a spectacular municipal monument: an axe, claimed to be the world's largest double-bitted axe, twenty feet from edge to edge. It goes on. The double-bitted axe, with its aura of power and myth, was born to fame and endures as a North American symbolic storehouse of heroic memories.

Many, many centuries ago something very similar transpired in prehistoric Crete and in classical Greece, where the double axe was both a favored tool and a powerful and mystifying cultural symbol. Perhaps it was to be expected that it would achieve a like destiny when it appeared again in the North American forest. Who can say? Such potential for drama and exhibitionism, even for mysterious layers of meaning, may be lodged in the very nature of the double-bitted form. Or in ourselves. Or both.

There is much that we do not know and never will: some things are inscrutable. But we know that after the Civil War North American loggers, first by the thousands and then by the hundreds of thousands, would gladly purchase a new axe that was perfectly balanced, smoothly aerodynamic, and versatile. With it they would make logging history. And we know that their outlook as frontier Americans was sharply framed by certain historical circumstances: it was, in the first place, a moment of triumphant novelty and experimentation in toolmaking and tool using, and in some fields, axe making included, America became the world's leader; these were times, secondly, of massive timber industries and rapidly expanding crews of experienced and experimenting loggers, men strong and proud, dedicated to their tools and on the lookout for better ones. And we know, finally, that they lived in a culture aware and fond of its love affair with the felling axe as a noble national weapon in what was callously seen as a saga of wilderness conquest—a catalytic element, this, whose potency was imaginative and symbolic. We may be confident that cultural conditions as complex as these interact and reinforce each other in many ways, and that they deeply engage and shape human psychology: its curiosity, ambition, imagination, and all the unfathomable ingredients of inventiveness. So we speculate about what new technologies may have sprung from such fertile matrices. Coming long after, we ransack the records and the archives for the tracks of the creator(s) and first users and improvers of the double-bitted axe, eager for the testimony or even the identity of those who bore the presumed scoffs of traditionalists and still persisted and then prevailed. But they are mostly nameless and silent, faded into the woodwork, leaving us with only historical probabilities and likelihoods. It is unlikely that the double-bitted axe appeared in nineteenth-century North America in a flash of one man's sudden inspiration. Of course, it might have. It could have come about like the Colt revolver or the telegraph, or even like barbed wire or the lowly peavey; the inventor might even have been suddenly inspired by a Roman double axe excavated in Germany or England, or by the double axes he saw on a Greek vase found in an Italian tomb and displayed in an American museum.[56] But no trail of known evidence points to anything so exciting as that. If there was a Eureka! moment—in a dream, in a shop, in a forest—we have lost track of it, probably forever. In its American origins the thing is finally almost as inscrutable as it was successful.

The lack of a known inventor, the absence of verifiable origins in time and place, the lack of a patent, the absence of revolutionary fanfare—these may yet gesture in a certain direction. Do they suggest that the double-bitted axe was known as an experimental design for some time, maybe decades, while its radical novelty wore off in a land in love with new things? From the earliest days everything was, literally, in the hands of the loggers themselves, not a notably articulate tribe, whose conversations rarely reached the ears of editors. They merely loved their double-bitted axe and lived by it, and they have left no readily accessible lode of raw material or hearsay that, for example, lumber historians might have drawn upon, built upon, or at least repeated; so historians have until now told us almost nothing on the subject. No discoverable record indicates that there ever was a standard opinion as to how this novel thing first came about and where and why and when—as, for example, there has always been a common understanding that the less spectacular logger's peavey was invented in Stillwater, Maine, by Joseph Peavey in 1858.

Although it embodied timeless technological virtues—perfect balance, effective aerodynamics, exquisite versatility—such as could justify its manufacture and use in almost any time and place, it was always unlikely that the double-bitted axe would reenter the modern forest on its technological credentials alone; it would wait in the wings for that moment when further cultural conditions were simultaneously present on stage. The required conditions were never present in Europe and did not converge in North America until about the time of the Civil War. When the moment was ripe, the Collins Company and others would gamble on making the double-bitted axe in quantity and supplying it to wholesalers. In such an atmosphere, and within an intensely competitive industry, other axe makers and other tree choppers would see the light quickly and follow where it led. It led to a new chapter in America's romance with the axe.[57]

Notes

1. *Stillwater Messenger*, 5 June 1867.

2. Most conspicuously, Steven Lubar and W. David Kingery, eds., *History From Things: Essays on Material Culture* (Washington, D.C., and London, 1993). Of special relevance are the contributions by Prown, by Gordon, and by Lubar. See also W. David Kingery, ed., *Learning From Things: Method and Theory of Material Culture Studies* (Washington, D.C., and London, 1996), especially the essays in part 2.

3. American axes are treated expertly but briefly in Paul B. Kebabian, *American Woodworking Tools* (Boston, 1978). Two well-illustrated handbooks are Henry J. Kauffman, *American Axes* (Brattleboro, Vt., 1972), and Allan Klenman, *Axe Makers of North America* (Victoria, B.C., 1990). Kauffman is especially rich on manufacturing and Klenman on manufacturers; both focus on the appearance, variety, and styles of axes and their makers more than on history and context. Carl Russell, *Firearms, Traps and Tools of the Mountain Men* (Albuquerque, N.M., 1967), includes a good chapter on early American trade axes. Short articles on axes occasionally appear in the *Chronicle*, the magazine of the Early American Industries Association.

4. David C. Smith, *History of Lumbering in Maine: 1861–1960* (Orono, Me., 1972), 17.

5. Deborah Fitzgerald, review of *Regulation and the Revolution in United States Farm Productivity*, by Sally H. Clarke, *Technology and Culture* 37 (1996): 851–53.

[A large portion of the notes have been omitted.]

56. A Roman double axe, found in 1848, is in the Mainz Museum, Germany; the British Museum holds other examples. Many double axes are painted on Greek vases: the collections of the Boston Museum of Fine Arts contain several good examples, one showing a blacksmith shop with the axes on the wall. Minoan bronze working double axes cannot be implicated: archaeological discovery of them (now

nearly 200 specimens) did not begin until after the double axe had been reinvented in North America.

57. There is a robust confusion of terminology and spelling in the axe world. The reader will have noticed that among the quotations in this essay there is no consistency on the spelling of "ax" and "axe." Shakespeare and most of his contemporaries wrote "axe," and that spelling got imported to America and more or less standardized. But near the end of the nineteenth century the *Oxford English Dictionary* (OED) mounted an "ax" bandwagon (the shorter spelling had pretty well died out in the fifteenth century) and the cause was taken up by others, which has confused things for a century or so. By the early twentieth century "ax" was widespread in England—except for the companies that made and sold axes, which universally shunned that spelling!—while "axe" remained wide-spread in America. Editors and stylebook guides continue to make their own decisions, for reasons never apparent. No known stylebook appeals to what might be the most relevant authority: the spelling used throughout the last century and a half by the hundreds of axe manufacturers in both England and America. There, "axe" is the overwhelming choice; it remains to be seen if this will impress the current OED editors. It is also the spelling uniformly chosen by tool manufacturers in Sweden and Germany when they use English.

Long ago, Angles and Saxons were wont to beat up their trees and sometimes each other with a tool they variously spelled "aex," "echxe," "exe," "ex," "eax," and several other ways (see the OED). The spelling "ax" was sometimes used by Middle English writers, Chaucer among them, but at that time the word "axe" was usually conscripted for the meaning ask (a sense derived from Old English), which seems to be the reason for the late medieval and early modern use of "ax" for the tool. Still earlier, Saxons and Franks both took (or were given) their tribal name from what was in their language their favorite tool and weapon, namely, the axe, that is, the saxon or frank or francisca. The Celts started all this: they called an axe a "celt." For what it is worth, Celts, Saxons, and Franks were all people of the axe. Incidentally, even toolmakers (never mind dictionaries and style books) took more than a century to reach an imperfect consensus on the spelling of "bit," and on whether "double-bitted" deserves a hyphen. By the time they largely agreed (on the uses employed here), most of them were about ready to give up on the axe business.

Tracing the Work of Two Students

Research Paper in CMS Note Style

The conflict over the War Powers Act goes far back into America's history, and Halley Fishburn explores in this paper the conflict between Congress and the White House on matters of authority in times of war. Fishburn traces the act from James Madison's writings in 1781 to the Iraqi War of 2003.

Note: Fishburn used the computer settings, which uses a raised numeral with both in-text citations and the footnotes.

Halley Fishburn

History 1020

Professor Gildrie

April 22, 1003

Military Provisions of the U.S. Constitution

The War Powers Act is not a relic of history; it is a vibrant and throbbing document that rattles down the halls of the Capitol building and the White House on a regular basis. James Madison in 1781 was well intentioned in the desire to have the army answerable to the government, but he established a never-ending conflict between the commander in chief, who orders the forces into battle, and Congress, who must approve the action.

This discord surfaced again in 2003 when Senator Russell Feingold questioned President George W. Bush's power to declare war on Iraq.[1] The debate centers on the so-called "use of force" joint resolution that both Houses of Congress passed after the September 11 terrorist attacks at the World Trade Center and the Pentagon. Feingold and others say the resolution empowering the president to act was limited to action against "nations, organizations or persons [the president] determines planned, authorized, committed or aided the terrorists . . . or harbored such organizations or persons, in order to prevent any future acts of international terrorism."[2]

Aristotle is often quoted for having said that decisions of a leader "backed by a standing army" would be different from those made by a leader "awed by the fear of an armed people." The founding fathers of the United States Constitution realized this and thus created a document which allowed the governmental bodies power over the military. James Madison suggested early in 1781 that the Articles of the Confederation be changed to give Congress full authority to call forth the forces of

---

[1]Russell Feingold, quoted in Jules Witcover, "What about the War Powers Act? *Baltimore Sun* May 1, 2002, http://www.commondreams.org.\views02/o501-07.htm.
[2]Ibid.

the United States in order to enforce its decisions;[3] however, it was not until the outbreak of Shays's Rebellion in April of 1787 that the major necessity lacking in the Articles of the Confederation—federal governmental power to suppress insurrections and domestic violence—became obvious.[4] Furthermore, the rebellion proved that Congress would not declare a state of insurrection existed, Congress could not raise, support, or even govern armies, and the secretary of war working as commander of the armed forces could not execute the laws of the land.[5] These realizations lead to the formation of the War Powers of the Constitution.

In Article I, Section 8, of the Constitution, Congress is given power to provide for the common defense and general welfare, declare war, raise and support armies (but not appropriate money to support any army for longer than two years), to provide and maintain a navy, to make rules for the regulation of land and naval forces, and to arm, discipline, govern, and call forth the militia. Since Congress has almost complete control over the peace-time military, it "was damned by officers and soldiers as the chief root of evil and has been so damned ever since.[6] However, if these clauses which define the War Power of Congress had been omitted from the Constitution, they might have been claimed, by analogy to the British constitution, for the president, creating a dictatorship.[7] Congress was purposely granted War Powers as a direct check upon the executive branch whose head is designated commander in chief of the armed forces.[8]

---

[3]Quoted in Harry Ward, The Department of War 1781-1795 (Pittsburgh: University of Pittsburgh Press, 1962), 93.

[4]Richard Brandon Morris, *The Forging of the Union: 1781-1789* (New York: Harper and Row, 1987), 265.

[5]Ward, 80-81.

[6]Merrill Jensen, *The New Nation: A History of the United States during the Confederation* (New York: Vintage Books, 1950), 29.

[7]Edwin S. Corwin, *The Constitution and What It Means Today* (Princeton: Princeton University Press, 1958), 71.

[8]Francis D. Wormuth and Edwin B. Firmage, *To Chain the Dog's of War: The War Powers of Congress in History and Law* (Dallas: Southern Methodist University Press, 1986), 179.

The president of the United States is also given War Power in Article 2, Section 2, of the Constitution as commander in chief of the Army and Navy of the United States and of the militia of the states when called into actual service of the nation. Alexander Hamilton summed up his idea of the office of president: "[The presidency] would amount to nothing more than the supreme command and direction of the military and naval forces as first General and Admiral to the Confederacy."[9] Modern conception of "the power of the Commander-in-Chief in wartime" stems from Lincoln's example.[10] Today, War Powers have tilted in favor of the president.[11] The president employs forces of the United States and declares martial law (Article 4, Section 4, of the Constitution), decides whether or not an insurrection exists or invasion threatens,[12] and possesses almost unlimited power to direct a war once Congress declares it.[13] Modern presidents, such as Nixon, have even displayed the ability to abuse war powers by not seeking Congressional authorization.[14] Senator William Fulbright elaborated on this when, during an interview, he said:

> The current restraints imposed by Congress are utterly insufficient
> to the task. All they really do is to provide the Administration with an
> excuse for doing anything and everything that is not explicitly
> forbidden—and, as we have seen, all it takes to transfer some
> contemplated military action from the prohibited category to the
> permissible is a certain agility of semantics and an extraordinary
> contempt for the Constitutional authority of Congress.[15]

---

[9]Alexander Hamilton, John Jay, and James Madison, *The Federalist* (New York: Modern Library, 1941), No. 69, 446.

[10]Corwin, 100.

[11]Timothy Boylan, "War Powers, Constitutional Balance, and the Imperial Presidency Idea at Century's End" *Presidential Studies Quarterly* 29 (June 1999), 232.

[12]Corwin, 15.

[13]Wormuth, 179.

[14]Bernard Brodie, *War and Politics* (New York: Macmillan, 1973), 215-22.

[15]William Fulbright, quoted in Elizabeth Drew, "Washington," *Atlantic Monthly*, April 1971, 14.

The separation of powers has been a hotly debated subject since the Lincoln administration. The fact that most of the War Powers are bestowed upon Congress does not override the fact that Congress is explicitly given authority to "declare" war not "conduct" war. That is reserved for the commander in chief, the president.[16]

The Constitution also assures that individual states have no War Powers. Article 1, Section 10, asserts that states shall not keep troops or ships of war or engage in war without the consent of Congress. Furthermore, Article 4, Section 4, assures that the United States as a nation will defend individual states, giving them no need to employ means of defending themselves. Madison writes, "Protection against invasion is due from every society to the parts composing it. The latitude of the expression here used seems to secure each state, not only against foreign hostility, but against ambitious or vindictive enterprises of its more powerful neighbors."[17] Hamilton also writes to reassure those supporters of states' rights, "The operations of the federal government will be most extensive and important in times of war and danger; those of the state governments in t imes of peace and security. As the former periods will probably bear a small proportion to the latter, the state governments will here enjoy another advantage over the federal government. The more adequate, indeed, the federal powers may be rendered to the national defense, the less frequent will be those scenes of danger which might favor their ascendancy over the governments of the particular states."[18]

Proposals to reform the Constitution began immediately.[19] However, the Bill of Rights as adopted, contrary to Madison's intent, imposed restrictions only upon the

---

[16]Boylan, 238.

[17]Hamilton, No. 43, 312.

[18]Hamilton, No. 46, 328-9.

[19]Marshall Smelser, *The Democratic Republic: 1801-1815* (New York: Harper and Row, 1968), p. 15.

federal government.[20] The primary significance of the Bill of Rights is seen most clearly in what it does not include[21]—it does not apply to states.[22] Thus, the militia called for in the Second Amendment was totally at the mercy of the states and of little real use to the federal government until the National Defense Act of June 3, 1916, defined "the militia of the United States" as consisting of "all able-bodied male citizens of the United States" between the ages of 18 and 45.[23] This limited a state's power to grant service by indemnity and allowed Congress the ability to call forth a greater number of men for military service.

The War Powers of Congress and the president along with the lack of War Powers granted to the states has given the United States a government "backed by a standing army" with the ability to call forth more recruits yet balanced by the separation of powers. These military provisions of the Constitution have helped make the United States the great military power it is today.

More recently, Senator Russell Feingold (D-Wisc.) made a critical distinction in saying that Congress's "use of force" joint resolution after Sept. 11, 2001, was very limited in that it approved only actions clearly responsive to those attacks.[24] Congressional sources say the administration at first sought an open-end resolution in the nature of the 1964 Gulf of Tonkin resolution that then-President Lyndon Johnson took as a blank check for whatever military action he chose to initiate in Vietnam.

It was to undo this legislative mistake that Congress in 1973 enacted the War Powers Act. It requires regular consultation with Capitol Hill in contemplating

---

[20]Morris, 319.

[21]Mont Judd Harmon, *Essays on the Constitution of the United States* (Port Washington, N.Y.: Kennikat Press, 1967), 32-48.

[22]Charles Fairman, Stanley Morrison, and Leonard Williams Levy, *The Fourteenth Amendment and the Bill of Rights: The Incorporation of Theory* (New York: Da Capo Press, 1970), 222-25.

[23]Corwin, 72-73.

[24]Feingold, quoted in Witcover.

military action, written notification within 48 hours of such action and its "estimated scope or duration," and congressional consent through either a declaration of war or "specific statutory authorization." If such approval is not granted in 60 days, the president is supposed to withdraw U.S. forces within 30 days.[25] Jules Witcover makes this observation:

> The details of the War Powers Act, however, have usually been honored in the breach. But in this latest case, Congress wrote the empowering resolution specifically confining military action against "nations, organizations or persons [the president] determines planned, authorized, committed or aided the terrorists . . . or harbored such organization or persons, in order to prevent any future acts of international terrorism" by them.[26]

Such language, says Witcover, made it imperative that unless the administration could establish some kind of Iraqi complicity in 9/11, the administration would need new authorization from Congress for any invasion of that country. Meanwhile, Deputy Assistant Attorney General John Yoo argued that the president was not bound by the War Powers Act requiring specific congressional approval because he was constitutionally empowered as commander in chief.[27]

Here's the question: Should Congress go back and create a new War Powers Act for future relations with the White House or should Congress learn to write joint resolutions in which the wording is absolutely clear in its authorization to the commander in chief?

Probably, history will continue to repeat itself.

---

[25] Witcover, ibid.
[26] Ibid.
[27] Ibid.

References

Boylan, Timothy. "War Powers, Constitutional Balance, and the Imperial Presidency Idea at Century's End." *Presidential Studies Quarterly* 29 (June 1999), 232-53.

Brodie, Bernard. *War and Politics*. New York: Macmillan, 1973.

Corwin, Edwin S. *The Constitution and What It Means Today*. Princeton: Princeton University Press, 1950.

Drew, Elizabeth. "Washington." *Atlantic Monthly*, April 1971.

Fairman, Charles, Stanley Morrison, and Leonard Williams Levy. *The Fourteenth Amendment and the Bill of Rights: The Incorporation of Theory*. New York: Da Capo Press, 1970.

Hamilton, Alexander, John Jay, and James Madison. *The Federalist*. New York: Modern Library, 1941.

Harmon, Mont Judd. *Essays on the Constitution of the United States*. Port Washington, N.Y.: Kennikat Press, 1967.

Jensen, Merrill. *The New Nation: A History of the United States during the Confederation*. New York: Vintage Books, 1950.

Morris, Richard Brandon. *The Forging of the Union, 1781-1789*. New York: Harper and Row, 1987.

Smelser, Marshall. *The Democratic Republic: 1801-1815*. New York: Harper and Row, 1968.

Ward, Harry. *The Department of War 1781-1795*. Pittsburgh: University of Pittsburgh Press, 1962.

Wormuth, Francis D., and Edwin B. Firmage. *To Chain the Dogs of War: The War Powers of Congress in History and Law*. Dallas: Southern Methodist University Press, 1986.

Witcover, Jules. "What about the War Powers Act?" *Baltimore Sun*, May 1, 2002, http://www.converge.org.nz/pma/cra0440.htm.

Writing a Paper Using
APA Style

I n some of your college courses, you may be asked to write a research paper in the
style advocated by the American Psychological Association (APA) and described in
its *Publication Manual of the American Psychological Association* (2001). This style
has gained wide acceptance in the social sciences, and versions similar to it are used in
the biological sciences, business, and the earth sciences. It features the name and year
system—that is, your citations will name the authority followed immediately by the
year of publication and then by a paraphrase or quotation concerning the research:
Marshall (2003) has identified three types of homeless people.

WEB LINK
to Chapter 12
Related Web
Destinations
http://www.
ablongman.com/
lester

Writing in the social sciences and physical sciences requires you to think in scientific terms, to concern yourself with a hypothesis that you must investigate. Following
formal scientific methods, you will be testing, surveying, observing, and looking always
for the implications of what you have found. Thus, your approach to the topic will be
an objective one, without outward signs of personal involvement—unlike the approach
you have used in humanities disciplines to examine ethical standards or the quality of
life and art. This is not to say that you cannot be personally motivated, but in the sciences the focus is on the facts and data more than subjective moral issues.

Considering an Academic Approach
to the Subject Matter

Perhaps the goal here is not so much *finding* a topic as it is *approaching* the subject in a scientific manner. Earlier in the text, we described the role of the thesis sentence as a controlling agent for a paper, for example:

Nutritional foods can become an economic weapon in the battle against rising
health care expenses.

However, in scientific writing, the thesis statement (see page 421) usually appears as a *hypothesis, statement of principle,* or an *enthymeme.* The *hypothesis* is a theory that needs testing and analysis, which you will do during your research. It is an idea expressed as a truth for the purpose of argument and investigation and testing. Put another way, it makes a prediction based upon a theory. Here is an example:

Certain nutritional foods can prevent disease.

The task of the scientist is now clear—to examine certain foods to determine their preventive value against certain diseases. A laboratory test would probably become much more specific if the scientist were to test, let's say, the herb Saw Palmetto for its effects on the urinary tract. It's unlikely you'll engage in such research as an undergraduate, but you should understand the direction of scientific inquiry.

Also, even though you are not going into a laboratory, you can nevertheless examine the theoretical implications of a hypothesis. Techniques for writing the theoretical paper are discussed on pages 421–422.

In similar fashion, a *statement of principle* makes a declarative statement in defense of an underlying but unstated theory:

The most effective recall cue is the one that is encoded within the event that is to be remembered.

Your report would attempt to prove the principle on the basis of testing, observation, interviews, and other methods of field research.

On this point, see pages 311–314 of Chapter 9, which also discusses the hypothesis, including these types: relational hypothesis, conditional hypothesis, and the causal hypothesis. See the tip box on page 313 about the advantages of using the hypothesis.

You may also employ the *enthymeme,* which is an incomplete logical structure that depends on one or more unstated assumptions to reach a resolution or to be complete. It serves as the beginning position for writing a theoretical paper. Most enthymemes include a *because* clause. Here is an example:

Little league sports are good for children because they promote discipline.

Unstated is the assumption that discipline is good for children. Your project will require the design of a plan for testing the assertion and reporting your results.

Hyperactive children need medication because ADHD is a medical disorder, not a behavioral problem.

Here, you will need to examine the unstated assumption that medication alone will solve the problem and also examine the literature for theories about behavioral problems in hyperactive children.

Health-conscious Americans should eat functional foods because they protect against cancer and heart problems.

Again, you will need to examine the literature carefully to prove the validity of the theory, especially the assumption that diet alone will produce good health.

EXERCISE 12.1
FRAMING A HYPOTHESIS OR AN ENTHYMEME

Listed below are a mixture of thesis sentences, hypotheses, and enthymemes. Identify each and be prepared to defend your answers. Remember, the thesis sentence has a built-in conclusion, the hypothesis expresses a theory to be tested and researched, and the enthymeme tests a theory with an incomplete logical structure and unstated assumptions.

1. The federal income tax system works well because citizens fear reprisals by the IRS.
2. Methods of keyboarding at a computer is a predictor of successful writing.
3. Same-gender schools affect the marital prospects of the graduates.
4. A soil sample is a predictor of gardening success with roses.
5. Junk food at school lunch programs endangers children because it has no nutritional balance.
6. State legislators have shifted their budgets to help the medical profession rather than, as in the past, the educational programs of K–12 and the colleges.
7. Because the average rainfall is well below the norm this year, the burley tobacco crop will be minimal but prices for the farmers will be higher.
8. An external zip drive is more reliable than an external hard drive.
9. A graduate's employment opportunities are affected by his or her grade point average.
10. Birth rates by teenagers have increased because of the early onset of puberty in girls.

Designing a Paper in APA Style

In the social sciences your assignment is likely to be a:

• Theoretical article
• Review article
• Report on empirical research

Each of these types has a special design and content.

WEB LINK
to Reading
12.1
http://www.
ablongman.com/
lester

Writing a Theoretical Article

As an undergraduate student, you will be asked by some instructors to write a theory paper, which is an essay that draws upon existing research to trace the development of a theory or to make a comparison of theories. A theoretical analysis will examine the current thinking about a social topic, such as criminal behavior, dysfunctional families, class size for effective learning, or learning disorders. The theoretical paper, in most instances, will have four major ingredients:

1. It will identify a problem or hypothesis that has historical implications in the social science community. For example, it might examine this hypothesis: *Cutters, usually young women, slice their arms, legs, and torsos to match damaged physique with damaged psyches.*

2. It will trace the history and evolution of the theory. The task for the researcher is to gather all available literature on the subject, such as articles on the phenomenon of cutters. Some articles will be highly technical but others might be personal narrations, magazine and newspaper articles, and statistical data from empirical studies.

3. It will provide a systematic analysis of the articles that explore the problem. The theory paper will trace the various issues, not so much in chronological order but in relation to issues that you will have identified in your introduction. That is, you are not writing a history but an analysis of the problem as discussed in the literature.

4. It will arrive at a judgment and discussion of the prevailing theory. Usually, the writer will advance one theory as more valid than another. In the case of the hypothesis about cutters, the study may disprove the hypothesis in favor of a different theory.

Introduction

The theoretical paper should be arranged much like a typical research paper with the additional use of headings to divide the sections, although no heading is necessary for the introduction. If the topic is "cutters," you will want to introduce the subject, indicate that it merits examination, and show how prevalent the practice has become and how it is affecting the lives of more and more young women. You may want to discuss some background information to relate the practice, if appropriate, to other practices, such as tattooing, branding, and piercing.

The introduction should provide a very brief review of the key literature while keeping in mind that in the body of the paper you will provide in-depth analysis of the findings. This early review might quote an authority or two, for scholarly quotations will set the academic tone of the piece.

Your introduction should establish the problem under examination by giving the hypothesis or theory to be examined. You will need to discuss its significance to the scientific community to provide a rationale for your study. You may give your initial perspective on the issue and, in an undergraduate paper but not a graduate paper, you might explain your personal interest in the subject—for example, a roommate or a good friend, you have discovered, is a cutter.

Body

The body of your paper will trace the various issues, and each may be listed under its own heading. Under each issue you would establish a prevailing theory and examine the literature. Other arrangements are available, however. You might establish a historical perspective, moving from past to present to examine the contemporary perspectives in light of the previous history. In the body you can also compare and analyze the various aspects of the theories.

Throughout, you should cite extensively from the literature on the subject. Let the experts, and sometimes the patients, speak for themselves. Do not pretend to be the expert, just the messenger. Your task is analysis not detailed explanation, reporting not investigative research, classification of the issues not providing a solution. Don't take on a task greater than you can handle without the tools and skills of empirical research.

Conclusion

The conclusion of the theoretical paper will need several ingredients. You might again explain the significance of the issue and give a general overview of the prevailing theories. In many cases the writer will defend one theory as it grows from the evidence in the body by discussing rather fully the implications of the theory. In some cases, if appropriate, you may suggest additional research work that might be launched in pursuit of more answers to the problem or issue.

Note: See pages 490–497 for an example of a theoretical essay.

Writing a Review Article

A common assignment in some courses is a "review of the literature," a paper in which you make a critical analysis of a set of articles and books on a common topic. The purpose of such a review is to examine the state of current research to determine, in part, if additional work might be in order. The review article serves several purposes:

1. It summarizes existing research on a topic and examines the implications made by the researchers. In doing so, it defines a problem to clarify the working hypothesis.

2. It analyzes the literature to show the research being done in a particular area.

3. It reviews articles and books relating to the same general subject, distinguishing each for its contributions.

4. It may recommend additional research that might grow logically from the work under review.

The review article is usually a short paper because it examines published work without extensive research on the part of the writer of the review.

Introduction

The opening of the review article should identify the problem or the subject under study and its significance. It might provide a very brief summary of the articles and books under review, but remember that the body itself will be a complete review. The introduction might also establish the hypothesis at work.

Body

The body of the review should provide a systematic analysis of the research findings that were examined. That means, usually, a series of quotations to illustrate the researchers' basic positions and findings. Search out and explain the findings made and, perhaps, their significance. Compare the views of two or more authors.

Conclusion

The closing section of the review should discuss the implications made by the research. The conclusion should show and comment on the apparent significance of each article and book.

Writing a Report on Empirical Research

Empirical research requires one to conduct original research in the field or lab. It might mean stimulating a nest of laboratory rats, testing all the well water on a section of land, or observing the behavior of cardinals in a controlled winter environment. Thus, empirical research is not the kind of work you would typically perform as an undergraduate. Nevertheless, you should understand its implications for work in the social, physical, and applied sciences.

WEB LINK to Reading 12.2
http://www. ablongman.com/ lester

You should understand also that a report on empirical research may take the form of a proposal to explain a hypothesis and method of study *even though you will not actually conduct the study*. Typically, an empirical study:

1. Introduces a problem or hypothesis under investigation and explains the purpose of the work.

2. Describes the design and methodology of the research.

3. Reports the results of the investigation or test.

4. Explains, interprets, and explores the implications of the findings.

As an undergraduate, you would need to work closely with an instructor to accomplish each of these stages.

Model for a Report on Empirical Research

The basic design for a report on empirical research takes this form, although elements will differ according to the nature of the study.

Introduction:

- Present the point of your study.
- State the hypothesis and how it relates to the problem.
- Provide the theoretical implications.
- Explain the manner in which your study relates to previously published work.

Method:

- Describe the subject (what was tested, who participated, whether human or animal, and where the field work was accomplished).
- Describe the apparatus to explain your equipment and how you used it.
- Summarize the procedure and the execution of each stage of your work.

Results:

- Summarize the data you collected.
- Provide statistical treatment of your findings with tables, graphs, and charts.
- Include findings that conflict with your hypothesis.

Discussion:

- Evaluate the data and their relevance to the hypothesis.
- Interpret the findings as necessary.
- Discuss the implications of the findings.
- Qualify the results and limit them to your specific study.
- Make inferences from the results.
- Suggest areas worthy of additional research.

EXERCISE 12.2

EXAMINING A SCIENTIFIC ABSTRACT

Shown below is an abstract of a scholarly article accessed through PsycInfo. Your task is to describe in a brief list several pieces of information that you can learn from this abstract.

What are the author's qualifications?

How recent is the article?

What problem or issue was researched?

How was the research conducted?

How was participation of peers a factor in the research?

What is the significance of the study, as stated in the abstract?

Was the article published in a scholarly journal?

How might the descriptors and key concepts at the end help another researcher?

AUTHOR: *Yip,-Kam-shing*; *Ngan,-Mee-yuk*; *Lam,-Irene*
AUTHOR AFFILIATION: Yip,-Kam-shing: Hong Kong Polytechnic U, Dept of Applied Social Studies, Hong Kong
TITLE: An exploration study of peer influence and response to adolescent self-cutting behavior in Hong Kong.
PUBLICATION YEAR: 2002
SOURCE: *Smith-College-Studies-in-Social-Work.* 2002 Jun; Vol 72(3): 379–401
ABSTRACT: This paper reports on a qualitative study of peer responses to self-cutting of secondary school adolescents in Hong Kong. Through semi-structured in-depth interviews with 3 **adolescent self-cutters** (aged 14–16 yrs), their family members, and their peers, the peers' response to adolescents' self-cutting was explored. The findings show that different peers had different types of influence, as well as different responses to self-cutting. Close and supportive peers were usually the first to discover the self-cutting. They were a source of help, communicating with parents, friends, teachers, and the adolescents themselves. In contrast, non-supportive peers, especially boyfriends or girlfriends, created conflicts that seemed to provoke self-cutting. The findings' significance for social work intervention is also discussed. (PsycINFO Database Record (c) 2002 APA, all rights reserved)
KEY CONCEPTS: *peer influence*; *peer response*; *adolescent self-cutting*; *Hong Kong*
MAJOR DESCRIPTORS: ˙*Interpersonal-Influences*; ˙*Peer-Relations*; ˙*Self-Inflicted-Wounds*

Handling Text Citations in APA Style

Citing sources in the text of your paper requires that you use the verb tense appropriate for APA style, and that you effectively blend the source information into your text.

Using the Correct Tense

Scientists, in general, work with small bits of data that can be manipulated, tested, and observed. They usually test a hypothesis or examine a theory to prove it or disprove it. Either conclusion is acceptable because even negative results permit scientists to move on to the next experiment. When an examination is finished, it is put into the past as something accomplished. Consequently, scientists refer to their findings in the past tense (Johnson proved) or in the present perfect tense (Johnson has demonstrated).

Thus, verb tense is an indicator that distinguishes papers in the natural and social sciences from those in the humanities. MLA style, as shown in Chapter 10, requires phrasing such as "Johnson *stipulates*" or "the work of Elmford and Mills *demonstrates*," while APA style requires "Johnson *stipulated*" or "the work of Elmford and Mills *has demonstrated*."

Notice how this passage employs the APA style for its verb tense.

> Vacha and Marin (1993) **surveyed** hosts of doubled-up families and concluded that a lack of space and, in particular, crowding of bathrooms and kitchens, was the main problem for the hosts. They **proposed** that funds should be allocated directly to the providers to help them offset the costs of hosting a sub-family, which would be far cheaper than housing a family in a welfare hotel. At the very least, welfare rules should be rewritten so as not to actively discourage this living arrangement.

The APA style does not require past tense all the time. It expects present tense when you discuss the results of your research (*the results confirm* or *the study indicates*) and when you mention established knowledge (*the therapy offers some hope* or *salt contributes to hypertension*). This example shows correct usage for APA style:

> The danger of steroid use **exists** for every age group, even youngsters. Lloyd and Mercer (2000) **reported** on six incidents of liver damage to 14-year-old swimmers who used steroids.

Blending Sources Effectively in APA Style

In your text citations, use only the last name of the author whose work you are citing. In the entries for your References section, use only initials with the last name (Williams, R. K.). Of course, you should use the full name for notable people that you mention in your text.

> Rollins (2003) has identified and codified the slave records of Thomas Jefferson.

T I P   *Year of Publication*

APA style places the year of publication immediately after the source's name, unlike MLA and CMS styles, which list the date only in the bibliography or in a footnote. APA insists on the date to indicate the timeliness of the source material. A paper on nerve damage with all citations to works in the 1990s would be out of date.

Citing Last Name Only and the Year of Publication

> Montague (2003) has advanced the idea of combining the social sciences and mathematics to chart human behavior.

One study has advanced the idea of combining the social sciences and mathematics to chart human behavior (Montague 2003).

Providing a Page Number

WEB LINK
to Exercise
12.1
http://www.
ablongman.com/
lester

The APA style does not require (but does encourage) including a page number for summaries and paraphrases. The page number is required for direct quotations. Use "p." before a page number, and "pp." before page numbers.

Montague (2003) advanced the idea of "soft mathematics," which is the practice of "applying mathematics to study people's behavior" (p. B4).

T I P   *Punctuation*

For information on punctuating your citations, see Chapter 10, pages 353–356, where you will find details about using ellipsis points, brackets, parentheses, and other marks.

Using a Long Quotation

Present a quotation of 40 words or more as a separate block, indented one-half inch from the left margin. Because the quotation is set off from the text in a distinctive block, do not enclose it with quotation marks. Do not indent the first line of the quotation; however, if the quotation is more than one paragraph, indent the first line of any additional paragraphs one-half inch. Set parenthetical citations after the last period.

> Albert (2000) reported the following:
>> Whenever these pathogenic organisms attack the human body and begin to multiply, the infection is set in motion. The host responds to this parasitic invasion with efforts to cleanse itself of the invading agents. When rejection efforts of the host become visible (fever, sneezing, congestion), the disease status exists. (pp. 314-315)

Citing a Work with More Than One Author

When one work has two or more authors, use *and* in the text but use an ampersand (&) in the parenthetical citation.

Werner **and** Throckmorton (2003) offered statistics on the toxic levels of water samples from six rivers.

It has been reported (Werner & Throckmorton, 2003) that toxic levels exceeded the maximum allowed each year since 1983.

For three to five authors, name them all in the first entry (e.g., Torgerson, Andrews, Smith, Lawrence, & Dunlap, 2003), but thereafter use just the first author's name with "et al." (e.g., Torgerson et al., 2003). For six or more authors, employ just the first author's name with "et al." in the first and in all subsequent instances (e.g., Fredericks et al., 2003).

Citing More Than One Work by an Author

To identify two or more works published in the same year by the same author, use lowercase letters after the date (Thompson, 2003a) and (Thompson, 2003b). Be sure to include those letters in the corresponding entries in the References section of your paper.

Including Additional Information in a Citation

In the parenthetical citation you can direct the reader to a particular page for special attention, or point to a work that contrasts with the source you have just cited.

Horton (2003; cf. Thomas, 2001a, p. 89, and 2001b, p. 426) suggested an intercorrelation of these testing devices. But after multiple-group analysis, Welston (2003, esp. p. 211) reached an opposite conclusion.

Citing Indirect Sources

You may want to mention a work that you have not directly consulted but that was cited in one of your sources. Mention the earlier work in your text discussion, but in the parenthetical reference, cite only the source you directly consulted.

In other research, Massie and Rosenthal (as cited in Osterling & Dawson, 2003) studied home movies of children diagnosed with autism, but determining criteria was difficult due to the differences in quality and dating of the available videotapes.

Citing from a Textbook or Anthology

If you make an in-text citation to an article or chapter in a textbook, casebook, or anthology, refer only to the author of the article or chapter you cite. The list of references will further clarify your source:

One writer stressed that two out of every three new jobs in this decade will go to women (Ralph 2003).

Abbreviating Corporate Authors in the Text

The name of a corporate author may be abbreviated after the initial full reference:

One source questioned the results of the use of aspirin for arthritis treatment in children (American Medical Association [AMA], 2003).

Thereafter, refer to the corporate author by the abbreviation: (AMA, 2003).

Citing a Work with No Author or an Anonymous Author

When a work has no author listed, use the title (or the first few words of the title) in your citation. The source will be listed by title in the References section.

> The cost per individual student has continued to rise rapidly ("Money Concerns," 2000, p. 2).

However, if a work's author is designated on the title page as "Anonymous," use this form:

> It has been demonstrated that peer pressure can improve or discourage adolescent posture (Anonymous, 2003).

Citing Electronic Sources

Material from electronic sources presents different challenges when you are citing in APA style. Here is a basic rule: Omit page or paragraph numbers unless the Web site or database reproduces the original pagination of the printed material or original paragraph numbers. Do not count pages on the screen, do not use the page numbers on your printouts, and do not count paragraphs yourself. Just omit the page number. Readers who wish to locate a quotation in an article can use the computer's "Find" feature.

Paragraph Numbers

If the source has original paragraph numbering, use this form:

> The most common type of diabetes is non-insulin-dependent diabetes mellitus (NIDDM), which "affects 90% of those with diabetes and usually appears after age 40" (Larson, 2003, para. 3).

Page Numbers

Use this next form if the Web site or database reproduces original pagination:

> One source has argued the merits of Chekhov's subtext and its "psychological nuances of the words" (Ward, 2003, p. 18).

Web Site

Mention the name of a site or home page if it contributes to a reader's understanding that the source is electronic and therefore has no page number for the quotation, but this is an option.

At the web site Office of Personnel Management, Dove (2003) has made the distinction between a Congressional calendar day and a legislative day, noting, "A legislative day is the period of time following an adjournment of the Senate until another adjournment."

Abstract

Indicate your citation of an abstract as opposed to the article itself.

"Psychologically oriented techniques used to elicit confessions may undermine their validity" (Kassin, 2003, abstract).

HyperNews Posting

Though not required, signaling the type of online source can serve the reader.

In an online posting Ochberg (2000) commented on the use of algae in paper that "initially has a green tint to it, but unlike bleached paper which turns yellow with age, this algae paper becomes whiter with age."

Online Magazine

There's often a difference in the content of a print magazine, such as *Business Week*, and its counterpart on the Web, *BusinessWeekOnline*. Be sure you identify which one is your source.

BusinessWeekOnline (2001) reported that Napster's idea of peer-to-peer computing is a precursor to new web applications, even though the courts might close them down.

Government Document

Naming the federal government sites that you have consulted will serve your reader.

The Web site *Thomas* (2003) has provided since the 93rd Congress a "Bill Summary and Status" to keep citizens as well as members of Congress up to date on legislative activities.

E-mail and Electronic Mailing Lists

Personal communications, which others cannot retrieve, should be cited in the text only and not mentioned at all in the References section. However, electronic chat groups have gained legitimacy in recent years, so in your text you might wish to give an exact date and provide the e-mail address *only* if the citation has scholarly relevance and *only* if the author's address is public and open to correspondence.

One technical writing instructor has bemoaned the inability of hardware developers to maintain pace with the ingenuity of software developers. In his E-mail message, he indicated that educational institutions cannot keep pace. Thus, "students nationwide suffer with antiquated equipment, even though it's only a few years old" (ClemmerJ@apsu.edu, personal communication, March 8, 2003).

If the e-mail is part of an electronic mailing list (or listserv), a network, or an online journal, it *may* be listed in the References section. In such cases, use the form shown next and see the bibliography form on page 441.

Camilleri (2003, May 7) has identified the book *Storyteller* for those interested in narrative bibliography.

FTP Site

Not every site will need mention in the text; for instance, the References list will have full information on Kranidiotis, cited here:

Kranidiotis (2003) has shown in the following graph that perceptually "all the sounds corresponding to the points on the curve have the same intensity: this means that the ear has a large range where it is nearly linear (1000 to 8000 Hz), achieving better results on a little domain."

CD-ROM

Compton's Interactive Encyclopedia (2002) explained that the Abolition Society, which originated in England in 1787, appears to be the first organized group in opposition to slavery. Later, in 1823 the Anti-Slavery Society was formed by Thomas Fowell Buxton, who wielded power as a member of Parliament.

EXERCISE 12.3
WRITING TEXT CITATIONS IN APA STYLE

Shown below are five statements. Your task is to write a sentence that features correct APA citation form for each one.

1. Paraphrase of Rachel M. Thurston, 2003, page 67: The resistance of American drivers to mass transit eliminates any hopes that high-speed electric trains will be economically feasible.

2. Paxton Morris and Emily C. Rawling, 2003, page 256: "The tests determined that herbal supplements, a healthy diet, and regular exercise enabled 47.6 percent of the subjects to reduce their drug dependency."

3. The Wellness Foundation, 2003, issued a statement on its Web site to describe non-drug treatments for hyperactive children, asking for "drug-free playgrounds" in a play on words.

4. Marcus C. Washington, professor of sociology at the Bingham institute, 2003, pages 34–35, studied the mothers of children diagnosed with autism to chart their disbelief, their dismay, their ultimate acceptance.

5. P. C. Widmer, 2003, p. 23: "The federal prison system is depending more and more on small city jails to house federal inmates, and the small cities have bought into the plan in order to produce income."

GUIDELINES

Blending Sources in APA Style

- Use only the last name of an author whose work you are citing.
- Use the past tense of the verb or the present perfect tense in citations.
- Try to achieve variety in your choice of verbs—*found, discovered, proved, offered, has demonstrated, has shown, has tested*, and so forth.
- Try to establish your position early in the paragraph before beginning citations. In that way you will not be moving from one source to another without the context of your own presentation.
- Blend more than one source into a paragraph to show how several different authorities agree or disagree on the topic of discussion.
- Quote the sources with precision.
- Provide a page number for quotations. Paraphrases and summaries require no page number, but APA style encourages including that information.

Formatting the APA Paper

Place your materials in this order:

1. Title page
2. Abstract
3. Text of the paper
4. References
5. Appendix

Title Page

In addition to the title of your paper and your name and academic affiliation, the title page should establish your running head that will appear on every page preceding the page number.

Abstract

You should provide an abstract with every paper written in APA style. An abstract is a quick but thorough summary of the contents of your paper. It is read first and may be the only part read by others researching your topic, so it must be accurate, self-contained, concise, non-evaluative, and coherent. For theoretical papers (see pages 421–422), the abstract should include:

- The topic in one sentence, if possible.
- The purpose, thesis, and scope of the paper.
- A brief reference to the sources used (e.g., published articles, books, and so forth).
- The conclusions and the implications of the study.

For the report of an empirical study (see pages 423–424), the abstract should include the four items listed above for theoretical papers with the addition of three more:

- Description of the subjects (e.g., species, number, age, type).
- Description of the methodology, including procedures and apparatus.
- The findings produced by the study.

Text of the Paper

Double space throughout your paper. In general, use centered headings in roman type for the major divisions of your paper. Use flush left headings in italic type for sub-headings within the major divisions.

Method

Subjects

Instrumentation

Procedure

Results

Discussion

Most instructors will give you some freedom with regard to fonts, margins, and other desk-top publishing features. For the three basic types of papers in the social sciences and their respective components, see pages 421–424. Each type of paper requires a different arrangement of the various parts.

References

Use the title "References" for your bibliography section. Alphabetize the entries and double space throughout. Every reference used in your text should appear in your alphabetical list of references at the end of the paper. Prepare your list of references with a hanging indention, as shown in the sample References section that follows.

References

Aber, J. L. (1993, November). The effects of poor neighborhoods on children, youth and families: Theory, research and policy implications (Background memorandum for Policy Conference on Persistent Urban Poverty). Washington, DC: Social Science Research Council.

Arbuckle, J. (1995). *Amos user's guide.* Chicago: Smallwaters.

Arbuckle, J. (1996). Full information estimation in the presence of incomplete data, In G. A. Marcoulides & R. E. Schumacker (Eds.), *Advanced structural equation modeling* (pp. 243-277). Hillsdale, NJ: Erlbaum.

Attar, B. K., Guerra, N. G., & Tolan, P. H. (1994). Neighborhood disadvantage, stressful life events, and adjustment in urban elementary-school children. *Journal of Clinical Child Psychology, 23,* 391-400.

Bulman, R. J., & Brickman, P. (1980). Expectations and what people learn from failure. In N. T. Feather (Ed.), *Expectancy, incentive and action.* Hillsdale, NJ: Erlbaum.

Burton, L. M., & Jarrett, R. L. (2000). In the mix, yet on the margins: The place of families in urban neighborhood and child development research. *Journal of Marriage and the Family, 62,* 1114-1135.

Coley, R. L., & Hoffman, L. W. (1996). Relations of parental supervision and monitoring to children's functioning in various contexts: Moderating effects of families and neighborhoods. *Journal of Applied Developmental Psychology, 17,* 51-68.

Compas, B. E., Malcarne, V. L., & Fondacaro, R. M. (1988). Coping with stressful events in older children and young adolescents. *Journal of Consulting and Clinical Psychology, 56,* 405-411.

Appendix

An appendix is the appropriate place for material that is not germane to your text but nevertheless has pertinence to the study. Here you can present graphs, charts, study plans, observation and test results, and other matter that will help your reader understand the nature of your work.

Writing the References Entries in APA Style

WEB LINK
to Reading
12.3
http://www.
ablongman.com/
lester

Use the hanging indention for all entries. Authors are identified by last name and one or more initials. Provide the publication date and other information at detailed in the sections that follow.

> Ante, S. E. (2001, August 14). How the music-sharing phenom began, where it went wrong, and what happens next. *BusinessWeek Online*. Retrieved August 13, 2003 from http://www.businessweek.com/2000/00_33/b3694001.htm

Books

Basic Form for a Book

> McGraw, P. C. (2000). *Life strategies: Doing what works, doing what matters*. New York: Hyperion.

List the author (surname first with initials for given names). Give the year of publication within parentheses. The title of the book is italicized or underscored, with only the first word of the title and any subtitle capitalized (but do capitalize proper nouns). Give the place of publication, and publisher. In the publisher's name omit the words *Publishing, Company,* or *Inc.*, but otherwise give a full name: Florida State University Press; HarperCollins. List chronologically two or more works by the same author; for example, Fitzgerald's 2001 publication would precede his 2003 publication.

> Fitzgerald, R. F. (2001). Water samples . . .

> Fitzgerald, R. F. (2003). Controlling . . .

Multiple works by the same author in the same year are alphabetized by title and marked with lowercase letters—a, b, c—immediately after the date:

> Cobb, R. A. (2003a). Circulating systems . . .

> Cobb, R. A. (2003b). Delay valves . . .

Entries of a single author precede multiple-author entries beginning with the same surname, without regard for the dates:

> Fitzgerald, R. F. (2003). Controlling . . .

> Fitzgerald, R. F., & Smithson, C. A. (1999). Mapping . . .

Entries with the same first author and different second or third authors should be alphabetized by the surname of the second author:

Fitzgerald, R. F., & Smithson, C. A. (2003). Mapping . . .

Fitzgerald, R. F., & Waters, W. R. (2002). Examining micro carbons . . .

Book Edition

Oldham, R., Massey, C. Y., & Winston, P., Jr. (2003). *Field guide for observation* (3rd ed.). New York: Mason.

Alphabetized Work, Encyclopedia or Dictionary

Begin with the title to an entry if no author is listed.

Kiosk: Word history. (1992). In *The American heritage dictionary of the American language* (3rd ed., 1 vol.). Boston: Houghton Mifflin.

Moran, J. (1998). Weather. In *World book encyclopedia* (Vol. 21, pp. 126–139). Chicago: Field Enterprises.

Joseph. (1999). In *Who was who in the Bible.* Nashville: Nelson.

Book with Corporate Author

The institution that acted as author of a work will sometimes be the publisher as well.

American Council of Education. (2000). *Annual report on remedial education.* Washington, DC: Author.

American Medical Association. (1998). *Essential guide to menopause.* New York: Pocket.

Book with No Author

American heritage dictionary of the English language (3rd ed.). (1992). Boston: Houghton Mifflin.

Book in Several Volumes Published in Different Years

Show the years of publication and the number of volumes.

Murphy, S. Y., Sr. (1999–2003). *Psychology: The science and the art* (Vols. 1–3). New York, Wilson.

Chapter of a Volume in a Series

Use this entry as a general guide for including a number of different contributors. This example shows the chapter authors and title, the series editor, the volume editor, the name of the series, and the name and number of the volume.

WEB LINK to Exercise 12.2
http://www.ablongman.com/lester

> Maccoby, E. E., & Martin, J. (1983). Socialization in the context of the family: Parent-child interaction. In P. H. Mussen (Series Ed.) and E. M. Hetherington (Vol. Ed.), *Handbook of child psychology: Vol. 4. Socialization, personality, and social development* (4th ed., pp. 1–101). New York: Wiley.

Part of an Edited Book

List author, date, chapter or section title, editor (with name in normal order) preceded by "In" and followed by "(Ed.)" or "(Eds.)," the name of the book (underscored or italicized), page numbers to the specific section of the book cited (in parentheses), place of publication, and publisher.

> Hill, R. (1999). Repatriation must heal old wounds. In R. L. Brooks (Ed.), *When sorry isn't enough* (pp. 283–287). New York: New York University.

Periodicals

Article in a Journal

After the author's name and date of publication, give the title of the article, without quotation marks around it. Capitalize the first word in the title and any subtitle, and capitalize any proper nouns. The name of the journal is underscored or italicized, with all major words capitalized. The volume number is underscored or italicized, and inclusive page numbers are *not* preceded by "p." or "pp."

> Deardorff, J., Gonzales, N. A., & Sandler, I. N. (2003). Control beliefs as a mediator of the relation between stress and depressive symptoms among inner-city adolescents. *Journal of Abnormal Child Psychology 31,* 205–218.

Article in a Magazine

Provide the year of publication, the month without abbreviation, and the specific day for magazines published weekly, fortnightly (every two weeks), and monthly. Use "p." or "pp." with the inclusive page numbers when you do not furnish a volume number. If a magazine prints the article on discontinuous pages, include all page numbers.

> Lakey, S. (2000, September). Privacy, please. *Business Nashville, 4,* 26, 28, 30.

> Pompili, T. (2000, September 1). Exchange topples domino. *PC Magazine,* p. 47.

> Selim, J. (2002, November). The bionic connection. *Discover, 23,* 49–51.

Article in a Newspaper

Remember to provide a specific date and section numbers as well as discontinuous page numbers. You cannot use "B7 + " as in MLA style.

Kemper, T. D. (2000, August 11). Toward sociology as a science, maybe. *Chronicle of Higher Education,* pp. B7, B9–B10.

Article Retrieved from a Server (InfoTrac, SilverPlatter, ProQuest)

Wakschlag, L. S., & Leventhal, B. L. (1996). Consultation with young autistic children and their families. *Journal of the American Academy of Child and Adolescent Psychiatry, 35,* 963–965. Retrieved September 2, 2003, from InfoTrac database.

Abstract as the Original Source

Cite from the article itself, not an abstract, if at all possible.

Rosen, G. (2000). Public school alternatives: The voucher controversy [Abstract]. *Current, 423,* 3.

Abstract of an Unpublished Work

Burton, B. A. (1999). Telling survival stories: Trauma, violence, family and everyday life in an American community [Abstract]. Unpublished manuscript.

Abstract Retrieved from a Server (InfoTrac, SilverPlatter, ProQuest)

Compare this entry with the Deardorff entry, page 437.

Deardorff, J., Gonzales, N. A., & Sandler, I. N. (2003). Control beliefs as a mediator of the relation between stress and depressive symptoms among inner-city adolescents. *Journal of Abnormal Child Psychology 31,* 205–218. Abstract retrieved September 2, 2003, from InfoTrac database.

Review

Foley, M. (2002, November). Measured deception: The metric system is the precise embodiment of human error [Review of the book *The measure of all things: The seven-year odyssey and hidden error that transformed the world*]. *Discover, 23,* 77.

Reports, Proceedings, and Nonprint Works
Report

> McCroskey, J. (2000). Taxation to subsidize the tourism business (Report No.
>   2000-K). Golden, CO: Independence Institute.

Nonprint Material

Provide within brackets a description of the medium, such as television series, motion picture, CD, and so forth.

> Corcoran, R. L. (2000, May 22). "Interpreting dreams: Subconscious reflections
>   and realities" [Interview]. Macon, GA.

> Ford, B., & Ford, S. (Producers). (1998). *Couples dance instructional videos:*
>   *Robert Royston & Laureen Baldovi* [Videotape]. Antioch, CA: Images in
>   Motion.

> *Gold Rush 1.0.* (1999). [Computer program]. Columbia, MD: WisdomBuilder.

> African American history: Abolitionist movement. (2000). *Encarta encyclopedia*
>   *2000* [CD]. Redmond, WA: Microsoft Corporation.

> Morgan, C. (Producer). (2003, May 4). *60 minutes* [Television series episode]. New
>   York: CBS News.

Proceeding

If you cite an unpublished paper that has been presented at a meeting, use this form:

> Lanktree, C., & Briere, J. (1991, January). Early data on the Trauma
>   Symptom Checklist for Children (TSC-C). Paper presented at the meeting
>   of the American Professional Society on the Abuse of Children, San
>   Diego, CA.

If you cite from a published contribution to a conference, use this form:

> Deci, E. L., & Ryan, R. M. (1991). A motivational approach to self: Integration in
>   personality. In R. Dienstbier (Ed.). *Nebraska Symposium on Motivation: Vol.*
>   *38. Perspectives on motivation* (pp. 237–288). Lincoln: University of
>   Nebraska Press.

Electronic Sources

When citing Internet sources in APA style, in the References section, provide this information if available:

1. Author or editor's last name, followed by a comma, the initials, and a period.

2. Year of publication, followed by a comma, then month and day for magazines and newspapers, within parenthesis, followed by a period.

3. Title of the article, not within quotations and not underscored, with only the first word of the title and any subtitle and proper nouns capitalized, followed by the total number of paragraphs within brackets only if that information is provided. This is also the place to describe the work within brackets, as with [Abstract] or [Letter to the editor].

4. Name of the book, journal, or complete work, underscored or italicized, if one is listed.

5. Volume number, if listed, underscored or italicized.

6. Page numbers only if you have that data from a printed version of the journal or magazine. If the periodical has no volume number, use "p." or "pp." before the numbers; if the journal has a volume number, omit "p." or "pp."

7. The word *Retrieved*, followed by the date of access, followed by the word *from*.

8. The URL (URLs can be quite long, but you must provide the full data for other researchers to find the source). Do not place a period at the end of the URL.

Article from an Online Journal

> Young, Michael E. (1998). Are hypothetical constructs preferred over intervening variables? *Psycholoquy, 9*, Article 9. Retrieved April 3, 2003, from
> http://psycprints.ecs.soton.ac.uk/archive/00000558/

Article from a Printed Periodical Reproduced Online

Many articles online are the exact duplicates of their print versions, so if you view an article in its electronic form and are confident that the electronic form is identical to the printed version, add within brackets *Electronic version*. This allows you to omit the URL.

> Bowler, D. M., & Thommen, E. (2000). Attribution of mechanical and social causality to animated displays by children with autism [Electronic version]. *Autism, 4*, 147–172.

Add the URL and date of access if page numbers are not indicated, as shown in this next entry:

> Leahy, M. (2000). Missouri's savannas and woodlands. *Missouri Conservationist, 61*. Retrieved August 30, 2003, from http://
> www.conservation.state.mo.us/conmag/2000/08/l.htm

Abstract

Parrott, A. C. (2000). Does cigarette smoking cause stress? *American Psychologist, 55*. Abstract retrieved October 13, 2003, from http://www.apa.org/journals/amp/amp5410817.html

Article from an Online Magazine, No Author Listed

Benefits of electric load aggregation. (2003, May). *PMA Online Magazine*. Retrieved November 3, 2000, from http://www.retailenergy.com/articles/loadagg.htm

Article from an Online Newspaper

Gallagher, S. (2003, August 11). Fires in west imperil ancient sites. *Atlanta Journal-Constitution Online*. Retrieved August 11, 2003, from http://www.accessatlanta.com/partners/ajc/epaper/editions/today/

Bulletins and Government Documents

Murphy, F. L. (2000). The beneficial effects of fish oil on coronary heart disease. Retrieved October 19, 2003, from Preventive Health Center web site: http://www.mdphc.com/nutrition/beneficial-effects-of-fish-oil.htm

U.S. Cong. Senate. (1999, February 3). A bill to amend the Indian Gaming Regulator Act. Senate Bill 339. Retrieved October 8, 2003, from http://thomas.loc.gov/cgibin/bdquery

Hypernews Posting

Forster, A. (2000, May 18). The best paper of all. Message posted to Recycling Discussion Group electronic mailing list, archived at http://www.betterworld.com/BVvDiscuss/get/recycleD/26.html

Discussion Group

Nelder, C. (2000). Envisioning a sustainable future. [Msg 42]. Message posted to Better World discussion topics at http://www.betterworld.com/BWZ/9610/coverl.htm

News Groups, Telnet, FTP Sites

Haas, H. (2000, August 5). Link checker that works with cold fusion. Message posted to impressive.net/archives/fogo/200000805113615.AI4381@w3.org

Library Databases

University servers give you access to many sources stored in large databases, such as PsycInfo, ERIC, and netLibrary. Use this next form, which gives the date of your retrieval, the name of the database, and if readily available the item number within parentheses. If you cite only from the abstract, mention that fact in your References entry (see the Kang entry below).

Coleman, L., & Coleman, J. (2002). The measurement of puberty: A review. *Journal of Adolescence, 25,* 535–550. Retrieved April 2, 2003, from ERIC database (EJ655060).

Kang, H. S. (2002). What is missing in interlanguage: Acquisition of determiners by Korean learners of English. *Working Papers in Educational Linguistics, 18.* Abstract retrieved April 2, 2003, from ERIC database.

EXERCISE 12.4
WRITING ENTRIES FOR THE REFERENCES SECTION

Write a bibliography entry in APA style for each of the sources listed below.

1. **Author:** *Dennis W. Johnson*
   Title: Elections and public polling: Will the media get online polling right?
   Source: *Psychology and Marketing.* 2002 Dec; Vol 19(12): 1009–1023
   Special Issue: Political marketing.

2. **Author:** *James G. Gimpel*
   Title: Packing heat at the polls: Gun ownership, interest group endorsements, and voting behavior in gubernatorial elections
   Source: *Social Science Quarterly.* 1998 Sep; Vol 79(3): 634–648

3. **Author:** *Robert R. Brischetto, Richard L. Engstrom*
   Title: Cumulative voting and Latino representation: Exit surveys in fifteen Texas communities
   Source: *Social Science Quarterly.* 1997 Dec; Vol 78(4): 973–991

4. **Accession number:** 1997-07247-002
   Author: *Robert H. Binstock*
   Title: The 1996 election: Older voters and implications for policies on aging
   Source: *Gerontologist.* 1997 Feb; Vol 37(1): 15–19
   Abstract: In Database: PsycINFO 1996–1997.

5. **Author:** *Toshio Nidaira*
   Title: Exit polls in Japanese elections: The methods used by the Japan Broadcasting Corporation
   Source: *Japanese Journal of Behaviormetrics.* 1996 Mar; Vol 23(1): 20–27
   Special Issue: Accuracy in social research.

6. **Author:** *George F. Bishop, Bonnie S. Fisher*
   Title: "Secret ballots" and self-reports in an exit-poll experiment
   Source: *Public Opinion Quarterly.* 1995 Win; Vol 59(4): 568–588

Chapter Review

The primary purpose of this chapter detailing the basic elements of APA style has been to explain the style and format required for papers in the social sciences. Your professors in education, psychology, sociology, social work, political science, and others will expect the APA format.

WEB LINK
to Chapter 12
Related Web
Destinations
http://www.
ablongman.com/
lester

To write papers in this style, you should know several styles of research protocol. You will need to design your paper for a theoretical study, a review, or empirical research. Then, as you write, you can blend your sources according to the APA standards.

Remember to use the past tense or present perfect tense for introducing your sources and to include the year of publication to show currency.

Chapter 12 Assignment: Writing a Paper in APA Style

This assignment asks you to write a research paper in APA style. Reproduced below are six short articles treating a common subject. Your task is to read critically the articles, making marginal annotations, highlighting material, and writing notes. In addition, as described in Chapter 9, you will need to summarize the major issues, chart them carefully, and match your summaries and notes to the chart or outline. First, based on the sources gathered here, form a theory or hypothesis that your paper will explore. Then, produce the paper, with fidelity to the APA style of writing. Cite from the articles in your paper and prepare a References list for it.

Obesity and Risk of Mental Disorders

C Lamertz; C Jacobi; A Yassouridis; K Arnold; A Henkel.
Nutrition Research Newsletter, Dec 2002 v21 i12 p15

In most industrialized nations an elevated body mass index (BMI) is not only associated with an increased risk for physical health problems and mortality but also with social stigma and severe penalties. In addition, some theories assume that the negative view of being overweight in our society contributes not only to psychological distress but also to an increased risk for defined mental disorders in obese individuals. Depending on differences in sampling, diagnostic criteria, diagnostic coverage, age composition, and culture, numerous clinical studies demonstrate almost consistently up to 4.8 times higher prevalence rates of mental disorders as well as an elevated general psychopathology in obese patients compared with non-obese non-patients. The current epidemiological survey focused on the following aspects: the examination of the association between obesity and mental disorders in a large representative sample of the general population of adolescent and young adults; the use of both an internationally validated clinical structured interview for Diagnostic and Statistical Manual IV (DSM-IV) diagnoses and clinical scales for the assessment of general psychopathology; to control the potential confounding effect of a lifetime diagnosis of eating disorders.

The results of this study represent cross-sectional data from the first wave of The Early Developmental Stages of Psychopathology (EDSP) study. The study was designed to estimate prevalence, risk factors, comorbidity, and course of mental disorders in the German youth population. The overall design of the study was prospective, consisting of a first wave and two follow-up surveys. The EDSP sample was drawn from the 1994 official population register of all residents in metropolitan Munich. All registrants who were 14 to 24 years of age during the first half of 1995 were eligible for inclusion. A total of 3021 interviews were completed. The majority of respondents were living with their parents, and were middle class. After subjects with classified eating disorders, and subjects with missing data were excluded, 2939 remained in the study.

Diagnostic assessments were based on the computer-assisted personal interview (CAPI) version of the Munich-composite International Diagnostic Interview (M-CIDI), a modified version of the World Health Organization CIDI, supplemented by questions to cover DSM-IV and International Classification of Diseases (ICD-10) criteria. The M-CIDI allows for the assessment of symptoms, syndromes, and diagnoses of 48 mental disorders and provides information about onset, duration, and clinical and psychosocial severity.

Analyses of cross-tabulations demonstrate no significant associations between BMI categories and mental disorders for both adolescents and young adults. Anxiety, mood, substance, and somatoform disorders were not found to be significantly more or less frequent in obese than in average or underweight subjects. These findings apply to both age groups and genders as well as to both partitions. The results of this study support the findings of other studies that general psychopathology is not significantly associated with obesity in the general population. Overweight and obese young adults and adolescents in the present study were found to be as mentally healthy or unhealthy as the age-matched non-obese individuals in the general population.

Obesity and Health-Related Quality of Life in Men

William S. Yancy Jr.; Maren K. Olsen; Eric C. Westman. Nutrition Research Newsletter, Nov 2002 v21 i11 p4

Overweight is an increasing problem in the United States; recent estimates classify over 50% of Americans as either overweight or obese. Plenty of research shows the health burdens of being overweight and obese, such as type 2 diabetes, hypertension, coronary artery disease, and others, but now there is a growing body of literature describing the effect that being overweight has on lower health-related quality of life (HRQOL) as well.

Several studies have shown that overweight persons have lower HRQOL, especially in the physical aspects of daily life, compared with their normal-weight counterparts. However, these findings may not apply to the medical outpatient population. In addition, the inverse relationship between body weight and HRQOL is established for women, the association is not as clear in men. To help clarify these issues, a recent study measured the independent relationship between body weight and HRQOL in a population of Veterans' Affairs male outpatients while considering comorbid illness.

This cross-sectional study examined 1168 male outpatients from Durham Veterans' Affairs Medical Center. The Medical Outcomes Study Short Form 36 (SF-36) was used to measure HRQOL. The SF-36 is a self-administered measure that contains brief indices of the following domains: Physical Functioning, Role Limitations due to Physical Functioning (Role-Physical), Bodily Pain, General Health, Vitality, Social Functioning, Role Limitations due to Emotional Functioning (Role-Emotional), and Mental Health. The Kaplan-Feinstein Comorbidity Index was used to assess the presence and severity of comorbid illnesses, while the Center for Epidemiological Studies Depression Scale (CES-D) was used to evaluate for depressive symptoms. Lastly, the Framingham Physical Activity Index was used to evaluate daily physical activity.

The subjects had a mean age of 54.7 years; 69% were white and 29% were African American. Mean scores on each SF-36 subscale for the entire sample and for each BMI group were lower than the US norms. Subjects with a BMI > 40 kg/[m.sup.2] had significantly lower scores compared with normal-weight individuals on 5 of the 10 subscales (Physical Functioning, Role-Physical, Bodily Pain, Vitality, and Physical Component Summary). Lower scores were observed at BMI > 35 kg/[m.sup.2] on the physical functioning and Physical Components subscales, while on the Bodily Pain subscale, lower scores were observed at BMI > 25 kg/[m.sup.2]. Two significant interactions existed. Increased BMI had a greater negative association with General Health and Vitality when the physical activity score was low compared with when the physical activity score was high.

The results show an inverse relationship between BMI and physical aspects of HRQOL exists in a population of male outpatients. Because the cohort analyzed did not include patients with diabetes and because the study controlled for other comorbid illnesses, the results are very likely to reflect the independent association between obesity and HRQOL. However, it must be acknowledged that there is likely an attenuation of the association between body weight and HRQOL in this population because SF-36 scores were low regardless of body weight. Further research is necessary but the findings emphasize that obesity not only increases a person's risk of morbidity and mortality, but also may significantly impact individuals' daily lives.

Obesity Linked to Attention Disorder

New Scientist, Oct 19, 2002 v176 i2365 p26

Many obese adults may be finding is hard to stick to diets or exercise plans because they suffer from attention deficit hyperactivity disorder (ADHD).

Behavioural psychiatrist Jules Altfas from the Behavioral Medical Center for Treatment and Research in Portland, Oregon, studied 215 obese adults and found that 27.4% of them had ADHD, compared with only 4.7% of the general US population. And when the group with the most extreme form of obesity took part in a weight-loss plan, those who didn't have ADHD lost more than twice as much weight as those with ADHD, he reports in BMC Psychiatry (www.biomednetcentral.com/1471-244X/219).

"The ADHD sufferers couldn't remember their diet plans. . . . They were disorganised and ate impulsively," says Altfas. Treating the ADHD could help them lose weight, he suggests.

Secret: Most Thin People Don't Eat Whatever They Want.

Tufts University Health & Nutrition Letter, July 2002 v20 i5

"When I was in kindergarten," says Susan Roberts, "all of the kids brought in cupcakes for the class on their birthdays. On my own birthday I offered the teacher one of the lavishly frosted chocolate cupcakes my mother had given me to hand out. The teacher, a thin woman, refused it. She just was not moved to eat a cupcake mid-morning, no matter how good it looked."

Four decades later, Dr. Roberts, chief of the Energy Metabolism Lab at Tufts, knows why—and can say in scientific terms why her teacher was thin. She had a low disinhibition score. That is, even if there was something delicious to eat or that other people were having, she did not partake unless she was hungry herself. The sights and smells of good-tasting foods or of other people digging in did not affect what or how much she consumed.

Thinness is part and parcel of low disinhibition. In looking at the disinhibition scores of more than 600 women in their 50s and 60s, Dr. Roberts and Nicholas Hays, PhD, found that the lower a person's disinhibition, the less she tended to weigh. In fact, all those with low and medium disinhibition scores were at healthy weights. But the lowest Body Mass Index for someone who was highly disinhibited was 28—163 pounds for someone who's 5 feet 4 inches. Highly disinhibited women had also gained the most weight since they were in their 30s—often as much as 35 pounds. Based on the results, which were very strong statistically, Dr. Roberts maintains that someone's level of disinhibition is the "strongest predictor of whether she or he will be fat that you're ever going to see."

Unfortunately, disinhibition is hard to "fix." And it's pretty common in this country. In fact, "the US is a culture of disinhibition," Dr. Roberts says. "It encourages it. We have large portions and menu items called Death By Desert. The possibilities for what we in the field call opportunistic overeating—cues to eat more even when you're not hungry—are overwhelming."

That's one of the reasons, says Dr. Roberts, that "it's not easy to go about teaching somebody to be disinhibited. Disinhibition is very ingrained."

Any possible solutions?

The silver lining Dr. Roberts saw in her research is that using dietary restraint—consciously eating less than you want to, say, by counting calories, putting down your fork before you're full, eating less the next day to make up for a large meal the night before, or simply avoiding certain foods most of the time—can counteract the effects of disinhibition to some degree.

In other words, being in a constant state of caloric vigilance can help keep the disinhibition in check. Consider that the unrestrained, disinhibited women in the study were obese, with Body Mass Indices averaging 31 (about 180 pounds for a woman 5 feet 4 inches tall). But the disinhibited women who were restrained eaters had Body Mass Indices closer to 28—which made them, on average, some 15 pounds thinner.

Some researchers have called restrained eating neurotic. They say that people should eat the amount that's right for them and let the chips fall where they may rather than constantly try to hold back. But others, like Dr. Roberts, say that conscious restraint may be called for in a country where it's so easy to go overboard. "In America," she comments, "maybe you have to be just a little neurotic to keep from availing yourself of all the temptations out there. Most people who are thin can't eat everything they want when they want."

Dr. Roberts herself is a somewhat disinhibited eater who is also restrained. "If I buy grasshopper [mint and chocolate] cookies," she says, "I will eat them whether or not I'm hungry for them." That's the disinhibited part. "But," she continues, "every week at the supermarket, I pass them up." That's the restrained part—which helps keep the 5-foot 6-inch researcher at a Body Mass Index of 22—132 pounds.

Disinhibited, Restrained, or Both?

From "The Eating Inventory" by Stunkard & Messick (1985) in the *Journal of Psychosomatic Research, 29,* 71–83

Disinhibition Index

Respond, true or false, to the following statements. The more to which you respond "true," the more likely you are to be a disinhibited eater, and the more likely to be at a higher-than-healthy weight.

1. When I smell a sizzling steak or see a juicy piece of meat, I find it very difficult to keep from eating, even if I have just finished a meal.
2. I usually eat too much at social occasions, like parties and picnics.
3. Sometimes things just taste so good that I keep on eating even when I am no longer hungry.
4. Being with someone who is eating often makes me hungry to eat also.
5. When I see a real delicacy, I often get so hungry that I have to eat right away.

Restrained Eating Index

Respond, true or false, to the following statements. The more that are true, the more likely you are to counteract the effects of disinhibition with restrained eating and remain thinner than you would be otherwise.

1. When I have eaten my quota of calories, I am usually good about not eating anymore.
2. I deliberately take small helpings as a means of controlling my weight.

3. While on a diet, if I eat food that is not allowed, I consciously eat less for a period of time to make up for it.

4. I often stop eating when I am not really full as a conscious means of limiting the amount I eat.

5. I pay a great deal of attention to changes in my figure.

Factors Related to Self-Perception of Overweight

Nutrition Research Newsletter, June 2002 v21 i6 p7

Obesity continues to be a public health problem in the United States, with a steady increase in prevalence and with a trend that varies across population groups. The prevalence of overweight and obesity is higher in racial-ethnic minority populations, especially African-American women, than in whites. The prevalence of obesity may also vary across socioeconomic classes; low socioeconomic status is usually associated with obesity in most Western populations, at least in women. Given the sex, racial, and socioeconomic differences in overweight and obese in the population, the researchers focused their attention on the self-perception of overweight and the difference in this perception among population groups. It is believed that sociocultural factors drive the standards of desirable body weight within cultures, which in turn drive the behaviors such as dieting. Differences in the perception of body weight between African-American and white women has been well documented. Less is known about the differences in self-perception of body weight among men and among individuals in different socioeconomic classes such as education level. The current study sought to compare the self-perception of overweight in the study population according to sex, race/ethnicity, and socioeconomic status and to compare the self-perception of overweight among individuals classified as normal weight, overweight, and obese.

Data from 5440 adults who participated in the 1994 to 1996 Continuing Survey of Food intakes by Individuals and the Diet and Health Knowledge Survey conducted by the US Department of Agriculture were analyzed. Data for analysis included self-perceived weight status, self-reported weight and height, and demographic and socio-economic data.

One-half of the samples were women. Approximately 57% of the individuals were classified as having lower income. Overall, 47% of the sample reported that they were overweight. Self-perceived overweight was significantly higher in women than in men and in whites compared to blacks and Hispanics. The proportion of self-perceived overweight was higher in persons with higher income and higher education.

Self-perception of overweight was more common in women compared with men and in whites compared with blacks or Hispanics. Both the correct and incorrect perception of overweight was more common in normal weight and overweight white women compared with African-American women. More overweight and obese white men correctly perceived their overweight status compared with African-American men.

Self-perceived overweight was found to vary by sex, race/ethnicity, and socioeconomic status. In the present study, more than one-half of the overweight and approximately 20% of obese African-American men and women believed that they were of normal weight. Erroneous perception of body weight may have important health and behavioral implications. In particular, a considerable proportion of overweight individuals may be at risk of obesity if they continue to perceive themselves as having normal weight.

Appendix A

Writing an Essay Examination Answer

WEB LINK
to Appendix A
Related Web
Destinations
http://www.
ablongman.com/
lester

Writing an essay that will answer an examination question differs somewhat from other writing assignments that have been described in the chapters of this text. The examination essay will have time constraints, a different purpose, and only one critical reader—your instructor. In five minutes, twenty minutes, or fifty minutes, you must display your knowledge about a specific issue in your essay answer. You must argue a position and support it with evidence. In many cases there is no absolutely correct answer, but you must create a convincing formulation of ideas.

Your essay answer will accomplish several things:

- Address the problem.
- Explore the issues.
- Illuminate a solution.
- Defend a supposition.
- Make a justification.
- Discuss implications and alternatives.

In addition, good essay answers are not plot summaries of a story, not a quick list of ideas, and not a mere recitation of facts as might be called for in a short-answer quiz. The essay answer calls for, at the very least, a full-blown paragraph that establishes a thesis sentence and defends it.

Your instructor, then, is asking you to demonstrate your ability in three vital areas:

- Comprehension of both the material and the wording of the question.
- Synthesis to pull together ideas from the instructor's lectures, the textbook chapters, and any outside reading you might have done.
- Presentation that demonstrates your mastery of the material as well as your ability to think clearly and logically.

451

Writing essay examination answers has four important stages: reading the entire test to get a quick overview, planning specific answers, writing the essays, and reviewing the paper. Prior to the test, of course, you will have formulated notes on major issues, learned the terminology, and pinpointed key issues that will likely appear on the test.

Reading the Test

Once you have the examination in your hands, take time to examine everything on it in a summary fashion. What must you do? How many questions are there? How much time do you have for each answer? Will the answers be judged differently for value? After this review, and only after it, should you begin working on the first essay answer. Pace yourself and allot time for each essay answer. Remember to save five minutes or more at the end for proofreading.

Planning Your Answer

Instructors are usually looking for certain kinds of answers, and they supply the clue in the wording of the question. Consider the question carefully and try to formulate quick answers to these two questions:

What does the question ask me to do?

What does the instructor anticipate?

Begin jotting down ideas as you consider the language of the question, which will suggest the direction to take in your essay. This language falls into distinct categories. Each carries its own mode of development.

Classification and Analysis

In particular, classification divides and analysis examines; you may be asked to do both. The question might say, rather innocently, "List the issues in the debate on cloning." Beware the temptation to write a list; this is an essay examination, remember, so the instructor expects a full essay that first classifies several issues and then provides your analysis, which examines each in depth, as based on your time allotment. Anything can be analyzed by a systematic separation of the subject into distinct parts. You can then explore underlying principles, reasons, scientific factors, and even historical precedents.

Key words in the language of the question will signal the classification and analysis modes of development. Some of them are: *identify, list, consider, distinguish, catalog, define,* as well as *classify* and/or *analyze.*

Interpretation

A kind of analysis, interpretation generally asks you to explain the meaning of a work of art, a musical composition, a novel, a poem, or something similar. An examination question might request your views on an event in history, a social issue, or even a physical or psychological problem. In essence, your instructor wants your response to your reading on the subject. The question can be specific, such as, "What is your interpretation of German unification after the fall of the Berlin Wall?"

Key words in the language of the question will prompt you to write an interpretation. Some of them are: *interpret, explain, review, explore, discuss, define, elucidate,* and *analyze.*

Evaluation

A question that asks you to evaluate requires interpretation, as discussed above, and something more. It expects appraisal based on a set of criteria that you establish. "Evaluate the behavior of the stock market during the last quarter" requires your assessment of the ebb and flow of economic indicators, which you will have been studying, surely, in the course. Similarly, you may need, based on your studies in the course, a set of criteria for judging a poem, for evaluating nursing home standards, or for judging the merits and failures of a state's gambling laws.

Key words in the language of the question will prompt you to write an evaluation. Some of them are: *justify, prove, disagree with, appraise, assess, judge, criticize,* and *pass judgment on.*

Description

In many cases, the word *describe* asks you for a description of a process, such as "Describe the development of a frog." Your essay would trace and explain a phenomenon of nature. The examination question might ask you to describe the Heimlich maneuver. It might ask you to examine a historical process, as with "Describe the growth of the old gum-shoe detective stories to the modern suspense novel." However, within the context of an essay examination question, *describe* often means *define* or *analyze,* so read the question carefully. For example, if the direction is "Describe the stock market crash of 1939," the instructor does not expect a description of stockbrokers leaping from their 15th-floor windows. Nor does he or she want a description of the general poverty and bread lines on the streets. The instructor *does* want you to explain, define, and analyze the events leading up to the crash and the reasons for it. Consequently, the word *description* can be tricky.

Key words in the language of the question will indicate description should be the basis of your answer. Some of them are: *describe, list, outline, illustrate, condense, summarize, sketch,* and *demonstrate.*

Comparison and Contrast

The words *compare* and *contrast* mean completely different things. To compare means to show similarities: "Explain in 400 words or less how all wars have the same characteristics" or "Defend this statement: Every bear market of Wall Street begins with similar indicators." The word *contrast* means to show differences: "Explain how the Persian Gulf War in 1991 differed demonstrably from the U.S.-Iraq conflict of 2003" or "What is the difference between the NASDAQ Index and the Dow Jones Industrial Average?" Perhaps the first thing you should ask yourself is this: Does the question require comparison, contrast, or a combination of both?

Key words in the question will indicate an approach: *compare, contrast, show similarities, describe differences, distinguish,* or *what associations can you make?*

Cause and Effect

Instructors use the words *cause* and *effect* when they want you to explain why, to give reasons, to examine outcomes, and to predict consequences. In more simple terms, the instructor is asking, "Why did this happen?" and "What can we now expect?" You will see these kinds of questions in all kinds of courses:

Science: Why do stars twinkle?

History: Why are history books focused on the deeds of men?

Sociology: Trace the social effects of the birth control pill.

Economics: What has been the consequence of Europe's conversion to the euro?

Anthropology: Why did the Aztecs practice human sacrifice? How did Hernando Cortez use the practice to his advantage in conquering Montezuma's army?

Study the examination question carefully to determine if you should give reasons why or explain the effects and results. Of course, you might need to discuss both.

Key words in the language of the question will indicate if your response should address causes, effects, or both. Some of them are: *why, how, what led to, trace, consequences of, causes of, results of, causes and effects.*

Discussion of Implications

You may be presented with one or more facts, figures, charts, studies, or lab results and be asked to discuss the implications. For example, "What are the implications of the study on K–3 math instruction in the Rockwell school district?" This type of question can also be used to elicit your reaction to a written passage or essay, as in "What are the implications of Janet C. Hall's proposed revision of the Electoral College?" It can also be used with interpretation: "What are the implications of Huckleberry Finn's preference of life on the raft over life in the river towns along the Mississippi?"

Key words in the language of the question will prompt you to discuss what the source material means in a broader contest. Some of them are: *implications, sugges-*

tions, what inferences can you draw, examine the insinuations, explore this proposition, or *what are the connotations of.*

GUIDELINES

Writing the Essay Examination Answer

- Perform an initial overview of the entire exam to set priorities and allot your time for the different parts.
- Determine the nature of each question to be certain that you know what the instructor expects.
- Before beginning to write, make a few notes, even a rough outline of ideas that you wish to examine. Whenever you have a thought that you want to pursue a little later in the answer, write it down immediately in the margin. Otherwise, it might be lost forever.
- Use the terminology of the course, with words spelled correctly. You might commit to memory a list of key words.
- Remember to include specific bits of information, such as dates; names of characters, authors, and important persons; titles of people and the names of books, documents, articles, and events of history.
- Cite the textbook and other sources from your studies to give evidence of your conscientious reading.
- Structure the essay according to plan. See the discussion about planning your answer in response to the language of the question.
- Review your answer and proofread before submitting the paper to the instructor.

Writing the Essay Examination Answer

Develop your answer logically and thoroughly, using your own variation on this basic plan:

1. Give a quick answer to indicate that you know the material.
2. Develop the passage with an examination of each issue along with your rationale and evidence.
3. Lay out your final conclusions clearly.

Of course, every answer must find its own way, and the instructor's question will often signal the design of your essay answer.

Let us now consider three hypothetical questions for an essay examination and discuss methods for designing and writing the short essay answer.

WEB LINK
to Reading
A.1
http://www.
ablongman.com/
lester

A Question on an Ethical Issue

Let us look at an essay question that includes a portion of a scientific article. Then we'll look at formulating an effective answer. The question below is somewhat technical, but you should now be ready for this kind of challenge.

Examination Question

Reproduced below is part of an article that appeared in the November 2001 issue of JAMA, the *Journal of the American Medical Association*. The title of the article is "Informed Consent for Population-Based Research Involving Genetics." Address the challenge mentioned in the second paragraph and suggest your solutions.

Article Excerpt

The Human Genome Project has produced an explosion of genetic information. Unfortunately, the gap is immense between gene discovery and our ability to use genetic information to improve health and prevent disease. Bridging this gap with population-based knowledge about the contribution of gene variants and gene–environment interactions to disease requires that genetics be integrated into the public health research agenda. The likely outcome of this research will be more effective and targeted medical and public health interventions.

A significant challenge in pursuing these scientific aims is satisfying the basic ethical principles of respect for persons, beneficence, and justice. How these principles are best applied depends on the nature of the risks and potential benefits of a particular study. Genetic research is typically considered sensitive because much of it has been directed toward the investigation of highly predictive mutations in families with a heavy burden of disease. Investigating BRCA1/2 mutations among families that have multiple members affected with breast or ovarian cancer, for example, arouses grave concerns about the psychological and social harms that could result from uncovering information that has significant implications for the health of family members. These concerns are intensified when only limited or unproven interventions are available. Thus, recommendations for the protection of genetic research participants typically call for close scrutiny by an Institutional Review Board (IRB), detailed informed consent procedures, and professional genetic counseling, sometimes both pre- and post-test.

Okay, nothing's ever easy, but this assignment has a built-in answer, and the instructor surely knows it. The first sentence of the second paragraph gives you the classification of three items—respect for persons, beneficence (which means the state or quality of being kind), and justice. Thus, the instructor is asking you for classification and analysis (see page 452), and the essay itself has established the three classifications.

But that's not all, the passage also provides the answers in the last sentence:

Thus, recommendations for the protection of genetic research participants typically call for close scrutiny by an Institutional Review Board (IRB), detailed informed consent procedures, and professional genetic counseling, sometimes both pre- and post-test.

These three considerations match the three issues raised above. The instructor has tossed you a home run pitch, but you still face the task of fleshing out your answer.

If you have about fifteen minutes or less for writing the answer, it would be wise to use this basic design:

1. Give a quick answer to indicate that you know the material.
2. Develop the passage with an examination of each issue along with your rationale and evidence.
3. Present your final conclusions clearly.

Here is student Ralph Conover's opening:

> Medical scientists have improved their genetic information tremendously as a result of the Human Genome Project, but they face some ethical issues as they target the human population for interventions, which, some fear, might be considered interference by the human subjects.

Next, the student introduces the three issues and begins a brief analysis:

> There are three issues that this article examines with regard to ethics—the respect for individuals who participate in the program, their treatment as patients, and the judicial, legal considerations. The target will be toward families that have multiple members afflicted with cancer, and how medical teams want to examine other members of the same family, which quite naturally will cause fear, trauma, and distress in those survivors. Thus, the medical teams must operate within ethical and legal boundaries to protect the integrity of the scientific program as well as the mental well-being of family members.

The student then brings things to a conclusion in order to go to the next question on the test.

> On which side should the balancing scale tilt—toward medical research or interventions for the health of family members. This program recommends protection of participants in three categories. First, provide close examination by a Review Board of the institution. Second, provide consent forms that are fully explained to participants. Third, establish a program for counseling before and after any testing for genetic mutations. That might give a win-win situation for both the medical community and the participants who have volunteered for testing.

In fifteen minutes, this answer is about as much as any student can develop.

A Question on a Social Problem

Instructors expect you to confront the issues of the day, and they will often challenge you to discuss current social problems that affect students on campus as well as the world at large. Here is one such challenge by a professor.

Examination Question

WEB LINK
to Reading
A.2
http://www.
ablongman.com/
lester

Even with the end of most of the totalitarian regimes of the 20th century, like Soviet Russia, the ideology of intrusive government or the Welfare State remains a political philosophy. Sociologist Jack D. Douglas has summarized the growth of intrusive government in his book *The Myth of the Welfare State* (1989), and a passage from his book is printed below. Read the passage and then write a brief essay on one, just one, aspect of your life that has been affected by the new bureaucracy following 9/11. In particular, discuss the pros and cons of that intrusion.

Book Excerpt

America today is ruled by an immense imperial state bureaucracy headed by an imperial president, imperial legislators, and imperial courts, all of which strive mightily every day to extend their powers over our lives. We have drifted blindly, in the quest for the deceitful lures of utopian ideals and greed, into the tyranny of the majority which the founding fathers saw as the greatest danger to the System of Natural Liberty. America today is a government-dominated society in which all of us are controlled in innumerable ways directly and, far more, indirectly by vast and still-proliferating regulatory agencies issuing a torrent of administrative laws, by untold thousands of planning commissions and committees, by soaring police powers, by a tidal wave of legislative laws and activities, and by a tumultuous sea of injudicious court decisions in which revolutionary ukasi [edicts, as by a czar] are masked in the rhetoric of constitutional precedents, rational interpretation, and due process. Interlocking layers of our huge government bureaucracies now dictate minute details of our lives and enforce these dictates with vast police powers. There is literally no realm of life that is still free from massive intrusions by government legislative, regulatory, and judicial fiat.

By examining the question, you should quickly realize that it will require, in part, a personal reaction to events since the September 11, 2001, terrorist attacks but also a comparison and contrast discussion on conditions prior to 9/11 and circumstances after that date, especially with regard to government intrusion and its consequences. Here's how one student, Kamitha Thomas, opened her essay.

Sociologist Jack Douglas has said, "There is literally no realm of life that is still free from massive intrusions by government legislative, regulatory, and judicial fiat." And he was writing this in 1989, well before the tragic events of 9/11. Today, the issue of government intrusion, especially for our protection from terrorism, has been a blessing and interference. We expect the federal government to protect us, and we welcome it, but legislation like the Patriot Act and the formation of Homeland

Security just opens our private lives to public scrutiny. I don't want government agents sniffing around my home or planting wires to listen in on my privacy.

This opening has accomplished several things. It cites from the reading, demonstrating a comprehension of the passage. It relates the issue of intrusion to the 9/11 incident, as required. It answers the question and sets up the comparison/contrast issue to be explored in the conclusion. It mentions current legislation that the government has enacted, showing knowledge of the topic. Next, the student moves to personal experience, as required by the question.

Have I been affected by government intervention in my life? Wow, did you ask the right person! My husband serves in the Army at Fort Campbell, Kentucky, as part of the 101st Airborne Division. Guess what? He was locked down after 9/11, and I didn't see him for four days. I couldn't even go on base. I was scared, and he was frightened for me and the kids. The security in and out of the base is unbelievable. But now, my experience gets even worse—he's in Iraq to fight terrorism there. So yes, my family has been affected deeply by the terrorism of 9/11.

The student provides her personal anecdote about the effects on her life after 9/11. Other students discussed the harassing delays and checks at airports, the new problems with visas and travel abroad, the cancellation of study abroad programs, tighter controls on financial aid, and other similar matters.

However, the student still has one more task—discussing the pros and cons of the matter. Here's how she closed her essay answer.

Despite the inconvenience that clamped a lid on our freedoms and took my husband to Iraq, I still support the President in his fight on terrorism. Until that long-term war is over, I will endure without complaint the hardships, or as Douglas calls it, the "intrusions" on my marriage. For my children's sake, let's protect America, but on the converse side, let's not give away our freedom and liberty to government. We must be vigilant against unnecessary regulations disguised as features for our safety but which in fact control us and snoop into our homes undetected. Our classroom discussions on the Patriot Act—government access to our private Google searches and a new system of nationwide roving wiretaps—these alarm me in spite of my staunch support of the war on terrorism.

The student completes her brief essay by showing both sides of the issue—the intrusions and the necessity. She completes the assignment with her comparison and contrast discussion of her positive feelings about legislation to protect the populace and also with her negative feelings about the power of agencies now operating under the Patriot Act.

A Question on Literature

WEB LINK to Reading A.3
http://www.ablongman.com/lester

The same basic design will prevail for an essay in the humanities, where you address the subject, answer it quickly, build a body of analysis on the primary work, and then focus your conclusion on the artist. This classic paradigm will serve you well. Let's look at an examination question on a literary work and one student's answer.

Examination Question

The narrator Nick Carraway in F. Scott Fitzgerald's novel *The Great Gatsby* has been labeled by some literary critics as a vital feature of the novel, almost as important as Jay Gatsby himself. Major characters often have what is called an "epiphany," which is a life-altering awakening. With that in mind, trace the development of Nick Caraway's character in the novel.

This is how one student, Aimee Claire Beaudoin, responded:

In <u>The Great Gatsby</u> Nick Carraway changes throughout the novel because of the moral questions he faces. Although he is not the main character, Carraway remains at the center of the novel as the narrator, and he experiences both internal and external conflicts that force him to examine his values and to become a more compassionate person.

In the beginning Carraway is a carefree Midwesterner with the morals of an Easterner during the 1920s. His beliefs and desires—drinking heavily, smoking, using women, and wasting money—are typical for the setting of the novel. The only compassion Carraway possesses is for himself. He wants to become wealthy and have fun at the same time. Social standings are more important than values. Not able to realize the severity of the crimes around him, he awakens too late to help anyone but himself. He awakens only after it's too late, after Gatsby is dead.

Carraway buys his women everything they desire, yet he cannot maintain a happy life with women, who also lack human compassion. Nevertheless, after numerous parties, uncaring affairs, and devastating debts, Carraway still has enough human compassion to change drastically. He realizes that love and money do not ensure happiness by observing Gatsby and Daisy and her husband, Tom. Daisy and Tom have affairs that lead to two deaths, one of them the death of an innocent woman. Carraway decides there is no justice in the world. Yet he does not become fully aware until an "innocent victim" is blamed for the woman's murder and, thus, Gatsby is murdered.

As Carraway gazes upon his murdered friend, his desire for wealth and material items collapses. It is a bitter "epiphany." Carraway buries his lack of values when he buries his buddy, and he sets off to find happiness with love, not with money. Fitzgerald uses Nick Carraway to justify the lifestyle he, himself, led while writing the novel, perhaps in the hope of making his own life change, just as Carraway's life changes.

This student has presented an efficient and straightforward answer to the question. The writer opens with an answer to the question, saying conflicts in Carraway's life "force him to examine his values and to become a more compassionate person."

Next, the student gives the vital and necessary analysis of the novel, which has its focus on the narrator Carraway, as required by the question. She does not drift into long discussions of the plot, nor does she get sidetracked by commentary on Gatsby or Daisy, the love interest of Gatsby. Carefully, the student has traced the growth of Carraway and the changes that begin to occur in his character.

Then the student closes with the image of a new Nick Carraway, and she relates her thesis of a changed man to the author himself, F. Scott Fitzgerald.

Reviewing Your Examination Paper

WEB LINK to Exercise A.1
http://www.ablongman.com/lester

Here are a few suggestions for the final moments of the examination period.

- If at all possible, leave time at the end of the period to proofread your answer. Be sure that you have clearly expressed your essay with supporting information and data from the text.

- Correct in the margins any mistakes or omissions that you find. Touching up your draft with corrections is expected. Don't try to rewrite the entire answer.

- Do not leave any question unanswered. Write something! Start by rewording the question and bringing into the paragraph whatever comes to mind. Make connections to ideas you do recall. Even if your answer is incomplete, you still give your instructor an option of granting you a few points instead of the zero he or she must record if you leave the space blank.

- Remain confident. If you have read each question carefully, roughed out a design for the answer, filled the space with a reasonable essay answer for the time allotted, and proofread your answer, you can only relax as you await the paper's return in a few days.

Appendix B

Writing a Scientific Paper: CSE Style

The Council of Science Editors (CSE) sets the standards for writing in the physical and applied sciences, such as

WEB LINK
to Appendix B
Related Web
Destinations
http://www.
ablongman.com/
lester

- chemistry
- computer science
- engineering
- physics
- health
- medicine
- nursing
- biomedicine

It may be a few semesters before you venture into these disciplines, yet health, computer science, chemistry, and physics may be on your schedule sooner than you think. Therefore, this short section on CSE style is supplied as a short guideline for you. If you know the basic note system (see Chapter 11), you can adapt easily to the scientific style.

Handling Citations

The disciplines of the applied sciences use a verb tense similar to APA style, as described on pages 425–426 of Chapter 12. That is, citations usually require the past tense or the present perfect tense, as shown in this next example:

It should be noted that a recent study[3] **has raised** many interesting questions related to photosynthesis, some of which **were answered** by Tucker and Levenson.[4]

A variation on this style is shown here:

The results of the respiration experiment published by Jones (5) had been predicted earlier by Smith (6).

In each case above, the numbers refer to footnotes or a numbered reference citation.

The Scientific Approach

In a science class almost any subject is available to you, but you will approach it in a distinctive manner. Let's see how a medical student might write on the topic of organ donations. You can compare this version with the one on page 387 in Chapter 11, which shows a humanist's approach to the subject.

Taddonia has shown that human tissue can be used to correct many defects.[1] Barnill offered evidence to show that more than 400 people receive corneal transplants each month.[2] Yet the health profession needs more donors. It has been shown[3-6] that advanced care directives by patients with terminal illnesses would improve the donation of organs and tissue, and it would relieve relatives of making any decision. Patients have been encouraged to complete organ donation cards[7] as well as to sign living wills,[8] special powers of attorney,[5] and DNR (Do Not Resuscitate) Orders.[8] It is encouraged that advanced care directives become standard for the terminally ill.

The scientist makes an objective approach without signs of personal commitment, shows a preference for the passive voice and the past tense, and willingly lets a number represent the literature that will be cited in a References section. The applied scientist keeps a focus on the subject at hand, not the authorities. There's even a reluctance to quote from the sources.

Thus, this scientific style carries a certain detachment. The writer does not get personally involved, and the sources are not intrusive in the discussion. Purposely so, it is a style far removed from the personal essay that you are probably accustomed to. However, it is a style you will discover more and more as you work your way through your academic program.

Note: See pages 490–497 for an essay that displays the CSE format.

Designing a Paper in CSE Scientific Format

In the applied sciences, like the social sciences, you will be writing theory, reporting test results, or writing a review. The elements of these designs are explained more fully in Chapter 12, pages 420–424, but here's a quick overview.

Theory in the Applied Sciences

A theoretical analysis in the applied sciences—let's say it's computer science—might, for example, examine these types of subjects:

- intelligent user interfaces
- natural language interaction
- human factors of multimedia systems

- human and social factors of virtual reality
- computer-supported collaborative work
- hypertext and hypermedia
- studies of user behavior
- the psychology of programming
- systems theory and foundations of human-computer interaction
- user interface management systems

Reporting on Empirical Research in the Applied Sciences

Sometimes it's hard to imagine how the sciences contribute to our way of life, but if we combine organic chemistry, physics, and the study of food, we discover some interesting discoveries. For example, Pringles potato chips require a special process, an engineering design, to get each chip the same shape and taste. NASA scientists invented the drink Tang. In truth, foods comprise complex chemical matter, and the convenience foods that you snack on instead of a vegetable-laden lunch are the result of chemical development. Granted, as an undergraduate you will not be conducting scientific investigations anytime soon, but you should understand the nature of such work.

Reviewing the Literature in the Applied Sciences

Pages 422–423 of Chapter 12 establish for you the standards for making a critical evaluation of a published article or book. The titles and subject matter will have their special slant in the applied sciences, just as they do in the social sciences. In chemistry, for example, you might examine and review such articles as "Over-the-Counter Medicines: What's Right for You?" and also "Child-Resistant Packaging for Medicines."

Documenting the Applied Science Paper

WEB LINK
to Reading
B.1
http://www.
ablongman.com/
lester

Use the basic form and style shown in Chapter 11 for endnotes or footnotes and the References list. Of course, the entries have a scientific slant, but the format remains almost the same. A note will look like this:

1. M. Ervin, Autism spectrum disorders: Interdisciplinary teaming in schools, *ASHA Leader,* 2003; 8:4.

The reference entry would appear in this form:

Ervin, M. Autism spectrum disorders: Interdisciplinary teaming in schools.
ASHA Leader, 2003; 8:4-9.

Appendix C

Readings

The eighteen widely diverse readings in this appendix offer you not only sources for writing additional essays but also the opportunity to see in use the major topics of your text—identifying the rich assortment of sources that are available; summarizing, paraphrasing, and quoting passages; evaluating an argument; formulating your own argument; and avoiding plagiarism by practicing academic integrity.

Many of the complete readings and excerpts in the text include helpful marginal notes that relate material to a specific text topic or explain a writing principle. Here, too, each reading includes at least one marginal note that links the selection to a topic in a specific section of one of the twelve chapters (for example, "See Chapter 7, Quoting and Paraphrasing with Precision"). Of course, within the readings you will recognize numerous other opportunities to link a personal story, an argument, an ironic statement, a group of citations, to the topics you have become acquainted with as you have learned to compose from sources.

On Video Games, the Jury Is Out and Confused

Katie Hafner

1   Victoria Taplin of Chevy Chase, Md., has struggled for years with the question of whether to let her two sons, Russell, 11, and Paul, 8, play video games.

2   Ms. Taplin's concerns have traversed miles of psychological terrain mapped closely to what she has heard and read over the years: Games encourage obsessive behavior and rob boys of time for homework and other activities like sports and music; boys who play video games become socially isolated, their only friends existing on a computer screen. Her worst fear? That violent games might somehow bring out aggressive, even violent, impulses in her sons.

In blending a variety of quotations (Chapter 6), the author is able to include a number of contrasting opinions about children and video games; see also Chapter 3, Finding and Evaluating a Writer's Argument

3   Although she has read about a report from researchers at the University of Rochester that playing action video games can have a positive effect by improving visual attention skills, Ms. Taplin remains wary.

WEB LINK
to Exercise
C.1
http://www.
ablongman.com/
lester

4   "The increased peripheral vision business is fine," she said of the study, which was published last week in the journal *Nature*. "But it doesn't address my concerns about violence and what happens to their attention span."

5   Ms. Taplin continued, "With all those images that flicker and flash, how will they be able to sit down and work with something that takes time to understand?"

6   Being a parent has never been easy, and armfuls of literature on the topic of video games aren't making it any easier. Sorting out the debate about the effects of electronic games on children and deciding on a set of guidelines can be an endless, and thankless, task.

7   Even experts disagree. One prominent group consisting mainly of censorship opponents has said that much of the research that links video games to violent behavior is flawed; it joined a court fight against a St. Louis law that barred minors from buying or renting violent games. The law was overturned by a federal appeals court on Tuesday.

8   News reports haven't always been helpful. Much of the news coverage of the Rochester study focused on the fact that a game used in the experiments was Medal of Honor, which requires players to kill or maim enemies. But the study's co-author, Daphne Bavelier, an associate professor of brain and cognitive sciences, said those reports were misguided.

9   "I'm just pulling my hair," said Dr. Bavelier. "It's not about the killing." Nonviolent games would have worked for the study, she said, as long they demanded quick reflexes and pinpoint accuracy.

10   In the face of contradictory, inconclusive or just plain confusing evidence, some parents, like Ms. Taplin, agonize over what limits to set. Others agonize less, but are not always comfortable with what their children are doing or might be doing. Many parents rely on their own instincts and their knowledge of their children to set limits and construct rules.

11   "Parents are the best judges of their children and what they can handle," said Stephanie Greist, communications director for the Free Expression Policy Project, a nonprofit research group in New York that opposes censorship of media violence.

12   For some parents, the latest study was reassuring, if only in a fleeting way. Deborah Jospin, a friend of Ms. Taplin's who lives in Chevy Chase and has a consulting practice working with nonprofit organizations, said she and others in her circle of friends who struggle with the video game issue felt temporarily "forgiven" last week when they heard there were some benefits to video game playing.

13   "Everyone was saying, 'Phew, there's some value, they're not just a mindless, ridiculous waste of time,' " said Ms. Jospin, the mother of two boys, Jonathan and Matthew Dutko, 10 and 8. At the same time, she said, "we all sort of laughed about it, because they'll be trained to look out of the corner of their eye for someone with a gun."

14   Patricia Greenfield, a professor of psychology at the University of California at Los Angeles and director of the Children's Digital Media Center there, said the Rochester study corroborated work that she and colleagues published in 1994. "The cognitive effects are clear," she said. "Video games develop selective visual attention such as skill in monitoring more than one location simultaneously."

15   Professor Greenfield emphasized that nonviolent video games can develop the same visual skills. "Just because a violent game develops visual skills doesn't mean a parent would want their child to play, because it can also stimulate aggression and hostility," she said.

16   Richard Maddock, a psychiatrist at the University of California at Davis whose 13-year-old son plays video games, follows literature on the subject and read the article in *Nature*.

17   "I thought the results were persuasive and made a good case that certain kinds of skills are improved by these video games," Dr. Maddock said. "I don't find it surprising, because most mammals play when they're young, and the purpose of that is the acquisition of skills they're going to need to survive as adults."

18   Lee Stremba, a lawyer who lives in Manhattan with his wife and two children, ages 5 and 12, said he found the study thought-provoking.

19   "I think the games can have a favorable impact," Mr. Stremba said. "We stay away from games of violence, but when it's not games of violence, I do think they get some benefit from games that require hand-eye coordination. I find it pretty amazing what little kids can do with these complicated games."

20   For many parents, the latest study won't do much to change the limits they've spent years working to establish. Dr. Maddock, for example, has worked out a complex set of time restrictions, confining game time to two hours a day and using the games as an incentive to finish homework. His 13-year-old son, Michael, does not own a game device and plays all his games on the family computer.

21   The time restriction is essential, said Dr. Maddock, who worries about what Michael would do if given his druthers. Without the time limit, "he would choose playing video games over almost any other activity," he said.

22   "For me," Dr. Maddock said, "the risk of the games is that they are so compelling that a child, if left to his own devices, might fail to play in other ways and fall behind in the acquisition of other kinds of skills."

23   Ms. Taplin and her husband have set strict conditions on Russell's video game playing.

24   For years, despite Russell's pleas, Ms. Taplin resisted buying him a video game machine. She finally "caved," as she put it, when Russell turned 10 and he was the only one in his peer group without a machine.

25   "They love going to each other's houses, and I didn't want my son to be the only who didn't have video games," said Ms. Taplin. "I didn't want him to be an oddball child, marginalized socially." The first purchase was a Nintendo. Now the family owns a GameCube.

26   When they bought Russell the Nintendo, Ms. Taplin and her husband, Ben Delancy, both lawyers, drew up a contract and had Russell sign it. An excellent student, the boy agreed that he would not let his grades falter. If they did, he agreed, the games would be taken away. He also agreed to respect time limits set by his parents.

27   Ms. Taplin said that there are also restrictions against acquiring games that contain killing and other graphic violence. She said she paid attention to the ratings on a game:

she will not buy it unless it is rated E for everyone, meaning the game is for ages 6 and up. "I go for anything under T," she said, referring to games considered suitable for teenagers.

28   Yet even the E-rated sports games she allows her children to play emphasize violence. The Delancy boys' collection includes Blitz 2002, a football game with more than the usual amount of tackling, and Soccer Slam. The latter, said Andy Reiner, executive editor of *Game Informer Magazine*, "is more like 'American Gladiators' playing soccer."

29   Ms. Taplin said her children sometimes traded games at school. "Sometimes I find these T-rated games in my house that I haven't bought," she said. "I should be cracking down on this a little bit more."

30   Furthermore, she said, "My husband is a little hard to control. Sometimes he lets them rent games with little figures on top of buildings trying to shoot each other off." One is Super Smash Bros. Melee, a T-rated game in which characters battle with swords and laser guns.

31   Ms. Jospin and others say they could not keep tabs on what their children did at friends' houses. "We've all been trained to ask if a friend's parents have guns, but it's kind of invasive to ask the friend's parents, 'And what kinds of video games will they be playing?'" said Shirley Sagawa, Ms. Jospin's business partner, who lives in Alexandria, Va., with her husband and three sons, ages 3, 8 and 10.

32   Enforcing the rules even at home can be tricky. Russell Delancy has a computer in his room but no Internet connection, and he frequently uses his mother's PC to go online to chat with friends.

33   A couple of weeks ago, Ms. Taplin said, she came home and found Russell and a friend in her office using her computer. "I saw a lot of blood," she said. "Someone had just been shot. It was a violent, awful image." She ordered them off the computer immediately. "Since then, I've been watching more closely," she said.

34   Although they might not be well versed in the particulars of the video games their children play, many parents strive for a general balance in a child's day.

35   "Parents need to think about what is being displaced when kids play video games, and balance any possible improvement in visual attention with that," said Jeanne Funk, a professor of psychology at the University of Toledo who has conducted several studies on the effects of video game violence.

36   Although experts continue to disagree on the long-term effects of violent video games, Dr. Funk said that her research suggests that immediately after playing a violent video game, people have more aggressive thoughts, feelings and behaviors.

37   "That doesn't mean they're going to go out and shoot somebody, but it might mean that they're going to be meaner to the people in their life and that they're going to look for the negative," Dr. Funk said.

38   This certainly proved to be the case for Costas Stavrou, an appliance repairman in Minneapolis who for years would not let his two sons, Geovanni, 14, and Johnny, 11, own a Playstation. Eventually, though, for Christmas in 2000 he and his wife gave in, figuring that at least if the children played at home and not at friends' houses, they could be monitored. One of the first games they got was a James Bond game.

39   The results were not pleasant. Mr. Stavrou noticed that each time the boys played, they fought with each other. Johnny grew especially aggressive, Mr. Stavrou said. "It's like he turns into the character of whatever games he's playing," he said.

40   After a few weeks, the Stavrous started to limit the boys to no more than 30 minutes at a time and an extra half-hour if they read for 15 minutes beforehand. The boys no longer play shooting games he said, only car racing and sports games.

41   "Once we put a limit on that stuff, it's been helping with Johnny's behavior," Mr. Stavrou said.

42   To provide balance in her children's lives, Ms. Sagawa of Alexandria said she and her husband employed a "keep them busy" strategy, with enough sports and homework to keep the children's minds off the games. Ms. Sagawa said she has found games useful as both incentive and punishment.

43   "They're too little to take the keys to the car away," she said. "But you can take away the Game Boy."

44   Others cope by banning video games altogether. Joseph Gault a 6-year-old in Palo Alto, Calif., is not allowed to play video games, even at friends' houses. Instead, he is encouraged to read comic books. His father, Nick Gault, said he was comfortable with that decision. "You do see the natural interest in anything violent, but there are so many enjoyable means of media available that just not providing that doesn't seem like we're depriving him of anything," he said.

45   Somehow, though, when Joseph accompanies his father to Best Buy, he knows how to play the video games. "He's picking it up from somewhere" Mr. Gault said.

The End of Work

Jeremy Rifkin

1   From the beginning, civilization has been structured, in large part, around the concept of work. From the Paleolithic hunter/gatherer and Neolithic farmer to the medieval craftsman and assembly line worker of the current century, work has been an integral part of daily existence. Now, for the first time, human labor is being systematically eliminated from the production process. Within less than a century, "mass" work in the market sector is likely to be phased out in virtually all of the industrialized nations of the world. A new generation of sophisticated information and communication technologies is being hurried into a wide variety of work situations. Intelligent machines are replacing human beings in countless tasks, forcing millions of blue and white collar workers into unemployment lines, or worse still, breadlines.

> This finely crafted essay relies on many sources to make its points; see Chapter 2, Searching the Library and Its Sources, and Chapter 9, Writing the Multi-Source Essay

WEB LINK to Exercise C.2
http://www.ablongman.com/lester

2   Our corporate leaders and mainstream economists tell us that the rising unemployment figures represent short-term "adjustments" to powerful market-driven forces that are speeding the global economy into a Third Industrial Revolution. They hold out the

promise of an exciting new world of high-tech automated production, booming global commerce, and unprecedented material abundance.

3   Millions of working people remain skeptical. Every week more employees learn they are being let go. In offices and factories around the world, people wait, in fear, hoping to be spared one more day. Like a deadly epidemic, inexorably working its way through the marketplace, the strange, seemingly inexplicable new economic disease spreads, destroying lives and destabilizing whole communities in its wake. In the United States, corporations are eliminating more than 2 million jobs annually.[1] In Los Angeles, the First Interstate Bankcorp, the nation's thirteenth-largest bank holding company, recently restructured its operations, eliminating 9,000 jobs, more than 25 percent of its workforce. In Columbus, Indiana, Arvin Industries streamlined its automotive components factory and gave out pink slips to nearly 10 percent of its employees. In Danbury, Connecticut, Union Carbide re-engineered its production, administration, and distribution systems to trim excess fat and save $575 million in costs by 1995. In the process, more than 13,900 workers, nearly 22 percent of its labor force, were cut from the company payroll. The company is expected to cut an additional 25 percent of its employees before it finishes "re-inventing" itself in the next two years.[2]

4   Hundreds of other companies have also announced layoffs. GTE recently cut 17,000 employees. NYNEX Corp said it was eliminating 16,800 workers. Pacific Telesis has riffed more than 10,000. "Most of the cuts," reports *The Wall Street Journal*, "are facilitated, one way or another, by new software programs, better computer networks and more powerful hardware" that allow companies to do more work with fewer workers.[3]

5   While some new jobs are being created in the U.S. economy, they are in the low-paying sectors and generally temporary employment. In April of 1994, two thirds of the new jobs created in the country were at the bottom of the wage pyramid. Meanwhile, the outplacement firm of Challenger, Gray and Christmas reported that in the first quarter of 1994, layoffs from big corporations were running 13 percent over 1993, with industry analysts predicting even steeper cuts in payrolls in the coming months and years.[4]

6   The loss of well-paying jobs is not unique to the American economy. In Germany, Siemens, the electronics and engineering giant, has flattened its corporate management structure, cut costs by 20 to 30 percent in just three years, and eliminated more than 16,000 employees around the world. In Sweden, the $7.9 billion Stockholm-based food cooperative, ICA, re-engineered its operations, installing a state-of-the-art computer inventory system. The new laborsaving technology allowed the food company to shut down a third of its warehouses and distribution centers, cutting its overall costs in half. In the process, ICA was able to eliminate more than 5,000 employees, or 30 percent of its wholesale workforce, in just three years, while revenues grew by more than 15 percent. In Japan, the telecommunications company NTT announced its intentions to cut

[1]"When Will the Layoffs End?" *Fortune*, September 20, 1993, p. 40.
[2]Ibid., pp. 54–56.
[3]"Retooling Lives: Technological Gains Are Cutting Costs, and Jobs, in Services," *Wall Street Journal*, February 24, 1994, p. A1.
[4]"Strong Employment Gains Spur Inflation Worries," *Washington Post*, May 7, 1994, pp. A1, A9.

10,000 employees in 1993, and said that, as part of its restructuring program, staff would eventually be cut by 30,000—15 percent of its workforce.[5]

7   The ranks of the unemployed and under-employed are growing daily in North America, Europe, and Japan. Even developing nations are facing increasing technological unemployment as transnational companies build state-of-the-art high-tech production facilities all over the world, letting go millions of laborers who can no longer compete with the cost efficiency, quality control, and speed

> For a discussion of when formal citation is not necessary, see Chapter 7, Common Knowledge Exceptions

of delivery achieved by automated manufacturing. In more and more countries the news is filled with talk about lean production, re-engineering, total quality management, post-Fordism, decruiting, and downsizing. Everywhere men and women are worried about their future. The young are beginning to vent their frustration and rage in increasing antisocial behavior. Older workers, caught between a prosperous past and a bleak future, seem resigned, feeling increasingly trapped by social forces over which they have little or no control. Throughout the world there is a sense of momentous change taking place—change so vast in scale that we are barely able to fathom its ultimate impact. Life as we know it is being altered in fundamental ways.

Substituting Software for Employees

8   While earlier industrial technologies replaced the physical power of human labor, substituting machines for body and brawn, the new computer-based technologies promise a replacement of the human mind itself, substituting thinking machines for human beings across the entire gamut of economic activity. The implications are profound and far-reaching. To begin with, more than 75 percent of the labor force in most industrial nations engage in work that is little more than

> See Chapter 2, Accessing Online Newspapers, for additional source suggestions

simple repetitive tasks. Automated machinery, robots, and increasingly sophisticated computers can perform many if not most of these jobs. In the United States alone, that means that in the years ahead more than 90 million jobs in a labor force of 124 million are potentially vulnerable to replacement by machines. With current surveys showing that less than 5 percent of companies around the world have even begun to make the transition to the new machine culture, massive unemployment of a kind never before experienced seems all but inevitable in the coming decades.[6] Reflecting on the significance of the transition taking place, the distinguished Nobel laureate economist Wassily Leontief has warned that with the introduction of increasingly sophisticated computers, "the role of humans as the most important factor of production is bound to diminish in the same way that the role of horses in agricultural production was first diminished and then eliminated by the introduction of tractors."[7]

---

[5]"Siemens Plans New Job Cuts as Part of Cost Reductions," *New York Times*, July 6, 1993, p. D4; "On the Continent, a New Era Is Also Dawning," *Business Week*, June 14, 1993, p. 41; "NTT's Cut of 10,000 Jobs Could Pave Way for Others," *Financial Times*, September 1, 1993, p. 5.
[6]"Stanching the Loss of Good Jobs," *New York Times*, January 31, 1993, p. C1.
[7]Wassily Leontief, *National Perspective: Definition of Problems and Opportunities*, paper presented at the National Academy of Engineering Symposium, June 30, 1983, p. 3.

9   Caught in the throes of increasing global competition and rising costs of labor, multinational corporations seem determined to hasten the transition from human workers to machine surrogates. Their revolutionary ardor has been fanned, of late, by compelling bottom-line considerations. In Europe, where rising labor costs are blamed for a stagnating economy and a loss of competitiveness in world markets, companies are hurrying to replace their workforce with the new information and telecommunication technologies. In the United States, labor costs in the past eight years have more than tripled relative to the cost of capital equipment. (Although real wages have failed to keep up with inflation and in fact have been dropping, employment benefits, especially health-care costs, have been rising sharply.) Anxious to cut costs and improve profit margins, companies have been substituting machines for human labor at an accelerating rate. Typical is Lincoln Electric, a manufacturer of industrial motors in Cleveland, which announced plans to increase its capital expenditures in 1993 by 30 percent over its 1992 level. Lincoln's assistant to the CEO, Richard Sobow, reflects the thinking of many others in the business community when he says, "We tend to make a capital investment before hiring a new worker."[8]

10   Although corporations spent more than a trillion dollars in the 1980s on computers, robots, and other automated equipment, it has been only in the past few years that these massive expenditures have begun to pay off in terms of increased productivity, reduced labor costs, and greater profits. As long as management attempted to graft the new technologies onto traditional organizational structures and processes, the state-of-the-art computer and information tools were stymied, unable to perform effectively and to their full capacity. Recently, however, corporations have begun to restructure the workplace to make it compatible with the high-tech machine culture.

Re-engineering

11   "Re-engineering" is sweeping through the corporate community, making true believers out of even the most recalcitrant CEOs. Companies are quickly restructuring their organizations to make them computer friendly. In the process, they are eliminating layers of traditional management, compressing job categories, creating work teams, training employees in multilevel skills, shortening and simplifying production and distribution processes, and streamlining administration. The results have been impressive. In the United States, overall productivity jumped 2.8 percent in 1992, the largest rise in two decades.[9] The giant strides in productivity have meant wholesale reductions in the workforce. Michael Hammer, a former MIT professor and prime mover in the restructuring of the workplace, says that re-engineering typically results in the loss of more than 40 percent of the jobs in a company and can lead to as much as a 75 percent reduction in a given company's workforce. Middle management is particularly vulnerable to job loss

---

[8]"Businesses Prefer Buying Equipment to Hiring New Staff," *Wall Street Journal*, September 3, 1993.
[9]"Price of Progress: Re-engineering Gives Firms New Efficiency, Workers the Pink Slip," *Wall Street Journal*, March 16, 1993, p. 1.

from re-engineering. Hammer estimates that up to 80 percent of those engaged in middle-management tasks are susceptible to elimination.[10]

12   Across the entire U.S. economy, corporate re-engineering could eliminate between 1 million and 2.5 million jobs a year "for the foreseeable future," according to *The Wall Street Journal*.[11] By the time the first stage of re-engineering runs its course, some studies predict a loss of up to 25 million jobs in a private sector labor force that currently totals around 90 million workers. In Europe and Asia, where corporate restructuring and technology displacement is beginning to have an equally profound impact, industry analysts expect comparable job losses in the years ahead. Business consultants like John C. Skerritt worry about the economic and social consequences of re-engineering. "We can see many, many ways that jobs can be destroyed," says Skerritt, "but we can't see where they will be created." Others, like John Sculley, formerly of Apple Computer, believe that the "reorganization of work" could be as massive and destabilizing as the advent of the Industrial Revolution. "This may be the biggest social issue of the next 20 years," says Sculley.[12] Hans Olaf Henkel, the CEO of IBM Deutschland, warns, "There is a revolution underway."[13]

13   Nowhere is the effect of the computer revolution and re-engineering of the workplace more pronounced than in the manufacturing sector. One hundred and forty-seven years after Karl Marx urged the workers of the world to unite, Jacques Attali, a French minister and technology consultant to socialist president François Mitterrand, confidently proclaimed the end of the era of the working man and woman. "Machines are the new proletariat," proclaimed Attali. "The working class is being given its walking papers."[14]

14   The quickening pace of automation is fast moving the global economy to the day of the workerless factory. Between 1981 and 1991, more than 1.8 million manufacturing jobs disappeared in the U.S.[15] In Germany, manufacturers have been shedding workers even faster, eliminating more than 500,000 jobs in a single twelve-month period between early 1992 and 1993.[16] The decline in manufacturing jobs is part of a long-term trend that has seen the increasing replacement of human beings by machines at the workplace. In the 1950s, 33 percent of all U.S. workers were employed in manufacturing. By the 1960s, the number of manufacturing jobs had dropped to 30 percent, and by the 1980s to 20 percent. Today, less than 17 percent of the workforce is engaged in blue collar work. Management consultant Peter Drucker estimates that employment in manufacturing is going to continue dropping to less than 12 percent of the U.S. workforce in the next decade.[17]

> See Chapter 11 for details on writing with footnotes

---

[10]"Conference Stresses Job Innovation," *Washington Post*, July 21, 1993, p. D5.; "A Rage to Re-engineer," *Washington Post*, July 25, 1993, p. H1.

[11]Cited in "Into the Dark: Rough Ride Ahead for American Workers," *Training*, July 1993, p. 23.

[12]"Price of Progress."

[13]"Germany Fights Back," *Business Week*, May 31, 1993, p. 48.

[14]Jacques Attali; *Millennium: Winners and Losers in the Coming World Order* (New York: Random House, 1991), p. 101.

[15]Donald L. Barlett and James B. Steele, *America: What Went Wrong?* (Kansas City: Andrews and McMeel, 1992), p. xi.

[16]"Germany Fights Back," p. 49.

[17]Barlett and Steele, p. 18; Peter F. Drucker, *Post-Capitalist Society* (New York: Harper-Collins, 1993), p. 68.

15   For most of the 1980s it was fashionable to blame the loss of manufacturing jobs in the United States on foreign competition and cheap labor markets abroad. Recently, however, economists have begun to revise their views in light of new in-depth studies of the U.S. manufacturing sector. Noted economists Paul R. Krugman of MIT and Robert L. Lawrence of Harvard University suggest, on the basis of extensive data, that "the concern, widely voiced during the 1950s and 1960s, that industrial workers would lose their jobs because of automation, is closer to the truth than the current preoccupation with a presumed loss of manufacturing jobs because of foreign competition."[18]

16   Although the number of blue collar workers continues to decline, manufacturing productivity is soaring. In the United States, annual productivity, which was growing at slightly over 1 percent per year in the early 1980s, has climbed to over 3 percent in the wake of the new advances in computer automation and the restructuring of the workplace. From 1979 to 1992, productivity increased by 35 percent in the manufacturing sector while the workforce shrank by 15 percent.[19]

17   William Winpisinger, past president of the International Association of Machinists, a union whose membership has shrunk nearly in half as a result of advances in automation, cites a study by the International Metalworkers Federation in Geneva forecasting that within thirty years, as little as 2 percent of the world's current labor force "will be needed to produce all the goods necessary for total demand."[20] Yoneji Masuda, a principal architect of the Japanese plan to become the first fully computerized information based society, says that "in the near future complete automation of entire plants will come into being, and during the next twenty to thirty years there will probably emerge . . . factories that require no manual labor at all."[21]

18   While the industrial worker is being phased out of the economic process, many economists and elected officials continue to hold out hope that the service sector and white collar work will be able to absorb the millions of unemployed laborers in search of work. Their hopes are likely to be dashed. Automation and re-engineering are already replacing human labor across a wide swath of service related fields. The new "thinking machines" are capable of performing many of the mental tasks now performed by human beings, and at greater speeds. Andersen Consulting Company, one of the world's largest corporate restructuring firms, estimates that in just one service industry, commercial banking and thrift institutions, re-engineering will mean a loss of 30 to 40 percent of the jobs over the next seven years. That translates into nearly 700,000 jobs eliminated.[22]

19   Over the past ten years more than 3 million white collar jobs were eliminated in the United States. Some of these losses, no doubt, were casualties of increased international

[18]Paul Krugman and Robert Lawrence, "Trade, Jobs and Wages," *Scientific American*, April 1994, pp. 46, 47.
[19]"The Myth of Manufacturing's Decline," *Forbes*, January 18, 1993, p. 40; John Judis, "The Jobless Recovery," *The New Republic*, March 15, 1993, p. 22.
[20]William W. Winpisinger, *Reclaiming Our Future* (Boulder: Westview Press, 1989), pp. 150–151.
[21]Yoneji Masuda, *The Information Society as Post-Industrial Society* (Washington, D.C.: World Future Society, 1980), p. 60.
[22]"Price of Progress."

competition. But as David Churbuck and Jeffrey Young observed in *Forbes*, "Technology helped in a big way to make them redundant." Even as the economy rebounded in 1992 with a respectable 2.6 percent growth rate, more than 500,000 additional clerical and technical jobs simply disappeared.[23] Rapid advances in computer technology, including parallel processing and artificial intelligence, are likely to make large numbers of white collar workers redundant by the early decades of the next century.

20   Many policy analysts acknowledge that large businesses are shedding record numbers of workers but argue that small companies are taking up the slack by hiring on more people. David Birch, a research associate at MIT, was among the first to suggest that new economic growth in the high-tech era is being led by very small firms—companies with under 100 employees. At one point Birch opined that more than 88 percent of all the new job creation was taking place in small businesses, many of whom were on the cutting edge of the new technology revolution. His data were cited by conservative economists during the Reagan-Bush era as proof positive that new technology innovations were creating as many jobs as were being lost to technological displacement. More recent studies, however, have exploded the myth that small businesses are powerful engines of job growth in the high-tech era. Political economist Bennett Harrison, of the H. J. Heinz III School of Public Policy and Management at Carnegie-Mellon University, using statistics garnered from a wide variety of sources, including the International Labor Organization of the United Nations and the U.S. Bureau of the Census, says that in the United States "the proportion of Americans working for small companies and for individual establishments . . . has barely changed at all since at least the early 1960s." The same holds true, according to Harrison, for both Japan and West Germany, the other two major economic superpowers.[24]

21   The fact is that while less than 1 percent of all U.S. companies employ 500 or more workers, these big firms still employed more than 41 percent of all the workers in the private sector at the end of the last decade. And it is these corporate giants that are reengineering their operations and letting go a record number of employees.[25]

22   The current wave of job cuts takes on even greater political significance in light of the tendency among economists continually to revise upward the notion of what is an "acceptable" level of unemployment. As with so many other things in life, we often adjust our expectations for the future, on the basis of the shifting present circumstances we find ourselves in. In the case of jobs, economists have come to play a dangerous game of accommodation with steadily rising unemployment figures, sweeping under the rug the implications of an historical curve that is leading inexorably to a world with fewer and fewer workers.

23   A survey of the past half-century of economic activity discloses a disturbing trend. In the 1950s the average unemployment for the decade stood at 4.5 percent. In the 1960s

---

[23]David Churbuck and Jeffrey Young, "The Virtual Workplace," *Forbes*, November 23, 1992, p. 186; "New Hiring Should Follow Productivity Gains," *Business Week*, June 14, 1993.
[24]Bennett Harrison, *Lean and Mean: The Changing Landscape of Corporate Power in the Age of Flexibility* (New York: Basic Books, 1994), pp. 45–47, 51.
[25]U.S. Bureau of Census, 1987 Enterprise Statistics, Company Summary (Washington, D.C.: U.S. Government Printing Office, June 1991), Table 3.

unemployment rose to an average of 4.8 percent. In the 1970s it rose again to 6.2 percent, and in the 1980s it increased again, averaging 7.3 percent for the decade. In the first three years of the 1990s, unemployment has averaged 6.6 percent.[26]

24   As the percentage of unemployed workers edged ever higher over the postwar period, economists have changed their assumptions of what constitutes full employment. In the 1950s, 3 percent unemployment was widely regarded as full employment. By the 1960s, the Kennedy and Johnson administrations were touting 4 percent as a full employment goal. In the 1980s, many mainstream economists considered 5 or even 5.5 percent unemployment as near full employment.[27] Now, in the mid-1990s, a growing number of economists and business leaders are once again revising their ideas on what they regard as "natural levels" of unemployment. While they are reluctant to use the term "full employment," many Wall Street analysts argue that unemployment levels should not dip below 6 percent, lest the economy risk a new era of inflation.[28]

25   The steady upward climb in unemployment, in each decade, becomes even more troubling when we add the growing number of part-time workers who are in search of full-time employment and the number of discouraged workers who are no longer looking for a job. In 1993, more than 8.7 million people were unemployed, 6.1 million were working part-time but wanted full-time employment, and more than a million were so discouraged they stopped looking for a job altogether. In total, nearly 16 million American workers, or 13 percent of the labor force, were unemployed or underemployed in 1993.[29]

26   The point that needs to be emphasized is that, even allowing for short-term dips in the unemployment rate, the long-term trend is toward ever higher rates of unemployment. The introduction of more sophisticated technologies, with the accompanying gains in productivity, means that the global economy can produce more and more goods and services employing an ever smaller percentage of the available workforce.

A World Without Workers

27   When the first wave of automation hit the industrial sector in the late 1950s and early 1960s, labor leaders, civil rights activists, and a chorus of social critics were quick to sound the alarm. Their concerns, however, were little shared by business leaders at the time who continued to believe that increases in productivity brought about by the new automated technology would only enhance economic growth and promote increased employment and purchasing power. Today, however, a small but growing number of business executives are beginning to worry about where the new high-technology revolution

---

[26]U.S. Department of Labor, Bureau of Labor Statistics, *Employment and Earnings*, January 1994, p. 182; Mishel Lawrence and Jared Bernstein, *The Joyless Recovery: Deteriorating Wages and Job Quality in the 1990s* (Washington, D.C.: Economic Policy Institute, Briefing Paper).

[27]Wallace C. Peterson, *Silent Depression: The Fate of the American Dream* (New York: W. W. Norton, 1994), p. 33.

[28]"The Puzzle of New Jobs: How Many How Fast?" *New York Times*, May 24, 1994, p. D1.

[29]U.S. Bureau of Labor Statistics, *Current Population Survey*, 1993.

is leading us. Percy Barnevik is the chief executive officer of Asea Brown Boveri, a 29-billion-dollar-a-year Swiss-Swedish builder of electric generators and transportation systems, and one of the largest engineering firms in the world. Like other global companies, ABB has recently re-engineered its operations, cutting nearly 50,000 workers from the payroll, while increasing turnover 60 percent in the same time period. Barnevik asks, "Where will all these [unemployed] people go?" He predicts that the pro-portion of Europe's labor force employed in manufacturing and business services will decline from 35 percent today to 25 percent in ten years from now, with a further decline to 15 percent twenty years down the road. Barnevik is deeply pessimistic about Europe's future: "If anybody tells me, wait two or three years and there will be a hell of a demand for labor, I say, tell me where? What jobs? In what cities? Which companies? When I add it all together, I find a clear risk that the 10% unemployed or underemployed today could easily become 20 to 25%."[30]

28   Peter Drucker, whose many books and articles over the years have helped facilitate the new economic reality, says quite bluntly that "the disappearance of labor as a key factor of production" is going to emerge as the critical "unfinished business of capitalist society."[31]

29   For some, particularly the scientists, engineers, and employers, a world without work will signal the beginning of a new era in history in which human beings are liberated, at long last, from a life of backbreaking toil and mindless repetitive tasks. For others, the workerless society conjures up the notion of a grim future of mass unemployment and global destitution, punctuated by increasing social unrest and upheaval. On one point virtually all of the contending parties agree. We are, indeed, entering into a new period in history—one in which machines increasingly replace human beings in the process of making and moving goods and providing services. This realization led the editors of *Newsweek* to ponder the unthinkable in a recent issue dedicated to technological unemployment. "What if there were really no more jobs?" asked *Newsweek*.[32] The idea of a society not based on work is so utterly alien to any notion we have about how to organize large numbers of people into a social whole, that we are faced with the prospect of having to rethink the very basis of the social contract.

30   Most workers feel completely unprepared to cope with the enormity of the transition taking place. The rash of current technological breakthroughs and economic restructuring initiatives seem to have descended on us with little warning. Suddenly, all over the world, men and women are asking if there is a role for them in the new future unfolding across the global economy. Workers with years of education, skills, and experience face the very real prospect of being made redundant by the new forces of automation and information. What just a few short years ago was a rather esoteric debate among intellectuals and a small number of social writers around the role of technology in society is now the topic of heated conversation among millions of working people. They wonder

[30]"Apocalypse—But Not Just Now," *Financial Times*, January 4, 1993, p. D1.
[31]Drucker, p. 68.
[32]"Life on the Leisure Track," *Newsweek*, June 14, 1993, p. 48.

if they will be the next to be replaced by the new thinking machines. In a 1994 survey conducted by *The New York Times*, two out of every five American workers expressed worry that they might be laid off, required to work reduced hours, or be forced to take pay cuts during the next two years. Seventy-seven percent of the respondents said they personally knew of someone who had lost his or her job in the last few years, while 67 percent said that joblessness was having a substantial effect on their communities.[33]

31   In Europe, fear over rising unemployment is leading to widespread social unrest and the emergence of neo-fascist political movements. Frightened, angry voters have expressed their frustration at the ballot box, boosting the electoral fortunes of extreme-right-wing parties in Germany, Italy, and Russia. In Japan, rising concern over unemployment is forcing the major political parties to address the jobs issue for the first time in decades.

32   We are being swept up into a powerful new technology revolution that offers the promise of a great social transformation, unlike any in history. The new high-technology revolution could mean fewer hours of work and greater benefits for millions. For the first time in modern history, large numbers of human beings could be liberated from long hours of labor in the formal marketplace, to be free to pursue leisure-time activities. The same technological forces could, however, as easily lead to growing unemployment and a global depression. Whether a utopian or dystopian future awaits us depends, to a great measure, on how the productivity gains of the Information Age are distributed. A fair and equitable distribution of the productivity gains would require a shortening of the workweek around the world and a concerted effort by central governments to provide alternative employment in the third sector—the social economy—for those whose labor is no longer required in the marketplace. If, however, the dramatic productivity gains of the high-tech revolution are not shared, but rather used primarily to enhance corporate profit, to the exclusive benefit of stockholders, top corporate managers, and the emerging elite of high-tech knowledge workers, chances are that the growing gap between the haves and the have-nots will lead to social and political upheaval on a global scale.

33   All around us today, we see the introduction of breathtaking new technologies capable of extraordinary feats. We have been led to believe that the marvels of modern technology would be our salvation. Millions placed their hopes for a better tomorrow on the liberating potential of the computer revolution. Yet the economic fortunes of most working people continue to deteriorate amid the embarrassment of technological riches. In every industrial country, people are beginning to ask why the age-old dream of abundance and leisure, so anticipated by generations of hardworking human beings, seems further away now, at the dawn of the Information Age, than at any time in the past half century. The answer lies in understanding a little-known but important economic concept that has long dominated the thinking of both business and government leaders around the world.

---

[33]"From Coast to Coast, from Affluent to Poor, Poll Shows Anxiety Over Jobs," *New York Times*, March 11, 1994, p. A1.

Taming the Road Warrior

Janet B. Goehring

1   People out there are driving like nuts," says Maryland State Delegate Timothy Murphy.

2   Congestion coupled with a growing "me first" attitude is creating havoc on the roads as impatient drivers react to stress and tempers flare. Their driving becomes erratic and dangerous—the phenomenon known as aggressive driving or, in its most extreme form, road rage. Drivers know it when they see it. Cars racing down a crowded road, darting in and out of lanes, tailgating, and drivers yelling, honking, and gesturing at others are all behaviors that are recognized as aggressive driving. University of Hawaii psychologist Leon James claims "aggressive driving is not extreme any more; it has become a cultural norm on the highway."

> *Chapter 7, Quoting and Paraphrasing with Precision, gives guidelines as to when you may use only names rather than formal references*

Reason for Fear

WEB LINK
to Exercise
C.3
http://www.
ablongman.com/
lester

3   And drivers are afraid. In a recent member survey by the American Automobile Association Potomac office, motorists named aggressive driving as their top concern on the roads. Drivers fear the aggressive driver (44 percent) more than the drunk driver (31 percent). Ninety percent say they witnessed aggressive driving behavior within the last year, and half said they had seen an extreme example in the past week. Not only are these drivers seeing anger on the roads, they are participants as well. Almost two out of three people in the survey admitted to driving aggressively in the last year. Some of the behaviors admitted to included speeding, gesturing, tailgating, and slowing down and speeding up to get even with another driver.

4   Other surveys point to an epidemic of aggressive driving, and the problem is increasing. Reported incidents of aggressive driving have increased by 7 percent every year since 1990, according to the American Automobile Association Foundation for Traffic Safety. The group studied 10,037 separate incidents reported in police records and newspaper articles between January 1, 1990, and September 1, 1996. David K. Willis, foundation president, warns that "for every aggressive driving incident serious enough to result in a police report or newspaper article, there are hundreds or thousands more which never got reported to the authorities."

5   The National Highway Traffic Safety Administration (NHTSA) reports 41,901 people died and more than 3 million more were injured in police-reported crashes in 1996. NHTSA Administrator Ricardo Martinez estimates that "about one-third of these crashes and about two-thirds of the resulting fatalities can be attributed to behavior associated with aggressive driving."

Solutions Sought

6   Growing concerns about these drivers and the hazards they create on the roads has led to a flurry of activity by safety groups, law enforcement officials, mental health professionals, and legislatures. NHTSA plans a variety of programs to combat aggressive driving including an education and awareness program and a demonstration project to examine effective enforcement.

7   Citizens Against Speeding and Aggressive Driving (CASAD) was formed last February in response to the many dangerous driving incidents in the Washington, D.C., region. According to Lisa Sheikh, its founder and executive director, citizens need "to organize around the problem of speeding and aggressive driving just as they did with drunk driving in the '80s." The group's goals are to slow down traffic, reduce aggressive driving, and increase safety on the roads.

8   Also in the Washington, D.C., area, a coalition of 14 law enforcement agencies and safety groups have organized a program called "Smooth Operator." Their goal is to raise drivers' awareness of dangerous behaviors on the road and to reduce the number of incidents through education and enforcement. The enforcement component occurs in one-week "waves" where heightened patrols specifically target aggressive driving. More than 28,000 "enforcement contacts" were made during the first two waves.

9   Another component of Smooth Operator was the use of a special cellular phone number to help identify aggressive drivers. Motorists who see an incident dial #77 to report it directly to local law enforcement agencies. Bob Wall of the Fairfax County police department says "we raised awareness" of the dangers of aggressive driving and received "a lot of positive feedback from the public."

Zero Tolerance

10   The Arizona Highway Patrol and the Governor's Safety Office teamed together two years ago to start an enforcement effort aimed at aggressive drivers. Patrol officers in unmarked vehicles travel the roads specifically looking for egregious driving behavior such as speeding 20 to 30 mph over the limit, erratic lane changes, and tailgating. Offending drivers get zero tolerance. Everyone pulled over in this program receives a reckless driving or similar ticket.

11   Lieutenant Gary Zimmerman of the highway patrol says that "people have been very supportive" and that they have had good success even though it is hard to measure the effects. Zimmerman says officers have found that they are making a lot of arrests for other crimes in these particular traffic stops. He believes the "aggressive driver has no respect for law enforcement whatsoever."

12   Legislators in Virginia and Maryland struggled with ways to address aggressive driving in the 1997 session. Although none of the bills passed, their introduction increased the visibility of the issue.

13   Virginia Delegate Joe May says that almost everyone in the legislature agrees that aggressive driving is a problem of increasing magnitude. But the behavior is difficult to define and even harder to prosecute. The 1997 bills were a first step to addressing the

problem, and May predicts similar bills will be introduced this coming session. It may take "many approaches to tackle the problem," he says.

14 One of May's approaches was a bill calling for driver improvement programs to add curriculum on aggressive driving. When the Department of Motor Vehicles learned of the bill, it agreed to implement the new curriculum administratively, without legislation.

15 May's second approach failed in the judiciary committee because of constitutional problems, so it will need some changes before he reintroduces it. The bill attempted to give judges the option to convict someone charged with reckless driving with the more serious offense of aggressive driving if circumstances warrant. It would have added a section to the motor vehicle code specifically related to the offense of aggressive driving

> Support for an argument is vital.
> See pages 101–103 for details

and set penalties to be imposed for a conviction. It described aggravating factors that elevated the level of the offense, including actions that cause intentional danger to life, limb and property. Delegate May drafted this language because he sees aggressive driving as a "deliberate act to place someone in danger."

Filling a Void

16 Maryland's Delegate Murphy wants to create an offense of aggressive driving to fill a void that he sees in existing law. His attempt also died in the judiciary committee, but he plans to reintroduce a similar bill this coming session. Murphy says the level of intent for reckless driving, wanton disregard, is difficult to prove in court, and many cases might be lost. The negligent driving charge, he believes, is "too soft" to address the seriousness of aggressive driving behavior. He believes Maryland needs a specific aggressive driving charge that falls between the other two offenses. His original bill stated "an individual is guilty of aggressive driving if the individual drives a motor vehicle in a belligerent, contentious or antagonistic manner that endangers the safety of persons or property." Murphy would like to see fines up to $500 and imprisonment for up to two months. He also would have five points assessed against the violator's driving record.

17 Delegate David Rudolph plans to try again with a bill to impose a cumulative assessment of points and fines against a driver's record when convicted of three or more moving violations arising out of a single traffic incident. Under current Maryland law, if a driver is charged with multiple offenses, he can be convicted and penalized for only the most serious offense. Rudolph hopes to solve the problem of drivers getting away with several offenses when they could be convicted on only one of them. Often aggressive driving incidents involve a series of infractions such as speeding, following too closely, and illegal lane changes.

18 Maryland Delegate Barrie Ciliberti convened a conference on aggressive driving in May 1997. He brought together traffic safety experts, law enforcement officials and politicians to discuss the issues and raise awareness of the problem. Ciliberti prefers to call aggressive driving "deadly driving." He sees the conference as a first step. His goals are to continue momentum by holding conferences, raising awareness, defining the problem, and letting people know they cannot get away with aggressive driving.

The Well-Dressed Dead

Bob Brier

WEB LINK to Exercise C.4
http://www.
ablongman.com/
lester

1   Much of my career has been spent studying mummies, working with cadavers from the ancient and not so ancient past. I am comfortable in the presence of the deceased, but some mummies can still be unnerving, like the two thousand or so in the centuries-old crypts beneath the Capuchin monastery in Palermo, Sicily. There, the dehy-drated dead are clothed in their finest attire—priests wear their robes, military officers their uniforms, and society men and women are dressed as if expecting to attend a dinner or ball. Many of the mummies are stretched out in niches carved into the limestone, but because space was at a premium, others are hung from hooks on the walls. The great majority of them are little more than skeletons today, and their jaws have been loosely wired in place so they appear to be gaping at you.

> Note how the author of this fascinating article on mummies weaves personal experience with outside sources; see Chapter 1, Writing to Combine Personal Ideas with Those of the Sources

2   During a recent visit, I found myself wondering what it was about these mummies that made them so eerie. Perhaps it was their clothes and upright postures. We have always had separate realms for the living and the dead. Call it heaven, the nether-world, or just the graveyard, there's a place where the dead belong and it's not among the living, all dressed up for a day's work or an evening out. The Palermo mummies are ghoulish because they are not doing what they are supposed to be doing—they play at being alive.

3   The Palermo catacombs consist of four long halls cut into the limestone to form a rectangular passageway: the hall of men runs into the hall of women which leads to the hall of professionals, which connects with the hall of monks (a separate hall parallel to this is for priests). The mummies have been grouped according to age and social status. Dozens of long-dead infants, still in their baby clothes and many still in their cribs, keep each other company. Suspended from their hooks, lawyers and physicians congregate in the hall of professionals. Normally one thinks of death as the great equalizer; not so in the catacombs of Palermo. Here class still has its privileges, a kind of Club Dead.

4   The Palermo mummies are not unique. Beneath many of Italy's cathedrals and monasteries are crypts that hold mummies. Most are naturally preserved because of atmospheric conditions that allow bodies to dry out before decaying. Italy also has a long tradition of "Incorruptibles"—saints and religious people who, the faithful believe, were so holy, so pure, that their bodies did not decay. Some are on display as objects of veneration—nuns in their habits and priests in their robes—to reassure us that they are still present.

5   The Capuchins outgrew their original cemetery, begun in 1534, and started excavating the crypts to accommodate the growing numbers of dead brethren. The first inhabitant of the new crypts was Brother Silvestro of Gubbio, who died in 1599. Over the centuries other monks were preserved and interred beneath the monastery in this space, which was initially reserved for them. Eventually, wealthy and influential towns-people, especially monastery benefactors, and their children were permitted to be buried alongside the monks, so they could be visited by family members who would pray for their souls. The last cleric interred here was Brother Riccardo, who died in 1871, but

citizens continued to be placed here for another fifty years. Among the notables spending eternity in Palermo are a son of the king of Tunis, who converted to Catholicism (d. 1622), and the Spanish painter Velasquez (1599–1660).

6   By the nineteenth century, Palermo's mummies were on the tourist map. John Lloyd Stephens, who along with artist Stephen Catherwood popularized the ruins of Mesoamerica, recorded his reaction to the Palermo mummies in his *Incidents of Travel in Egypt, Arabia Petra and the Holy Land* (1837):

7   In the vault of the convent at Palermo I had seen the bodies of nobles and ladies, the men arranged upright along the walls, dressed as in life, with canes in their hands and swords by their sides; and the noble ladies of Palermo lying in state, their withered bodies clothed in silks and satins, and adorned with gold and jewels; and I remember one among them, who, if then living, would have been but twenty, who two years before had shone in the bright constellation of Sicilian beauty, and, lovely as a light from heaven, had led the dance in the royal palace; I saw her in the same white dress which she had worn z the ball, complete even to the white slippers, the belt around her waist, and the jewelled mockery of a watch hanging at her side, as if she had not done with time forever; her face was bare, the skin dry, black, and shrivelled, like burnt paper; the cheeks sunken; the rosy lips a piece of discoloured parchment; the teeth horribly projecting; the nose gone; a wreath of roses around her head; and a long tress of hair curling in each hollow eye.

> The author has decided to display several lengthy quotes; see Chapter 6, Place Long Quotations in an Indented Block

8   Today, Stephen's Sicilian beauty no longer has her watch, and the mummies' clothes are in tatters. The reason can be found in the account of John Ross Browne, an American newspaper reporter and travel writer who devoted an entire chapter of his 1853 book, *Yusef: Or the Journey of the Frangi: A Crusade in the East*, to the Palermo catacombs. According to the "ghostly-looking" monk who led Browne through the crypts, the deceased were visited by relatives once a year who came "to pray for the salvation of their souls, and deck the bodies with flowers." Browne also recorded a mercenary aspect of the Palermo catacombs:

9   From the conversation of the monk, I learnt that these catacombs are supported by contributions from the relatives of the deceased, who pay annually a certain sum for the preservation of the bodies. Each new-comer is placed in a temporary niche, and afterward removed to a permanent place, where he is permitted to remain as long as the contributions continue; but when the customary fees are not forthcoming the corpses are thrown aside on a shelf, where they lie till the relatives think proper to have them set up again.

10   Now, hundreds of tourists a year pay the monks a small entrance fee to see the catacombs' occupants, but family members no longer visit, and there's no one to mend a torn dress or reset a dislocated jaw. The mummies have come by their long-forgotten look honestly.

11   There are no records detailing how the Palermo mummies were preserved, but dehydration was certainly the central process. Small dehydrating rooms were carved out of

the limestone off to the sides of the large halls. There, the newly deceased were placed on racks of ceramic pipes so body fluids would drip onto a thick layer of limestone gravel covering the floor. As far as I could determine, no other procedure was involved. Once a mummy was considered sufficiently dehydrated, it was placed in the crypts with other members of this strange community.

12 Not all of the mummies in the Palermo crypt are ghoulish. One of my favorites is the vice consul to the United States, Giovanni Paterniti, who died here in 1911. He's been dead for more than three quarters of a century and, with his handsome mustache, still looks distinguished. But the undisputed star of the catacombs is Rosalia Lombardo, a seven-year-old girl who died in 1920. Reposing in a glass-topped coffin, Rosalia looks as if she were sleeping. With her pink bow on her head and her long eyelashes still intact, she is one of the best-preserved mummies in the world. How she was prepared is a secret that went to the grave with her embalmer. Rosalia was prepared soon after her death by Professor Alfredo Salafia, a native of Sicily who had studied chemistry and developed a method of embalming that yielded remarkable long-term results. Years before Rosalia's death, Salafia gained a considerable reputation as a master embalmer. In 1905, he prepared the body of Italian Prime Minister Francesco Crispi. When the coffin, in Palermo's Pantheon, was reopened in 1910 for a celebration of fifty years of Sicilian independence, there was no visible change in the body, according to family members who had seen it five years earlier. The same year as the celebration, Salafia sailed for New York to market his services and his secret embalming fluid.

13 To demonstrate the effectiveness of his method, he embalmed an unclaimed body at the Eclectic Medical College of New York, injecting it with several gallons of his secret fluid via the carotid artery. The body was then left unrefrigerated for six months and then was dissected before a group of physicians and morticians. All the tissues were well preserved, firm, and dry, and no odor except that of the embalming fluid was noticeable. For the next decade Salafia advertised his embalming solutions in various journals of the undertaking profession. He never patented his fluid, so when he died in Palermo on January 31, 1933, he took his secret with him. Almost certainly Rosalia was embalmed by arterial infusion of the solution, and there are several strong candidates for the primary ingredient. Arsenic was commonly used in preserving bodies in the nineteenth century, but bichloride of mercury is also a possibility and is still legal as embalming fluid in Italy. The mystery could easily be solved through analysis of a tissue sample, but it is unlikely that the monks of the Capuchin monastery will ever permit anyone to sample Rosalia. I wonder if somewhere, on a back shelf in an embalmer's laboratory, there isn't an old forgotten bottle of Salafia's solution.

14 Although Rosalia is the best preserved of all the mummies in the Palermo crypts, from a scientific point of view, she is far from the most important. Those ghoulish dressed-up skeletons hold a vast amount of information about life and death in Palermo in the seventeenth, eighteenth, and nineteenth centuries. A careful study of their clothing could provide fascinating details about changing fashions. Stripped of their clothing and studied, the mummies would not only lose their eerie appearance but would also tell us about infant mortality, occupational hazards, medical treatment, and life expectancy in Palermo of long ago. But for now they rest in their crypts, safe from the scalpels of inquisitive scholars.

Love Online

Adam Rogers and Kevin Platt

1   Boston journalist Judith Forman first laid eyes on Toronto actor Andrew Pifko after he performed in a play one recent Friday night. But the two were already practically going out. Three months before their first meeting, Forman, 24, and Pifko, 30 had been brought together by that increasingly popular cyberyenta known as JDate.com—the Jewish-singles network. The pair met randomly on one of the site's chat rooms, and before long they were engaged in an intense cross-border flirtation. She sent him photos and a David Gray CD. He sent her a personalized CD mix and flowers. She faxed him at work so he could see her hand-writing. He called her late at night and they would talk for hours. So when Forman flew 550 miles to Toronto and finally met Pifko in the theater lobby after his show, the relationship was a powder keg ready to send fireworks crackling across the Canadian sky. "He picked me up and twirled me around," Forman recalled giddily of their first encounter. "The chemistry was there."

> *Here the authors combine information that is common knowledge (see Chapter 7, Understanding the Common Knowledge Exceptions) with a variety of personal quotes, no doubt from the World Wide Web (see Chapter 2, Searching the Internet and Its Sources)*

WEB LINK to Exercise C.5
http://www. ablongman.com/ lester

2   There's an unexpected denouement to this Boston-Toronto love connection, but we don't want to bum you out just yet. This week, as the world endures another Valentine's Day, 80 million American singles require comfort in the face of the annual assault on their self-esteem. Fortunately, they can take heart: online dating has finally come of age. Membership at the match-making sites is dramatically up, while the blush factor of telling your friends that you're meeting HotPants243 for a latte is significantly down. There are also more sites catering to niche demographics, from CatholicSingles to Good-Genes.com, an introduction service for hoity-toity Ivy League graduates. But the big question—the one that everyone wants answered—is whether meeting your eventual spouse on the Net is more likely than in the real world. For folks like the 34-year-old New Yorker who calls herself Emma324 online, it doesn't matter; online dating is more convenient and comfortable than scouring dreary Manhattan bars and haranguing friends to set her up. "As you get older, you know fewer and fewer people who aren't married," she says. "But go online and there are hundreds of people who are single. It makes you feel a lot less alone."

> *Could there be a bit of irony here also? See Chapter 4, Summarizing a Paragraph That Contains Irony*

3   Connecting people was the original purpose of the Internet. While the first e-mail on the Defense Department's Arpanet in 1971 read "qwertyuiop"—the top line of let-ters on the keyboard—"What are you wearing?" was probably not far behind. By the early '90s, couples were hooking up, breaking up or getting hitched by way of the earli-est AOL chat rooms and Usenet bulletin boards, the hundreds of discussion groups ori-ented around particular topics. But the current online-dating sites now fully mine the matchmaking potential of computers. Sign up with one of these services and you're asked to describe your history, hobbies and personal preferences in a mate. (The weirdest sign-up question, via offbeat TheSpark.com: which would you rather kill, Puppy or Kitten?) Then the sites go to work, pumping your data into software that automatically matches

you with those who share like-minded proclivities (or depravities). Most sites offer the option of adding a photo to your profile.

4   The larger sites, like Matchmaker.com, SocialNet.com and Match.com, boast a tech-savvy, slightly male-skewed audience who are typically in their 20s and 30s and concentrated around major cities. The online-research firm Media Metrix says that the number of people regularly using such sites increased from 3.4 million in December 1999 to 5 million in December 2000. Moreover, the sites report that membership rolls are swelling as V-Day approaches: Matchmaker.com, for instance, reports that its membership jumped 110,000 in the last two weeks. Its smaller counterparts are growing, too, with many niche players like JDate, Altmatch.com (for gays and lesbians) and Singles of Palm Beach catering to specific groups or localities. Since most sites charge users about $20 a month, these services are among the few dot-coms that can claim healthy revenues.

5   Internet dating has also entered the daily fabric of life abroad. In China the practice is helping to break down the centuries-old tradition of parents' or politicians' selecting their children's spouses. One million people have signed up for Club Yuan, the dating section of Chinese portal Sina.com. In Britain, Richard Scase of the University of Kent predicts that one in five single Brits uses the Net or offline dating agencies to date, and expects that number to "explode" over the next five years as globalization brings American-length workdays to the rest of the world. According to Trish McDermott, "VP of Romance" at Match.com, "More and more people are moving from home, putting their career first and getting married later. We bring people together who share core values and a lifestyle but who otherwise would never have met."

6   The whole thing may reek of desperation to teens and the college-age crowd, but older singles may have no other ways to find dates. Gays and lesbians in big cities, in particular, have few social recourses if they don't enjoy the club scene, and fewer still in rural areas, where they might be nervous about picking up the local gay publication. Single parents can also find themselves isolated. "I don't know where I'm supposed to meet men, given that none of them are coming by to see if I want to go out," says Roxanne Fonder Reeve, a 40-year-old working mom from Seattle. She joined Match.com three years ago after splitting up with her husband, and started going on dates nearly every night. Today she's more selective but still finds matches online while maintaining a strict "don't ask, don't tell" policy with her befuddled parents.

7   More mature singles have embraced the trend too. Sixty-one-year-old Dyane Roth of Nashville, Tenn., has been dating on the Net ever since her ex-husband introduced her to it about a year ago. Since then, she's met 11 men in person—after putting their names into Internet sites that check criminal records, just to be sure. Her matches have run the gamut, from a man who severely understated his weight, to a retired Fortune 500 exec with homes in three countries. Now she's working on a book on online dating for seniors. "Most single seniors are either widowed or divorced," she says. "There just aren't that many places to meet people."

8   The potential downside, of course, is that a seemingly perfect match on paper—or in this case on-screen—may not fly in the real world. Or, as McDermott of Match.com puts it, "What we can't measure is chemistry." One problem appears to be false advertising: someone can describe herself online as "a sensuous hybrid of Jennifer Lopez and

Seven of Nine," but in person come off more like Gorgo the Smog Monster in a bad mood. Experienced Net daters urge honesty in all endeavors, since the truth will always out in the end, but many confess to small exaggerations here and there.

9   Perhaps that's why the actual number of known Net-facilitated marriages appears so paltry. Match.com, for instance, claims credit for 1,100 weddings in its six-year existence. On the other hand, those same sites are always touting the heartwarming stories of folks like Mark, a dot-com programmer from Valley Forge, Pa. He

> In effect, this essay is a summary of online dating. See Chapter 4, Writing a Summary

went online after moving to town, met a woman who lived nearby and got married last fall. He says he waited until the last minute to tell friends and family that he had met his fiancee on the Net, but to his surprise, no one made much of a fuss.

10   Skeptical observers of online dating say that the odds of duplicating Mark's feat are long. They argue that the Internet doesn't convey the overall gestalt of a person, that impalpable physical essence that either carbonates your hormones or leaves them flat. Without any information besides the text of e-mail, readers project their own fantasies onto other people. Worse still, says Joseph Walther, a professor at New York's Rensselaer Polytechnic Institute who studies online relationships, users can carefully edit their e-mails and present themselves in the most flattering way. At the same time, the Net's limitations—no raised eyebrows or sarcastic smiles—can induce users to interpret e-mail more positively, while the anonymity of the medium tends to provoke premature personal confessions ("Let me tell you about my divorce"). The result is a positive-feedback loop: they seem nice and interested in you, so you're nice and interested in them. "It doesn't take much to get a dynamic going." Walther says, and the feelings of intimacy often don't translate into the real world.

11   That's what may have happened to George Howard and Becky Ta, who carried on a New York–San Francisco flirtation for a month and a half, complete with frequent e-mailing, phone calls at 5 in the morning and $100 mobile-phone bills. Eventually Howard headed West for their big date. They had a nice weekend, winding their way through Napa Valley wineries on a four-hour train ride and sampling Bay Area restaurants. But it ultimately didn't work out, in part because they disagreed on how serious a commitment each wanted in their lives. "There was an incompatibility that was overshadowed by the intensity of the buildup to the meeting," Howard says.

12   But perhaps both the naysayers, and the proselytizers who promise love online, are just taking the whole thing too seriously. For many participants, virtual dating simply provides the thrill of a chase, a jolt of hormonal caffeine during a long workday or a lonely night. For women on the male-dominated services, it's also a flattering source of instant attention, and some take robust advantage of it. A 31-year-old New Yorker who calls herself Strawberry212 online went on only two "regular" dates in the two years after the breakup of a serious relationship. Then she stuck her profile on the Web and started going on three dates a week while corresponding with two dozen men at a time. When she enthusiastically relayed those figures to one guy she met online, he called her a "cyber-hussy."

13   Guys are just as likely to play the cyberscoundrel. One New Yorker, who calls himself BigBigBigBoy in one of his online accounts, has a technique called "triangulation" that he has shared with friends. First he meets someone online, gets her in a chat room and finds out all her likes (say, Shakespeare and horses) and dislikes (football). Then he

abruptly breaks off contact. Later he logs on using a different name and starts up a new conversation, assuming all the traits she favors ("I love reading 'Hamlet' while riding my Shetland pony when my friends are watching the Super Bowl"). Big . . . Boy writes in an e-mail, "If you're going to meet the person, you can't change who you are, but you can always claim to be someone else."

14   Seasoned online daters say that a satisfying way to pursue love on the Net necessitates a wholesale lowering of expectations. Deidra Reid, 39, joined a host of services last year because she found the African-American community in Silicon Valley to be small and dispersed. Online, she was able to score a date every other night—but that wasn't necessarily a good thing. "I was wearing myself out emotionally, thinking every guy was the one," she says. Now she prefers to exchange a few e-mails with a potential boyfriend, then arrange a quick coffee to see if there are any sparks. Many other veterans follow the same blueprint.

15   So is there hope for finding a match online after all? Most definitely—although sadly, the promised conclusion to the Toronto-Boston love connection is a bit anticlimactic. One week after returning from her trip to Toronto, Judith Forman got a phone call from Andrew Pifko. Forman suspected what was coming, got into bed and pulled her white, flowered comforter over her head. "I've had a few long-distance relationships, and they've all been unsuccessful," he told her, before letting her down gently. Forman was crushed. "The reality is the Internet brings you close, but can't keep you close," she says. Still, Forman is now back on JDate.com, looking for love within her own area code. Which should tell us that Internet dating, despite the hang-ups, is here to stay.

Everything in Entire World Now Collectible

1   In this suburb of Seattle [Kirkland] a man stops off for bread and milk on his way home from work. He's excited about his purchases, but not because he's hungry.

2   "This is awesome," said Marvin Humboldt, 46, lovingly holding his grocery purchases. "I've finally got the full run of the Wonder Bread 'NFL Legends' bags. And this gallon of 2% milk has a red dot on the cap, which means it's a first-run factory proof."

WEB LINK
to Exercise
C.6
http://www.
ablongman.com/
lester

3   Halfway across the country, in Des Moines, IA, 34-year-old Janine Tompkins buys a bucket of Dutch Boy interior paint. She's not planning to do any home redecorating, though.

> This unauthored article uses numerous sources to support its amusing argument that today almost anything is collectible; see Chapter 8 on Writing the Multi-Source Essay

4   "This is the semi-gloss latex," Tompkins said. "Dutch Boy only made 12,500 of these in eggshell white this year. This one's definitely going straight into the display cabinet."

5   According to a report issued Monday by the North American Collector's Association, every single thing currently being manufactured is officially categorized as a collectible.

6   "It used to be that only certain particularly noteworthy or rare items, like *Fantastic Four* # 1 or a 1952 Topps Mickey Mantle card, were considered valuable collector's items.

That's no longer the case," NACA president Bob Gunther said. "If you have any objects of any kind in your home, in your garage, or on the floor of your car, don't throw them away. They could be worth big money someday. In fact, they're probably worth a lot of money right now."

7   Do you have a Taco Bell "Defeat The Dark Side . . . And Win!" cardboard cup-top playing piece from the restaurant's 1999 tie-in sweepstakes for *Star Wars: Episode I* lying around some-where? Chances are you do, because more than 80 million of them were made. But don't throw it out: According to the March issue of *Game-Piece Buyer's Guide*, it's worth $295.

> See Chapter 5 for details on using quotations in your writing and punctuating them properly

8   What about those free postcards handed out at record stores promoting bands nobody's ever heard of and who were dropped from their labels weeks after their debut releases flopped? They're netting big money on eBay. And anything put out before 1980—whether a toy, a set of flatware, or even an unopened roll of toilet paper found in a back cupboard of your grandfather's RV—is a bona fide antique worth anywhere from $100 to millions.

9   "See, normally, things that fall under the category of plentiful, undesirable junk would be worthless, simply due to the laws of supply and demand," said Fred Franks, a Parsippany, NJ, dealer specializing in 1970s-era sponges. "But nobody wants to sell what they collect, anyway: They just want to keep it and hoard it because it's so valuable. So, in this business, we're not talking about demand anymore, just supply, and lots of it. This has caused the value of even mundane, everyday objects to go through the roof. See this lint on my jacket here? That's at least eight, nine bucks worth of lint there. I have Internet quotes to prove it."

10   Manufacturers have caught on to the trend, releasing mundane products such as cigarettes, beer, and snack chips in special collector's "platinum" editions at marked-up prices. As collector mania spreads, even items like floor polish, paper plates, and rubber bands are becoming prohibitively expensive for many Americans.

11   Rarity, once a prerequisite for an item to have collector's value, is no longer relevant. An early sign of this shift occurred in the early '90s, when Marvel Comics encouraged fans to pre-order multiple copies of the much-hyped "Todd McFarlane's *Spider-Man* # 1" because of the book's anticipated collector's value. The issue sold more copies than any comic book in history, but fans still hoarded multiple copies in special dust-proof Mylar bags, in part because of its unique status as the least rare comic book ever.

12   "Rarity is nothing. Do you have any idea how many Beanie Bables are out there?" asked Barbara Mason, editor of *Beanie Baby Illustrated*. "Let's put it this way: There are approximately twice as many Scoop The Pelican Beanie Babies on the planet Earth than there are actual pelicans. And they're worth more, too."

13   Age, once the other major determining factor in an item's worth, is no longer important, either. Items used to only get valuable over long periods of time. Not so anymore, says TransUniverse Collectibles, makers of the official *Star Trek: Voyager* Officers' Club individually wrapped toothpick assortment, which retails for $79.95 and is sold directly to collectors.

14   "Old? Are you kidding? Everything we sell here at TransUniverse goes straight to collectors with no middlemen the day we make it, because these Trekkle types insist on buying [the items] the first day they're out," TransUniverse co-founder Wayne Spoeri said. "We don't need to wait for it to become a collector's item over time—we just print the words 'Collector's Item' right on the package. They're valuable because we only make a limited run of, say, 500,000. Okay, more, but still."

15   With everything on the planet officially collectible, collectors have more items to choose from than ever. Objects such as plastic twist ties from speaker-wire packaging, the tin-foil lining of chewing-gum wrappers, and the little rubbery residue left in magazines when attachments are removed have all jumped sharply in value—and investors see no signs of a slowdown.

16   "I just sold some guy 3,000 gallons of factory runoff from a waste-processing plant in central Illinois," said collectibles dealer Gary Hammond of Louisville, KY. "The government tried unsuccessfully to get the stuff zoned for burial in three states, but now it's in this guy's basement in a glass case. Why? Because it was banned in three states, so now it's collectible. That's the beauty of this business—even stuff that absolutely nobody wants, somebody wants."

The Supreme Court and Physician-Assisted Suicide—The Ultimate Right

Marcia Angell

1   The U.S. Supreme Court will decide later this year whether to let stand decisions by two appeals courts permitting doctors to help terminally ill patients commit suicide.[1] The Ninth and Second Circuit Courts of Appeals last spring held that state laws in Washington and New York that ban assistance in suicide were unconstitutional as applied to doctors and their dying patients.[2,3] If the Supreme Court lets the decisions stand, physicians in 12 states, which include about half the population of the United States, would be allowed to provide the means for terminally ill patients to take their own lives, and the remaining states would rapidly follow suit. Not since *Roe* v. *Wade* has a Supreme Court decision been so fateful.

WEB LINK to Exercise C.7 http://www. ablongman.com/ lester

This reading and one that follows use two very different styles—academic formality and personal experience—to discuss the same complex topic: assisted suicide. Here, see Chapter 11, CMS style

2   The decision will culminate several years of intense national debate, fueled by a number of highly publicized events. Perhaps most important among them is Dr. Jack Kevorkian's defiant assistance in some 44 suicides since 1990, to the dismay of many in the medical and legal establishments, but with substantial public support, as evidenced by the fact that three juries refused to convict him even in the face of a Michigan statute enacted for that purpose. Also since 1990, voters in three states have considered ballot initiatives that would legalize some form of physician-assisted dying, and in 1994 Oregon became the first state to approve such a measure.[4] (The Oregon law was stayed pend-

ing a court challenge.) Several surveys indicate that roughly two-thirds of the American public now support physician-assisted suicide,[5,6] as do more than half the doctors in the United States,[6,7] despite the fact that influential physicians' organizations are opposed. It seems clear that many Americans are now so concerned about the possibility of a lingering, high-technology death that they are receptive to the idea of doctors' being allowed to help them die.

3   In this editorial I will explain why I believe the appeals courts were right and why I hope the Supreme Court will uphold their decisions. I am aware that this is a highly contentious issue, with good people and strong arguments on both sides. The American Medical Association (AMA) filed an amicus brief opposing the legalization of physician-assisted suicide,[8] and the Massachusetts Medical Society, which owns the *Journal* [*New England Journal of Medicine*], was a signatory to it. But here I speak for myself, not the *Journal* or the Massachusetts Medical Society. The legal aspects of the case have been well discussed elsewhere, to me most compellingly in Ronald Dworkin's essay in the *New York Review of Books*.[9] I will focus primarily on the medical and ethical aspects.

4   I begin with the generally accepted premise that one of the most important ethical principles in medicine is respect for each patient's autonomy, and that when this principle conflicts with others, it should almost always take precedence. This premise is incorporated into our laws governing medical practice and research, including the requirement of informed consent to any treatment. In medicine, patients exercise their self-determination most dramatically when they ask that life-sustaining treatment be withdrawn. Although others may sometimes consider the request ill-founded, we are bound to honor it if the patient is mentally competent—that is, if the patient can understand the nature of the decision and its consequences.

5   A second starting point is the recognition that death is not fair and is often cruel. Some people die quickly, and others die slowly but peacefully. Some find personal or religious meaning in the process, as well as an opportunity for a final reconciliation with loved ones. But others, especially those with cancer, AIDS, or progressive neurologic disorders, may die by inches and in great anguish, despite every effort of their doctors and nurses. Although nearly all pain can be relieved, some cannot, and other symptoms, such as dyspnea, nausea, and weakness, are even more difficult to control. In addition, dying sometimes holds great indignities and existential suffering. Patients who happen to require some treatment to sustain their lives, such as assisted ventilation or dialysis, can hasten death by having the life-sustaining treatment withdrawn, but those who are not receiving life-sustaining treatment may desperately need help they cannot now get.

6   If the decisions of the appeals courts are upheld, states will not be able to prohibit doctors from helping such patients to die by prescribing a lethal dose of a drug and advising them on its use for suicide. State laws barring euthanasia (the administration of a lethal drug by a doctor) and assisted suicide for patients who are not terminally ill would not be affected. Furthermore, doctors would not be required to assist in suicide; they would simply have that option. Both appeals courts based their decisions on constitutional questions. This is important, because it shifted the focus of the debate from what the majority would approve through the political process, as exemplified by the Oregon

initiative, to a matter of fundamental rights, which are largely immune from the political process. Indeed, the Ninth Circuit Court drew an explicit analogy between suicide and abortion, saying that both were personal choices protected by the Constitution and that forbidding doctors to assist would in effect nullify these rights. Although states could regulate assisted suicide, as they do abortion, they would not be permitted to regulate it out of existence.

7   It is hard to quarrel with the desire of a greatly suffering, dying patient for a quicker, more humane death or to disagree that it may be merciful to help bring that about. In those circumstances, loved ones are often relieved when death finally comes, as are the attending doctors and nurses. As the Second Circuit Court said, the state has no interest in prolonging such a life. Why, then, do so many people oppose legalizing physician-assisted suicide in these cases? There are a number of arguments against it, some stronger than others, but I believe none of them can offset the overriding duties of doctors to relieve suffering and to respect their patients autonomy. Below I list several of the more important arguments against physician-assisted suicide and discuss why I believe they are in the last analysis unpersuasive.

8   *Assisted suicide is a form of killing, which is always wrong. In contrast, withdrawing life-sustaining treatment simply allows the disease to take its course.* There are three methods of hastening the death of a dying patient: withdrawing life-sustaining treatment, assisting suicide, and euthanasia. The right to stop treatment has been recognized repeatedly since the 1976 case of Karen Ann Quinlan[10] and was affirmed by the U.S. Supreme Court in the 1990 *Cruzan* decision[11] and the U.S. Congress in its 1990 Patient Self-Determination Act.[12] Although the legal underpinning is the right to be free of unwanted bodily invasion, the purpose of hastening death was explicitly acknowledged. In contrast, assisted suicide and euthanasia have not been accepted; euthanasia is illegal in all states, and assisted suicide is illegal in most of them.

9   Why the distinctions? Most would say they turn on the doctor's role: whether it is passive or active. When life-sustaining treatment is withdrawn, the doctor's role is considered passive and the cause of death is the underlying disease, despite the fact that switching off the ventilator of a patient dependent on it looks anything but passive and would be considered homicide if done without the consent of the patient or a proxy. In contrast, euthanasia by the injection of a lethal drug is active and directly causes the patient's death. Assisting suicide by supplying the necessary drugs is considered somewhere in between, more active than switching off a ventilator but less active than injecting drugs, hence morally and legally more ambiguous.

10   I believe, however, that these distinctions are too doctor-centered and not sufficiently patient-centered. We should ask ourselves not so much whether the doctor's role is passive or active but whether the *patient's* role is passive or active. From that perspective, the three methods of hastening death line up quite differently. When life-sustaining treatment is withdrawn from an incompetent patient at the request of a proxy or when euthanasia is performed, the patient may be utterly passive. Indeed, either act can be performed even if the patient is unaware of the decision. In sharp contrast, assisted suicide, by definition, cannot occur without the patient's knowledge and partic-

ipation. Therefore, it must be active—that is to say, voluntary. That is a crucial distinction, because it provides an inherent safeguard against abuse that is not present with the other two methods of hastening death. If the loaded term "kill" is to be used, it is not the doctor who kills, but the patient. Primarily because euthanasia can be performed without the patient's participation, I oppose its legalization in this country.

11   *Assisted suicide is not necessary. All suffering can be relieved if care givers are sufficiently skillful and compassionate, as illustrated by the hospice movement.* I have no doubt that if expert palliative care were available to everyone who needed it, there would be few requests for assisted suicide. Even under the best of circumstances, however, there will always be a few patients whose suffering simply cannot be adequately alleviated. And there will be some who would prefer suicide to any other measures available, including the withdrawal of life-sustaining treatment or the use of heavy

> In effect, these italicized statements are thesis sentences. See "Framing an Initial Statement of Opinion," pages 311-314

sedation. Surely, every effort should be made to improve palliative care, as I argued 15 years ago,[13] but when those efforts are unavailing and suffering patients desperately long to end their lives, physician-assisted suicide should be allowed. The argument that permitting it would divert us from redoubling our commitment to comfort care asks these patients to pay the penalty for our failings. It is also illogical. Good comfort care and the availability of physician-assisted suicide are no more mutually exclusive than good cardiologic care and the availability of heart transplantation.

12   *Permitting assisted suicide would put us on a moral "slippery slope." Although in itself assisted suicide might be acceptable, it would lead inexorably to involuntary euthanasia.* It is impossible to avoid slippery slopes in medicine (or in any aspect of life). The issue is how and where to find a purchase. For example, we accept the right of proxies to terminate life-sustaining treatment, despite the obvious potential for abuse, because the reasons for doing so outweigh the risks. We hope our procedures will safeguard patients. In the case of assisted suicide, its voluntary nature is the best protection against sliding down a slippery slope, but we also need to ensure that the request is thoughtful and freely made. Although it is possible that we may someday decide to legalize voluntary euthanasia under certain circumstances or assisted suicide for patients who are not terminally ill, legalizing assisted suicide for the dying does not in itself make these other decisions inevitable. Interestingly, recent reports from the Netherlands, where both euthanasia and physician-assisted suicide are permitted, indicate that fears about a slippery slope there have not been borne out.[14,15,16]

13   *Assisted suicide would be a threat to the economically and socially vulnerable. The poor, disabled, and elderly might be coerced to request it.* Admittedly, overburdened families or cost-conscious doctors might pressure vulnerable patients to request suicide, but similar wrongdoing is at least as likely in the case of withdrawing life-sustaining treatment, since that decision can be made by proxy. Yet, there is no evidence of widespread abuse. The Ninth Circuit Court recalled that it was feared *Roe* v. *Wade* would lead to coercion of poor and uneducated women to request abortions, but that did not happen. The concern that coercion is more likely in this era of managed care, although understandable, would hold suffering patients hostage to the deficiencies of our health care system. Unfortunately, no human endeavor is immune to abuses. The question is not whether a

perfect system can be devised, but whether abuses are likely to be sufficiently rare to be offset by the benefits to patients who otherwise would be condemned to face the end of their lives in protracted agony.

14   *Depressed patients would seek physician-assisted suicide rather than help for their depression. Even in the terminally ill a request for assisted suicide might signify treatable depression, not irreversible suffering.* Patients suffering greatly at the end of life may also be depressed, but the depression does not necessarily explain their decision to commit suicide or make it irrational. Nor is it simple to diagnose depression in terminally ill patients. Sadness is to be expected, and some of the vegetative symptoms of depression are similar to the symptoms of mental illness. The success of antidepressant treatment in these circumstances is also not ensured. Although there are anecdotes about patients who changed their minds about suicide after treatment,[17] we do not have good studies of how often that happens or the relation to antidepressant treatment. Dying patients who request assisted suicide and seem depressed should certainly be strongly encouraged to accept psychiatric treatment, but I do not believe that competent patients should be required to accept it as a condition of receiving assistance with suicide. On the other hand, doctors would not be required to comply with all requests; they would be expected to use their judgment, just as they do in so many other types of life-and-death decisions in medical practice.

15   *Doctors should never participate in taking life. If there is to be assisted suicide, doctors must not be involved.* Although most doctors favor permitting assisted suicide under certain circumstances, many who favor it believe that doctors should not provide the assistance.[6,7] To them, doctors should be unambiguously committed to life (although most doctors who hold this view would readily honor a patient's decision to have life-sustaining treatment withdrawn). The AMA, too, seems to object to physician-assisted suicide primarily because it violates the profession's mission. Like others, I find that position too abstract.[18] The highest ethical imperative of doctors should be to provide care in whatever way best serves patients' interests, in accord with each patient's wishes, not with a theoretical commitment to preserve life no matter what the cost in suffering.[19] If a patient requests help with suicide and the doctor believes the request is appropriate, requiring someone else to provide the assistance would be a form of abandonment. Doctors who are opposed in principle need not assist, but they should make their patients aware of their position early in the relationship so that a patient who chooses to select another doctor can do so. The greatest harm we can do is to consign a desperate patient to unbearable suffering—or force the patient to seek out a stranger like Dr. Kevorkian. Contrary to the frequent assertion that permitting physician-assisted suicide would lead patients to distrust their doctors, I believe distrust is more likely to arise from uncertainty about whether a doctor will honor a patient's wishes.

16   *Physician-assisted suicide may occasionally be warranted, but it should remain illegal. If doctors risk prosecution, they will think twice before assisting with suicide.* This argument wrongly shifts the focus from the patient to the doctor. Instead of reflecting the condition and wishes of patients, assisted suicide would reflect the courage and compassion of their doctors. Thus, patients with doctors like Timothy Quill, who described in a 1991

Journal article how he helped a patient take her life,[20] would get the help they need and want, but similar patients with less steadfast doctors would not. That makes no sense.

17   *People do not need assistance to commit suicide. With enough determination, they can do it themselves.* This is perhaps the cruelest of the arguments against physician-assisted suicide. Many patients at the end of life are, in fact, physically unable to commit suicide on their own. Others lack the resources to do so. It has sometimes been suggested that they can simply stop eating and drinking and kill themselves that way. Although this method has been described as peaceful under certain conditions,[21] no one should count on that. The fact is that this argument leaves most patients to their suffering. Some, usually men, manage to commit suicide using violent methods. Percy Bridgman, a Nobel laureate in physics who in 1961 shot himself rather than die of metastatic cancer, said in his suicide note, "It is not decent for Society to make a man do this to himself."[22]

18   My father, who knew nothing of Percy Bridgman, committed suicide under similar circumstances. He was 81 and had metastatic prostate cancer. The night before he was scheduled to be admitted to the hospital, he shot himself. Like Bridgman, he thought it might be his last chance. At the time, he was not in extreme pain, nor was he close to death (his life expectancy was probably longer than six months). But he was suffering nonetheless—from nausea and the side effects of antiemetic agents, weakness, incontinence, and hopelessness. Was he depressed? He would probably have freely admitted that he was, but he would have thought it beside the point. In any case, he was an intensely private man who would have refused psychiatric care. Was he overly concerned with maintaining control of the circumstances of his life and death? Many people would say so, but that was the way he was. It is the job of medicine to deal with patients as they are, not as we would like them to be.

19   I tell my father's story here because it makes an abstract issue very concrete. If physician-assisted suicide had been available, I have no doubt my father would have chosen it. He was protective of his family, and if he had felt he had the choice, he would have spared my mother the shock of finding his body. He did not tell her what he planned to do, because he knew she would stop him. I also believe my father would have waited if physician-assisted suicide had been available. If patients have access to drugs they can take when they choose, they will not feel they must commit suicide early, while they are still able to do it on their own. They would probably live longer and certainly more peacefully, and they might not even use the drugs.

20   Long before my father's death, I believed that physician-assisted suicide ought to be permissible under some circumstances, but his death strengthened my conviction that it is simply a part of good medical care—something to be done reluctantly and sadly, as a last resort, but done nonetheless. There should be safeguards to ensure that the decision is well considered and consistent, but they should not be so daunting or violative of privacy that they become obstacles instead of protections. In particular, they should be directed not toward reviewing the reasons for an autonomous decision, but only toward ensuring that the decision is indeed autonomous. If the Supreme Court upholds the decisions of the appeals courts, assisted suicide will not be forced on either patients or doctors, but it will be a choice for those patients

who need it and those doctors willing to help. If, on the other hand, the Supreme Court overturns the lower courts' decisions, the issue will continue to be grappled with state by state, through the political process. But sooner or later, given the need and the widespread public support, physician-assisted suicide will be demanded of a compassionate profession.

For more details on the CSE style see Appendix B

References

1. Greenhouse L. High court to say if the dying have a right to suicide help. *New York Times.* October 2, 1996:A1.
2. *Compassion in Dying* v. *Washington*, 79 F.3d 790 (9th Cir. 1996).
3. *Quill* v. *Vacco*, 80 F.3d 716 (2d Cir. 1996).
4. Annas GJ. Death by prescription—the Oregon initiative. *N Engl J Med* 1994;331:1240–3.
5. Blendon RJ, Szalay US, Knox RA. Should physicians aid their patients in dying? The public perspective: *JAMA* 1992;267:2658–62.
6. Bachman JG, Alcser KH, Doukas DJ, Lichtenstein RL, Corning AD, Brody H. Attitudes of Michigan physicians and the public toward legalizing physician-assisted suicide and voluntary euthanasia. *N Engl J Med* 1996;334:303–9.
7. Lee MA, Nelson HD, Tilden VP, Ganzini L, Schmidt TA, Tolle SW. Legalizing assisted suicide—views of physicians in Oregon. *N Engl J Med* 1996;334:310–5.
8. Gianelli DM. AMA to court: no suicide aid. *American Medical News.* November 25, 1996:1, 27, 28.
9. Dworkin R. Sex, death, and the courts. *New York Review of Books.* August 8, 1996.
10. *In re: Quinlan*, 70 N.J. 10, 355 A.2d 647 (1976).
11. *Cruzan* v. *Director, Missouri Department of Health*, 497 U.S. 261, 110 S. Ct. 2841 (1990).
12. Omnibus Budget Reconciliation Act of 1990, P.L. 101–508, sec. 4206 and 4751, 104 Stat. 1388, 1388-115, and 1388-204 classified respectively at 42 U.S.C. 1395cc(f) (Medicare) and 1396a(w) (Medicaid) (1994).
13. Angell M. The quality of mercy. *N Engl J Med* 1982;306:98–9.
14. van der Maas PJ, van der Wal G, Haverkate I, et al. Euthanasia, physician-assisted suicide, and other medical practices involving the end of life in the Netherlands, 1990–1995. *N Engl J Med* 1996;335:1699–705.
15. van der Wal G, van der Maas PJ, Bosma JM, et al. Evaluation of the notification procedure for physician-assisted death in the Netherlands. *N Engl J Med* 1996;335:1706–11.
16. Angell M. Euthanasia in the Netherlands—good news or bad? *N Engl J Med* 1996;335:1676–8.
17. Chochinov HM, Wilson KG, Enns M, et al. Desire for death in the terminally ill. *Am J Psychiatry* 1995;152:1185–91.
18. Cassel CK, Meier DE. Morals and moralism in the debate over euthanasia and assisted suicide. *N Engl J Med* 1990;323:750–2.
19. Angell M. Doctors and assisted suicide. *Ann R Coll Physicians Surg Can* 1991;24:493–4.

20. Quill TE. Death and dignity—a case of individualized decision making. *N Engl J Med* 1991;324:691–4.
21. Lynn J, Childress JF. Must patients always be given food and water? *Hastings Cent Rep* 1983;13(5):17–21.
22. Nuland SB. *How we die*. New York: Alfred A. Knopf, 1994:152.

Last Right

Carrie Carmichael

WEB LINK to Exercise C.8
http://www.ablongman.com/lester

1   Last fall, a friend asked if she could jump out my 11th-floor window. She had esophageal cancer and was planning ahead. If the chemotherapy didn't shrink her tumor, and if surgery didn't offer her continued life, she wanted something "swift and certain." Pills wouldn't be an option if she couldn't swallow anymore. She didn't have a doctor to assist her dying, so injectible morphine would be harder to get. Five years ago, she was hit by a vehicle in Mexico. "The impact didn't hurt," she told me, and she figured that hitting the ground wouldn't either.

This reading and the previous one use two very different styles to discuss the same complex topic. Here, see Chapter 1, Using Personal Experience As a Source for Writing

2   We had been very close for decades and shared the major events of adult life: children's births, divorce, career crises. Nursing her husband through his protracted death from colon cancer had galvanized her. She did not want to hang on to life after the prognosis was hopeless and her pain became unrelenting. We had just sat down to a lunch I had made for us when she asked. She wanted to jump out my window because she lived in a brownstone. Her chemo-necessitated wig, picked up that morning at a shop in my neighborhood, sobered me. This was not one of our hypothetical suicide conversations—this one was real. It took my breath away, I put down my fork and said, "Let's take a look."

3   My bedrooms and living room look out on West 72nd Street. In the master bedroom, I threw up the sash. A sidewalk covering in place during some building restoration had just been removed. She was glad it was gone, she said. Nothing to break her fall. But nothing to protect pedestrians either.

4   "You couldn't be in the apartment," she ordered. "The doorman would see you leave. I would have to be here alone." She didn't want me suspected of criminal behavior.

5   "We'll see what the chemo does," I said. "And then we'll talk more." I was devastated that a woman I loved was threatened with imminent death. I wanted to be a good friend, but asking me to help her commit suicide changed everything.

6   After she left, I had second thoughts about my swift acquiescence. This was hardly a casual request. Could I sleep in my room after my friend plunged to her death from my window? Could I enter and leave passing the place where her crumpled body had lain? Which of my neighbors, which of the toddlers in strollers and kids on scooters, would see her fall?

7   On the phone a few days later, when I told her that I was waffling, she said just the offer was comforting. She felt calmer. We talked about other tall buildings with

windows that open, as well as other options. Neither of us had experience with pills, injectible drugs or morphine suppositories. Nor did we know how much help she might need with any of them.

8   A few months passed and her life shrank. She moved south to live with her daughter's family. She slept much of the time, was racked with coughing and in more and more pain. My friend felt that as long as her pleasure in life was greater than her pain, she would choose to live. But she didn't want to wait until she didn't have the strength to take her own life. In February, I traveled to see her for what I knew would be the last time. "I've found a hotel with balconies," she told me during my visit. "Will you drive me there?" And I agreed. Since her family would inherit her estate, she didn't want them accused of hastening her death.

9   On the day we chose, her bag was packed and she was ready to go. As I drove onto the block, her daughter and family were saying goodbye. After they pulled away, we walked to the car. I opened the door for her. We put our seatbelts on. When we pulled up at the hotel, with the car in park, we hugged. Exchanged "I love you's." "If you change your mind, just call," I reminded her. We wept, and she waved goodbye as I turned and left. The ordinary act of dropping off a friend at a hotel was made extraordinary by her intention. I was the last person who loved her to see her alive.

10   When her friends heard how she had taken her own life, reaction was mixed. Shock at her method. Admiration of her courage. How could she do that? they asked angrily. What a legacy for her family. Thoughtless. Why didn't she cut her wrists in a warm bath? Why didn't somebody duct-tape her to her bed and find a better way? I kept quiet.

11   For my own part, I have asked myself why I did what I did. I didn't want to let her down. Although I gave her permission to take her own life, I feel guilty that I did not find an easier way for her to die. At the same time, I'm angry that she didn't use a gentler method, one with a more peaceful end. Something easier for her. Something much easier for me.

12   So far, no punishments. No rewards. But I am haunted. I'm not at peace. Will I ever be? I know my friend is where she wanted to be, on her own terms. She had the right to take her own life, and her loved ones were right to help her, but there should have been a better way. I am left with the legacy of my friend's desperation and the prospect of my own.

I'm with the Band: A Short Cultural History of Wedding Rings

Nita Rao

1   One day not long ago, Herman Rotenberg, who owns a place called 1,873 Unusual Wedding Rings on West 47th Street, was asked to engrave grape leaves on matching platinum bands for a guy who peeled off the label from his favorite bottle of red wine and

> This essay uses multiple sources. See Chapter 9

**WEB LINK
to Exercise
C.9**
http://www.
ablongman.com/
lester

brought it into the shop. "Buying a wedding band is not like buying a pair of shoes," says Rotenberg, whose business dates from 1947. (The name is a bit of a misnomer: The shop actually stocks over 3,000 rings with price tags between $50 and $5,500.) "It's the most important part of the wedding, at least in terms of what marriage really means."

2   Rotenberg has plenty of history to back him up. The roots of his business actually reach 4,800 years, to the ancient Egyptians, who are generally credited with the genesis of wedding band exchanges when they started twisting reedy plants like hemp into rings. These, they believed, were linked to supernatural, immortal love, a circle with no end. The Romans upgraded to iron. (Revoltingly enough, though, for Roman women, bands signified a binding legal agreement of ownership by their husbands, who regarded rings as tokens of purchase.) Both the Egyptians and Romans wore bands on the fourth finger of the left hand because they swore the *vena amoris*, or love vein, connected directly from that finger to the heart, thereby joining a couple's destiny.

3   Puzzle rings, with their labyrinthine, twining bands, came next. The rings, which first showed up in Asia more than 2,000 years ago, followed early trade routes to the Middle East, where they were commonly used as wedding bands, especially by sultans and shelks who required each of their wives to wear one as a pledge of devotion. Sterling silver poesy rings caught fire during the Renaissance and remained a wedding band option for Europeans throughout the 17th century. Poesy bands were etched with verse and frequently cited in Shakespeare's plays. ("Is this a prologue or the poesy of a ring?" asks Hamlet.)

> *Though these are the exact words spoken by Hamlet, you might want to paraphrase rather than quote more difficult phrases from the past; see Chapter 5, Paraphrasing Archaic Language*

4   Meanwhile, in the United States, the Puritans renounced wedding bands altogether, because they considered jewelry decadent frippery. Colonial Americans traded wedding thimbles instead of rings, arguing that thimbles were acceptable because they were practical (After marriage, women often sliced off the bottom of the thimble and—vollà!— created a wedding band.)

5   Victorians lavished their rings with whimsical "twin hearts" and flowers; the Edwardians mooned over intricate patterns of leaves and delicate filigree. The art deco movement, with its simple, abstract, modern lines, ruled wedding band designs in the 1920s and 1930s. For the first time, during World War II, it became the regular custom for men to wear rings as a reminder of wives back home.

6   Not every society started off exalting the concept of the ring, though. Indians, Pakistanis, and Bangladeshis, for instance, "picked up wedding bands from Western culture," said Ayesha Hakki Niazl, editor of *Bibi*, a Houston-based bridal and fashion magazine targeting South Asian communities. "People just follow according to wherever they're living."

7   If they are living in America in the 21st century, what they want, according to Rotenberg, is platinum. But then again, Rebecca Silva of the incredibly rarefied antique jewelry store Fred Leighton says there's also "a trend toward color: thin ruby bands and sapphires. You don't want to do what your mother did." *Bibi's* Hakki Niazi notes that rose-colored gold is hot, as is estate jewelry. "You get more character, so you and 50 other people might not have the same ring."

8   For some couples, even personalized grape leaves aren't intimate enough. They want a truly indelible symbol of their love. After "Pamela and Tommy Lee did all that business," tattoo artist Mike Bellamy of Triple X Tattoo on West 36th Street says, he was solicited by three or four couples anxious to ink their fingers with initials or Celtic knots in Ileu of wedding bands. Bellamy warns that this is a complicated process. "The difficult way a finger heals up makes it unpredictable," says Bellamy. "It might look blurry or spread out." And of course, unlike a diamond, which, if things turn sour, can always find its way to the pawnshop, it may take some creative thinking to modify the permanent art on your digit. Still, ingenious solutions are possible: When Pamela Anderson and Tommy Lee split up, she altered her "Tommy" wedding band tattoo to a "Mommy" winding around her finger.

Sorenstam Fails to Conquer, but Wins Fans on the Way

Jere Longman

WEB LINK
to Exercise
C.10
http://www.
ablongman.com/
lester

1   The talk-show hosts set up behind the 18th green kept referring to the opening round of the Colonial golf tournament as Annika Sorenstam's first rodeo.

2   If she could not quite stay on the bull today, at least she had grabbed it by the horns. And she was definitely not one of the clowns.

This article about a recent first-time sports event mixes common knowledge (see Chapter 7, Understanding the Common Knowledge Exceptions) with quotations that necessitate appropriate citation (see Chapter 6, Following the Conventions for Quoting Others in Your Text)

3   Sorenstam did not make the cut today in her first PGA tournament, failing to qualify for the final two rounds after shooting a five-over-par 145 over the first two days.

4   But if she disappointed herself slightly, she did not seem to disappoint the tens of thousands who packed the course, 5 deep along the fairways, 10 deep around the greens, to see her make history, if not enough putts.

5   This year's Colonial caused the biggest clamor in Fort Worth since Pete the Python escaped from the local zoo in 1954, said the novelist Dan Jenkins, a longtime resident of the city and a former golfing partner of Ben Hogan's. On a street across from the course, people turned their lawns into parking lots, some charging as much as $60 a car.

6   Todd Wiseman, a college student on summer vacation, said he could not in good faith ask for more than $30. Still, he stood to make $500 or $600 on the day. "It beats working at Chili's," he said.

7   People climbed into trees to watch Sorenstam play the fourth hole, and two women danced and shimmied when she drove her tee shot 20 feet from the pin. Across the fairway, spectators stood outside the course and peered through the fence as if watching a construction project, which, in a social engineering sense, this was.

8   Sorenstam had said this was a personal challenge, not a skirmish of gender politics, but she became a mirror in which any number of agendas were reflected.

9   "Merrill Lynch discriminates against women," said a sign towed over the course by a plane.

10   In some ways, this seemed like a battle in a war that had already been won. Title IX has mandated equal opportunity in collegiate athletics for three decades, and women in the United States have their names on the marquee above men in tennis, figure skating, soccer and track and field.

11   When Gabriela Andersen-Scheiss, a resident of Idaho representing Switzerland, staggered to the finish line of the marathon at the 1984 Los Angeles Olympics, women won the right to exhaust themselves in public. The 1999 Women's World Cup final, played before 90,000 people in the Rose Bowl and 40 million American television viewers, demonstrated that people would shower big money and big attention on women's sports.

12   Billie Jean King's campy tennis victory over Bobby Riggs in 1973 provided symbolic proof that women could compete against men. Riggs, though, was well over the hill. It was left to Sorenstam to demonstrate that the best woman golfer could compete head to head against the best men.

13   David Blair of Burleson, Tex., said that most of his golfing buddies believed that Sorenstam did not belong here. "They feel threatened," Blair said as he stood near the ninth fairway. "It's more macho to think the best woman can't beat the worst man."

14   Yet again, Texas provided the front line in the war between the sexes.

15   Babe Didrikson Zaharias, who in 1945 became the last woman to play on the PGA Tour, was from Beaumont. King defeated Riggs in Houston's Astrodome. This, too, is the home state of President George W. Bush, whose administration, many advocates of women's sports fear, will soon dilute Title IX.

16   The burning question this week was this: Would Sorenstam hold her own, or would she become the biggest monument to defeat since the Alamo?

17   Her one-over-par 71 on Thursday, played amid extreme pressure, appeared to have proved her point. She seemed mentally fatigued today, and her success here could at best be called modified. But it hardly mattered to the gallery.

18   "She showed that women can compete," said Kelly Hearn of Grapevine, Tex.

19   Donna Lopiano, the executive director of the Women's Sports Foundation, said in a recent interview that male and female athletes should be appreciated in the same light as boxers in different weight classes. Just because a lightweight cannot defeat a heavyweight does not make him any less of a boxer, she said. Nor should a woman be considered deficient if she cannot defeat most men, she said.

20   Given increased opportunities to compete, and no longer shunned for having muscles, women are now pushing against the physiological barrier that, scientists say, gives men a 10 to 15 percent advantage in athletic performance because of increased muscle mass and oxygen-carrying capacity. Paula Radcliffe of Britain has pushed the women's marathon record as close as it has ever been to the men's. And Sorenstam showed she belonged here.

21   "She got here with intense desire and talent," Penny Pulz, a former L.P.G.A. player, said today as she held up a sign that said "Go Annika Go." "God didn't say, 'This is men's-only talent.' "

22　　What happens next? Geno Auriemma, who has coached the Connecticut women's basketball team to four N.C.A.A. championships, has often said that too many people expect too little of female athletes, that the "good try" is often considered sufficient.

23　　Some golf experts have suggested that Sorenstam should urge the L.P.G.A. to toughen its courses. Perhaps with greater challenges, the thinking goes, women will respond with greater performances.

24　　Julie Foudy, captain of the national women's soccer team, said on "Nightline" Thursday that she was somewhat saddened by Sorenstam's appearance here. Not that Sorenstam was playing, but that she had been a dominant golfer for so long but received great attention only when she played against men.

25　　To be sure, prejudices and skepticism must still be overcome.

26　　Peter Kostis, a CBS golf analyst, seemed to suggest Thursday on ESPN's *Outside the Lines* that Sorenstam's need to seek a challenge against men implied that the women's tour was inferior. On the same show, Debbie Schlussel, a conservative political commentator, called Sorenstam's presence a publicity stunt similar to Bill Veeck's use of a midget, Eddie Gaedel, to bat in the major leagues in 1951.

27　　Carl Tiderius, an orthopedic surgeon who, like Sorenstam, is from Sweden, carried a miniature Swedish flag as he watched today. He said that the qualities that made Sorenstam a great golfer also made some Swedes temper their regard for her.

28　　"Don't get too big, don't think you are something," he explained of the egalitarian Swedish attitude. "Some think she is too tough, too much of an individualist. But that's why we find her here."

29　　And her presence seemed to render critical remarks by golfers like Vijay Singh and Nick Price churlish and petulant. Singh was personally lambasted on the course by a man here who wore a hat shaped like a chicken. If Singh did not have the courage to show up, Sorenstam did.

30　　"I really tested myself," she said. "That's why I'm here. I have a lot to be proud of."

Designer Babies

Sharon Begley

1　　It is only a matter of time. One day—a day probably no more distant than the first wedding anniversary of a couple who are now teenage sweethearts—a man and a woman will walk into an in vitro fertilization clinic and make scientific history. Their problem won't be infertility, the reason couples now choose IVF. Rather, they will be desperate for a very special child, a child who will elude a family curse. To create their dream child, doctors will fertilize a few of the woman's eggs with

> This essay demonstrates the methods for using summary, paraphrase, and quotation to build an essay on a complex topic. See Chapters 4–6

her husband's sperm, as IVF clinics do today. But then they will inject an artificial human chromosome, carrying made-to-order genes like pearls on a string, into the fertilized egg. One of the genes will carry instructions ordering cells to commit suicide. Then the doctors will place the embryo into the woman's uterus. If her baby is a boy, when he becomes an old man he, like his father and grandfather before him, will develop prostate cancer. But the cell-suicide gene will make his prostate cells self-destruct. The man, unlike his ancestors, will not die of the cancer. And since the gene that the doctors gave him copied itself into every cell of his body, including his sperm, his sons will beat prostate cancer, too.

2   Genetic engineers are preparing to cross what has long been an ethical Rubicon. Since 1990, gene therapy has meant slipping a healthy gene into the cells of one organ of a patient suffering from a genetic disease. Soon, it may mean something much more momentous: altering a fertilized egg so that genes in all of a person's cells, including eggs or sperm, also carry a gene that scientists, not parents, bequeathed them. When the pioneers of gene therapy first requested government approval for their experiments in 1987, they vowed they would *never* alter patients' eggs or sperm. That was then. This is now. One of those pioneers, Dr. W. French Anderson of the University of Southern California, recently put the National Institutes of Health on notice. Within two or three years, he said, he would ask approval to use gene therapy on a fetus that has been diagnosed with a deadly inherited disease. The therapy would cure the fetus before it is born. But the introduced genes, though targeted at only blood or immune-system cells, might inadvertently slip into the child's egg (or sperm) cells, too. If that happens, the genetic change would affect that child's children unto the nth generation. "Life would enter a new phase," says biophysicist Gregory Stock of UCLA, "one in which we seize control of our own evolution."

3   Judging by the 70 pages of public comments NIH has received since Anderson submitted his proposal in September, the overwhelming majority of scientists and ethicists weighing in oppose gene therapy that changes the "germline" (eggs and sperm). But the position could be a boulevard wide and paper thin. "There is a great divide in the bioethics community over whether we should be opening up this Pandora's box," says science-policy scholar Sheldon Krimsky of Tufts University. Many bioethicists are sympathetic to using germline therapy to shield a child from a family disposition to cancer, or atherosclerosis or other illnesses with a strong genetic component. As James Watson, president of the Cold Spring Harbor Laboratory and codiscoverer of the double-helical structure of DNA, said at a recent UCLA conference, "We might as well do what we finally can to take the threat of Alzheimer's or breast cancer away from a family." But something else is suddenly making it OK to discuss the once forbidden possibility of germline engineering: molecular biologists now think they have clever ways to circumvent ethical concerns that engulf this sci-fi idea.

4   There may be ways, for instance, to design a baby's genes without violating the principle of informed consent. This is the belief that no one's genes—not even an embryo's—should be altered without his or her permission. Presumably few people would object to being spared a fatal disease. But what about genes for personality traits, like risk-taking or being neurotic? If you like today's blame game—it's *Mom's fault* that you inherited her temper—you'll love tomorrow's: she intentionally stuck you with that personality quirk. But the child of tomorrow might have the final word about his genes, says UCLA geneticist John Campbell. The designer gene for, say, patience could be paired with an on-off switch, he says. The child would have to take a drug to activate the patience gene. Free to accept or reject the drug, he retains informed consent over his genetic endowment.

5   There may also be ways to make an end run around the worry that it is wrong to monkey with human evolution. Researchers are experimenting with tricks to make the introduced gene self-destruct in cells that become eggs or sperm. That would confine the tinkering to one generation. Then, if it became clear that eliminating genes for, say, mental illness also erased genes for creativity, that loss would not become a permanent part of man's genetic blueprint. (Of course, preventing the new gene's transmission to future generations would also defeat the hope of permanently lopping off a diseased branch from a family tree.) In experiments with animals, geneticist Mario Capecchi of the University of Utah has designed a string of genes flanked by the molecular version of scissors. The scissors are activated by an enzyme that would be made only in the cells that become eggs or sperm. Once activated, the genetic scissors snip out the introduced gene and, presto, it is not passed along to future generations. "What I worry about," says Capecchi, "is that if we start messing around with [eggs and sperm], at some point—since this is a human enterprise—we're going to make a mistake. You want a way to undo that mistake. And since what may seem terrific now may seem naive in 20 years, you want a way to make the genetic change reversible."

6   There is no easy technological fix for another ethical worry, however: with germline engineering only society's "haves" will control their genetic traits. It isn't hard to foresee a day like that painted in last year's film "Gattaca," where only the wealthy can afford to genetically engineer their children with such "killer applications" as intelligence, beauty, long life or health. "If you are going to disadvantage even further those who are already disadvantaged," says bioethicist Ruth Macklin of Albert Einstein College of Medicine, "then that does raise serious concerns." But perhaps not enough to keep designer babies solely in Hollywood's imagination. For one thing, genetic therapy as done today (treating one organ of one child or adult) has been a bitter disappointment. "With the exception of a few anecdotal cases," says USC's Anderson, "there is no evidence of a gene-therapy protocol that helps." But germline therapy might actually be easier. Doctors would not have to insinuate the new gene into millions of lung cells in, say, a cystic fibrosis patient. They could manipulate only a single cell—the fertilized egg—and still have the gene reach every cell of the person who develops from that egg.

7   How soon might we design our children? The necessary pieces are quickly falling into place. The first artificial human chromosome was created last year. The Human Genome Project decoded all 3 billion chemical letters that spell out our 70,000 or so genes. Animal experiments designed to show that the process will not create horrible mutants are underway. No law prohibits germline engineering. Although NIH now refuses to even consider funding proposals for it, the rules are being updated. And where there is a way, there will almost surely be a will: none of us, says USC's Anderson, "wants to pass on to our children lethal genes if we can prevent it—that's what's going to drive this." At the UCLA symposium on germline engineering, two-thirds of the audience supported it. Few would argue against using the technique to eradicate a disease that has plagued a family for generations. As Tuft's Krimsky says, "We know where to start." The harder question is this: do we know where to stop?

How We Got to Two Million: How Did the Land of the Free Become the World's Leading Jailer?

Vince Beiser

1   In the heart of Los Angeles, just a few blocks from the downtown commuter hub of Union Station, stands a pair of massive concrete towers. Tinted in bland desert tones of beige and dull rose, the angular, unapologetically functional buildings could be some big corporation's headquarters, or a hospital, or perhaps a research facility. Only the windows—nearly all of them narrow, vertical slits through which nothing can be seen from the outside—give a clue to what the complex really is: the Twin Towers Correctional Facility, which happens to be the world's biggest jail.

> What position is the author taking in this reading about incarceration in the United States? The topic of Argument is discussed at length in Chapter 3; see Finding and Evaluating A Writer's Argument, and Looking for Support to an Argument

2   Linking the towers is a low-lying structure called the Inmate Reception Center. This is the first stop for every inmate taken into custody by the Los Angeles Country Sheriff's Department. Each day, as many as 6,000 prisoners pass through the IRC's vast labyrinth of hallways and holding areas. It takes a staff of 800 just to log, sort, and monitor them, from booking and fingerprinting to locking them up in cells crowded with other inmates.

**WEB LINK
to Exercise
C.11**
http://www.
ablongman.com/
lester

3   Local taxpayers spent nearly $400 million to build the Towers in the early '90s because older jails were overflowing with arrestees. The jails, in turn, serve as gateways for the 21 new prisons the state has built since 1980. Over the past two decades, the number of inmates in those prisons has grown sevenfold, to more than 160,000. It cost California taxpayers nearly $5.3 billion to build the new lockups — and it costs another $4.8 billion every year to keep them running.

4   California is no anomaly; over the last 20 years, the number of prisoners has surged in every state in the country. While the nation's population has grown by only 20 percent, the number of Americans held in local, state, and federal lockups has doubled — and then doubled again. The United States now locks up some two million people. That's far more than ever before, and more than any other country on earth. And the number is still growing.

5   Most Americans never even see, let alone become ensnared in, the nation's vast correctional system. But the unprecedented prison boom is incurring unprecedented costs—economic, social and ethical—that are being paid, one way or another, by everyone in this country. The MotherJones.com Incarceration Atlas, and the articles that accompany it, tally up part of the bill. Drawing on records from a wide range of federal and state agencies, the Atlas provides a state-by-state look at the growing expense of our penal system. It details how many residents of each state are currently imprisoned compared with 1980, the soaring number of nonviolent drug offenders, and the increasing racial disparity in imprisonment. It also shows how the bill for prisons has grown six times

faster per capita than spending on higher education, which has actually dropped or remained stagnant in many states.

6   How did this happen? How did a nation dedicated to the principle of freedom become the world's leading jailer? The answer has little to do with crime, but much to do with the perception of crime, and how that perception has been manipulated for political gain and financial profit. From state legislatures to the White House, politicians have increasingly turned to tough-on-crime policies as guaranteed vote-getters. That trend has been encouraged by the media, which use the public's fearful fascination with crime to boost ratings, and by private-prison companies, guards' unions, and other interests whose business depends on mass-scale incarceration.

7   Prisons certainly aren't expanding because more crimes are being committed. Since 1980, the national crime rate has meandered down, then up, then down again—but the incarceration rate has marched relentlessly upward every single year. Nationwide, crime rates today are comparable to those of the 1970s, but the incarceration rate is four times higher than it was then. It's not crime that has increased; it's punishment. More people are now arrested for minor offenses, more arrestees are prosecuted, and more of those convicted are given lengthy sentences. Huge numbers of current prisoners are locked up for drug offenses and other transgressions that would not have met with such harsh punishment 20 years ago.

8   In return for spending so much more on prisons today—a nationwide total of some $46 billion annually—taxpayers might reasonably expect a corresponding drop in crime. But most experts agree that prisons have done little to make communities safer. A recent study by the University of Texas estimates that while the number of inmates has grown by more than 300 percent since the late 1970s, that growth is responsible for no more than 27 percent of the recent drop in crime. Indeed, many states with the fastest increases in prison populations received no commensurate payback in crime reduction. In West Virginia, for example, the incarceration rate ballooned by 131 percent over the past decade—but crime dropped by only 4 percent. Meanwhile, in neighboring Virginia, incarceration rose just 28 percent, but crime dropped 21 percent.

9   Locking up more people only reduces crime if those being locked up are serious criminals, experts say. "If it's a serial rapist, that makes an impact on crime," explains Marc Mauer, assistant director of the Sentencing Project, a research and advocacy group based in Washington, D.C. "But if it's a kid selling crack on the corner, that just creates a job opening for someone else." Most experts agree that a combination of other factors, including the until-recently strong economy, more effective policing, and the decline of the crack trade have done far more than incarceration to cut crime.

10   The fuse of America's prison explosion was lit in the late 1960s. With a war raging in Vietnam, riots sweeping major cities, and protests rolling college campuses, middle America was hungry for action to restore law and order. In 1968, Congress responded with a major anti-crime bill that doled out millions of dollars to local police and increased the federal government's involvement in local law enforcement. Crime had never been much of an issue in federal politics before, but Richard Nixon made it a central campaign theme that year. Shortly after his election, Nixon added narcotics to the list of America's leading enemies, sounding the call to a national war on drugs. "The abuse of

drugs has grown from essentially a local police problem into a serious national threat to the personal health and safety of millions of Americans," he declared.

11   Around the same time, states began eliminating the flexibility that judges and parole boards had long exercised in deciding how to punish offenders and when to let them out of prison. Liberals denounced the old system as rife with racial discrimination; conservatives slammed it for being too lenient. Both called for fixed, mandatory sentences for specific crimes. In 1973, New York governor Nelson Rockefeller set a new standard by pushing through what are still some of the nation's harshest sentences for drug crimes, including mandatory 15-year prison terms for possessing small amounts of narcotics. The concept caught on: By now, nearly every state and the federal government have some form of mandatory sentencing.

12   Mandatory sentencing leaves judges little room to maneuver: Those found guilty are automatically locked up for predetermined amounts of time. "With the power of release taken away from parole authorities, and judge's discretion also removed, it was left by default to the legislatures to set sentencing policy," says Franklin Zimring, a criminologist at the University of California at Berkeley. "Punishment became a political decision." Even archconservative US Supreme Court Justice William Rehnquist thinks these laws have more to do with politics than criminology. "Mandatory minimums," he has said, "are frequently the result of floor amendments to demonstrate emphatically that legislators want 'to get tough on crime.' "

13   Throughout the 1980s, lawmakers competed with one another to introduce ever-harsher penalties. States like California ratcheted up their anti-drug efforts, deploying helicopters in paramilitary crackdowns on marijuana growers. President Reagan doubled the FBI's budget, boosted spending on federal prisons, and expanded drug prosecutions—even though crime rates were falling. The crusading spirit was so contagious that even liberals like Walter Mondale, Reagan's opponent in the 1984 election, advocated using the armed forces to fight drugs.

14   The battle against drugs erupted into full-scale war when a new drug called crack began spreading in the inner cities, bringing with it a surge of violent crime—and an epidemic of fevered media coverage. "In the summer of '86, members of Congress were literally elbowing each other aside for TV time to talk about drugs," recalls Eric Sterling, who served then as counsel to the House Judiciary Committee. A new wave of laws boosting penalties still higher for drug offenders soon followed. Drugs were taking the place of the Cold War as an issue on which politicians could try to out-posture each other. "In the mid-1980s, there was general prosperity and the Soviets were not a threat," adds Zimring. "We were running out of enemies. Crack was the narcotic equivalent of the H-bomb scare."

15   A clear lesson had emerged: For politicians, crime pays. George Bush proved it in 1988, when he summoned the specter of paroled rapist Will Horton to haunt Michael Dukakis out of the election. Bill Clinton topped him in 1992 by leaving the campaign trail to personally deny clemency to a mentally retarded man on death row in Arkansas.

16   Punishment had become a solidly bipartisan issue. In 1994, with crime on the decline for four years, Congress approved yet another major anti-crime package, raising drug penalties and providing billions of dollars for more prisons and police. In the early

1990s, the federal government and 23 states ratcheted up the mandatory-minimum concept another notch, by passing "three strikes" laws dictating prison sentences of 25 years to life for third felonies. These laws have undoubtedly taken some violent offenders out of circulation—but they have also handed out life sentences to thousands of people for petty crimes from possessing a stolen bicycle or stealing a spare tire.

17   By now, federal surveys show there are more than 236,000 drug offenders in state prisons—more than 10 times the 1980 figure. The surge in the number of drug prisoners has leveled off in recent years, but prison populations continue to grow, thanks in large part to increases in sentencing. Now, "it's less about more people going in than about people staying longer," says Allen Beck, chief of correctional statistics at the federal Bureau of Justice Statistics.

18   Locking up so many inmates is not cheap. *Design-Build*, a construction trade magazine, estimates that 3,300 new prisons were built during the 1990s at a cost of nearly $27 billion, with another 268 in the pipeline valued at an additional $2.4 billion. And construction costs are only the beginning. In Los Angeles, the Twin Towers complex sat empty for over a year after it was completed because the county had run short of money to operate it.

19   Housing each prisoner costs taxpayers around $20,000 per year—money that often comes at the expense of other social programs. Between 1980 and 1996, prison spending shot up in every state, while spending on higher education declined in 19 states. In May, Colorado lawmakers diverted $59 million earmarked for improving colleges and universities into paying for prison expansion.

20   The prison boom has also exacted a tremendous social cost. Blacks, Hispanics, and Native Americans are all incarcerated at rates far higher than that for whites. On any given day, nearly a third of all young black males are in prison, on probation, or on parole. Blacks are more likely than whites to be arrested, convicted, and given longer sentences for drug offenses—despite surveys showing that whites use drugs at the same rate as blacks do.

21   There are signs, however, that America may finally be sobering up from its two-decade incarceration binge. "Drug courts" that allow judges to order offenders into treatment rather than jail are gaining favor across the country. New York is looking at rewriting its harsh drug laws. Voters in many states have approved medical-marijuana initiatives in recent years. And many political leaders, including conservatives like New Mexico governor Gary Johnson, are calling for a less-punitive approach to drugs. Perhaps partly as a result, in the past few years prison populations have declined slightly in 11 states.

22   At the same time, a grassroots anti-prison movement is flowering across the country, from student campaigns to force campus caterer Sodexho-Marriott to divest their holdings in private prisons, to advocacy groups like Families Against Mandatory Minimums. "In the '80s all the prison activists were aging '60s people like me," says Ruthie Gilmore, a veteran organizer in California. "But now there are many more young people and families of prisoners, especially mothers, involved. It's still much smaller than, say, the '80s anti-apartheid movement, but it's going in that direction."

23   But while there are more critics of prisons today, there are also more interest groups with a financial stake in the incarceration complex—groups with a powerful incentive to

ensure that the influx of inmates continues. Private, for-profit prison corporations are a multibillion dollar industry. Other companies reap hundreds of millions of dollars annually by providing health care, phones, food, and other services in correctional facilities. Many small towns and rural communities, their traditional industries in decline, lobby for new prisons in their areas. Such forces are working actively to increase the number of citizens being locked up. Private prison companies contribute to a policy group called the American Legislative Exchange Council that has helped draft tougher sentencing laws in dozens of states, and the California prison guards union doles out millions every election to tough-on-crime candidates.

24   The media, especially television, also have a vested interest in perpetuating the notion that crime is out of control. With new competition from cable networks and 24-hour news channels, TV news and programs about crime—dramatic, cheap to produce, and popular—have proliferated madly. According to the Center for Media and Public Affairs, crime coverage was the number-one topic on the nightly news over the past decade. From 1990 to 1998, homicide rates dropped by half nationwide, but homicide stories on the three major networks rose almost fourfold.

25   Such saturation coverage has a direct impact on public perceptions. In one 1997 survey, 80 percent of those polled said that news stories about violent crime increase their fear of being victimized. As a result, it has become "impossible to run an election campaign without advocating more jails, harsher punishment, more executions, all the things that have never worked to reduce crime but have always worked to get votes," concludes George Gerbner, former dean of University of Pennsylvania's Annenberg School of Communications and one of the nation's foremost experts on the media. "It's driven largely, although not exclusively, by television-cultivated insecurity."

26   While prison growth has slowed in the last couple of years, it's a long way from stopping. From mid-1999 to mid-2000, the number of people behind bars nationwide rose by 56,660. And the Bush administration has made clear that it is committed to continuing the push for more prisons. After all, as governor of Texas, George W. Bush oversaw a correctional system that locks up residents at a higher rate than any other state except Louisiana. The new attorney general, John Ashcroft, and the new drug czar, John Walters, are both renowned hard-liners. And in its very first budget proposal, the Bush team laid out an explicit priority: more money for federal prisons, to the tune of $1 billion.

Two Cheers for Consumerism

James Twitchell

1   Of all the strange beasts that have come slouching into the 20th century, none has been more misunderstood, more criticized, and more important than materialism. Who but fools, toadies, hacks, and occasional loopy libertarians have ever risen to its defense? Yet the fact remains that while materialism may be the most shallow of the 20th century's variousisms, it has been the one that has

> Here, you might review Chapter 3, *Discovering a Writer's Intentions*, as you determine the position taken by the author

WEB LINK to Exercise C.12 http://www. ablongman.com/ lester

ultimately triumphed. The world of commodities appears so antithetical to the world of ideas that it seems almost heresy to point out the obvious: Most of the world most of the time spends most of its energy producing and consuming more and more stuff. The really interesting question may be not why we are so materialistic, but why we are so unwilling to acknowledge and explore what seems the central characteristic of modern life.

2   And why is the consumer so often depicted as powerless? From Thomas Hobbes in the mid-17th century ("As in other things, so in men, not the seller but the buyer determines the price") to Edwin S. Gingham in the mid-20th century ("Consumers with dollars in their pockets are not, by any stretch of the imagination, weak. To the contrary, they are the most merciless, meanest, toughest market disciplinarians I know"), the consumer was seen as participating in the meaning-making of the material world. How and why did the consumer get dumbed down and phased out so quickly? Why has the hypodermic metaphor (false needs injected into a docile populace) become the unchallenged explanation of consumerism?

3   Much of our current refusal to consider the liberating role of consumption is the result of who has been doing the describing. Since the 1960s, the primary "readers" of the commercial "text" have been the well-tended and tenured members of the academy. For any number of reasons—the most obvious being their low levels of disposable income, average age, and the fact that these critics are selling a competing product, "high culture" (which is also coated with its own dream values)—the academy has casually passed off as "hegemonic brain-washing" what seems to me, at least, a self-evident truth about human nature: We like having stuff.

4   In place of the obvious, they have substituted an interpretation that they themselves often call vulgar Marxism. It is supposedly vulgar in the sense that it is not as sophisticated as the real stuff, but it has enough spin on it to be more appropriately called Marxism lite. Go into almost any cultural studies course in this country and you will hear consumerism condemned: What we see in the marketplace is the result of the manipulation of the many for the profit of the few. Consumers are led around by the nose. We live in a squirrel cage. Left alone, we would read Wordsworth, eat lots of salad, and meet to discuss Really Important Subjects.

5   The idea that consumerism creates artificial desires rests on a wistful ignorance of history and human nature, on the hazy, romantic feeling that there existed some halcyon era of noble savages with purely natural needs. Once we're fed and sheltered, our needs have always been cultural, not natural. Until there is some other system to identify and satisfy those needs and yearnings, capitalism—and the culture it carries with it—will continue not just to thrive, but to triumph.

6   In the way we live now, it is simply impossible to consume objects without consuming meaning. Meaning is pumped and drawn everywhere throughout the modern commercial world, into the farthest reaches of space and into the smallest divisions of time. Commercialism is the water we all swim in, the air we breathe, our sunlight and shade. Currents of desire flow around objects like smoke in a wind tunnel.

7   This isn't to say that I'm sanguine about material culture. It has many problems that I have glossed over. Consumerism is wasteful; it is devoid of other-wordly concerns. It is heedless of the truly poor, who cannot gain access to the loop of meaningful information that is carried through its ceaseless exchanges. On a personal level, I struggle

daily to keep it at bay. For instance, I fight to keep Chris Whittle's Channel One TV and all place-based advertising from entering the classroom; I contribute to PBS in the hope that they will stop slipping down the slope of commercialism (although I know better); I am annoyed that Coke has bought all the "pouring rights" at my school and is now trying to do the same to the world; and I just go nuts at Christmas.

8 But I also realize that while you don't have to like it, it doesn't hurt to understand it and our part in it. We have not been led astray. To some degree, the triumph of consumerism is the triumph of the popular will. You may not like what is manufactured, advertised, packaged, branded, and broadcast, but it is far closer to what most people want most of the time than at any other period of modern history.

9 We have not been led into this world of material closeness against our better judgment. For many of us, especially when we're young, consumerism is not against our better judgment. It *is* our better judgment. And this is true regardless of class or culture. We have not just asked to go this way, we have demanded. Now most of the world is lining up, pushing and shoving, eager to elbow into the mall. Woe to the government or religion that says no.

10 Getting and spending have been the most passionate, and often the most imaginative, endeavors of modern life. We have done more than acknowledge that the good life starts with the material life, as the ancients did. We have made stuff the dominant prerequisite of organized society. Things "R" Us. Consumption has become production. While this is dreary and depressing to some, as doubtless it should be, it is liberating and democratic to many more.

Starbucks to Begin Sinister "Phase Two" of Operation

WEB LINK
to Exercise
C.13
http://www.
ablongman.com/
lester

1 After a decade of aggressive expansion throughout North America and abroad, Starbucks suddenly and unexpectedly closed its 2,870 worldwide locations Monday to prepare for what company insiders are calling "Phase Two" of the company's long-range plan.

2 "Starbucks has completed the coffee-distribution and location establishment phase of its operation, and is now ready to move into Phase Two," read a statement from Cynthia Vahlkamp, Starbucks' chief marketing officer.

> After reading this satiric piece from The Onion, see Chapter 5, Exploring a Writer's Irony

"We have enjoyed furnishing you with coffee-related beverages and are excited about the important role you play in our future plans. Please pardon the inconvenience while we fortify the second wave of our corporate strategy."

3 Though the coffee chain's specific plans are not known, existing Starbucks franchises across the nation have been locked down with titanium shutters across all windows. In each coffee shop's door hangs the familiar Starbucks logo, slightly altered to present the familiar mermaid figure as a cyclopean mermaid whose all-seeing eye forms the apex of a world-spanning pyramid.

4 Those living near one of the closed Starbucks outlets have reported strange glowing mists, howling and/or cowering on the part of dogs that pass by, and

electromagnetic effects that cause haunting, unearthly images to appear on TV and computer screens within a one-mile radius. Experts have few theories as to what may be causing the low-frequency rumblings, half-glimpsed flashes of light, and periodic electronic beeps emanating from the once-busy shops.

5   In addition, newly painted trucks marked with the nuclear trefoil, the biohazard warning symbol, and various mystic runes of the Kaballah have been spotted rolling out of Starbucks distribution warehouses.

6   A spokesman for Hospitality Manufacturing, a restaurant-supply company that does business with Starbucks, provided some insight as to what Phase Two might entail.

7   "This week, they cancelled their usual 500,000-count order of Java Jackets and ordered 1.2 million Starbucks-insignia armbands instead," Hospitality Manufacturing's Jasper Hennings said. "They also called off their standing order for restaurant-grade first-aid kits, saying they had a heavy-duty source for those now. And, most ominous of all, they've stopped buying stirrers altogether."

8   "I don't like the looks of this," added Hennings before disappearing late Monday night.

9   No Starbucks employees were available for comment, as those not laid off in January's "loyalty-based personnel restructuring" or hospitalized in the series of freakish, company-wide milk-steamer malfunctions that severely scalded hundreds of employees, have been sent to retraining centers.

10   Remaining Starbucks employees earmarked for retraining are being taught revised corporate procedures alongside 15,500 new hires recently recruited from such non-traditional sources as the CIA retirement program, Internet bulletin boards frequented by former Eagle Scouts, and the employment section in the back of *Soldier of Fortune* magazine.

11   More insight into Phase Two was provided by the company's most recent quarterly stockholders' report, which features a map of North America showing the location of every existing Starbucks. Lines drawn between the various stores form geometric patterns across the U.S., including five-pointed stars, Masonic symbols, and, in the Seattle area, the image of a gigantic Oroborous serpent wrapped around an inverted ziggurat.

12   Starbucks management has been tight-lipped regarding the upcoming changes. No upper-level executives have been seen in public since the first of the month, and no details seem to be forthcoming. Visitors to the Starbucks web site, however, are greeted with a letter from Starbucks founder Howard Schultz reading in part:

13   "To our valued Starbucks customer: Just wait until you see the exciting changes we've got in store for you as part of our new Phase Two. When you finally see what we've got brewing here at Starbucks, you'll have no choice but to love it."

It's Time to Start the Slow School Movement

Maurice Holt

1   When the young Cole Porter left his elementary school in Indiana for a prep school on the East Coast, his mother gave his age as 12, although he was in fact two years older.

WEB LINK
to Exercise
C.14
http://www.
ablongman.com/
lester

She had always encouraged his musical gifts and evidently decided that two more years at home, practicing the piano and entertaining passengers on the passing riverboats, was a better way of fostering his songwriting abilities.[1] We should all be grateful for her foresight.

> Note how the author uses formal citation style here; see Chapter 11 for specifics on CMS Style for both text and Works Cited. Other academic articles may use MLA style (Chapter 10), APA style (Chapter 12), or CSE style (Appendix B)

2   In today's school climate, Kate Porter's deception appears both unlikely and unwise. The pressure to proceed from one targeted standard to another as fast as possible, to absorb and demonstrate specified knowledge with conveyor-belt precision, is an irresistible fact of school life. Parents are encouraged to focus on achievement, not self-realization. A present-day Porter would soon be labeled a nerdy slow learner if he flunked the math test and preferred the keyboard to a baseball bat. It's curious that, in an age when the right of adults to shape their own lifestyle is taken for granted, the right of children to an education that will help them make something of themselves is more circumscribed than ever.

3   This curriculum straitjacket is the price exacted for believing that education is about assessed performance on specified content. The march toward ruthless conformity began in the 1970s, as the Cold Warriors blamed schools for the supposed deficiencies in American technology. It gained momentum in the 1980s, when, as Arthur Levine has noted, the generation born after World War II became young urban professionals, and "the education of their children became the baby boomers' and the nation's preoccupation."[2] The 1983 Reagan-era report *A Nation at Risk* set the agenda for all that has followed. Influenced on the one hand by the idea that education is an atomistic, science-like activity, and on the other by the output-led simplicities of supply-side economics, schools in America have been in the grip of some form of standards-based reform for nearly 20 years.

4   The current Administration of George W. Bush has pushed through the idea of universal standards-based tests to be given each year in grades 3 through 8, a requirement that undermines the independence of the states and is widely thought to be unworkable. History may show, as is so often the case, that this ultimate adornment to the edifice of standards may mark the very moment when its foundations begin to crumble. The 33rd Phi Delta Kappa/Gallup poll shows a rising trend in favor of school-based assessment and of public schooling in general.[3] The results of state testing in English and mathematics, far from offering new insights, merely confirm that the chief determinants of performance are parental income and the level of school resources—in short, the affluence of the neighborhood. Conservative columnist George Will puts it more brutally: "The crucial predictor of a school's performance is the quality of the children's families."[4]

5   But this is not a law of nature: it reflects the tendencies of tests to reflect culturally embedded concepts of student "quality" and of school funding systems to offer least to those who need most. To excel in high-stakes tests, even schools in sleek suburbs are prepared to distort their curriculum, as Billie Stanton observes in a revealing report on the effects of standards-led reform in Colorado: "Even parents in an affluent Boulder neighborhood . . . are questioning whether private school may not be preferable, since watching their fourth-graders return home dazed and drained from being drilled again and again in how to write a 'power paragraph.' "[5]

6   In borderline schools, Stanton writes, there is "a narrowing of curriculum, a trend that sucks all enrichment and love of learning out of education while creating a 'drill and

kill' focus on reading, writing, and math to the exclusion of everything else." Colorado rates schools on a bell curve, with the threat of intervention for those that "fail," creating a climate of fear that encourages recourse to dubious practices—not least by the state itself. Astonishingly, a state recommendation points out that a school can raise its rating and avoid humiliation merely by getting "three more kids to prove proficient on third-grade reading and five more on fifth-grade reading."[6] The pursuit of "tough standards" can corrupt everything it touches—not least, the results.

A Fresh Perspective

7   There has to be a better way of understanding what schools should be about and how to improve them. For some, charter schools are the answer, but the recent RAND research offers little encouragement for this view, and privatized schools have fared no better.[7] A report on an Edison school in Michigan hardly inspires confidence: standardized tests are administered by computer every few weeks, and "inside the classroom, the teachers follow a curriculum . . . which provides daily lesson plans that are scripted down to the questions that the teachers are to ask students about particular stories."[8] The default discourse of the classroom has become command rather than conversation. Little wonder that students have become as restless as their teachers. It is time we devised a fresh scenario that will help our legislators to get their feet on the ground again.

8   I suggest that for guidance we turn, in the first instance, not to educational theory but to a different setting where thought and action are closely connected. We need to move away from mechanical models, where the ends are defined from above and the appropriate means are applied from below. We need to think instead about how people come together to examine and improve an activity which, like education, depends in its most realized form on the unexpected and the unpredictable. Learning and teaching are often at their richest when the moment gives rise to an expected insight, when what Dewey called the collateral experience can generate a new end and set in train new means to achieve it.

9   Something of this kind began to happen in 1986, when a McDonald's hamburger franchise opened its doors in the Piazza di Spagna in Rome. Carlo Petrini—then a journalist for a weekly magazine—made a joke that turned into a movement: "We said, there's fast food, so why not slow food?"[9] Now the International Slow Food Congress meets annually; there are American slow food convivia in New York, California, and North Carolina; and Italy has its first slow city. The founding manifesto declared: "A firm defense of quiet material pleasure is the only way to oppose the universal folly of Fast Life."

10   As the movement has grown, its main concerns have emerged: it is, "above all, a movement for cultural dignity," it is "a battle against a way of life based solely on speed and convenience," and it seeks to save "the cultural inheritance of humanity."[10] Preserving the variety of different kinds of food, challenging legislation that restricts small producers, and making good, cheap ingredients available to all have become particular issues, while of course encouraging ways of living that find time for agreeable meals and quiet reflection.

11   Some similarity is already evident with the ends of education, in which respect for our cultural inheritance and for a variety of ways of interpreting it goes hand in hand with an emphasis on the long-term implications of schooling rather than short-term rewards. We remember from our schooldays not the results of tests but those moments when a teacher's remark suddenly created a new perception. As Michael Oakeshott put it, "Not the cry, but the rising of the wild duck impels the flock to follow him in flight."[11] You are not a mere observer, a passive consumer—you become part of an experience, savoring the moment and benefiting from its intensity.

12   It is helpful to identify some aspects of the slow food movement that underpin its approach. First, it expresses a definite *philosophical position*—that life is about more than rushed meals. Second, it draws upon *tradition* and *character*—eating well means respecting culinary knowledge and recognizing that eating is a social activity that brings its own benefits. A respect for tradition also *honors complexity*—most sauces have familiar ingredients, but how they are combined and cooked vitally influences the result. And third, slow food is about *moral choices*—it is better to have laws that allow rare varieties of cheese to be produced, it is better to take time to judge, to digest, and to reflect upon the nature of "quiet material pleasure" and how everyone can pursue it.

> An argument like this one requires that you know the basics of logic, as discussed in Chapter 3, especially pages 100–111

13   These attributes are not chosen at random; they are prominent in the writings of the curriculum theorist Joseph Schwab, and William Reid has suggested that they mark out what Schwab termed "the practical" approach to curriculum activity.[12] In "The Practical: A Language for Curriculum," Schwab argues that this view of social action itself embodies theoretical constructs such as tradition, character, and context and is fundamentally different from action conceived as "practice" and divorced from "theory."[13] The slow food movement is entirely concerned with the language of the practical; it is all about real people eating, arguing, and legislating in ways that take account of particular issues, informed by the three crucial elements of philosophical grounding, tradition and character, and moral choice.

14   The alternative view, which currently dominates the scene, draws a distinction between theory and practice. Because theory, Reid argues, tends to be seen in education as "abstract and refined in character," it follows that practice "is conceived as concrete and mundane." Practice then becomes "the deployment of knowledge and skills," such as management, presentation, and implementation.[14] By the same token, practice becomes value free: "Good practice is simply that which works. The idea of the practical, on the other hand, represents practice as deeply implicated with considerations of a social, cultural, and political nature that . . . confront problems of moral choice."[15] In sum, the prevailing view of practice is not philosophically grounded, is independent of tradition and character, and is unconcerned with moral issues.

Developing the Metaphor

15   I suggest that conventional fast food expresses this narrow conception of practice. There is no philosophy behind the concept of a hamburger—only the theory that a beef-filled bun is tasty and relieves hunger. Neither does its preparation draw upon tradition and character, as does, for example, the preparation of sole meunière or a Genoese sponge

cake. Fast food involves only rudimentary skills, which can be taught to employees without any knowledge of the culinary arts. The fact that virtually the same hamburger sells in Paris and Moscow demonstrates its supremely decontextualized nature. And the sourcing of its ingredients is not a matter of morality; in a hamburger, one kind of salt is as good as another.

16   There is assuredly a place for both fast food and slow food in the world. There is nothing intrinsically objectionable in hamburger practice. If one is in business to make hamburgers, the fast food model—theory and practice—makes perfect sense. It is wholly appropriate to the nature of the problem, which is uncomplicated and procedural. But this is not the case if one has in mind a meal that is at once eclectic, imaginative, and socially stimulating. Judgment, finesse, tradition, and ambience all have a part to play, since the taste of food on the palate is just as important as a full stomach. And indeed, it is possible to produce a quick meal within the slow food canon: an omelet takes less time to prepare than the average burger.

17   In the context of education, the form of schooling espoused under the banner of standards demonstrates the same deterministic thinking that governs the production of fast food. What is sought is a conception of educational practice that can be defined in terms of content and sequence and assessed in terms of agreed-upon ends capable of numerical expression. The engagement between teacher and learner should be as predictable as possible, and variation between one teacher and another can be offset by scripting the learning encounter and tightening the form of assessment. If the purpose of schooling is to deliver the knowledge and skills that business needs, this approach cuts costs, standardizes resources, and reduces teacher training to a school-based process. Above all, the efficacy of the operation can be measured and the results used to control it and its functionaries—the teachers.

18   But if schools exist to equip students with the capacity to address the unpredictable problems of adulthood and to establish themselves in a world of growing complexity, then crucial disadvantages emerge. Classroom practice becomes a boring routine, teachers feel de-skilled, and, though what is learned is measurable, its educative value is diminished. The "fast school" offers a static conception of education that has more in common with training. And how can this kind of practice be improved? Since it derives from an impoverished view of theory, distinct from practice, only practice itself can guide improvement. Hence the emphasis on defining "best practices" or "what works," based on the dubious assumption that practice is context-free. But can it ever be?

19   Commitment to standards-led school reform means creating a system of schools geared solely to the product—test results—and not to the process of creating educative experiences. Gerald Bracey has offered a few of the personal attributes that standardized tests cannot measure—attributes crucial to the cultivation of the virtues and the formation of moral agents: "creativity, critical thinking, resilience, motivation, persistence, humor, reliability, enthusiasm, civic-mindedness, self-awareness, self-discipline, empathy, leadership, and compassion."[16] But these are as remote from the activity of fast schools as is gastronomic pleasure from fast food.

20   The result of creating fast schools is institutional indigestion, and signs of discomfort are now appearing. Even Advanced Placement courses in mathematics and science are not immune. A study commissioned by the National Science Foundation and the U.S. Department of Education is critical of "the curriculums that most of those courses

cover and the way they are taught. . . . The courses crammed in too much material at the expense of understanding."[17]

21   Standards supporters have always claimed that, if better tests are used, the quality of teaching will improve. The Maryland School Performance Assessment Program (MSPAP) is therefore of particular interest, since it has been rated "the best in the nation."[18] But the February 2002 MSPAP results were so misleading that the latest eighth-grade version has been "all but scrapped." What went wrong? It turns out that the MSPAP tests, devised to "emphasize critical thinking," were difficult to grade—"the process was rushed and subjective."[19] And in any case, all the state wanted was "content-based exams" and simple tests to match. The implication is clear: however much time is spent improving tests, the problem lies elsewhere—in the mistaken belief that tests and targets should drive the curriculum.

22   A school system based on testing content and basic proficiencies is better than none at all, and developing nations can afford to do little more. What is surprising is that the richest country in the world is hell-bent on doing exactly this.

23   It was certainly not meant to be so; the slow school requirement for philosophical grounding was very evident in the conclusions of the committee set up in 1918 by the National Education Association to develop the high school curriculum. Its members rejected continental models and decided to forge a uniquely American settlement. They took account of the earlier efforts of the Committee of Ten, of the writings of John Dewey, and of pressure from manufacturers who wanted school leavers to have the skills that would help them compete with European rivals. They took account of cultural tradition, too, and believed, like post-revolutionary France, that the success of the republic depended on schooling that was well conceived, free from sectarian bias, and equally accessible to all. But it was to be local rather than national. You went to high school to become an American, but you took a chance on what sort of Americans were running the school board.

24   The result in the U.S. was, and is, a system in which the language of the practical still lingers, but it is now in competition with an emphasis on deterministic doctrines that threaten to drive it underground. In part, this reflects the growing strength of the industrial lobby in American politics, but it also owes much to psychometric influences which, over the years, have persuaded Americans that numbers are everything: if you can't measure it, you can't manage it. Nothing, as W. Edwards Deming remarked, could be further from the truth: "The most important figures needed for management of any organization are unknown and unknowable."[20]

25   The system of local school boards was intended to frustrate federal interference, but the political prominence given to education since the 1960s has made such interference inevitable. Yet, unlike France, America has no tradition of education as a national construct. Indeed, the local character of the U.S. system was to be its strength. The current scenario could lead to the worst of both worlds: the individual character of schools undermined by national legislation based not on deliberation but on dogma. The more education is seen as a commodity, the less its power to animate the emotional attachment of students. The day may come when one goes to high school not to become an American but to acquire the technical skills of globalism.

26   The dissatisfaction of parents with fast schools is beginning to surface. One alternative is home schooling; another is to use a private school—some of which offer radical solutions. In Woodstock, New York, for example, a "Sudbury School" has opened,

with no classrooms and no grades, based on the proposition that "there is no right way to learn, no time by which a student should have mastered a given skill."[21] A study of students attending a similar school in Massachusetts found that 87% went on to higher education, but much of the interest in the Woodstock enterprise "has come from middle-class children's parents,"[22] which is not irrelevant; these students are better able to cope with unstructured formats and benefit from family resources as well. But in the public sector, a slow school must have the practical underpinning to make it an enriching vehicle for students from all social and cultural backgrounds.

Toward the Slow School

27   What would a slow school look like, and would parents make use of a school with such a counterintuitive name? How might Schwab's three principles of philosophical grounding, tradition and culture, and moral judgment play out in practice? The first point to make is that several American initiatives designed to reform public schools over the last two decades or so have much in common with the principled underpinnings of the slow school. And variety should be encouraged. There ought not to be a canonical slow school, any more than there can be standardized slow food. Commonality of approach does not imply uniformity of practice.

28   It's reasonable to suppose that Theodore Sizer's Horace would be happy to work in a slow school.[23] The idea that "less is more" fits exactly with an emphasis on intensive rather than extensive experience. Better to eat one portion of grilled halibut than three king-sized burgers. Better to examine in detail the reasons why Sir Thomas More chose martyrdom or why Alexander Hamilton argued for a strong federal government than to memorize the kings of England or the capitals of the states of the union. The slow school is a place where understanding matters more than coverage; one takes time to see what Newton's concepts of mass and force might imply, to appreciate their abstract nature and the intellectual leap they represent. Then the usual algorithms fall into place quickly and securely. The slow school offers the intellectual space for scrutiny, argument, and resolution.

29   These are all essential to practical inquiry, and it would seem that the Paideia schools established in Chattanooga demonstrate the value of such strategies, since they manage to incorporate Mortimer Adler's commitment to Socratic dialogue while satisfying Mammon's need for good test results.[24] Indeed, the supreme irony of the slow school is that precisely because it provides the intellectual nourishment students need and puts curriculum first, good test results follow. Success, like happiness, is best pursued obliquely.

30   Equally relevant is the work of Deborah Meier, who has shown how a school, given the autonomy to do so, can construct a demanding curriculum that engages students from widely varied environments and can carry them forward into higher education.[25] What all these schools have in common is the power to improve themselves, and this is the singular virtue of any school curriculum that uses the language of the practical. Because ends and means are allowed to interact, improvement stems naturally from the deliberation that arises from this interaction. Improvement is not, as legislators have come to believe, a matter of extrinsic pressure; it is an intrinsic property of the school itself, precisely because "the practical" embodies theory within its practice.

31   Is this the time to start the slow school movement? I believe it is an idea whose time has come. At a stroke, the notion of the slow school destroys the idea that schooling is about cramming, testing, and standardizing experience. It legitimizes a range of admirable yet hitherto marginal strategies for schooling and brings them into the mainstream of argument, using a philosophical basis that is supple enough to accommodate a variety of reform programs, yet tough enough to resist the counterarguments of the standards movement.

32   The slow approach to food allows for discovery, for the development of connoisseurship. Slow food festivals feature new dishes and new ingredients. In the same way, slow schools give scope for invention and response to cultural change, while fast schools just turn out the same old burgers. If we think about the future of education, we assuredly want a more satisfying and stimulating approach than the present sad state of affairs. Only slow schools hold out that kind of promise.

33   The idea of the slow school, therefore, is more than a new metaphor; its foundation in the notion of the practical gives it great scope for development. It would seem to be desirable to form an association that could exchange ideas and establish the slow school concept as a distinctive institutional strategy for schooling in the new millennium: an approach that combines agile pedagogy and responsive structure with an imaginative grasp of knowledge and understanding.

34   The putative Slow School Association would help parents, legislators, and administrators understand not only what a slow school is, but also what it is not. It is important to establish the intellectual credentials of the slow school, since it would be necessary to agree to certain preconditions with legislators and administrators. For example, frequent testing (as opposed to informal teacher monitoring) is inimical to the philosophy of the slow school. Once slow school students have demonstrated their ability to do well with fewer tests, the movement would acquire political clout and could help rein in the senseless over-testing that currently threatens schools and students.

35   One can suppose, for example, that a slow school would make use of computers as aids to learning, but without attributing to them the numinous educative powers that figure in the rhetoric of many politicians. Equally, the language of the practical, as the deliberative underpinning of curriculum thinking, has nothing to do with postmodernist flights of fancy of the kind espoused by some educational theorists, nor with the notion of basing a curriculum solely on practical work or students' transient needs and interests. Rather, the slow school philosophy, as expressed through the language of the practical, affirms an eclectic approach to schooling that addresses the question put by Robert Dearden: "Why should everything be judged by the standards appropriate to mathematics and science?"[26] The language of determinism, given brutal expression in the standards movement, obliges us to recall Aristotle's caution: "It is the mark of an educated man that in every subject he looks only for so much precision as its nature permits."[27] Between the precision of tests and the raw variety of classroom life lies a vast gulf.

36   Recent developments in Japan have a bearing on this issue. Starting in the 2002–03 school year, Japan's public schools will pursue a radically different curriculum that offers students much more free time—a deliberate departure from the extreme formality and relentless drilling so admired a decade ago as the paradigmatic example of what American schools should be like if the U.S. were to regain its lead in the global

economy. A senior official of the Japanese Ministry of Education, Ken Terawaki, has a convincing explanation: "Our current system, just telling kids to study, study, study, has been a failure. Endless study worked in the past, when . . . Japan was rebuilding. . . . But that is no longer the case . . . telling them to study more will no longer work. . . . We want to give them some time to think."[28] There is concern "that an orderly and unimaginative school system excels at producing pliant, disciplined workers . . . but is failing to produce the problem solvers and innovators of the future."[29] By pursuing a punitive, outdated model of schooling rather than encouraging U.S. schools to individualize, innovate, and fulfill their historical purpose, America has become stuck in a time warp.

37   There is no reason why the phrase "slow school" should not acquire the cachet associated with "slow food." In many aspects of life, doing things slowly is associated with profound pleasure. Fast sunbathing is not regarded as particularly enjoyable. If we want to understand a striking baseball catch, we replay it in slow motion. Why try to absorb the treasures of Florence in a brief guided tour, if you can spend a month appreciating them for yourself? If we want our children to apprehend the variety of human experience and learn how they can contribute to it, we must give them—and their teachers—the opportunity to do so. Let the slow times roll!

> See Chapter 11 on footnoting your sources

Works Cited

1. William McBrien, *Cole Porter* (New York: HarperCollins, 1998), p. 18.
2. Arthur Levine, "An Endgame for School Reform," *Education Week*, 12 December 2001, p. 52.
3. Lowell C. Rose and Alec M. Gallup, "The 33rd Annual Phi Delta Kappa/Gallup Poll of the Public's Attitudes Toward the Public Schools," *Phi Delta Kappan*, September 2001, pp. 44, 54.
4. George F. Will, "'Fixing' Education," *Boston Globe*, 7 January 2002, p. A-15.
5. Billie Stanton, "Education Reform Causes Major Fallout," *Denver Post*, 11 November 2001, p. 12.
6. Ibid.
7. Brian Gill et al., *Rhetoric Versus Reality: What We Know and What We Need to Know About Vouchers and Charter Schools* (Santa Monica, Calif.: RAND Corporation, 2002), chap. 2.
8. Jacques Steinberg, "Buying In to the Company School," *New York Times*, 17 February 2002, p. 17.
9. David Auerbach, "Carlo Petrini's Digestive System," *Civilization*, February/March 1998, p. 27.
10. Ibid.
11. Michael Oakeshott, "Teaching and Learning," in Timothy Fuller, ed., *Michael Oakeshott on Education* (New Haven, Conn.: Yale University Press, 1989), p. 62.
12. William A. Reid, *Curriculum as Institution and Practice* (Mahwah, N.J.: Erlbaum, 1999), p. 8.
13. Joseph J. Schwab, "The Practical: A Language for Curriculum," in Ian Westbury and Neil Wilkof, eds., *Joseph J. Schwab: Science, Curriculum, and Liberal Education* (Chicago: University of Chicago Press, 1978), pp. 287–321.

14. Reid, p. 8.
15. Ibid.
16. Gerald W. Bracey, "The 11th Bracey Report on the Condition of Public Education," *Phi Delta Kappan*, October 2001, p. 158.
17. Karen W. Arenson, "Study Faults Advanced-Placement Courses," *New York Times*, 15 February 2002, p. 15.
18. Nurith C. Aizenman, "Once-Lauded MSPAP Undermined by Format," *Washington Post*, 11 March 2002, p. B-1.
19. Ibid.
20. Quoted in Henry Neave, *The Deming Dimension* (Knoxville, Tenn.: SPC Press, 1990), p. 151.
21. Claudia Rowe, "In Woodstock, a Nonschool with Nonteachers," *New York Times*, 20 February 2002, p. 16.
22. Ibid.
23. Theodore Sizer, *Horace's School* (Boston: Houghton Mifflin, 1992).
24. Anne Wheelock, "Chattanooga's Paideia Schools: A Single Track for All—And It's Working," *Journal of Negro Education*, vol. 63, 1994, pp. 77–92.
25. Deborah Meier, "The Big Benefits of Smallness," *Educational Leadership*, September 1996, p. 12.
26. Robert Dearden, *The Philosophy of Primary Education* (London: Routledge, 1968), p. 68.
27. Ibid.
28. Quoted in Howard W. French, "More Sunshine for Japan's Overworked Students," *New York Times*, 25 February 2001, p. 18.
29. Ibid.

The Patient Predator

Kevin Patterson

WEB LINK
to Exercise
C.15
http://www.
ablongman.com/
lester

1   The creature arrived in the arctic as it had spread itself around the world. It lay dormant in the lungs of someone apparently healthy enough to undertake such a journey, and then, when he was weakened, perhaps by hunger, or cold, or simple loneliness, it revived itself explosively. The sailor, or the missionary, or the trader found himself coughing paroxysmally and febrile, in some little iglu or tent, the bacterium streaming through his blood, to all his organs, and then a local Inuk had the misfortune to enter the shelter and leave. In Arviat, one of the Inuit communities that hug the shore of Hudson Bay, lives a woman I will call Therese Oopik, who carries the descendants of the creature within her. I visit Arviat in my work as an internist and she is my patient. We have been acquainted for a decade. Mostly we have had quiet conversations about contraception and bladder infections; these days we talk about this infection that seems likely to claim her.

> This reading and the two that
> follow offer three very different
> sources on the topic of
> tuberculosis; see Chapter 9 on
> Writing the Multi-Source Essay

2   She was beautiful when I first knew her, with a full-faced smile and glowing from the cold, but for two years now she has lost weight steadily and she looks as emaciated as a New York City fashion model. We joke about this. When I next visit there, she suggests, I might find a job for her.

3   Arviat is populated by 1,800 people, almost all Inuit, and it clings to the low rocks that stretch into the Arctic water like a collection of brightly painted aluminum-sided mollusks. The wind scours this place. Everyone knows everyone else and most of their problems. There have been episodic outbreaks of tuberculosis here, as in all the little communities in this part of the Canadian Arctic, ever since that first coughing sailor or missionary arrived. Tuberculosis has smoldered on notwithstanding the advent of antibiotics. The disease is primarily an expression of poverty and its consequences, especially overcrowding, and in the Arctic, these are usual. Latent infection endures in almost everyone older than 40. It revives itself regularly and seeps through the community; by the time a new outbreak is recognized there are usually dozens of new infections, some apparent, most already gone dormant.

4   Therese is 27 and does not know from whom she caught her illness. There are nearly as many possibilities as there are people around her. Half her left lung is taken up by a giant cavity full of the organism. Every time her sputum has been analyzed in the last two years, it has been found to be packed with the little rods of Mycobacterium tuberculosis that stain crimson when examined under the microscope. She coughs constantly and is so thin she is cold even inside, wrapped in blankets. After months of unsuccessful treatment in Arviat, she spent much of last winter in a hospital in southern Canada, but she continued to lose weight steadily. Her sputa remain resolutely positive. Finally, she insisted on going home, to her children, and to the tundra.

5   She has the cachectic facies of a painting of a Victorian consumptive, Munch's Sick Child, perhaps. It is an uncomfortable feeling to find in her sickness the conventions of beauty—boniness and pallor. She is suspicious of doctors and nurses and takes her medication only episodically. People worry aloud about her children. This is a catastrophe in formation. A slow-moving freight train.

6   This catastrophe threatens to erupt on a vastly larger scale than Arviat, to involve the entirety of North America. For the past 12 years I've treated patients in TB hot zones such as the Arctic, the Pacific Islands, inner-city America. What I and others on the front lines have to report is that TB is migrating out of these geographically remote or economically isolated communities and into the mainstream.

The New Front in the Battle against TB

Sarah Kershaw

WEB LINK
to Exercise
C.16
http://www.
ablongman.com/
lester

1   A decade after a tuberculosis epidemic gripped New York City, raging through Harlem at a rate not seen since the early 1900's, the disease has taken another turn in the circle of its history. While overall numbers have declined, tuberculosis is now most prevalent in the immigrant neighborhoods of Queens, where it poses a growing public health threat.

> Note that, like common knowledge (Chapter 7), federal, state, and local government data do not need formal citation

2   In Corona, immigrants from the countries most ravaged by the disease—including China, Ecuador, Haiti, India, Mexico, Bangladesh and Pakistan—have settled in droves over the last decade. The city's Department of Health runs one of the busiest tuberculosis clinics in the country there, one that treated 37,000 patients last year.

3   The rate of tuberculosis in Corona was the highest in the city in 2001—36.1 cases per 100,000 people, more than double the citywide average of 15.7 cases and at least seven times the national average. For the first time, the incidence of tuberculosis in Corona surpassed the rate in Central Harlem, for decades the epicenter of tuberculosis in the city.

4   Tuberculosis, an airborne lung infection that kills 2 million people a year worldwide, was largely brought under control in New York City after the epidemic peaked in 1992, when it was fueled by AIDS and homelessness. City health officials have reported a steady decline since then in new tuberculosis cases among New Yorkers born in the United States.

5   The disease's shift to immigrants reflects a kind of turning back of the clock to the turn of the 20th century, when tuberculosis rippled through the city's immigrant population, spreading rapidly through tenements and windowless factories.

6   "It's a dramatic change in the disease," said Sonal Munsiff, assistant commissioner for the Tuberculosis Control Program at the New York City Department of Health. She added, "We are no longer in crisis mode, but in certain places, case rates are many, many times more than they should be."

7   While the change has occurred in cities around the country, it is most striking in New York, which has the highest rate of tuberculosis in the nation. In 1992, only 18 percent of the new tuberculosis cases were among foreign-born New Yorkers, according to the Department of Health. In 2001, 64 percent of the 1,261 new tuberculosis cases were among immigrants.

8   And so, Queens is now the front line of the city's aggressive battle, which commands an annual budget of $37.5 million. Most worrisome to health officials is that people with an active infection, which typically festers in the lungs, shutting them down with wrenching pain if untreated, can be highly contagious.

9   The disease is most likely to spread through the air in enclosed or crowded spaces. On average, a person with an active infection will spread the disease—through coughing or sneezing—to 15 to 20 other people in a year's time, according to the World Health Organization.

10   A team of health workers based in Corona fan out through the borough to find and treat patients. The workers often comb remote places like a junkyard in the shadow of Shea Stadium, and not long ago they stumbled on an apartment crammed with Ecuadorean immigrants. In all, more than 60 people who had lived there were infected.

11   "This is a tough bug to kill," said Errol Robinson, director of the Queens Network for the city's tuberculosis program, who oversees the Corona Chest Center.

12   Mr. Robinson, who began working in the program 14 years ago, used to spend much of his time working in homeless shelters, at encampments under bridges or in the streets of Harlem and the South Bronx. Now his staff works with immigrants, knocking on their doors before they head to work, and he relies on translators or bilingual workers to communicate with patients.

13   While the incidence of the disease in Corona is still far below the case rate in Central Harlem at the epidemic's zenith in 1992—240 cases per 100,000 people—it has nevertheless sounded an alarm.

14   For one thing, the Corona tuberculosis rate reflects only those patients who have been tested at the city's newly renovated clinic on Junction Boulevard or by other area doctors. Health officials say that countless more are likely to be infected but untouched by the city's campaign to track them down and treat them with a course of medication that takes six to nine months to complete.

15   Lloyd Walker, one of the public health workers, sees an average of 13 patients a day. He zooms through the streets of Queens in his blue Ford Taurus with a medication log and a bottle of hand cleanser for patients who need to wash up before taking their pills. His job is part of a treatment for tuberculosis known as Directly Observed Therapy, which was credited with bringing the epidemic under control and drastically reducing the number of cases of Harlem and other hot zones. Under the treatment, patients are observed taking their daily medication, usually five days a week.

16   At the beginning of treatment, a patient must take as many as four different drugs every day. And it is often a challenge to get patients who work up to 14 hours a day, drift from home to home or leave and re-enter the country, to stick to the regimen.

17   If they do not complete the treatment, which cures the disease but does not prevent contracting it again, patients can build up immunity to the drugs and then face years of treatment. And drug resistant strains have been on the rise.

18   Each day about noon, Santos Rodriguez, who lives in the junkyard near Shea, meets Mr. Walker in the back of an auto body shop. The men who work in the nearby auto parts shops know Mr. Walker, and they usually help him find Mr. Rodriguez, a 42-year-old Salvadoran immigrant.

19   Mr. Rodriguez said he became ill with tuberculosis last year, experiencing night sweats, fatigue, loss of appetite, a severe cough—all symptoms of the disease—and was hospitalized for more than two months.

20   "Santos!" the men called the other day, when they saw Mr. Walker's car pull up to the shop on Willets Point Boulevard. A few minutes later, Mr. Rodriguez walked to a cabinet where he keeps his bottles of medication, in a drawer full of wrenches and bolts. In the back of the shop, Mr. Walker put down two pieces of paper towel on a plank of plywood. Mr. Rodriguez, who does odd jobs in the shops, washed the grease off his hands with the cleanser Mr. Walker gave him and took six pills.

21   Mr. Rodriguez has missed his medication several times and once lost his three bottles, he said, but he has been observed five days a week for the past month. For that, he has reaped regular rewards from the health workers, including coupons for Kentucky Fried Chicken and juice. "I know I have to do this," he said in Spanish.

22   Many immigrants are arriving with the dormant form of tuberculosis, which can either develop into an active infection if the immune system is weakened or never lead to illness, according to experts and several medical studies. Screening for tuberculosis is common among immigrants arriving legally, but many others make their way to New York City without ever being tested.

The TB Epidemic from 1992 to 2002

Mario C. Raviglione

Abstract

1   In 1992, less than 20 countries were implementing a sound TB control strategy. At the same time, TB was being resurrected as a major public health problem world-wide after two decades of neglect. Awareness of upward trends in the industrialized countries and MDR-TB outbreaks in large cities were driving forces behind the re-emergence of TB in the international health agenda. New evidence, and consequent estimates, suggested that the situation in developing countries, especially in sub-Saharan Africa, was deteriorating rapidly. Similarly, major increases were observed in the former USSR. It was estimated that some 7–8 million new cases and 2–3 million deaths were occurring annually in the world. The global targets of reaching 85% cure rates and 70% case detection among infectious cases were established by the World Health Assembly in 1991. Both the WHO declaration of TB as a global emergency in 1993 and the launch of the five-element DOTS strategy in 1994–1995 resulted in countries adopting DOTS in encouraging numbers. In fact, in 2000, 148 countries including all 22 highest burden countries (HBC) responsible for 80% of cases world-wide, had adopted the new DOTS strategy. Nevertheless, progress in case detection remained slow due to incomplete geographical coverage or need to widen detection and notification capacity with innovative schemes. The major constraints to TB control became increasingly clear, and a global Stop TB Partnership was eventually established to address such constraints. A Global DOTS Expansion Plan revealed the needs and the gaps to achieve the global targets in 2005. Today, in 2002, the top priority remains that of expanding DOTS, as rapidly as possible, using a number of new approaches to increase case detection and notification while maintaining high cure rates. These must involve collaboration with the private sector and communities, as well as strengthening of primary care services. Similarly, crucial is the rapid identification of solutions to TB/HIV and MDR-TB.

See Chapter 4, Writing an Abstract, for details about building your own abstract and when one is required

WEB LINK to Exercise C.17
http://www.ablongman.com/lester

The Nature of Cuba

Eugene Linden

WEB LINK to Exercise C.18
http://www.ablongman.com/lester

1   On a winding road not far from the vibrant colonial city of Santiago de Cuba, we stop to admire a particularly stunning coastline of cliffs, coves and beaches that seems to stretch to infinity. And just inland are the towering Sierra Maestra. The lower slopes are a patchwork of grasslands and trees that give way at higher altitudes to dense forests. Clouds form, disperse and tatter around the peaks.

Note how the author mixes personal experience with a history of the nature of Cuba; see Chapter 1, Writing To Combine Personal Ideas with Those of Sources

2   The road is empty, and no passing car disturbs the sounds of the surf and wind. "If I were a developer," I say to Antonio Perera, and ecologist and former director of the Cuban government agency that oversees protected lands, "this is where I would site my hotel."

3   "In that case," he says, "I'd be fighting you." Chances are, he'd win: Perera once helped defeat a plan to widen and straighten this very road.

4   During a recent 1,000-mile trip through Cuba to see its wildlands at this pivotal time in its history, I saw a lot of unspoiled territory that is largely a monument to battles that Perera and his colleagues have won: swamps bursting with wildlife, rain forests and cloud forests, grasslands and lagoons. Perera says 22 percent of Cuba's land is under some form of protection. The percentage of safeguarded environment in Cuba is among the highest of any nation, says Kenton Miller, chairman of the Switzerland-based World Commission on Protected Areas.

5   As wildlife and habitat have disappeared from the region, Cuba's importance as an ecological bastion has steadily risen. As one scientist put it, Cuba is the "biological superpower" of the Caribbean. The island has the largest tracts of untouched rain forest, unspoiled reefs and intact wetlands in the Caribbean islands. Cuba also is home to many unique, or endemic, species, including the solenodon, a chubby insectivore that looks rather like a giant shrew, and the bee hummingbird, the world's smallest bird, weighing less than a penny.

6   Condos and hotels carpet large parts of the Caribbean. Population pressures and poverty have turned much of Haiti into a denuded moonscape that bleeds topsoil into the ocean every rainy season. Cuba's environment, too, has in the past suffered the ill effects of unchecked logging, the conversion of lowlands into sugarcane fields, urban overdevelopment and pollution in Havana Bay. Still, with its anachronistic rural life and largely healthy ecosystems, the island is a sort of ecological Brigadoon, offering a vision of the Caribbean of long ago. Neat thatch-roofed villages line quiet roads; litter-free highways connect provincial cities whose approaches are graced by tamarind or guaiacum trees. Large populations of migratory birds flock to Cuba—ducks, vireos, sapsuckers and woodpeckers—and wetlands hold a gorgeous profusion of warblers, egrets, herons and flamingos.

7   Whether Cuba can continue to remain a holdout is, of course, a great question. Much of the nation's ecological health can be chalked up to planning by Fidel Castro's regime, to be sure; but Cuba is an elysian vision also by default. Roads are unlittered partly because there's nothing to litter. During the Soviet era, which ended in 1991, Cuban industry and agriculture, boosted by Soviet support, proved highly polluting, but now many factories and fields are idle. Population pressure is not a problem; indeed, thousands risk their lives each year to flee. A recent analysis by the Heritage Foundation and the *Wall Street Journal* ranked Cuba as the world's second most repressive economy, behind only North Korea.

8   But unlike North Korea, Cuba seems on the verge of change. Commerce abhors a vacuum, and it appears that this beguiling island cannot indefinitely resist development. Spanish, Canadian, Dutch, Swedish, Norwegian, German, French and other investors have taken advantage of the 43-year-old U.S. trade embargo to forge their own trade relationships with Castro's government. And the pressure to develop the island is likely to increase if—or when—Cuba resumes trade with the United States.

9   John Thorbjarnarson, a zoologist with the Wildlife Conservation Society in New York, has worked in Cuba for several years. He says that although development poses a threat to Cuba's ecology, the nation "stands head and shoulders above anywhere else in the Caribbean in terms of government support for conservation."

10   Once out of the Holguín airport, where we started our improvised ecotour, we seem to travel back in time. Oxcarts and bicycles abound, and evidence of modern construction or technology is scarce. Very little in the way of consumer goods manages to get into Cuba, partly because the government is broke but also because officials micromanage decision making about imports to a grinding halt.

11   Alexander von Humboldt National Park, in the eastern part of the island, covers almost 300 square miles on the border of Holguín and Guantánamo provinces. Driving there, we go through what must be one of the least built-up parts of the Caribbean, and the experience is disorienting. The few cars we see are well-preserved relics, long gone from their country of origin: DeSotos, Studebakers, Willys, Nashs and many other extinct models. If Cuba is a center of endemism for wildlife, it might be called a center of end-upism for cars.

12   Along the road, billboards stand vigil. "Socialism or Death." "Men Die, the Party Is Immortal." The slogans might seem outdated four decades into Castro's regime, but for many Cubans the Communist fervor still runs strong. Accompanying Perera and me on this leg of the journey is Alberto Pérez, a white-haired information officer with the United Nations Development Programme (UNDP). He says that he grew up rich in Cuba, that his father owned 16 houses and that his family lost virtually everything when Castro took power. But he swears it was all worth it because of what Castro has done for the poor. Apparently, not everyone in his family agrees. His sister fled to Florida.

13   We pass through a village and Pérez sees *anon*, knobby pink-fleshed fruit also known as sugar apples, at a stand by the side of the road. We buy a bunch of them as well as cups of fresh sugarcane juice. The fruit has a vanilla-like flavor and would make excellent ice cream. The sugarcane juice is cool and refreshing, not overly sweet. Around a neatly trimmed fence post made of the cactuslike euphorbia, or milk bush, we watch an old man pull pieces of sugarcane through a metal device that strips off the outer layer. He's wiry and fit and cheerfully offers his age—81—adding that "the work isn't hard, but this hangover is."

14   Pérez buys out the stand's supply of sugar apples for friends back in Havana. On the road, we go through Marcané and Cueto, villages immortalized in song by the 95-year-old guitarist and singer, Company Segundo, known to many Americans from the *Buena Vista Social Club* movie and sound track.

15   Having traveled through many poor rural villages in Africa, Asia and Latin America, I'm amazed at the cleanliness, orderliness and the seeming functionality of these towns. Luis Gómez-Echeverri, former director of the UNDP mission in Cuba, says the poorest Cubans have a better standard of living than poor people in any of the 82 countries he has visited. Though Cubans have little economic freedom, the U.N.'s annual Human Development Report ranks Cuba among the top five developing countries in terms of education and access to clean water, medicine and housing.

16   At the same time, nowhere do people in elite professions such as medicine and science make less money than in Cuba. A physician typically earns no more than $100 a

month. Bartering is common. The Cuban term is *resolver* (to resolve), and the word might describe the juggling act by which a mother with a new baby will trade a dress for a hen to lay eggs, and then trade the eggs for goat's milk.

17   We stop for lunch in Moa at a *paladar* (a private home that sells meals). The house, simple in the extreme and spotless, would make an Amish farmhouse look like Trump Palace. A lunch of grilled swordfish for four people costs $12.

18   As we wend our way toward the Humboldt rain forest, Perera spots a rare plant by the road, *Dracaena cubensis*, which has adapted to a type of rocky, nutrient-poor soil called serpentine that contains levels of magnesium toxic to other plants. This shrub-like plant is so specialized to serpentine formations, Perera says, that botanists have not been able to grow it in the botanical garden in Havana.

19   Leaving the road and plunging into the park in the SUV, we ford a couple of streams and negotiate a dirt path. Perera and I then hike past thickets of delicate and seductively fragrant mariposa (Cuba's national flower, a designation that disturbs Perera because it is not native to the island) until we come to a ledge where I see a vista of rain forest-carpeted slopes punctuated by waterfalls. Some parts of the park are so remote that they have not been systematically explored.

20   Perera was largely responsible for the park's creation. While most of the nations that attended the United Nation's 1992 Earth Summit in Rio de Janeiro forgot about its commitments to halt the destruction of species, reduce poverty and prevent climate change not long after their jets left the runway, Perera and the Cuban delegation have sought to preserve the island's biodiversity. And the logical place to start was in the eastern forests that became Humboldt. With 905 plant species, Humboldt contains 30 percent of Cuba's endemic plants, and also has the most plant diversity in the Caribbean. The park also provides habitat to many birds, including the bee hummingbird. Most intriguing, if the ivory-billed woodpecker still exists anywhere on earth, it is likely to be atop the plateau deep inside the park. The large black-and-white bird has near mystical status among ornithologists, not least because it may have gone extinct despite feverish efforts to save it. The last confirmed sighting of the ivory-billed woodpecker in the United States was five decades ago. But scientists working in eastern Cuba came upon a pair of the birds in 1987, and the government moved to protect the area, setting aside forest that would become the core of Humboldt Park, named after Alexander von Humboldt, who explored the island 200 years ago.

21   Whether or not ivory-billed woodpeckers live in Humboldt Park, there's little doubt that the government's actions to save the bird highlight an environmental approach that differs from that of Castro's predecessor, the plunder-minded president Fulgencio Batista. Since Castro seized power in 1959, forest cutting has slowed markedly, according to Perera; forest cover has increased from about 14 percent in 1956 to about 21 percent today.

22   The headquarters for this section of Humboldt Park sits above Taco Bay. A couple of rangers take us for a spin around the lagoon in search of a manatee family that divides its time between Taco Bay and another lagoon nearby. In a dinghy, powered by an impossibly small outboard, we put-put across the placid waters, stopping first in a channel that becomes a tunnel as it passes under mangrove boughs—one of the few places in the world

where pine forests meet mangrove swamps, Perera says. We encounter no manatees, but Taco Bay still looks like a wonderful ecotourism spot. Though the ranger station has a small bunkhouse for visitors, little seems to have been done to enhance such sites. Perera, speaking carefully (all Cubans speak carefully when touching on official matters), says the government has trouble delegating the authority for the planning and design of ecotourist ventures, making it difficult for entrepreneurs to get started.

23   Tact is especially valuable in a country where a verbal misstep can land one in jail. In its latest human rights assessment, Amnesty International reported in 2002 that a significant but unspecified number of Cubans were imprisoned for their personal beliefs and political dissidence. (In 1997, for instance, Cuban journalist Bernardo Arévalo Padrón was sentenced to six years in prison for saying in an interview that Castro lied and broke promises to respect human rights.) This past March, the Castro regime reportedly arrested at least 75 Cubans for alleged dissident activity—the largest roundup of political activists in decades—after a number of them had met with a member of the U.S. diplomatic mission to Cuba. A U.S. State Department spokesman said the arrests were a reaction to "independent individuals and groups which are willing to take a few more risks these days and express their opposition to, or independence from, the government."

24   Islands showcase the capricious paths of evolution: their very isolation acts as a filter, minimizing somewhat the coming and going of species that make terrestrial ecosystems so diverse and complex. From an ecological point of view, Cuba is strategically situated between North and South America, with flora and fauna drawn from both continents. And it's a big island—750 miles long and up to 150 miles wide—the 15th largest on the planet. Arrayed around the main island are more than 4,000 other islands; some, like the Isle of Youth (890 square miles), are quite large. Many, according to Michael Smith, of Conservation International in Washington, D.C., serve as important refuges for endangered species.

25   Cuba's living world can be traced to the geological forces that created the place. Its mammals have a particularly South American accent, for instance. Most experts argue that South American primates, sloths and other animals reached Cuba on rafts of floating vegetation. Ross MacPhee, a mammalogist at the American Museum of Natural History in New York, has a different idea. He theorizes that a ridge, a part of which is now 6,000 feet below the Caribbean between the West Indies and South America, rose above the ocean surface 33 million years ago. For a little less than a million years, the bridge allowed animals to reach Cuba, which was then united with Puerto Rico and Hispaniola as one great peninsular mass contiguous with today's Venezuela. Evidence for this, he says, is the presence of ferric oxide, or rust, in the Aves Ridge seabed; the compound is formed when iron-containing soil is exposed to atmospheric oxygen.

26   However they got there, the island's animals and plants make for an eccentric mixture. Mammal species are scarce, though there's the tree-dwelling rodent, the hutia, and the insectivorous solenodon. Perhaps not surprisingly, the one mammal that flourishes on Cuba (and many other islands) has wings: bats. Plants that can float (or have seeds that float) also have become established. Cuba has a great diversity of palm trees— roughly 100 species. Reptiles, like the iguana and the crocodile, are well represented,

too, perhaps because their capacity to estivate, or wait out the summer heat in a torpor akin to hibernation, suits them to ocean voyages on tree trunks and the like. Cuba ranks tenth in the world in reptile diversity, with some 91 different species.

27   Geology continues to shape island life. An abundance of limestone-rich terrain is heaven for mollusks, particularly snails, which fashion their shells out of the mineral. In western Cuba, erosion has created steep-sided limestone hills called *mogotes*. A snail originating on a particular mogote is essentially limited to it, so snail evolution follows its own course on virtually each mogote, producing a great number of species. Cuba has hundreds of different snail species, including the gaudy polymita of the island's eastern region; it might be green, red, yellow or some combination of colors. Alas, the polymita is critically endangered because people collect its shell; the Cuban kite, a bird that feeds on the mollusk, is also disappearing.

28   In nature, one animal's absence is another's opportunity, which may partially explain a peculiarity of islands: disproportionate numbers of both gigantic and tiny creatures, such as the giant lizards and tortoises on some islands today, and the pygmy rhinos on Borneo. (Not to mention a 300-pound rodent, *amblyrhiza*, that once graced, if that is the word, Anguilla.) Cuba is home not only to the world's smallest bird but also the smallest scorpion (*Microtityius fundorai*), a big-voiced tiny frog (*Eleutherodactylus iberia*) and one of the world's smallest owls. There is a small insect-eating bat (*Natalus lepidus*) with an eight-inch wingspan as well as a gigantic, fish-eating bat (*Noctilio leporinus*) with a two-foot wingspan.

29   Why dwarfs and giants flourish on islands has long provoked debate among biogeographers. J. Bristol Foster of the University of British Columbia theorized in the early 1960s that reduced predation and competition on islands allow species to expand into unusual ecological niches. There can be powerful advantages to the extremes, researchers say. Gigantism may offer otherwise diminutive mammals like rodents access to new food sources. Dwarfism may give a large-bodied animal an edge in lean times, and on an island, where predators are few, a dwarf won't necessarily pay a penalty for its size.

30   Moreover, a key element of island biology is that, just as living things are suited to the extremes, they are especially susceptible to being wiped out when the environment to which they are so finely adapted is disrupted. So says E. O. Wilson, the Harvard biologist and pioneer of island biogeography, who points out that most of the major extinctions caused by humans have occurred on islands.

31   Human beings settled Cuba about 5,500 years ago, many thousands of years after they established themselves on the continents. Humanity's relatively recent appearance in Cuba may explain why some animals persisted longer there than on the mainland. The giant sloth, for instance, vanished from South America roughly 11,000 years ago, presumably after being hunted to extinction, but held on another 5,000 years in Cuba. Numerous endemic Cuban species are threatened by human activity, biologists say. Among them are the solenodon, whose numbers have been reduced by feral dogs, and the hutia, which is illegally hunted for food. The Zapata wren is endangered largely because of habitat destruction, the Cuban pygmy owl because of logging, and the Cuban parrot because of a thriving illegal pet trade. Ross MacPhee says the Cuban government can't afford to enforce environmental regulations, but most environmentalists

I spoke with disagreed with that assessment, saying the government backs up its conservation laws.

32   Continuing along the northeast coast to Baracoa, we stop at a church to see a remnant of the cross said to have been left by Christopher Columbus in 1492. (When Columbus landed he reportedly said, "This is the most beautiful land that human eyes have ever seen.") The cross, shown by radiocarbon dating to be about 500 years old, is made of coccoloba, a relative of the sea grape. Originally more than six feet tall, it has been whittled to half its size by relic seekers. Given the island's tumultuous history of invasions, wars and pirates, not to mention atheistic Communists, it's something of a miracle that even a splinter of the cross remains.

33   From Baracoa we head over the mountains toward the south coast, passing Cubans hawking goods to tourists. Among the items are protected species—polymita snails and Cuban parrots. The parrots have drab green feathers, modeled, it would appear, on the fatigues favored by Castro. Pérez, seeing the contraband sales, wants to stop. But Perera says no. "If we stopped," he says, "I would feel obligated to denounce the sellers and have them arrested, and we would spend the rest of the day on this."

34   Traversing the pass through the Nipe-Sagua-Baracoa Mountains, we leave the range's rain shadow, and the tropical forest soon gives way to desertlike dryness. Along the southeast coast are remarkable marine terraces, including the most dramatic, at Punta Caleta. The limestone formations look like giant steps, the risers formed by cliffs dozens of yards high. Exposed by geologic uplifting, they offer an extraordinary record of past sea levels. Geophysicists flock here to "read" the climate record encoded in these marine terraces, which are said to be the oldest, largest, most elevated and least altered on the planet.

35   As we pass Guantánamo on our way to Santiago de Cuba, Perera remarks sardonically that the DMZ surrounding the United States naval base—wrested from the Cuban government in 1898 and then leased for 99 years beginning in 1934—is the most protected environment in Cuba, because it is guarded by fences and armed sentries (and reportedly ringed by land mines that Cubans placed outside the fences). Maybe someday it will be a park, Perera speculates.

36   A site of historical significance to Cubans that is already a nature reserve is Desembarco del Granma National Park. It marks where Castro, upon returning from exile in Mexico on December 2, 1956, disembarked from the yacht *Granma* and began the revolution. Castro chose the spot for its remoteness. The area more recently captivated Jim Barborak, an American protected-area specialist with the Wildlife Conservation Society. His evaluation of the local geomorphology—marine terraces reaching from several hundred feet above sea level to deeply submerged reefs—helped get the park designated a U.N. World Heritage Site. Barborak wrote in his report that it was "one of the most impressive coastal landscapes in the Americas from the Canadian Maritimes to Tierra del Fuego."

37   What happened after Castro landed here, as Perera tells the story, would later bear on the government's approach to wildlands. Three days after Castro landed, Batista's troops took Castro's guerrillas by surprise in Alegría de Pío. Outgunned, the rebel force scattered. An illiterate farmer named Guillermo Garcia Frías assembled the survivors,

including Fidel and his brother Raúl, and led them into the Sierra Maestra, where they regrouped. For saving Castro's life and then leading the ragtag revolutionaries to safety, Castro made Garcia one of five comandantes of the revolution. He later became a member of the central committee and the politburo. A nature lover, Garcia turned to preserving the Sierra Maestra. He hired Perera in 1979 fresh out of the University of Havana's biology program to work on preserving biodiversity.

38   Mary Pearl, president of the Wildlife Trust, based in Palisades, New York, says that Garcia's ties to Castro established a strong environmental ethic for a generation of scientists and officials. As a result, says Pearl, coeditor of the book *Conservation Medicine: Ecological Health in Practice*, Cuba's ecosystems are in the best shape of all islands in the Caribbean.

39   The Florida Straits off Cuba have the greatest diversity of marine species in the hemisphere, according to a recent U.N.-sponsored study by Michael Smith. In addition, Cuba's wetlands have seen a dramatic reduction in the pesticide runoff that mars wetlands in other countries, as farmers turn from expensive chemicals to organic means of fertilizing and controlling pests. Though the shift probably would not have occured without the Soviet Union's collapse, which impoverished Cuba and limited its access to agrichemicals, it is an example of the sort of conservation-by-default that has benefited the island environment.

40   Now Cuba's ecology is increasingly a concern of outside organizations. The UNDP channels roughly $10 million a year in aid into Cuba, one-third of which goes into environmental projects such as supporting protected areas, cleaning Havana Bay and helping Cuba devise new coastal management plans.

41   Orlando Torres is a short, balding, middle-aged ornithologist and professor of zoology at the University of Havana. He has boundless energy. I don't think I've ever encountered anyone who enjoys his work more. He's not in it for the money; he earns $23 a month.

42   He's eager to show off Zapata Swamp National Park, another preserve with historical importance. Zapata encompasses the Bay of Pigs, where the 1961 CIA-assisted assault by Cuban exiles failed disastrously. The swamp covers about 1,900 square miles, or the size of Delaware, and remains sparsely populated, with only 9,000 permanent residents; 60 to 70 percent of its area is undeveloped.

43   The Hatiguanico River, which runs westward on the Zapata Peninsula, is largely untouched by industry and agriculture. Cesar Fernandez, the local park ranger, takes us down the river in an outboard-powered boat. The water is clear and teems with tarpon and other fish. The surrounding trees and swamp foliage are crowded with birds. As we move downstream, herons, egrets, kingfishers and other birds take flight ahead of us. Turtles, sunning themselves on branches, plunk into the river. At a shimmering pool, I dive in, and feel the cool springwater rising from the depths. Divers have so far probed as deep as 200 feet, Torres says, with no bottom in sight.

44   Torres keeps a tab of bird species. In the first hour he counts 25. Though hunting and poaching do occur, on the whole wildlife may be the beneficiary of the police state; the government restricts hunting and does everything it can to keep guns out of private hands.

45   That river trip was a mere appetizer for the visual feast we would encounter the next day. In an eastern part of the swamp, we walk along a path into the park near the head of the Bay of Pigs, stopping at Salinas, a salt flat that once supplied the mineral for trade but long ago reverted to a natural state. At a ranger station, we pick up a former forester and the park's premier guide, and head into the swamp. He and Torres name the birds they spot—here a broad-winged hawk, there, black-necked stilts on ridiculously spindly legs. The two are hoping to eye a trogon, Cuba's colorful national bird whose colors are red, white, blue and green—a palette that a Yankee environmentalist might see as saluting the island's proximity to its giant neighbor as well as its ecological good citizenship.

46   I see a tall bird with a white chest perched by itself on a tree stump in the wetland. But it flies off before I can ask the experts to identify it. Torres thrusts a bird book into my hands and asks me to point out the creature. After riffling through the pages a few times, I finger an ivory-billed woodpecker. Torres laughs. But hey, the bird really did look like the fabled relic.

47   Halfway to the coast, the guide leads us into a dry part of the swamp to a stand of dead palms. He studies the hollow stumps and then starts scratching on one. A moment later a tiny head appears and looks down at us with a combination of indignation and suspicion. Torres is ecstatic. It's a small screech-owl, *Otus lawrencii*. "This is a very good record," he says. "I spent a week looking for it with an English bird expert and failed to find one." Trying to convey the significance to a nonbirder, he says, "If a trogon is worth a dollar, the barelegged [or screech-] owl is one million dollars." Knowing Torres' salary, I get the picture.

48   Leaving Cuba, I was struck by the incongruity of so much pristine beauty so close to the Caribbean's many overdeveloped islands. For an American, this is a lost world a scant 90 miles from home. It was also hard to digest the irony that the forces that have worked to preserve nature in Cuba contradict so many tenets of conventional wisdom about conservation.

49   Trying to sort out my reactions I imagine a summit meeting on sustainable development, which is an approach to achieving economic growth without destroying natural systems. Asked to describe their dream of an environmental paradise, the sustainable development mandarins describe a land of high biodiversity with a stable, educated population; a government dedicated to protecting natural resources; a populace that wasted nothing; an agriculture that pursued organic methods and minimized toxic runoff.

50   Such a place aleady exists, I say.

51   "What's the standard of living?" the mandarins ask.

52   Well, I'd say, it's one of the poorest nations in its hemisphere, and the economy is so screwed up that doctors work as housekeepers because they can earn six times the hard cash they get for being a surgeon. Then I point out that the government is not a democratic republic but a Communist police state.

53   That, of course, is the rub. It is unlikely that there will be a stampede among nations to replicate Cuba's path toward sustainable development. In Cuba, Communism and poverty have not proved as disastrous for nature as they have elsewhere. In Soviet Russia, the need for productivity spurred central planners to pursue agricultural policies that poisoned rivers and destroyed lands on an epic scale. In contrast, Cuba's move toward

organic farming has had beneficial side effects on bird and fish populations. Farmers have learned to live with a trade-off in which they tolerate birds eating some of their crops as a type of wage for the birds' work controlling pests.

54   It is easy to be seduced by Cuba's beauty, but some ecologists temper their enthusiasm for Cuba's future. MacPhee wonders whether ecological trends in Cuba are as healthy as they seem at first blush, and contrasts the island's future with that of Puerto Rico, once a prime example of honky-tonk development. Cuba may have more of its original forests left, says MacPhee, but Cuba's poverty and dependence on agriculture means that wildlands remain under threat. In Puerto Rico, he says, the forests have staged a remarkable recovery since World War II as the economy has shifted away from crops.

55   In the United States, practically anything concerning Cuba arouses passion and even anger, and the island nation's environment is no exception. Sergio Díaz-Briquets, a consultant with the Council for Human Development, and Jorge Pérez-López, a U.S. Labor Department economist, have authored a recent book, *Conquering Nature*, arguing that socialism has harmed Cuba's ecosystems and that any recent "greening" of the Castro regime is cosmetic. They describe Zapata Swamp as a wounded ecosystem that faces dire threats from drainage schemes, peat extraction and wood cutting for charcoal.

56   But Eric Dinerstein of the World Wildlife Fund, the author of one study cited by Díaz-Briquets and Pérez-López, disputes their interpretation of the evidence. In fact, Dinersten says that the Zapata Swamp appears better off than wetlands elsewhere in the Caribbean. A new, unpublished edition of his study, Dinerstein adds, shows that Cuba is making progress by increasing the acreage of protected wetlands.

57   Likely as not, Cuba's natural areas will be buffeted by colossal forces when the nation, now on the threshold of a dizzying political and economic transition, opens up. Not all of Cuba's 11 million people necessarily share their leaders' austere ideology, and many may want to satisfy material aspirations. Conservationists fear that Cuban exiles will return to their homeland with grand development plans, undermining environmental safeguards. There are precedents. In Russia during the Soviet years, apparatchiks trampled forests and polluted rivers out of ignorance; now many of those same officials, turned capitalist, plunder nature for profit.

58   Cuba just might be different. A network of protected areas is in place, and the regime's singular blend of oppression, poverty and environmentalism has created an unusual wealth of wildlands. To me, that legacy was embodied in a ruined old estate in the forest overlooking Taco Bay. Before the revolution, the estate was owned by Americans remembered by locals today only as "Mr. Mike" and "Mr. Phil." The ghostly villas have no roofs, and strangler figs slowly crack apart the remaining walls of the crumbling building. To some, the sight is a sad reminder of a lost way of life. But it's also a sign that nature, given a chance, will prevail.

Credits

Angell, Marcia. Editorial: "The Supreme Court and Physician-Assisted Suicide—The Ultimate Right" by Marcia Angell. From *New England Journal of Medicine*, Jan. 2, 1997, Volume 336, pp. 50–53. Copyright © 1997 Massachusetts Medical Society. All rights reserved.

Atlanta Journal Constitution. Staff editorial: "English-only Work Rule Is Dumb in Any Language. As appeared in the *Atlanta Journal Constitution*. Reprinted by permission of Copyright Clearance Center.

Atlantic Online. First screenshot from website of *Atlantic Online* at http://www.theatlantic.com. Reprinted by permission of The Atlantic Monthly Group.

Barry, Dave. "Farm Security: The Mohair of the Dog that Bites You" by Dave Barry, published June 23, 2002. Copyright © Tribute Media Services, Inc. All rights reserved. Reprinted with permission.

Barzun, Jacques. From Prologue, pp. xx–xxi from *From Dawn To Decadence* by Jacques Barzun. Copyright © 2000 by Jacques Barzun. Reprinted by permission of Harper-Collins Publishers, Inc.

Beason, Larry. "Ethos and Error: How Business People React to Errors" by Larry Beason from *College Composition and Communication:* 53:1 (September 2001). Reprinted by permission.

Begley, Sharon. "Designer Babies" by Sharon Begley, from *Newsweek*, November 9, 1998, Newsweek, Inc. All rights reserved. Reprinted by permission.

Beiser, Vince. "How to Get to Two Million" by Vince Beiser. Originally published on *Mother Jones'* website as part of an interactive project on the U.S. Prison Population, © 2001, Foundation for National Progress. Reprinted by permission.

Berman, Bob. "Wrong Time, No Bang" by Bob Berman, *Astronomy* June 2002. Reproduced by permission, *Astronomy* Magazine, Kalmbach Publishing Co., © 2002.

Berry, Wendell. "Health Is Membership" from *Another Turn of the Crank* by Wendell Berry. Copyright © 1995 by Wendell Berry. Reprinted by permission of Counterpoint Press, a member of Perseus Books, L.L.C.

Beskow, Laura, et al. "Informed consent for population-based research involving genetics," *JAMA* 2001 286:2315–2321.

Binstock, Robert H. Abstract of article by Robert H. Binstock. Reprinted with permission of the American Psychological Association, publisher of the PsycINFO Database, all rights reserved. May not be reproduced without prior permission.

Bishop, George F., and Bonnie S. Fisher. Abstract of article by George F. Bishop and Bonnie S. Fisher. Reprinted with permission of the American Psychological Association, publisher of the PsycINFO Database, all rights reserved. May not be reproduced without prior permission.

Boot, et al. From "MDMA (Ecstasy) Neurotoxicity: Assessing and Communicating the Risks by Boot, McGregor, and Hall. *Lancet*, Vol. 355, 2000, pp. 1818. Reprinted with permission of Elsevier.

Boulet, Jim, Jr. Editorial: "Expect Host of Problems When Languages Collide" by Jim Boulet, Jr. Reprinted by permission of Jim Boulet, Jr.

Brier, Bob. "The Well-Dressed Dead," by Bob Brier, Volume 56, Number 3, pp. 32–35, 2003. Reprinted with permission of *Archaeology* Magazine, Volume 56 Number 3 (Copyright the Archaeological Institute of America, 2003)

Brishetto, Robert R., and Richard L. Engstrom. Abstract of article by Robert R. Brishetto and Richard L. Engstrom. Reprinted with permission of the American Psychological Association, publisher of the PsycINFO Database, all rights reserved. May not be reproduced without prior permission.

Burke, Kathleen. From "Notable Books for Children 2002," by Kathleen Burke, December 2002. Originally appeared in *Smithsonian*, December 2002. Reprinted by permission of the author.

Campbell, James. From "Travels with R.L.S." by James Campbell. Reprinted by permission of the author.

Carille, James, and Begala, Paul. "Miz Nippy and the Bass Boat." Reprinted with permission of Simon & Schuster Adult Publishing Group from *Buck Up, Suck Up . . . And Come Back When You Foul Up* by James Carville and Paul Begala. Copyright © 2002 by James Carville and Paul Begala.

Carmichael, Carrie. "Last Right" by Carrie Carmichael. Copyright © 2001 Carrie Carmichael. Reprinted by permission.

Carr, Caleb. From *The Lessons of Terror* by Caleb Carr, copyright © 2002 by Caleb Carr. Reprinted by permission of Random House, Inc.

Casmir, Fred L., and Kathryn Kweskin. Abstract of paper by Fred L. Casmir, Kathryn J.S. Kweskin. "Theoretical foundations for the evolution and testing of a chaos theory of communicating" from *World Futures*, 2001, Vol. 57, page 339. Reproduced by permission of Taylor & Francis, Inc., http://www.routledge-ny.com.

Chandarana, Rita. Paragraphs from Rina Chandarana: "Laws Must be Updated": Reuters News Service, "Canada's Cyber-Snooping Plans Raise Ire," Friday, September 27, 2002.

Cinquemani, Sal. Review of Justine Timberlake's "Justified Jive" by Sal Cinquemani in SlantMagazine.com, 2002. Reprinted by permission.

Corman, Steven R., et al. "Studying complex discursive systems: Centering resonance analysis of communication" abstract by Steven R. Corman; Timothy Kuhn; Robert D. McPhee; Kevin J. Dooley. Reprinted by permission of Oxford University Press.

"Ecstacy." From *Time*, April 3, 2000, Vol. 155 on the drug "ecstacy." Reprinted by permission.

Eliot, T.S. Lines 49–54 and 73–74 from "The Love Song of J. Alfred Prufrock" by T.S. Eliot.

Fields, Suzanne. "Bad Raps: Music Rebels Revel in Their Thug Life" by Suzanne Fields, *Insight*, May 21, 2001, p. 48. Reprinted with permission of *Insight*. Copyright © 2003 News World Communications, Inc. All rights reserved.

Friedman, Thomas. *Cuckoo in Carolina* by Thomas L. Friedman. Originally published in *The New York Times*, August 28, 2002. Reprinted by permission of *The New York Times* Co.

Follain, John, and Rita Cristofari. From *Zoya's Story: An Afghan Woman's Struggle for Freedom* by John Follain and Rita Cristofari. Copyright © 2002 by John Follain and Rita Cristofari. Reprinted by permission of HarperCollins Publishers, Inc.

Gilligan, Carol. From *The Birth of Pleasure* by Carol Gilligan, copyright © 2002 by Carol Gilligan. Used by permission of Alfred A. Knopf, a division of Random House Inc.

Index

541